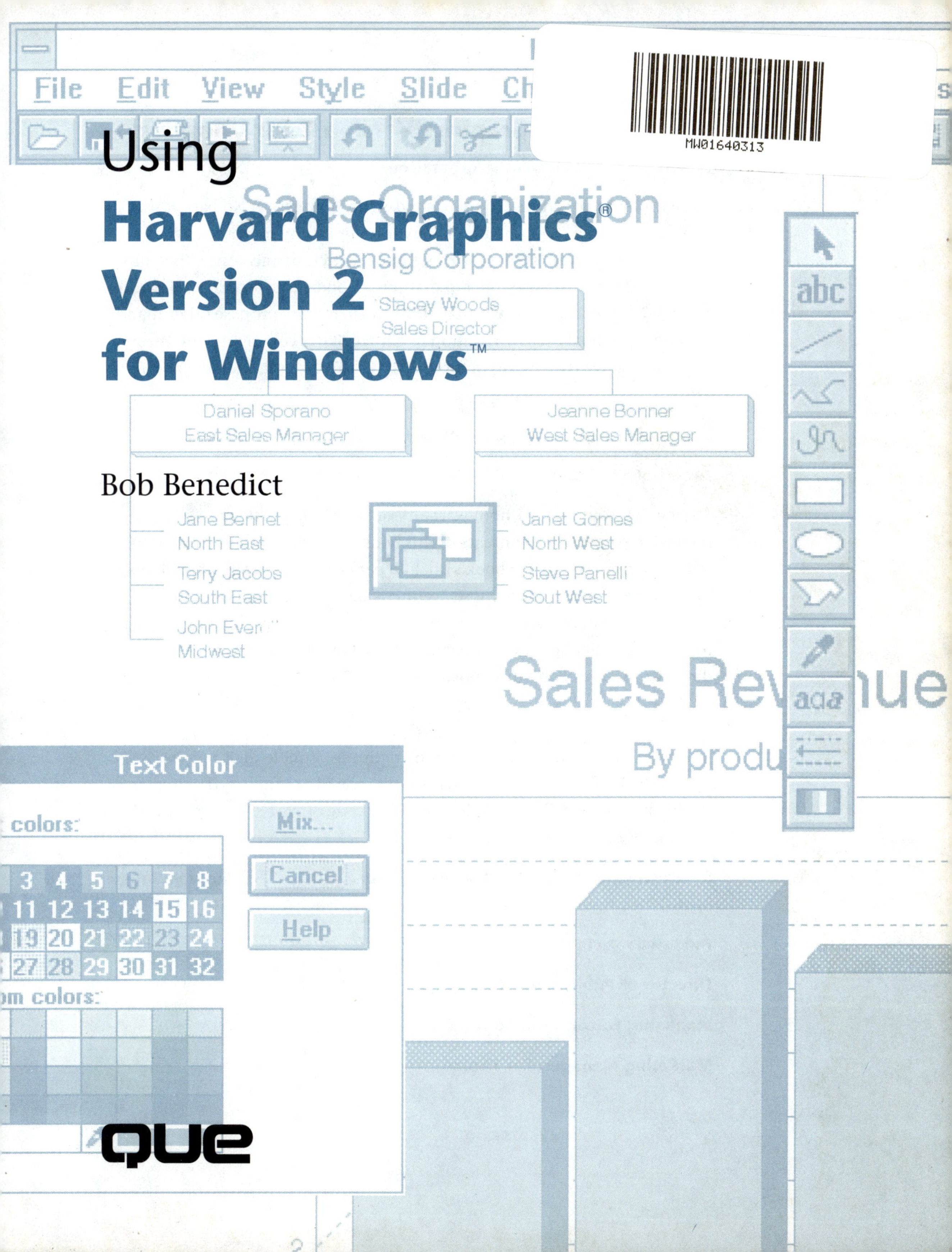

Using
Harvard Graphics® Version 2 for Windows™

Bob Benedict

QUE

Using Harvard Graphics Version 2 for Windows

Library of Congress Catalog No.: 93-86075

ISBN: 1-56529-122-0

95 94 93 6 5 4 3 2 1

Interpretation of the printing code: the rightmost double-digit number is the year of the book's printing; the rightmost single-digit number, the number of the book's printing. For example, a printing code of 93-1 shows that the first printing of the book occurred in 1993.

Screen reproductions in this book were created with Collage Plus from Inner Media, Inc., Hollis, NH.

Publisher: David P. Ewing

Director of Publishing: Michael Miller

Managing Editor: Corinne Walls

Marketing Manager: Ray Robinson

Credits

Publishing Manager
Thomas H. Bennett

Acquisitions Editor
Thomas F. Godfrey III

Product Development Specialist
Bryan Gambrel

Production Editor
Anne Owen

Editors
Heather Kaufman
Jo Anna Arnott
Christine Prakel

Technical Editor
Warren W. Estep

Book Designer
Amy Peppler-Adams

Cover Designer
Dan Armstrong

Production Team
Angela Bannan
Danielle Bird
Charlotte Clapp
Karen Dodson
Brook Farling
Joelynn Gifford
Michelle Greenwalt
Bob LaRoche
Beth Lewis
Caroline Roop
Amy L. Steed
Mary Beth Wakefield
Donna Winter
Lillian Yates

Graphic Image Specialists
Dennis Sheehan
Susan VandeWalle
Tim Montgomery
Teresa Forrester
Wilfred Thebodeau

Indexer
Johnna VanHoose

Composed in *Stone Serif* and *MCPdigital* by Que Corportion

About the Author

Robert C. Benedict, Jr., is a software engineer working in Silicon Valley. Prior to his current employment, Mr. Benedict was employed as an engineer for Software Publishing Corporation, working on the award-winning Harvard Graphics 3.0 project. His responsibilities on this project included presentations, macros, the Charting Gallery, directories, and templates. During this time, Mr. Benedict developed his knowledge of Harvard Graphics for Windows. *Using Harvard Graphics for Windows* was his first publication. Since writing this book, Mr. Benedict has published *Using Norton Utilities for the Macintosh* and *Quick and Dirty Harvard Graphics Presentations* for Que.

Mr. Benedict graduated from the University of California at Davis in 1988 with a B.S. in computer science. While attending school at Davis, he worked as an intern at Microsoft on Microsoft Excel 2.0.

Acknowledgments

I would like to thank Tom Godfrey for his help in finishing this project. Special thanks to Ron Holmes for his work on updating various chapters of the book and for helping to bring it in on schedule. My gratitude to Bryan Gambrel for his careful review of this edition. Thanks to Anne Owen for her complete edits and suggestion. And thanks to Wil Thebodeau for his work in making sure that the screen shots were complete and correct. Lastly, thanks to David Ewing, the publisher of Que Corporation, for deciding to update my first book.

Trademarks

Contents at a Glance

Contents

IV Using Advanced Techniques 361

15 Importing, Exporting, and Linking Data 363

16 Enhancing a Presentation 395

Introduction

Harvard Graphics for Windows is a program designed for creating business presentations. In the business environment, you typically give presentations in a conference room or lecture hall and use slides or overhead transparencies. A graphics art department sometimes produces the slides. With Harvard Graphics, you can create professional-looking slides on your desktop computer. After you have developed your presentation, you can use a projector to display the slides, or you can use Harvard Graphics to display the presentation on a computer screen.

Your ability to communicate information is directly related to your success as a business professional. Unfortunately, you don't always have the time you need to prepare for meetings and presentations. Harvard Graphics can help you increase the effectiveness of your presentations and can save you time. You don't have to be an expert user or a graphics artist to produce high-quality slides with this software. Your audience will remain focussed and attentive as you lead them through the information you have prepared.

Harvard Graphics has many features to help you create truly impressive presentations. The powerful charting capabilities of Harvard Graphics will help you reach your maximum potential as a communicator. With over a hundred different styles of charts from which to choose, you can find a style that accurately conveys your data to an audience. For each chart style, Harvard Graphics provides an assortment of options for you to enhance the appearance of your charts. You can change the colors for the different elements of a chart or add graphics objects, such as arrows or text, to draw viewers' attention to a particular area.

Beyond charting, Harvard Graphics has an extensive set of presentation enhancement tools. The Outliner helps you organize your thoughts before you begin entering data. In the Slide Sorter, you can preview work in progress and evaluate slides before presenting them to an audience. The Slide Editor is the drawing component of the product. You use the Slide Editor to add arrows and text, for example. Combined with high-quality output, these features make Harvard Graphics the ideal vehicle to translate your ideas into information you can present to any group of people.

What's New in Harvard Graphics for Windows?

This new version of Harvard Graphics is designed to run under Microsoft Windows 3.0. The product contains features found in most Windows applications. For example, you can cut, copy, and paste graphics objects inside the Slide Editor. Fonts and output devices developed for Windows are supported in Harvard Graphics. Slides and presentations are displayed in windows, which you can move and resize. You manipulate the different components of the product by clicking icons and by selecting items with a mouse. This version also includes an Outliner for creating presentations and a Slide Sorter for graphically arranging the slides in your presentation.

If you have been using a previous version of Harvard Graphics, you will find the same familiar components of the software in this version. You can add the same chart types you used in the previous version. The Slide Editor in Harvard Graphics for Windows contains the same basic functionality as the Draw feature of Harvard Graphics for DOS, Version 3.0. Both versions produce the high-quality output that is critical in presenting information in a professional work environment. Your overall productivity should only increase after you switch to the Windows version. In fact, this version imports files created in the DOS versions to help you retain information stored in those files.

What's New in Harvard Graphics 2.0 for Windows?

Harvard Graphics for Windows 2.0 is a significant upgrade over the previous version of the product with most changes improving the ease-of-use for end users. Most of the dialog boxes now display graphics images to help you understand how your changes will affect your presentation. For example, when modifying chart options, an image of a chart is displayed. As you move your mouse over different options, the image highlights the part of the chart affected by the option. All dialog boxes have been updated to be compliant with Windows 3.1 user interface guidelines, making the product more familiar to Windows users.

Other improvements to Harvard Graphics have changed features to make them more intuitive and user friendly. Presentation styles and templates are easier to create and use when building your presentation. Printing and printing options are easier to understand, and you can now edit and print speaker notes. A new icon bar provides quick access to common features.

Harvard Graphics now supports TrueType fonts. You can wrap text around a circle and fill the text with different colors. A few new features help you, the presenter, deliver your information. On-Screen Chalk allows you to emphasize parts of a slide while you present by drawing with the mouse. You can add sound for multimedia presentations and even present your slides across a network with the new presentation conferencing. With Version 2.0, Harvard Graphics for Windows has become a more powerful, yet easier-to-use, presentations package.

In the evolving computer market, multimedia and computer networks are two areas improving with more capable hardware and supporting software. Multimedia can richly enhance a presentation with flowing video images and moving stereo sound. Version 2.0 of Harvard Graphics for Windows supports sound files that are played while your viewers view your presentation. You can create a memorable slide with the sound of a big band triumphing in the background. For networks, the new conferencing feature allows you to share the ideas in your presentation with many viewers at the same time. You start a conference on your network that others then join to watch as you move from slide to slide. You can receive feedback on slides and brainstorm with your coworkers with system messaging while everybody views the same slide.

What's in This Book?

Using Harvard Graphics Version 2 for Windows is a guide to the many facets of this product. Each chapter is designed to provide helpful information, whether you are reading the book cover to cover or just learning about a particular feature. The book achieves this goal with clear explanations and informative examples.

The chapters in the book are grouped into the logical stages of learning a software package. The first part, "Creating a Presentation," is composed of introductory material intended to get you familiar with Harvard Graphics. Features described in these chapters are fundamental in creating the slides of a presentation.

Chapter 1, "Quick Start: Creating a Simple Presentation," gives you a guided tour of the basic steps you follow when creating a presentation. After reading this chapter, you should be able to prepare simple presentations using the default settings of the software.

Chapter 2, "Learning Harvard Graphics for Windows Basics," describes the different components of a presentation. You learn about the ways a slide or presentation can be enhanced and about how to use the Help feature to answer questions you have about the program.

Chapter 3, "Creating Text Charts," is the first chapter about creating slides. Text charts make up a significant portion of any presentation and are critical for clarifying your topics. This chapter teaches you how to choose a text chart type and how to enhance your chart.

Chapter 4, "Creating Organization Charts," explains how to use organization charts to graphically represent the members of a business or organization. You learn about the components of an organization chart and how to modify the appearance of the chart.

Chapter 5, "Creating XY Charts," covers the many different line and bar charts available in Harvard Graphics. This chapter teaches you how to pick the most effective style of XY chart for your data.

Chapter 6, "Creating Pie Charts," explains what comprises a pie chart and how you can use pie charts to communicate information.

Chapter 7, "Working with Text," presents techniques for enhancing the text on any slide. You learn how to change the font of your text and how to change text attributes.

The second section of *Using Harvard Graphics Version 2 for Windows* builds on your working knowledge of charts with information on how to improve your chart appearance. These chapters are filled with many chart examples that appear in the color insert in this book.

Chapter 8, "Quick and Dirty Chart Examples," contains effective examples of many different charts. You flip through these examples to find a chart that best suits your data and then follow simple instructions to transform your chart into the one in the book.

Chapter 9, "Chart Makeovers," takes a more general approach to improving charts by providing techniques for evaluating troubled charts. You see several examples of charts that are enhanced and improved in fully explained stages.

After you understand the basics of Harvard Graphics, you're ready to learn about features that really increase your productivity. The chapters in Part III, "Enhancing a Presentation," teach you how to add graphics objects to slides and how to work with an entire presentation.

Chapter 10, "Using the Slide Sorter," explains how to arrange the slides of a presentation within the Slide Sorter. In addition to moving and deleting slides, you also learn how to copy slides to another presentation.

Chapter 11, "Using the Outliner," teaches you how to create a presentation from an outline. The Outliner is a significant new feature that many users will employ as their primary means for building presentations.

Chapter 12, "Drawing in Harvard Graphics," is the first of two chapters dedicated to the Slide Editor. This chapter introduces the different parts of the Slide Editor and the graphics objects that can be added to a slide.

Chapter 13, "Enhancing Drawings and Objects," is the second chapter on the Slide Editor and covers the more advanced features. You will read about how to enhance the objects presented in Chapter 12.

Chapter 14, "Creating Output," explains how to transfer the slides you have previewed on-screen to some other media. You learn how to print a presentation on any printer supported by Microsoft Windows 3.1.

The final part of the book, Part IV, "Using Advanced Techniques," is dedicated to the advanced features of Harvard Graphics. You may not use these features during every session with the product. After you master the information in these chapters, you will be an experienced user of this product.

Chapter 15, "Importing, Exporting, and Linking Data," helps you connect Harvard Graphics to other software packages. You learn how to get information from other sources into Harvard Graphics and how to transfer data out.

Chapter 16, "Enhancing a Presentation," combines with the next chapter to cover features that affect entire presentations. This chapter is concerned with controlling the overall appearance of your presentation.

Chapter 17, "Creating ScreenShows and HyperShows," describes how to turn your presentations into interactive and animated shows. You learn how to control the flow of a presentation by using HyperShow links. You also learn how to add multimedia sound to your presentation and how to share your presentation with other network users with a conference.

Chapter 18, "Adding Symbols," covers the Symbol Library. This library contains professional drawings that you can add to any slide. You learn how to view the symbols and how to add symbols of your own to the library.

Appendix A, "Installing Harvard Graphics 2 for Windows," is a simple guide to installing Harvard Graphics on your hard disk.

Appendix B, "Speed Keys in Harvard Graphics," is a functional listing of the speed keys available within the product.

Appendix C, "Formulas," covers the formulas that can be entered into the data form for XY and pie charts.

Appendix D, "Working with the Icon Bar", explains how to work with the icon bar and set up a custom bar. You also see a list of all the available icons and what features they invoke.

Who Should Use This Book?

Using Harvard Graphics Version 2 for Windows is a reference guide for new users of Harvard Graphics and for people who are familiar with its features. If you're a new user, you will appreciate the linear organization of the chapters. The clear instructions within the book help you explore new features without feeling overwhelmed.

If you're somewhat experienced with Harvard Graphics, this book will help keep you productive while you use the software. The clear division of chapters and sections enables you to quickly find the information you need to understand a feature or complete an action within the product.

In addition to feature explanations, the book provides information on developing effective presentations. This information should benefit anyone who creates or delivers a presentation. The Design Notes will help you understand the issues you encounter when developing slides. The Tips present useful and efficient ways to achieve a desired result. You will also learn how to use the different features of the product to increase the effectiveness of individual slides.

While working with a feature, you may want to find out more about it or approach the task from a slightly different angle. The section titled "From Here..." at the end of each chapter provides valuable references to other sections in other chapters where you can find additional relevant information about that feature or task.

With the addition of the color inserts and charting examples, this book is helpful for people who are familiar with Harvard Graphics for Windows but still have problems creating effective charts. You simply flip through the inserts until you find the chart you need and then locate the example in one of these two chapters. Seeing the charts in full color will enable you to truly appreciate the extensive capabilites of this product.

How To Use This Book

You can use this book in several ways to increase your understanding of Harvard Graphics for Windows. The early chapters provide information that is fundamental to the product. Use this information while you're familiarizing yourself with the basic components of Harvard Graphics. In particular, the sections on creating slides explain the most common operations for building a presentation.

The later chapters of the book are best used when you need to learn how to work with a specific feature. These chapters help you become an experienced user of Harvard Graphics in a short period of time.

Before learning any Windows application, you should become familiar with the Windows environment. You don't have to be a Windows expert to be proficient with Harvard Graphics for Windows. If you understand the basics of the Windows environment, however, you will be more productive with all your Windows applications. Specifically, you should know how to use a mouse, how to click and drag with the mouse, and how to select icons and buttons. You should also be familiar with the different elements of the Windows desktop. This knowledge includes activating windows and selecting items from pull-down menus. If you need information on using Windows, take a look at *Using Windows 3.1*, Special Edition, published by Que.

The best way to use this book is to start reading. If you're new to Harvard Graphics, start with the Quick Start in Chapter 1 and the basics covered in Chapter 2. After reading these chapters and working with the product for just a short time, you will be amazed at how the intuitive interface of Harvard Graphics leads you through the simple features for creating and enhancing slides. If you're somewhat familiar with the product, you will find useful and interesting information in the middle and later chapters of the book. You will read Design Notes that explore different facets of a feature. You may also learn about features you're unfamiliar with and how these features can help you create effective presentations. Regardless of your experience level, *Using Harvard Graphics Version 2 for Windows* will serve as the ultimate companion reference for this powerful presentations software.

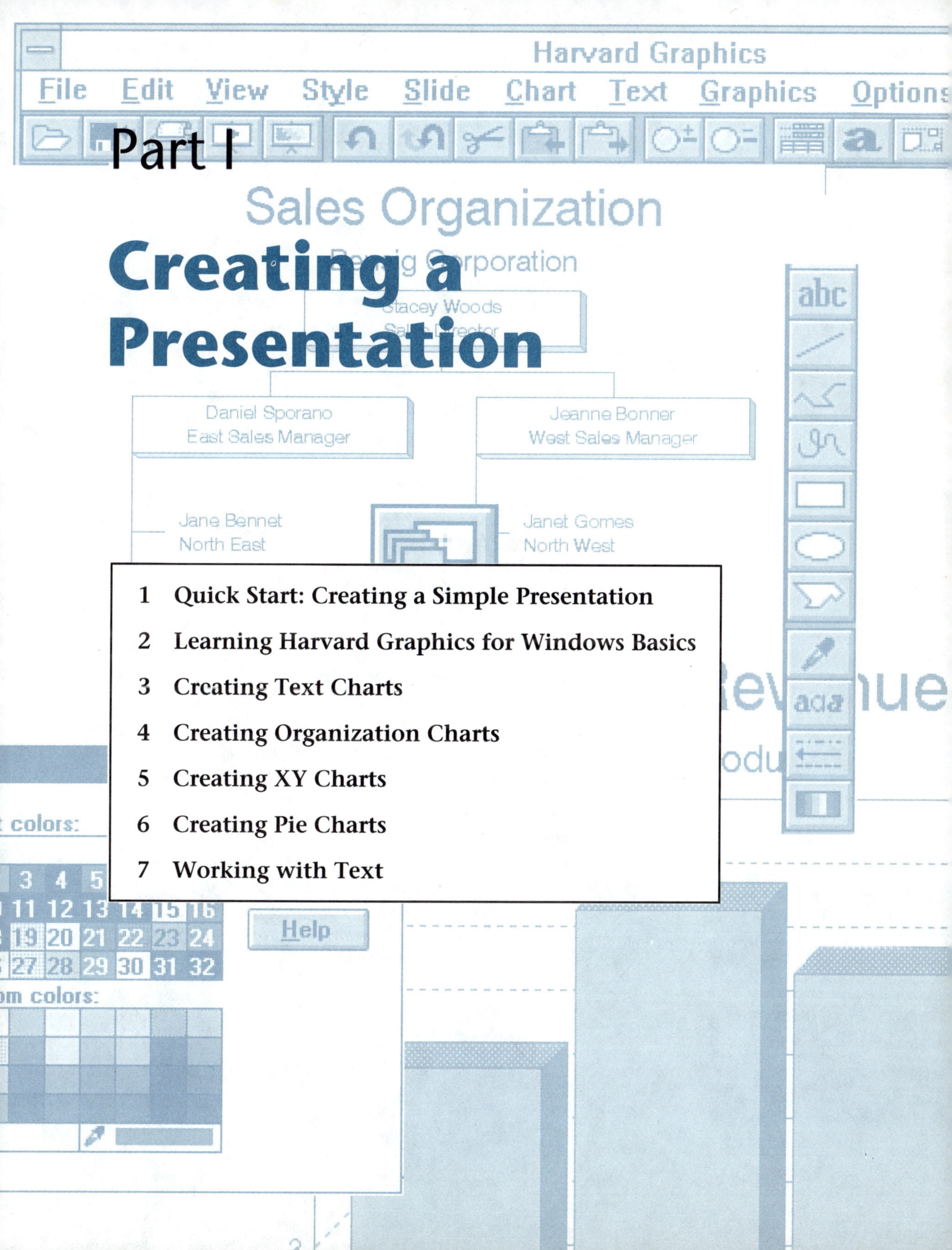

Part I

Creating a Presentation

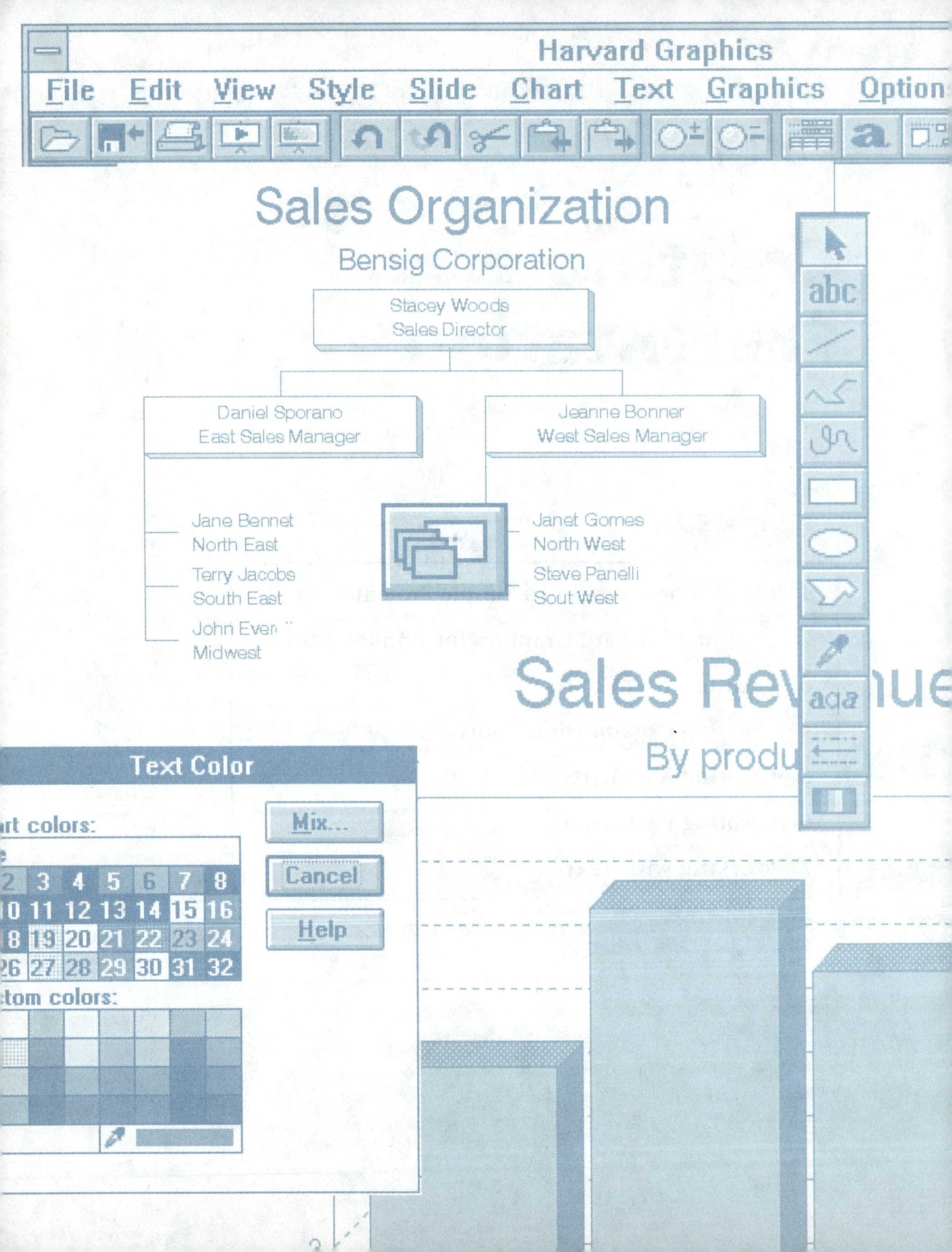

Harvard Graphics
File
Edit
View
Style
Slide
Chart
Text
Graphics
Option
Sales Organization
Bensig Corporation
Stacey Woods
Sales Director
Daniel Sporano
East Sales Manager
Jeanne Bonner
West Sales Manager
Jane Bennet
North East
Terry Jacobs
South East
Midwest
Janet Gomes
North West
Steve Panelli
Sout West
abc
Text Color
Mix...
Cancel
Help

Chapter 1

Quick Start: Creating a Simple Presentation

This quick start guides you through the basic steps and the most common features used to build a presentation in Harvard Graphics for Windows. When you finish this quick start, you will be ready for Harvard Graphics' more advanced features. You will be able to do the following:

- Create a new presentation
- Create a title chart
- Create a pie chart
- View a presentation in the Slide Sorter
- Preview a presentation
- Save a presentation

In this chapter, you learn how to do the following:

- Create a simple presentation
- Create a title and pie chart
- Save a presentation

Before you create slides for a presentation, you must have a topic or objective in mind. In determining the objective, consider the information to be communicated to your audience. In this quick start, your objective is to present the sales revenues for the Bensig Shoe Corporation. Specifically, you must show how much the sales of each product contributed to the total revenue.

Creating a Title Chart

To choose a type of chart for a slide, consider the slide's function. The first slide of a presentation contains the first image your audience sees. If you introduce your objective with this slide, your audience can view the remaining slides within the context of the objective and, consequently, can better understand the information you present and the relationship of the slides to the common theme. Title charts are ideal for introducing the topic of a presentation.

A title chart usually is divided into three regions: title, subtitle, and footnote. The title region appears at the top of the title chart and is the best place to present the topic. The subtitle, which appears below the title, provides secondary information about the topic. The footnote, which provides pertinent information about the topic, appears at the bottom of the chart. These three regions provide clear locations in which to present your topic and relevant information.

In this example, "Sales Revenue" is a good choice for your title because presenting the revenue is the main objective of the presentation. "Bensig Shoe Corporation" is a good choice for the subtitle because it informs the audience that the sales come from products of the Bensig Corporation. To indicate that the revenues are from the 1991 fiscal year, use "1991" as the footnote.

Starting the Program

Before you can create your chart, you must start Harvard Graphics and create a new presentation. Start Windows (if you haven't done so already) by typing **win** at the DOS prompt. After you start Windows, start Harvard Graphics by clicking the Harvard Graphics program icon.

Creating a New Presentation

When you start Harvard Graphics, you see the main Harvard Graphics window which provides an easy way for you to get started working on a new or previous presentation (see fig. 1.1). Follow these steps to create a new presentation and a title chart:

1. Click the Create New Presentation... button. Harvard Graphics displays the New Presentation dialog box for you to create the first slide of your presentation (see fig. 1.2).

2. To create the title chart, click the button next to Title in the Select a Slide Type: list.

3. Click the OK button.

   Harvard Graphics displays the data form in which you enter title chart information (see fig. 1.3). The data form contains three fields, one field for each of the three title chart regions (the title, subtitle, and footnote). The areas of gray text in the fields are placeholders that indicate the location of the text on the slide. If you create the chart without entering data into a region, the placeholder is displayed on the slide. The gray text does not show when you print your slides.

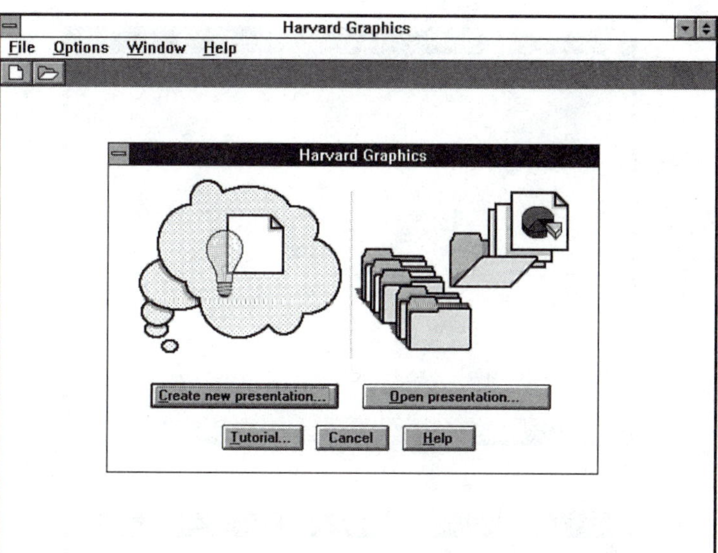

Fig. 1.1 The initial Harvard Graphics window.

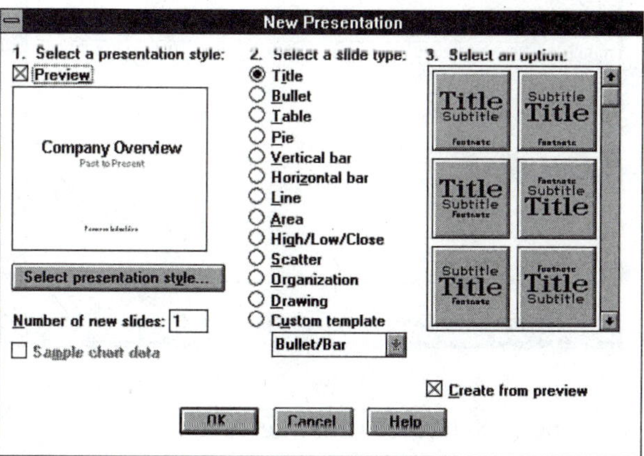

Fig. 1.2 The New Presentation dialog box.

4. Click the Title field. (You can move the pointer to a field by clicking it or by pressing the Tab key.)
5. Type **Sales Revenue** in the Title field.
6. Click the Subtitle field and type **Bensig Shoe Corporation**.

7. Click the Footnote field and type **1991**. The Title Chart data form should resemble figure 1.4.

8. Click the OK button. The slide appears in the Slide Editor (see fig. 1.5).

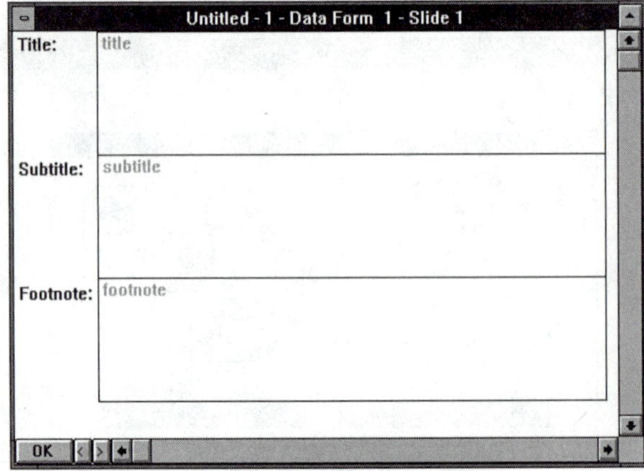

Fig. 1.3
The title chart data form.

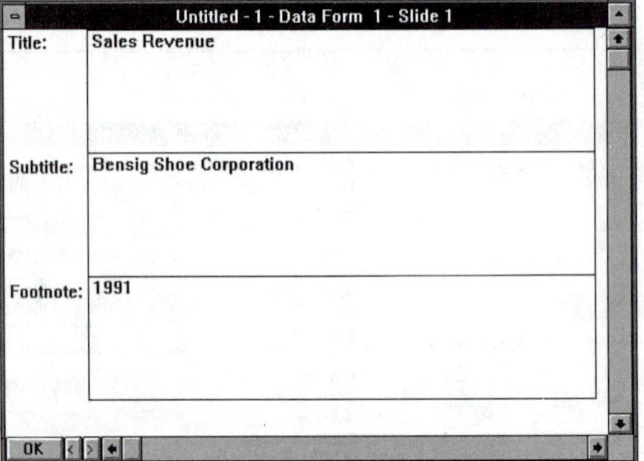

Fig. 1.4
The completed title chart data form.

You have created the first slide for your sales revenue presentation. In later chapters, you learn how to enhance slides within the Slide Editor, using arrows, text, and graphics objects.

Although you can see most of the chart in the Slide Editor, parts of the chart may be hidden beyond the window. Using the Slide Preview feature, you can view the entire chart without obstruction. You can press the F2 function key to preview a slide, or you can select Preview Slide from the View menu. Press any key to end the preview.

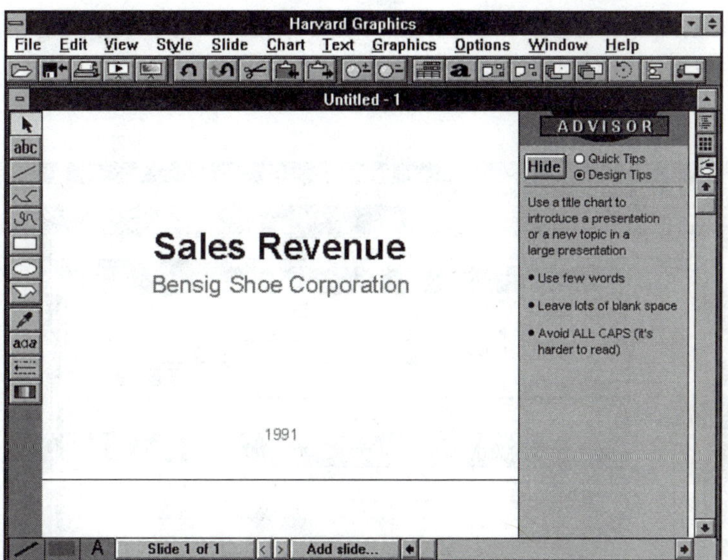

Fig. 1.5
The title chart in the Slide Editor.

Creating a Pie Chart

In this chapter, your objective is to present the product sales figures of the Bensig Shoe Corporation. You communicate your objective to the audience by using a title chart as the first slide. Following the title chart, you will display the slides that comprise the body of the presentation. These slides describe how the sales of individual products contributed to the total revenue.

In choosing the type of chart for the next slide, consider the information you must convey. In this example, the next slide contains numeric data. In addition, the individual product sales combine to form the total revenue. A *pie chart* is the most effective type of chart for this slide. Pie charts are so named because the bits of data are represented by slices of the pie. The size of a slice indicates how much the data contributed to the entire pie. Together, all the slices combine to make a complete pie.

Adding the Pie Chart

Before you add the pie chart slide to the presentation, you should view the presentation in the Slide Editor. To add the pie chart slide, follow these steps:

1. Click the Add Slide button at the bottom of the Slide Editor window.
2. In the Add Slide dialog box, click the Pie button in the Select a Slide Type: list. When you click, Harvard Graphics displays an example pie chart in the dialog box.
3. Click the OK button.

Harvard Graphics displays the pie chart data form in which you enter data (see fig. 1.6). Click the arrow in the upper right corner of the data form window to see more of the data form.

Fig. 1.6
The blank pie chart data form.

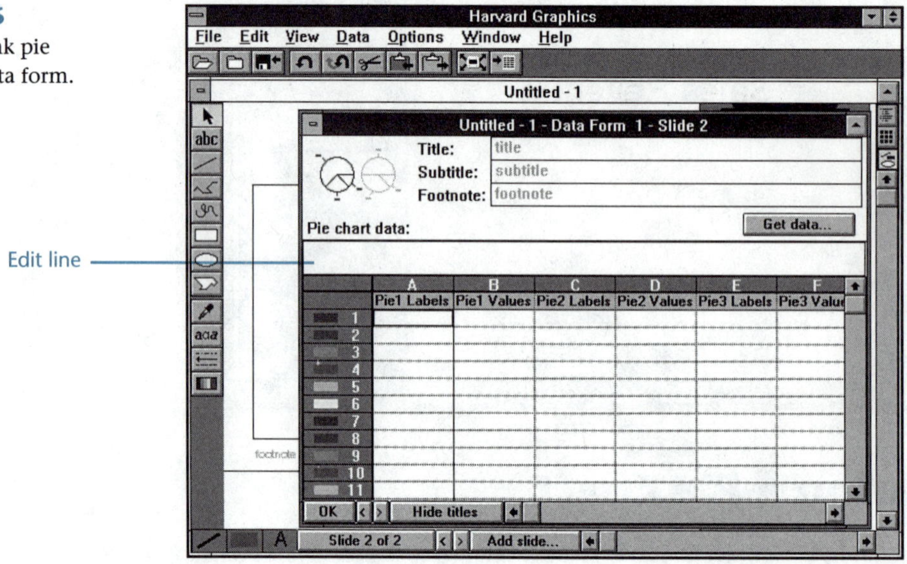

Edit line

Adding Slice Labels and Values

Each slice in the pie represents one of the four products—loafers, pumps, sneakers, and hikers—of the Bensig Shoe Corporation. The text that identifies a slice is the *slice label*. The data you enter for a slice is the *slice value*. As you enter data for a pie chart, the program displays the data in the *edit line*, which is above the actual pie data (refer to fig. 1.6). When you press the Enter key or click a different field, the program adds to the pie chart the data in the edit line.

Follow these steps to define the slice labels:

1. Click row 1 in the Pie1 Labels field and type **Loafers**.
2. Click row 2 in the Pie1 Labels field and type **Pumps**.
3. Click row 3 in the Pie1 Labels field and type **Sneakers**.
4. Click row 4 in the Pie1 Labels field and type **Hikers**.

To enter the slice values, follow these steps:

1. Click row 1 in the Pie1 Values field and type **12**.

2. Click row 2 in the Pie1 Values field and type **7**.
3. Click row 3 in the Pie1 Values field and type **9**.
4. Click row 4 in the Pie1 Values field and type **5**.

Entering the Title Information

In addition to the slice information, pie charts also have a title, a subtitle, and a footnote. The title of this pie chart is "Total Revenue." The subtitle is "By Product" to indicate to the audience that each slice represents a product. The footnote is "In millions" to inform your audience that the unit of measure for the chart's numeric data is millions.

Follow these steps to enter the title information into the pie chart:

1. Click the Title field in the pie chart data form and type **Total Revenue**.
2. Click the Subtitle field and type **By Product**.
3. Click the Footnote field and type **In millions**.
4. Click the OK button.

Figure 1.7 shows the completed Pie Chart data form in which you have defined four slices, one slice for each product. To see the entire chart, choose Preview Slide from the View menu or press F2. The slide is displayed filling the entire computer screen. Press any key to end the preview.

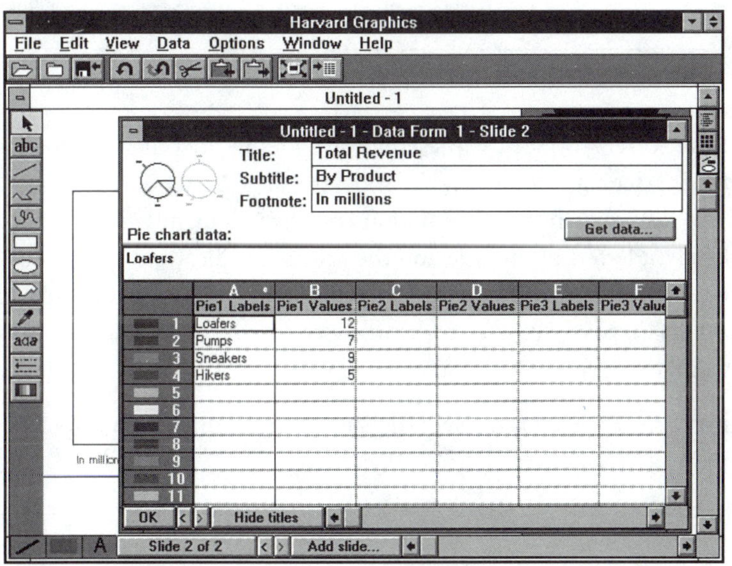

Fig. 1.7
The pie chart data form with the product sales data.

Viewing a Presentation in the Slide Sorter

Although the sales revenue presentation has two slides, you can see only one slide at a time within the Slide Editor. In the Slide Sorter, however, you can view many slides inside the same window. Observing your presentation in the Slide Sorter can give you an idea of how the slides combine to form the presentation. From the Slide Editor, you can see the presentation in the Slide Sorter by clicking the Slide Sorter icon or by selecting Slide Sorter from the View menu. Figure 1.8 shows the location of the icon in the Slide Editor.

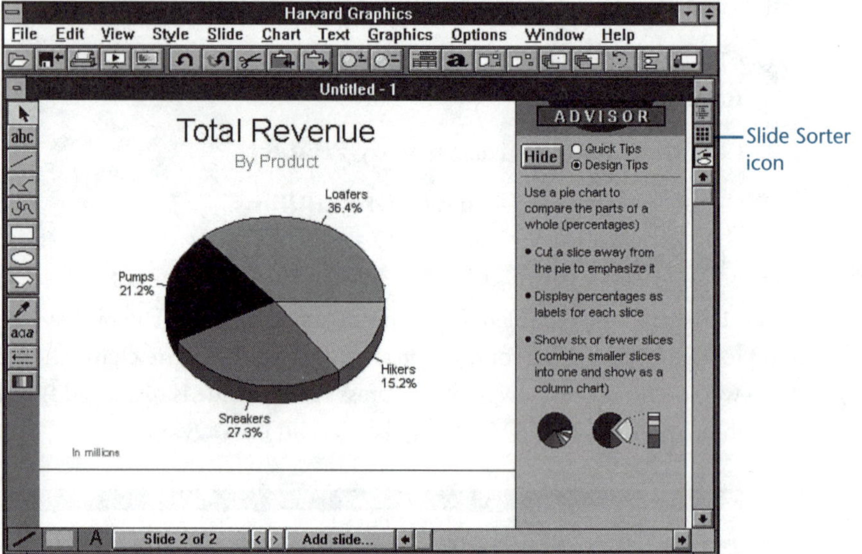

Fig. 1.8
The Slide Sorter icon beside the Slide Editor window.

In the Slide Sorter, you see the presentation slides in the order in which you created them (see fig. 1.9). Below the slide, the Slide Sorter displays the position of the slide within the presentation and the first eight letters of the slide title. The eight letters of the title and the position indicator distinguish slides that are similar in appearance. The slide highlighted with a box is the active slide in the Slide Sorter. You can perform specific editing operations—such as moving and deleting slides—on the active slide.

To return to the Slide Editor, select the Slide Editor icon, which is located below the Slide Sorter icon.

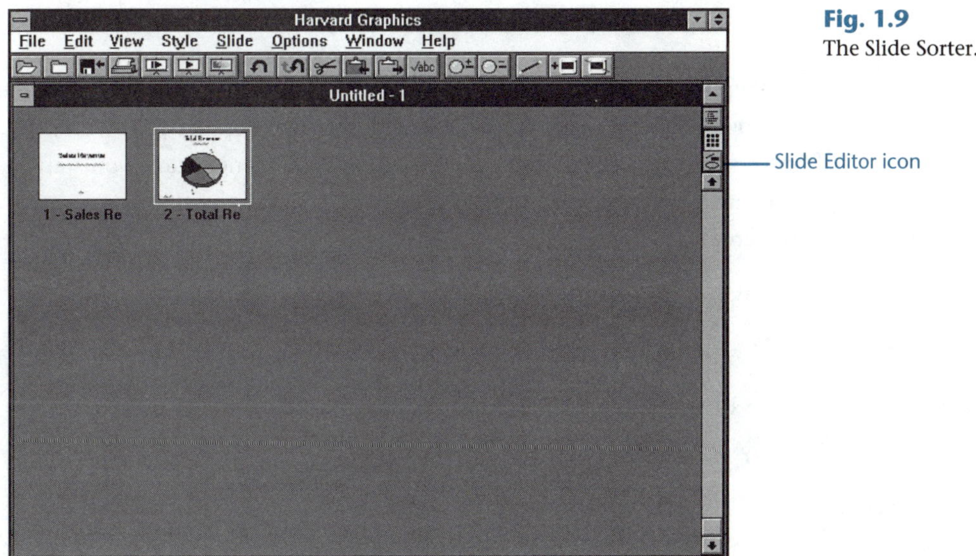

Fig. 1.9
The Slide Sorter.

Reviewing a Presentation

As you create and enhance presentations, you can use the ScreenShow feature to evaluate your work. ScreenShows are on-screen presentations in which the program displays each slide in order. As you view the slides, you can evaluate your presentation from an audience member's point of view. To review the presentation, follow these steps:

1. Choose ScreenS**h**ow from the File menu.

2. Choose From **B**eginning from the submenu.

   In a ScreenShow, each slide of your presentation remains on-screen until you press a key or click the right mouse button.

3. Press the space bar to display the next slide.

You can use the left-arrow key or the left mouse button to see the preceding slide. Pressing the Home key restarts the presentation from the beginning, and pressing the Esc key ends the ScreenShow.

Saving a Presentation

As you prepare slides in Harvard Graphics, your presentations exist inside the computer's memory only. To create a permanent copy of your work, you must save the presentation on your hard disk. The next time you start Harvard Graphics, you can load this file to continue working on your presentation.

To save your presentation, follow these steps:

1. Choose **S**ave from the **F**ile menu.

   Harvard Graphics displays the Save As dialog box (see fig. 1.10).

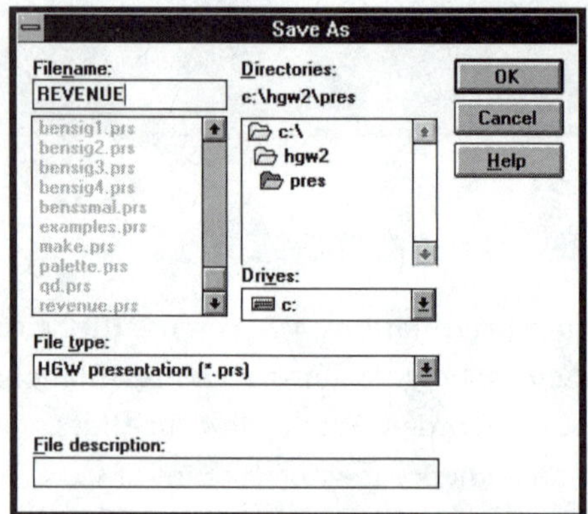

Fig. 1.10
The Save As dialog box.

2. Click the File**n**ame: text box and type **Revenue**.

3. Click the OK button.

   Harvard Graphics saves this file in the current directory (the directory displayed next to the Directory prompt). You should remember the directory name and the file name so that you can load this presentation the next time you're in Harvard Graphics.

Harvard Graphics has created a presentation file on your hard disk. Whenever you save a file, the program adds the extension PRS to the end of the file name.

After saving your presentation, you can continue to make enhancements and then save your changes to the file again. Use this technique to avoid losing data or to work with multiple copies of a presentation. You can save the presentation by using different file names to create unique copies for the slides.

From Here...

This quick start for creating a simple presentation familiarizes you with Harvard Graphics for Windows. You have learned how to create a presentation and how to add slides, using the default settings. You know how to add title and pie charts to a presentation, and you also have learned what to consider when choosing a style for each chart type.

The information in this quick start is a preview of what is to come in later chapters of the book. This information provides a foundation for learning the additional features of Harvard Graphics and for understanding how each feature relates to the process of creating a presentation.

Chapter 2

Learning Harvard Graphics for Windows Basics

Harvard Graphics for Windows is a powerful software package that has an extensive set of features to help you create effective presentations. If you try to master all the features at one time, you undoubtedly will feel overwhelmed. If you first learn the basic components of a presentation and the common operations used to create presentations, you will be better prepared to master the many features of the product. This chapter presents the basic components and operations of the program and explains how they relate to the process of creating a presentation.

The chapter begins by explaining how to work with an entire presentation. You learn how to create a new presentation and how to save the presentation on your hard disk. You also learn how to load the saved presentation into Harvard Graphics to make further enhancements. All these tasks are fundamental parts of working with a presentation. They enable you to create and enhance Harvard Graphics presentations.

After covering the basics of working with an entire presentation, this chapter explores the components within a presentation. The fundamental building block of a presentation is the slide. This chapter explains how to add a slide to a presentation and how to enter data for the chart displayed on the slide. You then learn about features that you use to enhance the slide and the chart on the slide.

In this chapter, you learn how to do the following:

- Open an existing presentation
- Add slides to a presentation
- Edit a presentation

The later sections in this chapter provide information on features that are helpful when you're working with a presentation. You may not use these features every time you use Harvard Graphics. However, these features address specific needs for working with a presentation. For example, you learn how to use the Slide Sorter or Outliner to change the order of your slides in the presentation. You learn how to move to a specific slide within the presentation to make enhancements to that slide. This chapter ends by covering the Help system, which provides valuable information on the features of Harvard Graphics.

When you have finished this chapter, you should have enough understanding of Harvard Graphics to create a simple presentation. Beyond creating slides and saving a presentation, you will also be able to determine what features of Harvard Graphics to use to make enhancements and changes.

Other chapters expand on the basics you have learned. The chapters on specific chart types, Chapters 3 through 6, provide more information on creating slides in a presentation and enhancing the charts displayed on the slides. The chapters on the Slide Sorter and the Outliner expand on the parts of this chapter that introduce you to editing an entire presentation. This chapter provides a foundation for the remaining chapters of the book.

Working with Presentations

A *presentation* is a collection of slides stored in computer memory or in a file on your hard disk. As you begin a presentation, you create a new presentation in memory. The following section teaches you how to start a presentation and how to add slides. "Saving a Presentation" explains how to transfer the slides you create from memory to a file you can retrieve later. "Opening an Existing Presentation" explains how to load a presentation from a file into memory. After you load the presentation, you can continue enhancing slides and creating new slides.

Creating a New Presentation

You must create a new presentation before you can prepare your slides. You should have in mind a theme for your presentation. If you don't have a theme, you should have a general idea of your presentation's content. A theme helps ensure that your slides are consistent; if they are consistent with the theme, they will be consistent with each other. A theme also helps you determine the order of your slides. You can arrange them in an order that emphasizes the theme by placing slides that lead up to the theme earlier in the presentation than slides that analyze or draw conclusions from the theme.

When you first start Harvard Graphics, it displays a start-up screen and a menu bar containing the File, Window, and Help menus along with the Main Harvard Graphics Window. The File menu contains commands—such as opening, saving, and printing—that you use to perform operations on presentations and presentation files. The Window menu contains commands you use to manipulate the windows owned by Harvard Graphics. You use the Help menu to access help information, including the index of help topics and keyboard help. You use the File menu for most of the tasks explained in this chapter. The Main Harvard Graphics window provides quick buttons to create a new presentation or open a previous one. Other menus and commands are explained as their operations are presented in the book.

To create a new presentation, do the following:

1. Start Windows if you haven't done so already.
2. Double-click the Harvard Graphics icon.
3. Click the Create New Presentation... button in the Main Harvard Graphics window.

After the program creates the presentation, Harvard Graphics displays the New Presentation dialog box, which is identical to the Add Slide dialog box, both of which allow you to add slides to a presentation (see fig. 2.1).

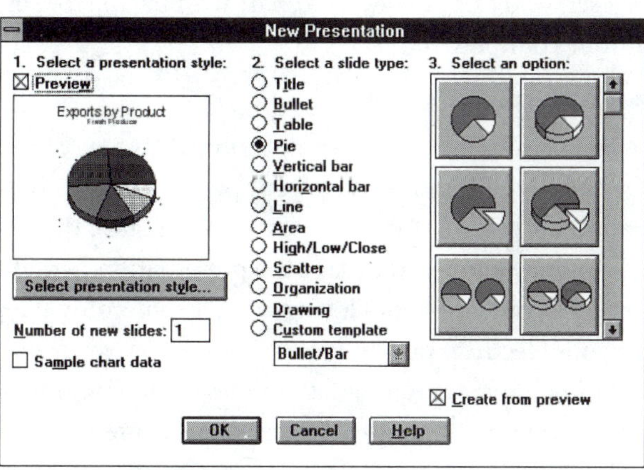

Fig. 2.1
The New Presentation dialog box.

You use this dialog box to create all the slides of a presentation. Step 1 in the dialog box is to Select a presentation style. Presentation styles control the overall appearance of a presentation. In most cases, you will create or use a style you feel is effective for the slides you typically present. The section "Working with Presentation Styles" in Chapter 16, "Enhancing a Presentation," explains how to create your own presentation style and how to use an existing one for step 1 of this dialog box. Step 2 of the dialog box is to select the type for the slide—in this case the first slide of your new presentation—that you are creating. You click the button next to the appropriate type. When you click the button, an example of the slide based on your presentation style is displayed in the Preview box on the left side of the dialog box. Click the Preview option in order not to show the preview if you are in a hurry. The Drawing button enables you to create a blank slide without a chart. The Custom Template button enables you to create a chart from a template. The available Templates are listed in the box below the option. (See the section "Working with Templates" in Chapter 16, "Enhancing a Presentation".)

Step 3 in the dialog box is to select an option or style of chart for your new slide. If the chart in the preview appears the same way you want your slide to appear, you can skip step 3 in the dialog box. The chart you create will use the same settings as the preview. To use one of the styles in the list, click the Create from Preview option to disable it, and then select the style you want to use. The Number of New Slides text box enables you to create many slides of the same type at one time. To create more than one slide, type the number in this box. You use the Sample Chart Data option to create a chart with an example data set. You can preview the chart with data before entering the actual data from your presentation.

Saving a Presentation

You use the File menu's Save and Save As commands to create presentation files on your hard disk. You must save your presentation before exiting Harvard Graphics if you want to continue working on or display the presentation later. You may also want to save the presentation periodically while you are working in order to avoid losing work if something happens to your computer or your electrical power. When you exit Harvard Graphics or close a presentation, the program removes the slides from memory; however, if you save the information in a file, you can load the presentation at any time in Harvard Graphics. If you exit Harvard Graphics or close a presentation and you do not save the information, the presentation is lost.

The Save command saves the presentation, using the current file name. The Save As command enables you to enter a new file name for the presentation. If you are saving a presentation for the first time, however, both the Save and Save As commands display the Save As dialog box, shown in figure 2.2, because you have not named the presentation. After the presentation has been saved, use the Save command to update the file with your latest changes. Use the Save As command to create a new file with a new name.

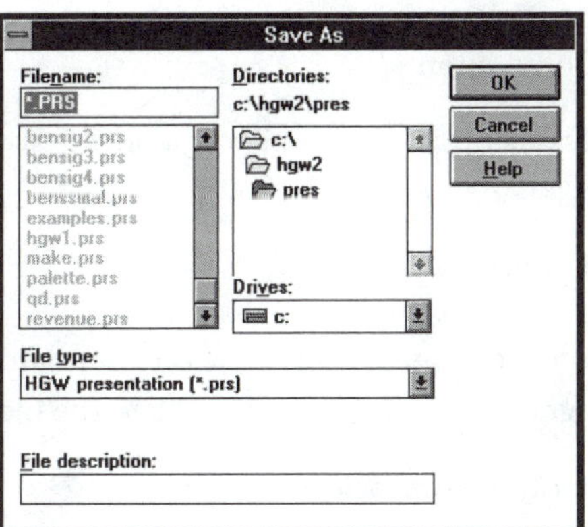

Fig. 2.2
The Save As dialog box.

The Save As dialog box contains the Filename text box, in which you type the name of your presentation. The program creates in the current directory a file with the name you enter. (The current directory name appears next to the Directory prompt.) You should remember the directory and the name of the file so that you can load this presentation the next time you are in Harvard Graphics. Other presentation files in the directory are listed in the Files list box. Other directories and drives on your hard disk are listed in the Directories/Drives list box. The setting in the File Type list box at the bottom of the dialog box determines the type of file that will be created. See "Exporting Data" in Chapter 15, "Importing, Exporting, and Linking Data," for information on the different file types. You use the File description field to enter a brief description about the presentation content. You use this description when opening an existing presentation to help you determine the correct presentation to open.

After you save the presentation, it remains in memory so that you can continue to make changes to the slides and then update the file with the Save command on the File menu.

Tip
When you choose a name for a file, use a name that in some way reveals the content of the slides.

To save a presentation, follow these steps:

1. Choose Save **A**s from the File menu to specify a new file name. (You can also choose Save to update a file without changing the name.)

2. Click the Filename text box and type the name of the file.

   Because the file name can contain eight letters only, you may need to abbreviate or use acronyms. The name *BensRev*, for instance, indicates that the presentation contains information concerning the revenues of the Bensig Corporation.

3. Click the File description box and type a brief description of your presentation content.

4. Click the OK button.

Harvard Graphics creates a presentation file on your hard disk. Whenever you save a file, the program adds the extension PRS to the file name.

Opening an Existing Presentation

When you start Harvard Graphics, you may not begin with a new presentation. At times, you may save your work in progress and resume the work later. As explained in the preceding section, when you save a presentation, Harvard Graphics creates on the hard disk the file with the name you specify. You use the Open dialog box to open the presentation (see fig. 2.3).

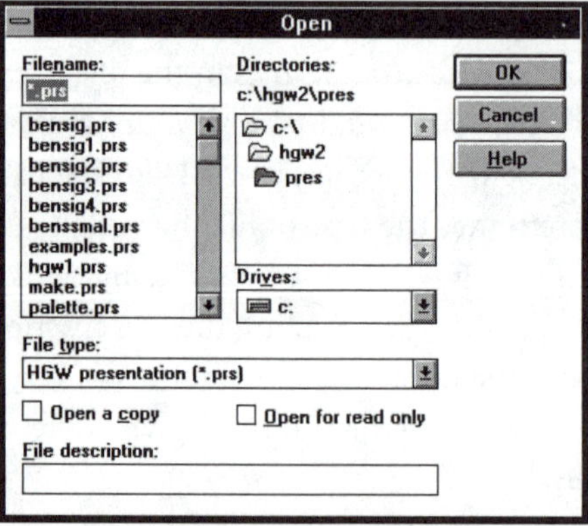

Fig. 2.3
The Open dialog box.

The Files list box in the Open dialog box lists all the files in the current directory. To load a file from the list, select the file by clicking the name, or type the name in the Filename text box. The current directory is listed next to the Directory prompt. The other available drives and directories on your system are listed in the Directories/Drives list box. You specify the type of file you are loading in the File Type list box. (See "Importing Data" in Chapter 15, "Importing, Exporting, and Linking Data," for information on opening files with different types.)

The Open a Copy option enables you to work with several copies of a presentation. The copy is opened as a new presentation and is completely separate from the original. In other words, changes made to one copy have no effect on the other. The Open for Read Only option is used to view presentations on a network. If another user is modifying a file on a network volume, use this option just to view the latest slides from the file.

To open an existing presentation, follow these steps:

1. Choose **O**pen from the File menu. The Open dialog box appears (refer to fig. 2.3).

2. Specify the file by typing the name of the presentation in the Filename text box of the dialog box and by clicking OK. Harvard Graphics searches the current directory for this file.

   Alternatively, you can load the file by double-clicking the file name in the Files list box. This box displays all the presentation files that the current directory contains.

The Directories/Drives list box displays the drives and directories available on your computer. If your file is saved in a directory other than the current directory, you must make the directory that contains the changed file the current directory. When you change the directory, Harvard Graphics displays the presentation files stored in that directory.

To change the current directory, you can double-click the drive or directory in the Directories/Drives list box. Alternatively, you can type the drive and directory names in the Filename field—do not type the presentation file name—and click the OK button. This step changes the directory and shows the current files in the Files list box.

If you are not sure which presentation to open, click files in the file list box to display your description of the presentation in the File description box.

Closing a Presentation

You can close the presentation on which you are working. Closing the presentation frees space on your desktop and frees the computer memory used to store the presentation.

> **Caution**
>
> Make sure that you save your slides before you close the presentation; otherwise, you lose all the changes made since you last saved the presentation.

When you exit Harvard Graphics, the program closes all presentations in memory. If you haven't saved a presentation after making changes, Harvard Graphics asks whether you want to save the presentation before closing. To close a presentation before exiting, select the File menu and choose Close.

Adding Slides to a Presentation

The basic element of every presentation is the slide. You present all your charts, text, and drawings on slides. Slides are defined by the images they present and by their location in the presentation. The first slide of a presentation usually introduces the presentation or the speaker, for example. You use the slides in the body of a presentation to communicate the most significant information to the audience, and the final slides generally present conclusions and draw the presentation to a close.

Before creating slides, you must determine the topic or theme of your presentation. To help the audience see the relationship among the slides, you must communicate your theme on one of the first slides, and each subsequent slide should relate to the theme. After you consider the theme of your presentation, you can create the slides.

Picking a Chart Type for a Slide

The primary step when you create a slide is picking a type for the chart that will be displayed on the slide. A *slide* presents data and images to the audience. A *chart* is one type of object that can be displayed on a slide to communicate the data. In most cases, each slide has one chart that is the primary focus, or reason, for the slide. You create this chart with the slide.

The following sections discuss the chart types that can be displayed on a slide. The section "Adding the Slide" explains how to create a slide and how to set the type for the chart. Every slide does not have to display a chart. One of the choices for the chart type is Drawing, which indicates that all the images on the slide will be created with the Slide Editor (see Chapter 12, "Drawing in Harvard Graphics"). You can also create many charts on a slide by using the information in the section "Adding Charts to Slides" in Chapter 12.

The four major chart types in Harvard Graphics are text charts, organization charts, pie charts, and XY charts. You learn how to create these chart types in the following sections.

Text Charts. You use text charts to present textual information, such as the presentation's title. On a text chart, you use words and phrases to communicate the information. Your audience reads the content of the slide as you speak. The three text chart types are the title chart, the bullet chart, and the table chart.

The following list explains the main uses of these text charts:

- The *title chart* is used primarily to communicate general information, such as the identity of the speaker or the theme of the presentation (see fig. 2.4).

Sales Revenue
Bensig Corporation
1991

Fig. 2.4
A title chart.

- The *bullet chart* is used primarily to present a list of topics or facts that you intend to discuss in the designated order (see fig. 2.5).
- The *table chart* is used primarily to present text or numeric data that is best shown in a table or columns (see fig. 2.6).

Fig. 2.5
A bullet chart.

Sales Goals

Bensig Corporation

- Increase Market Awareness
- Reach 110% of Quota
- Obtain 5 New Accounts Per Region
- Expand Sales Regions

Fig. 2.6
A table chart.

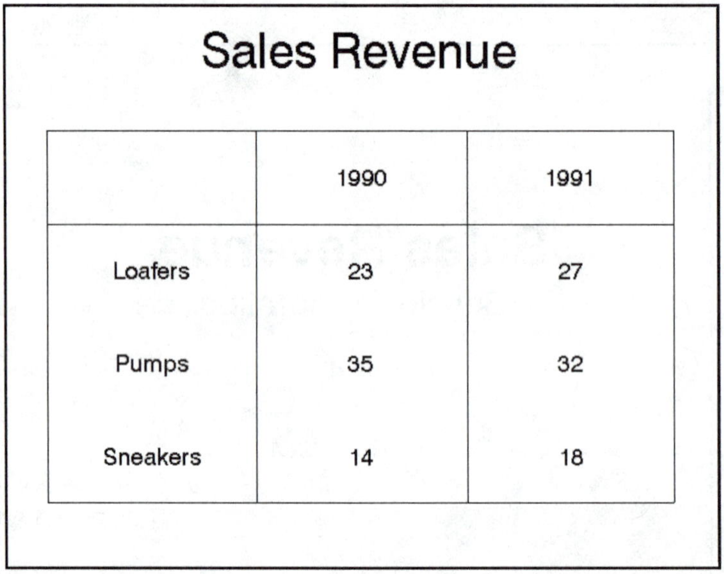

Sales Revenue

	1990	1991
Loafers	23	27
Pumps	35	32
Sneakers	14	18

For more information on text charts, see Chapter 3, "Creating Text Charts."

Organization Charts. You use organization charts to present graphically the members of a company or organization. Each box in the chart represents a member of the organization. You can enter a name, a title, and a comment about each member. Figure 2.7 shows an example of an organization chart. In Chapter 4, "Creating Organization Charts," you learn how to add, delete, and move members to new locations on the organization chart.

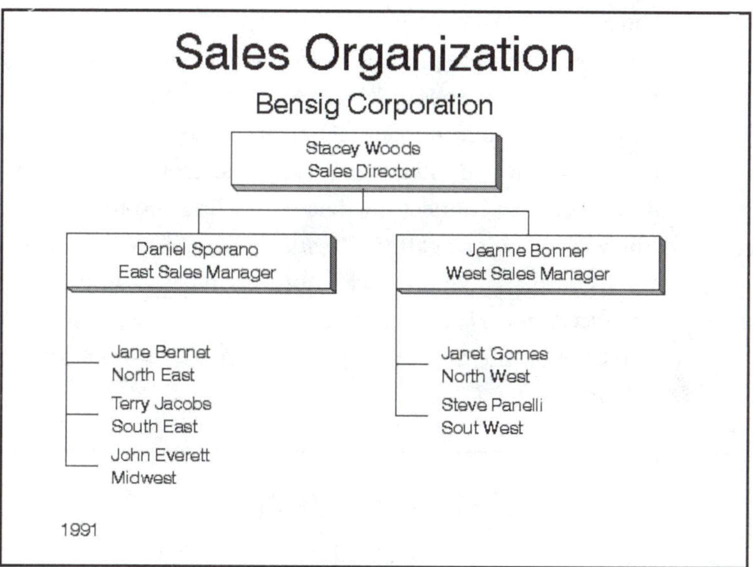

Fig. 2.7 An organizational chart.

Pie Charts. Pie charts are ideal for presenting numeric data. You determine the size of each slice of the pie chart by the corresponding data; larger values represent larger slices in the pie. Pie charts show the relationship between the parts (the slices) and the whole (the pie). With a pie chart, the audience easily can compare the information you convey in the slices. Figure 2.8 provides an example of a pie chart. Chapter 6, "Creating Pie Charts," explains the features you use to create and enhance a pie chart.

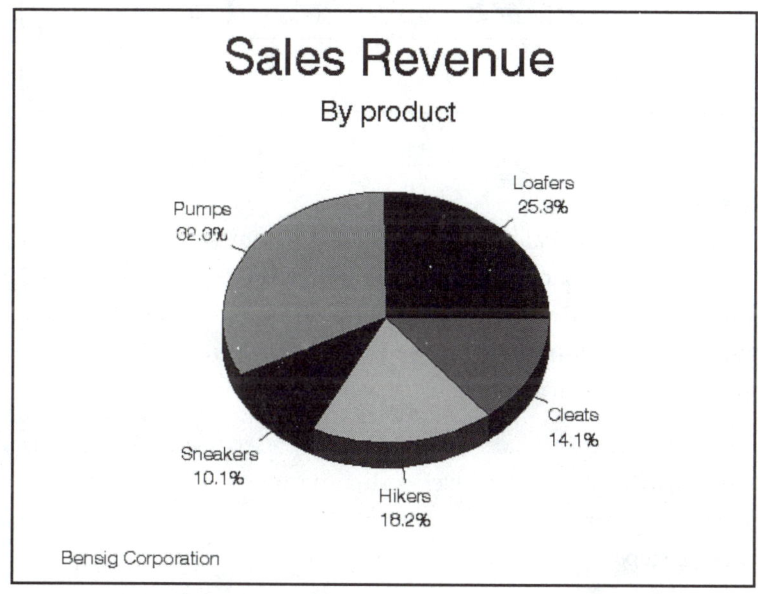

Fig. 2.8 A pie chart.

XY Charts. You also use XY charts for numeric data. This chart type graphs data on two axes, as if you were plotting coordinates on graph paper. Harvard Graphics supports several varieties of XY charts. The most common is the *bar chart,* which displays vertical or horizontal bars to represent the data. Figure 2.9 shows an example bar chart. *Line charts* draw lines from one point of data to the next. *Area charts* also connect the data with a line and then fill the area beneath the line with a color or pattern. *High/Low/Close charts* are a specialized variety of XY charts that graph stock information based on the different values for the stocks. *Scatter charts* represent each point with a single marker. For more information on the different types of XY charts, see Chapter 5, "Creating XY Charts."

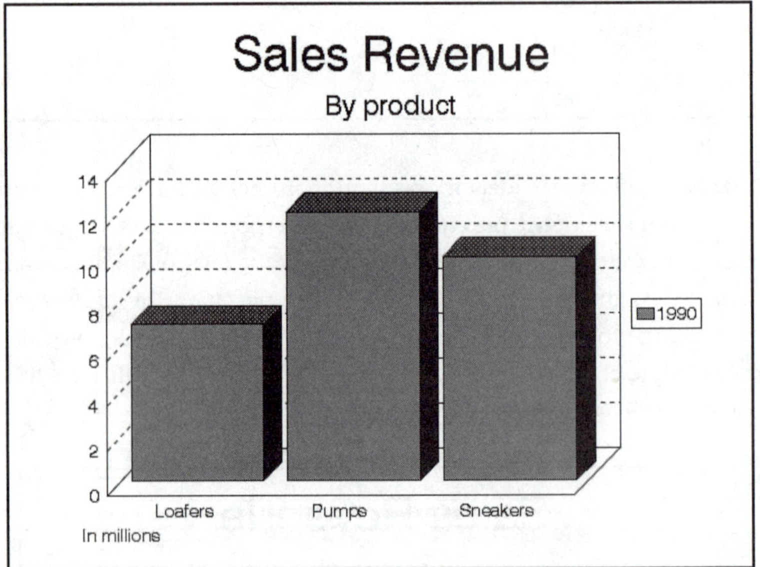

Fig. 2.9
A bar chart—the most common XY chart.

Adding the Slide

You use the Add Slide dialog box to add slides to a presentation (refer to fig. 2.1). If you create a new presentation, Harvard Graphics displays the New Presentation dialog box for you to create your first slide. Otherwise, you select Add Slide from the Slide menu in the Slide Editor or Slide Sorter to display the Add Slide dialog box.

After you determine the chart type that best represents your data, you can create the chart with the slide by choosing the appropriate button in the Add Slide dialog box. To create a slide with a vertical bar chart, for example, follow these steps:

1. Click the Vertical Bar button in the Select a slide type: list.

2. Click the OK button in the Add Slide dialog box.

   The data form for a bar chart is displayed for you to enter the data in the chart. See the following section for more information.

3. After you have entered your data, click the OK button at the bottom of the data form.

Entering Data

Each chart type provides a chart-specific data form in which you enter data. Figure 2.10 shows the XY chart data form, which is used to enter data for bar charts. The top part of the form contains the fields for chart titles, which clarify the information in the chart. The bottom portion of the form contains rows and columns where you enter data for the chart. The first column contains text that identifies the different sets of bars in the chart. The remaining columns contain the data values that determine the heights of the bars. See Chapter 5, "Creating XY Charts," for more information.

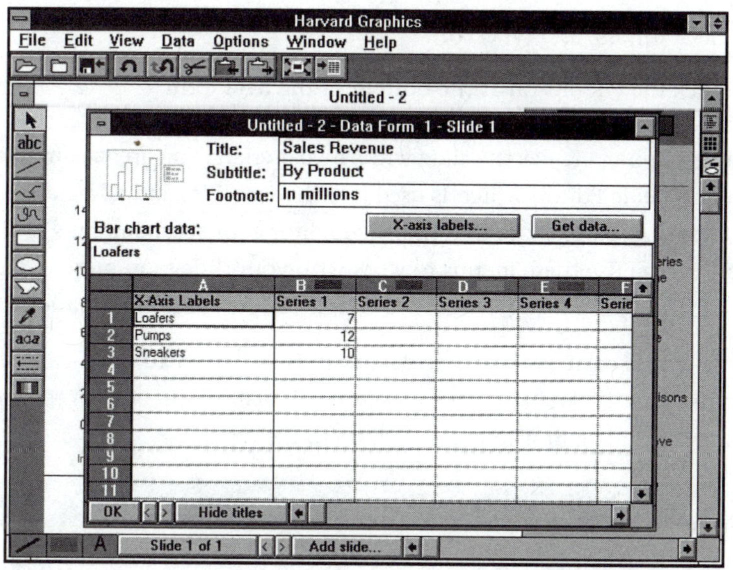

Fig. 2.10
The XY chart data form.

To enter information in a field on a data form, click the field. When you select a field, it is highlighted by a box to indicate that the field is active. As you type data, the information is entered in the active field. You can also use the Tab and Shift-Tab keys to make a field active. Follow these steps to enter data and title information to match the information in figure 2.10:

1. Click the Title field.
2. Type the title of the chart: **Sales Revenue**.
3. Click the Subtitle field.
4. Type the subtitle of the chart: **By product**.
5. Click the Footnote field.
6. Type the footnote of the chart: **In millions**.
7. Click cell A1.
8. Type the label of the first bar: **Loafers**.
9. Click cell B1.
10. Type the numeric value for the first bar: **7**.
11. Click cell A2, and type the label of the second bar: **Pumps**.
12. Click cell B2, and type the numeric value for the second bar: **12**.
13. Click cell A3, and type **Sneakers**.
14. Click cell B3, and type **10**.
15. Click the OK button at the bottom of the data form.

Harvard Graphics creates the slide with the bar chart. You are viewing the slide in the Slide Editor, which is used to enhance slides and add graphic objects (see fig. 2.11). Note that the Slide Editor adds several menus to the menu bar. You use these menus to work with your slides and presentations. See Chapter 12, "Drawing in Harvard Graphics," for more information.

When you first create a chart, the data form is displayed automatically. After you enter the initial data, you can use the Edit Data command on the Chart menu in the Slide Editor to make updates to the data.

Design Note

When entering data into a chart, make sure that you present the information in a way that your audience can easily understand. For text charts, limit the text to relevant and significant phrases. Remember that numeric charts become crowded if you enter too much data. The slices in your pie chart are difficult to distinguish if you create too many or too small slices, for example. Your audience may become disinterested if they are spending more time reading your slides than listening to you speak. Use the charts to enhance your presentation.

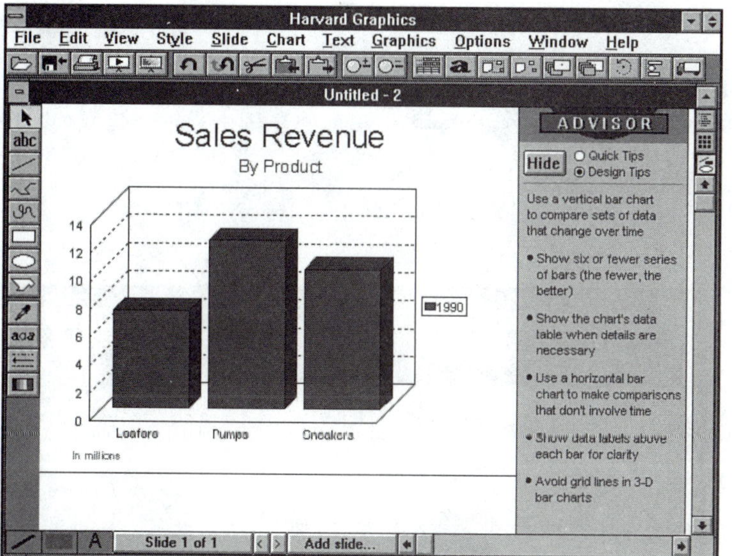

Fig. 2.11 The vertical bar chart in the Slide Editor.

Changing Chart Options

Harvard Graphics provides many features that enable you to enhance the appearance of your charts. These commands are available on the Chart menu in the Slide Editor. The Chart Options command on the Chart menu contains options that are specific to particular charts. For example, with bar charts, you can change the style and width of the bars. For more information on the options for specific chart types, see the chapters that explain how to create a chart of that type (Chapters 3 through 6).

In addition to the Chart Options command, the Chart menu contains other commands that are relevant to different chart types. For XY charts, you can modify the chart legend, grid, frame, and bars. In figure 2.12, the legend on the side of the chart points out that the values for the bars are taken from the statistics for the year 1990. The frame is displayed behind the chart and outlines the back, bottom, and left side of the chart, where the numbers are displayed. The grid is represented by the dotted lines within the frame. The frame and grid lines provide visual aids for evaluating the bars of the chart. All these options contribute to the effectiveness of the chart. For more information on these elements or on the options available for other chart types, see Chapters 3 through 6 on creating charts of each chart type.

> **Design Note**
>
> Your objective when you modify chart options is to create a chart that communicates the data. The audience must be able to interpret the slide's information with little or no explanation. The legend is an example of an option that can help your audience understand the slide.

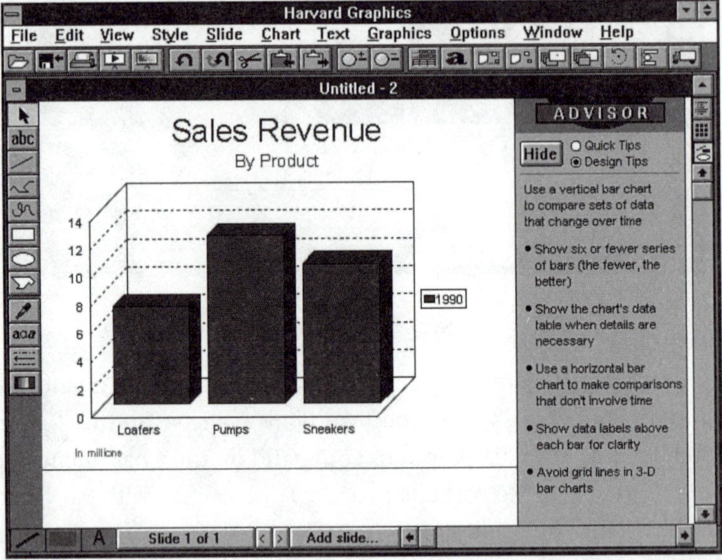

Fig. 2.12 A slide showing the grid, legend, and frame.

> **Design Note**
>
> The data in your chart must be easy to see from any location in the presentation room. A grid enables viewers to compare the height of the bars without reading the actual numeric values. You also can use large fonts that contrast with the background to make your slides easier to see.

You should work with the available chart options until you have created a chart that is visually appealing and clearly presents your information.

Previewing the Slide

The preview process is an important and often neglected part of creating a presentation. You can use Harvard Graphics' preview feature to evaluate the effectiveness of the changes you make to the chart. When you preview a slide, the images are shown using the entire screen without obstructions from windows or menu bars. As you examine your slides, consider the appearance of the slide and the relationship between the slide information and the theme. The Preview Slide command on the Slide menu enables you to view a slide unobstructed by windows, menus, or icons (see fig. 2.13).

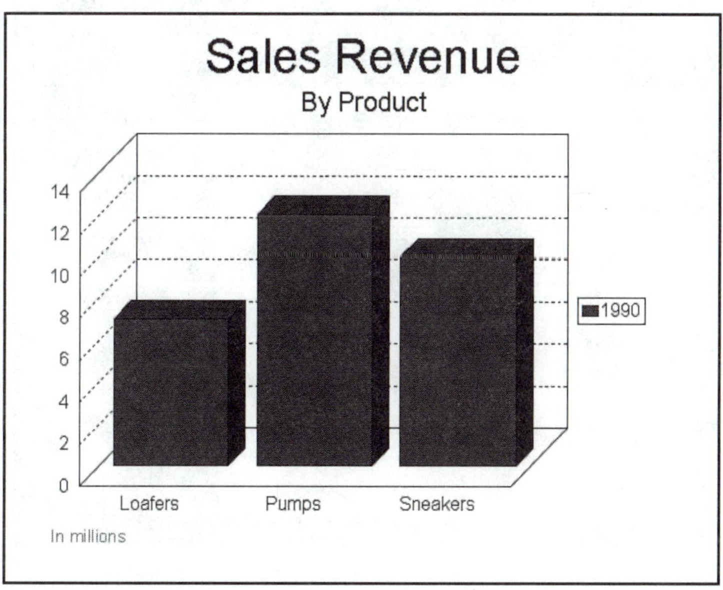

Fig. 2.13
A chart shown in Preview.

To preview a slide, choose Preview Slide from the View menu or press F2. You can press any key to end the preview.

Drawing on the Slide

In addition to changing options that control the appearance of your chart, you also can enhance slides with graphics objects. You use the Slide Editor to add graphics to a slide. To focus attention on a particular item on a slide, for example, you can add an arrow. In addition to arrows, you can add rectangles, circles, lines, polygons, text, and clip-art symbols. You add objects by clicking the icon that represents the object in the Slide Editor toolbox. Figure 2.14 shows the chart in the Slide Editor and the tool you use to add rectangles.

To add a rectangle to the bottom of the bar chart, follow these steps:

1. Click the Rectangle tool icon.
2. Click below Loafers and hold the mouse button.

3. Drag the cross-hair pointer to below Sneakers.

4. Release the mouse button. A rectangle is displayed below the chart (see to fig. 2.14).

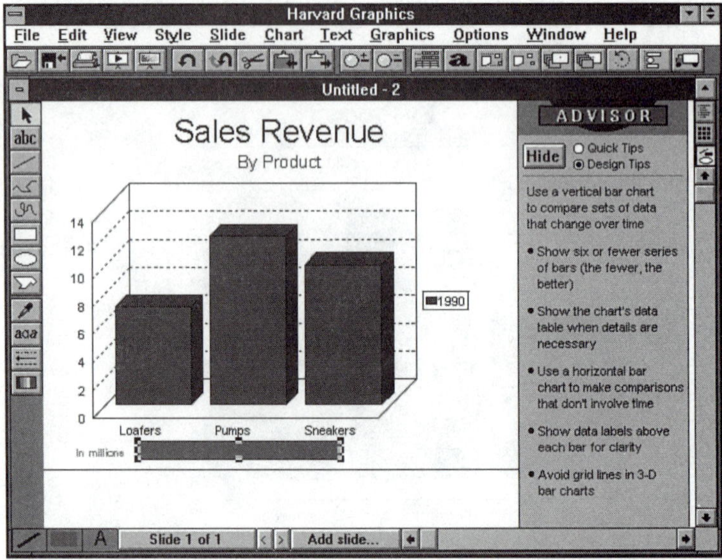

Fig. 2.14 The Slide Editor showing the bar chart and the added rectangle.

You have created an object by using the tools of the Slide Editor. You defined the rectangle by clicking one corner and dragging the pointer to the other corner. When you released the button, Harvard Graphics created the rectangle based on the two positions of the pointer. (See Chapter 12, "Drawing in Harvard Graphics," for more information.)

When you select a tool for drawing, the tool remains selected after you create an object so that you can create many objects at one time. To stop drawing, click the Selection tool icon, which is the icon with the arrow-shaped pointer, located in the top row of icons.

You also can use the Slide Editor to modify the text attributes for any text on a slide. Data from a title chart, the footnote in a pie chart, or the members of an organization chart are examples of text you can change by using the Slide Editor. Chapter 7, "Working with Text," explains how to add and modify the text of a slide; Chapter 12, "Drawing in Harvard Graphics," explains how to add graphics objects to a slide; and Chapter 13, "Enhancing Drawings and Objects," explains how to modify the appearance of the objects.

Creating Additional Slides

When you create a presentation, Harvard Graphics displays the Add Slide dialog box in which you create the first slide. The Add Slide button in the Slide Editor, shown in figure 2.15, also displays the Add Slide dialog box, in which you create additional slides. The program adds each new slide to the presentation following the slide you currently are viewing.

To create a new slide, click the Add Slide button to display the Add Slide dialog box. You also can use the Add Slide command on the Slide menu to display the dialog box.

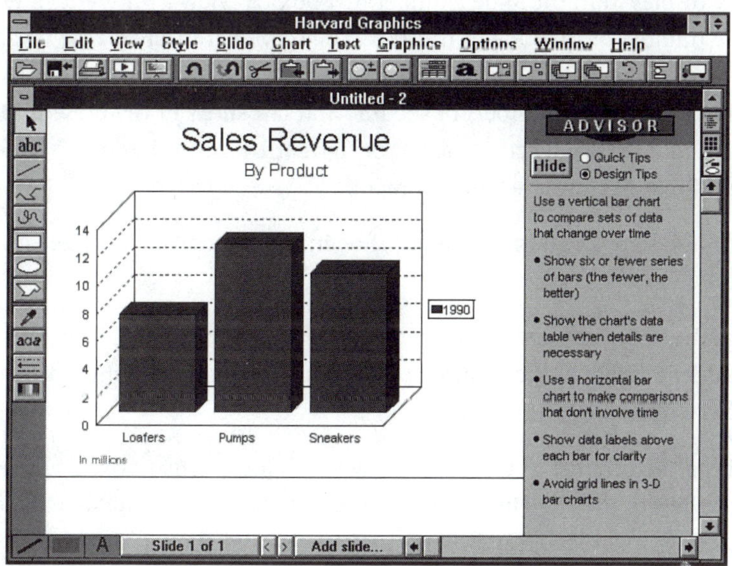

Fig. 2.15
The Slide Editor window and the Add Slide button.

Moving to Slides

In the Slide Editor, you can view only one slide in a presentation at a time. The button on the bottom left corner of the Slide Editor window indicates how many slides are in the presentation and which slide the Slide Editor is displaying. When you click this button, the program displays the Go to Slide dialog box, which enables you to view different slides of the presentation in the Slide Editor (see fig. 2.16).

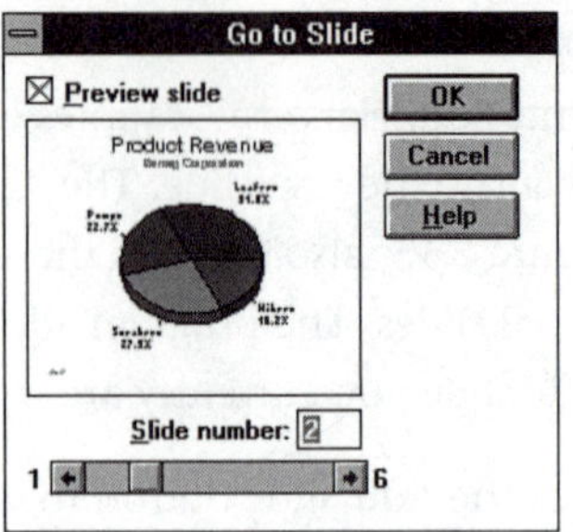

Fig. 2.16
The Go to Slide dialog box.

In the Go to Slide dialog box, the number of the current slide in the Slide Editor is displayed in the Slide Number text box. To view a different slide, type the number of the slide in this box. The scroll bar in the dialog box also enables you to move to a slide. The right and left ends of the scroll bar show, respectively, the slide numbers of the first and last slides in the presentation. To view a different slide, click the left or right arrow until the correct slide number shows in the Slide Number text box.

Follow these steps to go to a different slide in the presentation in the Slide Editor:

1. In the Slide Editor window, click the button that shows the current and total numbers of slides in the presentation. Harvard Graphics displays the Go to Slide dialog box.

2. Type the number of the slide in the Slide Number text box. You see a preview of the slide in the box in the middle of the Go to Slide dialog box. If you are in a hurry, click the Preview slide box to disable the preview.

3. Click the OK button.

Tip
If your presentation contains mostly text charts or if you develop your slides from an outline of the presentation content, you will benefit from the editing capabilities provided in the Outliner.

Editing a Presentation

As you create the slides of a presentation, you must evaluate the entire presentation for content and effectiveness. Harvard Graphics provides many features to help you with this task. You can change the order of the slides in the presentation, for example, by using the Slide Sorter and the Outliner. The Slide Sorter displays miniature images of the slides in your presentation; the Outliner shows the textual chart information, such as the body of a text chart and the title of a numeric chart.

Using the Slide Sorter

The Slide Sorter enables you to view many slides simultaneously. The Slide Sorter arranges the slides in order of creation. You can change the order of your slides by clicking and dragging a slide to a new location. You also can add, delete, and copy slides. Chapter 10, "Using the Slide Sorter," explains how to edit your presentations with this feature.

Tip

The Slide Sorter provides a graphical interface for editing a presentation, especially a presentation containing several numeric charts.

You have two ways to get to the Slide Sorter from the Slide Editor or Outliner. You can click the Slide Sorter icon on the right side of the Slide Editor window, or you can choose Slide Sorter from the View menu. Three icons are located on the right sides of the Slide Editor, Slide Sorter, and Outliner windows. The top icon resembles a simple outline and is used to switch to the Outliner. The second icon shows nine small squares that represent slides. This icon is for the Slide Sorter. The third icon, for the Slide Editor, has objects that are created in the Slide Editor, such as a circle or square. Figure 2.17 shows the icons you use to move between the Slide Sorter, the Slide Editor, and the Outliner.

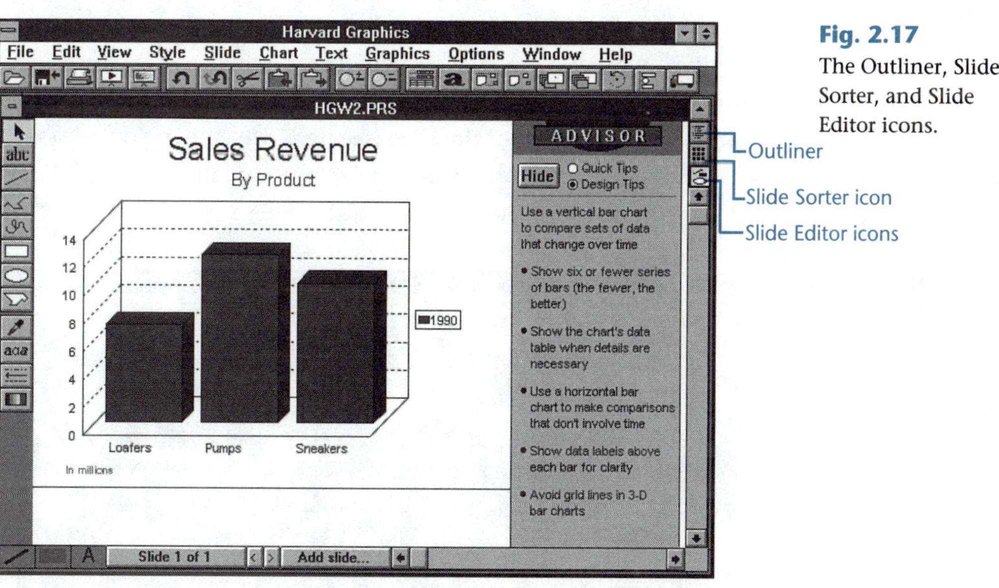

Fig. 2.17 The Outliner, Slide Sorter, and Slide Editor icons.

Figure 2.18 shows the Slide Sorter displaying five slides. The Slide Sorter represents these slides as scaled-down images. Although you cannot read the text in the slides, Harvard Graphics displays enough of the image to help you distinguish one slide from another. Harvard Graphics also displays the title of the slide below the image.

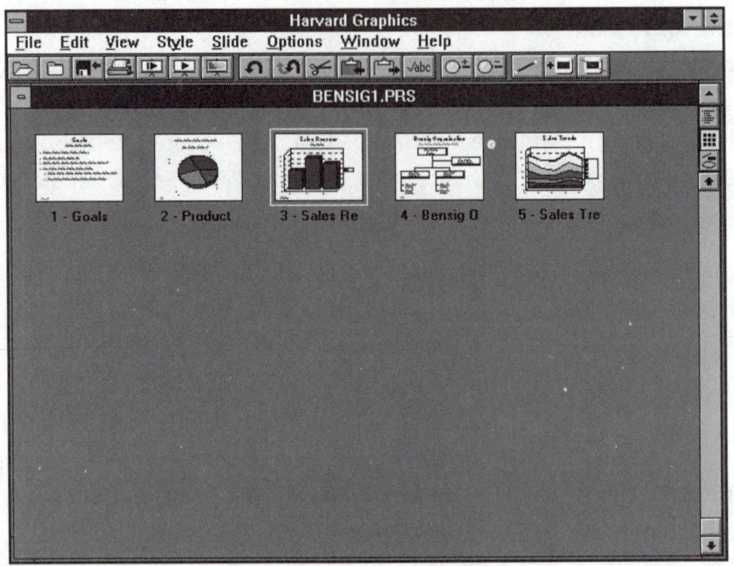

Fig. 2.18
The Slide Sorter window.

You move slides in the Slide Sorter by selecting and dragging the slide to a new position. When you select a slide, a highlight box appears around the slide, indicating that it is active. As you drag the slide, a *slide placeholder,* the image of a hand that points to the new location, appears between slides to indicate the new location of the slide (see fig. 2.19). When you release the mouse button, the slide appears in its new location, and the other slides adjust to make room for the relocated slide.

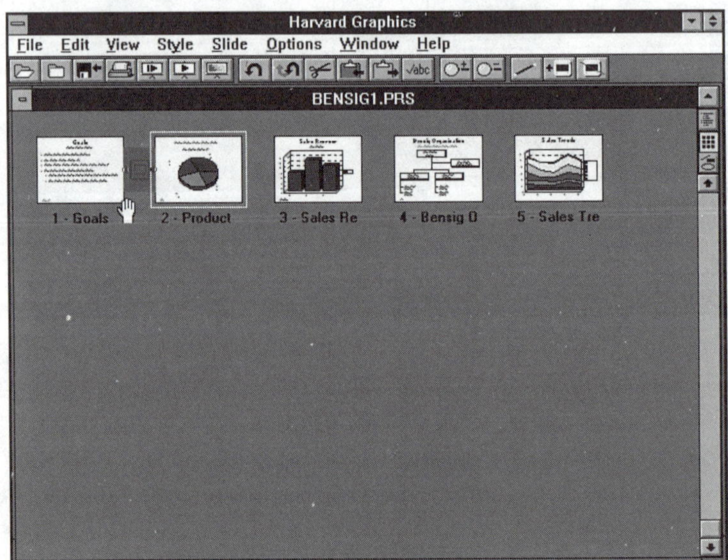

Fig. 2.19
The slide placeholder.

Suppose that you have the presentation shown in figure 2.18. To make the bar chart the second slide in this presentation, follow these steps:

1. Click the bar chart and hold the mouse button.

2. Drag the pointer until the slide placeholder appears between the first two slides of the presentation.

3. Release the mouse button.

The slides are now in the new order.

Using the Outliner

You use the Outliner to create and edit the slides of a presentation. An outline contains topics that represent the slides in the presentation. Topics also show the data in bullet, title, and organization charts. Figure 2.20 shows a presentation with four slides in the Outliner window. The icons on the left side of the outline indicate which topics are slides, as opposed to data from a chart. The top two slides are text charts, as indicated by the text chart icon. The second chart is a bullet chart. The topics indented below the slide topic are subtopics that comprise the data of the bullet chart. The bottom two charts are numeric data charts and have a small bar chart on the icon. Chapter 11, "Using the Outliner," discusses the features of the Outliner and explains how they are used to edit a presentation.

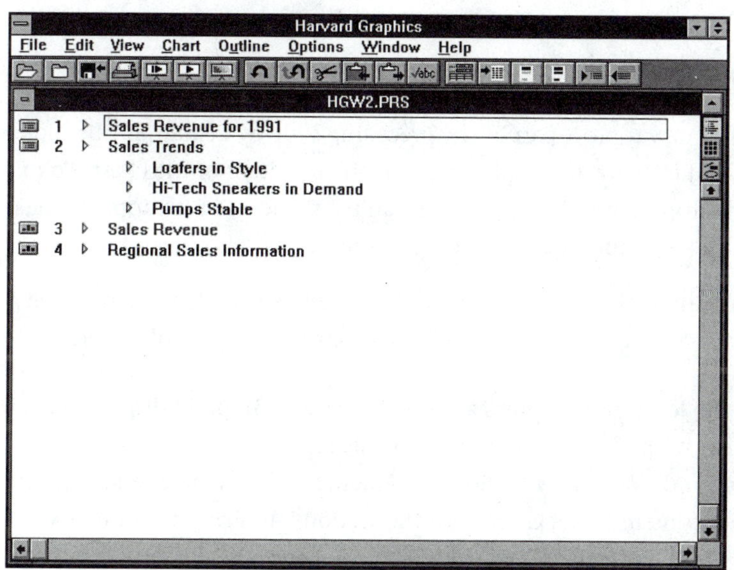

Fig. 2.20
Four slides in the Outliner.

Moving Slides in the Outliner. You can move the slides in your presentation by selecting the slide's topic and dragging it to a new location. When moving a slide, the Outliner displays the image of a hand that points to the new location. In addition to the placeholder, a red line also indicates the location of the new slide. Follow these steps to move a slide in the presentation:

1. Click the triangle next to the topic and hold the mouse button until the hand placeholder appears.

2. Drag the pointer to the location of the new topic.

3. Release the mouse button.

The new topic, and any subtopics that are indented below the topic, are now displayed in the new location.

Adding a Chart in the Outliner. You can use the Outliner to add text charts to a presentation. When you create a new topic, the program adds a new slide. The information you type under this new topic becomes the data for the chart.

Suppose that you want to add to the presentation in figure 2.20 a bullet chart on Sales Goals following the Sales Revenue slide. Follow these steps to create a new slide:

1. Click the triangle for the Sales Revenue topic.

2. Press Enter to create a new topic.

   The new topic is part of the preceding slide by default. If this slide were a bullet chart, this topic would be the first item of the chart. To make the topic a new slide, you must adjust the level of the topic to make this new topic equal to the other slides.

3. To adjust the level, press Shift-Tab to move the slide up one level. You can continue to press Shift-Tab to increase the level of a topic.

When the levels of the topics are equal, Harvard Graphics displays a chart icon next to the topic to indicate that this topic now represents a new slide. The icon indicates that the slide is a bullet chart. New slides added in the Outliner contain bullet charts. See the section "Adding a Chart to a Slide" in

Chapter 11, "Using the Outliner," for information on creating different chart types in the Outliner. The information you type into the topic of this chart is the title of the chart. The additional topics you enter below the title comprise the body of the bullet chart.

To add data to the new slide, follow these steps:

1. Click the topic that represents the new slide.
2. Type **Sales Goals** as the topic of this slide.
3. Press the Enter key to create the first item of the chart.
4. Type **Reach 100% of Quota**.
5. Press Enter to create a second item.
6. Type **Increase Sales Regions**.

Figure 2.21 illustrates the Outliner with the completed presentation.

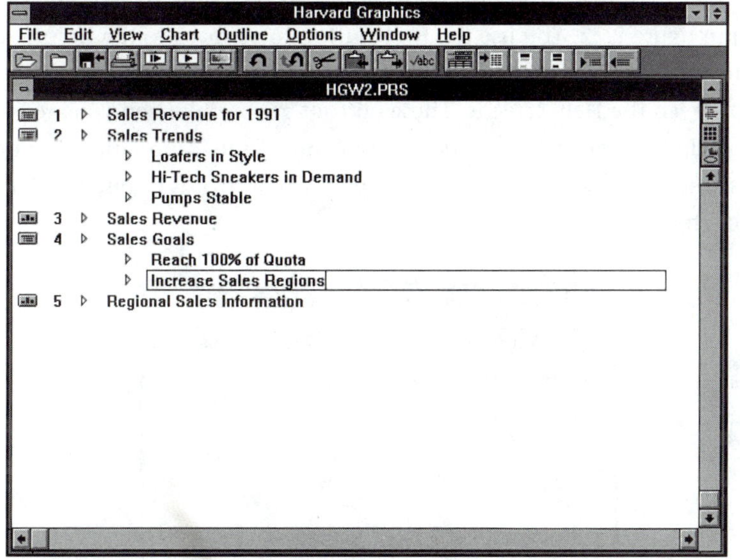

Fig. 2.21
The completed presentation in the Outliner.

To edit any of the individual slides from the Outliner, click the topic that represents the slide; then click the Slide Editor icon. To see all the slides in one window, click the Slide Sorter icon.

Getting Help

Harvard Graphics provides a complete Help system. The program displays the Help menu on every menu bar in the program. The items on the Help menu provide information about specific tasks and keys and about the active window. The Help menu also provides a selection to access a contents of help topics. The contents can guide you to the feature for which you need help. The Help system even provides information that teaches you how to use Windows Help.

When you choose any item on the Help menu, Harvard Graphics starts the Windows Help system with information pertaining to the item you selected. The first item on the menu shows the contents of help topics for Harvard Graphics. Figure 2.22 shows the Help window with the contents . After you learn how to manipulate the items on any Help window, you can use Windows Help to get the answers you need.

The buttons at the top of the Help window are the primary tools for finding help information. The Contents button displays the contents of topics, shown in figure 2.22. You use the Back button to get back to the Help screen you previously viewed. You use the Browse buttons to flip forward and backward between the Help screens. These buttons are useful when you are looking for help in a particular area but are not sure of the information you need. You use the Search button to search Help, based on words or phrases that describe the area.

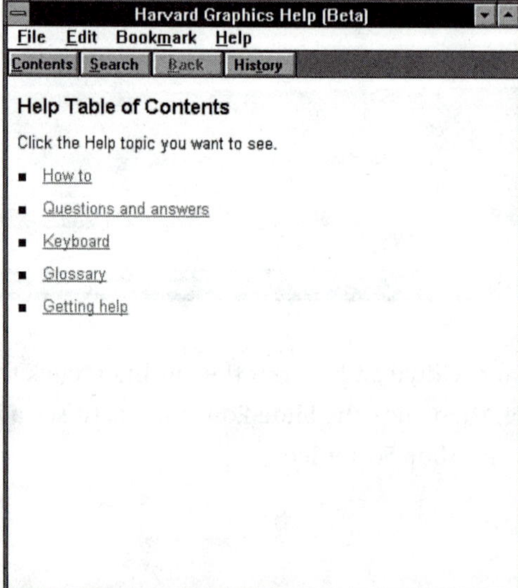

Fig. 2.22
The Help contents window.

In addition to these buttons, the Help text within the window contains topics you can choose to get information. The program displays these underlined topics in a different color within the text. When you move the pointer over a topic, the pointer changes to a hand to indicate that you can click the text. To get help on the Harvard Graphics commands, for instance, click the Commands keyword. To exit the Help system, choose E**x**it from the File menu in the Help window.

Using the Icon Bar

Harvard Graphics provides an Icon bar for quick access to commonly used features. When you're adding graphics in the Slide Editor, editing chart data, or working on your presentation in the many different views, the Icon bar places simple features for editing and enhancing within a simple mouse click. Figure 2.23 shows the Icon bar in the Slide Editor. Each icon represents a different feature. You use an icon simply by clicking on the icon in the bar. The first icon, for example, is used to open an existing presentation. To open the file, you could either click the icon or select Open from the File menu. To help you determine which icon you need, Harvard Graphics displays the name of each icon in the Window title when you first move the mouse over the icon. Figure 2.23 displays the name for the open presentation icon.

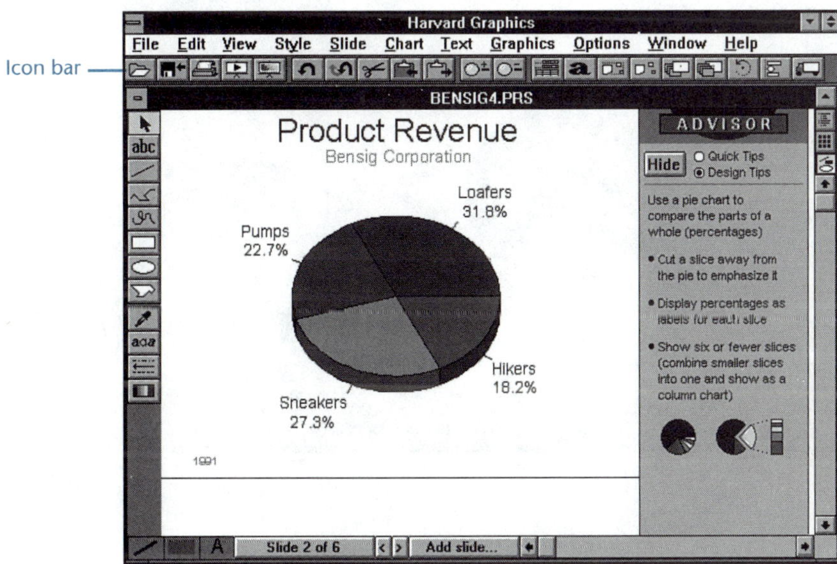

Fig. 2.23
The Slide Editor with the Icon bar.

Harvard Graphics comes with a set of default icon bars for the different parts of the product. You can use these bars as is or create a custom icon bar which displays icons for the features you use most often. Appendix D explains how to create a custom bar and also presents a list of the available icons. See individual chapters for information on the default icon bars available within Harvard Graphics.

Using the Advisor

The Harvard Graphics Advisor is displayed in the Slide Editor to provide Quick Tips that help you quickly achieve certain tasks. The Advisor also provides Design Tips that help you improve the appearance of your slide by suggesting options to modify and other changes you can make to a slide. Figure 2.24 shows the Advisor displaying Design Tips for a Pie chart. The tips explain how to emphasize an individual slice in the pie and how many slices you should display in the chart. To display Design Tips for a slide, click the Design Tips button. When viewing Design Tips, you click the Quick Tips button to display the Quick Tips again.

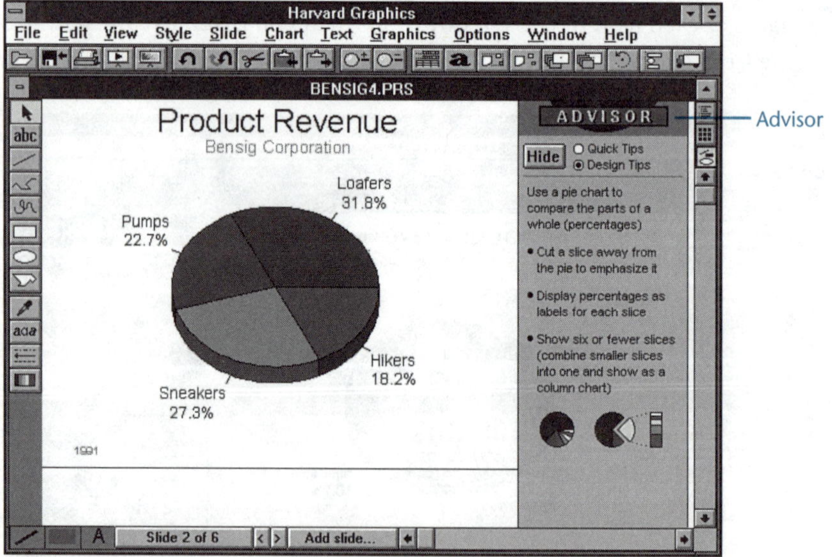

Fig. 2.24
The Advisor in the Slide Editor.

Running the Tutorial

Harvard Graphics provides a Tutorial called the 5-Minute Coach. The tutorial is designed to get you familiar with the basics of Harvard Graphics in a few minutes. The lessons are divided into four basic areas:

- Overview of Harvard Graphics covering slides and presentations
- Creating a presentation including adding a slide
- Enhancing a presentation including adding graphics to slides and making templates
- Managing presentations including using the Slide Sorter and Outliner

You start the tutorial by choosing Tutorial from the Help menu or by clicking the Tutorial... button on the Main Harvard Graphics window. When the tutorial is started, you see the Home screen, which is displayed in figure 2.25. You use the four large buttons in the middle of the screen to start one of the four lessons. For example, to get an overview of Harvard Graphics, click the Overview button.

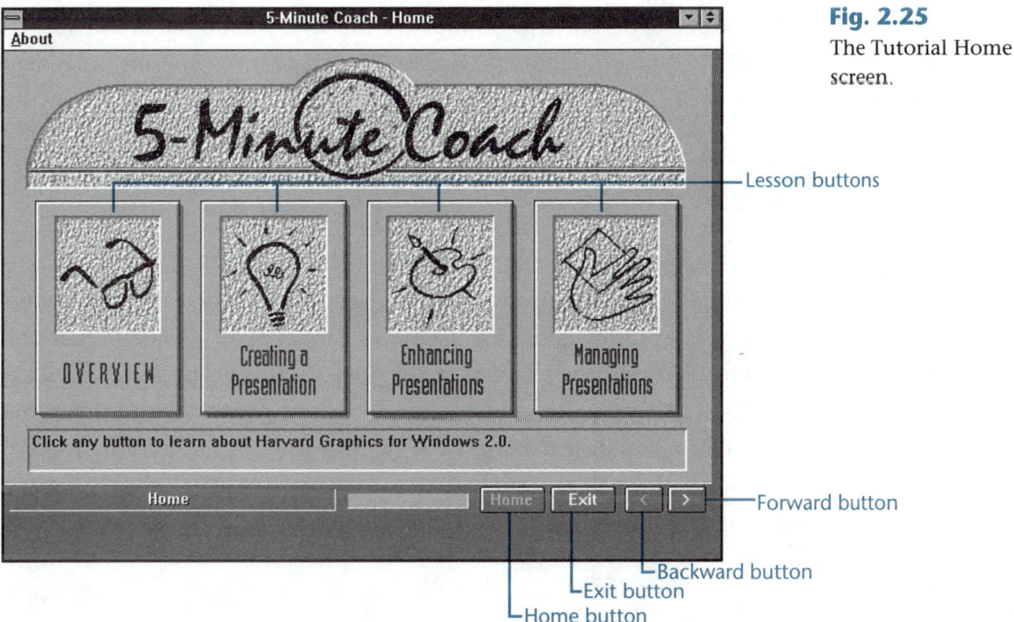

Fig. 2.25
The Tutorial Home screen.

Within each lesson, you click the forward button to advance to the next screen and the backward button to return to the previous screen. You click the Home button to return to the Home screen. Click the Exit button when you have finished viewing all the lessons or when you are ready to begin working with Harvard Graphics. Information and instructions are provided in yellow boxes or "cartoon" balloons. Some lessons also display animated graphics to help you understand the product. When the animation is complete, a balloon appears to inform you to click the forward button. Many lessons provide additional instructions based on the windows and dialog boxes available in Harvard Graphics. You should follow these instructions, which will help you learn the mouse clicks and key presses you must follow within Harvard Graphics

Exiting Harvard Graphics

To exit Harvard Graphics, you first must save the presentation; then choose the Exit command from the File menu. When you exit, the program removes all presentations from memory. For a presentation that you modified since you last saved it, the program displays a prompt, asking whether you want to save the presentation. This prompt ensures that you do not accidentally lose changes that you thought you had saved. Click the Yes button to save the presentation.

From Here...

To familiarize you with the basic components of a presentation and the features you use to create presentations, this chapter covers basic information on using Harvard Graphics for Windows. This chapter also builds a foundation for the remaining chapters of the book. In this chapter, you have learned how to create and save a presentation. You learned how to add slides to a presentation and how to choose the type for the chart displayed on the slide. You then learned about other features, which are used to enhance slides and edit an entire presentation.

The remaining chapters in this book expand on the general product areas presented here. Chapters 3 through 6 cover adding slides in greater detail by explaining more about charts that are displayed on slides. Chapter 7, "Working with Text"; Chapter 12, "Drawing in Harvard Graphics"; and Chapter 13, "Enhancing Drawings and Objects," explain how to create and enhance objects on a slide. Chapter 10, "Using the Slide Sorter," covers editing an entire presentation in the Slide Sorter. Chapter 11, "Using the Outliner," explains how to create and edit a presentation in the Outliner. All these features are introduced in this chapter on the basics of Harvard Graphics.

Chapter 3

Creating Text Charts

You can use text to communicate ideas and information on any type of chart; on a chart with primarily numeric data, for example, you can use text to present a specific observation on the chart. You can create *text charts*, though, which are charts that communicate information through words and phrases. Your audience silently reads the slide or follows along in the text as you discuss the slide. You can use a text chart to present department goals to the members of a group, for example. Each goal is an item of textual data that can be communicated only with words. The theme for a presentation is another example of information you may want to present to an audience with a text chart.

In this chapter, you learn how to do the following:

- Create text charts
- Enter data into charts
- Pick styles for charts

Harvard Graphics provides for three different types of text charts: title, bullet, and table. *Title charts* are composed of three regions in which the text of the chart appears. These distinct regions enable you to present small segments of easy-to-read text. You can use a *bullet chart* to display an organized list of text items to which your audience can refer as you discuss each item of data. *Table charts*, which look like spreadsheets, are useful for lining up rows and columns of text or numbers. Figure 3.1 shows examples of the three different types of text charts.

Creating Title Charts

Title charts have three regions—title, subtitle, and footnote—into which you enter information. The *title* region is usually the most prominent feature of the chart. By default, the text in this region is the largest and most noticeable. The *subtitle* region gives supporting information about the title and uses a font size smaller than the title but larger than footnote copy. By default, the *footnote* region of a title chart has the smallest text. Data entered into the footnote should be relevant to the title but less significant than the subtitle.

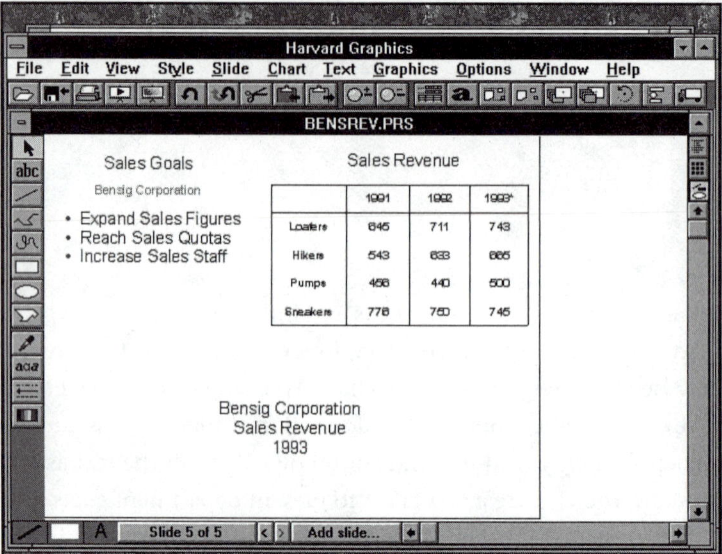

Fig. 3.1
A slide consisting of a title chart, a bullet chart, and a table chart.

Choosing a Title Chart Style

When you choose a chart type (title, pie, organization, and so on), Harvard Graphics presents the available styles for the chart type you selected. If you choose the vertical bar chart, for example, the available list of predesigned vertical bar chart options is presented, from which you can make your selection.

When you select title chart, Harvard Graphics displays the available title chart styles, which illustrate the possible placement of the three regions. To pick the style for your title chart, you must decide where the three regions of the chart should appear in relationship to each other; for example, you can present the title region at the top, in the middle, or at the bottom of the chart. You also can choose a style that uses only one or two of the regions. To select a style, simply click the style in the dialog box. The style you select determines the initial locations of the title, subtitle, and footnote of your title chart. (For information on moving objects in the Slide Editor, see Chapter 13, "Enhancing Drawings and Objects.")

To begin a new slide, follow these steps:

1. If you have not started a presentation already, choose **N**ew Presentation from the **F**ile menu or choose Create **N**ew Presentation from the initial Harvard Graphics screen. If you have already started a presentation, the Add Slide dialog box appears. If you have just started Harvard Graphics, the New Presentation dialog box appears.

2. Choose T**i**tle as the slide type. The predesigned title chart options appear (see fig. 3.2).

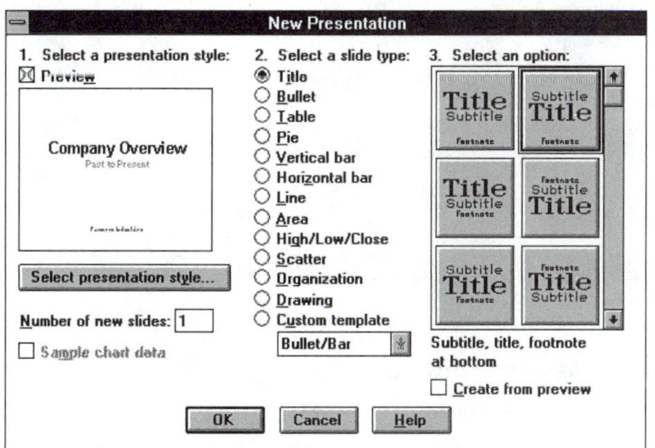

Fig. 3.2
The New Presentation dialog box, with the selection of predesigned options.

3. Select the style by clicking the appropriate icon. For the example in the tutorial that follows, you will create a title chart that shows the subtitle above the title; therefore, select the second chart in the first row.

4. Click OK.

The style of chart you select depends on the data you want to present. If the purpose of your chart is to introduce the topic of your presentation, use a title chart that displays the title region at the top of the chart, and enter the topic in this region.

Another way to organize your presentation is to use a title chart as the first slide in a "movie" presentation. In movie advertisements, the title of the film typically appears in the middle of the page. The company producing the film appears above the title with a phrase like *Bensig Films presents*. To display this information in a title chart, you can use a style that displays the subtitle above the title, as you did in the preceding instructions.

Entering Data into a Title Chart

After you select a chart style, Harvard Graphics displays the data form for the chart. You use the title chart data form to enter text into the title chart. Fields in the data form represent the three regions of a title chart (see fig. 3.3). You can move through the fields by clicking a field or pressing the Tab key.

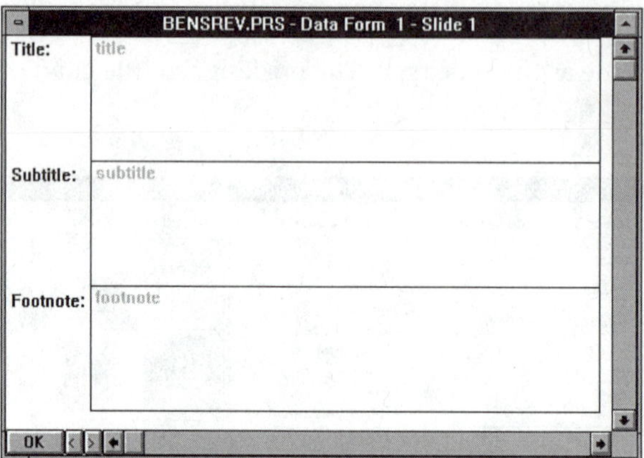

Fig. 3.3
The title chart data form.

A gray *text placeholder* indicates the information that belongs in the field. After you enter text in the field, Harvard Graphics removes the placeholder. The placeholder also shows the location of the field on the slide. As you enhance the slide in the Slide Editor, for example, the placeholders help you avoid placing graphics objects that may obstruct the chart's data. When you preview or print, the placeholders do not appear.

Within a field, you can edit the text by using the same keystrokes you use with a word processor. (You use the Backspace key to remove the character preceding the insertion point, and you use the Delete key to remove the character following the insertion point.) Use the mouse and the arrow keys to place the insertion point in different places within the field.

If you enter more words than can fit on a line, Harvard Graphics automatically moves the insertion point to the beginning of the next line; pressing Enter is not necessary. As you add and delete characters, the program automatically adjusts the lines, placing as much data as possible on the first line. The term for this process is *word wrap*. Harvard Graphics supports word wrap whenever you enter text into a slide.

The title chart communicates your topic to the audience. Be as creative as circumstances permit when you choose a title. For the example, the style for the title chart is intended to introduce a film produced by Bensig Films and directed by a notable director. Bensig, however, is a corporation that produces shoes, not films; the "movie" is actually a presentation on revenues, and the "director" is really the Regional Sales Director. The movie theme adds extra spice to the slides and helps keep the audience interested in the presentation.

To add the data to the title chart displayed in this tutorial, follow these steps:

1. Click the Title field.
2. Type the title. For the example, type **Sales Revenue for 1993**.
3. Click thc Subtitle field.
4. Type the subtitle. For the example, type **The Bensig Corporation presents**.
5. Click the Footnote field.
6. Type the footnote. For the example, type **by the Regional Sales Director**.
7. Click OK. You can see the completed title chart in figure 3.4.

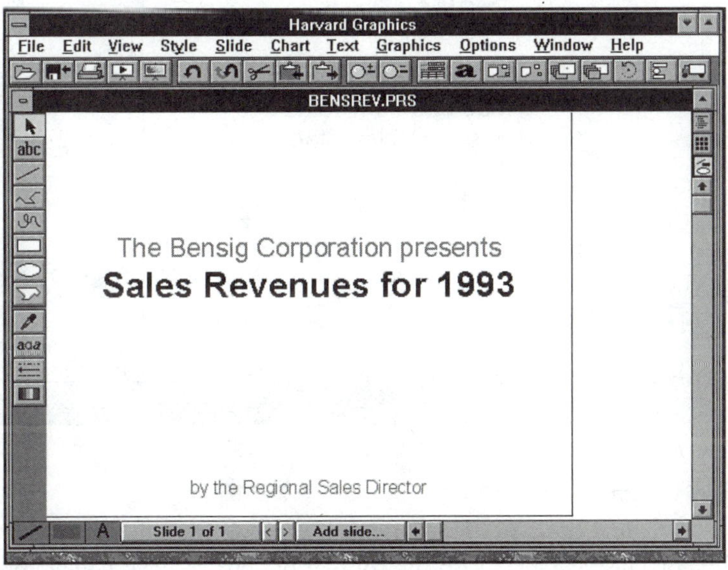

Fig. 3.4
The completed film title chart.

In addition to editing the data of a title chart, you can modify the text attributes of the data by using the text feature of the Slide Editor. Chapter 7, "Working with Text," teaches you how to enhance the text of a title chart.

Creating Bullet Charts

You use bullet charts to present textual information in an orderly list. In Harvard Graphics for Windows, a *bullet* is a round dot or other symbol displayed to the left of each item. The most significant characteristic of a bullet chart is the symbol you use. In Harvard Graphics, you can use round dots, squares, diamonds, triangles, arrows, dashes, or check marks for bullet symbols. You also can use numeric bullets in either Arabic or Roman notation, or you can create a chart that does not display any symbols. When you use numeric bullets, Harvard Graphics automatically updates the numbers as you add and remove bullet items. Figure 3.5 shows a bullet chart with a round dot for the symbol.

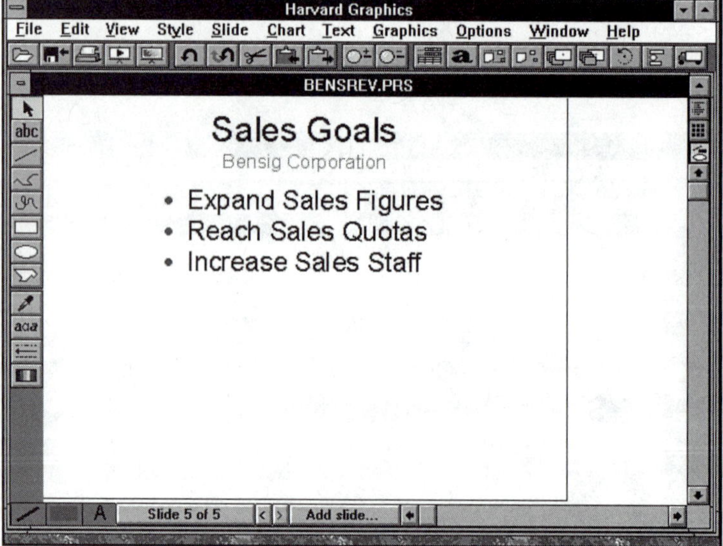

Fig. 3.5
Example of a bullet chart with round bullets.

Choosing a Bullet Chart Style

Harvard Graphics has six different types of symbols for bullet charts. The symbol you choose depends on the content of your items. If you are presenting the top five reasons that customers are buying your product, for example, you might use numbers for bullet symbols. As you discuss the reasons, you can then refer to the items by number.

In Chapter 1, "Quick Start: Creating a Simple Presentation," you created a presentation on the sales revenues for the Bensig Shoe Corporation. Suppose that after viewing the latest copy of the presentation, you decide to add a slide that reviews the sales goals defined at the end of the preceding year. Because check marks suggest the analogy of checking off each task you accomplish on your list of sales goals, you decide to use the check mark symbol in your bullet chart. Follow these steps to create the bullet chart:

1. Click the Slide Editor icon or choose Slide **E**ditor from the **V**iew menu. The current slide appears in the Slide Editor. The bullet chart you create will be added to the presentation following this slide.

2. Click the Add Slide button at the bottom of the Slide Editor window. Alternatively, you can choose **A**dd Slide from the **S**lide menu. The Add Slide dialog box appears.

3. To create a bullet chart on the slide, click the button for **B**ullet to specify the appropriate slide type. Harvard Graphics displays the styles of bullet charts from which you can choose (see fig. 3.6).

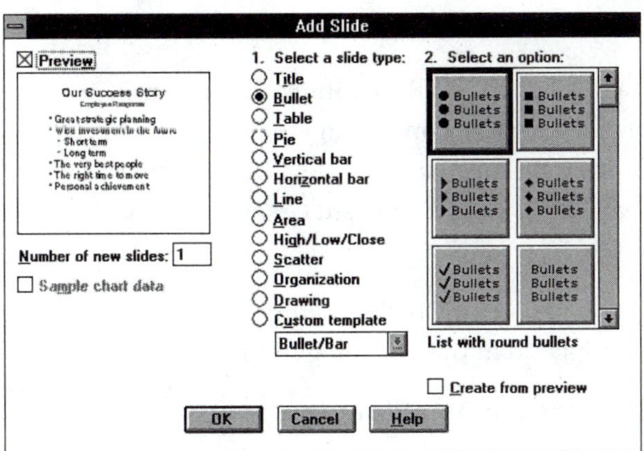

Fig. 3.6
The Add Slide dialog box with a bullet style selected.

The bullet symbols shown illustrate that the bullets do not differ much. Whether you choose round or square bullets is simply a matter of taste. In general, you should try to choose a bullet symbol that fits your data and provides a visual aid that enhances your discussion.

4. Click the title chart with check mark bullet symbols.

5. Click OK. The bullet chart data form, in which you enter the bullet items, appears (see fig. 3.7). You will use this data form in the following exercises.

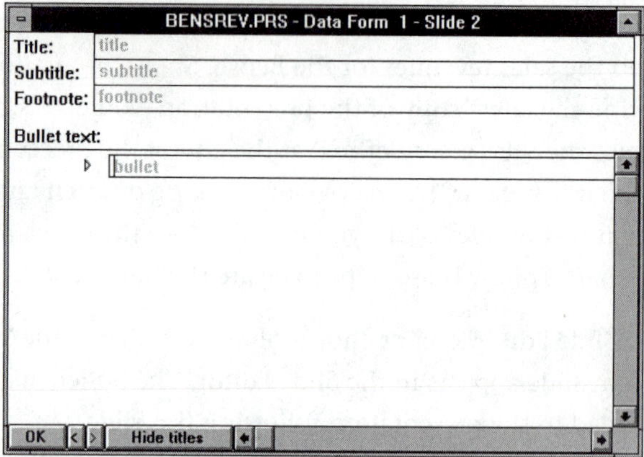

Fig. 3.7
The bullet chart data form.

Entering Data into a Bullet Chart

You can enter data into a bullet chart by using the bullet chart data form or the Outliner. The Outliner is a feature in which you can edit an entire presentation. In the Outliner, each slide is represented by a topic—a chart's title; because of the structure of a bullet or organization chart, you can edit all data from these chart forms in the Outliner. See Chapter 11, "Using the Outliner," for more information about the Outliner.

You enter data in a bullet chart by defining bullet items. You can create new bullet items by pressing Enter and typing the text for the item. Harvard Graphics adds the new bullet after the item that contains the insertion point. When you create a bullet chart, Harvard Graphics adds the first bullet item to the chart.

Follow these steps to enter the bullet chart data into the bullet chart data form that you displayed in the preceding steps:

1. Click the field for the first item.
2. Type the text for the first bullet. For the example, type **Increase Market Awareness**.
3. Press Enter to create a new bullet.
4. Type the text for the second bullet item. For the example, type **Expand Sales Regions**.
5. Press Enter to create a new bullet.
6. Type the text for the next bullet. For the example, type **Reach 110% of Quota**.

7. Press Enter to create a new bullet.

8. Type the text for the final bullet. For the example, type **Obtain 5 New Accounts Per Region**.

9. Click OK to create the slide. The Slide appears in the Slide Editor.

As you add bullet items, keep in mind that the chart has a limited amount of space in which to display each item. With five or more items, you may have to use a smaller font for the text (or use two consecutive charts). For information on changing the font, see Chapter 7, "Working with Text."

As you enter the data for a bullet item, you may need to include more text than can fit on one line. When you reach the end of the line, Harvard Graphics automatically wraps the next word to a new line. The text appears on two lines, but the chart displays only one bullet symbol for the item. To start a new line of text within a single bullet item before you reach the end of the line, press Ctrl+Enter.

Changing the Order of Bullet Items

You use the Edit menu commands to change the order of bullet items. If you have not selected any text in an item, choosing Cu**t** from the **E**dit menu removes the entire bullet item from the chart. When you paste this data back into the chart, Harvard Graphics places the new bullet after the active bullet item.

Suppose that when you create a bullet chart on sales goals, you decide all the items that discuss sales regions should be displayed together at the end of the chart. If you are not viewing the bullet chart data form, choose Edit **D**ata from the **C**hart menu, and then follow these steps to rearrange the bullet items into the new order:

1. Select the item you want to move. In the example, select the second item on the list, Expand Sales Regions.

2. From the **E**dit menu, choose Cu**t**.

3. Click the location where you want the cut item to appear, for the example, the last item on the list.

4. From the **E**dit menu, choose **P**aste topic(s).

   The cut item appears as the last item on the list.

Adding Sub-Bullets

Up to now, all the items in the bullet chart are the same level, and the bullet symbols are aligned evenly on the left side of the chart; however, you can add a second level of indented bullet items, or *sub-bullets*, to your chart. The indentation is a visual cue that these items are part of the preceding bullet and are not significant enough to be equivalent to the other bullet items.

Pressing the Enter key creates new bullet items in a bullet chart; pressing Tab changes the indentation of a bullet item. When you press Tab, the active item moves one place to the right. If you press Shift+Tab, the item moves one place to the left.

The level of the new item matches the level of the item immediately below it. To create sub-bullet items, you can change the level of the item by pressing Tab, or you can select a bullet item that has sub-bullets already and press Enter.

The last bullet item in the sample chart states the goal for expanding the sales regions. Suppose that after creating the slide, you remember that when you set up the goals, you were trying to expand in two specific regions. This information, although not as significant as the other items on the chart, is relevant to the last goal. To communicate the additional information, you can use sub-bullets after the goal. To add the sub-bullets, follow these steps:

1. Select the bullet item—the last bullet, for instance—to which you want to add the sub-bullets.

2. Press Enter to create the new item.

3. Press Tab to indent the item.

4. Type the text for the sub-bullet. For the example, type **Add New Cities in Chicago**.

5. Press Enter to create another sub-bullet.

6. Type the text for this entry. For the example, type **Start New Accounts in Kansas**.

When you complete these steps, your bullet chart data form should resemble the form shown in figure 3.8.

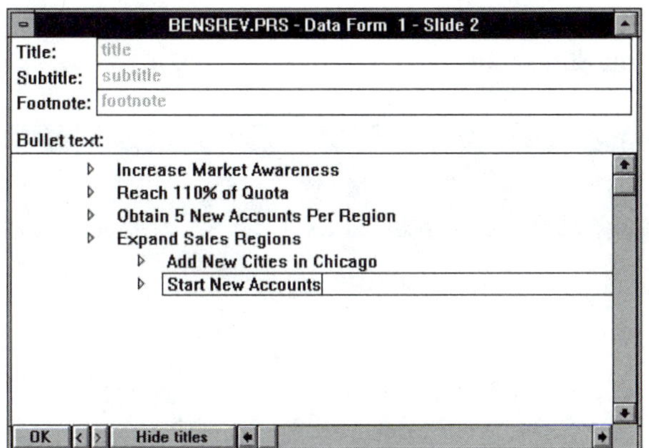

Fig. 3.8
The bullet chart with sub-bullets.

Adding a Title, Subtitle, and Footnote

To finish the chart, you need to add a title, a subtitle, and a footnote. Most of your charts will need this type of information to clarify the data. You add this information while you are still in the chart data form. Follow these steps to complete the chart you have been working on:

1. Select the Title field, and type the title **Goals**.
2. Select the Subtitle field, and type the subtitle **From 1993**.
3. Select the Footnote field, and type the footnote **Bensig Corporation**.
4. Click OK to create the chart and add the slide to the presentation.

Figure 3.9 shows the completed bullet chart. This chart is a good example of a text chart. The information in the chart is easy to read and understand, and you have added just enough text to explain the data without making the chart appear crowded.

Design Note

Set some basic guidelines for how much text to place on one line and what size to use for your font in your text charts. Chapter 7, "Working with Text," explains how to modify the text attributes for items in a chart.

Choosing Bullet Symbol Options

For any bullet chart you create, you can choose the Set **B**ullet Attributes item on the **T**ext menu to change the character, font, color, size, and spacing for the symbols in your bullet chart. To modify the bullet symbol, you must view the slide in the Slide Editor.

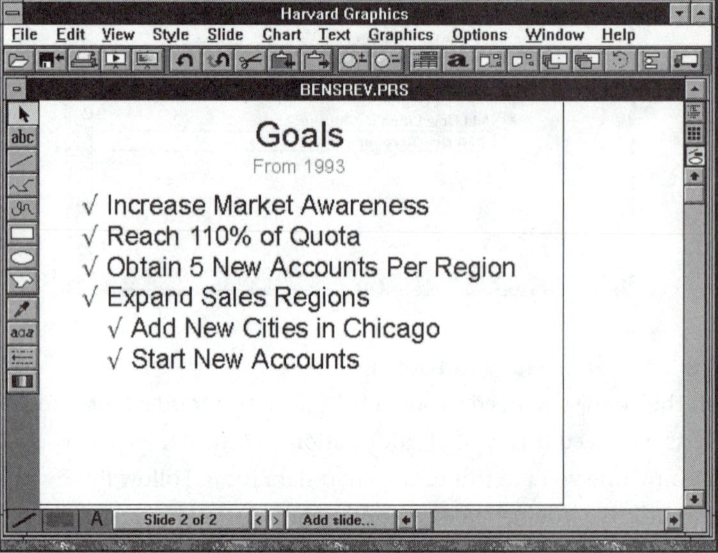

Fig. 3.9 The completed bullet chart.

In the bullet chart you created, suppose that you determine that check marks should be used for the top-level bullet items only. Because these items are the most significant items in your chart, you also decide to use a larger font for the symbols and to use a different symbol for the sub-bullets. You make these changes from the Bullet Attributes dialog box, shown in figure 3.10. Using the dialog box, you can modify the symbols for up to four levels of bullet and sub-bullet items. Any levels beyond the fourth assume the attributes of the fourth level.

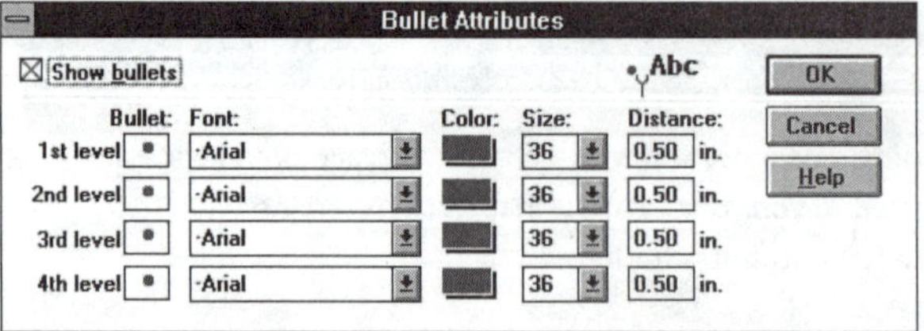

Fig. 3.10 The Bullet Attributes dialog box.

Figure 3.10 shows the settings for your chart on Bensig's sales goals and indicates that a check mark is the symbol for all the levels in the chart.

The Bullet Attributes dialog box contains five sets of boxes in which you set attributes (bullet, font, color, size, and distance) for each of the four bullet levels. The current settings for your slide's bullet chart appear in this dialog box. The following list explains these attributes:

- *Bullet.* This box shows the current bullet symbol displayed for the level. To see the available bullet symbols, click the symbol in one of the boxes; the Bullet Symbol dialog box appears.
- *Font.* The font for the symbol appears in this list box. To see the font choices, click the down arrow next to the list box; then use the up- and down-arrow keys to scroll through the list of available fonts. You can change the font by selecting a font from the list.
- *Size.* This list box contains the size of the font. As in the Font list box, you click the down arrow next to the list box and scroll through the list to see the available font sizes. You can change the size by selecting a font size from the list.
- *Color.* The Color box shows the color of the bullet symbol. Click the Color box to see other colors in the Text Color dialog box.
- *Distance.* This option sets the distance, in inches, between the symbol and the text of the item for each level. You can change the distance by typing a new value into the text box.

To make changes to the chart you created, display the slide in the Slide Editor and follow these steps.

1. From the **T**ext menu, choose Set **B**ullet Attributes. Harvard Graphics displays the Bullet Attributes dialog box (refer to fig. 3.10).
2. Click the Bullet symbol for the second level. The Bullet Symbol dialog box, from which you can select another bullet symbol, appears (see fig. 3.11).

   The dialog box contains 15 symbols. The first two columns contain symbols common to all same-level bullets. The last column contains letter or number bullet symbols available for the specified level. A first-level bullet would be the number 1 or the letter A, for example; the second level would be 2 or B, and so on. You can change the starting number or letter by entering a value in the Start **N**umbering At text box. The Continue from **P**revious Slide option enables you to number slides in sequential order. The items on one slide start with the number or letter just after the last number or letter on the preceding slide. The **C**haracter text box, in which you type a character, enables you to use a character from the keyboard as the bullet symbol.

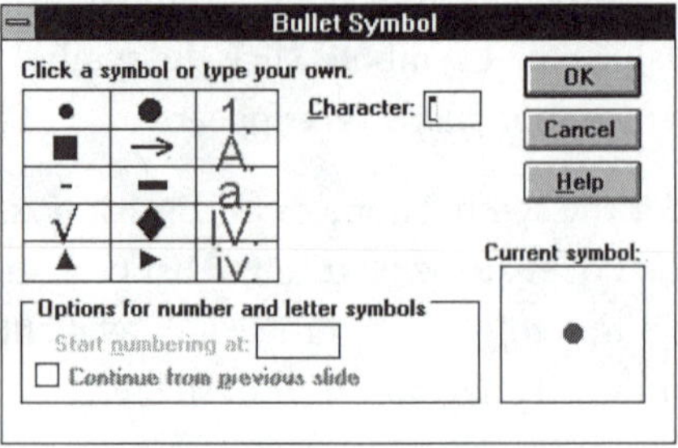

Fig. 3.11
The Bullet Symbol dialog box.

3. Select the hyphen symbol from the Bullet Symbol dialog box.
4. Click OK.
5. Click the down scroll arrow next to Size for the 1st Level.
6. Select 42 from the Size list.
7. Click OK.

Figure 3.12 shows the completed bullet chart.

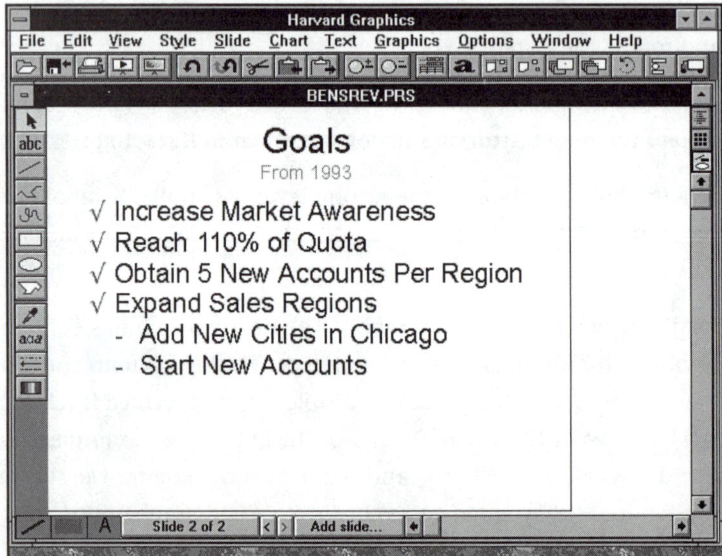

Fig. 3.12
The finished chart on sales goals.

Creating Table Charts

You use table charts to present text and numbers in a table of rows and columns. The advantage of using a table to present information is the ease with which you can organize your data. Your audience can easily find the row and column heading that describes any cell in the table. Figure 3.13 shows a table chart. In this chart, which is based on the Bensig Shoe Corporation's revenue figures, you can easily locate the sales information for sneakers sold in 1990, for instance.

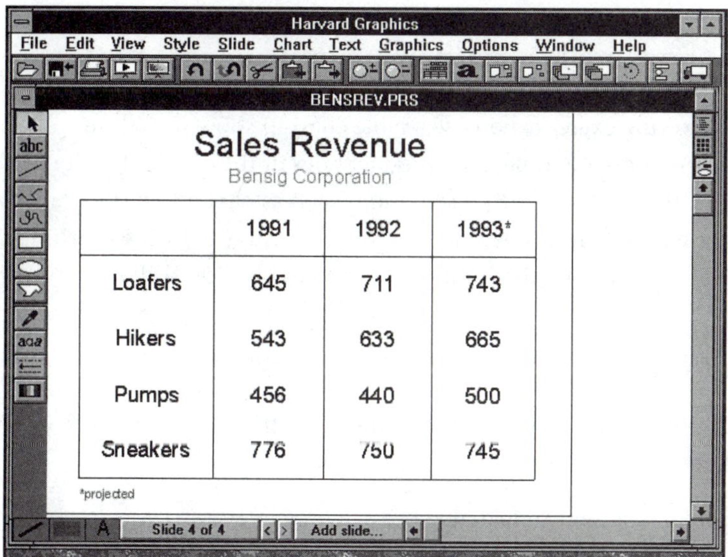

	1991	1992	1993*
Loafers	645	711	743
Hikers	543	633	665
Pumps	456	440	500
Sneakers	776	750	745

Fig. 3.13
An example table chart.

Choosing a Table Chart Style

The table chart styles differ mostly in the way the grid lines that separate cells of data appear. Figure 3.14 shows the table styles from which you can choose. The simplest style uses grid lines to separate the row and column headings from the rest of the chart. Other styles look more like spreadsheets, in that each value appears in a distinct cell enclosed by grid lines.

Design Note

When choosing a table chart style, think about the data you need to illustrate. Too many grid lines can make the chart look crowded, especially if you have many data values to display. On the other hand, grid lines can make a chart appear less sparse if the amount of data is limited. In general, you need to use an uncluttered style so that your data values are easier to read.

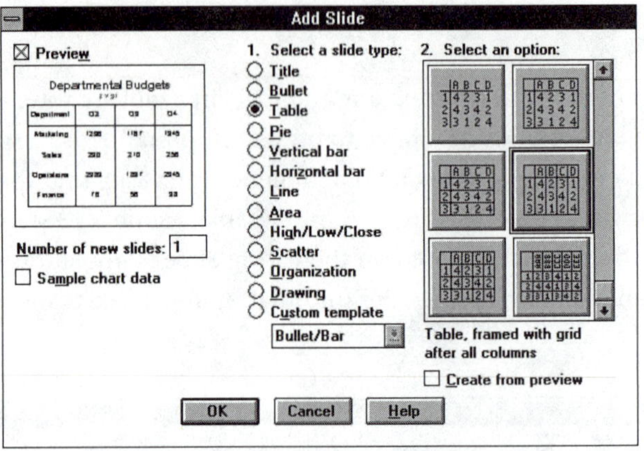

Fig. 3.14
The table chart style selected from the Add Slide dialog box.

In the following exercise, you use a table chart to show spreadsheet data for your presentation about Bensig's product sales in the different regions of the country. Other slides in the presentation, such as bar and line charts, show this information graphically, but you want the chart to look something like a spreadsheet, showing only numbers. To create this slide, follow these steps:

1. If you are not viewing the presentation in the Slide Editor, choose Slide Editor from the **V**iew menu.

2. Choose the Add Slide button at the bottom of the Slide Editor or choose Add Slide from the **S**lide menu.

   You see the Add Slide dialog box.

3. In the Add Slide dialog box, click the **T**able button for the slide type.

4. Select the table chart style you want. For the example, select the first table chart image in the second row (refer to fig. 3.14).

5. Click OK.

The table chart data form looks like a spreadsheet (see fig. 3.15). Table charts, however, do not support the functions of a spreadsheet. Chapters 5, "Creating XY Charts," and 6, "Creating Pie Charts," explain how to obtain spreadsheet functionality with an XY or pie chart.

Entering Data into a Table Chart

The table chart data form contains cells for each value in the chart. To add data, click the cell to make it active; then type the data. (You also can use the

Tab key and the up- and down-arrow keys to move through the different cells.) Unlike title and bullet charts, the organization of the data in a table chart is up to you. You can define the rows and columns in a way that best suits your data. In addition to the data, you can also enter a title, subtitle, and footnote for a table chart. The information in the following sections is an example of a strategy that can be adapted for many types of data.

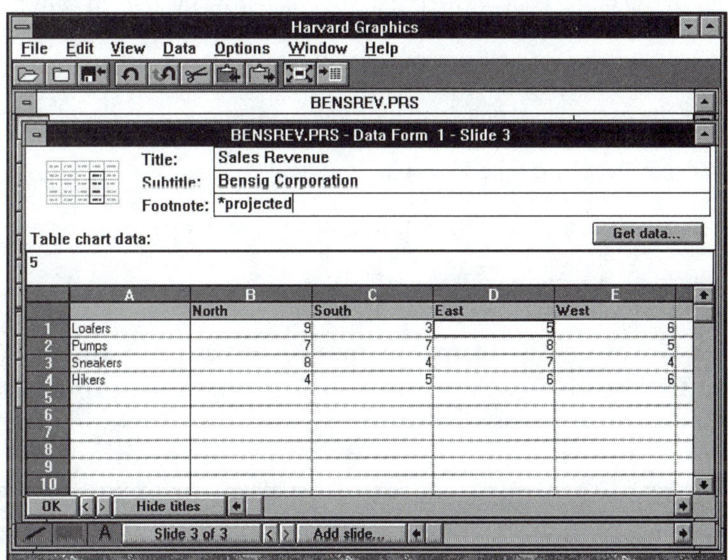

Fig. 3.15
The table chart data form.

Setting the Column Headers. You enter the headers for each column in the gray cells at the top of the form below the letters. For the sales region chart, the headers specify the different regions: North, South, East, and West. Follow these steps to enter the column headers:

1. Click the Window Expand arrow icon in the upper right corner of the data form window to see more of the data form.
2. Click the gray column-header cell for column B.
3. Type the header for column B. For the example, type **North**.
4. Click the column-header cell for column C.
5. Type the header for column C. For the example, type **South**.
6. Click the column-header cell for column D.
7. Type the header for column D. For the example, type **East**.

8. Click the column-header cell for column E.

9. Type the header for column E. For the example, type **West**.

Defining the Rows of a Table Chart. When you entered the column headers, you entered the first sales region in column B. To continue in this tutorial, you now use column A to enter the names of the products in the far left column of the table. Follow these steps to create row headers in column A:

1. Click cell A1 (the first row of column A).

2. For the example, type the row header **Loafers**.

3. Click cell A2 and type **Pumps**.

4. Click cell A3 and type **Sneakers**.

5. Click cell A4 and type **Hikers**.

Figure 3.16 shows the data form with the rows and columns defined. You can easily determine where to place the data values. For example, Loafer sales for the North go in cell B1.

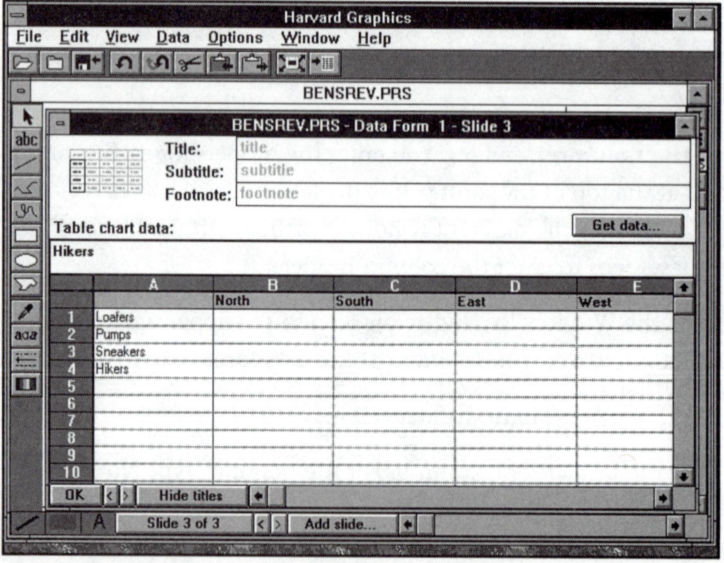

Fig. 3.16
A data form with rows and columns defined.

Entering the Data Values. Now that the rows and columns are defined, you are ready to enter the actual data values. Follow these steps to enter the data for the four regions:

1. Click cell B1 and type the value **5**.
2. Click cell B2 and type the value **7**.
3. Click cell B3 and type the value **8**.
4. Click cell B4 and type the value **4**.
5. Repeat steps 1 through 4 for columns C, D, and E, using any numbers you choose.

After you finish entering the data, your table chart data form should look like figure 3.17, with values in the cells for every combination of row and column.

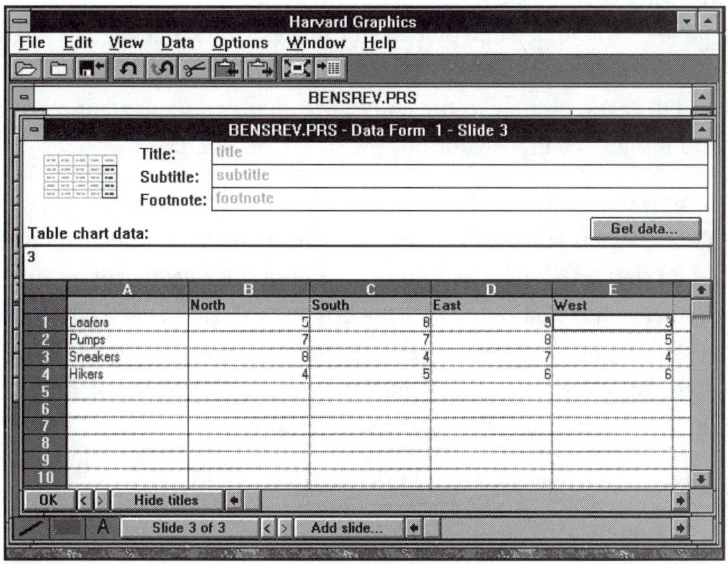

Fig. 3.17 The completed table chart data form.

Editing a Table Chart

In the table chart data form, you can edit the contents in a cell, or you can work with entire cells. When you click a cell or move the highlight to a cell, that cell becomes active. The information in the cell appears in the edit line above the data portion of the data form. If you start typing immediately, the new data completely replaces the previous data. If you click the edit line, the insertion point appears where you click. Harvard Graphics inserts any information you enter after the insertion point. You can press Backspace and Delete to remove characters before or after the insertion point. Follow these steps to add information to a cell:

1. In the data form, click the cell you want to change.

2. Click the edit line after the last character of the cell data.

3. Type the new information.

4. Press Enter to move to a new cell.

When you make a new cell active, Harvard Graphics copies the contents of the edit line to the previously active cell.

Selecting Data and Cells. Selecting information is an important part of editing table charts. In a cell, you can edit individual characters. To select a group of characters in the edit line, click before the first character you want to edit and drag the pointer to the end of the characters you want to edit. When you release the mouse button, the data is selected.

In addition to the contents of a cell, you can work with an entire cell or a block of cells. When you create a block of cells, you can rearrange large sections of data simultaneously instead of changing the cells one at a time. A single selected cell is highlighted with a box to indicate the active cell. The cells of a selected block appear in reverse video to indicate that all the cells are selected. To select a block, you click the first cell in the block, drag to the end of the block, and then release the mouse button.

Follow these steps to select cells B2 to D4 in the data form:

1. Click cell B2 and hold down the mouse button.

2. Drag to cell D4.

3. Release the mouse button. The cells are highlighted (see fig. 3.18).

Using a mouse is not the only way to select blocks of cells in the data form. By selecting the column heading, where the letter that identifies the column appears, you select the entire column. You can select a row in the same way; you click the cell in column A. By selecting the box on the far left side of the row that contains the column letters, you select all the data in your chart. You also can select all the data in your chart by choosing Select **A**ll in the **E**dit menu.

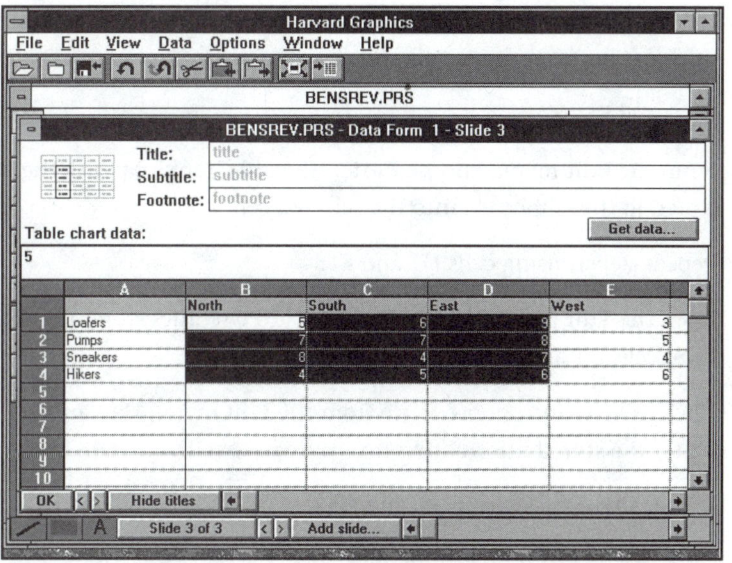

Fig. 3.18
A block of selected cells.

Editing with the Clipboard. You can use the **E**dit menu commands to edit the information in a table chart. When you use the Cu**t**, **C**opy, and **P**aste commands from the **E**dit menu, you use the Clipboard, which is a temporary storage place, provided by Windows, that you use to store and retrieve data and images.

To remove selected data from the table and store the information in the Windows Clipboard, use Cu**t**. To store the selected data in the Clipboard without removing the data from the table, use **C**opy. When you choose **P**aste from the **E**dit menu, the program inserts the information from the Clipboard (whether you have used Cu**t** or **C**opy) into the chart at the location of the insertion point. If you have selected a limited amount of text in the cell, the **E**dit menu commands affect only your selection. Otherwise, the commands operate on the entire cell.

Suppose that after you look over the data, you notice that you mistakenly entered into the North and South cells the values for the East and West Loafer sales. Likewise, the values for East and West belong to North and South. To switch the values, use the commands from the **E**dit menu and an unused part of the data form. Follow these steps to switch the values:

1. Click cell B1, drag to the right until cell C1 is highlighted, and release the mouse button. You have selected the two cells.

2. From the **E**dit menu, choose Cu**t**. Harvard Graphics removes the information from these cells and stores it in the Clipboard.

3. Click cell B5.

4. From the **E**dit menu, choose **P**aste. Harvard Graphics pastes the data stored in the Clipboard into the selected cell.

5. Repeat step 1, using cells D1 and E1.

6. From the **E**dit menu, choose Cu**t**. Harvard Graphics stores the data from cells D1 and E1 in the Clipboard.

7. Click cell B1, and choose **P**aste from the **E**dit menu. Harvard Graphics pastes the stored information into the active cell.

8. Repeat step 1, using cells B5 and C5.

9. Choose Cu**t** from the **E**dit menu.

10. Select cell D1, and choose **P**aste from the **E**dit menu. The final table chart data form is shown in figure 3.19.

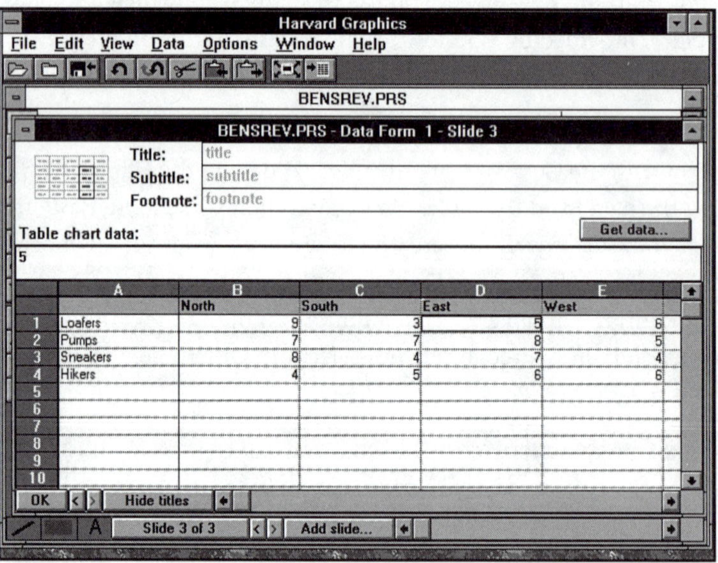

Fig. 3.19
The rearranged table chart data form.

Inserting Rows and Columns. The **D**ata menu contains additional commands to help you edit your chart data. The **I**nsert command inserts new rows and columns into your table chart to make room for additional data.

When you do an insert, the operation occurs on the active cell. Harvard Graphics inserts the new row or column at the location of the insertion point. To make room for the new row, Harvard Graphics shifts the existing rows and columns down or to the right, respectively.

The number of cells in the block you select determines the number of rows or columns affected by the operation. You can insert two new rows, for instance, by selecting cells in two different rows before executing an insertion. For example, you can use the Insert command to add a new item to the Bensig Corporation product line. Follow these steps to add Cleats to the data:

1. Click cell A3.
2. Choose **I**nsert from the **D**ata menu; then choose **R**ow from the pop-up menu. Harvard Graphics inserts a new row above the row containing Sneakers and shifts the Sneakers and Hikers rows down.
3. Click cell A3, and type **Cleats** to define the new product.
4. Click cell B3, and type **7**.
5. Click cell C3, and type **6**.
6. Click cell D3, and type **9**.
7. Click cell E3, and type **4**.

The new product is defined with the revenue for the four sales regions.

Deleting Rows and Columns. The **D**elete command on the **D**ata menu removes rows and columns from the data form. As with the **I**nsert command, the active cells determine which rows or columns Harvard Graphics deletes. When you delete a row, Harvard Graphics moves the following rows up to fill in the empty space; when you delete a column, Harvard Graphics shifts the remaining columns to the left. To remove data from the table chart data form, select cells in the rows and columns you want to delete; then choose **D**elete from the **D**ata menu. For example, to delete Cleats (the product you added in the preceding section) follow these steps:

1. Click cell A3.
2. Choose **D**elete from the **D**ata menu.
3. Choose **R**ow from the Delete pop-up menu.

Harvard Graphics removes the entire row from the chart.

Filling Data. The Fill commands on the Data menu are the quickest way to enter data into a table chart. The Fill Right and Fill Down commands operate on a block of cells. The Fill Right command copies data across the columns of a selected block of cells. If a cell has a value of 2 and you fill to the right, for example, all the selected cells to the right of the cell also will have a value of 2. The Fill Down command copies data from the top row to the rows below in the selected block. You should use the Fill commands if the row and column data in your chart is similar.

To fill cells in row 2 with data from row 1, follow these steps:

1. Select cells A1 to D2.
2. Choose Fill Down from the Edit menu.

The values in row 1 are filled into row 2.

Moving to Specific Cells. The Go to Cell option on the Data menu is the quickest way to select cells in the data form. The Go to Cell option is especially helpful when you are working with a large table chart. When you choose this command, the program displays the Go to Cell dialog box (see fig. 3.20). The Cell Location text box displays the cell that is currently active in the data form.

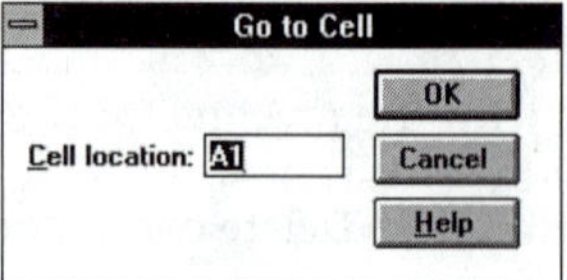

Fig. 3.20
The Go to Cell dialog box.

To select a new cell, follow these steps:

1. From the Data menu, choose Go to Cell.

   You see the Go to Cell Dialog box.

2. Type the cell reference in the Cell Location text box.
3. Click OK.

The cell you typed in the dialog box is highlighted in the data form.

Entering Title Information. Before you add the chart to the presentation, you should enter a title, subtitle, and footnote into the chart data form. To complete the chart and add it to the presentation, follow these steps:

1. Click the Title field.
2. Type **Regional Sales Information**.
3. Click the Subtitle field, and type **Bensig Corporation**.
4. Click the Footnote field, and type **1991**.
5. Click the OK button at the bottom of data form to create the slide with the table chart. The chart appears in the Slide Editor.

Figure 3.21 shows an example of a table chart with Bensig product sales information.

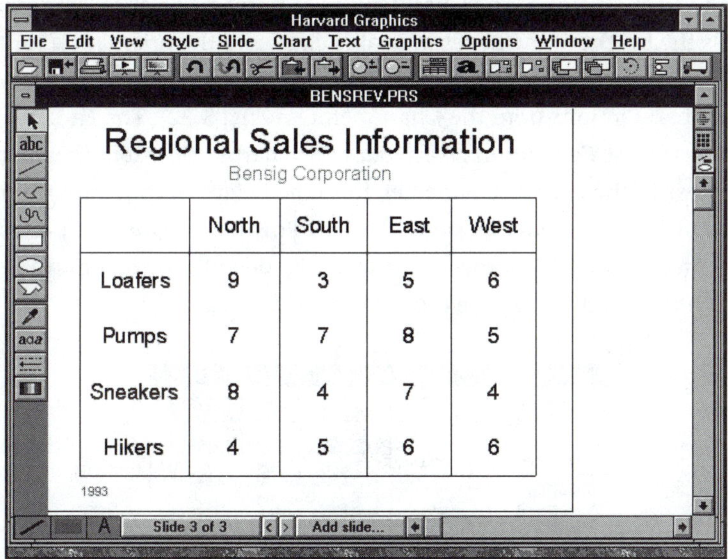

Fig. 3.21
The regional sales data in a table chart.

Modifying Table Charts

Once you have created a table chart, you may want to change something about its appearance. Whether you want the chart to appear in a different location on the slide, change the way the table fits on the slide, or modify the way numeric data will be formatted, options are available for meeting the desired outcome. If, for example, you want to increase or decrease the size of your table, follow these steps:

1. Select the table you want to resize.
2. Move the pointer to one of the eight handles surrounding the table. When the double-tipped arrow appears, press the mouse button and drag the handle until the table chart is the size you want.
3. Release the mouse button.

If you want to change the location of the table on the slide, follow these steps:

1. Select the table.
2. Move the pointer anywhere inside the table, press the mouse button, and drag the chart to its new location. Once the table is located where you want, release the mouse button.

Setting Chart Options. The Chart **O**ptions command on the **C**hart menu controls the height of the boxes in a table chart and the orientation for the text in the first row. The Table Chart Options dialog box appears when you choose Chart **O**ptions from the **C**hart menu (see fig. 3.22). The Fit Row Height to Largest **C**ell option gives your table chart a consistent look, making all the rows in the chart the same height as the height of the row with the largest cell. The Text Orientation in the First Row item enables you to change the orientation for the top row of the chart. By default, the text in this row appears horizontally along the top.

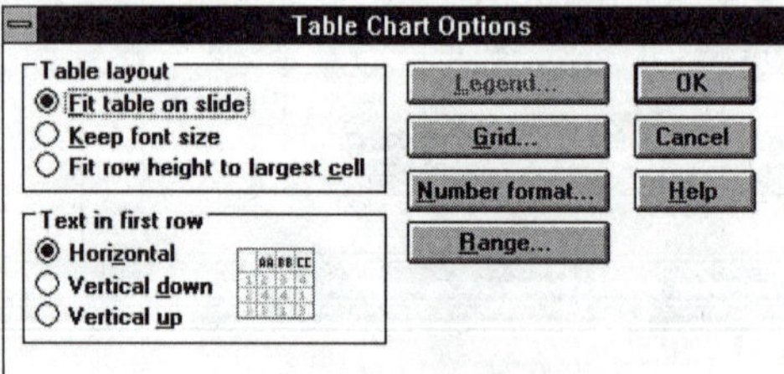

Fig. 3.22
The Table Chart Options dialog box.

To display the first row text vertically, follow these steps:

1. Choose Chart **O**ptions from the **C**hart menu. The Table Chart Options dialog box appears.
2. Choose the Vertical **D**own or Vertical **U**p in the dialog box.
3. Click OK button.

The text is now vertically oriented; you read the text up or down instead of from left to right (see fig. 3.23).

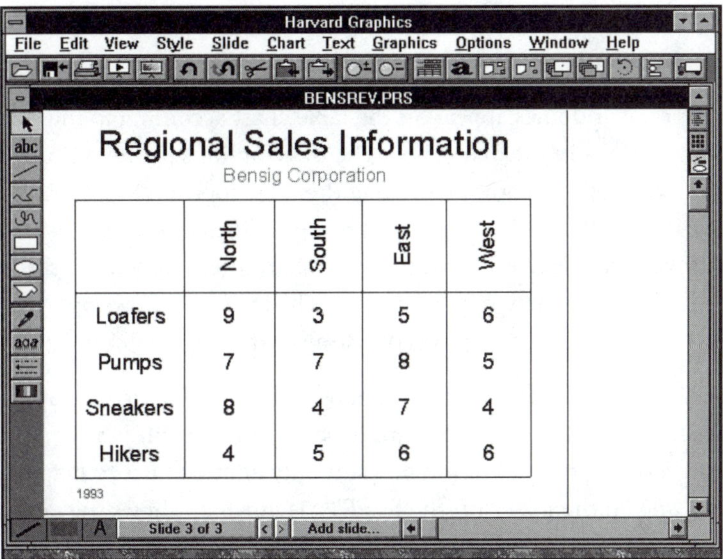

Fig. 3.23 Vertically oriented text in the first row.

Modifying Grid Lines. When you choose a table chart style, your most significant consideration is the grid lines. After creating a table chart, you can use the **G**rid command on the **C**hart menu to change the way the lines appear. Figure 3.24 shows the Table Chart Grid Options dialog box. This dialog box has two sets of options for the row and column grid lines. You use each set to determine how the row and column grid lines appear. Another option displays a frame around the data. If you choose the Show **F**rame around Table option on the dialog box, a box appears around the body of the chart.

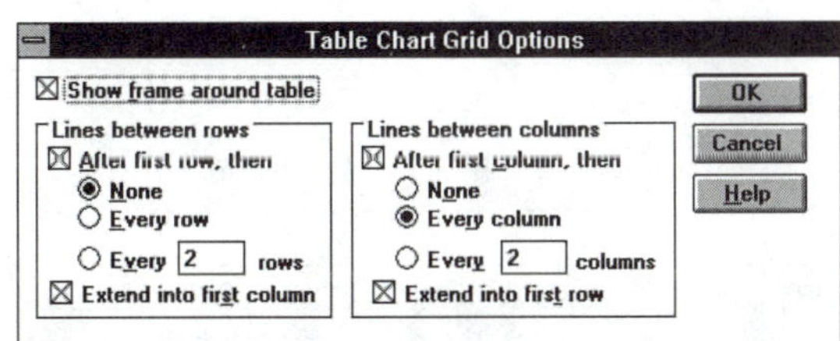

Fig. 3.24 The Table Chart Grid Options dialog box.

For both rows and columns, the first option (**A**fter First Row) determines whether grid lines separate the rows and columns. If you do not choose this option, the remaining options for the rows or columns cannot be used in the chart. If you enable **A**fter First Row, the chart contains a grid line separating the first row from the rest of the data. In the table chart you created for Bensig Corporation, this line separates the row containing the column headers from the rest of the values for the column.

Any additional grid lines appear on the table chart according to the status of remaining options in the dialog box. The three options (**N**one, **E**very Row, and E**v**ery *xxx* Rows) determine the way the lines appear. These options are exclusive. If you choose **N**one, the first row grid line is the only line displayed. If you choose **E**very Row, the table chart looks more like a spreadsheet, with grid lines drawn on every row. The E**v**ery *xxx* Rows option draws grid lines between groups of rows consisting of the specified number of rows.

On the revenue chart, for example, suppose that you want to display the grid lines in alternating rows and columns, rather than crowding the chart with lines for every row and column. You want only enough lines to help your audience line up the data with the headers. Figure 3.25 shows the table chart with alternating grid lines.

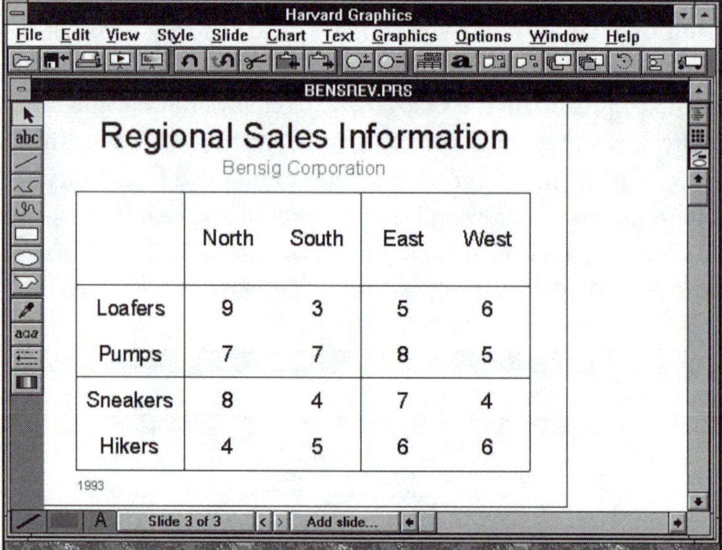

Fig. 3.25
A table chart with alternating grid lines.

To produce this chart, set the options in the following way:

1. Click **A**fter First Row so that an X appears in the box.

2. Click the E**v**ery *xxx* Rows option and type **2**.

3. Click After First Column so that an X appears in the box.
4. Click the Every *xxx* Columns option and type **2**.
5. Click OK.

The table chart with the alternate grid lines appears in the Slide Editor.

You can use the Every *xxx* Rows option to display grid lines at any interval of rows. The number you enter in the field between the words *Every* and *Rows* determines the size of the interval. To set the interval, click the Every *xxx* Rows text box and type the number. The Extend into First Column option of the dialog box causes the grid lines to be drawn from the bottom of the table chart all the way through to the top. At the top of the chart, the grid lines separate the headers in the same way the cells are divided. The Extend into First Row option displays grid lines between the row headings on the chart. Click this option to extend the grid lines.

Setting the Number Format. A variety of numeric format options allow you to determine exactly how numbers will appear in your table charts. The following list illustrates the available options:

- Currency displays the $ symbol
- Comma separates thousands with a comma
- Scientific Notation displays number in scientific notation
- Percent displays the % sign
- Negative Notation either precedes a negative number with a minus sign or encloses a negative number in parentheses
- Decimal places determines the number of decimal places
- Scaling factor is the scale used when dividing a numeric by a scale factor
- Leading text is the text preceding a number
- Trailing text is the text preceding a number

Note

The International settings associated with the Windows Control Panel determine which symbols represent currency, thousand separator, and decimal separator. Also worth noting here is the fact that, with the exception of the scale factor, you can apply number formatting to a single cell, or a range of cells.

To format a cell, or range of cells, follow these steps:

1. Select the cell or range of cells to which you want to apply a specific number format.

2. From the Table Chart Options dialog box, select all the formatting options you want to apply, and click OK.

From Here...

In this chapter, you have been introduced to the different text charts you can create with Harvard Graphics. You have learned about the advantages for using a title, bullet, or table chart. For each type of chart, you learned how to pick a style, and you learned what to consider when deciding on a style. You also learned how to enter data into your chart and how to use the **E**dit menu to modify the data.

In addition to entering data, you learned how to modify the appearance of a bullet or table chart. For bullet charts, you learned how to change the bullet symbol to emphasize the significant items in the chart. With table charts, you learned what effects grid lines can have on your chart and how to use lines to help your audience read the chart.

The next chapter, Chapter 4, "Creating Organization Charts," explains how to create and modify charts that you use to present the members and hierarchical structure of an organization.

Chapter 4

Creating Organization Charts

4

In this chapter, you learn how to do the following:

- Create organization charts
- Modify organization charts

You use organization charts to represent graphically the members of an organization or company and the relationships of the different positions. Each member has a name and a job title that describes the member's position. To help distinguish positions in the organization chart, Harvard Graphics displays each member's name and job title in an individual box.

Figure 4.1 is an example of an organization chart that uses three-dimensional boxes to identify members and job titles. In this chart, three levels are defined in the organization. Lines extend from the boxes on the top two levels of the organization chart to the boxes and names below. The top boxes represent managers, and the boxes and names below represent subordinate positions or work groups that are directly responsible to each manager. The box to the side of and below the top box represents a staff member who is directly responsible only to the manager and who has no subordinates.

Choosing an Organization Chart Style

The style of an organization chart is defined by the style of the boxes that enclose each entry and the way the last level of the organization is displayed. For boxes, you can choose between two-dimensional (2-D) and three-dimensional (3-D) boxes. Figure 4.1 shows an organization chart with 3-D boxes; figure 4.2 shows an organization chart with 2-D boxes.

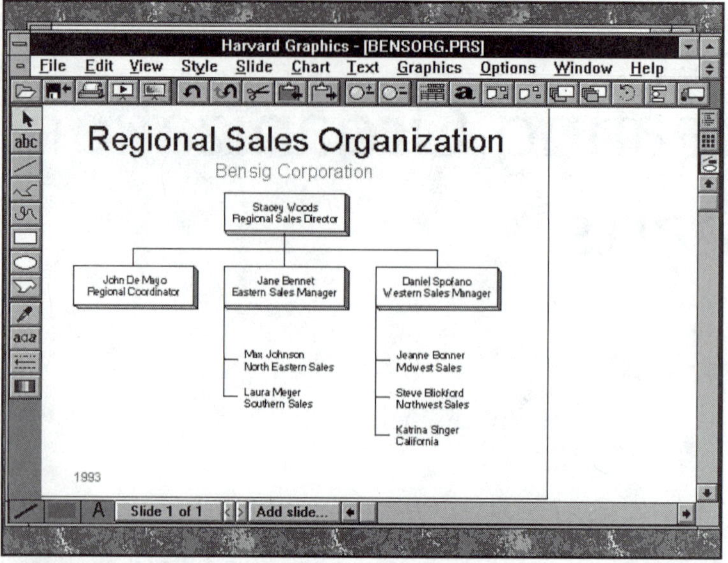

Fig. 4.1
An organization chart with managers, subordinates, and a staff position.

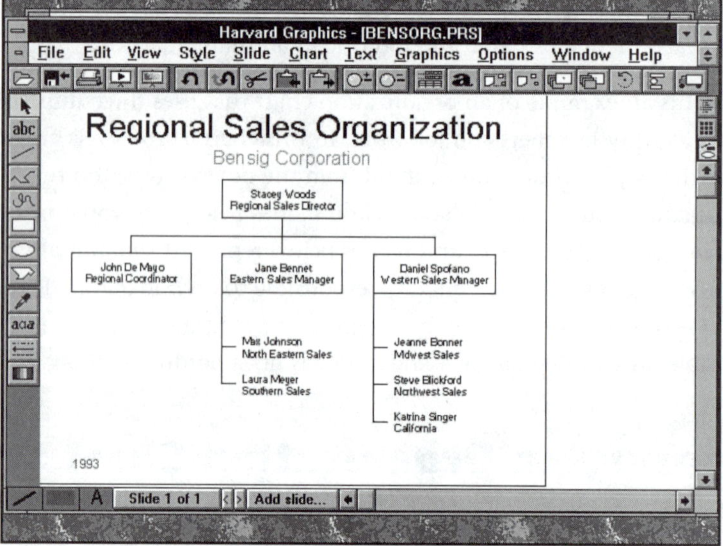

Fig. 4.2
An organization chart with 2-D boxes.

You can choose a vertical list of subordinate positions, which is connected by a line to the box representing the appropriate manager (refer to fig. 4.1), or you can choose to display the subordinate levels in horizontally aligned boxes (see fig. 4.3). The first choice leaves more room for member information, but the second choice may be more visually appealing because a box represents each member of the organization.

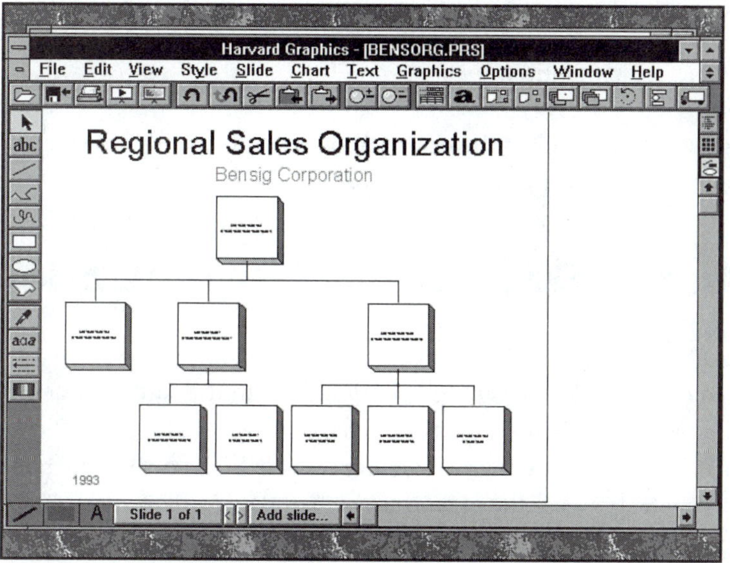

Fig. 4.3 An organization chart with horizontally aligned boxes.

To create an organization chart with 3-D style boxes, follow these steps:

1. From the **F**ile menu, choose **N**ew Presentation. The Add Slide dialog box appears.

2. Choose Organization as the slide type.

3. Harvard Graphics displays the options for organization charts (see fig. 4.4).

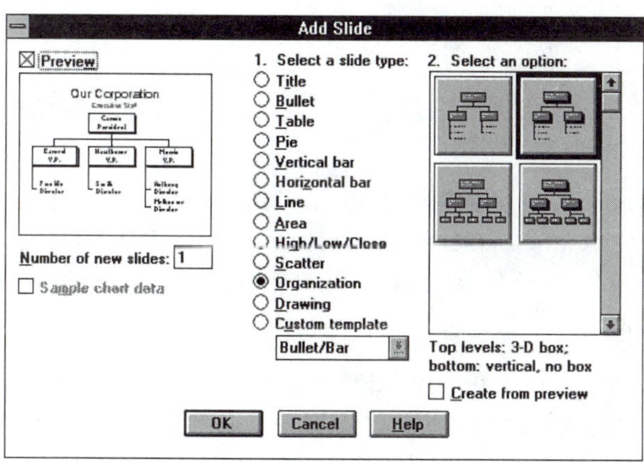

Fig. 4.4 The Add Slide dialog box showing the styles of organization charts.

4. Select the second organization chart diagram in the top row.

5. Click the OK button.

Harvard Graphics displays the organization chart data form, in which you define the positions of your organization.

Entering Data into an Organization Chart

You can enter the data for an organization chart in the data form or in the Outliner, which is discussed in more detail in Chapter 11, "Using the Outliner." The steps you follow in either case are the same. For the remainder of this chapter, you use the organization chart data form to enter your data (see fig. 4.5). By default, the top-level manager box appears when you open the data form. (Each chart can have only one top-level manager.)

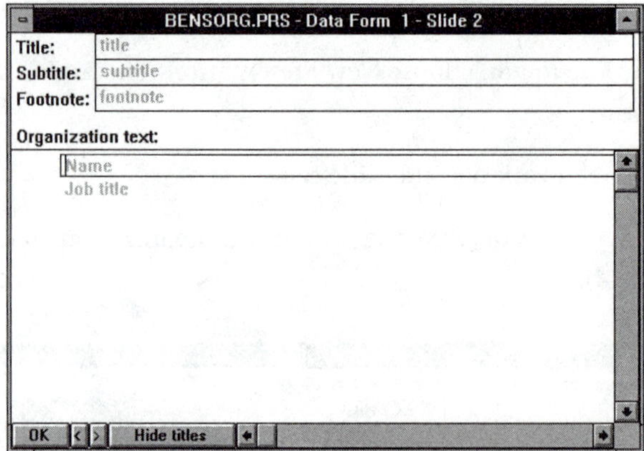

Fig. 4.5 The organization chart data form.

The organization chart data form is divided into two regions. The top of the form contains the title, subtitle, and footnote for the chart. You use the bottom portion, below the Organization Text prompt, to define the positions of the organization.

To enter the data into an organization member's box, you first must position the insertion point in the Name or Job Title field by using the mouse or the arrow keys. The field that contains the insertion point is the active field. After the insertion point is in the correct position, you can type the information directly into the field.

The chart shown in figure 4.1 represents the regional sales organization for Bensig Corporation. The highest manager is the regional sales director. To define the director as the top-level manager in the new chart, follow these steps:

1. Click the Name field in the data form.

2. Type the name for this box. For the example, type **Stacey Woods**.

3. Click the Job Title field.

4. Type **Regional Sales Director**.

   You have defined the top-level management position.

Adding Comments

Following the name and title of the organization member, you can add a comment that gives additional information about the member. To add a comment, you must create a new line in the Job Title field by pressing Ctrl+Enter. The insertion point moves to the beginning of the new line. In addition to comments, you can use this technique to display member information on more than one line.

To add a comment to the director's box, follow these steps:

1. Click the Job Title field for the top-level manager.

2. Press the End key to move to the end of the field.

3. Press Ctrl+Enter to start a new line.

4. Type the comment. For the example, type **Acting VP of Sales**.

Figure 4.6 shows the data form with the comment added to the management position.

Adding Subordinate Positions

The positions reporting to a manager are indicated in the organization chart by lines from the manager's box down to the boxes for the subordinate positions. (In this tutorial, the terms *manager* and *subordinates* are used. If an organization chart represents different divisions of a company, the division could be the manager, and different groups of the division the subordinates.)

On the organization chart data form, subordinates are identified by the way they are indented. Members with names indented under a manager's name are subordinates of (report to) that manager. In figure 4.7, Max Johnson and Laura Meyer are subordinates of Jane Bennet. The level of indentation is especially helpful when determining subordinates in a chart of more than two levels. In this case, members in the middle levels are managers of some members and subordinates of others. In figure 4.7, Jane Bennet and Daniel Sporano are both subordinates of the director, Stacey Woods, and managers of other members.

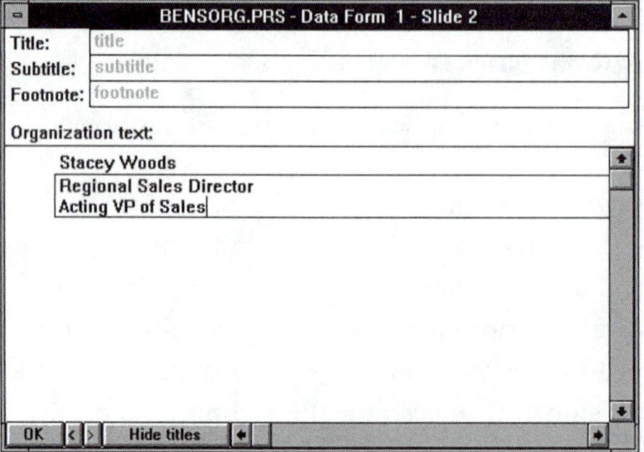

Fig. 4.6 The top-level management position with a comment added.

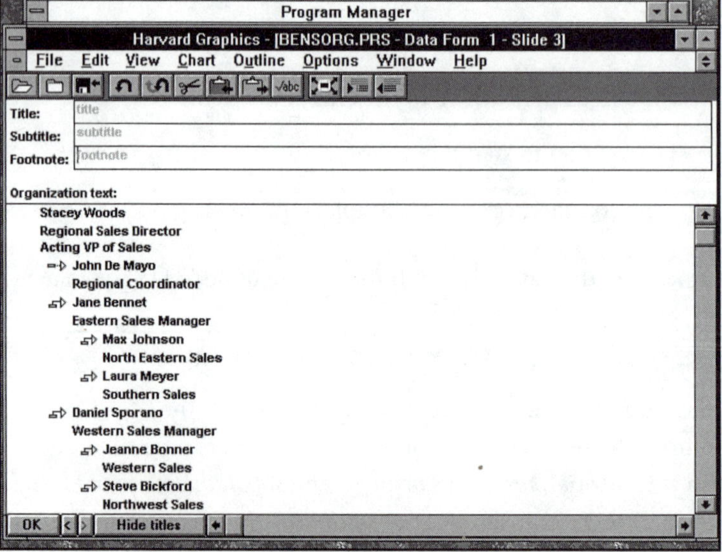

Fig. 4.7 An organization chart with many levels.

In Harvard Graphics, a *staff position* represents a staff member directly responsible only to a manager and with no subordinates. The levels of staff positions in an organization chart also are indicated by how they are indented in the data form. To distinguish between a subordinate and a staff position, each level of organization has a symbol displayed next to the name. Subordinates have a box symbol with a bent arrow at the top; notice Jane Bennet in figure 4.7, for example. The staff position symbol is a box with a straight arrow extending from the right side rather than the top. In figure 4.7, John De Mayo is a staff position under the regional director.

You can add subordinate positions to your organization chart. To add a subordinate for a manager, for example, you first must add a new field under the manager. To create a new field, select the Job Title field of the manager and press Enter.

Harvard Graphics adds the new position as a manager of the same level or as a subordinate, depending on the entry that appears below the manager in the data form. If the position below is another manager, the new position also will be a manager. If the position below is a subordinate, pressing Enter creates another subordinate. The one exception to this rule pertains to positions added after the first manager. Harvard Graphics adds these positions as subordinates because the chart can have only one top-level manager.

In the Bensig sales organization chart, you have already entered the information for the top-level manager. To enter the information for the remaining members of the organization, follow these steps:

1. Click the Job Title field for the regional sales director.
2. Press Enter to create a subordinate field. Harvard Graphics adds two new fields to the data form. You enter the name and job title of the new member in these fields.
3. Type **Jane Bennet**, and press Enter.
4. Type **Eastern Sales Manager**.
5. Press Enter to create a field for a new manager.
6. Type **Max Johnson**, and press Enter.
7. Type **North Eastern Sales**.

8. Follow the same steps to add the following managers:

Name	Title
Laura Meyer	Southern Sales
Daniel Sporano	Western Sales Manager
Jeanne Bonner	Midwest Sales
Steve Bickford	Northwest Sales
Katrina Singer	California

Figure 4.8 shows the data form with the members you created. All members appear at the same level as subordinates of the top-level manager. The following section, "Changing the Level of a Position," explains how to adjust the positions to illustrate the correct organization.

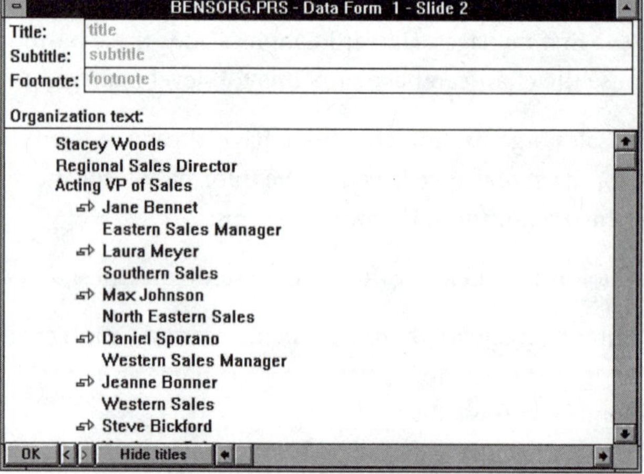

Fig. 4.8 All subordinates appear at the same level.

Changing the Level of a Position

The level of a position in the data form determines how the position appears in the chart. A position indented below the preceding position is one level lower in the organization and appears as a subordinate in the chart. After you enter the information for positions of the organization, you can change the level of any position to a higher or lower level. When you adjust the level of a manager, the manager's subordinates also change. The only restriction for changing levels is that each manager must have at least one subordinate. If only one subordinate position is below a manager, you cannot lower the level of that subordinate.

To lower or raise the position's level, you first must select the position. You can use the arrow keys to move the insertion point into the member's Job Title field, or you can select the member's name or job title with the mouse. After you select the position, you can use the Tab key to change the position's level. To lower the position on the organization chart, press the Tab key. To raise the level, press Shift+Tab (hold down the Shift key while you press Tab).

Another way to change the level of a position exists. You can use the mouse to drag the member's name right (to lower the level) or left (to elevate the level). When you drag a member's name, the mouse pointer changes to a hand to indicate that you are changing the level. See the section "Moving Positions" for more information on using the mouse to edit the chart's organization.

In the regional sales chart, Harvard Graphics added all the members as subordinates to the director. In the Bensig sales staff, however, members report to the East and West managers, who are the only members who report to the director. To adjust the subordinates of the two regional managers, follow these steps:

1. Click the name of the member you want to move. For the example, click Max Johnson.

2. Press Tab to move Max to a lower position in the organization.

3. Follow the preceding steps to move Laura Meyer, Jeanne Bonner, Steve Bickford, and Katrina Singer to lower positions.

Figure 4.9 shows the complete organization of managers and subordinates. From this figure, you can see that Jane Bennet and Daniel Sporano, who are managers, also are subordinates because they report to Stacey Woods. You also can see how others report to Jane Bennet and Daniel Sporano.

Adding a Staff Position

Any member of the organization can have two staff positions reporting to him or her. In the data form, staff positions are indented the same way subordinate positions are indented. To indicate that an indented position is a staff position, Harvard Graphics displays a staff-position symbol next to the name of the member. In the chart, staff positions appear more to the side of the manager than are the subordinates. The line from the manager box joins the staff position box at the side rather than at the top.

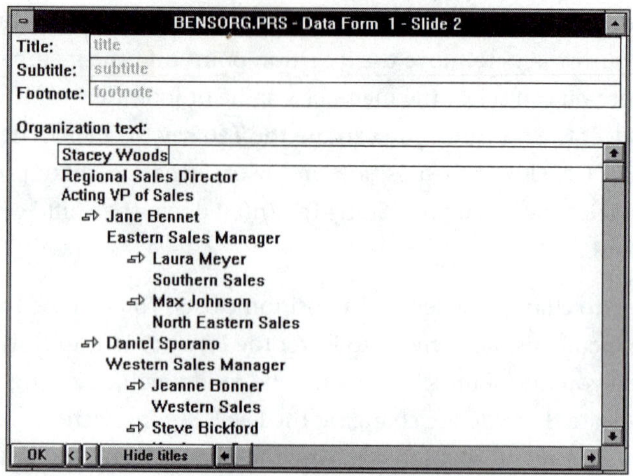

Fig. 4.9
The complete organization, with managers and subordinates.

You can find the command to add staff positions on the Organization Charts menu, which you access through the **C**hart menu. When you execute the **A**dd Staff Position command, Harvard Graphics adds a new position to the data form below the active position, and the staff position symbol appears next to the position.

Follow these steps to add a staff position under the regional director:

1. Click the box to which you want to attach the staff position. For the example, click Stacey Woods.

2. From the **C**hart menu, choose O**r**ganization Charts. The Organization Charts pop-up menu appears.

3. Choose **A**dd Staff Position from the Organization Charts pop-up menu. Harvard Graphics creates a staff position, in which you enter a name and job title, under the member.

4. Type the name of the person who holds the staff position. For the example, type **John De Mayo** in the Name field.

5. Click the Job Title field, or press Enter.

6. Type the job title. For the example, type **Regional Coordinator**.

Figure 4.10 shows the data form with the staff position. You can see in the figure that the symbol next to John De Mayo is a staff position symbol, which is different from the subordinate symbol that appears next to Jane Bennet.

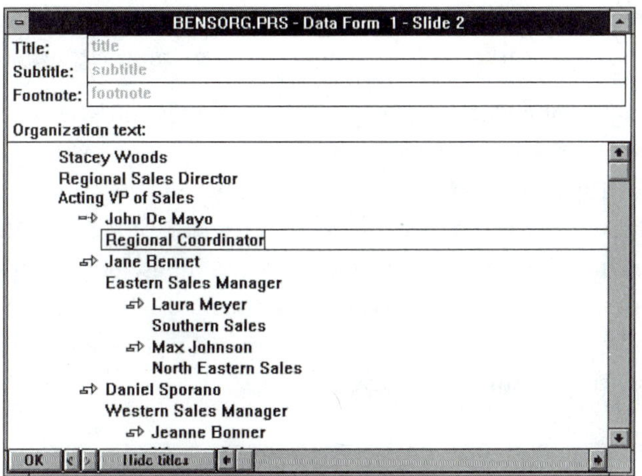

Fig. 4.10 The organization chart with a staff position.

Deleting Positions

To delete a position, you can use the Clear command from the Edit menu. Because editing commands affects the active position only, you must select the field you intend to delete. You can click the Name or Job Title field, or you can use the arrow keys to move the insertion point into the Name or Job Title field.

Suppose, for example, that the Northwest and Midwest sales regions have been combined into one region and that Jeanne Bonner is the employee responsible for the new region. Follow these steps to delete a position:

1. Click the name of the member whose position you want to delete. For this example, click Steve Bickford.
2. From the **E**dit menu, choose Cl**e**ar.

Harvard Graphics deletes the selected position.

Moving Positions

In addition to deleting or changing the level of a position, you can rearrange the positions in the organization. To move any position in the data form, you can use the mouse to drag the information to the new location.

When you select a position, the information for that position and all subordinates and staff positions below the position are highlighted. When you move a management position, you also move the associated subordinates and staff positions. To move a position without moving the associated subordinates, you must change the level of the subordinates so that they are no longer subordinates to the position you are moving. See the section "Changing the Level of a Position" earlier in this chapter for more information.

After you highlight a block of positions, the mouse pointer becomes a hand icon pointing to the location to which you are dragging the block. A red line that begins with a triangle in the data form shows the location and the level of the positions after you release the mouse. The end of the triangle is indented to match the new level. As you move the mouse pointer up and down to select a new location, you also can move the mouse left and right to change the level. Figure 4.11 shows an example of a placeholder that appears when you select a position to move.

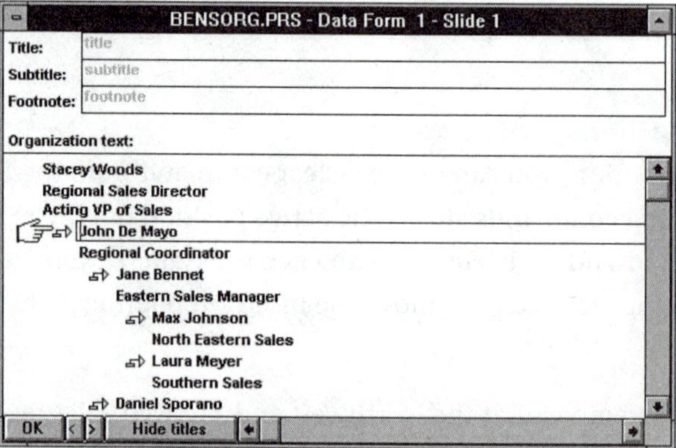

Fig. 4.11
The hand placeholder.

Suppose, for example, that you decide that you want to make one of the two sales managers in the Bensig Corporation the primary sales manager. To indicate this change in the organization chart, you make the Eastern Sales Manager a subordinate of the Western Sales Manager. To move a member from one level to another, follow these steps:

1. Click the subordinate symbol next to the name you want to change, Jane Bennet, for example. Hold down the mouse button.

   Jane Bennet and all subordinates are highlighted (see fig. 4.12). When you move Jane Bennet, all her subordinates move as well, and a red line appears above the name of the manager you are moving. (If you were to release the mouse button with the line position shown in figure 4.12, the manager would be the first subordinate of the director.)

2. Drag the mouse pointer until the red line is below the new job title—for the example, Western Sales Manager—and the triangle at the end of the

red line is aligned with the subordinate symbol in front of Jeanne Bonner.

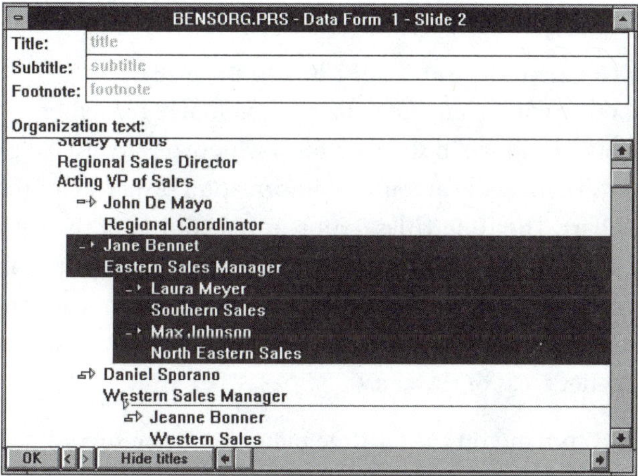

Fig. 4.12 The selected manager and subordinates.

3. Release the mouse button.

Figure 4.13 shows the data form after the move. You can see in the form that the Eastern Sales Manager is now a subordinate of the Western Sales Manager.

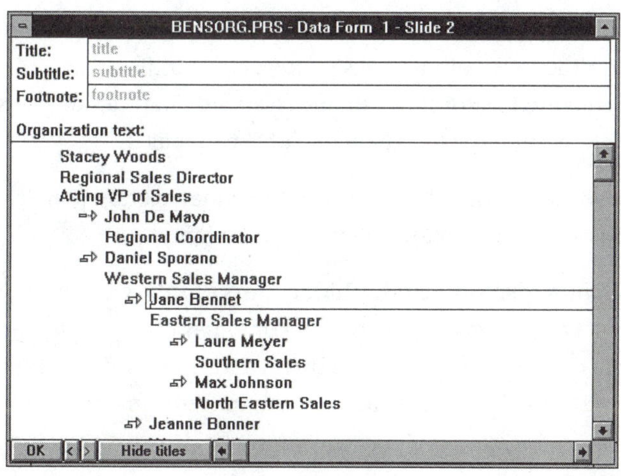

Fig. 4.13 The Eastern sales organization moved under Western sales.

You also can use the Cu**t**, **C**opy, and **P**aste commands on the **E**dit menu to move a member to another location in the chart. When you issue the **C**opy command, Harvard Graphics copies the selected position to the Clipboard, and the original remains in the data form. When you choose Cut, Harvard Graphics removes the original position from the data form and stores it in the Clipboard. Choose **P**aste from the **E**dit menu to copy the entry from the Clipboard back into the organization chart below the active member.

Working with Large Organizations in the Data Form

If you are working with a large organization, you may have more positions in the chart than you can see in the data form window. Harvard Graphics has two commands to limit the amount of information displayed in the data form for the chart. The Hide Titles option at the bottom of the data form removes the Title, Subtitle, and Footnote fields from the window, making more room to show member information. If you still cannot see positions in the organization chart, use the scroll bars on the side of the data form window to view other areas of the chart.

The Collapse command on the Outline menu hides the subordinates of the active position. To hide the subordinates of an active position, follow these steps:

1. From the Outline menu, choose Collapse. The pop-up menu appears.
2. Choose **T**opic, which is the only active option in the Collapse pop-up menu.

Figure 4.14 shows the organization chart in which you collapsed the subordinate levels for the two regional sales managers. To indicate that the managers represent a collapsed list of subordinates, Harvard Graphics displays a filled-in subordinate symbol next to the name of the manager.

You also can collapse the subordinates list of a manager by double-clicking the subordinate symbol next to the manager's name.

Harvard Graphics does not remove hidden lists of subordinates from the organization chart; instead, the program combines the subordinates and the manager into one item. As you move the manager around, the collapsed subordinate lists also move. If you cut the manager from the data form to the Clipboard, for example, Harvard Graphics also cuts the manager's subordinates.

You use the Expand command on the Outline menu to redisplay subordinates in the data form. In addition to the Expand command, you also can expand the subordinates by double-clicking the subordinate symbol next to the manager's name. To expand the chart, follow these steps:

1. From the **Outline** menu, choose **Expand**.

2. From the **Expand** menu, choose **All**.

Harvard Graphics expands the hidden list of subordinates.

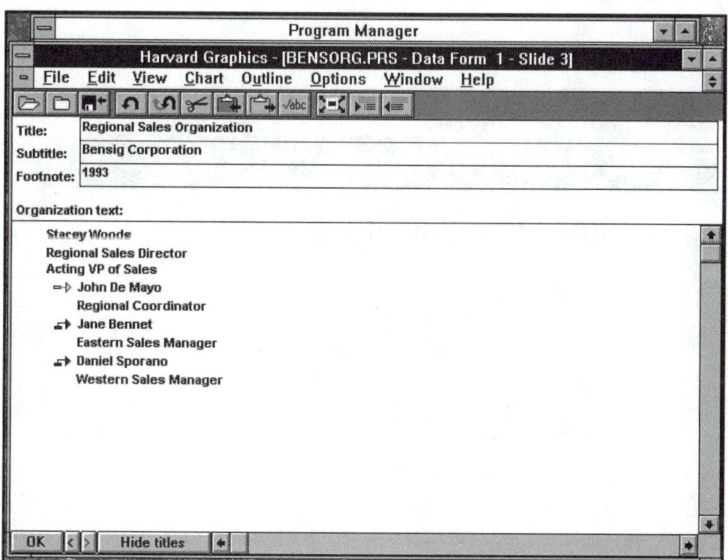

Fig. 4.14 Regional managers, with symbols, indicating collapsed subordinate levels.

Hiding the Job Title for a Position

The **Hide** Job Title command (on the **Organization** Charts menu under the **Chart** menu) hides a member's job title in both the chart and the data form. (Remember, the job title is hidden, not removed, from the chart.) The **Hide** Job Title command affects the active member. If more than one member is active, the job titles for all the selected members are hidden.

The **Hide** Job Title command differs from the Hide Titles button, discussed in the section "Working with Large Organizations in the Data Form," in that the **Hide** Job Title command affects the members of the organization. The Hide Titles button just removes the title, subtitle, and footnote from the data form.

Figure 4.15 shows the sales staff organization chart displaying only the member names.

To hide job titles, follow these steps:

1. To select the entire organization, click beside the name of the first member.

2. From the **C**hart menu, choose O**r**ganization Charts.

3. Choose **H**ide Job Title. Harvard Graphics hides the job titles.

To redisplay job titles that have been hidden, select the entire organizational chart, and then choose the **S**how Job Title command on the O**r**ganization Chart menu.

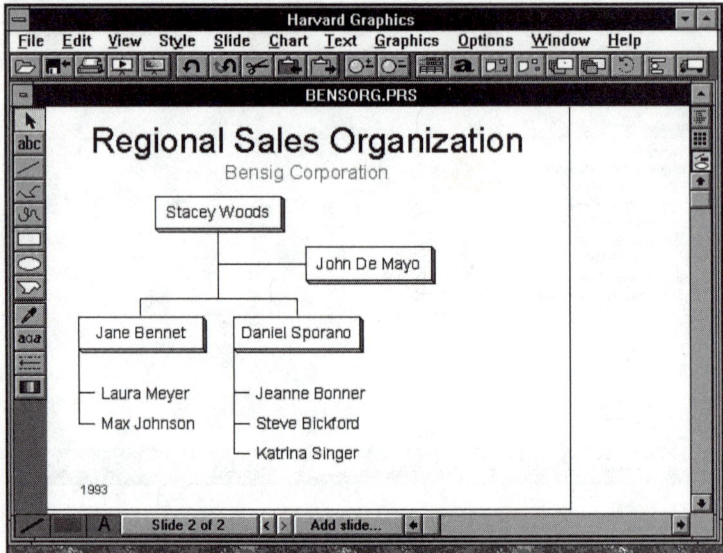

Fig. 4.15
The Bensig sales staff chart showing only the member names.

Adding Titles and Footnotes

To complete the chart, add a title, subtitle, and footnote to help clarify the information in the chart.

Follow these steps to fill out the title region of the organization data chart:

1. Click the Title field and type the title. For the example, type **Regional Sales Organization**.

2. Click the Subtitle field and type the subtitle. For the example, type **Bensig Corporation**.

3. Click the Footnote field and type the footnote. For the example, type **1993**.

4. Click the OK button at the bottom of the data form to accept the changes.

Harvard Graphics creates the organization chart slide.

Modifying the Appearance of the Chart

After you create an organization chart, you can use the Chart **O**ptions command on the **C**hart menu to modify the appearance of the boxes in the chart, the alignment of text in the boxes, and the style of the boxes themselves. Figure 4.16 shows the Organization Chart Options dialog box. The options in the dialog box show the settings for the Bensig sales staff chart. The Text alignment section indicates that text is centered in a box. In the Organization Chart Options dialog box, you chose to use 3-D boxes and to display the last level of the organization in a vertical list. Both choices are reflected in the dialog box.

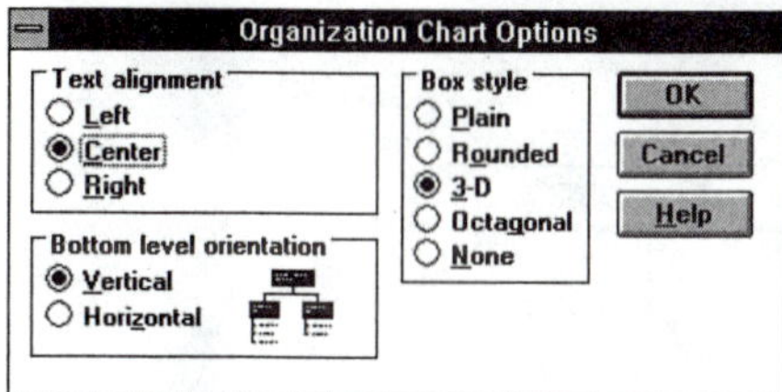

Fig. 4.16
The Organization Chart Options dialog box.

Figure 4.17 shows the completed chart in the Slide Editor. Chapter 13, "Enhancing Drawings and Objects," explains how to enhance the text and objects on a slide by using the Slide Editor tools.

The Organization Chart Options dialog box provides more choices for box styles. With the Box Style options in this dialog box, you also can select plain boxes, rounded boxes, octagonal boxes, or no box at all.

The Text alignment options in the dialog box enable you to align the text on the left, in the center, or on the right side of the box.

The Bottom Level Orientation options provide a choice between showing the last level of members in a vertical list or in boxes aligned horizontally.

Suppose that in the Bensig sales staff chart, you decide that you want boxes with rounded corners for all the members of the organization, including the last level. To make the information in the chart easier to read, you also want to align all the text on the left side of the box. To make these changes in the appearance of the chart, follow these steps:

1. From the **C**hart menu, choose Chart **O**ptions. The Organization Chart Options dialog box appears.
2. In the Text alignment section, choose **L**eft.
3. In the Box style, choose R**o**unded.

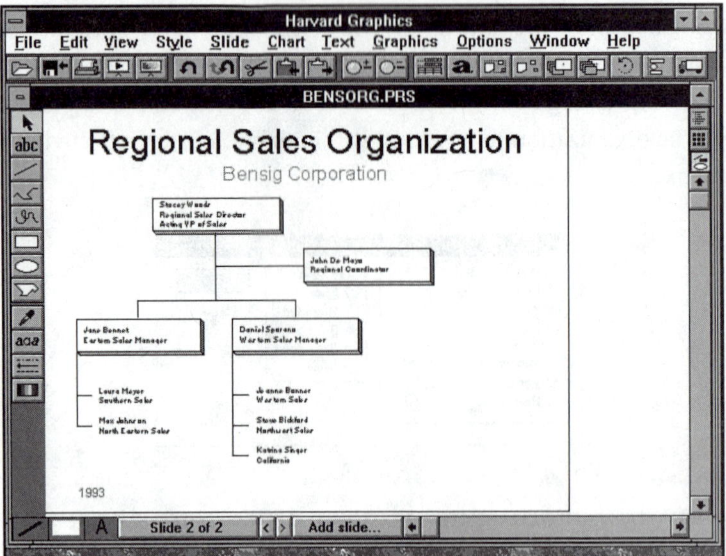

Fig. 4.17
The completed organization chart in the Slide Editor.

4. For the Bottom level orientation, choose Hori**z**ontal.
5. Click OK.

Harvard Graphics makes the specified changes, shown in figure 4.18.

You modify the attributes of the organization chart boxes, such as the color or the outline thickness, in the Slide Editor. In future chapters, you learn how to use the Slide Editor to change the size and color of the objects in a chart.

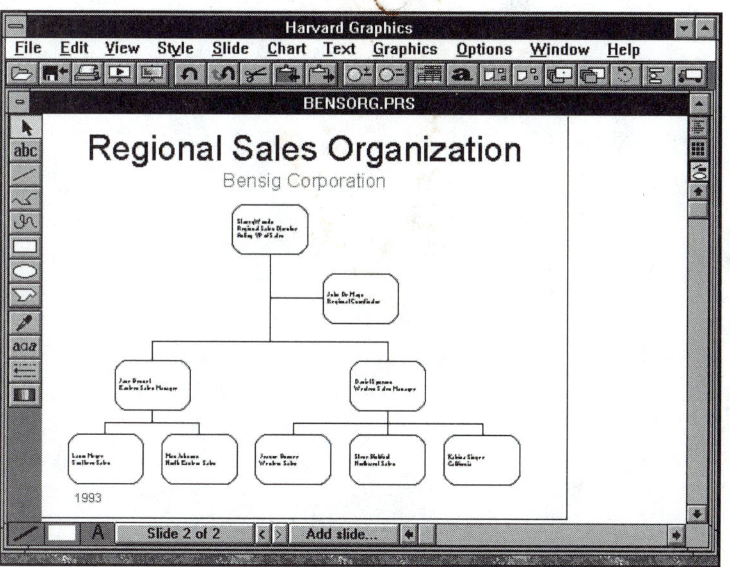

Fig. 4.18 The modified Bensig sales organization chart.

From Here...

In this chapter, you have been introduced to the basic elements of an organization chart. You learned how to create an organization chart. After you created the chart, you learned how to add subordinates and staff positions on the data form. You also learned how to move the positions in an organization and how to edit the chart data using the Windows Clipboard. After you added the chart to a presentation, you learned how to change the appearance of your chart and how to collapse the chart or to hide job titles.

In the next chapter, "Creating XY Charts," you learn how to create and edit XY charts.

Chapter 5

Creating XY Charts

You use XY charts to graph numeric data on a set of axes. The name for the XY chart comes from the Cartesian coordinate system in which all points of the system are represented by a pair of x- and y-coordinates. Each coordinate in the system is plotted on a separate axis. Much like the Cartesian system, the data in an XY chart is charted against two axes.

A typical focus in an XY chart, for example, may be the sales revenue for 1991. You use one axis to represent the years (1990, 1991, 1992, and so on) and the other axis to graph the revenue figures. The difference between a simple plot and an XY chart is that in an XY chart, you can represent the value with a point, a vertical bar, or some other graphical object.

Figure 5.1 shows an XY chart in which the horizontal axis represents years and the vertical axis represents the revenue. A three-dimensional bar represents each point on the graph. By comparing the sizes of the bars, the members of your audience can recognize easily that the company's revenues have increased significantly over the last few years.

This chapter explains how to create and enhance XY charts. You begin by learning about the different parts of an XY chart in the section "Understanding the Elements of an XY Chart." You then learn about the different styles of XY charts in "Choosing an XY Chart Style." The section "Entering Data into an XY Chart" explains how to define the axes for the chart and how to enter the numeric data values. The section "Changing the Appearance of an XY Chart" covers the options you can set to control the appearance of the chart and create the most effective charts.

In this chapter, you learn how to do the following:

- Create and edit XY charts
- Organize data forms
- Use legend, grid, and frame

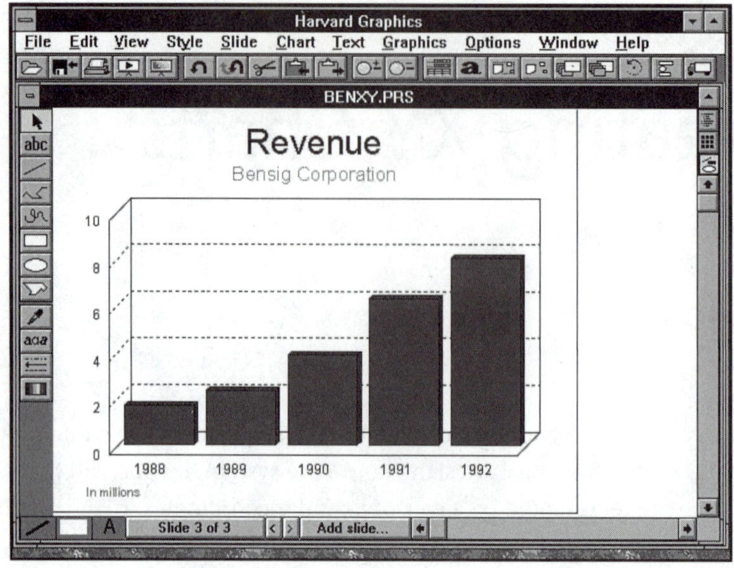

Fig. 5.1 A sample XY chart using vertical bars to graph numeric values.

Understanding the Elements of an XY Chart

XY charts support more features than any other chart type in Harvard Graphics. Before learning how to use these features, you must understand the basic elements of an XY chart. All the major components of an XY chart appear in figure 5.2.

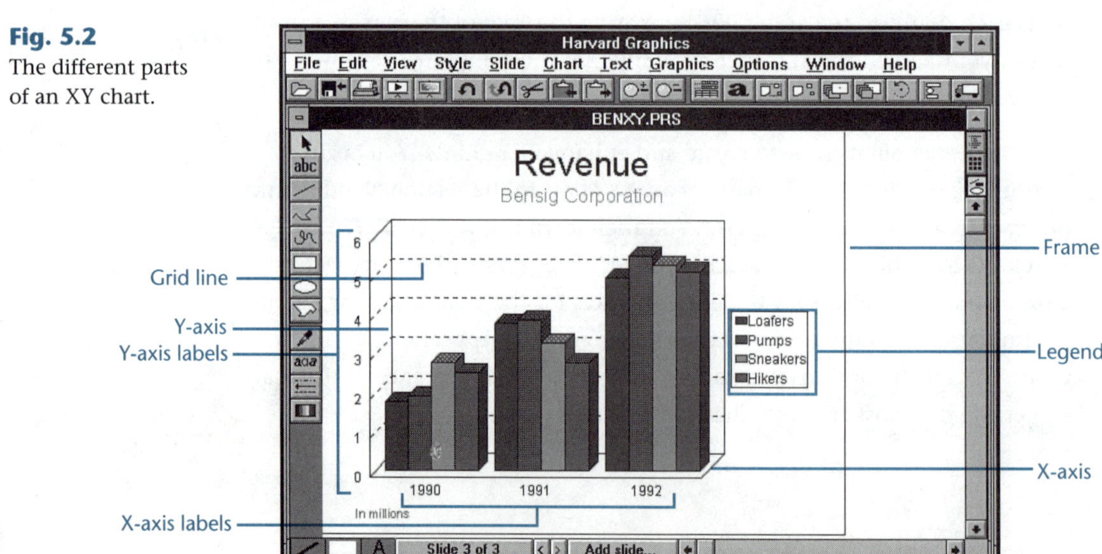

Fig. 5.2 The different parts of an XY chart.

The horizontal axis is the *x-axis*. In figure 5.2, the x-axis represents the years. Along the bottom of the chart, the years serve as the labels for the x-axis and are called *x-axis labels*.

The vertical axis is the *y-axis*. The *y-axis labels* are determined by the values of your data. If, for example, your values range from 1,000 to 10,000, Harvard Graphics uses y-axis labels that range from 1 to 12,000. The *frame* and *grid lines*, which help the audience compare the size of the bars against the axis, appear behind the chart.

You group the data in XY charts into *series*. A different color represents each series in the chart. Figure 5.2 shows four series of data illustrated with different color bars.

To help your audience interpret the data for a series, you can display a *legend*, which gives the names for the series. The legend shown in figure 5.2 illustrates that each of the four series represents a shoe product—loafers, pumps, sneakers, and hikers—of the Bensig Corporation. The Loafers series, for example, has gray bars, as indicated by the legend. The Pumps series bars are black.

Choosing an XY Chart Style

Choosing a style for your XY chart can be a difficult task, given the number of XY chart types available in Harvard Graphics: vertical bar, horizontal bar, line, area, high/low/close, and scatter. The following list explains these chart types:

- *Vertical and horizontal bar charts*. Figures 5.1 and 5.2 illustrate typical examples of a vertical bar chart. A different-colored bar represents each series in the chart. With the exception of transposed x- and y-axes, horizontal bar charts are the same as vertical bar charts.

- *Line charts*. Line charts use a continuous line to represent the data in a series. The line for a series passes through each data value in the series. Line charts are excellent for analyzing data. Your audience easily can see upward and downward sloping lines. Figure 5.3 shows a line chart with three series of data. Using the legend as a guide, you can see that Series 2 and Series 3 climb and Series 1 remains at nearly the same value.

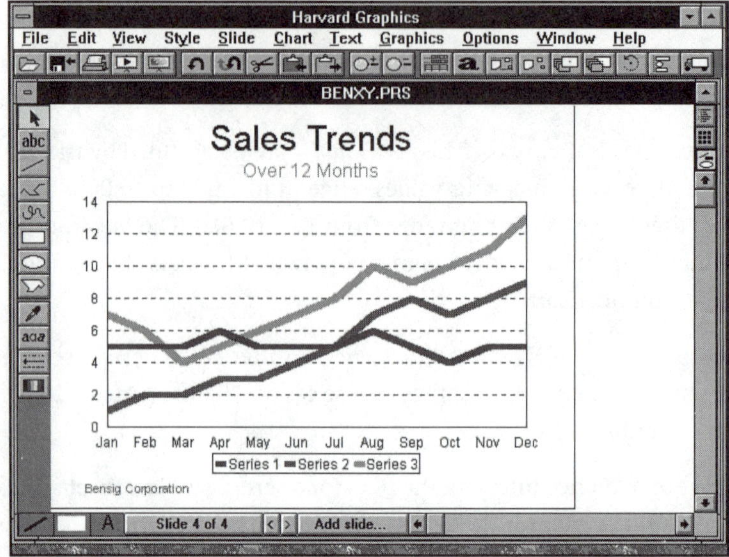

Fig. 5.3 A line chart with three series.

- *Area charts.* Area charts are similar to line charts in that a line connects the data values of a series. In an area chart, however, Harvard Graphics fills in the area between the line and the x-axis. The area for the series is the filled area under the line. In figure 5.4, the data of the graph shows the total sales for any one of the series during the months in the chart. The chart also shows the trends in the sales over the six-month period.

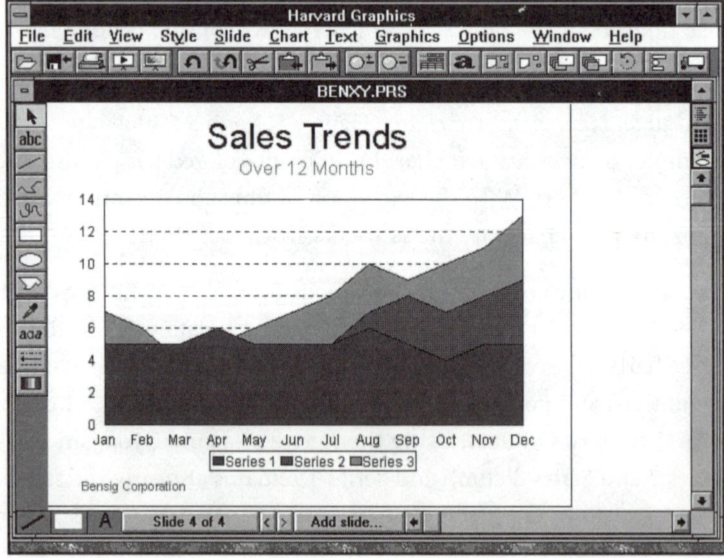

Fig. 5.4 An example area chart.

- *High/low/close charts.* You use high/low/close charts to graph stock information. The four series of this chart type combine to form one bar in the chart body for each time period you specify—day, week, month, and so on. The first series, the highest value for the stock for that period, determines the top of the bar. The low series specifies the lowest value for the period and determines the bottom of the bar. The next two series of a high/low/close chart represent the opening and closing values of the stock.

  The high/low/close marker for any time period is a single bar with tick marks on each side. Harvard Graphics creates the bar from the high and low values for the time period. The mark on the left side of the bar is the opening value, and the mark on the right is the closing value. Figure 5.5 shows a high/low/close chart spanning one week. From the chart, you can see that, on Wednesday, the stock ranged from a price of 3 to 7. The stock opened the day at 4 and closed up 2 points at 6.

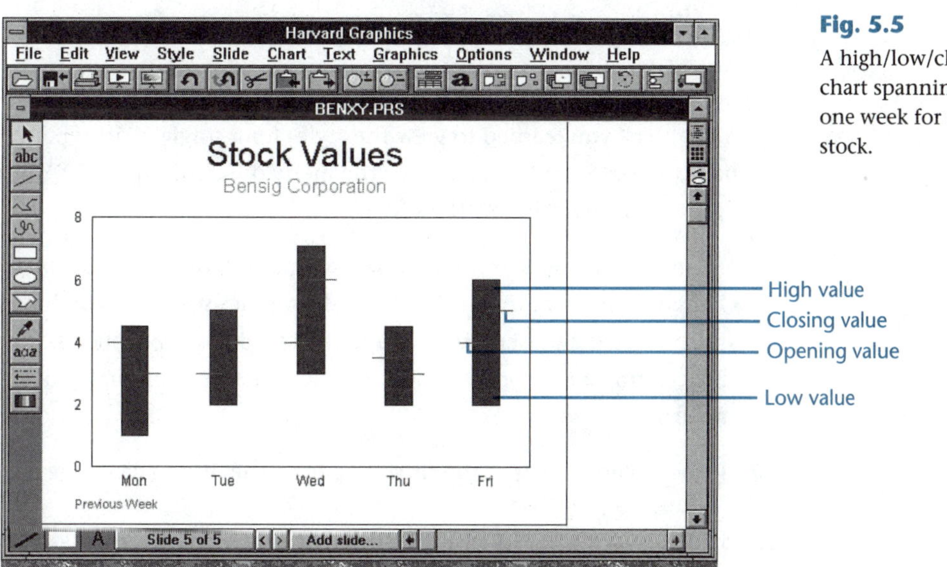

Fig. 5.5
A high/low/close chart spanning one week for a stock.

- *Scatter charts.* The last XY chart type is a scatter chart. This type is more like a traditional plot of x- and y-coordinates on a graph. A marker represents each data value in a scatter chart. With scatter charts, you can plot x- and y-coordinates by making both axes in the chart numeric. Figure 5.6 shows an example of a scatter chart. Scatter charts are good for graphing scientific data or mathematical functions.

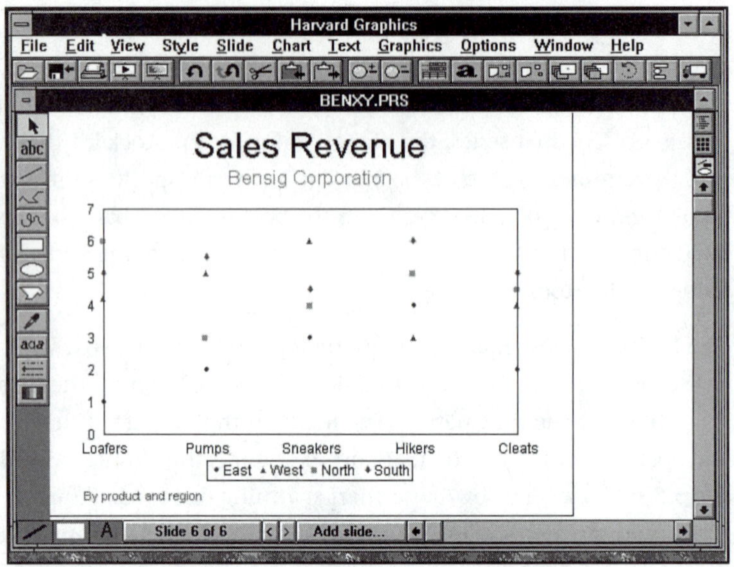

Fig. 5.6
A scatter chart.

Viewing Available Styles

Harvard Graphics helps you pick a style from the different chart types. In the earlier chapters, you learned to view the styles for a single chart type. With XY charts, you can see the images for the many different types of XY charts. To create an XY chart, follow these steps:

1. From the **F**ile menu, choose **N**ew Presentation, or choose Create New Presentation from the initial Harvard Graphics screen. If you have already started a presentation, the Add Slide dialog box appears. If you are creating a new presentation, the New Presentation dialog box appears.

2. Choose Vertical bar as the slide type from the Add Slide dialog box.

The dialog box with the styles for vertical bar charts appears (see fig. 5.7).

You can see the styles for the other XY chart types by clicking the button next to the name of the chart type. To see the chart styles for line charts, for example, click the button next to the line chart type; to see the chart styles for area charts, click the button next to the area chart type. You can also see the styles for a chart type by clicking the button for that type in the Add Slide or New Presentation dialog box.

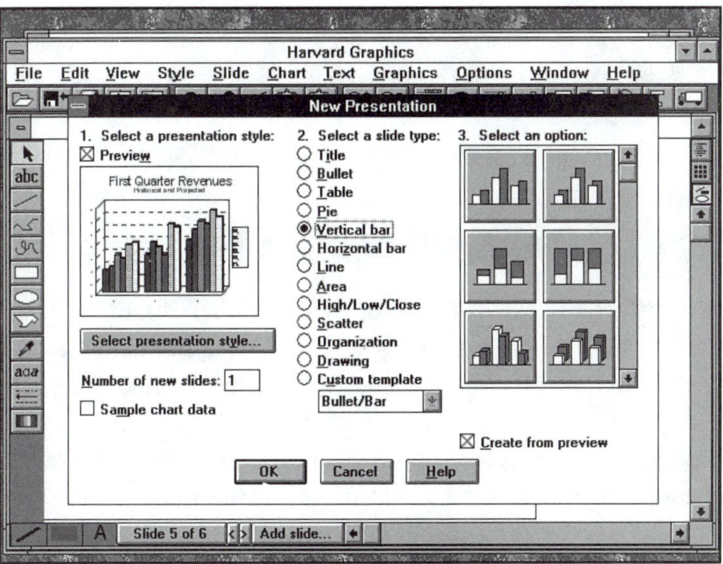

Fig. 5.7
Vertical Bar Chart options.

Selecting a Style

In earlier chapters, you created a slide presentation (including slides for the sales goals, organization, and revenue) for the Bensig Corporation. In this chapter, you create an XY chart that communicates the sales trends of products over the last few years. In this chart, the x-axis labels represent the last five years, and each product constitutes a series. For the representation of the data values, however, you are not sure whether a line or vertical bar chart will be the more effective. In the dialog box, you can browse through the styles for line and vertical bar charts.

Although line charts are ideal for showing trends, you decide on a three-dimensional vertical bar chart that displays the series in different depths. The term for this method of displaying the bars is *overlap*, which indicates that consecutive bars of the chart in one series overlap the next series. You also can use a cluster bar chart to display all the bars side-by-side. If after creating the chart, you decide that the style of chart you created is not effective with your data, you can always change the chart type by using the **C**hange Chart Type command on the **C**hart menu.

Follow these steps to create the three-dimensional overlapped vertical bar chart:

1. Click the Vertical bar button in the New Presentation or Add Slide dialog box to select vertical bar chart options.

2. Click the second image in the third row.

3. Click the OK button to create the chart.

You now see the XY chart data form, which you use to enter your data.

Entering Data into an XY Chart

You use the XY chart data form to enter data for an XY chart. The data form, shown in figure 5.8, is divided into two parts. The top portion of the form has fields to enter the title, subtitle, and footnote for the chart. The bottom part, below the `Bar Chart Data` prompt, contains the numeric values for the chart. You enter the x-axis labels in the first column of the data form. The next section, "Entering X-Axis Labels," describes how to enter labels in this column. You enter the names for individual series in the gray fields above each column (where the names Series 1, Series 2, and so on, are displayed). The section "Entering Series Names" discusses the series names and explains how they define the columns in the data form. The section "Entering Numeric Data" tells you how to enter the data values into the data form.

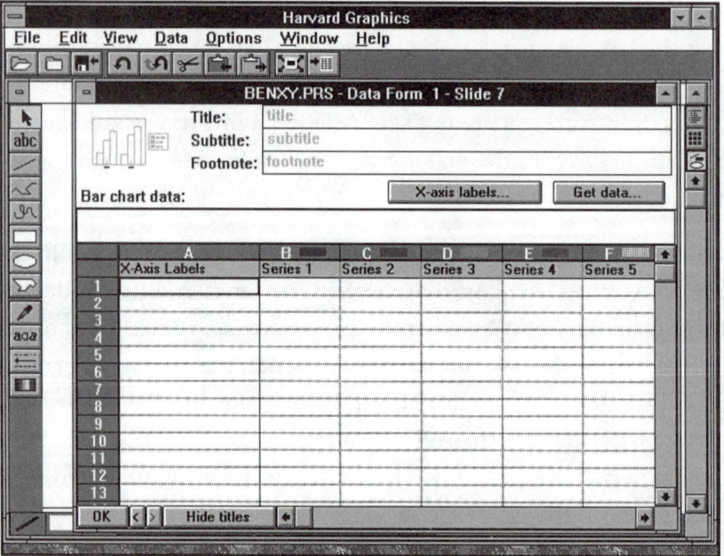

Fig. 5.8
The XY chart data form.

The data portion of the data form appears similar to a spreadsheet. You enter the data into the cells; a *cell* is the intersection of a row and a column. The column headings are the letters listed above the series names (A, B, C, and so on). The row headings are the numbers at the beginning of the rows (1, 2, 3, and on). You combine the column and row headings to form a *cell reference*, such as A1 for the first cell in the data form.

In the data form, Harvard Graphics provides some spreadsheet functions, such as the use of cell references and formulas. You can, for example, create a formula that adds the values from two different cells and displays the total in a third cell. *A1* + *B1* is an example of a formula that adds two cells. The section "Using Formulas in XY Charts" explains more about entering formulas in the XY chart data form.

The *active cell* in the data form is highlighted with a box. Editing operations, such as cutting and pasting, take place on the active cell. You click a cell to make it active. You also can press Tab to make the cell to the right active, Shift+Tab to make the cell to the left active, the up arrow to make the cell above active, and the down arrow to make the cell below active.

Before you can enter data values into the data form, you must define the rows and columns of the chart. The x-axis labels define the rows. You can enter these labels yourself, or you can use the X-Axis Labels feature to quickly enter sequential labels, such as days of the week or consecutive years. Series names define the columns. After you set the labels and series names, you can enter the data for the chart.

Entering X-Axis Labels

The x-axis labels appear in the first column of the data form and define the rows of data. You can, for example, enter the months in the year starting with January to chart values for each month. You can type the labels directly into the data form, or you can use the X-Axis Labels dialog box to enter labels automatically. To display the dialog box, click the X-Axis Labels button in the XY chart data form. Figure 5.9 shows the X-Axis Labels dialog box.

Before you define x-axis labels, you must decide on a label format. You can use the information in the Format scroll box to make your decision. To see a list of the available formats, scroll through the Format box. The Format scroll box contains only one selection for some formats, such as numeric or name format, and several selections for other formats, such as date and time formats.

You can use the other options available in the dialog box to enter a range of labels for any format other than the name format. You use a range to establish boundaries for your labels. To chart the daily donations received for a fund-raiser during a week's time, for example, you enter a range that spans only the given week and moves forward in increments of 1 (because you want daily contribution amounts).

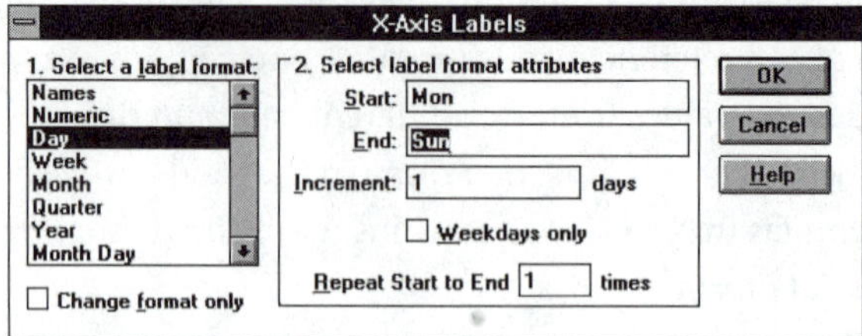

Fig. 5.9
The X-Axis Labels dialog box.

You use the **S**tart, **E**nd, and **I**ncrement text boxes to define the range. If you select a numeric format, you can define a range of labels from 1 to 10, for example, by entering **1** in the Start text box, **10** in the End text box, and **1** in the Increment text box. To display the days of the week, you select Day as the format. Then you enter **Monday** as the start, **Sunday** as the end, and **1** as the increment. To show every other day of the week, you enter an increment of 2.

Table 5.1 summarizes the options available in the X-Axis Labels dialog box.

Table 5.1 The X-Axis Labels Options

Option	Function
Format	A scroll list that contains the format choices available for labels
Start	Defines the beginning of a range
End	Defines the end of a range
Increment	Defines the increment value of the range
Weekdays Only	Affects date formats by showing only those dates that fall on a weekday
Repeat Start to End	Duplicates the range of labels in the data form for the specified number of times
Change Format Only	Enables you to change the format of your labels without changing the information in the labels

In the chart on product sales trends, you must enter labels for the last five years. Follow these steps to enter the labels:

1. Click cell A1 in the data form to make that cell active. When you use the X-Axis Labels dialog box, Harvard Graphics enters the labels, beginning at the active cell in the data form.
2. Click the X-Axis Labels button in the XY chart data form. The X-Axis Labels dialog box appears (refer to fig. 5.9).
3. Choose the Year format from the Format list box.
4. Click the Start text box and enter **1987** as the starting value.
5. Click the End text box.

   When you enter a start value, Harvard Graphics attempts to supply an appropriate ending value for the range. If this is not the correct end value, you must delete the information in this field and supply the correct information.
6. Press the End key to move to the end of the text box; then delete the incorrect information in the End text box by pressing the Backspace key until the text box is blank.
7. Type **1993**, the ending value.

   As with the original ending value, Harvard Graphics attempts to supply an increment for the starting and ending values. The value in this case is 1, which will increment consecutive years from 1987 to 1993.
8. Click the OK button.

Figure 5.10 shows the data form with the x-axis labels.

Entering Series Names

The series names define the series in the chart and the columns in the data form. Harvard Graphics displays the names you enter in the chart's legend. For any series, your audience uses the color of the bar or line as a key to the information in the legend. You enter series names in the top row (the gray row that begins with the X-Axis Labels cell) of the data form.

For the chart on trends in product sales, follow these steps to define the series for each product of the Bensig Corporation:

1. Click the gray cell in column B, and type the series name, **Loafers**.
2. Click the gray cell in column C, and type the series name, **Pumps**.

3. Click the gray cell in column D, and type the series name, **Sneakers**.

4. Click the gray cell in column E, and type the series name, **Hikers**.

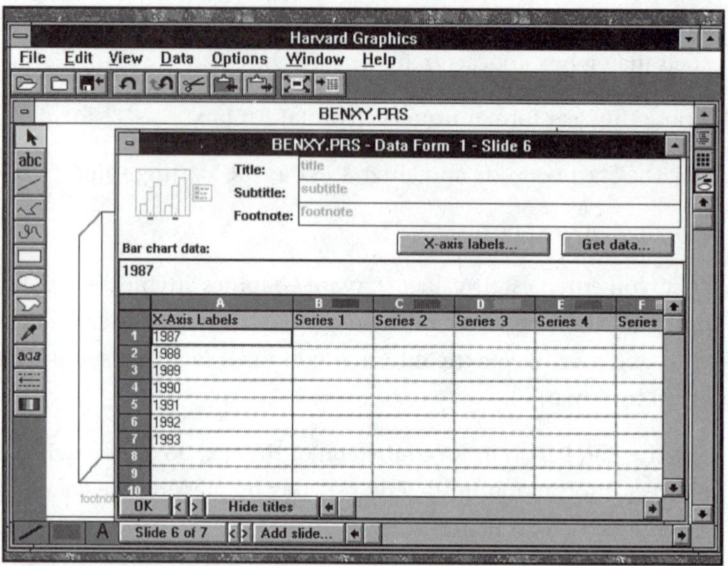

Fig. 5.10
The XY chart data form with x-axis labels.

The rows and columns are defined in the data form, as shown in figure 5.11. You can easily see in the figure where specific data values are entered. The value for loafer sales in 1990, for example, goes in cell B4. The next section explains how to enter data values into the data form.

Entering Numeric Data

You enter the actual data values of an XY chart after you define the x-axis labels and the series names. The labels and names will help you organize the rows and columns in preparation for the data. To enter the data into a cell, you must first make the cell active by selecting it. Harvard Graphics highlights the active cell with a box.

You type the value in the edit line, which is located above the data section of the data form (see fig. 5.12). When you change the active cell or press the Enter key, Harvard Graphics copies this information into the cell.

Figure 5.12 shows the data form for the XY chart. In the figure, you see the x-axis labels for the last five years. Along the top of the data section of the data form, you can see the series names, which define the information in the cells.

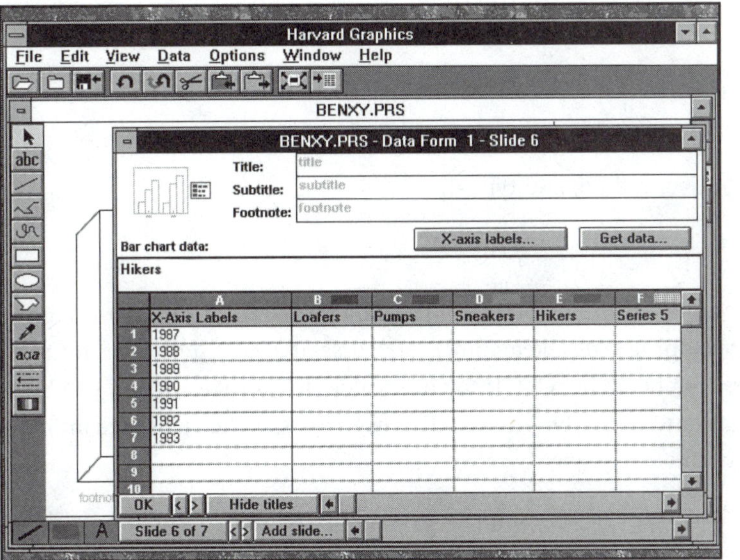

Fig. 5.11 The XY chart data form with defined rows and columns.

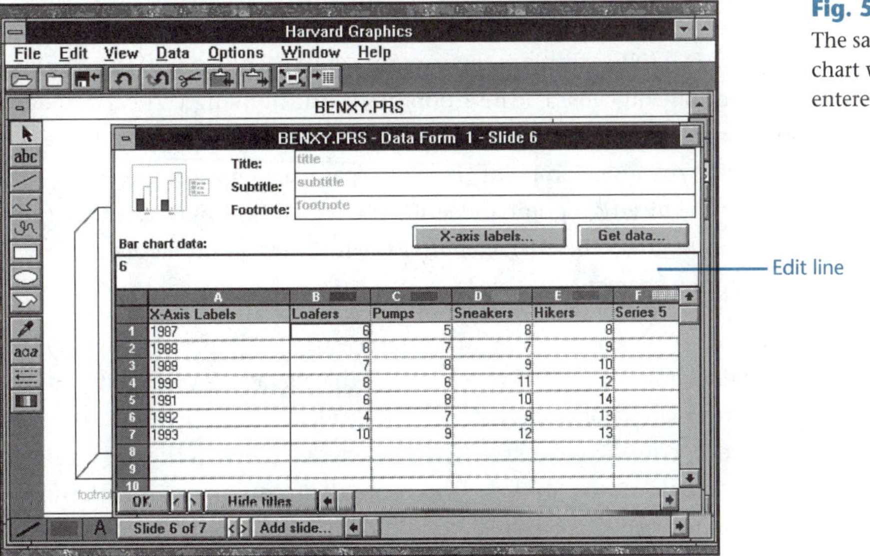

Fig. 5.12 The sales trends chart with data entered.

Follow these steps to complete the chart data:

1. Select the cell for loafers sales for 1987, cell B1, and type **6**.

2. Select the cell for loafers sales for 1988, cell B2, and type **8**.

3. Select cell B3, and type **7**.

4. Select cell B4, and type **8**.

5. Select cell B5, and type **6**.

6. Select cell B6, and type **4**.

7. Select cell B7, and type **10**.

To complete the data section of the data form, repeat steps 1 through 5 for the remaining series. Remember, of course, that to enter values for the Pumps series, you begin in cell C1; to enter values for Sneakers series, you begin in cell D1; and so on. Because, for this exercise, specific values are unimportant, you can make up your own values.

The data form is now complete with values, as shown in figure 5.12. The next section explains how to edit the data to correct mistakes or rearrange the values.

Editing in the Data Form

Harvard Graphics displays the contents of the active cell in the edit line, where you edit cells. The insertion point (the blinking vertical bar) determines the location of the edit in the edit line. Characters you type are inserted at the insertion point. The Backspace key removes the character to the left of the insertion point and shifts the remaining characters to the left. The Del key removes the character after the insertion point before shifting the remaining characters.

You can select characters with the mouse by clicking before the first character and dragging the pointer to the end of the characters you want to delete. The selected material is displayed in reverse video. With the keyboard, move the insertion point to before the first character by pressing the left- or right-arrow key. Hold down the Shift key and move the insertion point with the arrow keys to the end of the characters and then release the Shift key.

The **E**dit menu contains commands you use to edit, rearrange, and delete selected material. The Cu**t** command removes the selected data to the Windows Clipboard. When you execute a **P**aste command, Harvard Graphics inserts the Clipboard information after the insertion point in the edit line. To copy data from one cell to another, make a different cell active, and then choose **P**aste.

As with the data in a single cell, you can use the **E**dit menu to edit a block of cells. To select a block, you click the cell at the beginning of the block, drag to the end of the block, and release the mouse button. All the cells in the block are displayed in reverse video except the active cell, which is highlighted with a box.

When you highlight a block, all commands affect the entire block. If you press Del, for example, Harvard Graphics clears the values in the block. If you select **C**opy from the **E**dit menu, Harvard Graphics copies all the cells in the block to the Clipboard. When you select **P**aste, Harvard Graphics pastes all the cells from the block into the data form beginning at the active cell.

If, in entering the data for the sales chart, you realize that you entered the Pumps values in the Loafers series and the Loafers values in the Pumps series, you must switch the values to the appropriate columns. You use the commands from the **E**dit menu and the block-selecting technique you just learned.

To switch the values of the Loafers and Pumps series, follow these steps:

1. Click cell B1 and hold down the mouse button.
2. Drag the pointer to B7 (the last cell in the Loafers series).
3. Release the mouse button to select the cells.

   Figure 5.13 shows the data form for the sales trends chart with the cells for the Loafers series highlighted. To switch these values with the Pumps series, you must copy the Loafers series into an unused portion of the data form.

4. From the **E**dit menu, choose Cu**t**. Harvard Graphics removes the values from cells B1 through B7 and places them temporarily in the Clipboard.
5. Click cell F1 to make this cell active. If you cannot see column F, scroll through the data form by clicking the right arrow at the end of the scroll bar.
6. From the **E**dit menu, choose **P**aste cells to paste the information from cells B1 through B7 into column F.

   Because you moved the information from the Loafers series to column F, the Loafers series currently contains no values. Now you must move the values from cells C1 through C5 (from the Pumps series) to the Loafers series.

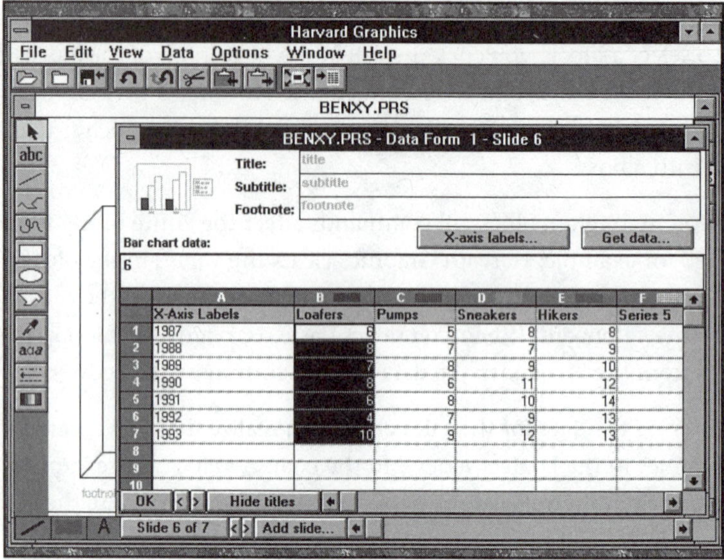

Fig. 5.13
An example of selected cells.

7. Select the block for the values in the Pumps series, and choose Cu**t** from the **E**dit menu. Harvard Graphics removes the selected cells.

8. Click cell B1 to make this the active cell.

9. From the **E**dit menu, choose **P**aste cells. Harvard Graphics pastes the information into the Loafers series.

To complete the exercise, you must move the information that is in column F to column C, the Pumps series. Follow the same procedures for selecting, cutting, and pasting.

Using Formulas in XY Charts

Formulas in an XY chart provide spreadsheet functionality in the data form. You can use formulas to add the values in a row or to average a row. You use a formula when data in your chart is dependent on or related to other data in the chart. For example, profit for a company is equal to the revenue generated by the company minus any internal costs. If you have the values for revenue and costs, you can use a formula to calculate the profit.

You use an equal (=) sign to indicate to Harvard Graphics that the data in the cell should be evaluated as a formula. Following the equal sign, you can enter any combination of cell references, simple operators, or predefined functions that follow the rules of basic algebra. The simple operators are listed in table 5.2. They perform mathematical operations, such as addition and subtraction. Predefined functions are a part of the Harvard Graphics program; functions perform specialized calculations, such as summing all the values in a column or averaging the data in a range.

Table 5.2 Simple Operators Used in Harvard Graphics

Operator	Function
+	Addition
-	Negative numbers or subtraction
*	Multiplication
/	Division
^, **	Exponent of a number
%	Percentage

You use parentheses to indicate the order in which Harvard Graphics evaluates the expressions in a formula, just as you use parentheses in algebraic formulas. Table 5.3 provides examples of formulas with cell references, parentheses, and simple operators.

Table 5.3 Examples of Cell Entries

Formula	Result
=C1+C2	Adds the contents of cells C1 and C2
=(F1+B2-A3)/D4	Adds the contents of cells F1 and B2; subtracts the contents of cell A3 from the total; divides the total by D4
=A3^2	Takes the contents of cell A3 to the second power

You can use predefined functions in a formula by themselves, or you can mix predefined functions with cell references and simple operators. Each function uses arguments that you provide to evaluate the value for the function. The arguments to a function are enclosed by parentheses and separated by commas. Each function takes a combination of values and cell ranges for the arguments. A value can be a number or a reference to a cell. The function ABS(–1), for example, gives the absolute value of –1, and the function ABS(C2) gives the absolute value of the contents of cell C2.

The first and last cells in the cell range specify the beginning and end of a group of cells. To indicate that cells are part of a range, you must enter one dot (.), two dots (..), or a colon between the references. When you enter the complete formula, Harvard Graphics changes all range indicators to the colon character.

Table 5.4 provides examples of formulas that use functions.

Table 5.4 Formulas Using Functions

Formula	Result
=SUM(C1:C4)	Adds the contents of cells C1 through C4
=(COS(B1)+C2)*6	Takes the cosine of cell B1 and adds it to the contents of cell C2 then multiplies the total by 6
=MAVG(F1:F4,2,4)	Calculates the moving average of cells F1 through F4, using the cells from 2 rows before the current cell to the cell 4 rows after the current cell

Appendix C provides a complete list of the predefined functions, explanations, examples, and lists of the arguments. To help you find the function you need, the appendix lists functions alphabetically as either algebraic or geometric functions.

When you edit the data form, some of the cells you copy and paste with the Clipboard may contain formulas with cell references. When you paste the formulas back into the data form, Harvard Graphics adjusts the references for the new cells. Suppose, for example, that in the formula in cell C2, you reference cell B2, which is in the same row; the formula might be something like =B2+5. When you paste this formula into cell C1, Harvard Graphics changes the reference B2 to B1, which is in the same row as the new cell C1. The new formula becomes =B1+5.

To avoid the adjustment of cell references when you paste formulas, you can use absolute referencing. An *absolute reference* indicates to Harvard Graphics that the reference in the formula is linked to a specific cell in the data form. For example, the formula in cell C2 is =B2+5, which refers to cell B2. Suppose that you want the formula to reference cell B2 no matter where you paste the formula. An absolute reference to cell B2 does not change when pasted. The $ character in a cell reference indicates an absolute reference, for example, B2. The formula =B2+5 does not change when pasted.

Entering Titles into an XY Chart

Every chart you create should have a title to clarify the information in the chart. You use the fields for the title, subtitle, and footnote to communicate relevant information about the data to the audience (refer to fig. 5.13). For the chart you are creating, you want to tell the audience that the topic of the chart is sales trends for the products of the Bensig Corporation. Follow these steps to enter the title, subtitle, and footnote for your chart:

1. Select the Title field and type **Sales Trends**, the title for the chart.
2. Select the Subtitle field and type **By Product**, the chart's subtitle.
3. Select the Footnote field and type **Bensig Corporation**, the chart's footnote.
4. Choose the OK button to add the chart to the presentation.

Figure 5.14 shows the completed data form.

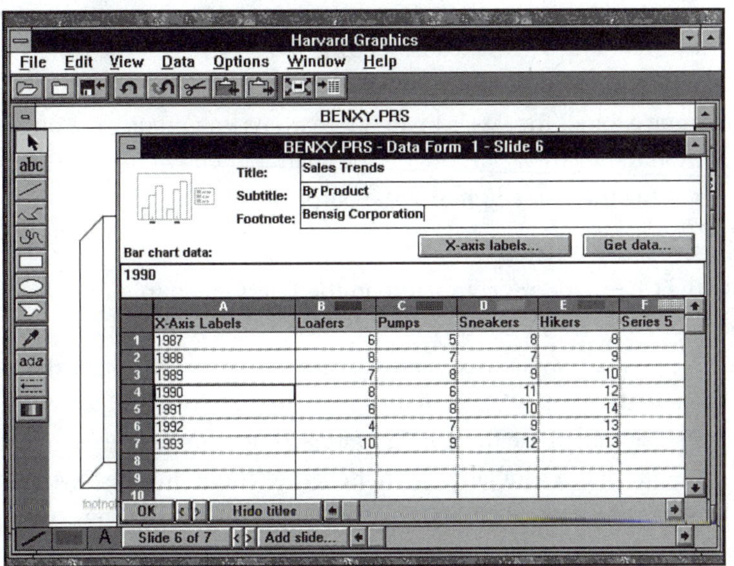

Fig. 5.14 The completed data form.

Changing the Appearance of an XY Chart

When you create an XY chart, the default settings for the chart options determine the appearance of the chart. You use the items on the **C**hart menu to change the appearance of the chart after it is created. You may want to change the appearance of a chart to increase its effectiveness and to enhance the overall appearance. For example, one option you can change is the width of bars in a bar chart. You can decrease the width on a chart crowded with many bars to make the chart look less busy. The grid lines, which appear behind the chart as a visual aid for comparing the heights of bars, also affect the appearance of the chart. You can change the grid lines with the **C**hart menu, too. You can increase the number of grid lines on the chart to help when comparing bars that are similar in height.

The following sections explore the options you can modify for an XY chart. The **C**hart menu options affect elements, such as the style of the bars in a bar chart or the width of the bars. The section "Setting XY Chart Options" explains how to use this command with XY charts. The **S**eries command on the **C**hart menu controls the appearance of individual series in the chart. This command is covered in the section "Setting XY Series Chart Options." The section "Modifying the Legend" tells you how to change the location and appearance of the legend with the **L**egend command. The A**x**is command enables you to add titles for the axis in the chart and to change their appearance. This command is discussed in "Setting Axis Options." The La**b**els command, covered in "Setting XY Chart Label Options," provides control over the appearance for all the labels in an XY chart. As you modify the options, keep in mind the focus or purpose for the chart and make changes that bring attention to the focus or emphasize the purpose.

Setting XY Chart Options

You use the Chart **O**ptions command on the **C**hart menu to modify the appearance for many of the chart types provided by Harvard Graphics. You use the Chart **O**ptions command to set the orientation of an XY chart, the bar style for bar and high/low/close charts, the dimension of the chart, and the parameters that determine the depths of objects in a three-dimensional chart. You also can display a data table in your chart to communicate to your audience the data values represented by the objects in the chart. Figure 5.15 shows the XY Chart Options dialog box, which you use to set these options. You can use the buttons along the right side of the dialog box (**S**eries, **L**egend, **F**rame, and so on) to gain quick access to the other items on the **C**hart menu.

Setting the Chart Orientation. You use the Chart Orientation options to change the orientation of the XY chart. The orientation determines the relative positions of different elements in a chart. Vertical orientation positions elements relative to the top and bottom of the chart. With XY charts, a vertical orientation displays the x-axis across the bottom and the y-axis vertically on the side of the chart. The bars of a bar chart start at the bottom of the chart and increase toward the top to represent greater data values. A horizontal orientation displays the y-axis across the bottom and the x-axis up the side of the chart. A horizontally oriented bar chart, as shown in figure 5.16, displays the bars of a bar chart from left to right horizontally. To change the orientation, choose the button next to Horizontal or Vertical.

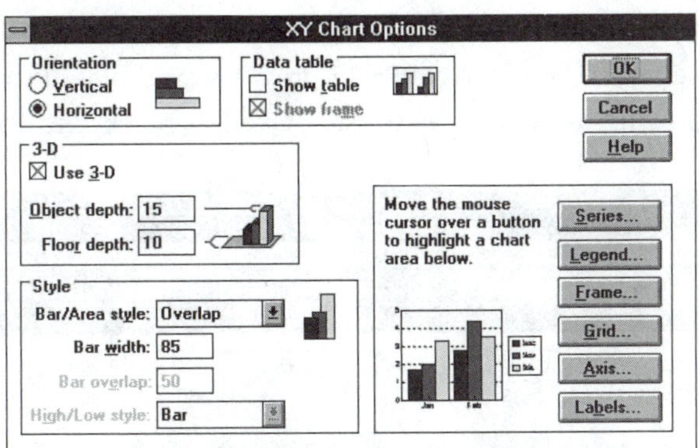

Fig. 5.15 The XY Chart Options dialog box.

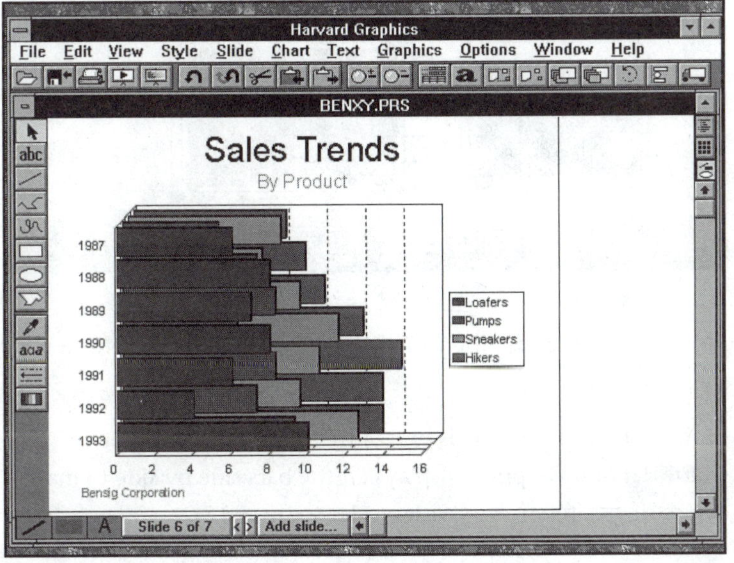

Fig. 5.16 A bar chart with a horizontal orientation.

Changing the Bar Appearance. Three options in the Chart Options (F8) dialog box enable you to modify the appearance of the bars in a bar chart.

The Bar/Area Style option determines how the bars of a series are displayed in relationship to each other. The choices for bar styles include Cluster, Overlap, Stack, Linked Stack, 100%, and Linked 100%. You can see these choices by clicking the down arrow next to the Bar/Area Style list box or by scrolling through the choices with the arrow keys. The Bar **W**idth option affects the appearance of the bars. This option controls the width of the bars. See the sections "Changing the Appearance of 2-D Bar Charts" and "Changing the Appearance of 3-D Charts" for more information on how the width affects the appearance of a chart. The Bar Overlap option determines how much the bars of one series overlap other bars. This option is also discussed in the sections on 2-D and 3-D charts. Figure 5.17 provides examples of the same chart using the following bar styles: the Cluster, Overlap, Stack, and 100% style.

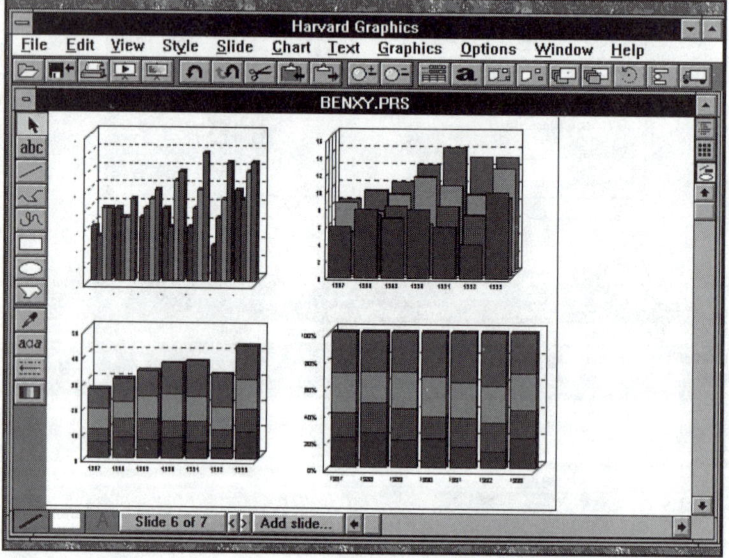

Fig. 5.17 Bar charts with cluster, overlap, stack, and 100% styles.

The following list describes the various Bar/Area Style options from which you can choose.

- *Cluster.* The Cluster style is one of the most common types for a bar chart. Harvard Graphics displays all the bars side by side to make comparing different bars easier (refer to fig. 5.17).

- *Overlap.* The Overlap style displays one series overlapped on top of the next series. As the number of series in your chart increases, distinguishing series in the back of the chart may become more difficult.

Distinguishing between series is especially difficult in a 2-D chart. In a 3-D chart, the overlapped bars take advantage of the added depth by displaying the series in rows of consecutive depths (refer to fig. 5.17).

- *Stack.* The Stack style combines the bars for each x-axis label into one bar. Stacked charts are ideal for illustrating how different series combine to form a single value (refer to fig. 5.17).

Design Note

In the sales trends chart, you can use a stacked bar to show how much revenue the combined products generated in a year and how much each product contributed to the total for that year.

- *100%.* The 100% style displays each bar in a stacked form with exactly the same height. The name for the style indicates that all the stacks are 100 percent of the common height. The individual parts of the bars represent percentages of the total (refer to fig. 5.17).

- *Linked Stack and Linked 100%.* For stack and 100% charts, you also can select a Linked Stack and Linked 100% style in which linked lines are drawn between the bars to connect the value for a series from one bar to the value in the next bar.

- *Paired.* The Paired style is useful only with an XY chart that has two y-axes. XY charts with two axes are covered later in the section "Creating Charts with Two Y-Axes."

Figure 5.18 shows examples of linked stack, linked 100%, and paired charts.

Changing the High/Low Style. The high/low style option in the Chart Options dialog box determines how Harvard Graphics represents in a chart of stock values the high and low values of a stock. This option is available only for high/low/close charts. You can use Error Bar or Area in addition to Bar to represent these values. Bars are solid rectangles (refer to fig. 5.5); and error bars are single vertical lines with a horizontal tick mark indicating the high and low (see fig. 5.19). In either case, the bar or line is drawn from the high to the low for each stock.

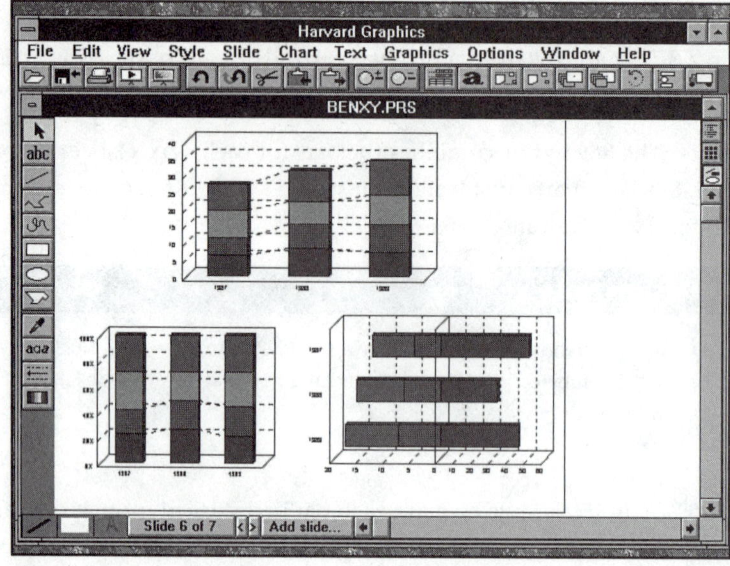

Fig. 5.18
Linked stack (top), linked 100% (lower left), and paired (lower right) charts.

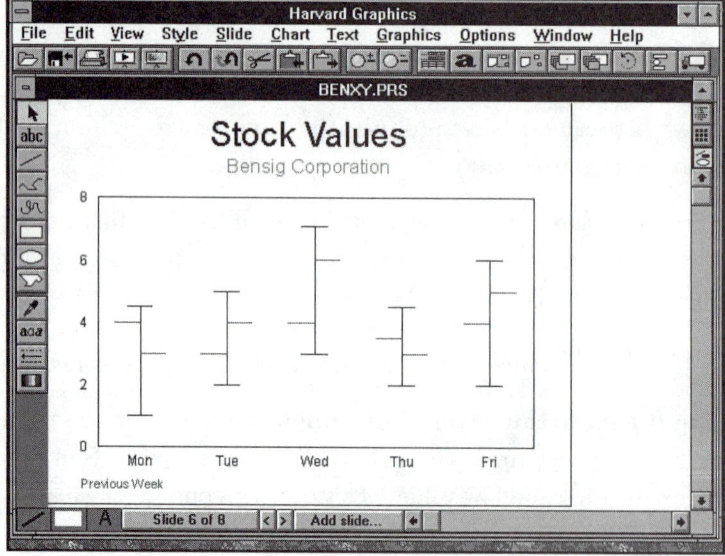

Fig. 5.19
A high/low/close chart with error bars.

The Area chart style connects the high and low for each stock by drawing a line. The area between the line of the high values and the line of the low values is filled. To change this option, you can use the arrow keys to scroll through the choices. To see all the high/low styles, click the down scroll arrow next to the list box. You can then select a style from the list with the mouse.

Switching between 2- and 3-D Charts. The dimension is one of the most visible changes you can make to a chart's appearance. You use the 3-D box on the Chart Options dialog box to change the dimension of the chart. A bar chart shown in three dimensions displays each bar as a box; in two dimensions, the bars appear as flat squares. Figure 5.20 presents a 2-D and a 3-D chart. The bars of the first chart, which uses a cluster style, are clearly visible because they appear side by side. The bars of the 3-D chart overlap. The overlap style adds to the effect of the 3-D chart by showing bars behind other bars.

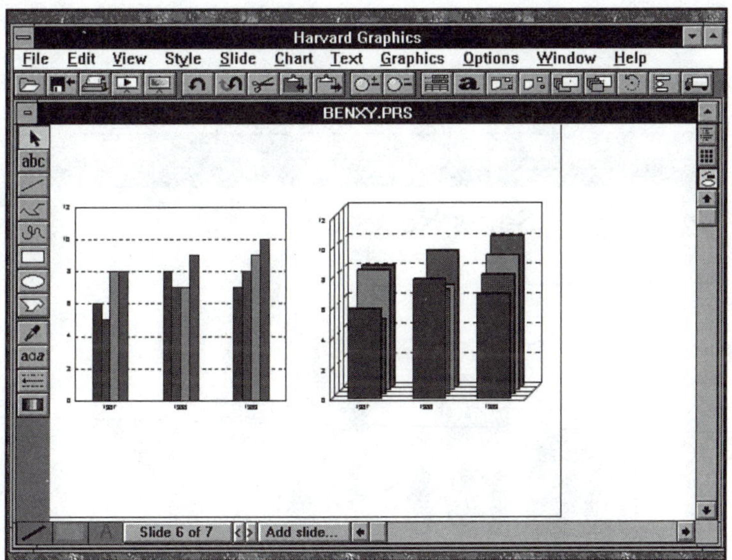

Fig. 5.20 Two- and three-dimensional charts.

To set the option to 3-D, click the 3-D box so that an X appears. The X indicates a 3-D chart. Click the X to remove it and set the option to 2-D.

Changing the Appearance of 2-D Bar Charts. For 2-D bar charts, the Bar Width and the Bar Overlap items in the Chart Options dialog box affect the size and the layout of the bars. The Bar Width determines how much of the available area reserved for the bars is used. The default for this field is 85, indicating that the bars use 85 percent of the area. In figure 5.21, the unused 15 percent of the chart area is the area between the groups of bars.

The Bar Overlap option indicates how much one bar overlaps the next. The default for the overlap is 50; 50 percent of the area of the bars in one series is visible from behind another series of bars. If you need to display a large number of series, you can increase the overlap to make room. A chart with just a few series can show more of each bar and will benefit from a smaller overlap. You can see an example of overlap in figure 5.21. Notice how the bars for the Loafers series overlap the Pumps series.

Design Note

The default setting for the bar width strikes a good balance for displaying bar charts. Although most of the chart is used to display the bars, enough room is reserved to keep the clusters in the chart distinct. To use more of the chart area, you can increase the value to 100 percent. The overlap default is also a good value for two-dimensional charts. Decreasing the overlap for the bars increases the visibility.

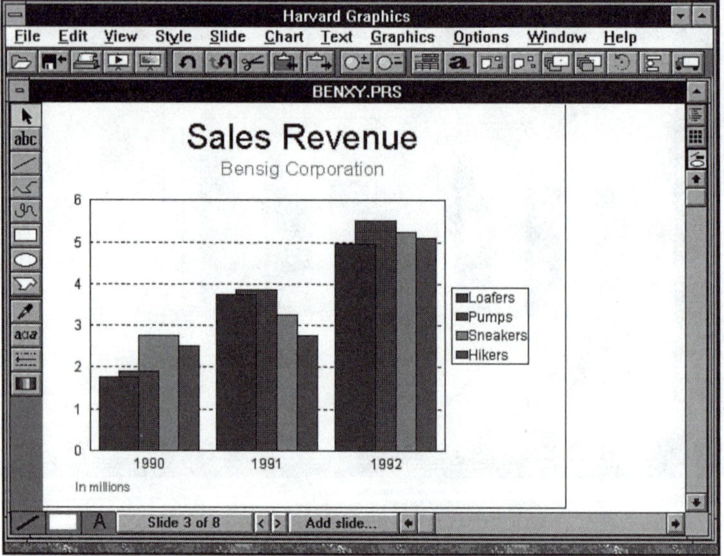

Fig. 5.21
An example two-dimensional chart.

Changing the Appearance of 3-D Charts. Several items on the Chart Options dialog box are helpful for modifying the appearance of a 3-D chart. In a chart, objects that appear behind other objects can become difficult to see. You can make the bars and other elements of the chart more visible by adjusting the Bar **W**idth, the **O**bject Depth, and the Floo**r** Depth for the chart.

The Bar **W**idth and **O**bject Depth combine to determine the size of the bars. The width controls the size of the front part of the bar. The depth determines the size for the side of the bar. This side is visible only in a 3-D chart. The actual data value determines the height of the bar, but you can decrease the width and depth to make seeing bars displayed behind bars easier.

The Floor Depth determines the depth of an entire 3-D chart. By increasing this depth, you increase the space between the series. This increase has the same effect as looking at a landscape from a greater distance. As you move backward, you can see more of the landscape.

Earlier in the chapter, you created a chart on sales trends for the Bensig Corporation. The chart was a 3-D, overlapped vertical bar chart. Figure 5.22 shows the sales trend chart with the default settings on the left and the same chart with a deeper floor and with thinner bars on the right. The thinner bars enable you to see between the series. The increased floor depth separates the bars of the different series to make the series in the back of the chart more visible.

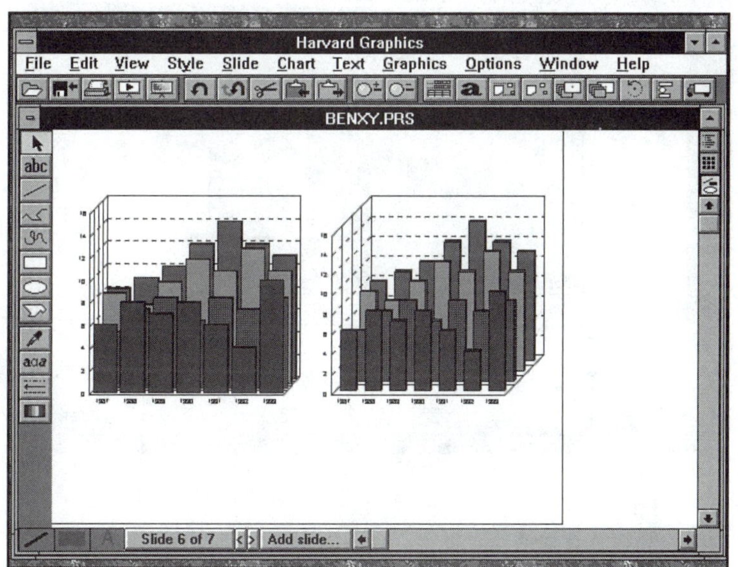

Fig. 5.22 The sales trend chart with the default settings (left) and the modified Bar Width and Floor Depth options (right).

Adding a Data Table. You use *data tables* to display, in a table at the bottom of the chart, the actual data values of an XY chart. A data table helps to present the data clearly. Use a data table if your audience will benefit from seeing the values. The data table may crowd the chart and cause it to shrink in size. Make sure, therefore, that the table adds to the effectiveness of the chart without making the chart too difficult to see.

You use the Show Table option in the Chart Options dialog box to display the table. If you activate Show Table (an X appears in the box next to it), Harvard Graphics draws your chart with a data table. To display the X, click the box. To turn off the data table, click the X. When you activate Show

Frame, Harvard Graphics surrounds the table by a frame, which helps to separate the table in the chart. Click the box to display an X and show the frame. Click the X not to show the frame. If you don't want a frame to surround your table, deactivate it by clicking the check-box to remove the X from the Show Frame.

Figure 5.23 shows the sales trends chart with a data table. The table looks similar to the XY chart data form. The columns and rows of the table are clearly defined to help your audience read the information.

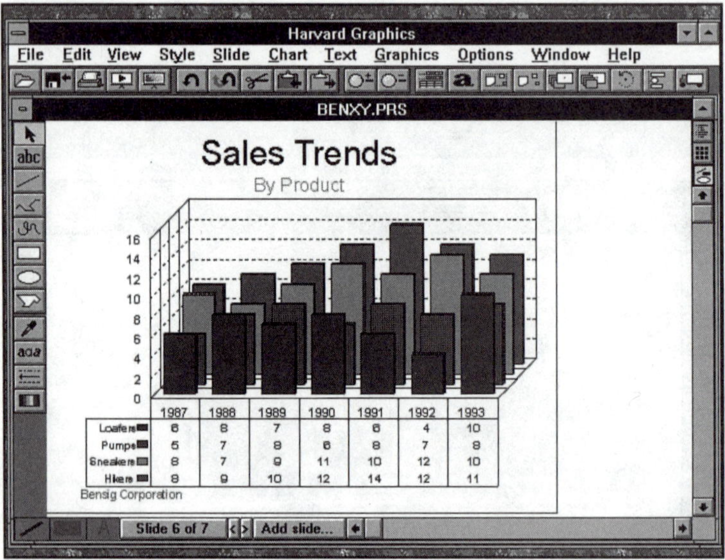

Fig. 5.23
A bar chart with a data table.

Setting XY Series Chart Options

You use the **S**eries command on the **C**hart menu to change the appearance of the individual series in an XY chart. When you choose **S**eries from the **C**hart menu, the XY Chart Series Options dialog box appears (see fig. 5.24). This dialog box contains the options available for changing the appearance of a series.

The S**e**ries list box on the left of the dialog box lists the names of the series in your chart. To change the options for a series, you first must select the name of the series. When you choose a series, the remaining options on the dialog box reflect the settings for the series. You then can change the settings for the series. You can change the settings for only one series at a time.

Showing and Hiding Series Information. You use the Show **S**eries option to indicate whether to display the selected series in the chart. This option enables you to view individual series in the chart without having to remove the data. If you decide not to display a series, the data remains in the chart. You use the Include Series in **D**ata Table option to indicate whether to display the series in the data table. You can show any series in the chart, in the table, in both, or in no part of the chart. The Show Cu**m**ulative Data option displays each bar in a series as the cumulation of the value for the bar plus the values for all the preceding bars.

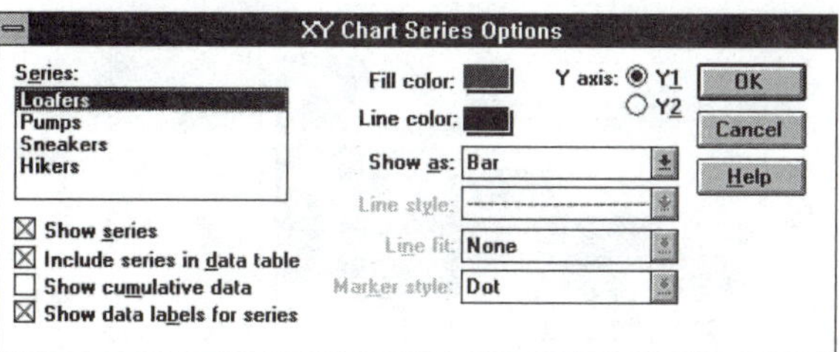

Fig. 5.24
The XY Chart Series Options dialog box.

Figure 5.25 shows a chart with one cumulative data series and a data table. All the values in the table are the same. Each bar is an accumulation of the values for that bar plus the preceding bar. The Show Data La**b**els for Series option ensures that the data labels for a series are not displayed. (For information on data labels, see the section "Setting XY Chart Label Options.")

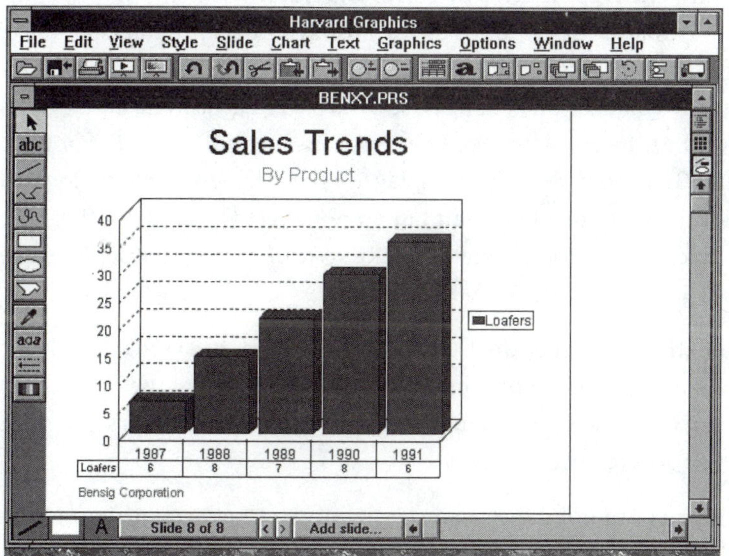

Fig. 5.25
A cumulative data bar chart.

Figure 5.26 shows the sales trends chart with the Show **S**eries option set for the Hikers series and the Include Series in **D**ata Table option set for all series. With this chart, you can display an individual series in chart form while you show the data for all the series in table form.

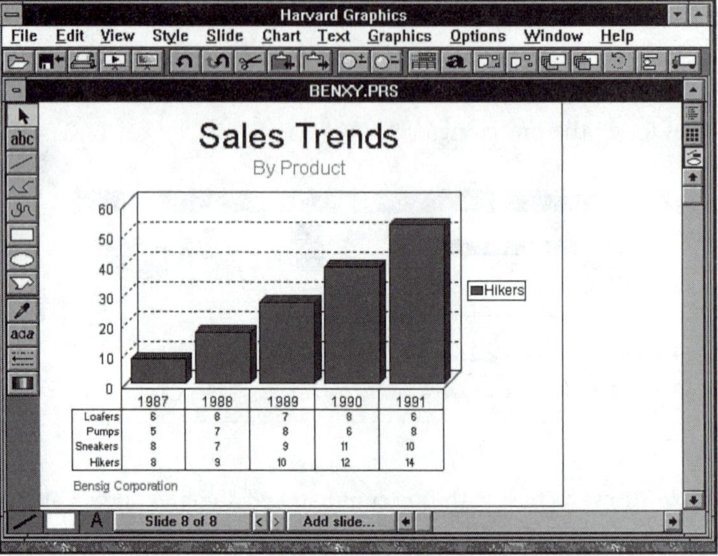

Fig. 5.26 The sales trend chart displaying bars for the Hikers series with the other series in a data table.

To display all the series again, reset the Show **S**eries option for each series.

Changing the Appearance of Series Displays. The items on the right side of the XY Chart Series Options dialog box affect the appearance of the objects used to represent a series in an XY chart. You use the Fill color options to change the colors of filled objects, such as bars or areas. The Line color options change the colors for the lines (such as the outline of a bar or the line in a line chart) that you use to display a series. The Line st**y**le options set the style for the series in a line chart but do not affect the lines of other objects. The Mar**k**er style options determine the style of marker that represents each point in a scatter chart.

The sales trends chart created earlier in the chapter is a vertical bar chart. The Fill color and Line color options affect the appearance of the series in this chart. Follow these steps to change the color for the Sneakers series of the chart you are creating:

1. If you have not done so already, from the **C**hart menu choose **S**eries. The XY Chart Series Options dialog box appears (refer to fig. 5.24).

2. Select the Sneakers series in the Series list box.

3. Click the Fill color list box to see the available colors. The colors are shown in the Fill color dialog box. (For more information about filling objects, see "Setting the Fill Style" in Chapter 13, "Enhancing Drawings and Objects.")

4. Choose a shade of green in the Fill Color dialog box.

   When you click the color, the Fill Color dialog box closes, and the Fill color field shows the color you selected.

5. To set the color of the bar outline, click the Line color list box to see the available colors. The Line Color dialog box is displayed for you to select a color.

6. Choose a darker shade of green in the Line Color dialog box. The dialog box closes, and the color appears in the Line color field.

7. Click the OK button in the XY Chart Series Options dialog box to accept the changes and return to the Slide Editor.

Setting the Line Fit for a Line Chart. The Line fit option in the XY Chart Series Options dialog box enables you to display line chart lines using different line fit formulas. The line fit determines the method Harvard Graphics uses to draw the line that connects the data in the chart. You can choose a method that ensures that the line passes through each point. You can also draw a line that is based on a calculation, such as the average of all the points. Figure 5.27 shows a chart with two different line fits. The line on top uses a None line fit, which means that the lines are connected without any calculation. The bottom line uses a Trend fit, which shows the general trend of the values and shows whether they are generally increasing or decreasing in value.

In addition to the Trend line fit, you can fit a line using a Step, Average, Exponential, Log Regression, or Power Regression formula. These formulas enable you to do specialized analyses based on standard mathematical formulas for the data values in the chart. The use of these formulas is beyond the scope of this book. For more information on the mathematics behind the formulas, consult the appropriate sections of the Harvard Graphics documentation. There are different ways to calculate the formulas, so make sure that you check the documentation before using the formula in the chart.

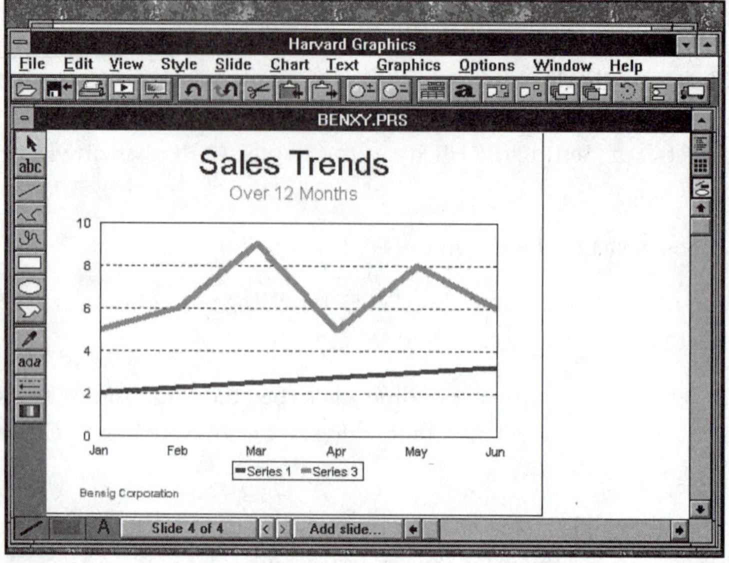

Fig. 5.27
A line chart using no line fit for the top line and a Trend line fit for the bottom line.

Creating Charts with Two Y-Axes. When you create an XY chart, the series in the chart use the same y-axis. To display values for different sets of data on the same chart, you can change the Y axis option in the XY Chart Series Options dialog box to display any series, using a second y-axis. The two available axes are titled Y**1** and Y**2**. After you select the series name in the Series list box, select the Y**1** or Y**2** button in the dialog box to change the y-axis you use for the series. Y1 is the default axis.

In the sales trends chart, you can use a second axis to display the profits generated by each product. If you display the profits (percentage of revenue) on the same axis as the revenue, the bars for the profits will be considerably smaller than the bars for the revenues; in fact, the profit bars might even be too small to view. If you use a separate axis to display the bars, however, Harvard Graphics sets the scale for the second axis based on the series that uses the axis. The bars for the series will be measured against the second axis, independent of the first axis. A relatively small value measured against the first axis may be an average or large value against the second axis. Harvard Graphics sets the size for the bar based on the scale of the axis so that the bar will be more visible.

Figure 5.28 shows the profits and revenues for loafers and sneakers. The revenues are measured against the Y1 axis on the left. The profits are measured against the Y2 axis on the right. The chart can be interpreted in two different ways. You can compare the revenues of loafers and sneakers with each other and the profits of the two products with each other. In the chart, you can see that loafers generated more revenue and profit. With the second interpretation, you can compare the revenue and profit for a single product. With both products, profits showed the same trends as the revenue.

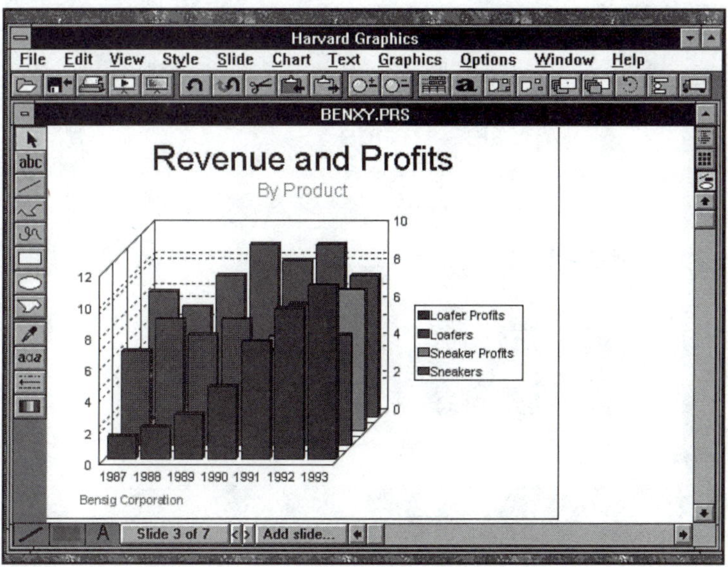

Fig. 5.28
An XY chart with two y-axes; one for profits and one for revenues.

If you change the y-axis for any of the series in your chart, you can use the Paired Bar style to display the series for both y-axes in a different part of the chart. With paired bars, Harvard Graphics displays the series for the Y1 axis to the left and the series for the Y2 axis to the right. (Remember, you set the bar style in the Chart Options dialog box.)

Creating Combination XY Charts. When you create an XY chart, all the series in the chart appear as the same type. You can use the Show **A**s option in the XY Chart Series Options dialog box to represent individual series in the same chart as bars, lines, curves, areas, or points. This option enables you to use the most effective method for displaying each series. For one series, bars in a bar chart may best represent the data. For another series, a line may be most effective. A chart that displays series with different types is a *combination chart.*

You can use the **S**eries command on the **C**hart menu to create a combination chart based on the sales trends chart you created earlier. Because you created your own values for certain series in the XY chart, the combination chart you create may look different from the completed combination chart, shown in figure 5.29; however, you follow the same technique. As you change the type for each series, you also will modify other options on the dialog box to enhance the appearance of the series.

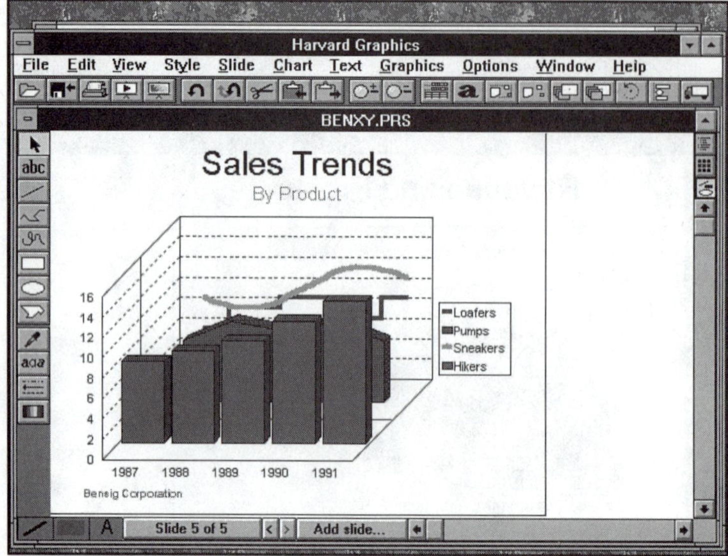

Fig. 5.29 An example of a combination chart.

Follow these steps to create the combination chart:

1. From the **C**hart menu, choose **S**eries. The XY Chart Series Options dialog box appears.
2. Choose Loafers in the Series list box. The options you change will affect only the Loafers series.
3. Choose the Show **A**s option, which controls the appearance of the series.
4. Use the down-arrow key to set the Show **A**s option to Line.
5. Select the Li**n**e fit list box.
6. Use the down arrow-key to set the Line fit to Step.
7. Choose Pumps in the Series list box.
8. Choose the Show **A**s option.
9. Use the down-arrow key to set the Show **A**s option to Area.

10. Choose Sneakers in the Series list box.

11. Choose the Show **A**s option.

12. Use the down-arrow key to set the Show **A**s option to Curve.

13. Click the OK button to accept the changes.

The series in the chart are displayed using the options you set. Loafers are shown in a Step series; the Pumps series is an area chart; the Sneakers series is displayed on a curve.

Modifying the Legend

The legend for an XY chart communicates the names of the series to the audience. You use the Legend Options dialog box, shown in figure 5.30, to change the location and appearance of the legend. To display the dialog box, choose **L**egend from the **C**hart menu. The first option, Show **L**egend, enables you to show or hide the legend. To use the remaining options in the dialog box, you must activate Show **L**egend. Below the Show **L**egend option, you enter a title for the legend. Harvard Graphics displays the title inside the legend box above the names of the series.

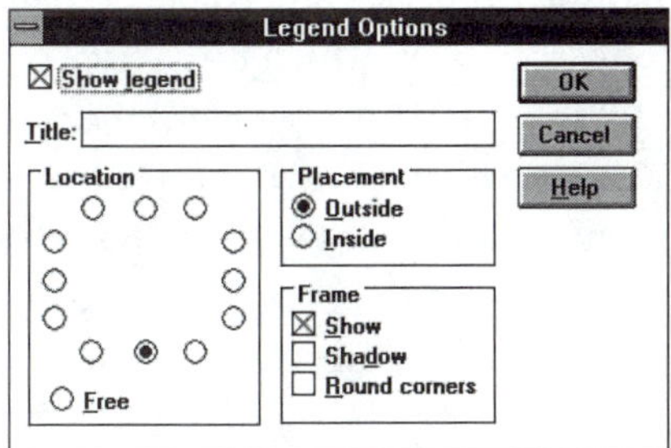

Fig. 5.30
The Legend Options dialog box.

The Location buttons enable you to place the legend in one of 12 predefined positions. You use the Placement field to place the legend **O**utside or **I**nside the frame of the chart. In the chapters that explain the Slide Editor, you learn how to move the legend and other elements of the chart with the mouse.

To change the appearance of the legend, you use the options in the Frame area. You activate the **S**how option to display a frame around the legend. With the Sha**d**ow option, you display a shadow behind the legend. You also can change the box style of the legend frame. If you choose the **R**ound Corners option, for example, Harvard Graphics places a box with rounded corners around the legend.

Design Note

The title and subtitle of the chart should provide enough information to identify the data, and the legend should complement the chart and provide information about the series. If your chart has only one series, a legend is not useful to the audience.

Design Note

By default, Harvard Graphics places the legend next to the chart, which may not be the best location for a chart with many data values. By moving the legend to the bottom of the chart, you can provide additional room to display the data.

Modifying the Chart Frame

You use the **F**rame option on the **C**hart menu to modify the appearance of the frame for an XY chart. By providing a background on which to contrast the items in the chart, the frame helps the audience evaluate the chart's information. Figure 5.31 shows the XY Chart Frame Options dialog box, which you access by choosing **F**rame from the **C**hart menu. You use this dialog box to alter the frame. You use the **S**tyle list box from the Select a Frame section to determine where to display the lines and colors of the frame. You can display the frame for only the x-axis, which is the back of the chart; or you can display the frame for the y-axis only, which is the side of the chart next to the y-axis. The default style is Full, which means that the x- and y-axis portions of the frame contain lines filled with the frame color. To display the frame for the y-axis only, you set this option to Y Only by clicking the arrow next to the list box and choosing Y Only from the list.

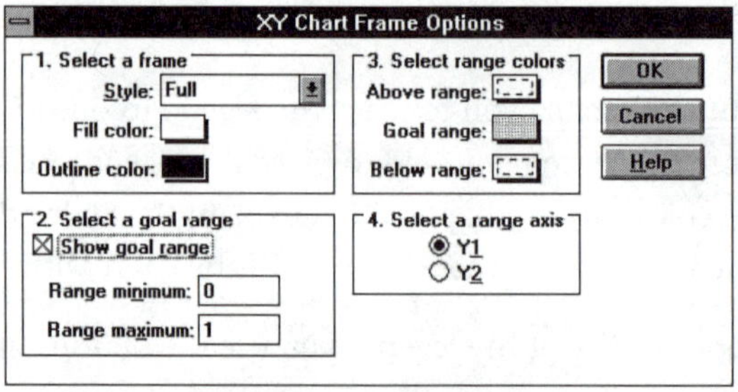

Fig. 5.31 The XY Chart Frame Options dialog box.

You use the Fill color and Outline color options from the Select a Frame section to control the colors of the frame. To see the available colors for either of these options, click the appropriate color option; then click the color from the Fill color or Outline color dialog box, both of which show samples of the colors.

You use the remaining items in the XY Chart Frame Options dialog box to define a goal range for a chart. The *goal range*, which Harvard Graphics displays in the frame of the chart, defines a range of data values that are significant to the audience. Harvard Graphics highlights the range with a filled box to illustrate the data values that fall in the range.

To define a goal range, you first must activate the Show Goal **R**ange option from the Select a Goal Range section of the dialog box. You enter the top and the bottom of the range into the Range maximum and Range minimum fields, respectively. After you define the range, you can change colors for the inside and outside of the range. The three fields in which you change the colors, which are located in the Select range options section, are the Above range, Goal range, and Below range fields. The Goal range option is the most important of these colors because the values inside the range appear against this color. Figure 5.32 shows a goal range highlighted with a color.

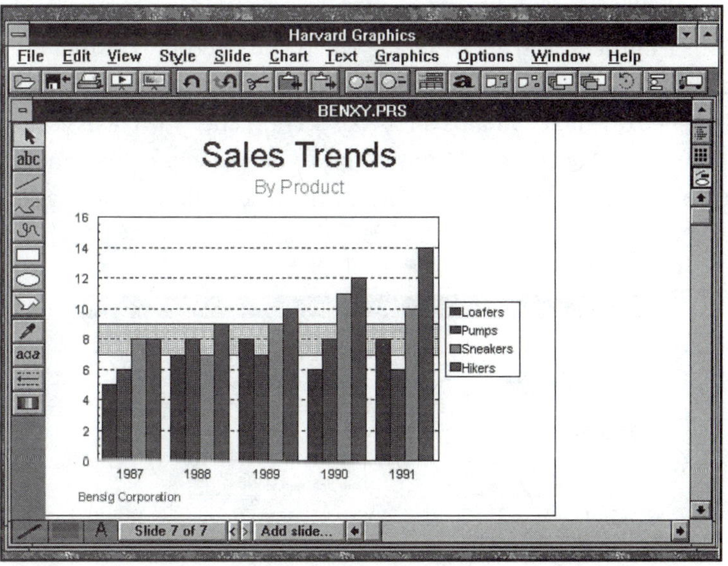

Fig. 5.32
An XY chart with a goal range.

Modifying the Grid Lines

The grid lines combine with the frame to provide a background for an XY chart. Grid lines are the horizontal or vertical lines your audience uses to determine the values for the objects in the chart. With a bar chart, for instance, the audience can compare the height of the bar to the nearest grid line to determine the value. The XY Chart Grid Options dialog box in figure 5.33 shows the options you can change for the grid lines of each axis. To show the grid lines of an axis, you first must indicate which grid lines to show by clicking Show **X**-axis grid or Show Y**1**-axis grid. The dialog box in the figure shows that grid lines will be displayed for the Y1 and Y2 axes.

Fig. 5.33
The XY Chart Grid Options dialog box.

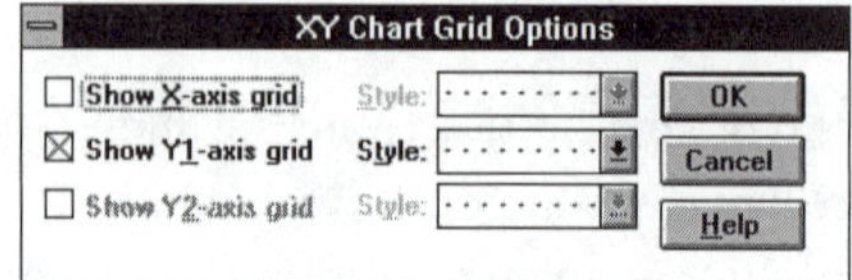

After setting the display option, you can select a style for the grid lines. The styles range from a solid line to a line consisting entirely of dots. To change the style, click the down scroll arrow in the appropriate Style list box to see the available styles; then select the style from the list.

Setting Axis Options

You use the A**x**is option on the **C**hart menu to change the scaling and the appearance of the axis in an XY chart. When you choose A**x**is from the **C**hart menu, the XY Chart Axis Options dialog box appears (see fig. 5.34). You use this dialog box, which contains an X Axis section and two Y Axis sections, to modify the axes. For the X, Y1, and Y2 axes, you can enter a title and set the scaling for each axis. You also can display the tick marks for the x- and y-axes.

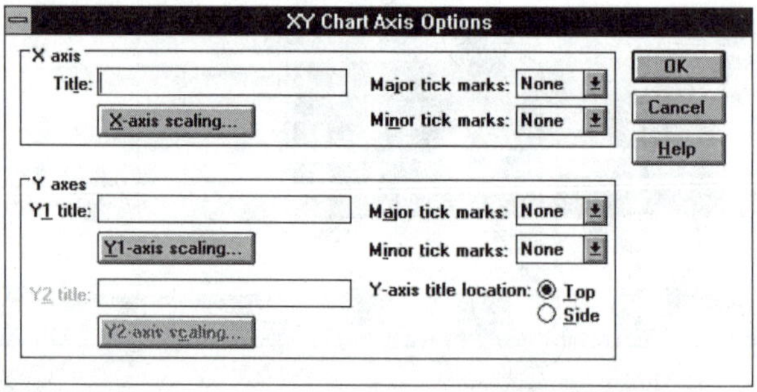

Fig. 5.34
The XY Chart Axis Options dialog box.

XY Chart Axis Options
X axis
Title:
X-axis scaling...
Major tick marks: None
Minor tick marks: None
OK
Cancel
Help
Y axes
Y1 title:
Y1-axis scaling...
Major tick marks: None
Minor tick marks: None
Y2 title:
Y2-axis scaling...
Y-axis title location: Top
Side

Changing the Scaling of an Axis. With the XY Chart Axis Options dialog box, you can change the scaling for any numeric axis. Although the y-axes are always numeric, you must set the x-axis to Numeric by using the X-Axis

Labels dialog box, explained in the section "Entering X-Axis Labels" earlier in this chapter. The scaling of an axis determines the size of the bars in a bar chart and the location of the points in a scatter chart. Click the **X**-axis scaling..., **Y**1-axis scaling..., or Y2-axis s**c**aling... button from the XY Chart Axis Options dialog box to show the desired Scaling Options dialog box. Figure 5.35 shows the Scaling Options dialog box.

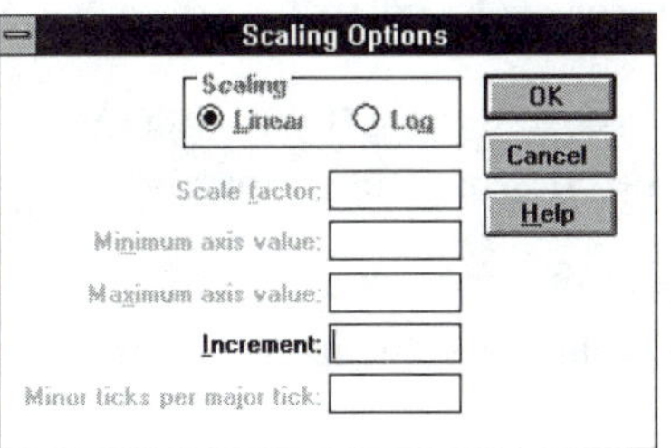

Fig. 5.35
The Scaling Options dialog box.

In the Scaling area of the Scaling Options dialog box, you can indicate whether to scale the axis on a linear or a logarithmic scale. A *linear scale* displays the bars evenly throughout the scale. The *logarithmic scale* is helpful for displaying XY charts with values of widely varying sizes. In a linear scale, for example, a bar with a data value of 2 would be very small next to a value of 10,000. Figure 5.36 shows these two values with an axis using a logarithmic scale. The labels on the side of the axis indicate accurately the actual values of the bars. With logarithmic scaling, both bars are clearly visible.

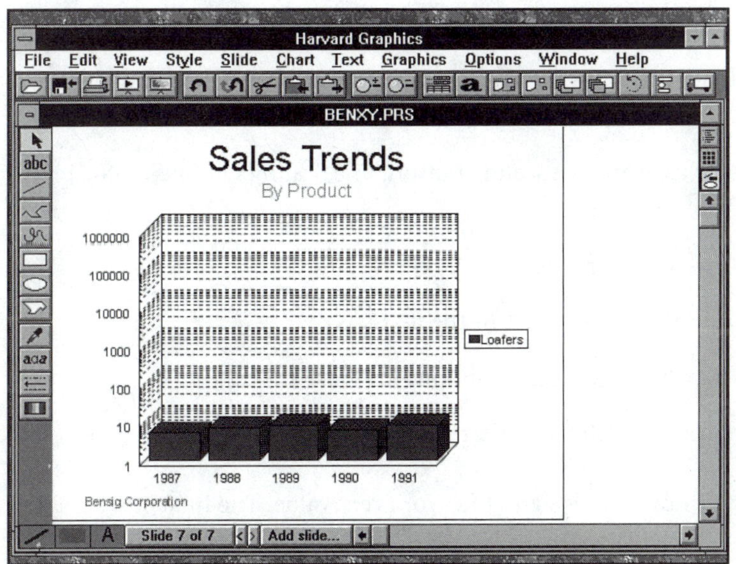

Fig. 5.36
A simple bar chart with logarithmic scaling.

After determining the type of scaling, you can use the remaining options in the Scaling Options dialog box to set the size of the scale and the interval of the grid lines on the axis.

You use the Scale **F**actor to scale down the values in the chart; the program divides the data values in the chart by the factor before displaying the data. With a factor of 100, for example, the program scales values that range from 100 to 1,000 to values between 1 and 10.

The Mi**n**imum Axis Value and the Ma**x**imum Axis Value settings determine the starting value and the ending value, respectively, for the axis.

By default, Harvard Graphics sets the starting value at 0 and the ending value large enough to show the largest value in the chart. These options override the automatic values set by the program. Make sure that the values you enter include all the data in the chart.

The **I**ncrement option determines the number of grid lines displayed between the minimum and maximum values. The Minor Ticks per Ma**j**or Tick option determines the number of tick marks displayed between the grid lines. Major ticks appear on the axis at the same places as the lines and are wider than minor ticks.

In the chart on sales trends, suppose that you decide that you need additional grid lines to help the audience compare bars. You can display lines for every possible data value in a linear scale by setting the increment to 1.

To display the additional grid lines, follow these steps:

1. From the **C**hart menu, choose A**x**is. The XY Chart Options dialog box is displayed.
2. Click the **Y**1-axis scaling button. The Scaling Options dialog box displays.
3. Click the **I**ncrement text box.
4. Type the increment **1** in the text box.
5. Click OK. The Scaling Options dialog box closes.
6. Click OK in the XY Chart Axis Options dialog box.

The chart now displays grid lines for every value. The final chart is shown in figure 5.37.

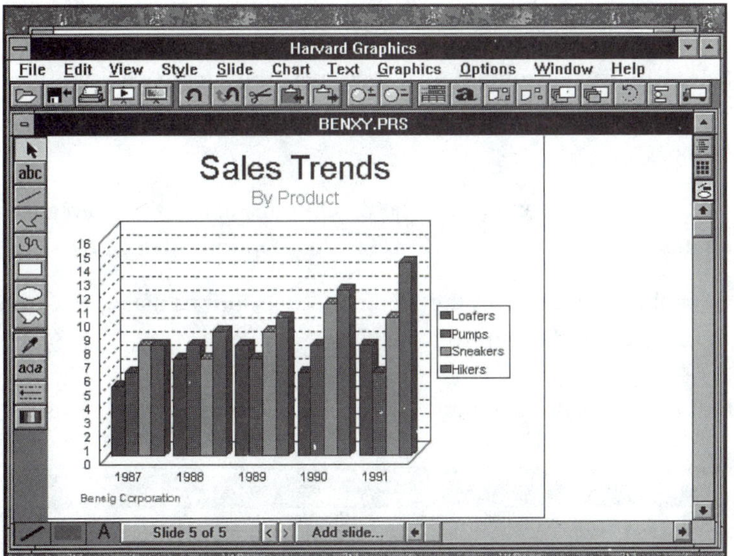

Fig. 5.37 The sales trends chart with additional grid lines.

Changing the Tick Marks of an Axis. Tick marks appear along the axis to help the audience compare the bars in a chart. Major tick marks appear at the same intervals as the grid lines; minor tick marks appear between the grid lines. For each axis, you use the options in the XY Chart Axis Options dialog box to show tick marks. The choices for major and minor ticks include In, Out, Cross, and None. The choices indicate locations relative to the axis. The In choice, for example, displays the tick marks in the frame on the inside of the axis. The Out option displays tick marks outside the axis; Cross displays tick marks on both the inside and the outside; and None displays no tick marks. Figure 5.38 shows the chart on sales trends with the major and minor tick marks displayed inside the frame.

Follow these steps to display the tick marks:

1. From the **C**hart menu, choose A**x**is. The XY Chart Axis Options dialog box appears.

2. Click the down scroll arrow next to the Ma**j**or Tick Marks list box for the Y axes.

3. Choose In from the list of tick mark locations.

4. Click the down scroll arrow next to the M**i**nor Tick Marks list box for the Y axes.

5. Choose In from the list of tick mark locations.

I Creating a Presentation

6. To set the scaling, click the **Y**1-axis scaling button.

7. Select the **I**ncrement text box; then press the Backspace key to clear the field. Clearing the text box enables you to see clearly both sets of tick marks.

8. Click the OK button on the Scaling Options dialog box to accept the changes and return to the XY Chart Axis Options dialog box.

9. Click the OK button on the XY Chart Axis Options dialog box to accept the changes and return to the chart.

The chart now displays major and minor tick marks inside the y-axis.

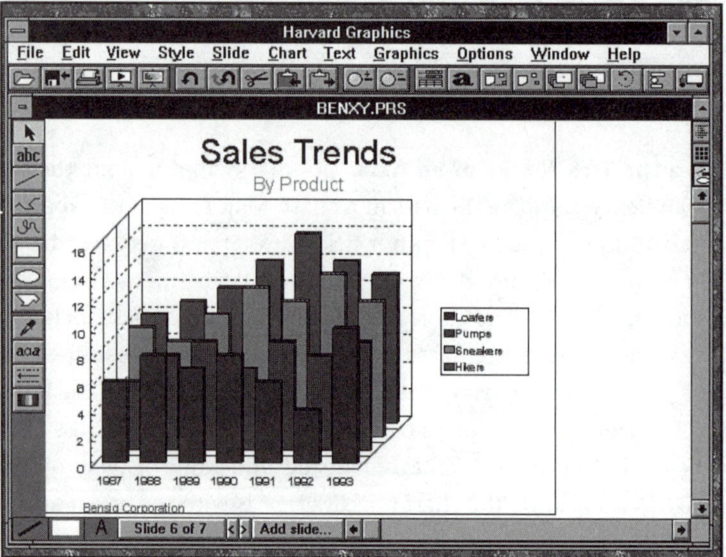

Fig. 5.38
The sales trend chart showing major and minor tick marks.

Setting XY Chart Label Options

You use the La**b**els item on the **C**hart menu to set the format and orientation for the labels on each axis and for the data labels in an XY chart. You can display numbers as currency or set the number of decimal places for a number to change the format of a label. For orientation, you can display the labels horizontally from left to right or vertically. When you choose La**b**els from the **C**hart menu, the XY Chart Label Options dialog box appears (see fig. 5.39).

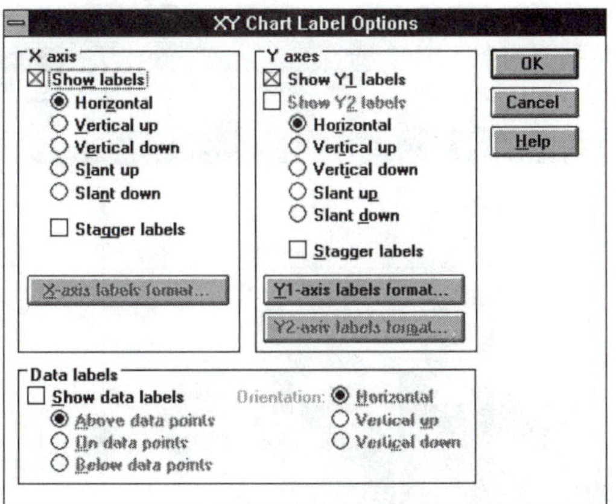

Fig. 5.39
The XY Chart Label Options dialog box.

To show the labels for an axis, you first must select the appropriate Show labels option (from either the X-axis or Y-axes areas) at the top of the dialog box. The Show Y**2** Labels option can be set only if your chart uses this axis (see the section "Creating Charts with Two Y-Axes" earlier in this chapter for information). To show the x-axis labels, for example, you click the box next to the X axis Sho**w** Labels option (an X appears); then you can use the remaining items in the dialog box to control the location and the format of the labels.

Changing the Label Orientation and Format. The choices for label orientation include Hori**z**ontal, **V**ertical Up, V**e**rtical Down, S**l**ant up, and Sla**n**t down. In addition to the orientation of individual labels, you can set the Stagger Labels option to alter the orientation of labels relative to each other. If you use the Stagger Labels option, you have more room to display the text of each label. Figure 5.40 shows the sales trends chart with slanted labels on the x-axis and staggered labels on the y-axis.

Follow these steps to slant the x-axis labels and stagger the y-axis labels:

1. From the **C**hart menu, choose La**b**els. The XY Label Chart Options dialog box appears.
2. Choose the S**l**ant up option under the X axis Show Labels option.
3. Choose the **S**tagger labels option under the Y axes Show labels option.
4. Click the OK button to accept the changes.

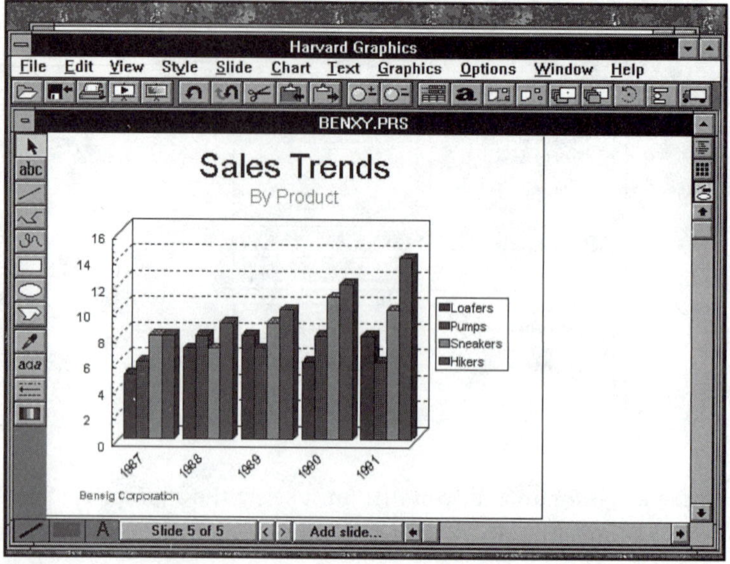

Fig. 5.40
The sales trends chart with staggered and slanted labels.

The chart now has slanted x-axis labels and staggered y-axis labels.

After you set the orientation, you can use the format buttons on the XY Chart Label Options dialog box to change the format for numeric x-axis and y-axis labels. If you choose **X**-Axis Labels Format or **Y**1-Axis Labels Format, for example, the Format Options dialog box appears (see fig. 5.41). You use this dialog box to set the format for the axis labels.

Format Options
Current format: 12345
Currency
Thousands separator
Scientific notation
Decimal places:
Leading text:
Trailing text:
OK
Cancel
Help

Fig. 5.41
The Format Options dialog box.

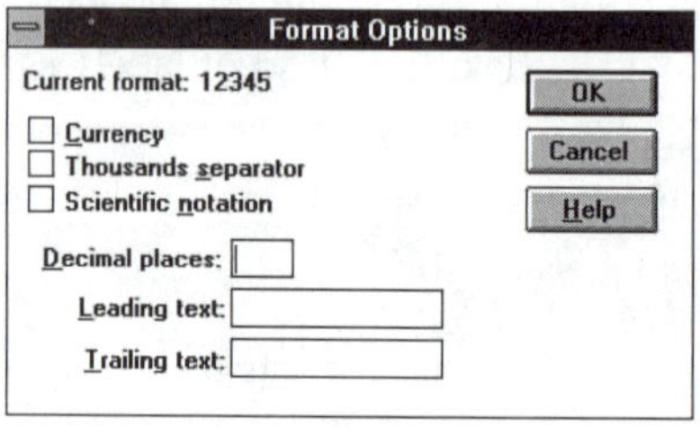

The options in the Format Options dialog box affect numeric labels only. The **C**urrency option indicates to Harvard Graphics that the data values in the chart are currency. The currency format and symbol are determined by the International settings of the Windows Control Panel. The Thousands **S**eparator option causes a thousands character to be displayed for numbers in the thousands. (You also can use the International settings to specify this character.) The Scientific **N**otation option displays the axis labels in scientific notation, a shorthand way of writing very large numbers. Because scientific notation is a shorthand for very large numbers, you can use this format option if you have large data values.

The **D**ecimal Places field controls the number of digits displayed after the decimal point of a number. With U.S. currency, for example, cents requires two digits after the decimal.

You enter text you want to precede or follow the labels on an axis in the **L**eading Text and **T**railing Text boxes. The leading text precedes the labels; the trailing text follows the labels. You can use these options, for example, to indicate the unit of measure used by your values. You can place **in.** or **lb.** as trailing text to communicate to the audience that the values are in inches or pounds.

Showing Data Labels. Data labels display the values for a series in the body of the chart. The objects in the chart, such as the bars of a bar chart, graphically represent data. Data values show the specific numeric values to help the audience interpret the data. Figure 5.42 shows data labels displayed on top of the bars for the series.

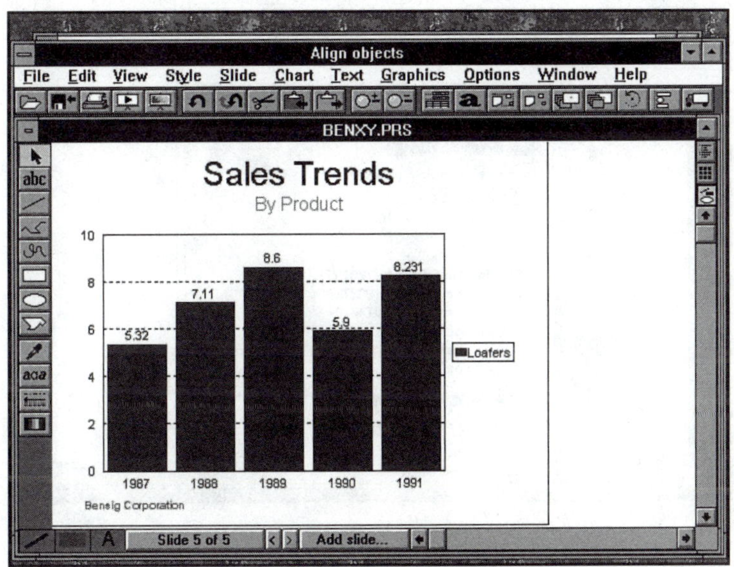

Fig. 5.42
An XY chart with data labels displayed on top of the bars.

In the XY Chart Label Options dialog box, you can specify that data labels be displayed above, on, or below the object that represents a data value. The three options—**A**bove data points, **O**n data points, and **B**elow data points—

control the location of the label. Make sure that the labels are visible and easy to read.

You set the orientation of the text in the label with the Orientation options. To display the text horizontally, choose **H**orizontal. For a vertical orientation, you can display the text upward by choosing Vertical **U**p, or you can display the text downward by choosing Verti**c**al Down.

Displaying Series Statistics

Series statistics allow you to examine the statistics for a selected series in an XY chart. The series statistics for the series of an XY chart can provide information that helps you analyze the data in the chart. To show the statistics, choose S**e**ries Statistics from the **C**hart menu. Figure 5.43 shows the Series Statistics dialog box for the Loafers series in the sales trends chart. You can view the information for any series by selecting the name of the series in the Statistics For field.

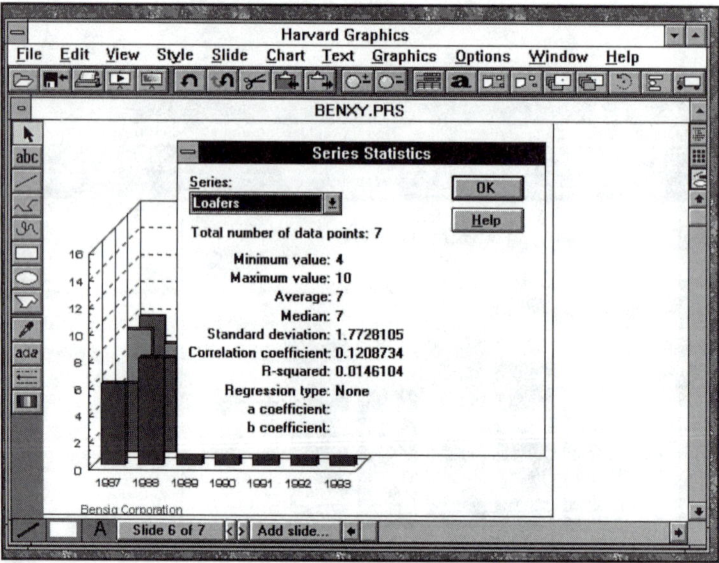

Fig. 5.43
Series Statistics dialog box for the Loafers series.

The information in this dialog box shows the minimum and maximum values for the data in the series. You also can see the average value, the median, and the standard deviation. For information on the formulas used to calculate the remaining values in the dialog box, consult the Harvard Graphics documentation.

You can use this information in several ways. You can, for example, use the total data points or minimum and maximum values to ensure that the data in the chart was entered correctly. Your audience might benefit from information such as the average or median of the data in a series, for instance.

From Here...

This chapter covers the many features of the XY chart type. In the beginning of the chapter, you are introduced to the elements of an XY chart and the different types of XY charts. You learned how to organize your data form with x-axis labels and series names. You also were presented material on using formulas to get spreadsheet functionality in the data form.

After entering the data into a chart, you learned how to modify the many XY chart options. You were guided through the items on the **C**hart menu, which you use to change the appearance of the elements in an XY chart. In particular, you learned how to modify the entire chart as well as individual series. You also learned how to use the legend, grid, and frame to help your audience evaluate the information in the chart.

Chapter 6

Creating Pie Charts

In this chapter, you learn how to do the following:

- Create and enhance pie charts
- Enter data into the pie chart data form
- Create and link multiple pie charts

Pie charts present information based on percentages and represented by a proportionally divided circle. If you cut a pie in half, each slice represents 50 percent of the total pie. In the same way, each data value in a pie chart becomes a section (a slice) of the circle. Figure 6.1 shows a pie chart with four slices. The slices communicate how much each of Bensig Corporation's products contributed to total revenue. The circle, or pie, represents total revenue of the Bensig Corporation for one year. The percentage each product contributed to the revenue is indicated by the size of the product's slice.

Understanding the Elements of a Pie Chart

The primary element of a pie chart is the *slice*. The pie chart in figure 6.2 shows labels, percents, and values for each slice. The *slice value* is determined by numeric data, the values of which are represented in the chart by the sizes of the slices. The *slice label* is the text that identifies the slice, and the *slice percent* is the percentage of the pie made up by that slice. To help your audience interpret the information in the chart, you can display all three items to indicate on your pie chart the numeric value of each slice and the percentage of the pie that each slice represents.

To focus attention on one segment of the pie, you also can "cut away" a slice from the other slices in the pie chart. In figure 6.2, the Loafers slice is cut away from the rest of the pie.

You can have more than one pie in a pie chart, and you can link the information in one pie to another pie. For instance, you might use two pies to represent two different sets of data, perhaps product revenues for two consecutive years. You link pies when the information in one pie relates to another.

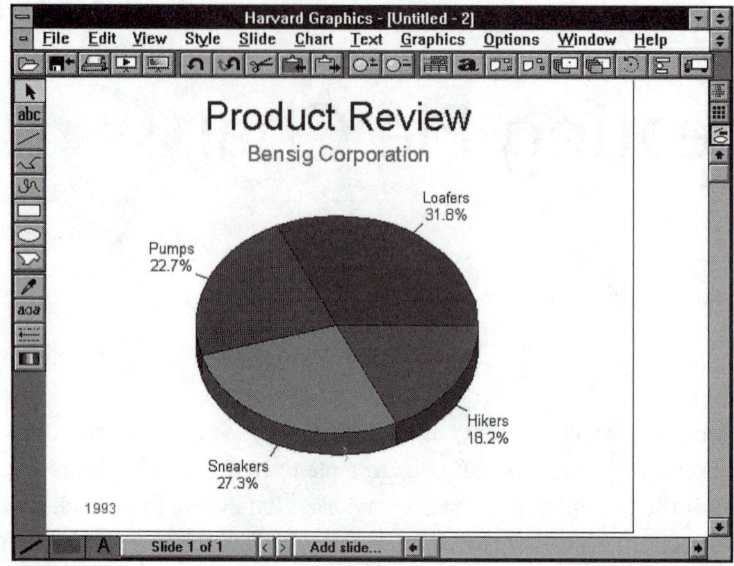

Fig. 6.1
A pie chart.

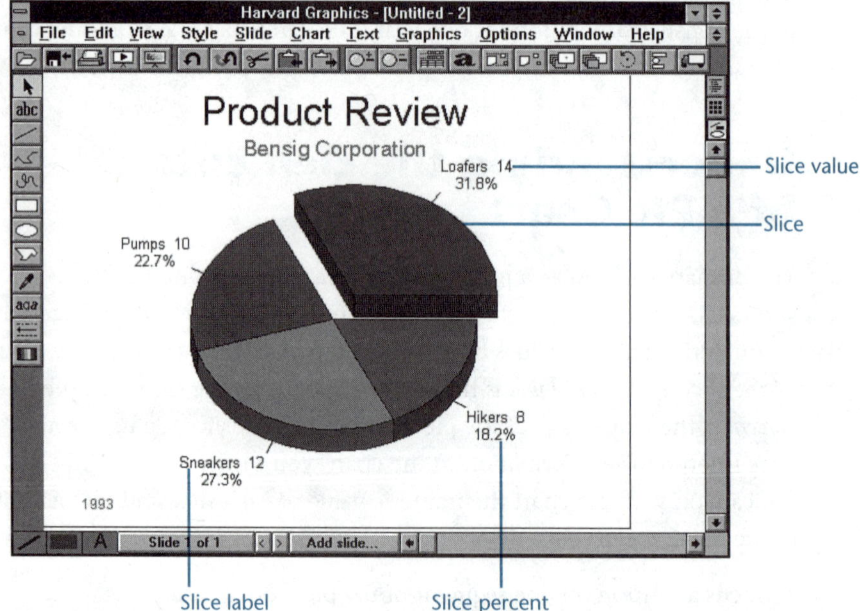

Fig. 6.2
A pie chart with one slice cut away.

Figure 6.3 shows a set of linked pies. The second "pie" in the chart is in the form of a *column chart*, in which data values are represented by sections of a column. You can display any pie in the chart as a column or a pie. The column chart shows the percentage of loafer sales accumulated in the four sales regions. As with a pie chart, the column sections combine to form a total value, with each section representing a percentage of the total.

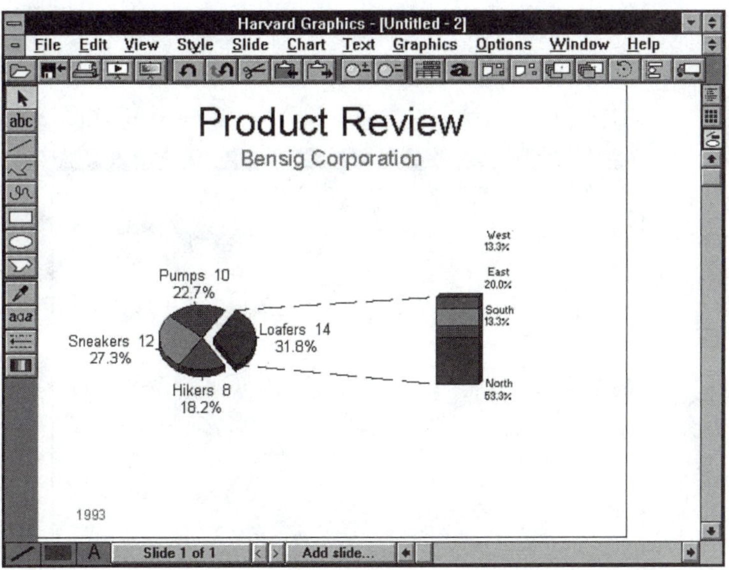

Fig. 6.3
Linked pie charts.

The column chart in figure 6.3 represents a breakdown of a selected slice in the first pie. The column chart is linked to the first pie chart with *link lines*, which are drawn from the top and bottom of the selected slice in the first pie to the ends of the column. The slices in the pie illustrate how much each product contributed to Bensig's total revenue. The sections of the column show how much sales in each of the four sales regions contributed to total loafer sales.

Choosing a Pie Chart Style

Harvard Graphics provides 12 pie chart styles from which to choose. These styles are presented in the New Presentation dialog box, shown in figure 6.4. When you create a new presentation, Harvard Graphics displays the New Presentation dialog box in which you can select a new slide type.

The first row of the Select an Option area of the New Presentation dialog box enables you to select the dimension of your pies. The second row gives you the option of specifying whether a slice of pie is cut away. (You can change the dimension of a pie and cut away additional slices after the chart is created.)

Design Note

Three-dimensional (3-D) pies add depth to your chart. If you have a large number of slices, however, individual slices are easier to distinguish in two-dimensional (2-D) pies.

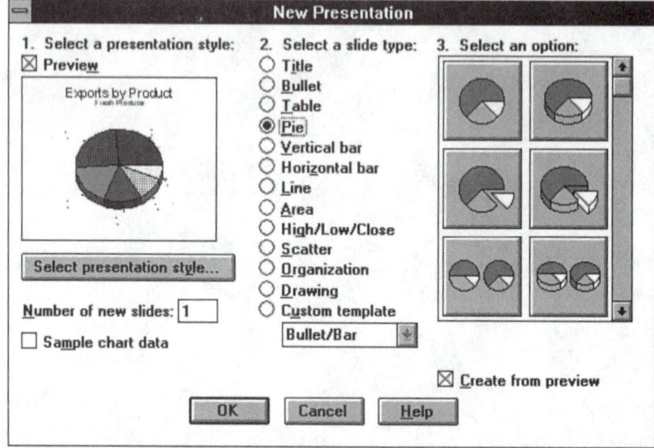

Fig. 6.4
The New Presentation dialog box with the pie chart styles.

The third row of the New Presentation gives you a choice of 2-D or 3-D charts, and the fourth row enables you to select linked pies (similar to fig. 6.3, except here the linked pie is an actual pie graph, not a stacked bar chart). In a linked pie chart, the second pie represents a breakdown of a slice in the first pie. For more information on linking pies, see "Creating Multiple Pie Charts" later in this chapter.

If you have multiple pies, you need to decide whether you want the second pie to be like the first pie, proportional to the first pie, or linked to the first pie as a pie or column chart. The New Presentation or Add Slide dialog boxes display all pie options (Select an option:) as the same size and type.

The fifth row of the New Presentation dialog box displays an option for a multiple pie chart—proportional pies. The size of each pie is determined by the ratio of the slice values. If, for example, the values in one pie are twice the quantity of the values in the second pie, the first pie is twice the size of the second. (For more information on proportional pies, see "Creating Proportional Pies" later in this chapter.) The last two styles, in the sixth row of the New Presentation dialog box are linked pies, with the second pie in each example displayed as a column chart (as you saw in fig. 6.3).

In this chapter, you develop pie charts to add to your presentation for Bensig Corporation, a leading manufacturer of shoes. You create a pie chart to illustrate how much each product of the company contributes to the total revenue. You also highlight the sales for loafers, the product that generates the most revenue for the company, by using a 3-D chart with a cut-away slice (the second pie chart option in the second row of the New Presentation dialog box).

To create a new presentation with a pie chart, follow these steps:

1. From the **F**ile menu, choose **N**ew Presentation. You see the New Presentation dialog box.

2. From the Select a slide type list, select Pie.

3. Select the style you consider most effective for your data. For the example, select the last pie in the second row for a 3-D pie chart with the first slice cut away.

4. Click OK in the New Presentation dialog box to show the pie chart data form.

Entering and Editing Data for a Pie Chart

In the pie chart data form, you can enter data for as many as six pie charts. The data form is divided into two parts. The top part of the form has space for title information. You normally add the title information after you have entered the data (see "Entering Title Information"). You enter data for the chart into the lower part of the form, with the data for each pie grouped into two consecutive columns. The first column of each pair contains the slice labels of the pie. The second column is for the slice values of the pie.

Figure 6.5 shows the pie chart data form. The columns for each pie chart are clearly titled to indicate where the labels and values are entered for each pie. Each cell in the data form is defined by row and column. Rows are numbered on the left side of the form, starting with the number 1. Columns have letter titles, beginning with the letter A. To enter the Pie1 Values for the second slice, you select cell B2. You enter the data for each pie into cells by selecting the correct cell and using the edit line, located just above the data portion of the form. The next section explains how to enter pie chart data into the pie chart data form.

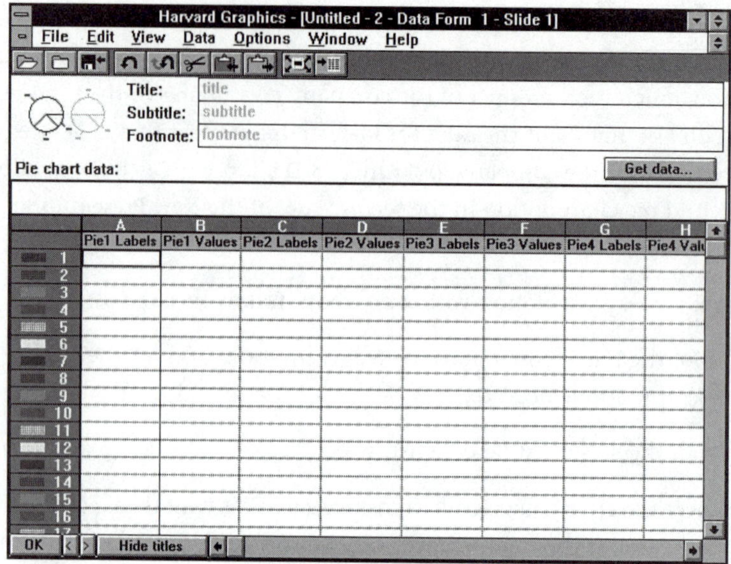

Fig. 6.5 The pie chart data form.

Entering Slice Labels and Values

You enter slice labels for each pie in the chart in the first column for that pie, and you enter slice values in the second column for that pie. The order of the slices becomes important when you format the chart. The first slice is the slice starting at the right-most horizontal location (3 o'clock). The position of the first slice is the *starting angle* for the pie. You can change the angle of the first slice through the Pie Chart Options dialog box. (These options are covered under "Modifying Pie Chart Options" in this chapter.) After the first slice has been defined, Harvard Graphics adds other slices to the pie in a counter-clockwise direction. The order of the slices in the data form determines the order of the slices in your chart. Figure 6.6 shows the default order for a pie with four slices. The Loafers slice is the first slice. The defaults for this chart were established in the section "Choosing a Pie Chart Style." The Loafers slice is the cut-away slice because it is the first.

Design Note

When you define the slices of a pie, enter the most significant information in the first slice. You have the most control over the location of this slice in the pie.

To enter the slice labels, select the Pie1 Labels cell for the first slice and type the information. To enter the value, select the adjacent Pie1 Values cell. To create a four-slice pie in the data form, follow these steps:

1. Select A1, the Pie1 Labels cell for the first slice in the pie.
2. Type the slice label. For this example, type **Loafers**.
3. Press Tab to move the highlight to the Pie1 Values cell for the first slice.
4. Type the slice value for the first slice. For this example, type **14**.
5. Select A2, the Pie2 Labels cell for the second slice in the pie.
6. Type the slice label; for the example, type **Pumps**.
7. Press Tab to move the highlight to the Pie2 Values cell, and type the slice value. For this example, type **10**.
8. Select cell A3, the Pie3 Labels cell for the third slice in the pie, and type **Sneakers**.
9. Press Tab to move the highlight to the Pie3 Values cell, and type **12**.
10. Select cell A4, the Pie4 Labels cell for the fourth slice in the pie, and type **Hikers**.
11. Press Tab to move the highlight to the Pie4 Values cell, and type **8**.

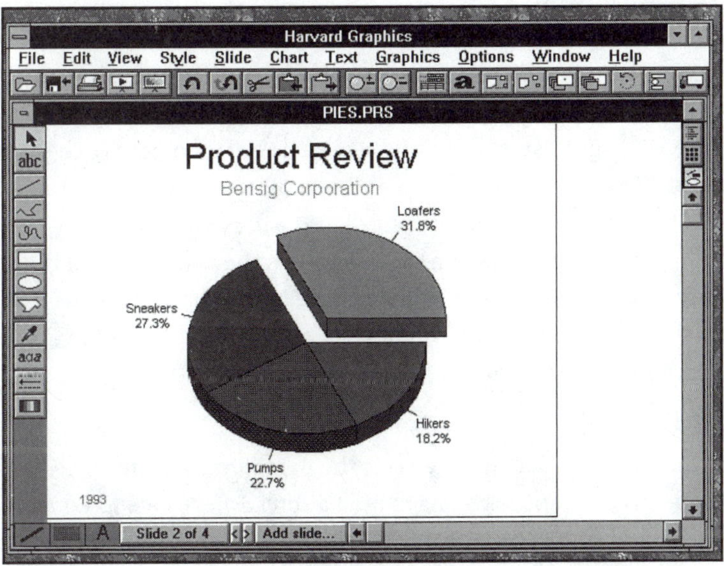

Fig. 6.6
The Loafers slice is the first slice.

Figure 6.7 shows a completed pie chart data form for product revenues of the Bensig Corporation. Each product is represented by a slice. Loafer shoes were the highest selling product for the year. When the chart is created, the Loafers slice will be cut away from the rest of the pie because the Loafers slice was entered as the first slice. Cutting away the slice draws attention to the loafers product. (The chart for this data is shown on the left side of figure 6.2.)

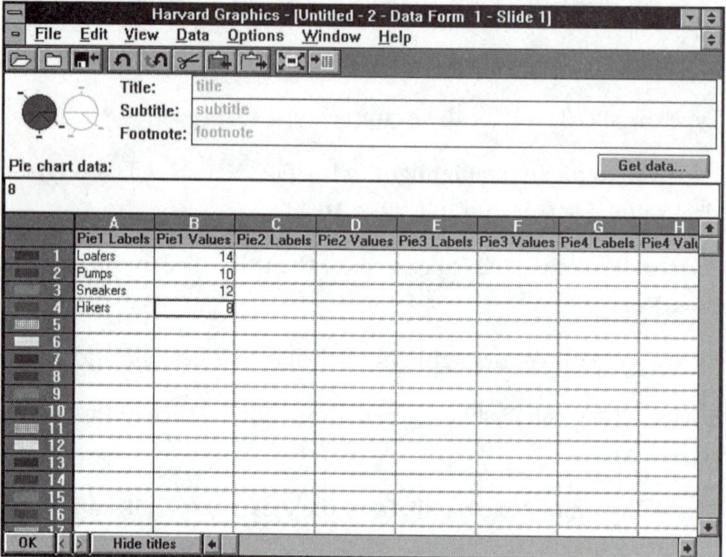

Fig. 6.7
The pie chart data form for product revenue.

The Fill commands on the **D**ata menu provide the quickest way to enter data into a pie chart. The Fill **R**ight and Fill Do**w**n commands operate on a block of cells. The Fill **R**ight command copies data across the columns of a selected block of cells. If a cell has a value of 3 and you fill to the right, for example, all the selected cells to the right of the cell also will have a value of 3. The Fill Do**w**n command copies data from the top row to the rows below in the selected block. You should use the Fill commands if you have the same data in consecutive cells of a row or column of your chart. (See Chapter 3, "Creating Text Charts," for more information about these commands.)

Editing Data

After you have entered data into cells on the data form, you may need to make changes to the data. If you have used a spreadsheet such as Lotus 1-2-3 or Microsoft Excel, then you are already familiar with the basic movements and commands of this chart. You can either use the mouse or the arrow and Tab keys to move to the desired cell. (You can also use the Enter key to move the highlight down one row and Tab and Shift+Tab to move the highlight right and left, respectively.)

To learn how to move the highlight from cell C3 to cell E1, using the keyboard, follow these steps:

1. Click C3 to make it the active cell.
2. Press the up arrow twice to move from row 3 to row 1.
3. Press Tab twice to move to column E.

When a cell is active, the contents of the cell are displayed in the edit line. When you type a character to enter data, Harvard Graphics clears the edit line before displaying the character. To accept your changes, press Enter. Press Esc to abort the changes and restore the previous value.

To edit the contents of a cell without losing the previous information, click the edit line at the point where you need to make changes. The insertion point appears in the edit line. As you type, the new data is added, beginning at the insertion point. When the insertion point is not displayed, Harvard Graphics assumes that you want to replace the entire contents of the cell.

To enter and edit information in cell A1, follow these steps:

1. Click cell A1.
2. Type **Laofers**. (Notice that you have misspelled the word.)
3. Press Enter to add the misspelled word to the chart in cell A1.
4. To correct the spelling mistake, click A1.
5. Click the edit line immediately following the *o* in *Laofers*, and press Backspace twice to remove the incorrect characters.
6. Type **oa**.
7. Press Enter when you have finished editing the cell to accept the changes.

Cutting, Copying, and Pasting Data

You use the commands on the **E**dit menu to edit the information in the data form. You use these commands to move, copy, or delete information. These commands operate on the contents of the active cell, which is displayed in the edit line, or on selected cells or blocks of cells.

You can copy a group of characters to the edit line and then paste them back into the same cell or into a different cell. In the edit line, the Edit commands affect selected characters. To select characters, position the insertion point to the left of the first character you want to select and drag the insertion point to the end of the characters and release the button. Then do one of the following:

- Choose Cu**t** from the **E**dit menu to move the data to the Windows Clipboard. Then position the insertion point in the edit line where you want to place the data and choose **P**aste. The data from the Clipboard is inserted to the right of the insertion point. To paste data into another cell, click the cell and click the insertion point in the edit line before choosing Paste.

- Choose **C**opy to copy the selected data in the edit line to the Clipboard without moving or changing the original contents. Click the insertion point where you want to copy the data. Then select **P**aste to insert the data after the insertion point. Choose Cl**e**ar to delete the selected characters. To paste data into another cell, click the cell and click the insertion point in the edit line before choosing **P**aste.

For example, to copy information from cell B2 to cell D3, follow these steps:

1. Select cell B2 in the data form.

2. Click the edit line to the left of the first character you want to copy and drag to the end of the characters in the B2 edit line. (The selected characters are displayed in reverse video.) Release the mouse button to select the data you have highlighted.

3. From the **E**dit menu, choose **C**opy.

4. Select cell D3.

5. Click in the edit line where you want to insert the data.

6. From the **E**dit menu, choose **P**aste. The characters from the Clipboard are inserted into the edit line at the insertion point.

7. Press Enter to accept the changes made to the contents of the cell.

To work with a block of cells, select the first cell of the block. Holding down the mouse button, move the insertion point to the end of the block and release the button. The Cu**t**, **C**opy, and Cl**e**ar commands affect the entire block.

The **P**aste command then copies cells from the Clipboard into the data form, starting at the active cell.

You can also clear an entire block of cells at one time. To clear a block of cells, follow these steps:

1. Drag to select the block.

2. From the **E**dit menu, choose Cl**e**ar.

Using Formulas

Formulas provide spreadsheet functionality in the pie chart data form. You can use formulas, for example, to add the values in a column or to take the average of a group or range of cells. An equal (=) sign in a cell tells Harvard Graphics to evaluate the data in the cell as a formula. Following the equal sign, you can enter any combination of cell references, simple operators, or predefined functions by following the rules of basic algebra.

To enter in cell A5 a formula that adds cells A1, A2, A3, and A4, for example, you select cell A5, and type **=A1+A2+A3+A4**.

Table 6.1 lists the simple operators for formulas.

Table 6.1 Simple Operators for Formulas

Operator	Function
+	Addition
–	Negative numbers or subtraction
*	Multiplication
/	Division
^ or **	Exponent of a number
%	Percentage

You use parentheses to determine the order in which expressions are evaluated in a formula. Table 6.2 gives examples of formulas that have cell references, parentheses, and simple operators.

Table 6.2 Examples of Formulas

Formula	Result
=C1+C2	Adds the contents of cells C1 and C2
=(F1+B2–A3)/D4	Adds the contents of cells F1 and B2, subtracts the contents of cell A3, and divides that total by contents of D4
=A3^2	Takes the contents of cell A3 to the second power

You can use *ranges* of cells in these formulas. A range of cells is a group, or block, of consecutive cells. Ranges of cells are specified by the first and last cell in the range. To indicate that cells are part of a range, you must enter either one dot (.), two dots (..), or a colon (:) between the references. When you enter the complete formula, Harvard Graphics changes all range indicators to the colon character.

In formulas, you can use predefined functions by themselves or combined with cell references and simple operators. Each function uses the arguments you provide to evaluate the value for the function. Table 6.3 provides examples of formulas that use functions. The arguments to a function are enclosed by parentheses and separated by commas. Each function takes a combination of values and cell ranges for the arguments. A value can be a number or a reference to a cell or range. For example, the function ABS(–1) gives you the absolute value of –1, and the function ABS(C2) gives the absolute value of the contents of cell C2.

Table 6.3 Functions in Formulas

Function	Result
=SUM(C1:C4)	Adds the contents of cells C1 through C4
=(COS(B1)+C2)*6	Takes the cosine of cell B1, adds the cosine to the contents of cell C2, and multiplies the total by 6
=MAVG(F1:F4,2,4)	Calculates the moving average of cells F1 through F4, using the cells from 2 rows before the current cell to the cell 4 rows after

The example earlier in this section (=A3+B3+C3) illustrates a formula to add three cells in the same row. Rather than typing each cell in the formula, you can use a sum function and a range to add the values. To enter the sum function and range, follow these steps:

1. Select cell A5.

2. Type **=SUM(A1:A4)**.

3. Press Enter to insert the formula into the cell. Cell A5 now contains and displays the sum of the contents of cells A1 through A4.

   If you do not want to add an extra slice to the pie you created in this chapter, press Esc instead of Enter to abandon the changes.

Appendix C, "Formulas," provides a complete list of predefined functions, with an explanation of each function, a list of the arguments, and an example of each function. To help you find the function you need, the functions are listed alphabetically in two groups: algebraic and geometric functions.

When you edit the data form, some of the cells you copy and paste with the Clipboard may contain formulas with cell references. When you paste the formulas back into the data form, Harvard Graphics adjusts the references for the new cells. In the formula for cell C2, for example, you reference cell B2, which is in the same row. When you paste this formula into cell C1, Harvard Graphics changes the reference to B2 to refer to cell B1, which is in the same row as the new cell, C1.

You can use absolute referencing to avoid the adjustment of cell references when you paste formulas. An *absolute reference* indicates to Harvard Graphics that the reference in the formula is linked to a specific cell in the data form. The $ character in a cell reference indicates that the cell is an absolute reference—one that will never be changed by the product. In the preceding example, the reference B2 would not have changed when pasted into cell C1 (see Chapter 5, "Creating XY Charts," for more information).

Entering Title Information

A chart should have a title to clarify the data for your audience. The subtitle and footnote support the title. When the chart is created, the title is displayed at the top of the chart, with the subtitle under the title. The footnote is displayed in a smaller font below the body of the chart. In the Slide Editor, you can change the position for any element on the slide, including the title. See "Moving Objects" in Chapter 13 for more information.

To enter title information for a pie chart data form, follow these steps:

1. Click the Title field.
2. Type the title for the chart; for the example, type **Product Revenue**.
3. Click the Subtitle field.
4. Type the subtitle; for the example, type **Bensig Corporation**.
5. Click the Footnote field.
6. Type the footnote; for the example, type **1991**.
7. Click OK to add the chart to your presentation.

Changing the Appearance of a Pie Chart

You use the options in the **C**hart menu to format and change the appearance of a pie chart. You can change the dimension of the chart, and you can modify the appearance of 3-D charts. You also can hide or show pies in a multiple pie chart and add a legend to slice labels.

Design Note

As you change different options, keep in mind that the audience should be able to understand the chart with little or no explanation on your part.

Modifying Pie Chart Options

The Chart **O**ptions command on the **C**hart menu changes the dimensions of a pie chart, changes the appearance of a 3-D chart, and defines relationships between multiple pies in a chart. Choosing Chart **O**ptions from the **C**hart menu displays the Pie Chart Options dialog box, which you use to change these options (see fig. 6.8). In the figure, the dialog box indicates that the chart is 3-D. The Pie depth and Pie tilt options determine the appearance of a 3-D chart. See the following section, "Changing the Appearance of 3-D Pies," to learn how to change these options.

The Share Pie Labels option, discussed in the section "Using Other Chart Options," uses the labels from the first pie for all the pies in the chart. The Make Pies Proportional option creates pies that are proportional to the slice values (see the section "Creating Proportional Pies" in this chapter). The third region, containing Link pies and Link *Slice x* of Pie 1 to Pie 2, enables you to create a link between Pie 1 and Pie 2 (see "Creating Linked Pies"). The buttons in the second region of the dialog box enable you to access other commands on the **C**hart menu. For example, to access the Series options, you click the Series button (instead of selecting **S**eries from the **C**hart menu, outside of the Pie Chart Options dialog box).

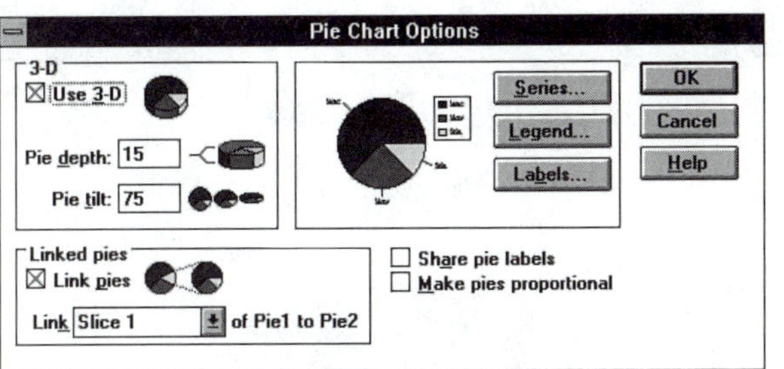

Fig. 6.8
The Pie Chart Options dialog box.

The remaining options on the dialog box may be dimmed. These options apply only to a chart with more than one pie.

Changing the Appearance of 3-D Pies. You use the Pie Depth and Pie Tilt options in the Pie Chart Options dialog box to change the appearance of 3-D pie charts. The Pie depth options determine the thickness of the pie. The values for the depth range from 1 to 100. As the thickness of the pie increases, the size of the pie is decreased to make room for the changing depth.

The Pie tilt determines the visibility of the top of the pie. The values for the tilt range from 1 to 75 (75 makes the slices the most visible to the audience). Decreasing the tilt rotates the front of the pie upward and the back of the pie downward, making the top of the pie less visible. Figure 6.9 presents a chart in which the depth has been decreased to make the pie look thinner. The tilt has also been decreased so that the top of the pie is less visible.

Design Note

The most important factor to consider when adjusting the depth and tilt is that the slices should always be clear to the audience. The default values for pie depth and pie tilt are set so that the audience can see the individual slices clearly and appreciate the three dimensions of the chart at the same time.

You can use the Pie Depth and Pie Tilt options to achieve special effects with your pie charts. If, for example, you are preparing a pie chart presentation for a group of coin collectors, you could decrease the depth to make the pies look like a coin. In contrast to this example, the pie chart in figure 6.10 has a depth of 75 and a tilt of 15. You might use this chart to represent a cake for a bakers' convention.

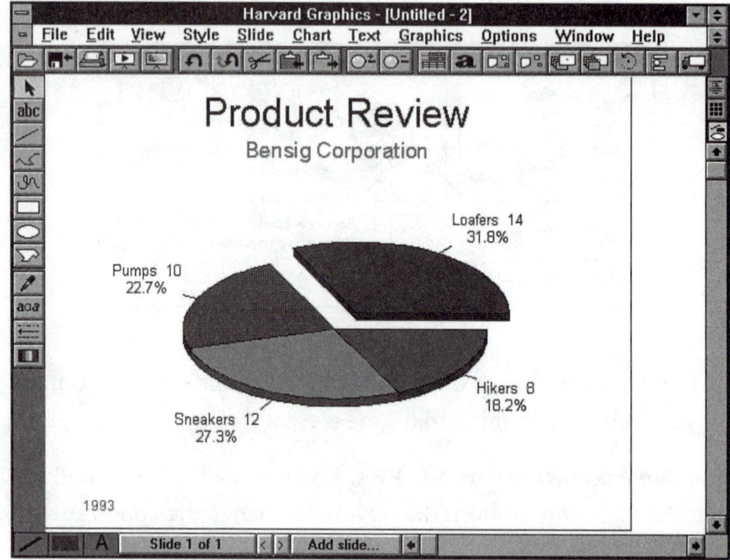

Fig. 6.9
The depth and the tilt have been decreased in this chart.

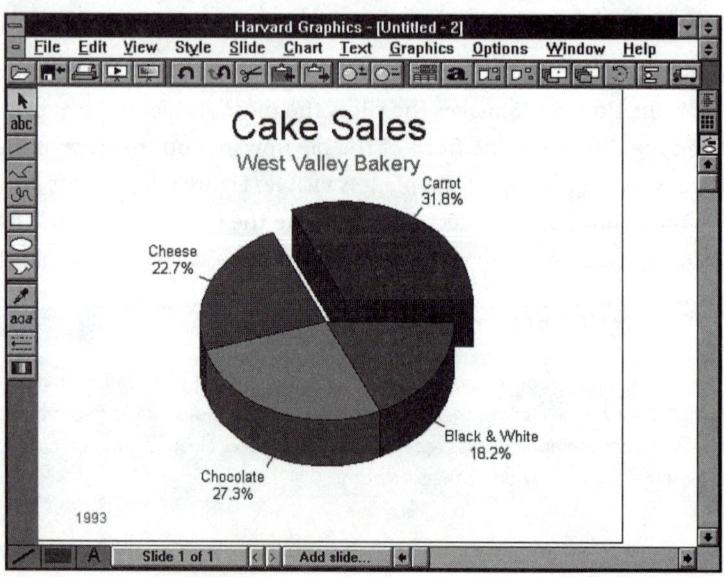

Fig. 6.10
An example of a modified 3-D pie chart.

To create the chart in figure 6.10, follow these steps to modify the depth and tilt:

1. From the **C**hart menu, choose Chart **O**ptions. Harvard Graphics displays the Pie Chart Options dialog box.
2. Click the Use 3-D option so that an X appears in the check box.
3. Click the Pie Depth field.
4. Press the Delete key until the previous value is removed.
5. Type **75**.
6. Click the Pie Tilt field, and delete the previous value.
7. Type **15**.
8. Click OK to accept the changes in the Pie Chart Options dialog box. The chart appearance changes to conform to the new settings.

Because the slices in the altered chart are difficult to see, you may want to reset these options back to the defaults. The remainder of the chapter assumes that the defaults have been restored.

Using Other Chart Options. The Share pie labels option in the Pie Chart Options dialog box saves you time when you enter multiple pies into the data form. If all your pies contain the same slices, you need to enter labels for only the first pie. When you choose the Share Pie Labels option, Harvard Graphics uses the Pie 1 labels for all the pies. The Make pies proportional option causes all pies to be displayed in proportion to the values in the slices. The discussion in the "Creating Proportional Pies" section in this chapter describes how this option affects the display of your pies.

The Link pies options create links between two pies in the chart. See "Creating Multiple Pie Charts" in this chapter.

Changing the Series Options

You use the Series option on the **C**hart menu to change the appearance of each pie in a pie chart. (You can also select the Pie Chart Series Options dialog box from the Series button on the Pie Chart Options dialog box.) The Pie Chart Series Options dialog box lists in the Pie list box all the pies in the chart (see fig. 6.11). To display this dialog box, select **S**eries from the **C**hart menu.

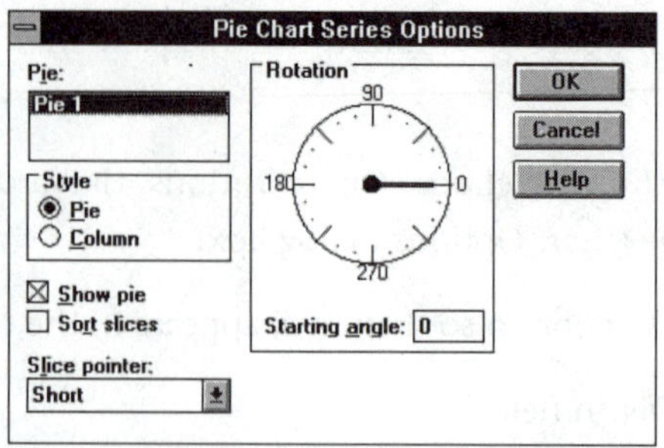

Fig. 6.11
The Pie Chart Series Options dialog box.

The Show pie option determines whether a pie is displayed in the chart. An X in the check box indicates that the option is selected. Showing the pies enables you to evaluate different sets of pies in the chart. You can decide, for example, whether all the pies look better in the same slide or in separate slides. The Sort Slices option sorts the slices of the selected pie according to the slice values. This feature is helpful for organizing the slices from the largest to the smallest value. For a chart on revenues, you could easily see which products contributed the most to the revenue. From the Style area, you can select to display the pie as a Pie or as a Column in the chart. A column chart is a different representation of the data. (See "Creating Linked Pies" for an example of how a column chart may be used.)

In the Rotation field, the dial and the Starting angle field determine where the first slice is drawn (see "Setting the Starting Angle" in this chapter).

The last item, the Slice Pointer drop-down list box, determines the length of the line drawn from the label to the slice. You can display a Long, Short, or Medium line. If this option is set to None, the slice pointer is not displayed (see "Setting the Slice Pointer Size" in this chapter).

To change the options for a pie, select the desired pie in the Pie list box. After you select the pie, changing the items in the dialog box affects that pie. To modify a pie in the chart, follow these steps:

1. From the **C**hart menu, choose **S**eries. The Pie Chart Series Options dialog box appears.
2. Choose the pie you want to modify in the Pie list box.
3. Click the Sort slices option so that an X appears in the check box.
4. Choose Column in the Style area.
5. Click OK to accept the changes.

Figure 6.12 shows two pies that have the same data. The pie on the left is a pie chart with unsorted slices. The pie on the right is a column chart with sorted slices (which you created with the preceding steps). The column on the right clearly shows the largest and smallest values in the data.

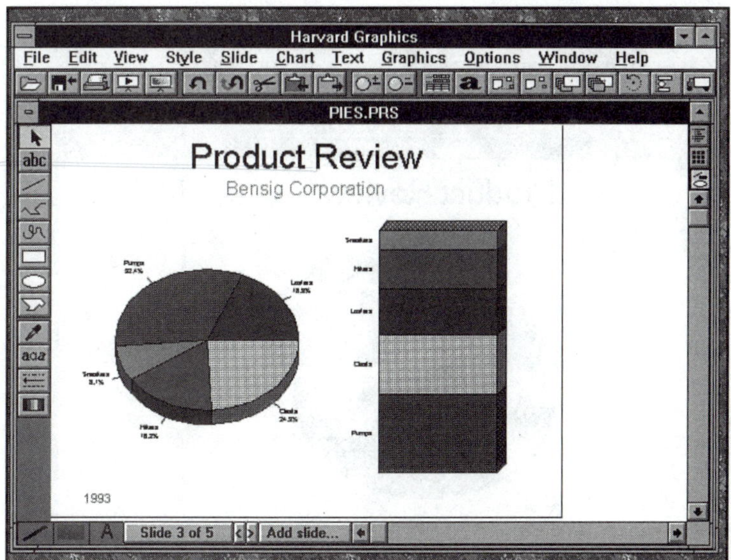

Fig. 6.12
The pie on the right was created from the pie on the left.

Setting the Slice Pointer Size. The Slice Pointer drop-down list box in the Pie Chart Series Options dialog box determines the size (length) of the slice pointer. The size of the pointer in turn determines how close to the slices of the pie the labels are displayed. Figure 6.13 illustrates short slice pointers.

Design Note

The complexity of the chart is the biggest factor to consider when setting the size of the pointer. For a pie with many slices, long pointers leave more room for the text of the pie. In a multiple pie chart, shorter pointers leave room for the pies.

To change the pointer size of a chart to short, follow these steps:

1. From the **C**hart menu, choose **S**eries. The Pie Chart Series Options dialog box appears.

2. Select the pie you want to change in the Pie drop-down list box. You cannot change the pointer size for a column chart. Change the Style option to Pie before setting the pointer size.

3. Click the down scroll arrow next to the Slice Pointer drop-down list box. Harvard Graphics displays the choices for pointer size.

4. Select Short from the list.

5. Click OK.

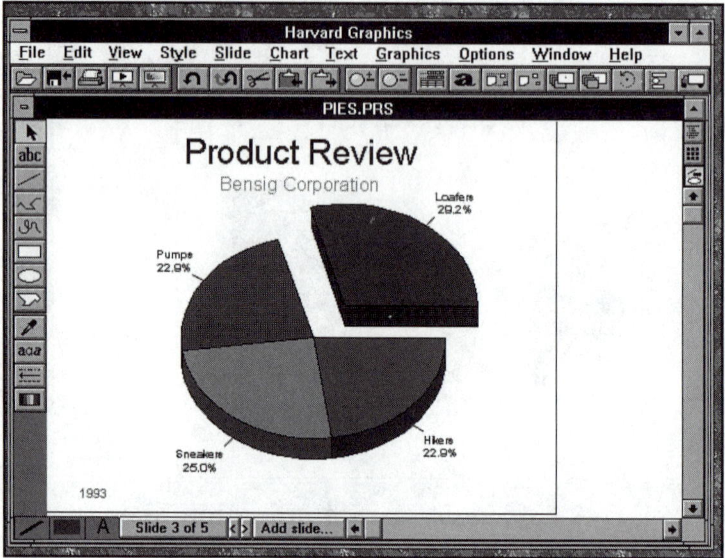

Fig. 6.13
Short slice pointers in a pie chart.

Setting the Starting Angle. The starting angle for a pie chart determines the location of the first slice. The starting angle is measured from the horizontal middle of the pie, starting on the right side (at 3 o'clock) and moving in a counterclockwise direction. The default value of 0 degrees displays the first slice from the right. A starting angle of 90 degrees places the first slice at the top of the pie chart. Figure 6.14 illustrates pie charts with 0 and 90 degree starting angles. For each pie, the Loafers slice is the first one in the pie.

Design Note

Decide the location of the first slice of a pie according to the emphasis you want to place on the parts of the chart. You can use the starting angle to display a slice in the front of a 3-D chart or along the top of a 2-D chart.

After you decide the location for your first slice of pie, type the degrees in the Starting angle text box of the Pie Chart Series Options dialog box. You can also use the dial to set the starting angle. The red pointer of the dial shows the current setting for the starting angle. The location of the pointer corresponds to the starting edge of the first slice. To change the angle, click the pointer and drag to the new angle. To set a 180-degree starting angle, follow these steps:

1. From the **C**hart menu, choose **S**eries. The Pie Chart Series Options dialog box appears.

2. Select the pie you want to change in the Pie list box.

3. Click the red pointer in the dial.

4. Drag the pointer to 180 degrees. As you drag the pointer, the Starting angle field reflects the current setting for the angle.

5. Release the mouse button and click OK.

The slices in the pie now start at the new angle.

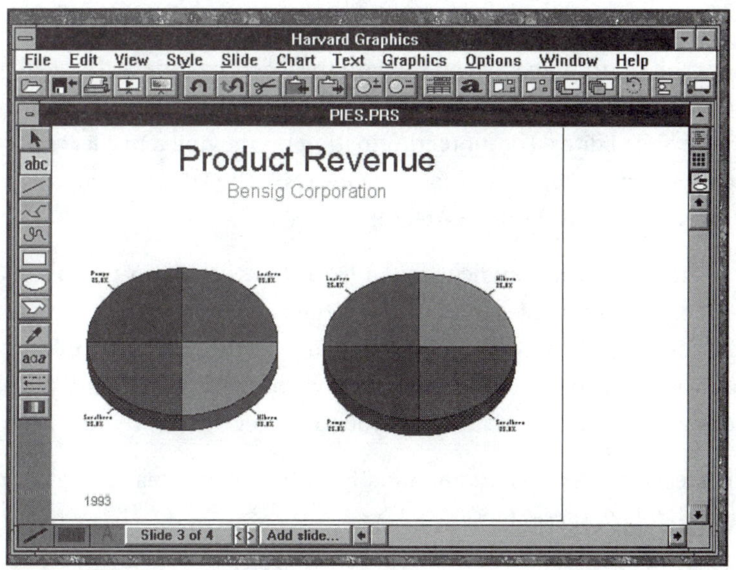

Fig. 6.14
Pie charts with 0 degree (left) and 90 degree (right) starting angles.

Adding a Legend

The legend is a different method for displaying slice labels. The legend for a pie chart interprets the slice labels to the audience. Rather than displaying labels on all sides of the pie, you can group labels in a legend. (The La**b**els option on the **C**hart menu hides and shows the slice labels in a pie chart.

For more information on the Labels command, see "Modifying Pie Labels" later in the chapter.)

The Legend Options dialog box, opened by choosing **L**egend from the **C**hart menu, is used to display and modify the chart legend (see fig. 6.15). The first option enables you to show or hide the legend. To enable the remaining options on the dialog box, you must choose the Show legend option. You can enter a title for the legend in the Title text box, below the Show legend option. The title is then displayed inside the legend box above the labels.

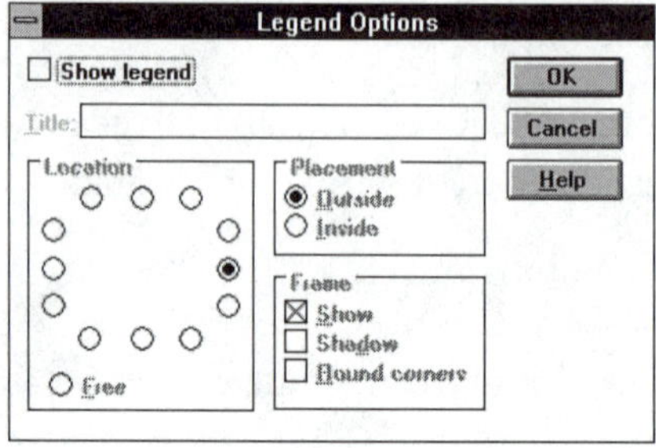

Fig. 6.15
The Legend Options dialog box.

The Location buttons enable you to place the legend in one of 12 predefined positions. The Free button enables you to control the placement of the Legend in the Slide Editor. For more information on moving a free legend, see Chapter 13, "Enhancing Drawings and Objects." The Placement options, which are grayed, affect only XY charts.

You can change the appearance of your legend in several ways. You can display a frame around the legend by setting the Show option in the Frame area. You can display a shadow behind the legend with the Shadow option in the Frame area. You also can change the box style of the legend frame. When the Round corners option is set, the box around the legend has rounded corners.

To add a legend to a pie chart and modify the settings to match the legend in figure 6.16, follow these steps:

1. From the **C**hart menu, choose the **L**egend option. The Legend Options dialog box appears.
2. Click the Show legend check box so that an X appears.
3. Click the Title text box.
4. Type the title for your legend; for the example, type **Products**.

5. Click the button in the middle of the bottom row of Location buttons. (This choice leaves more of the chart body available for the pie.)

6. Click the Shadow option in the Frame field so that an X appears.

7. Click OK to accept the changes to the legend. The chart now displays a legend.

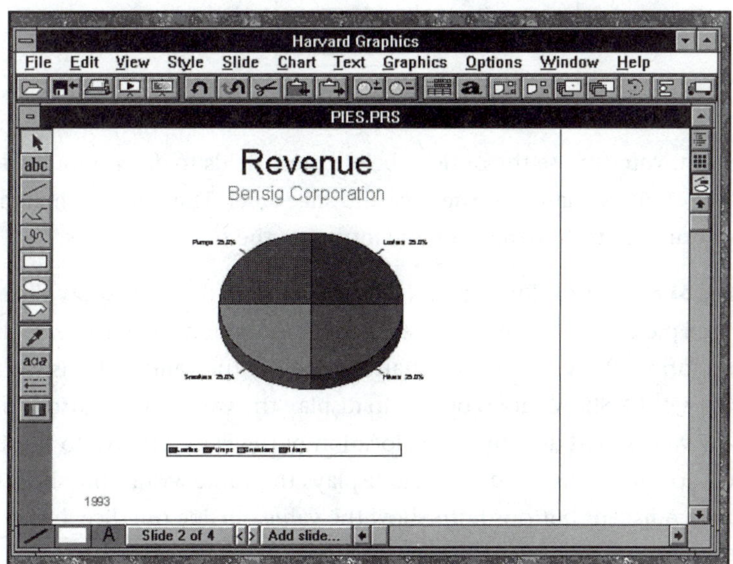

Fig. 6.16 A pie chart that uses a legend to communicate the slice labels.

In figure 6.16. the pie labels are not displayed in order to give emphasis to the information in the legend. The following section explains how to display and remove labels.

Modifying Pie Labels

You use the La**b**els option on the **C**hart menu to modify slice labels, slice values, and slice percents for a pie chart. The Pie Chart Label Options dialog box, shown in figure 6.17, lists the pies in a chart in the Edit box on the left side of the dialog box. When you select a pie in the list, the options in the dialog box reflect the settings for the pie. For slice labels, the Show slice labels option determines whether the labels are displayed. The Show values option controls the display of the slice values, and the Show percents option controls the percents. An X in the option to show that item indicates that the label, percent, or value will be displayed with the chart.

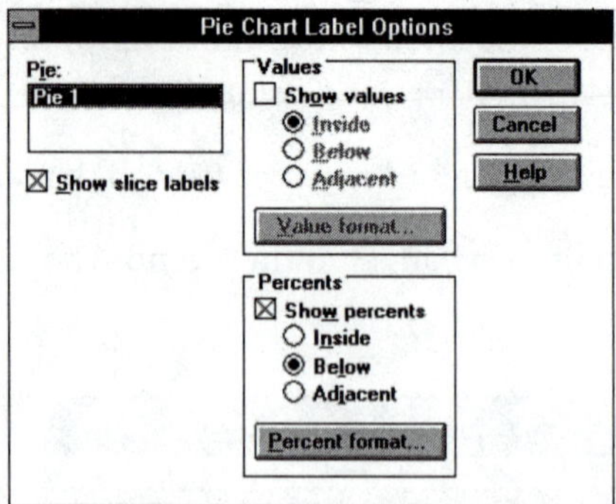

Fig. 6.17
The Pie Chart Label Options dialog box.

In addition, you can use the options below these fields to determine the locations of the values relative to the slice and slice label. The Value format and Percent format buttons determine the format of the numeric values.

Showing Slice Values. By default, Harvard Graphics does not show slice values in a pie chart. You use the Pie Chart Label Options dialog box to display and format the values in the chart. To modify the value options, you must first set the Show values option to display the values. The buttons below the Show values field determine the location of the value relative to the slice and the slice label. The Inside button displays the value within the slice. The Below and Adjacent buttons both show the value outside the slice, below or to the right of the slice label, respectively.

Design Note

For some color slices, the value may be difficult to read when displayed inside the slice.

To show slice values next to the label, follow these steps:

1. From the **C**hart menu, choose La**b**els. The Pie Chart Label Options dialog box appears.

2. Select the pie for which you want to show the values in the Pie list box.

3. Click the Show values option so that an X appears in the check box.

4. Click the Adjacent button below the Show values option.

5. Click OK to accept the changes.

Figure 6.18 shows a pie chart with slice labels, slice percents, and slice values next to the labels.

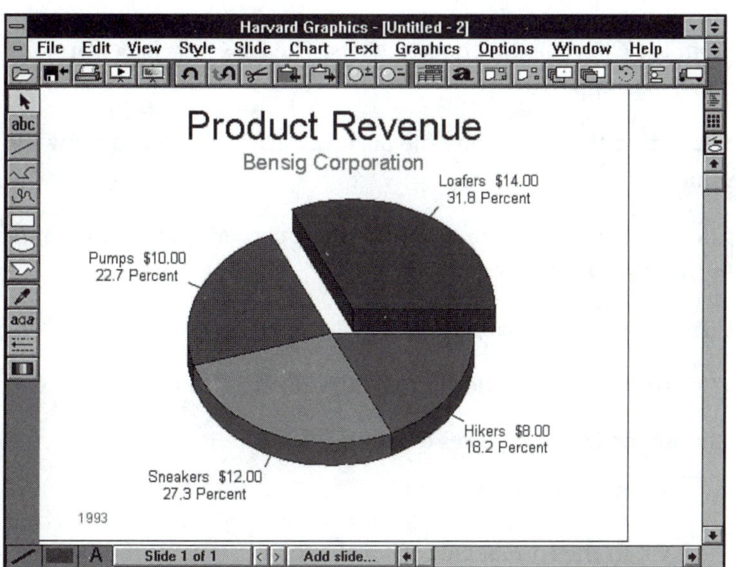

Fig. 6.18
A pie chart with slice labels, slice percents, and slice values beside the labels.

Specifying the Format of Numeric Values. The format for the values is set with the Format Options dialog box (see fig. 6.19). To show the dialog box, click the Value format button. The Currency option indicates that the values in the chart represent currency. The currency format and symbol are determined by the International settings of the Windows Control Panel. The Thousands separator option causes a thousands separator character to be displayed for numbers in the thousands. The International settings are used to set this character as well. The Scientific notation option displays values in a limited number of digits—a help when you are dealing with large values.

The Decimal places text box controls the number of digits displayed after the decimal point of a number. (For example, United States currency requires two digits after the decimal for cents.) The last two items in the Format Options dialog box enable you to include any text you want to display before or after the value. Leading text precedes a label, and trailing text comes after.

For example, you can use trailing text to communicate to the audience that values are in units like inches or pounds. To display slice values as currency, with two decimal places, follow these steps:

1. From the **Chart** menu, choose La**b**els. The Pie Chart Label Options dialog box appears.
2. Select from the Pie list box the pie on which you want to show the values.
3. Click the Show values option (if it is not chosen) so that an X appears in the check box.
4. Click the Value format button. The Format Options dialog box displays.
5. Click the Currency option so that an X appears in the check box.
6. Choose the Decimal places text box.
7. Type **2**.
8. Click OK in the Format Options dialog box to change the format.
9. Click OK in the Pie Chart Label Options dialog box to change the slice values.

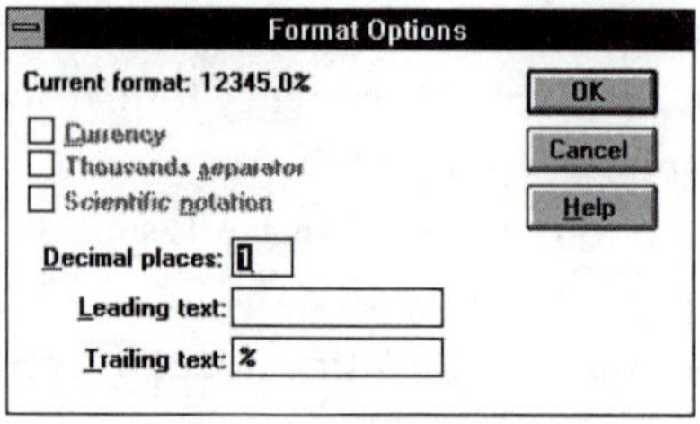

Fig. 6.19
The Format Options dialog box.

Figure 6.20 shows the chart with slice values displayed in the currency format.

Showing Slice Percents. By default, Harvard Graphics shows slice percents in a pie chart. You use the Pie Chart Label Options dialog box to hide the percents or to change the location and format of the slice percents. To modify the slice percents of a pie, you must first set the Show Percents option so that the values are displayed.

The buttons below the Show Percents option determine where the percent is placed relative to the slice and slice label: Inside, Below, or Adjacent.

The Inside button displays the percent within the slice. The Below and Adjacent options show the percent outside the slice, either below or to the right of the label, respectively.

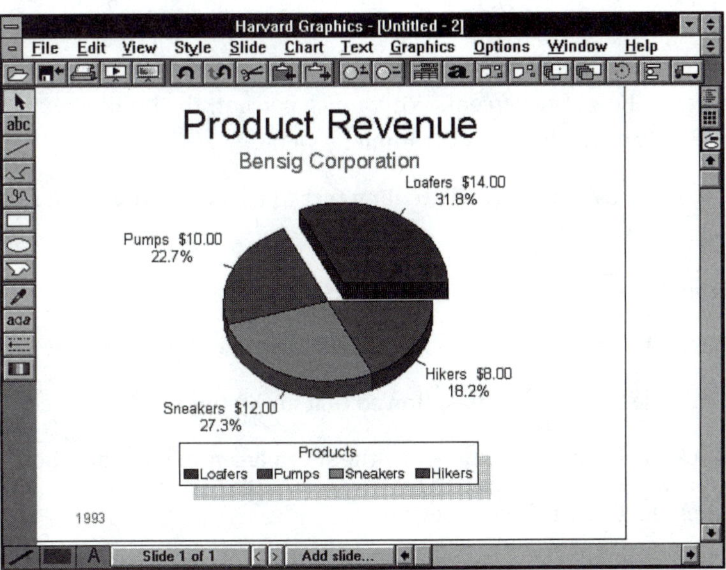

Fig. 6.20 The slice values shown in the currency format.

Design Note

For some color slices, the percent may be difficult to read inside the slice.

To show the slice percent next to the label, follow these steps:

1. From the **Chart** menu, select La**b**els. Harvard Graphics displays the Pie Chart Label Options dialog box.
2. In the Pie list box, select the pie for which you want to show the values.
3. If an X appears in the Show values check box, click it to clear the option and not show the values. This choice emphasizes the slice percents in the chart.
4. Choose the Show percents option.
5. Choose the Adjacent option below the Show Percents option.
6. Click OK.

To set the format for the percent, you use the Format Options dialog box (refer to fig. 6.19). With slice percents, the format of the number is already set. Only the last three options in the Format Options dialog box relate to displaying percents. These options are Decimal Places, Leading Text, and Trailing Text. The Decimal Places option controls the number of digits displayed after the decimal point, leading text comes before the percent, and trailing text follows the percent. With a slice percent, the trailing text contains the percent symbol after the numeric value.

Follow these steps to change the trailing text to use the word *Percent* instead of the percent symbol:

1. From the **C**hart menu, choose La**b**els.
2. Select the pie for which you want to show the values in the Pie list box.
3. Click the Show percents option so that an X appears in the check box.
4. Click the Below button to show the slice percent below the label.
5. Click the Percent format button.
6. Position the cursor in the Trailing text box to the right of the percent symbol.
7. Press the Backspace key to remove the symbol.
8. Type the word **Percent**.
9. Click OK on the Format Options dialog box to accept the changes.
10. Click OK on the Pie Chart Label Options dialog box to accept the modifications to the chart.

Figure 6.21 shows the finished chart.

Cutting Away Pie Slices

You can choose to cut away any slice in the pie chart you have created. The styles in the New Presentation dialog box enable you to cut only the first slice. In the Slide Editor, however, you can select any slice in a pie chart to cut away from the rest of the pie. You can separate a single slice or a group of slices from the remainder of the pie. To separate a group, you must cut away each slice one at a time. To cut away a slice, you move it away form the others. For more information on moving objects in the Slide Editor, see the section "Moving Objects" in Chapter 13.

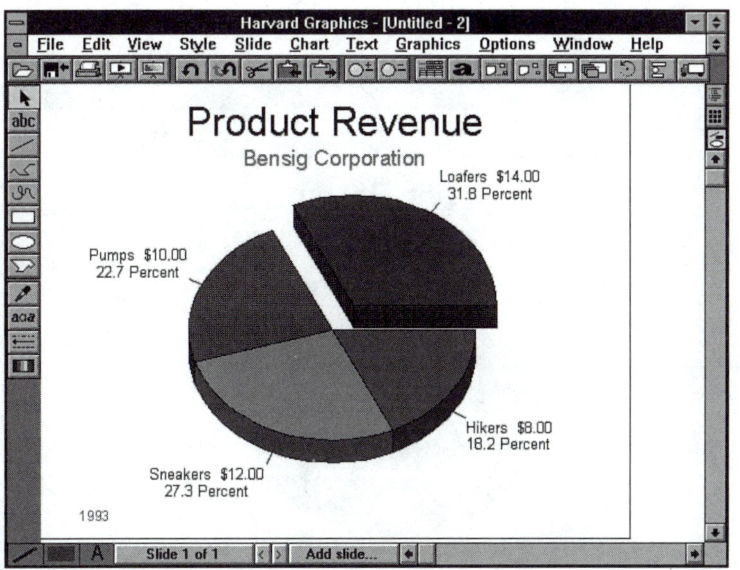

Fig. 6.21
A pie chart with the word Percent as trailing text.

Design Note

Cutting slices enables you to place emphasis on specific information in a pie chart.

You are still viewing the chart in the Slide Editor. To cut away any slice in a pie chart, follow these steps:

1. Click the slice to select the pie on the slide. A box appears around the slide to indicate that it is selected.

2. Click the slice a second time to select the individual slice within the pie. The handle appears in the center of the slide (see fig. 6.22).

3. Place the mouse pointer on top of the handle. The pointer changes from an arrow to the four-directional arrow that is used to move objects in the Slide Editor.

4. Drag the slice to the new location. As you drag, an outline of the slice indicates the position of the slice on the pie chart.

   You cannot drag the slice to any position on the slide. You can move the slice only toward or away from the center of the pie; the direction is based on the position of the slice in the pie. This restriction ensures that the slice fits with the others when not cut away.

5. Release the mouse button.

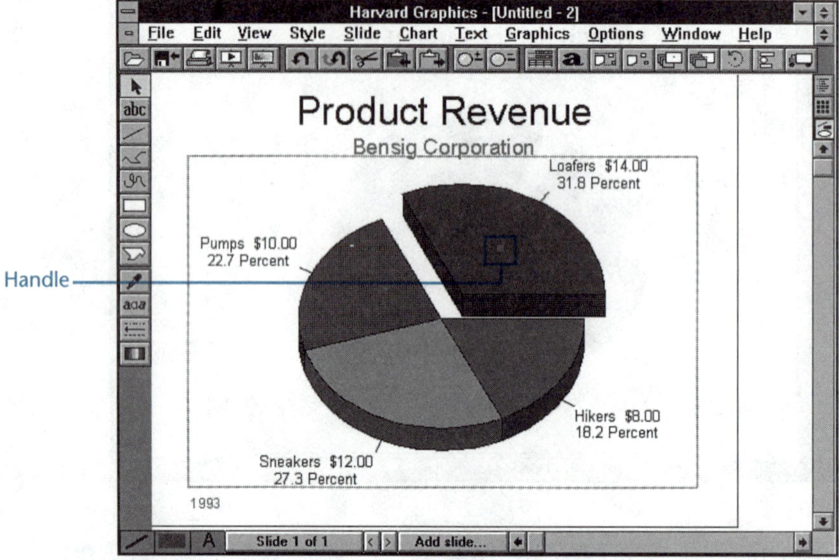

Fig. 6.22
Pie slices are cut within the Slide Editor.

The slice is now in the new location. To return the slice to the pie, follow the preceding steps, but drag the slice toward the center of the pie in step 4.

Modifying the Slice Color

You use the Slide Editor to change the color of a slice in a pie chart. The Fill tool sets the Fill Style and Fill Color for the objects on a slide. Figure 6.23 shows the location of the tool in the Slide Editor. For more information on the Fill tool, see "Setting the Fill Style" in Chapter 13.

Follow these steps to change the color of the slice:

1. Click the slice; the handle appears in the center of the slice. The current color for the slice is displayed to the right of the Fill tool.
2. Choose the Fill tool to display the Solid Color Fill dialog box. The colors from the color palette are shown in the Solid Color Fill dialog box.
3. Select the new color in the Solid Color Fill dialog box.
4. Click OK. The slice changes to the new color.

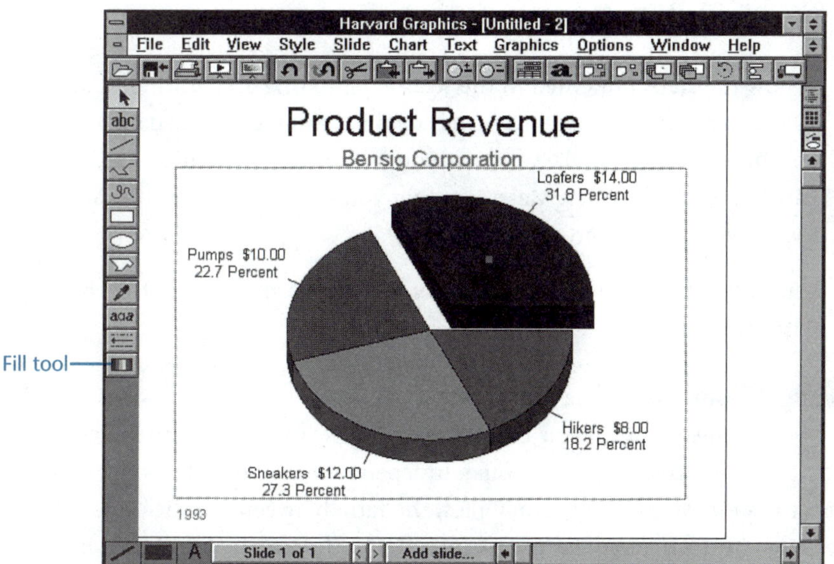

Fig. 6.23
Use the Fill tool to change the color of objects in the Slide Editor.

Creating Multiple Pie Charts

Harvard Graphics can display up to six pies in one chart. The pie chart data form has six sets of columns in which you enter the labels and values for each pie. The column titles indicate to which pie the data in a column belongs. After the chart is created, you can use the options on the **C**hart menu to modify the appearance of individual pies and of the entire chart.

Entering Data for Multiple Pies

For a single pie chart, you enter the data into the first two columns on the data form. You define additional pies in the columns following the first two columns. The order of the slices for each pie is independent of the order in any other pie. For example, you can make Loafers the first slice in one pie and third slice in another pie.

Follow these steps to create a pie chart with two pies:

1. Choose Add Slide from the **S**lide menu from within the Slide Editor. If you are not viewing the presentation in the Slide Editor, select Slide Editor from the **V**iew menu. Harvard Graphics displays the Add Slide dialog box.

2. Click the Pie button.

3. Click OK. Harvard Graphics displays the pie chart data form.

   Follow the steps presented in the section "Entering and Editing Data for a Pie Chart" in this chapter to enter data for two pies in the data form. For the second pie, make sure that you use the columns titled Pie 2 Labels and Pie 2 Values. Make sure that you enter a title, subtitle, and footnote for your chart.

4. Click the OK button at the bottom of the data form to create the chart with two pies.

Creating Proportional Pies

When you create a multiple pie chart, the diameters of the pies can be independent of each other or proportional. Independent pies are always the same size on the slide. With proportional pies, the ratio between the slice values is represented in the relative sizes of the pies. Proportional pies are shown in figure 6.24. The slice values are shown next to the slices to illustrate the differences in size. The values in the pie on the left range from 10 to 30. The values in the other pie range from 5 to 15. The first pie values are double the size of the second, and so the first pie is twice the size of the second pie.

Fig. 6.24 An example of proportional pies.

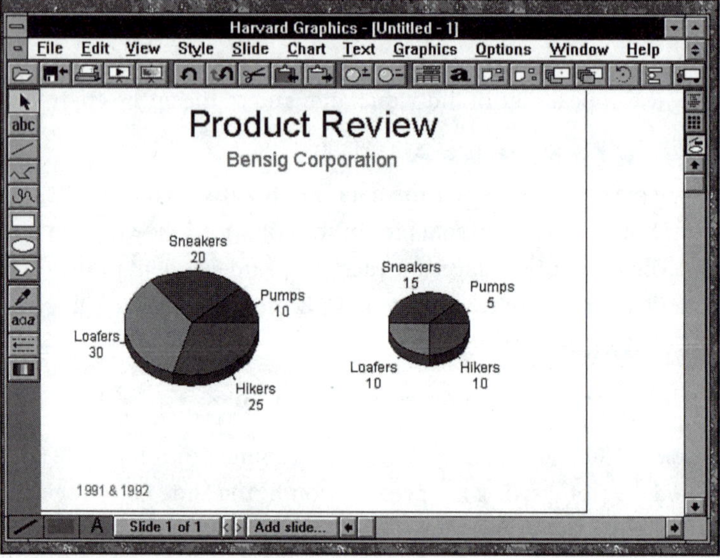

The Make pies proportional option in the Pie Chart Options dialog box is set for the pies in the figure. This option causes the first pie to be displayed as twice the size of the second. To create proportional pies for a chart with more than one pie, follow these steps:

1. From the **C**hart menu, choose Chart **O**ptions. Harvard Graphics displays the Pie Chart Options dialog box. If the Make proportional pies option is gray, the chart has only one pie, and the option has no effect on the chart.

2. Click the Make pies proportional option so that an X appears in the check box.

3. Click OK.

The pies in the chart are resized so that they are proportional.

Creating Linked Pies

Linked pies combine the information in one pie chart with the information in a second pie. The second pie is linked to a slice in the first pie and represents breakdown information about the slice. In figure 6.25, the column chart shows how much the sales throughout the country contributed to the sales of the product represented by the linked slice in the first pie. The second chart is displayed as a column chart to emphasize the relationship between the pies. You can display either pie in a linked pie chart as a column or a pie. Lines drawn from one pie to the other also can reinforce the relationship.

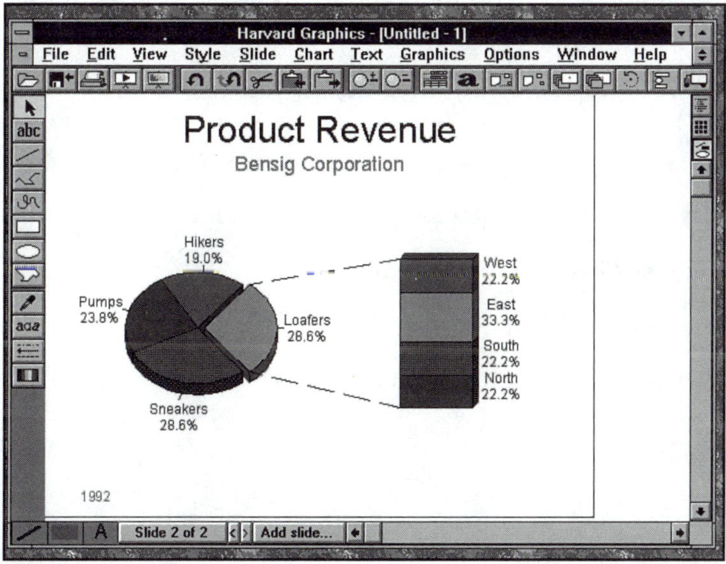

Fig. 6.25
Two linked charts in a pie chart.

When you create linked charts, a slice in Pie 1 is linked to Pie 2. When you enter the pie data into the data form, be sure to enter the breakdown information of a slice as the second pie in the chart. The Link Pies option in the Pie Chart Options dialog box determines whether the pies are linked, and the Link option determines which slice in Pie 1 is linked to the information in Pie 2. Figure 6.26 shows the Pie Chart Options dialog box, which you use to link pies.

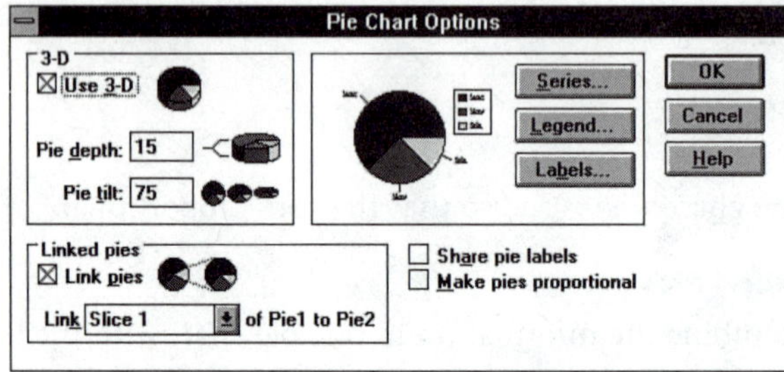

Fig. 6.26
The Pie Chart Options dialog box.

To create a linked pie chart, follow these steps:

1. From the **C**hart menu, select Chart **O**ptions. The Pie Chart Options dialog box displays.
2. Click the Link pies check box so that an X appears in the check box.
3. Click the down scroll arrow next to the Link *Slice x* of Pie 1 to Pie 2 option to see the slices available in the first pie.
4. From the drop-down list, select the slice you want to link.
5. Click OK.

To display the second pie chart as a column, follow these steps:

1. From the **C**hart menu, choose **S**eries.
2. Choose Pie 2 from the Pie list box.
3. Click the Column button for the Pie style.
4. Click OK.

From Here...

This chapter explains how to create and enhance pie charts. You learned the elements of a pie chart and ways to create different styles by using the Add Slide and New Presentation dialog boxes. You then learned how to enter data into the pie chart data form.

After creating the pie chart, you learned how to modify the appearance of 2-D and 3-D pie charts. You were shown how to change the starting angle for a pie chart and how to display a legend with the chart. At the end of the chapter, you learned how to create multiple pie charts and how to link two pies together.

Chapter 7

Working with Text

Text is an integral part of any chart. Title and bullet charts are made up entirely of text; XY and pie charts combine text with graphics to present data; and all labels and titles are communicated through text. Two types of text appear on a slide: text annotations and text that is associated with a chart (for example, the slide labels in a pie chart or the axis labels in an XY chart). The only difference between text annotations and text associated with a chart is the operations that you can perform in the Slide Editor.

This chapter covers the important text creation and editing capabilities of Harvard Graphics. Not only will you learn to understand the difference between text annotations and data text, you also will be able to add and edit text in your slides, using Harvard Graphics features. When you complete this chapter, you will be able to do the following:

- Add annotations to your slides
- Select text by using the appropriate tool from the toolbox
- Use the annotation ruler to set tabs and justify text
- Edit text annotations
- Move and anchor text in a slide
- Set type attributes
- Use the spell checking feature

In this chapter, you learn how to do the following:

- Work with text on a slide
- Add text annotations to a slide with the Text tool
- Select text with the Selection tool and Text tool
- Change text attributes

Adding Text Annotations

An *annotation* is text that you add to a slide in the Slide Editor. Usually, you use a text annotation to emphasize or draw attention to particular data.

To add text annotations and modify text attributes, you must view a presentation in the Slide Editor. If you have not done so already, create a presentation by choosing **N**ew Presentation from the **F**ile menu; you also can open an existing presentation by choosing **O**pen from the **F**ile menu. Then choose Slide **E**ditor from the **V**iew menu.

When you add a text annotation to your slide, you must indicate the location of the annotation, which you do by choosing a tool from the toolbox and clicking the appropriate location in the Slide Editor window. The two primary tools that you work with in this chapter are the Text tool and the Selection tool (see fig. 7.1). You must use the Text tool to add an annotation.

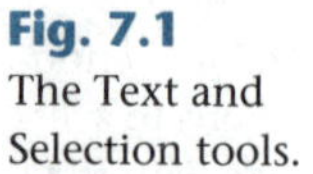

Fig. 7.1
The Text and Selection tools.

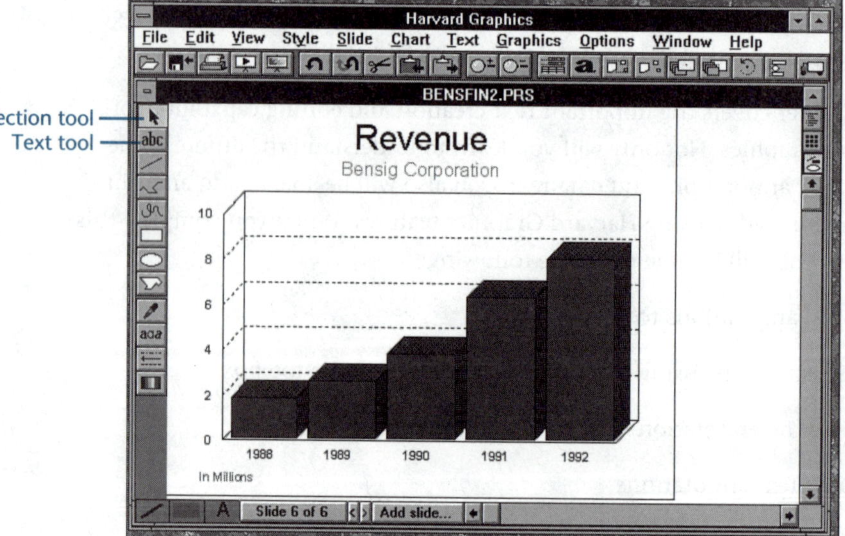

When you add an annotation, a text box, with an insertion point in the box and a ruler above the box, appears (see fig. 7.2). This text box extends from the location you clicked to the edge of the slide and determines how many words appear on one line in the annotation. The characters you type are entered after the insertion point, and when you reach the end of the line, Harvard Graphics wraps the text to a new line. (You can start a new line before you reach the end by pressing Enter.) The height of the text box is determined by the font, as well as the size and the number of lines of text. The section "Resizing a Text Box" in this chapter teaches you how to change the size of the text box.

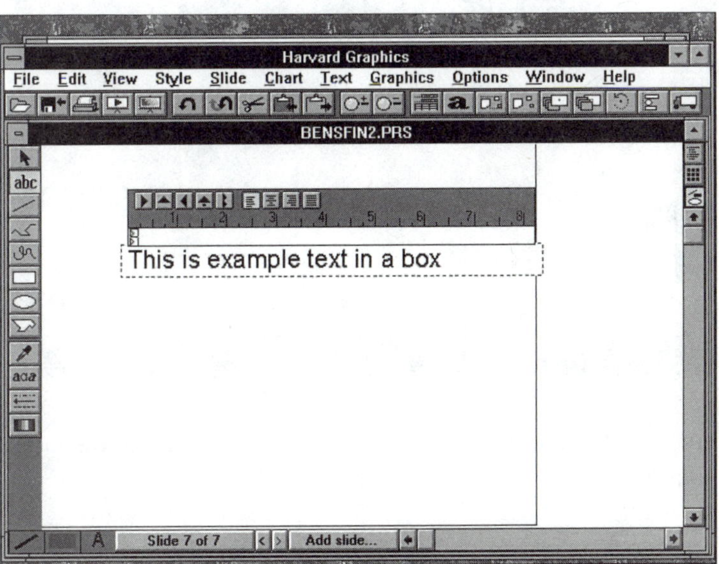

Fig. 7.2
The text box and ruler for adding text annotations.

You use the ruler above the text box to set the tabs and justification for the annotation. The measurements of the ruler help you judge the size of your text in the slide. You learn more about the ruler in the section "Using the Annotation Ruler" in this chapter.

If you are not currently viewing the slide in the Slide Editor, choose Slide **E**ditor from the **V**iew menu; then follow these steps to create the annotation on the current slide:

1. Select the Text tool.
2. In the slide, click where you want to add the text annotation.

   Grayed text appears to show the current text size and location. The grayed text is a placeholder that disappears when you enter text. The text you enter appears at this point.
3. Type the text of the annotation. As you type, the characters appear at the insertion point. Figure 7.3 shows a text annotation after the word *text* is entered.

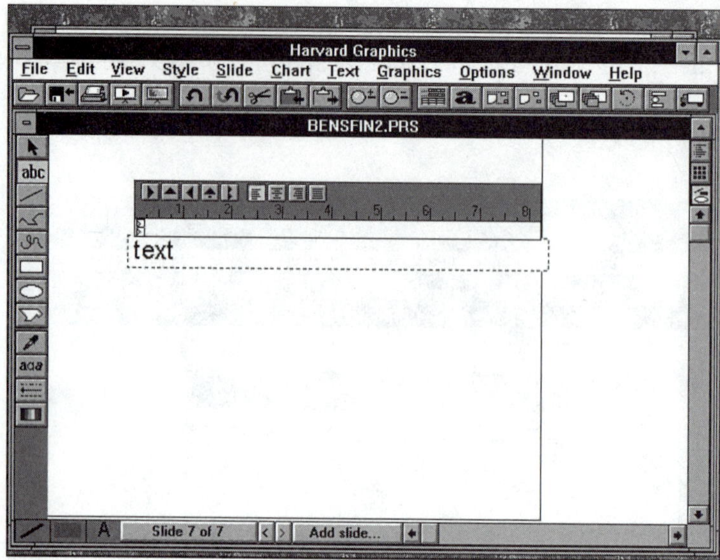

Fig. 7.3
A text annotation.

4. Press Esc. Harvard Graphics adds the text to the slide at the location you specified.

In addition to pressing Esc, you can select a new tool or click a different place in the slide to complete the current annotation and start a new one. Pressing the right mouse button is equivalent to pressing Esc. If you click the slide, you begin a new annotation. While the Text tool is selected, you can continue adding text to a slide until you select a new tool or press Esc.

Understanding Different Types of Text

In regards to editing a Harvard Graphics slide, you have two basic types of text. Both types of text in a slide look the same when you are displaying and printing the slide. The difference is determined by what operation—editing or modifying—you can perform on the text in the Slide Editor. You can edit (delete or change the characters of the text) and modify (change the text attributes, such as color or size) one type of text in the Slide Editor; the other type of text you can modify only.

You can modify and edit text annotations and title and bullet chart text in the Slide Editor. (If you edit the text that pertains to a chart in the Slide Editor, the changes appear in the chart data form.) Although you can modify the attributes of other text—such as the XY chart labels— in the Slide Editor, you cannot edit this text in the Slide Editor; instead, you must edit this text in the chart data form. Table 7.1 lists the editing options available for the type of text in the Slide Editor.

Table 7.1 Editing Options for Text in the Slide Editor

Edit and Modify Appearance	Modify Appearance Only
Bullet chart data	Text in XY charts
Title chart data	Text in pie charts
Organization chart data	
Text annotations	
Chart title information	

Selecting Text

Before you can edit text or change the attributes of text, you must select it in the Slide Editor. You can use the Selection tool or the Text tool to select text. Which tool you use, however, depends on the text that you need to select.

With the Selection tool, you can select blocks of text, not individual characters; for example, you can use the Selection tool to select an entire text annotation, but you cannot use it to select a single word in the annotation. You also can use the Selection tool to select an object that has text in it, such as a chart. When you use the Selection tool to select an object, handles appear around the object. If you change the attributes, all the text in the object changes.

You can use the Text tool to select text that can be edited in the Slide Editor; for example, to change the color of particular line in the text, you select the text by dragging the Text tool across it. When you select text with the Text tool, the text box and ruler for the text appear. As mentioned earlier, you also must use the Text tool to add text annotations. (If you click text that cannot be edited in the Slide Editor, such as the labels in a pie chart, Harvard Graphics assumes that you are adding a new text annotation to the chart.)

To select a text block or a chart on a slide, follow these steps:

1. In the Slide Editor window, click the Selection tool.
2. Click the text in the slide. You can click a text annotation or an object with text. Handles appear around objects you select.

If you want to change attributes for specific characters, you can select only the appropriate characters, rather than the entire text block, by using the Text tool. Follow these steps to select text in an annotation:

1. From the Slide Editor window, select the Text tool from the toolbox.
2. Click the text annotation. The text box and ruler appear around the text.
3. To select characters in the text annotation, place the mouse pointer, which has changed to an I-beam, in front of the first character, click the mouse button, and drag until all the text is highlighted.
4. Release the mouse button. The selected text appears in reverse video (see fig. 7.4).

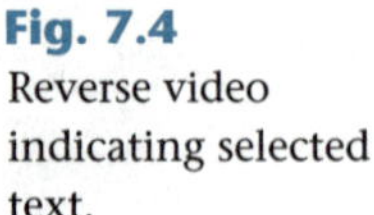

Fig. 7.4
Reverse video indicating selected text.

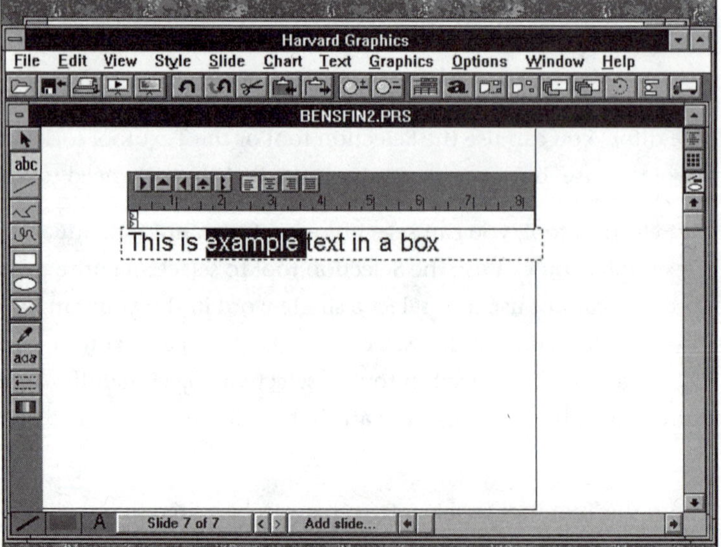

Design Note

For text that can be edited in the Slide Editor, you should use the Text tool only to edit the characters or to modify the attributes of only a portion of the text. To change the entire object, select the text with the Selection tool.

Using the Annotation Ruler

You use the ruler displayed above the text annotation box to set the tabs and justification for the text in the box. To see the ruler, you must use the Text tool to select the text. A selected object is outlined by the text box, and the ruler appears above the text box. Selected text appears inside the box. The changes you make to the ruler affect only the selected text.

Justifying Text with the Ruler

The justification of text determines how the lines of text are aligned inside the text box. In Harvard Graphics, text justification can be set to left, center, right, or full. Figure 7.5 illustrates the four justifications. Left-justified text aligns on the left side of the box. Right-justification aligns text on the right side. Centered text is centered between the two sides of the box. Full justification spreads the text throughout the line so that the first word is aligned on the left edge of the box, and the last word is aligned on the right.

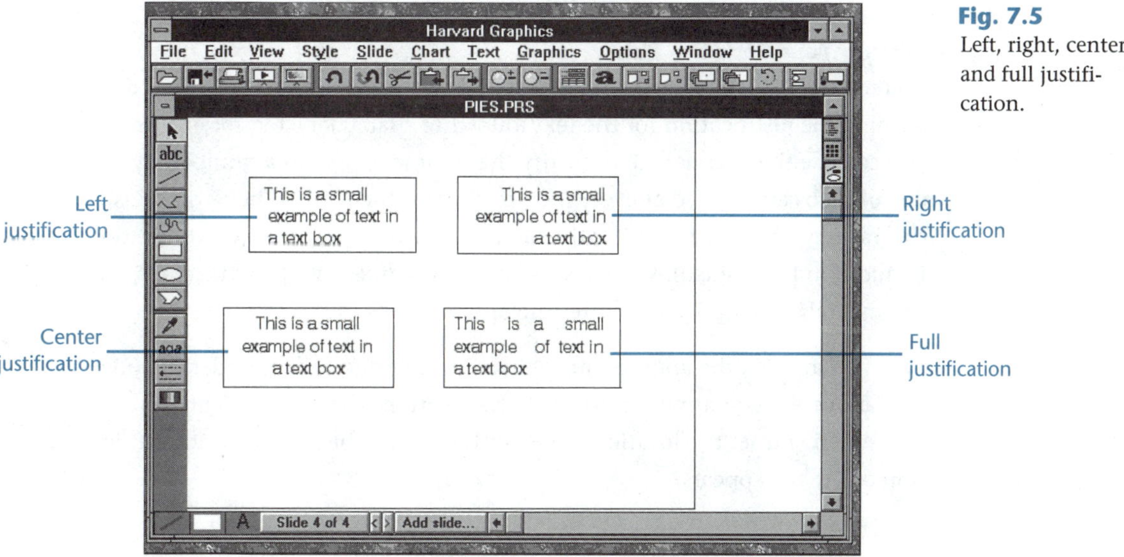

Fig. 7.5
Left, right, center, and full justification.

To change the justification for a text annotation, choose the Text tool in the Slide Editor, and then click the text annotation. The ruler and text box appear. Click one of the four justification icons shown in figure 7.6. To center all the text in a text box, for example, click the Center icon. You use this technique to choose a justification style for a text annotation. To learn how to choose a justification style for any text on a slide, see the section "Setting Text Justification" later in this chapter.

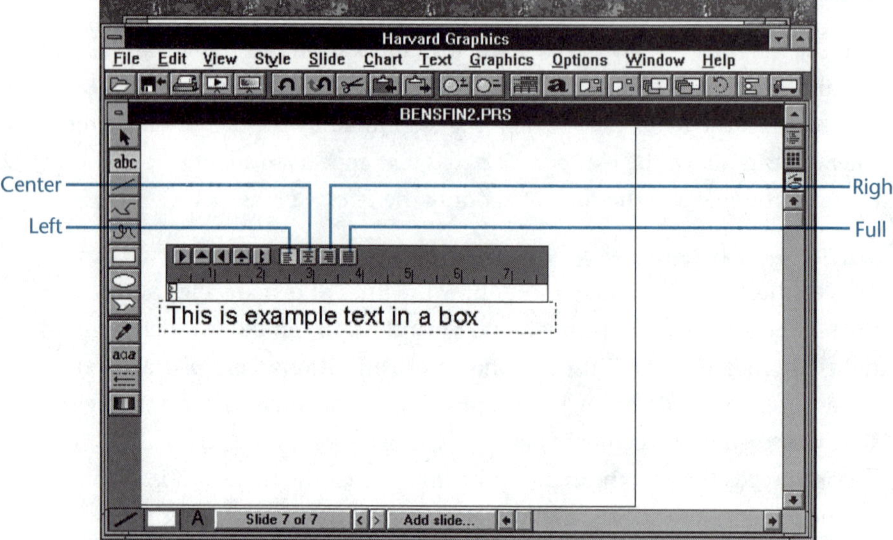

Fig. 7.6
The justification icons.

Setting Tabs with the Ruler

You use the tab icons on the ruler to set tabs for a text annotation. Tabs determine the justification for the text following a tab character; for example, you can use the decimal tab to justify the decimal places in a number. By default, tabs are located at every inch marker on the ruler. When you press the Tab key, the text following the tab is left-justified at the next tab location. In addition to left-justified tabs, you can use the ruler to set right, center, and decimal tabs. Figure 7.7 illustrates the different tabs in the ruler.

To set a tab, click the appropriate tab icon on the ruler; then, under the ruler (but above the text annotation), click the location where you intend to set a tab. When you set the location, an icon that shows the location and justification of the tab appears.

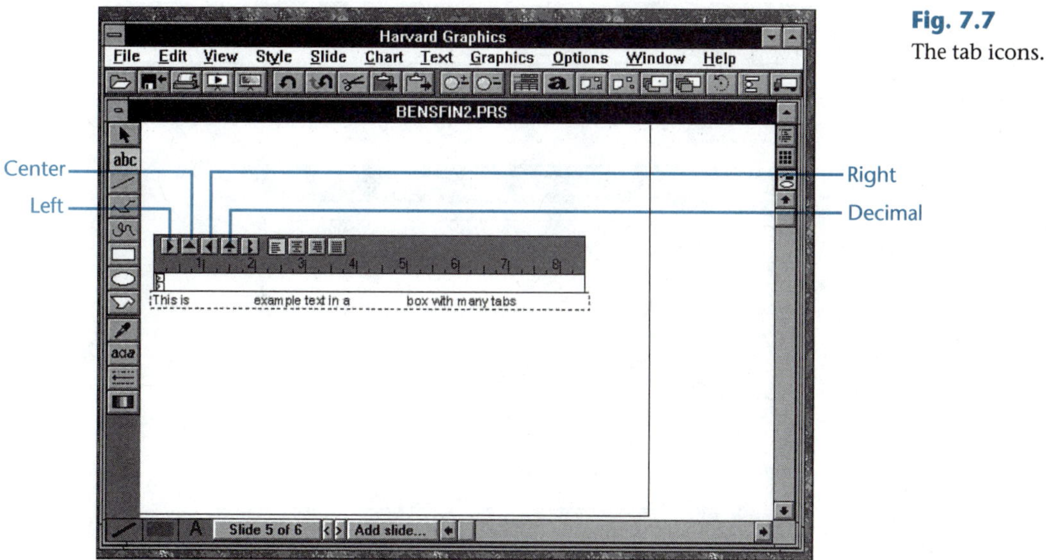

Fig. 7.7
The tab icons.

Follow these steps to set a right-justified tab at the 3-inch mark of a text annotation:

1. Click the icon for the right-justified tab.

2. Click directly under the 3-inch mark of the ruler. The tab icon for a right-justified tab appears at the specified location.

To remove a tab from the ruler, click the tab icon under the ruler and drag the icon above the ruler.

Changing the Paragraph Indent

The paragraph indent is determined by the location of the two clear triangles just below the ruler. The top triangle sets the indent for the first line of a paragraph. The bottom triangle sets the indent for the remaining lines. By default, all the lines of a paragraph are indented to the far left side of a text box. Figure 7.8 shows an annotation in which both indents have been moved. The first line is indented a little more than the others to show where the paragraph begins.

Fig. 7.8
A text box with different indentations for the lines of a paragraph.

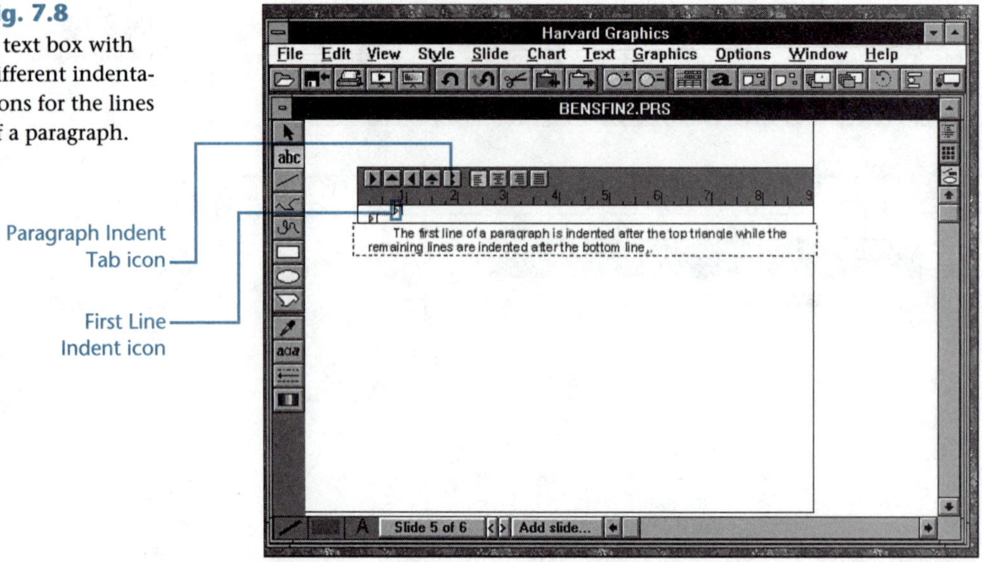

Paragraph Indent Tab icon

First Line Indent icon

To change the paragraph indentation, click the top or bottom triangle and drag the marker to the new location. If you select the bottom triangle, both icons move. Follow these steps to set the indentation to resemble figure 7.8:

1. Click and hold down the mouse button on the bottom icon.
2. Drag the icon to the first 1/4-inch tick mark. Both icons move as you drag the mouse.
3. Release the button.
4. Drag the top icon to the 3/4-inch tick mark. Only the top icon moves.
5. Release the button.

Your indent icons should resemble the icons in figure 7.8.

Design Note

Although Harvard Graphics sets a default indentation for sub-bullets in a bullet chart, you can change the indentation by using the Paragraph Indent Tab icon. To change the indentation of sub-bullets, select this icon and choose a new indentation setting.

Editing Text Annotations

Depending on the type of text in your chart, you can edit the text in the Slide Editor or in the chart data form. (For information on editing chart data, see Chapters 3 through 6, which cover the different chart types.) To edit text in the Slide Editor, select the text with the Slide Editor's Text tool. When you select text with this tool, the text box, ruler, and insertion point appear for the text.

The insertion point determines where the editing will take place. Additional text is inserted after the insertion point. Pressing the Backspace key removes the characters that precede the insertion point. The Del key removes the characters at the insertion point.

In addition to the Backspace and Del keys, you also can use the commands on the **E**dit menu to cut and paste selected text in a text annotation. The commands on the **E**dit menu operate on the highlighted text. The Cu**t** command removes the text and stores it in the Windows Clipboard; the **C**opy command leaves the original object in the slide and stores a copy of it in the Clipboard. The **P**aste command inserts the text stored in the Clipboard into a text annotation at the insertion point.

Follow these steps to copy text between annotations:

1. From the Slide Editor window, click the Text tool. (Remember, you must use the Text tool to select characters you intend to edit in the text annotation.)
2. Select the first annotation with the Text tool. The text box and ruler appear.
3. Select the appropriate text in the annotation by clicking in front of the text you intend to modify and dragging the Text tool to the end of the text. When you release the mouse button, Harvard Graphics displays the selected text in reverse video.
4. From the **E**dit menu, choose **C**opy. Harvard Graphics stores a copy of the text in the Clipboard; the original text remains intact.
5. Select the second annotation; the text box appears.
6. Click where you want to insert the information from the Clipboard.

7. From the **E**dit menu, choose **P**aste text. Harvard Graphics pastes the text from the Clipboard into the target annotation.

8. Press Esc to accept the change you made to the annotation.

You also can cut (or copy) text from one slide and paste it onto another slide. Follow these steps to transfer a text annotation from one slide to another:

1. From the Slide Editor window, click the Selection tool. (Remember, you use the Selection tool to select the entire text annotation instead of characters in the annotation.)

2. Click the text annotation. Handles appear around the text.

3. From the **E**dit menu, choose Cu**t**. Harvard Graphics removes the annotation from the slide and places it in the Clipboard.

4. Choose **G**o to Slide from the **S**lide menu. The Go to Slide dialog box appears (see fig. 7.9).

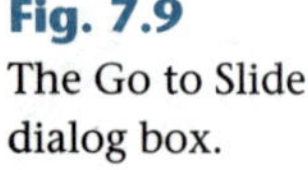

Fig. 7.9
The Go to Slide dialog box.

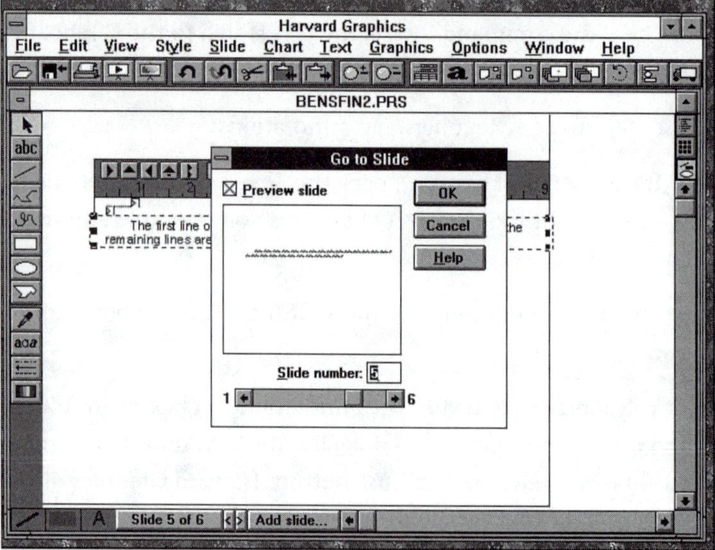

5. Type the slide number of the new slide in the Slide number text box.

6. Click the OK button. The new slide appears in the Slide Editor.

7. From the **E**dit menu, choose Paste **S**pecial. In the Paste Special dialog box, choose Text, then click Paste.

Harvard Graphics adds the material stored in the Clipboard to the specified location in the new slide.

For more information on editing objects with the Clipboard, see Chapter 13, "Enhancing Drawings and Objects."

Moving Text Annotations

You can move objects, such as text annotations, in the Slide Editor. To move an object, select the object with the Selection tool and drag the object to the new location. Follow these steps to move a text annotation:

1. From the Slide Editor window, click the Selection tool.
2. Click and hold down the mouse button in the middle of the text annotation; handles appear around the annotation, and the mouse pointer changes to a four-directional arrow (see fig. 7.10).

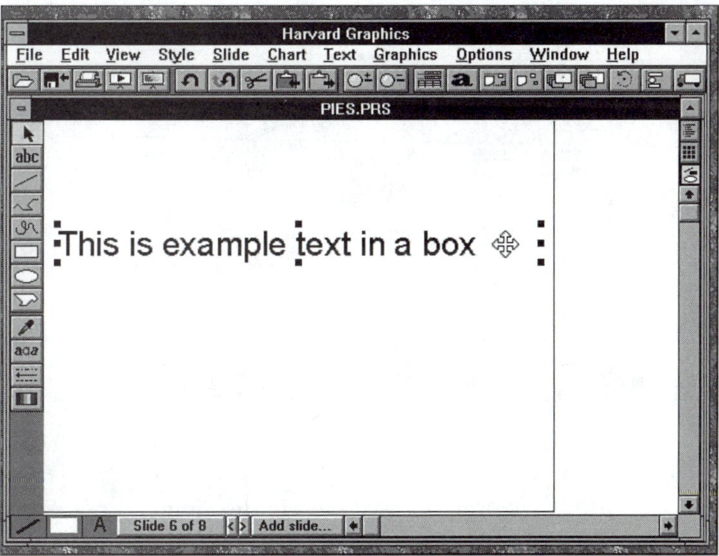

Fig. 7.10
A selected annotation with a four-directional arrow cursor.

3. Drag the text to the new location.
4. Release the mouse button. The text annotation appears in its new location.

For more information on moving objects in the Slide Editor, see Chapter 13, "Enhancing Drawings and Objects."

Setting Text Attributes

You use the items on the **T**ext menu to modify the appearance—the *attributes*—of the text on a slide. You can change the font, size, color, and style of the text. To change these attributes, select the text in the Slide Editor. If you do not select text before you set these attributes, the options on the **T**ext menu affect any new text annotation you add to your slide.

The **T**ext menu has commands that set each attribute individually, or you can use the A**l**l Attributes command to modify all parts of the text at the same time. Figure 7.11 shows the Text Attributes dialog box, which appears when you choose the All Attributes command. This dialog box also appears when you click the Text Attributes tool, also shown in figure 7.11.

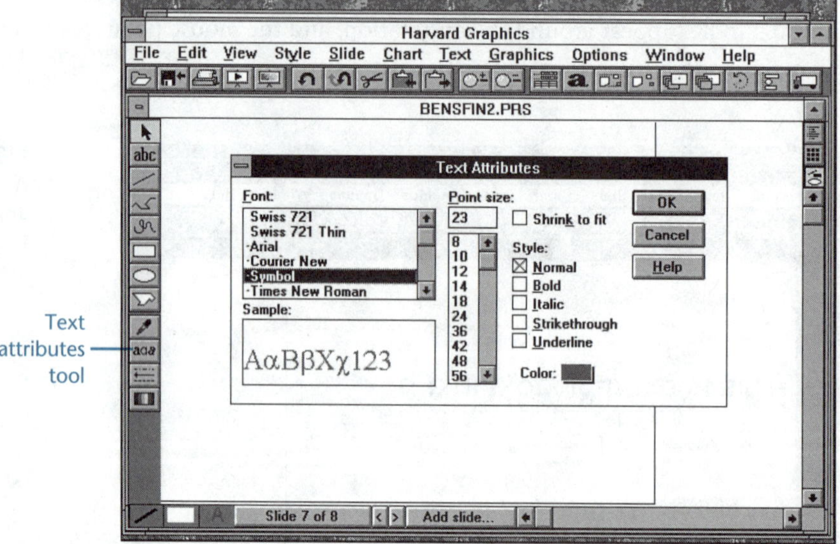

Fig. 7.11
The Text Attributes dialog box.

If you select text, this dialog box shows the attributes for the text; otherwise, the settings indicate the attributes for text annotations. For more information on the individual attributes, see the following sections in this chapter.

The Font scroll box lists all available fonts on your system. To select a font, click a font from this list. The current font size appears in the Point size text box. You can select another point size by clicking a size in the scroll box in the middle of the dialog box or by typing another point size in the Point size text box. See the section "Changing the Font" for more information.

The Color box shows the current color of the text annotation. Click the Color box to see other available colors. The Style check boxes enable you to set specialized text attributes, such as underline or boldface. If an X appears in the check box, the attribute is selected. To remove the attribute, click the check box so that the X disappears. In the Sample text box, you can see how the text looks with the current settings.

Follow these steps to modify the attributes of selected text, using the Text Attributes dialog box:

1. From the Slide Editor window, click the Selection tool.
2. Select the text annotation that you want to change.
3. Choose **All** Attributes from the **T**ext menu to display the Text Attributes dialog box. Alternatively, you can click the Text Attributes icon to display the dialog box.
4. From the Font scroll box, select the new font. You may have to scroll through the list to find a suitable font.
5. Select the size in the Size list box below the Point size text box. You also can type the size directly in the Point size text box.
6. Click the Color box to see the available colors. The Text Color dialog box appears as shown in figure 7.12.

Tip
The biggest advantage in using the Text Attributes dialog box to modify your text is that the Sample text box in the dialog box displays an example of the font for the current settings. As you change the settings, the text in the Sample box reflects your changes.

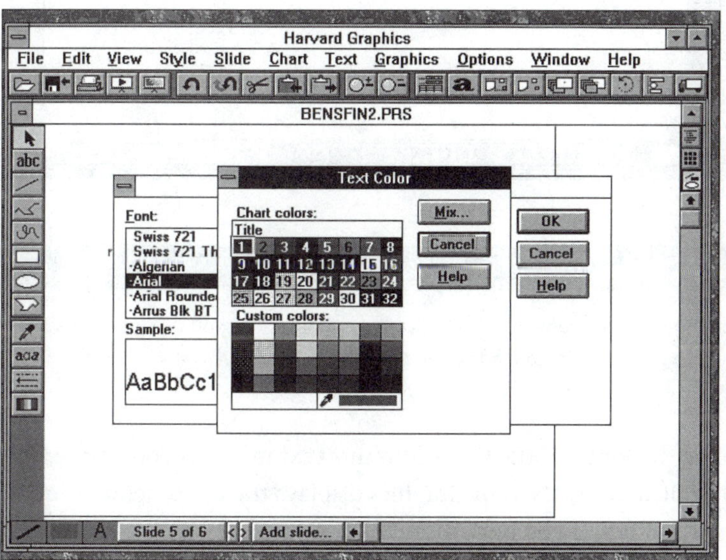

Fig. 7.12
The Text Color dialog box.

7. Click a new color in the dialog box.

8. Select the desired Style options. To enable a style, click the check box next to the style so that an X appears in the box.

9. Click OK.

The selected text changes to match the options you set in the Text Attributes dialog box.

Changing the Font

The **F**ont command on the **T**ext menu changes the font for the selected text in the Slide Editor. Figure 7.13 shows examples of Harvard Graphics fonts. Each font name represents its font style.

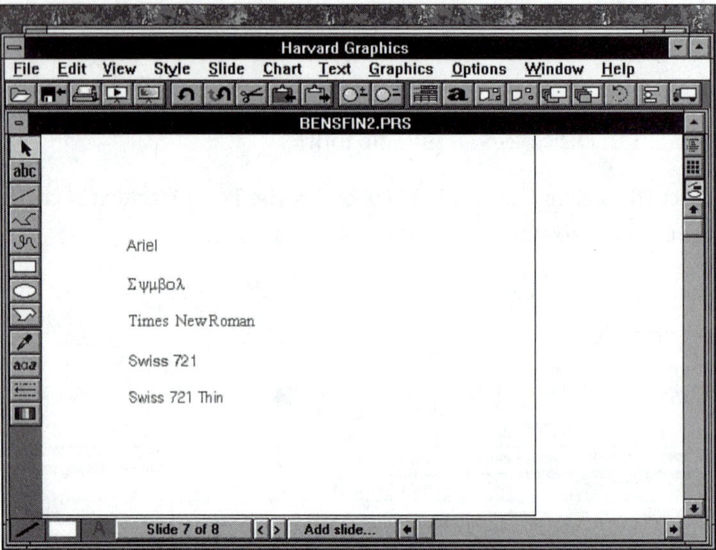

Fig. 7.13 Examples of Harvard Graphics fonts.

Design Note

Changing the font is one of the most visible modifications you can make to a slide. Be sure to use fonts that are attractive and easy to read.

To change the font, choose **F**ont from the **T**ext menu. If you have 25 or fewer installed fonts, Harvard Graphics displays the **F**ont menu, from which you choose a font. If you have more than 25 fonts, the Select Font dialog box, which can list an unlimited number of fonts, appears. To change the font, you choose the new font from the menu or the list in the dialog box. You also can use the Text Attributes dialog box, explained in the preceding section, to change the font and other text attributes.

Follow these steps to change the font for a text annotation, using the **F**ont command on the **T**ext menu:

1. From the Slide Editor window, click the Selection tool.
2. Select the text that you intend to change. Handles appear around the selected text.
3. Choose **F**ont from the **T**ext menu. A pop-up menu or a dialog box containing all available fonts appears.
4. Choose the new font from the menu or the dialog box.

The selected text in the Slide Editor window changes to reflect the new font.

Harvard Graphics combined with Windows provides a wide variety of fonts. Bitstream Typefaces fonts come with Harvard Graphics and are fully supported throughout the product. Harvard Graphics fonts are installed when you install the program. Fonts from Windows include packages like Adobe Type Manager. Your output device may supply additional hardware fonts, which look smoother in your output and usually print faster. See Appendix A, "Installing Harvard Graphics for Windows," for more information on the installation of fonts.

You can rotate, flip, and resize Windows fonts in the Slide Editor. If you rotate, flip, or resize the text of hardware fonts, however, Harvard Graphics changes the hardware font to the Bitstream font closest in appearance. In the **F**ont menu, hardware fonts begin with a bullet character.

Changing the Text Size

The size setting for your text determines the height of the characters. For the scalable fonts provided with Harvard Graphics, you can set the size to any value, and the fonts still look smooth in a slide.

You use the **S**ize command on the **T**ext menu to change the size of your text. When you choose Size, Harvard Graphics displays the Size menu with values ranging from 12 through 72. These values are the most common font sizes used in Harvard Graphics. If your text is set to one of these sizes, the item in the menu is marked with a check mark. To change the size of text, select the text with the Selection tool; then choose **S**ize from the **T**ext menu. A pop-up menu, from which you choose another size, appears.

To set the text size to a value not available on the **S**ize menu, you must use the A**l**l Attributes command on the **T**ext menu. Refer to figure 7.11 to see the Text Attributes dialog box, which appears when you choose A**l**l Attributes from the **T**ext menu. The section "Setting Text Attributes" explains how to set all the options in the dialog box.

Follow these steps to change the text annotation size, using the Text Attributes dialog box:

1. From the Slide Editor window, click the Selection tool.
2. Select the text you intend to change.
3. Choose A**l**l Attributes from the **T**ext menu. The Text Attributes dialog box appears.
4. Click the beginning of the Point size text box.
5. Press and hold the Delete key until the previous value is removed.
6. Type the new text size. For the example, type **45**.
7. Click OK.

The text in the slide changes to the new size.

Changing the Text Style

The text on your slides can be enhanced with many different styles. The most common text styles are boldface, italic, underline, and strike through. Figure 7.14 shows examples of each style. With these styles, you can underline the reference to a book or italicize the name of a magazine. You also can apply more than one attribute to the selected text; for example, you can apply both italic and boldface.

To change the text style, select the text in the Slide Editor. When you choose St**y**le from the **T**ext menu, you can see the current style settings for the selected text. A check mark next to the item in the Style list indicates that the text uses that style. If Normal is checked, no style is applied to the selected text. To apply a style, select the style from the list. You also can use the Text Attributes dialog box to set the style for your text. See the section "Setting Text Attributes" for more information.

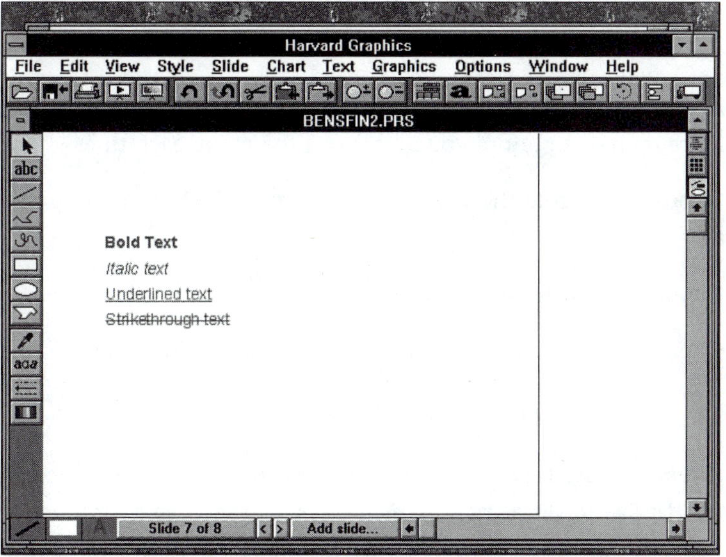

Fig. 7.14 Examples of different text styles.

Follow these steps to boldface and underline the text:

1. From the Slide Editor window, click the Selection tool.
2. Select the text you want to change; selection handles appear.
3. Choose Style from the **T**ext menu. A menu listing all available styles appears; the menu also indicates the current styles of the selected text (see fig. 7.15).

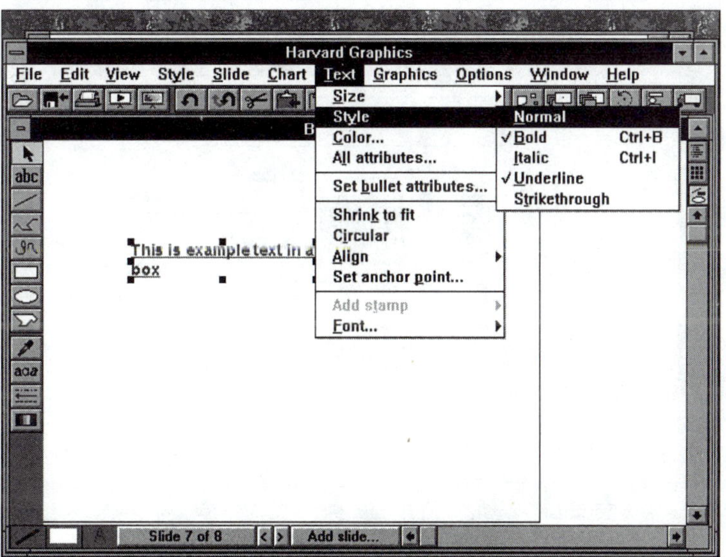

Fig. 7.15 The Style pop-up menu indicating the selected styles.

4. If a check mark does not appear next to Normal, choose Normal to disable any previous styles.

   After you choose an option on this menu, the menu closes. To choose more than one option, you must open the menu each time.

5. Choose Style from the Text menu to display the Style pop-up menu again.

6. Choose Bold from the menu.

7. Choose Style from the Text menu; then choose Underline.

Each style you choose on the Style pop-up menu appears in the selected text.

You also can use the Text Attributes dialog box to set the style options for your text. Unlike the Style pop-up menu, you can set several style attributes at one time in this dialog box. You also can see an example of your changes before you accept them. For more information on using the Text Attributes dialog box, see the section "Setting Text Attributes" in this chapter.

Changing the Text Color

You can use the Color command on the Text menu or with the Fill tool to modify the color of your text. When you choose Color from the Text menu or click the Fill tool, the Text Color dialog box, which shows the available colors, appears (see fig. 7.16).

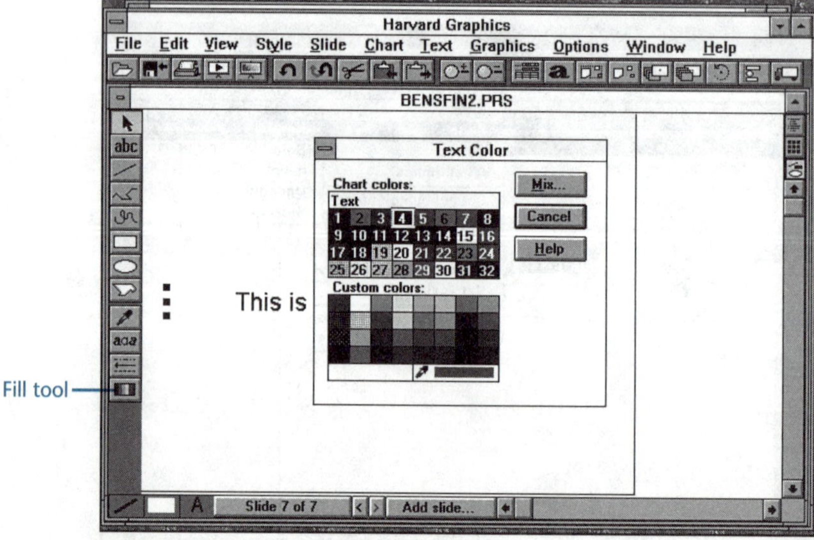

Fig. 7.16
The Fill tool and the Text Color dialog box.

Follow these steps to change the color of your text:

1. From the Slide Editor window, click the Selection tool.
2. Select the text you want to change; handles appear.
3. Click the Fill tool. The Text color dialog box, in which you select a color, appears.
4. Select a new color in the Text Color dialog box.

The selected text changes to the specified color.

When modifying the text color, make sure that you verify the appearance of your slides in your final output medium. If you are displaying a presentation on a color computer screen, evaluating the text in the Slide Editor is sufficient. If you are printing your presentation on a black-and-white device, however, make sure that you preview the printed slides to ensure that all the text is clear and readable.

Setting Text Justification

The **A**lign command on the **T**ext menu changes the justification for any of the text on a slide. Harvard Graphics can left-, right-, center-, and full-justify text. (Figure 7.5 illustrates the four justifications.) The Alignment command affects text you select with the Selection tool.

In the section "Justifying Text with the Ruler," you learned how to change the justification of text annotations. (You used the Text tool to select text to be modified with the ruler. See the section "Selecting Text" earlier in the chapter.) The **A**lign command on the **T**ext menu affects text you select with the Selection tool.

Follow these steps to change the text justification:

1. From the Slide Editor window, click the Selection tool.
2. In the slide, select the text you intend to change.
3. Select the Text tool. The ruler appears, containing the justification icons (left, center, right, and full).
4. Select the appropriate justification from the menu.

The selected text changes to the specified justification.

Resizing a Text Box

The text box determines the amount of text displayed on one line in a text annotation. The width of the box is set when you add the annotation to the chart. When the text you enter reaches the end of the box, Harvard Graphics wraps the text to a new line. You can change the amount of text that fits on the line by resizing the box.

To change the width of the text box, click the text with the Selection tool. When you select the annotation, handles appear around the text (see fig. 7.17). To change the width of the text box, click the handles on either side of the box and drag the box in or out.

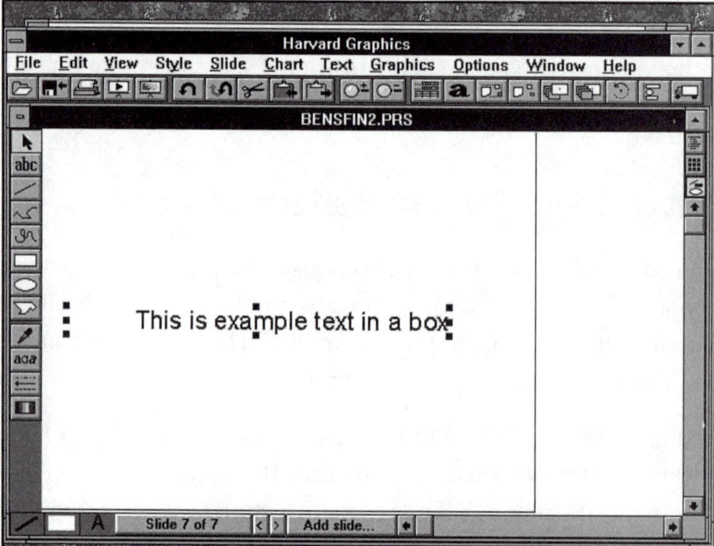

Fig. 7.17
The handles for resizing a text box.

After you adjust the size of the box, Harvard Graphics rewraps the text and changes the height of the box as necessary. You can change only the width of the box, not the height. The height is determined by the number of lines of text and by the font and size of the text. When you decrease the width, you increase the number of lines of text; if you increase the width, more text can fit on one line, and the text box has fewer lines. If you change the height of a text box by dragging the handles, Harvard Graphics snaps the box back to enclose the lines of text.

Follow these steps to shrink the width of a text box:

1. From the Slide Editor window, click the Selection tool.

2. Select the text you intend to change.

3. Click and hold down the mouse button on the handle in the middle of the right side of the box. When you select the handle, the mouse pointer turns into a two-directional arrow. If your cursor is a four-directional arrow, you have not selected the handle.

4. Drag the box inward to the new width.

5. Release the mouse button.

Harvard Graphics adjusts the text to fit the new box. The text box in figure 7.17 has been resized (see fig. 7.18). Because the text box width has been decreased, fewer characters appear on each line, but there are more lines of text.

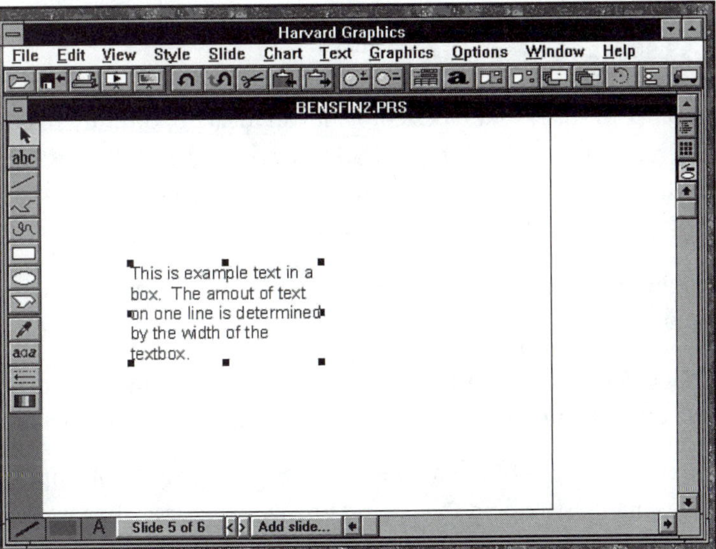

Fig. 7.18
The text box resized.

Note

In the section "Adding Text Annotations," you learned how to add text by clicking in the Slide Editor. Harvard Graphics creates a text box that extends from the point you clicked to the edge of the slide. If you know the size of text box you need for your annotation, you can size the box before entering the text. By sizing the text box in advance, you can avoid resizing it after you enter text. This technique is useful if you have a limited amount of space in which to display your text.

Shrinking Text to Fit

Circumstances may dictate that text fit in the boundaries of a text box. In other words, the text box should not grow as words wrap. By using the Shrin**k** to Fit option from the **T**ext menu, the text size decreases as more lines of text are added. As text is deleted, the text size in adjusted accordingly to bring it in line with its original size.

Creating Circular Text

The capability to shape text blocks provides an ideal opportunity to embellish your presentations. Harvard Graphics addresses such possibilities with the ability to flow text in a circular pattern. Follow these steps to create circular text:

1. From in the Slide Editor, select the text you want to apply a circular pattern to.
2. Choose C**i**rcular from the **T**ext menu. Once you apply this circular style, your text block will appear similar to that shown in figure 7.19.

If two lines of text exist in the text box, the first line of text will appear as the half of the circular style, and the second line will appear as the lower half.

Design Note

If more than two lines of text exist in a text block, all but the first two lines will be ignored. Further, if the length of the text exceeds the circumference of the circle, the text will overwrite itself.

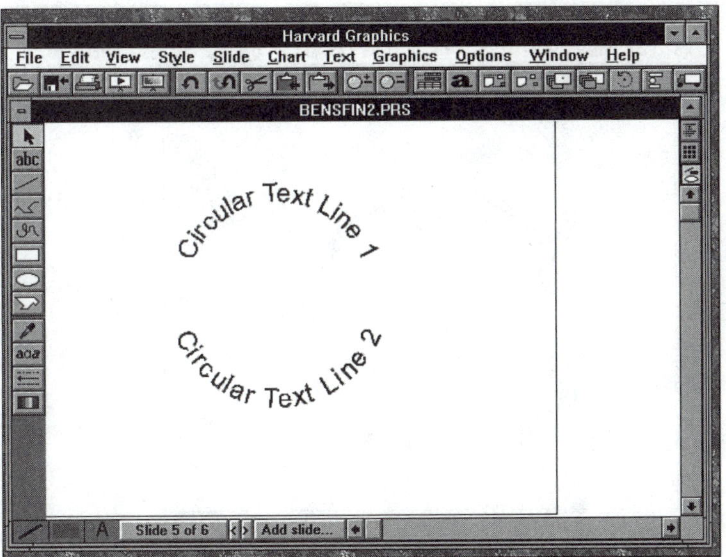

Fig. 7.19
Circular style applied to a text block with two lines of text.

Initially, a single line of text will appear in the top half of the circles circumference. Although this may be acceptable, you might want to have your text form a complete circle. To accomplish this task:

1. Select the text block you want to change. Be certain that the circular style has been applied.

2. With the pointer on one of the corner handles, drag the handle toward the opposite corner. Once the text flows to the desired position, release the mouse button. Figure 7.20 illustrates this concept.

Changing the Text Anchor Point

A template predefines the location of items—such as text annotations or a chart—on a slide. When you use a template with a presentation, annotations on different slides may have different amounts of text. The *anchor point* determines which direction the annotation will grow or shrink to adjust to the differences in size.

Anchor points are useful when you are creating templates for a presentation in which the textual items for each chart may differ in size. You use the Set Anchor **P**oint item on the **T**ext menu to modify the anchor point.

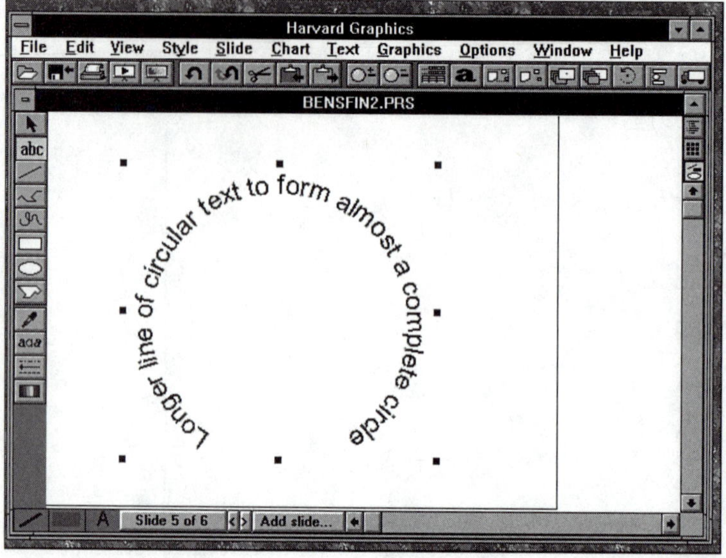

Fig. 7.20 Text block in a circle.

Figure 7.21 shows the Anchor Point dialog box, which indicates the current anchor point of your selected text annotation. The dotted lines in the dialog box show the height and width directions where the object will grow. You see the anchor point in the dialog box only; anchor points do not appear in the slide.

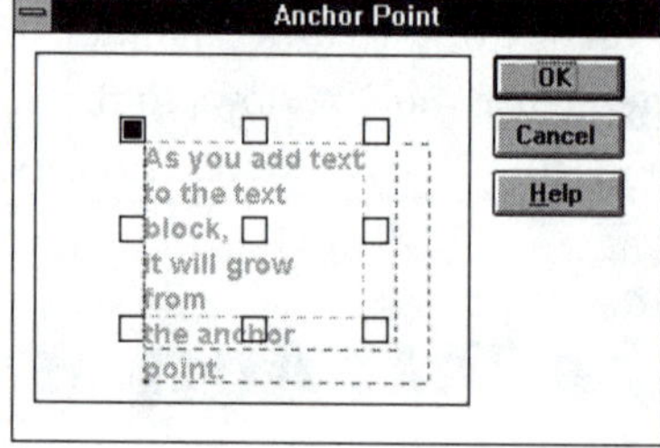

Fig. 7.21 The Anchor Point dialog box.

Follow these steps to change the anchor point of a text object:

1. From the Slide Editor window, choose Set Anchor **P**oint from the **T**ext menu. The Anchor Point dialog box appears.

2. Click the new anchor point in the dialog box. As you select different points, the dialog box reflects the new directions.

3. Click the OK button.

The anchor point is set for the text in the slide. If you use this slide to create a template, the anchor point controls the annotations on different slides that use the template.

Spell Checking Text

You can check the spelling for the text on a single slide or for an entire presentation. In addition to misspelled words, Harvard Graphics also checks for incorrect capitalization and consecutively repeated words (*the the*, for example). You even can define a personal dictionary to add words specific to your work with Harvard Graphics.

To spell check a slide or presentation, choose Check spelling from the **E**dit menu. You see the Check Spelling dialog box, shown in figure 7.22. To check a single slide, click the This Slide radio button in the dialog box. To check a presentation, click the Entire Presentation radio button. You use the Ignore words in ALL CAPS option to avoid checking words that are typically not found in the dictionary. If this option is set, Harvard Graphics does not check words in which all the letters are capitalized.

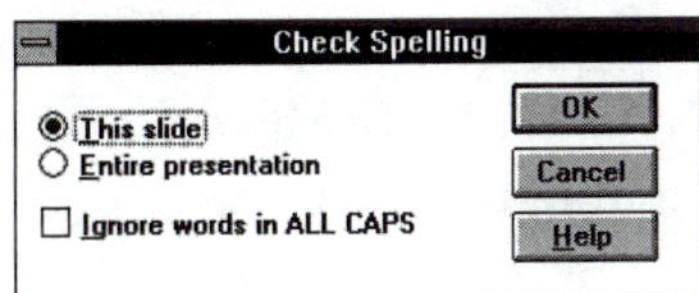

Fig. 7.22
The Check Spelling dialog box.

To check the spelling of an entire presentation from any location in the presentation, follow these steps:

1. Choose Chec**k** Spelling from the **E**dit menu. The Check Spelling dialog box appears.

2. Click the Entire Presentation button.

3. Click the OK button.

When Harvard Graphics encounters a mistake, the program displays the Correct Spelling dialog box (see fig. 7.23). The first line in the top left provides the slide number where the mistake was found. The second line highlights the misspelled word and shows the context in which the word was used. The Suggestions list box—which Harvard Graphics retrieves from its dictionary—

below the misspelled word presents a list of alternatives from which you can choose another spelling. You have several choices for handling a misspelling. You can make a correction, ignore the misspelling, add the word to a personal dictionary, or stop the spell checker altogether.

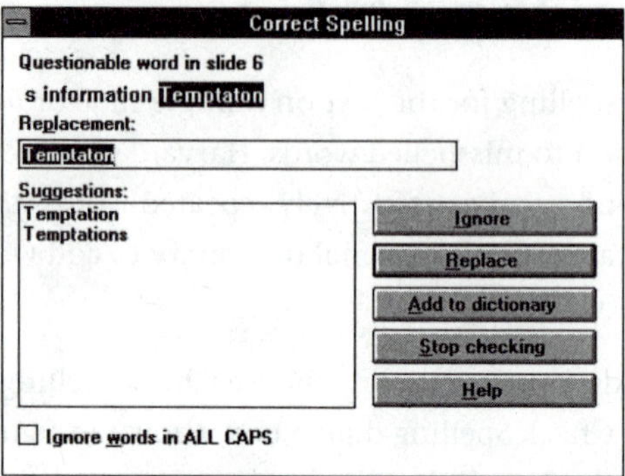

Fig. 7.23 The Correct Spelling dialog box.

Correcting a Mistake

You enter the correct spelling of the word in the Replacement text box on the right side of the dialog box. If you know the correct spelling, you can type the word in this box. If you select a word in the Suggestions list box, the selected word appears in the Replacement box. When the correct spelling is in the Replacement box, click the Replace button to change the word in the chart. Harvard Graphics continues to spell check.

Skipping a Word

Harvard Graphics presents any word not found in the dictionary as misspelled. In some cases, as with a company name, the word is spelled correctly but is not a word you find in a dictionary. To accept a word, click the Ignore button in the Correct Spelling dialog box.

If you frequently use a significant number of words that are not in the Harvard Graphics dictionary, you can add the words to the personal dictionary with the Add to dictionary button. See the section "Using a Personal Dictionary" to learn how to work with the personal dictionary.

Correcting a Repeated Word

As Harvard Graphics checks the spelling in a slide, the spelling checker also watches for repeated words in the text. If you typed the same word twice by accident, you can use the Repeated Word dialog box, shown in figure 7.24, to correct the mistake. This dialog box appears when Harvard Graphics finds repeated words in the same text object. The repeated words appear in the field near the top of the box, and the second word is highlighted. The slide number is indicated above the field.

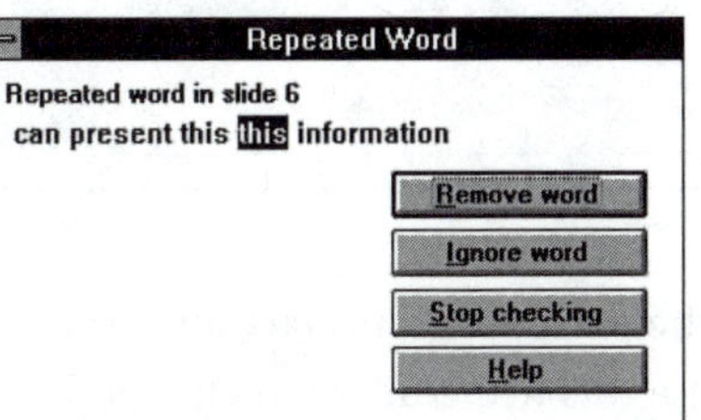

Fig. 7.24 The Repeated Word dialog box.

To delete a repeated word, click the Remove button in the Repeated Word dialog box. If the two words are correct, click the Ignore button to leave the text unchanged.

Stopping the Spell Checker

When you reach the end of a slide or presentation, Harvard Graphics displays the Spell Check Complete message, shown in figure 7.25. Click OK to remove the message box.

Fig. 7.25 The Spell check complete message box.

(You can stop the spelling check before Harvard Graphics has checked the entire presentation, however, by clicking the Stop Checking button in the Correct Spelling dialog box.)

Using a Personal Dictionary

Harvard Graphics has a personal dictionary in which you can store correctly spelled words that are not found in a standard Harvard Graphics dictionary; for example, the name of a company. When the correctly spelled word appears in the Correct Spelling dialog box, click the Add to Dictionary button to add the word to the personal dictionary.

You can use the Personal **D**ictionary command on the **E**dit menu to edit the words in this dictionary. To display the personal dictionary, choose Personal **D**ictionary from the **E**dit menu. The Personal Dictionary dialog box appears (see fig. 7.26). You use this dialog box to add and delete words.

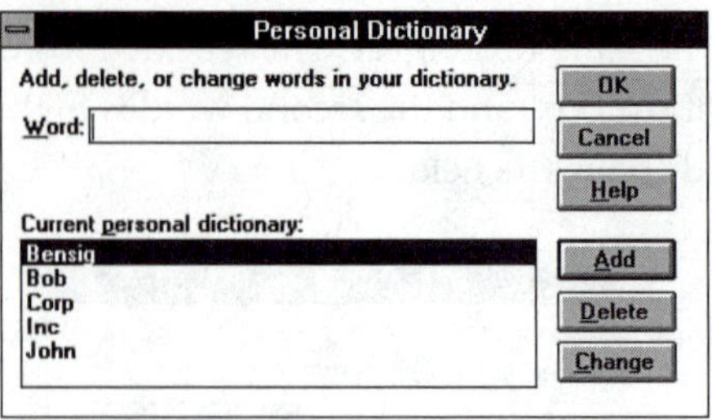

Fig. 7.26 The Personal Dictionary dialog box.

The words stored in the personal dictionary appear in the list box below the Word text box. You use this list to add and change words in the personal dictionary. To add a word, type the word in the Word text box and click the Add button. To change a word, click the word in the list. The selected word appears in the Word text box. After you modify the word, click the Change button to store the updated word. To remove a word, select the word in the list and click the Delete button. When you are finished with your changes, click the OK button.

Harvard Graphics allows you the opportunity to maintain multiple personal dictionaries. If, for example, you create presentations for multiple purposes (legal, medical, and so on), you might want to create and maintain a dictionary for each discipline. To create a new personal dictionary, follow these steps:

1. Using Windows File Manager, rename the file WINUSER.LEX. You might want to give the name ORIGINAL.LEX to indicate this is your original personal dictionary.

2. Once you return to Harvard Graphics, choose Personal Dictionary from the **E**dit menu. You are asked whether you want to create WINUSER.LEX. Choose Yes.

3. Add the words appropriate for the personal dictionary you are creating.

4. Once the personal dictionary contains the applicable words, you may want to rename it to something descriptive of what it represents. For example, LEGAL.LEX, indicating that the words contained in this dictionary file are for legal presentations. Repeat Step 1 to rename your dictionary.

Setting the Dictionary and Personal Dictionary File

The location of the dictionary files are, by default, stored in the subdirectory where Harvard Graphics resides. If you accepted all the default settings when installing the software, the supplied dictionary as well as your personal dictionary are located in the HGW subdirectory. Should you ever have reason to change the location of these files, or want to maintain multiple personal dictionaries, you must make the appropriate changes in Harvard Graphics. To initiate such a change, follow these steps:

1. From the **O**ptions menu, choose **P**aths.

2. Tab to or click the appropriate dictionary field and type a new path or file name. The dictionary file you use must have LEX as its extension. For example, MEDICAL.LEX might indicate a medical dictionary is to be used when spell checking the current presentation.

From Here...

This chapter explains how to work with the text on a slide. You learned about the different types of text and what operations can be performed on the types in the Slide Editor. You learned how to add text annotations to a slide with the Text tool and how to edit text. You also learned how to select text with the Selection and Text tools.

After entering text on a slide, you learned how to change the attributes of the text. You also learned how to change the font, size, color, style, and justification of your text. Finally, you learned how to spell check the text in a slide or presentation and how to work with a personal dictionary.

In the next chapter, "Using the Slide Sorter," you learn how to edit an entire presentation.

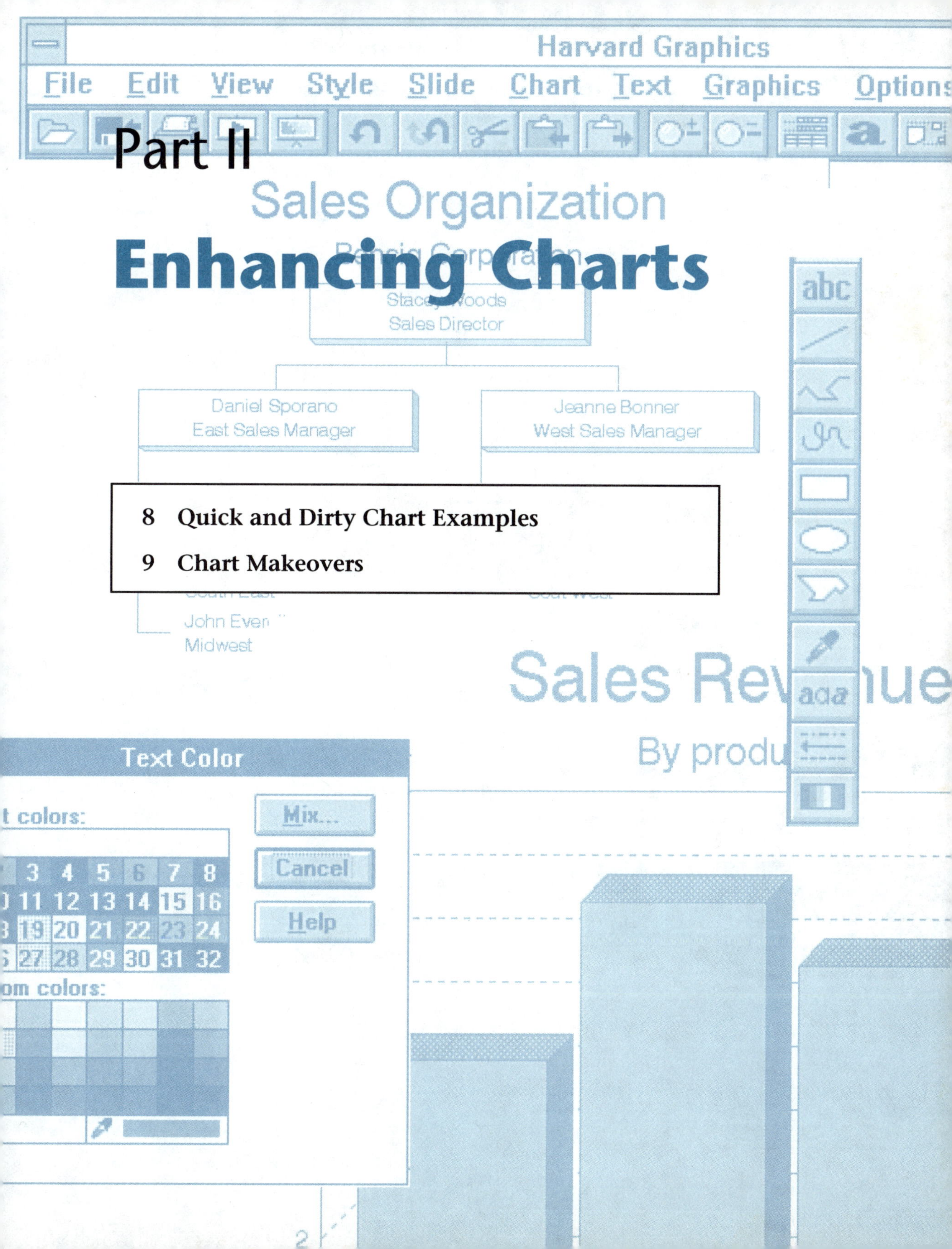

Part II

Enhancing Charts

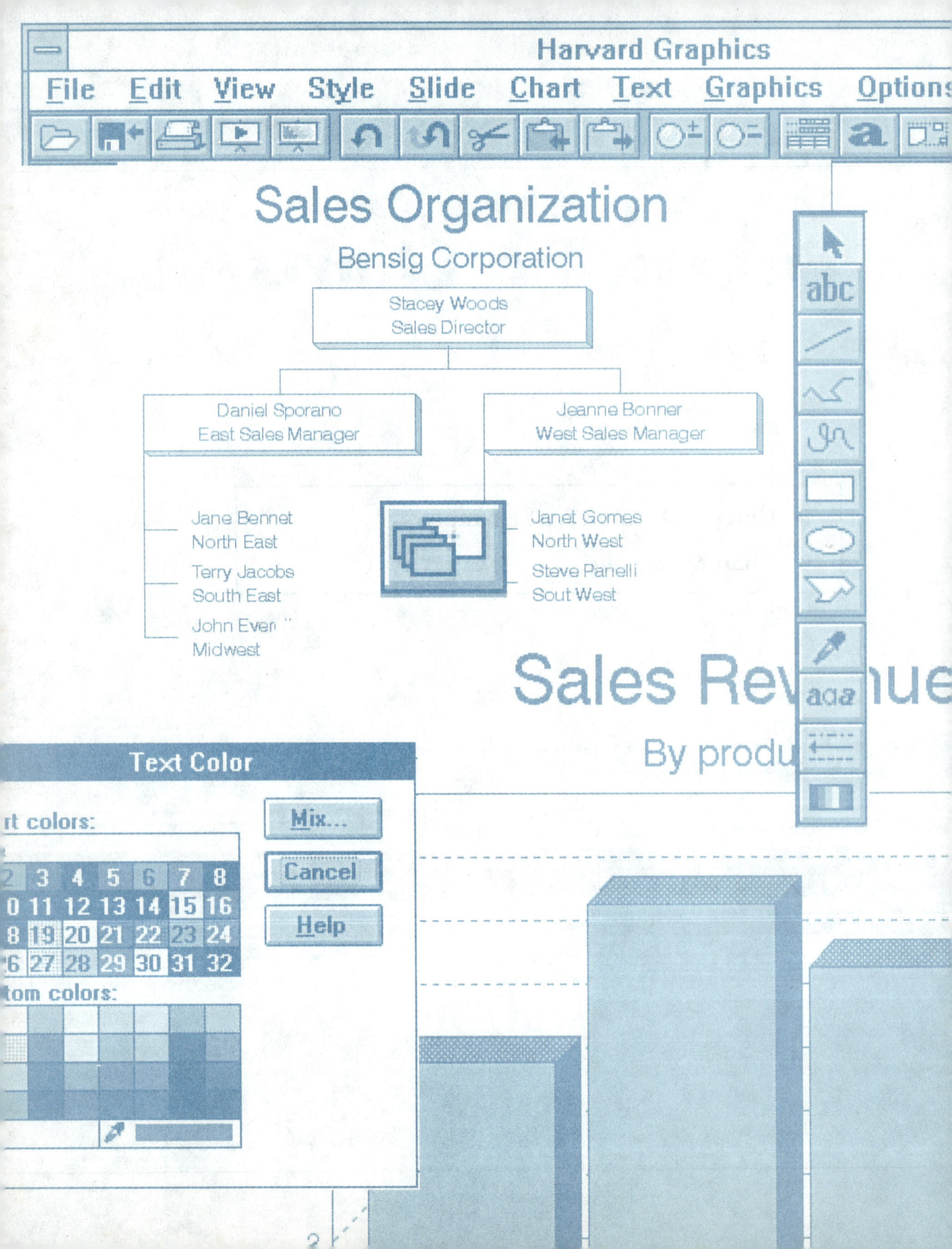
Harvard Graphics
File Edit View Style Slide Chart Text Graphics Options
Sales Organization
Bensig Corporation
Stacey Woods
Sales Director
Daniel Sporano
East Sales Manager
Jeanne Bonner
West Sales Manager
Jane Bennet
North East
Terry Jacobs
South East
Midwest
Janet Gomes
North West
Steve Panelli
Sout West
abc
Text Color
Mix...
Cancel
Help

With Harvard Graphics for Windows, you can create slide shows with graphic effects, such as the title slide shown here with a sweep effect. (See Chapter 8, Fig. 8.1.)

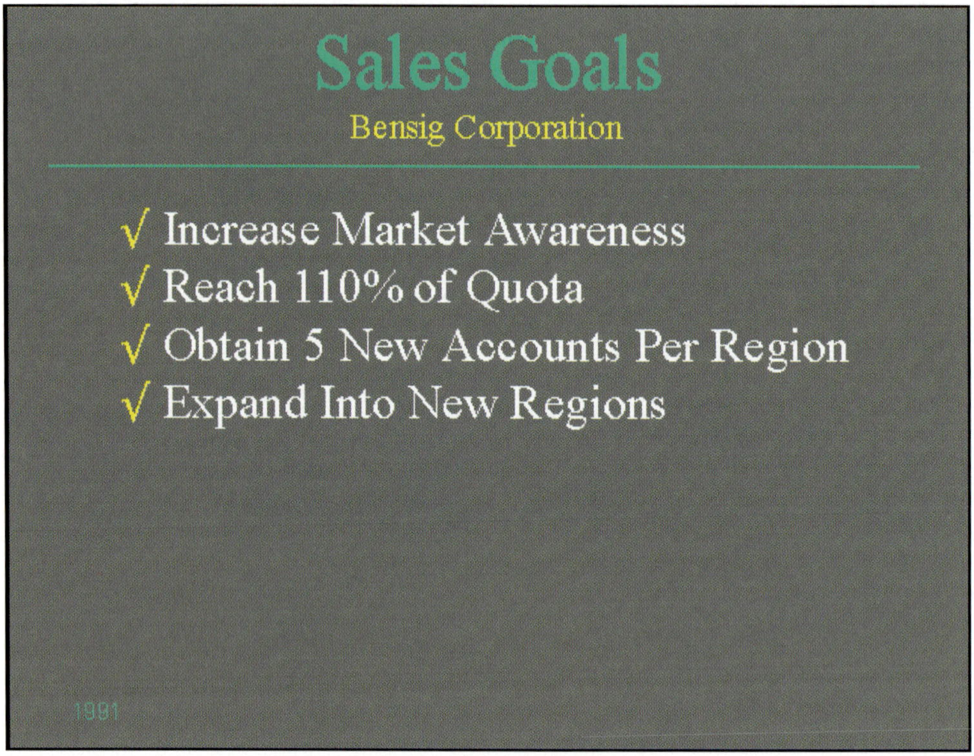

Create eye-catching lists with special effects, such as the bullet chart shown here. (See Chapter 8, Fig. 8.2.)

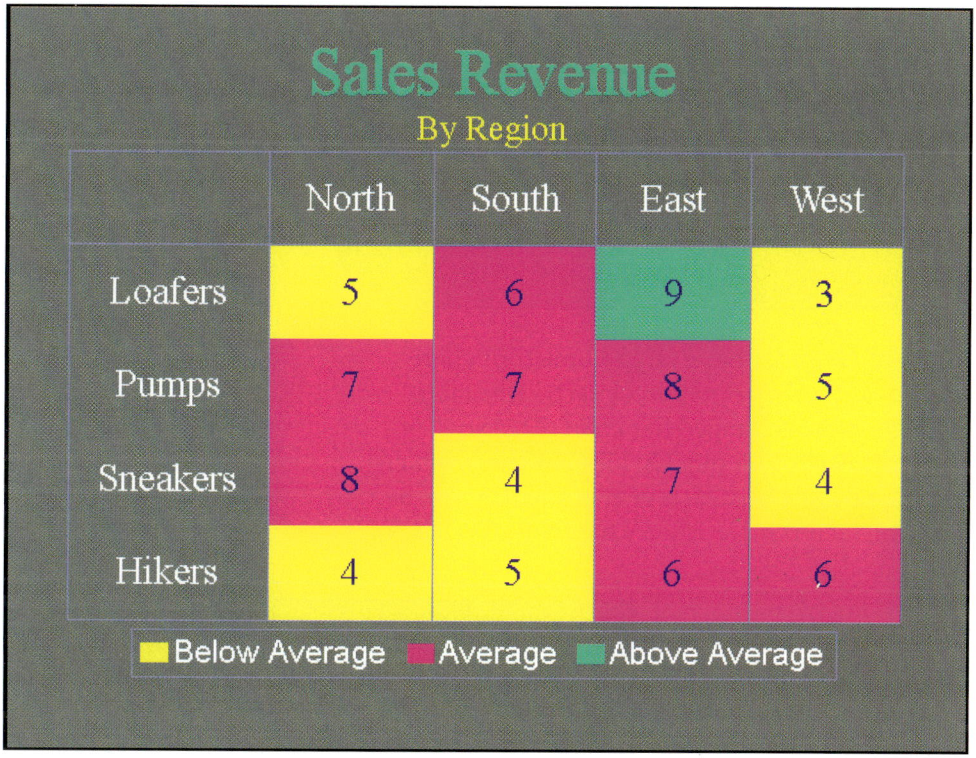

Sales Revenue

By Region

	North	South	East	West
Loafers	5	6	9	3
Pumps	7	7	8	5
Sneakers	8	4	7	4
Hikers	4	5	6	6

Below Average Average Above Average

Turn boring table charts into colorful masterpieces, such as the vivid sales revenue chart with colored regions shown here. (See Chapter 8, Fig. 8.3.)

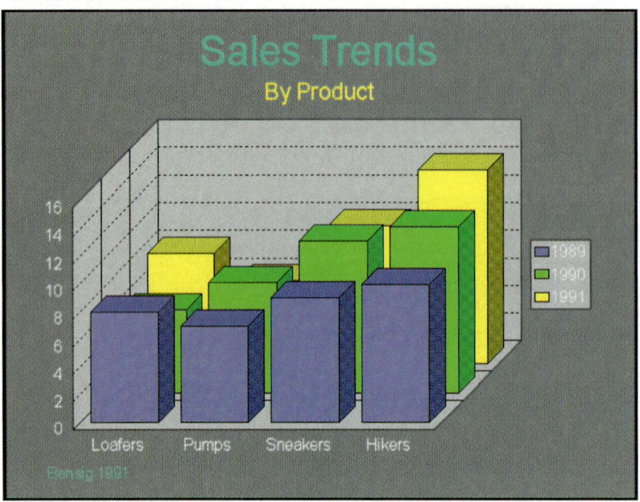

Harvard Graphics has a large number of chart styles—and many options for each. This chart shows a 3-D overlapped bar chart. This style of chart allows you to quickly identify the products that performed best each year or identify the best year for each product. (See Chapter 8, Fig. 8.5.)

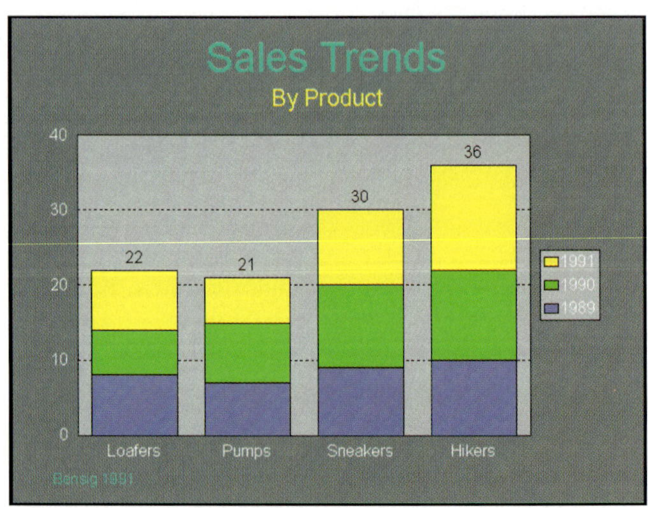

Here you see a 2-D stacked bar chart. This chart is used here to compare the performances of the three product lines over a three year period, but still allows you to see the sales from each individual year. (See Chapter 8, Fig. 8.6.)

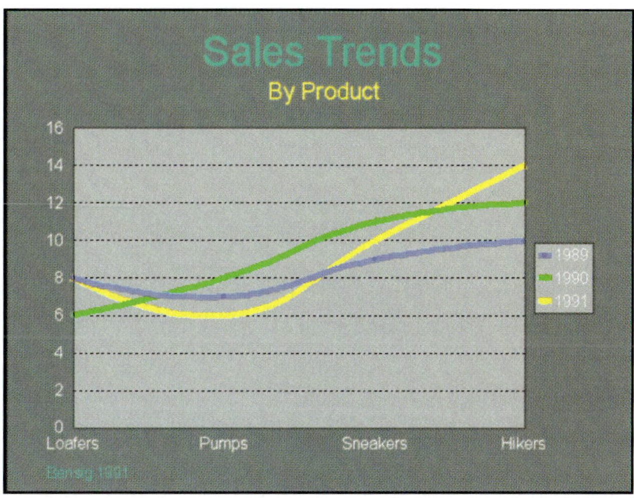

The line chart with curved lines, shown here, emphasizes the increasing sales trends of each product line. (See Chapter 8, Fig. 8.7.)

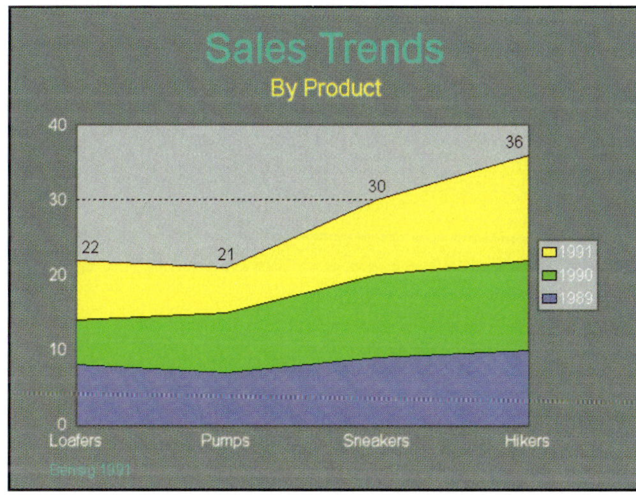

This stacked bar chart with data labels emphasizes the continual growth in each product line but places the most emphasis on the growth in the entire company. (See Chapter 8, Fig. 8.8.)

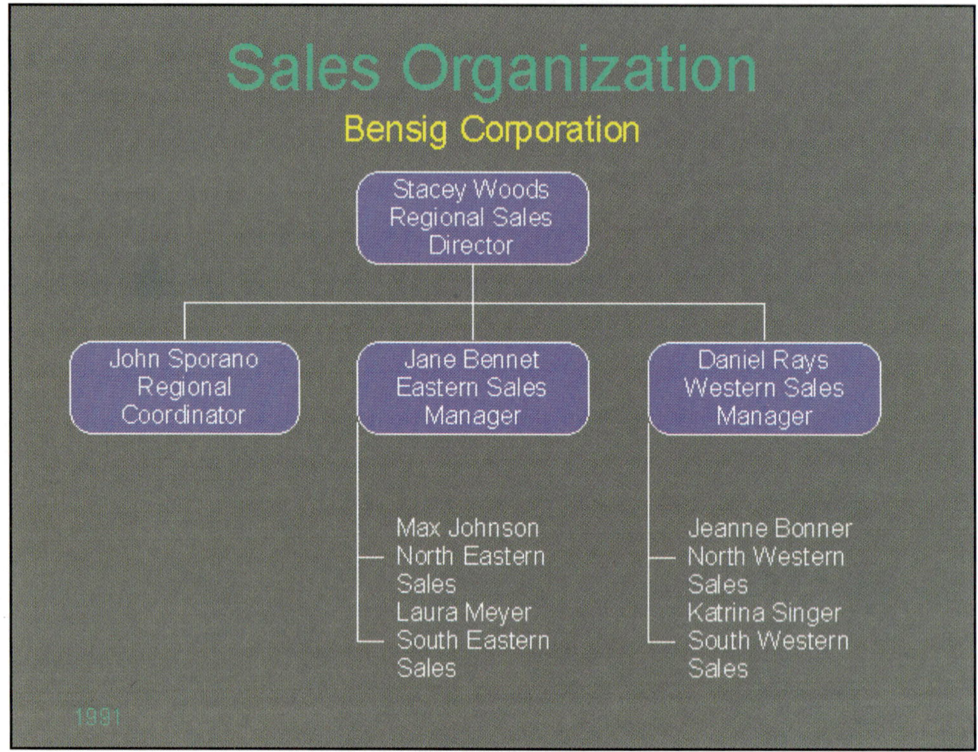

You can create organization charts that show both vertical and horizontal hierarchies. This chart uses rounded boxes for a special effect. (See Chapter 8, Fig. 8.4.)

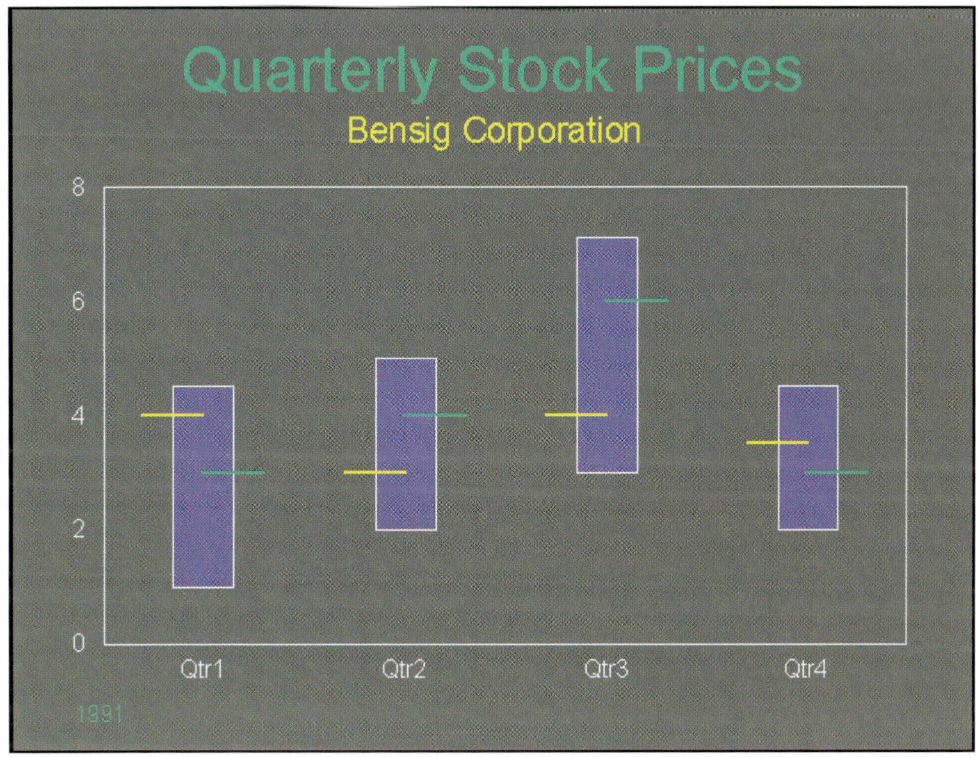

The high/low/close chart without gridlines is ideal for showing changes in two numbers, such as stock prices shown here. (See Chapter 8, Fig. 8.9.)

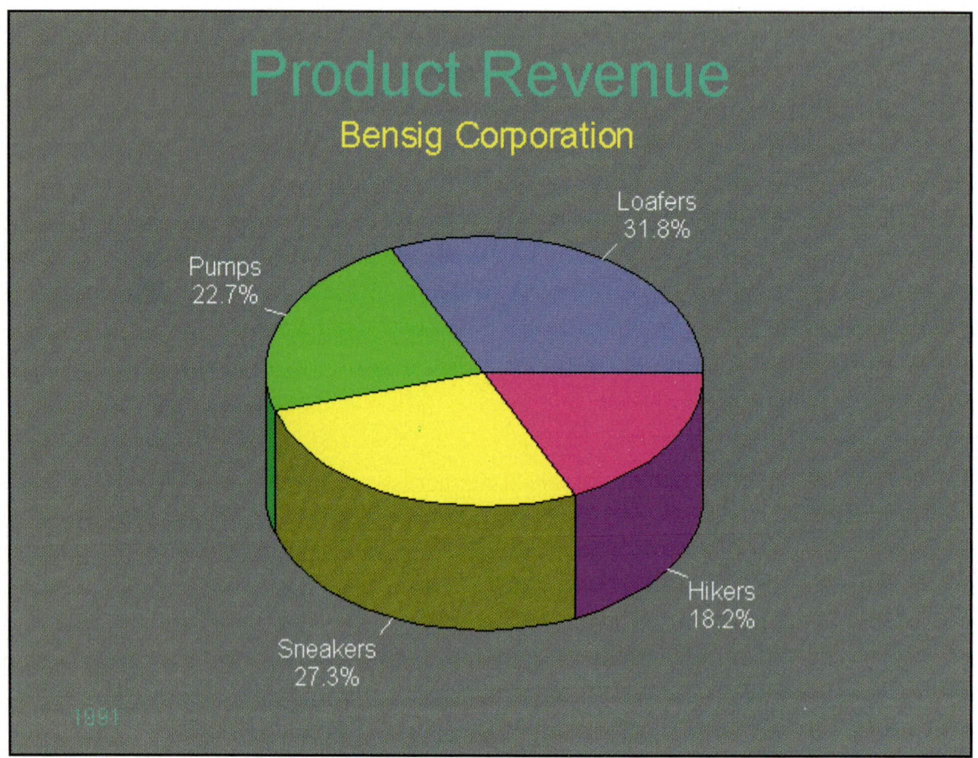

You can create pie charts, such as the one shown here, that break down larger numbers into their relevant parts. Notice how Harvard Graphics for Windows allows you to increase the depth of the pie for emphasis. (See Chapter 8, Fig. 8.11.)

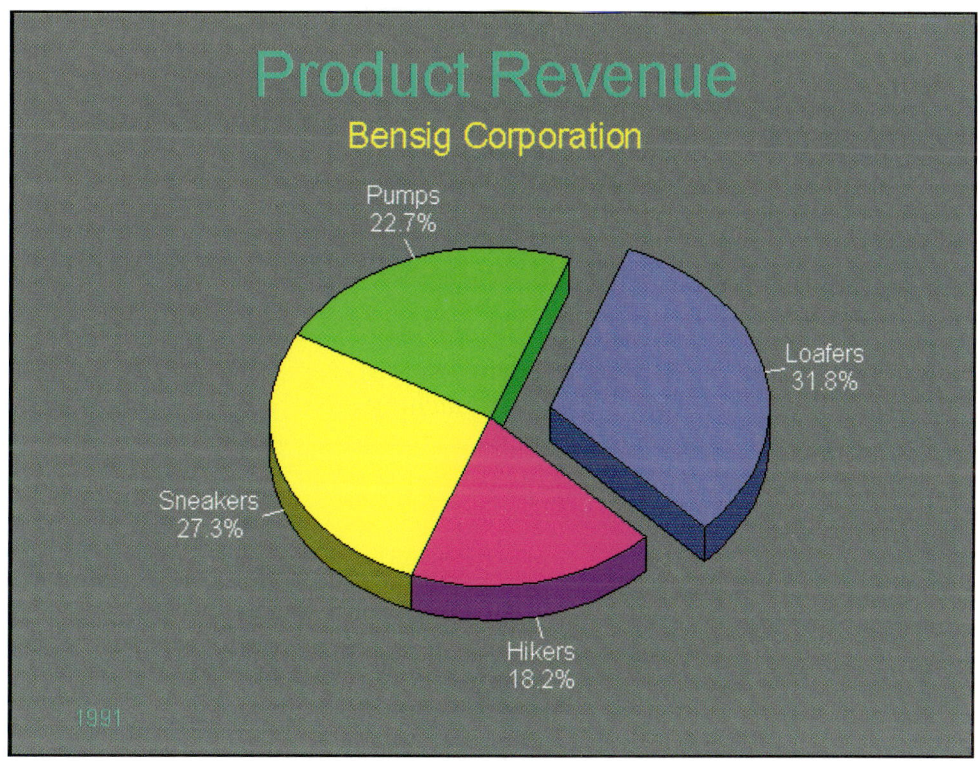

You can also create pie charts with a cut slice, as shown here. In this case, the cut slice emphasizes the Loafer division, which is the largest revenue producer for the company. (See Chapter 8, Fig. 8.10.)

Sales Goals For The Bensig Corporation

For The Year 1991

- Increase Market Awareness For All Products
- Reach 110% of Sales Quota
- Obtain 5 New Accounts Per Region Of The Country
- Expand Into New Regions Throughout The Country

Harvard Graphics for Windows can help you turn an unappealing bullet chart into an eye-catching slide. This bullet chart is much too difficult to read. (See Chapter 9, Fig. 9.1.)

Sales Goals

Bensig Corporation

- Increase Market Awareness
- Reach 110% of Quota
- Obtain 5 New Accounts Per Region
- Expand Into New Regions

1991

This is the same bullet chart with reduced text. It's already much easier to read quickly. (See Chapter 9, Fig. 9.2.)

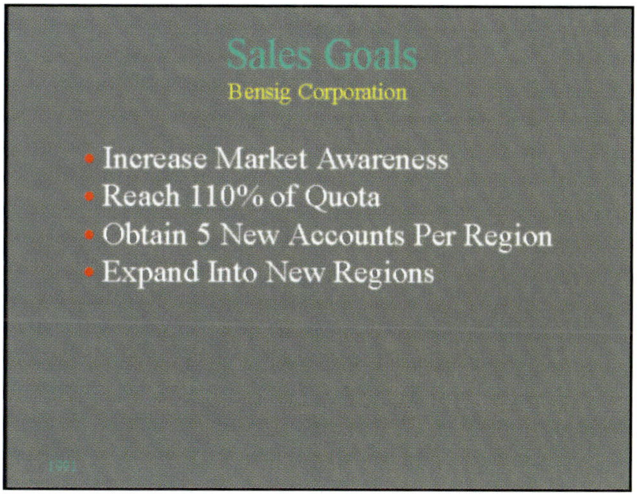

Sales Goals
Bensig Corporation

- Increase Market Awareness
- Reach 110% of Quota
- Obtain 5 New Accounts Per Region
- Expand Into New Regions

By changing the background and text colors, the text fonts, and font sizes, you can make the same chart much more pleasing to read. (See Chapter 9, Fig. 9.3.)

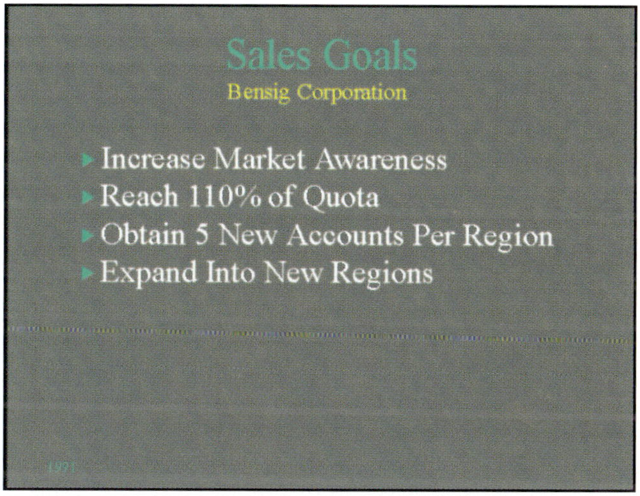

Sales Goals
Bensig Corporation

- Increase Market Awareness
- Reach 110% of Quota
- Obtain 5 New Accounts Per Region
- Expand Into New Regions

Here is the finished bullet chart complete with interesting bullets. Just a few minutes of tweaking with your chart will make your completed product look much more polished and professional. (See Chapter 9, Fig. 9.4.)

Here is a boring bar chart; it illustrates the desired point, but it's not easy to read and understand. Harvard Graphics offers so many different chart styles. There is almost always one that will make your point clearly and attractively. (See Chapter 9, Fig. 9.5.)

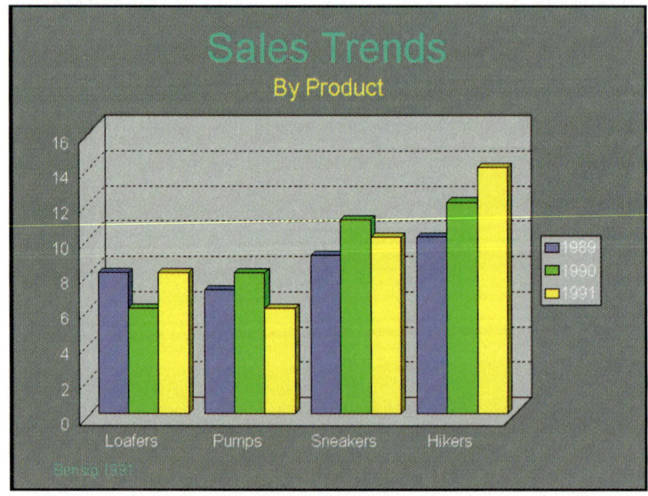

Here is the same bar chart with altered background and text colors. You should choose the colors in your legend so that your chart is visibly appealing and your point is easily understood. (See Chapter 9, Fig. 9.6.)

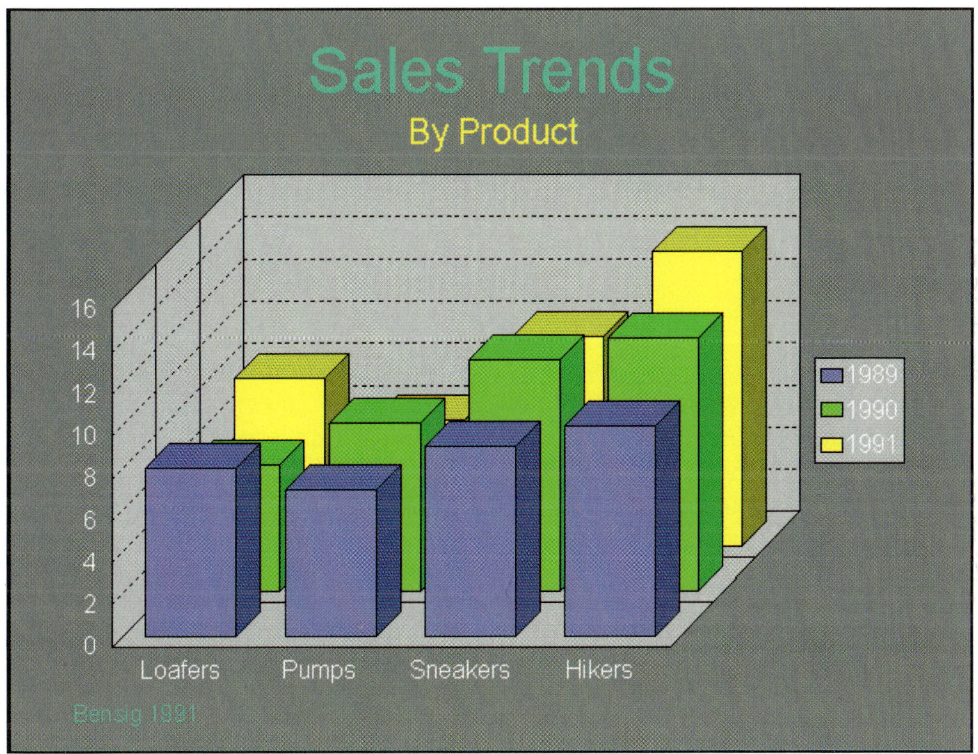

The finished chart has been turned into a 3-D bar chart to best emphasize the creator's point: sales trends by product. This chart allows the reader to easily compare any category to any other category, in any particular year. As with a pie chart, you can also increase or decrease the depth of your 3-D bar charts. (See Chapter 9, Fig. 9.7.)

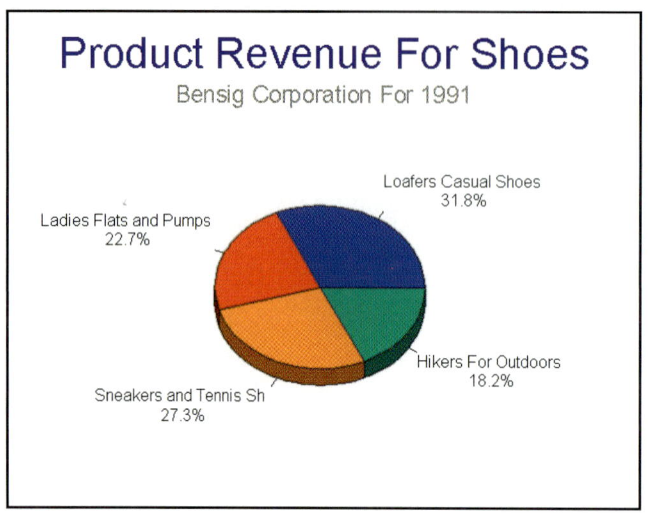

Here is a crowded pie chart with too much text. You should use Harvard Graphics to create charts that jump out at the reader. You're probably using Harvard Graphics because you want readers to just glance at your chart and understand the general point of your presentation. This way they don't have to read and decipher your charts while you speak. Harvard Graphics allows you to create just such a chart. (See Chapter 9, Fig. 9.8.)

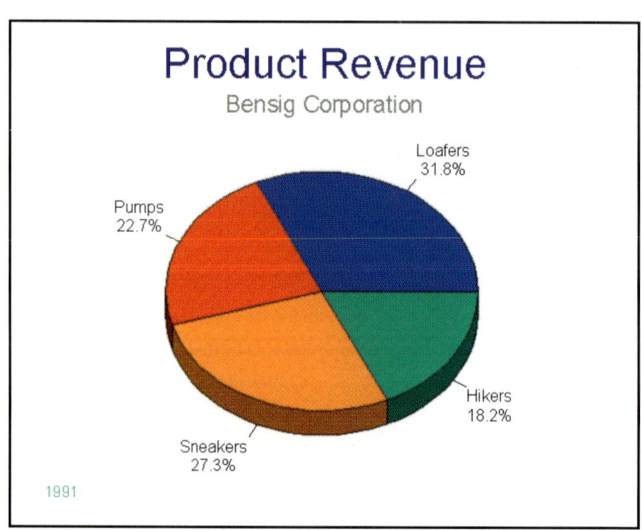

Simply increasing the size of the chart and reducing the amount of text can improve your pie chart, but it's still somewhat bland. (See Chapter 9, Fig. 9.9.)

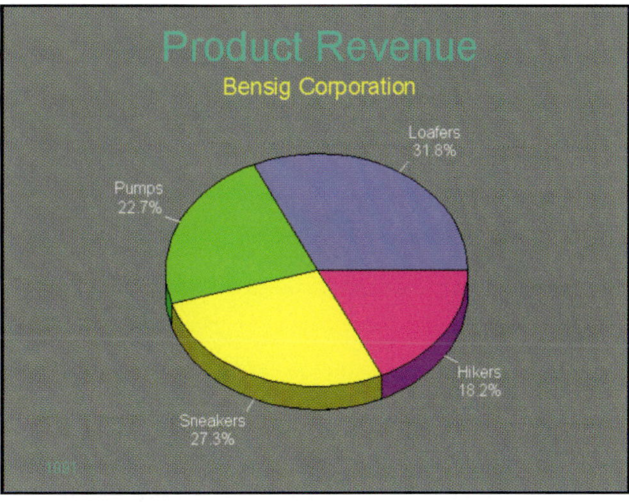

Use mellow background colors and vivid foreground colors to emphasize the pieces of the pie you want to stand out the most. A sharp pie chart with eye-catching colors, such as this, can be worth a thousand words. (See Chapter 9, Fig. 9.10.)

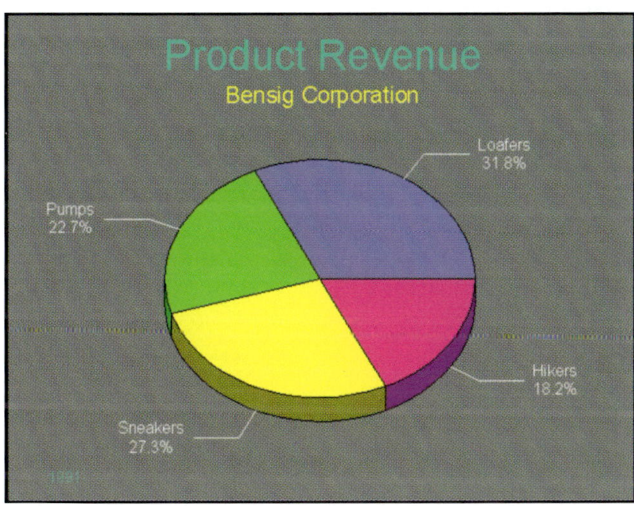

As a finishing touch, you can add extended pointers to your chart to make it appear less crowded. This finished chart will get the point across to your readers at a glance. (See Chapter 9, Fig. 9.11.)

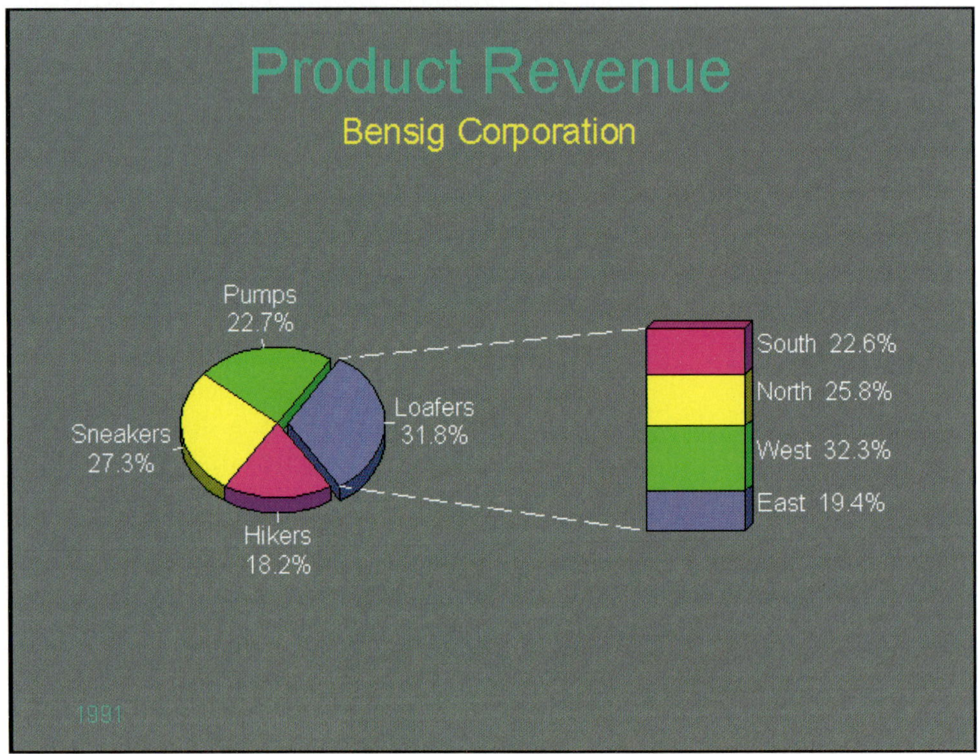

Harvard Graphics also allows you to link two charts together. In this case, the second chart is a breakdown of Loafer sales by region. You can create sharp, professional graphs with ease by using Harvard Graphics special effects. (See Chapter 8, Fig. 8.12.)

Chapter 8

Quick and Dirty Chart Examples

Harvard Graphics is a feature-rich graphics product with an abundant set of chart and slide options. You can create a variety of charts and slides, and enhance your images with color, graphics, and text. Knowing how to set options and add graphics is only part of creating effective presentations. Knowing when to modify options depends on your creative ability and your complete understanding of the effects of your changes. If you do not have the time to study the product and take a few graphic art courses, this chapter is for you.

In this chapter, you learn how to do the following:

- Create many different styles of charts
- Effectively modify charting options

"Quick and Dirty Chart Examples" presents some eye-catching examples of charts you can create with Harvard Graphics. You can learn ways to enhance text with special effects, use charting options to stack bars in a bar chart, and link pies in a pie chart. The best way to use this chapter is to glance through the examples and look for different elements you like in the charts. Along with each example, you see a brief description of when you can use the example and what options were modified to create the chart. Even if the different examples do not fit your precise needs, the charts may give you other ideas for improving your charts.

To help you better evaluate the charts in this chapter, examples of each chart appear in the color insert in this book. The same charts from the insert are displayed in black and white along with the steps and descriptions in this chapter. As you glance through the examples, you may want to refer to the color charts to appreciate how the different options can exemplify your information.

Using Special Effects To Enhance Text

Most charts contain text in various forms, including bullet items, pie labels, and slide titles. The conventional way to change text is to modify text attributes such as the font, text size, and color. Harvard Graphics provides other means for modifying graphics, such as the **S**pecial effects... command on the **G**raphics menu. Figure 8.1 shows a sweep effect applied to the title of a title chart. A title chart often is the first chart that sets the theme of a speaker's presentation. With the chart in figure 8.1, your viewers notice that your presentation is more than a basic presentation created with simple option defaults. For information on text attributes, see Chapter 7, "Working with Text." Special effects are covered in Chapter 13, "Enhancing Drawings and Objects."

Fig. 8.1
A title chart with a sweep effect.

Using Special Bullets To Emphasize Bullet Items

The chart in figure 8.2 illustrates some ways to improve a bullet chart. The most obvious change is the use of check marks for the bullet symbols. You can use different symbols to add style to your chart and to provide cues to enhance your presentation. The chart in the figure presents sales goals.

You could refer to the marks as checks indicating the goal was achieved. In addition to the bullet symbols, a line separates the slide title from the bullet items. Graphic separators help your viewers organize information on a chart and follow along with your presentation. See Chapter 3, "Creating Text Charts," for information on changing the bullet symbols. See Chapter 12, "Drawing in Harvard Graphics," for information on adding graphics to your slides.

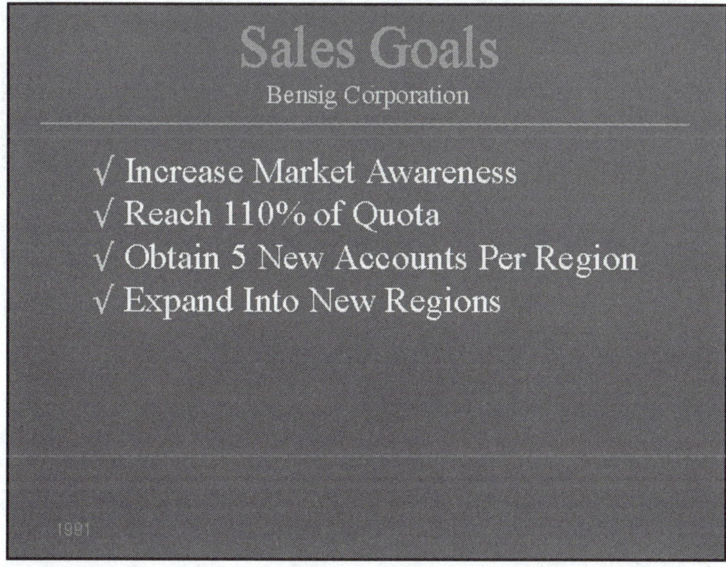

Fig. 8.2
A bullet chart with special bullets.

Using Ranges To Emphasize Trends in a Table Chart

Table charts present numeric and textual data very similar to a spreadsheet. The data is organized into rows and columns. Viewers interpret the data based on the rows and columns. Trends in the data, such as a row with above-average values or a column with lower values, are difficult to see unless you use colored ranges to emphasize these trends. Figure 8.3 uses three colors to emphasize average, above-average, and below-average values. You can see that the East enjoys high revenues but the West does not. See the section "Defining Ranges" in Chapter 3, "Creating Text Charts," for more information.

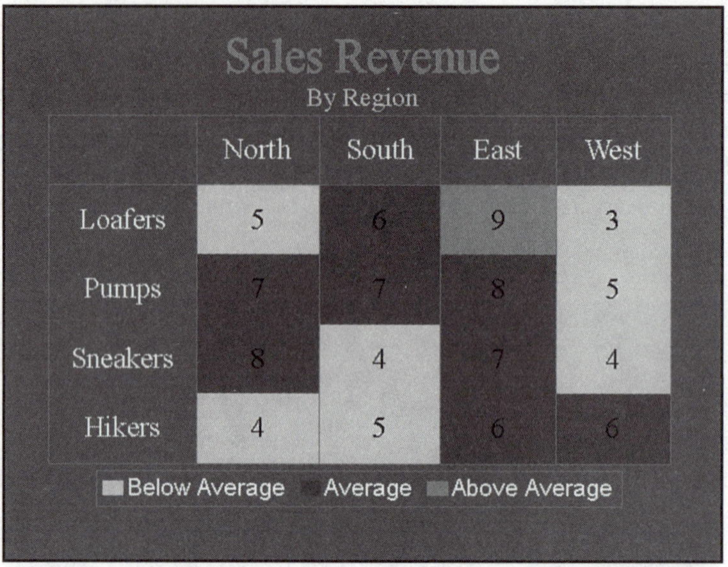

Fig. 8.3
A table chart with colored regions.

Changing the Box Style of an Organization Chart

Organization charts are some of the most difficult charts to lay out on a slide. Lines link together the members of a group or company to show how it is organized, and as the number of boxes increases, the available space between boxes decreases, thus making the chart crowded and difficult to read.

One way to conserve space is to use two-dimensional boxes rather than three-dimensional boxes, as with the chart in figure 8.4. The boxes are rounded rather than square to help keep the chart graphically appealing. See the section "Modifying the Appearance of the Chart" in Chapter 4, "Creating Organization Charts," for more information.

Using 3-D Overlapped Bars To Compare Data

The chart in figure 8.5 uses the overlapped bar style, which creates two methods for comparison. You can examine product sales for any given year by comparing from left to right. You also can compare a single product over three years by comparing front to back. Using the overlapped style allows you to spot different trends or comparisons in the data, which you may not see with a two-dimensional chart or a cluster chart that displays the bars in a flat row. In addition to changing the style, the floor depth in figure 8.5 has been increased and the bar width and depth have been changed to help make all the bars in the chart more visible. See the section "Changing the Appearance of 3-D Charts" in Chapter 5, "Creating XY Charts," for more information.

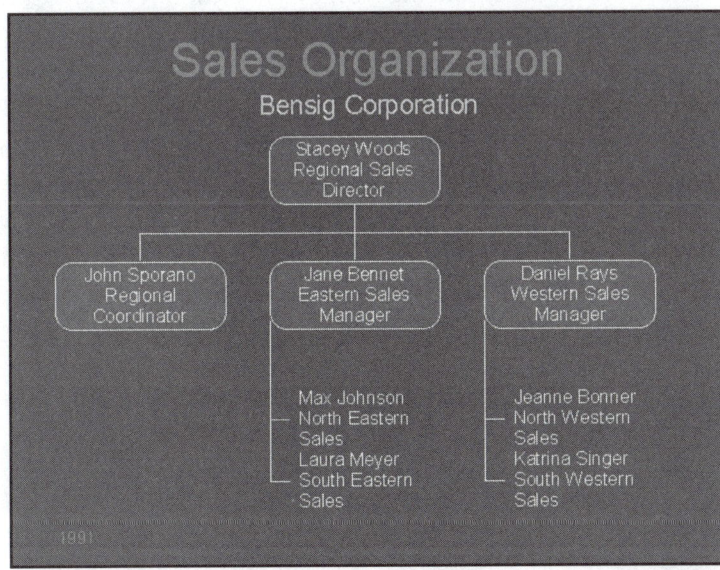

Fig. 8.4
An organization chart with rounded boxes.

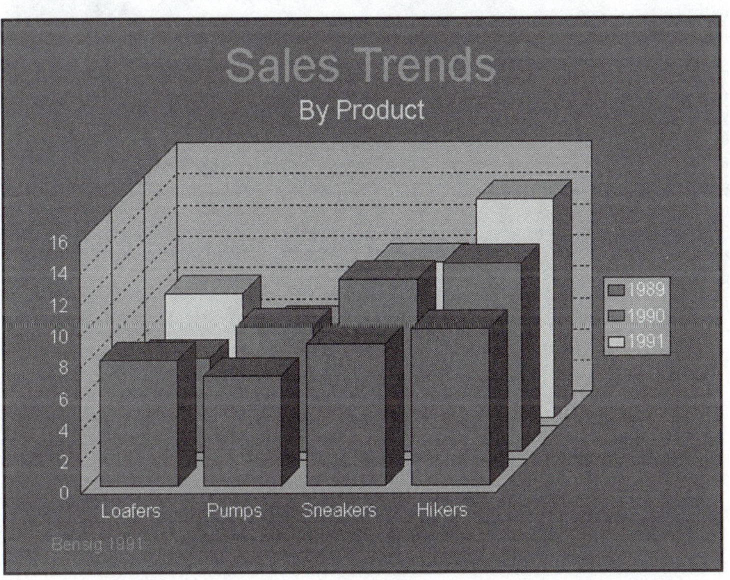

Fig. 8.5
A 3-D overlapped bar chart.

Showing Cumulative Data in a Bar Chart

The preceding example showed you how to modify a bar chart to create different comparisons of the same data. Looking at the example, you cannot easily tell which product has sold the most over the last three years. During some years, one product has sold well but the same product did not sell as well in another year. A stacked bar chart presents cumulative data by stacking bars on top of each other as in figure 8.6. In this chart, you can see that Hikers were the top seller for the three-year period, and Pumps and Loafers were very similar. Data labels have been added above the bars to help compare bars close in height. See the section "Showing Data Labels" in Chapter 5, "Creating XY Charts," for more information. If the goal of your slide is to evaluate cumulative data, see the section "Setting XY Chart Options" in Chapter 5, "Creating XY Charts," for more information.

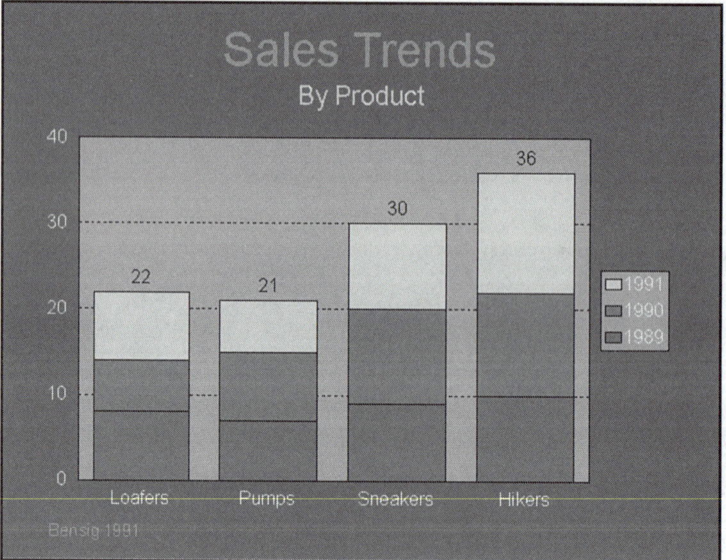

Fig. 8.6
A 2-D stacked bar chart.

Using Curved Line Charts To Emphasize Trends

Line charts connect the data values of a chart with straight line segments. Viewers see the values at the point where these segments intersect and watch for trends with upward and downward sloping lines. The chart in figure 8.7

is a variation on line charts that presents the trends without charting the precise data points. In this chart, your viewers can see only the trends, which may be more important than the actual data. See the section "Setting the Line Fit for a Line Chart" in Chapter 5, "Creating XY Charts," for more information.

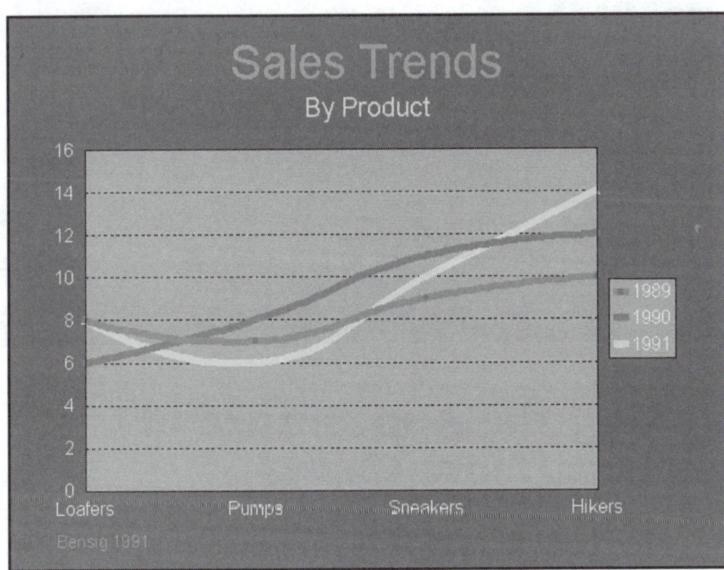

Fig. 8.7
A line chart with curved line fits.

Using Stacked Area Charts To Show Cumulative Data

Area charts show topographical data by filling areas of the chart below data values. Stacking the areas illustrates cumulative data, like the chart in figure 8.8. This chart shows you how much of each product was sold in the past three years. You could communicate the same point with the stacked bar chart discussed in the previous section, "Showing Cumulative Data in a Bar Chart." The advantage of the area chart is that you see trends in the changes in the areas from point to point. For example, in 1989, sales for all four products were relatively the same, but over the years, athletic shoes such as Hikers and Sneakers have done better. Data labels have been added above the areas to help compare different areas. See the section "Showing Data Labels" in Chapter 5 for more information. See the section "Creating XY Charts" in Chapter 5 for more information on creating an XY chart.

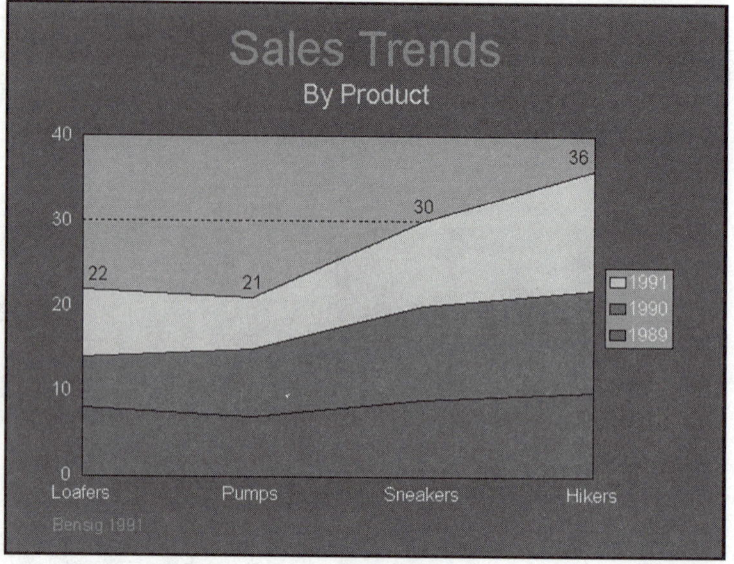

Fig. 8.8
A stacked area chart with data labels.

Changing the Appearance of High/Low/Close Charts

Figure 8.9 presents an interesting high/low/close chart. The chart does not display any gridlines behind the bars in the chart. Gridlines normally serve as measurement guidelines to help viewers determine the exact value of a bar. If you remove the gridlines, your viewers can make only general evaluations, such as determining which quarters the open price (the yellow line) was lower than the closing price (the blue line). See the color insert and the section "Modifying the Grid Lines" in Chapter 5, "Creating XY Charts."

Emphasizing a Single Slice in a Pie Chart

The Loafers slice in the pie chart in figure 8.10 is separated from the other slices. This slice is the largest in the pie, which is the main reason the slice was chosen to be separated. You cut away a slice to focus attention on it—for example, if the slice is the largest, smallest, or more significant information on the chart. Your viewers still can compare all the slices against the separated slice. See the section "Cutting Away Pie Slices" in Chapter 6, "Creating Pie Charts," for more information.

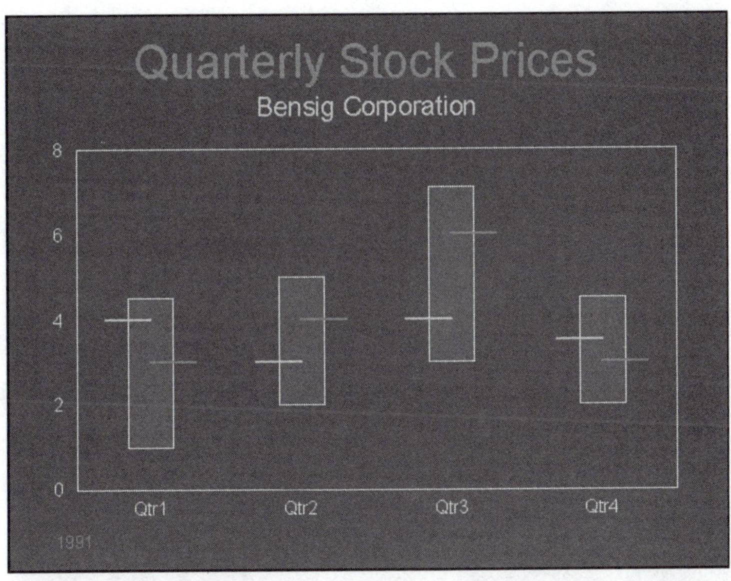

Fig. 8.9
A high/low/close chart without gridlines.

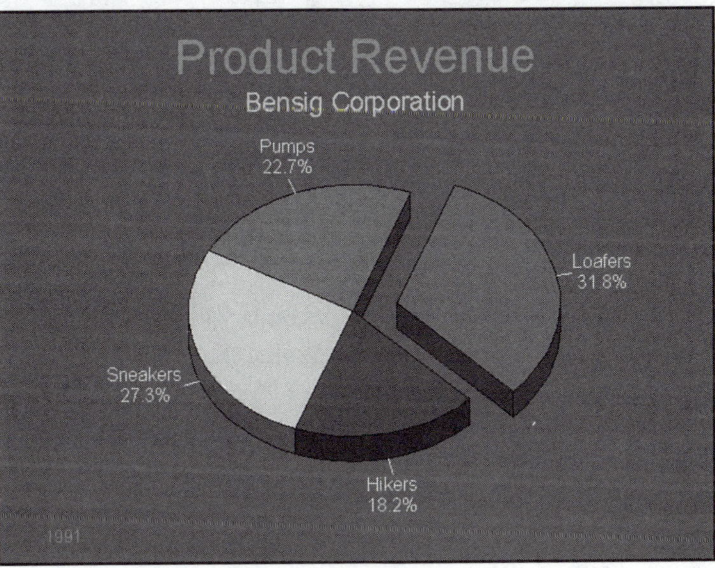

Fig. 8.10
A pie chart with a separated slice.

Achieving Different Looks for Pie Charts

The thickness of a pie chart supports interesting metaphors when discussing information in the chart. For a coin company, a thin pie chart could symbolize a coin. The thick pie chart may represent data for a bakery or wedding cake baker. Using metaphors when discussing charts supplies additional cues to help your viewers remember the information you presented. You also can use the cues to make the discussion more interesting and more relevant to your particular audience. See the section "Modifying Pie Chart Options" in Chapter 6, "Creating Pie Charts."

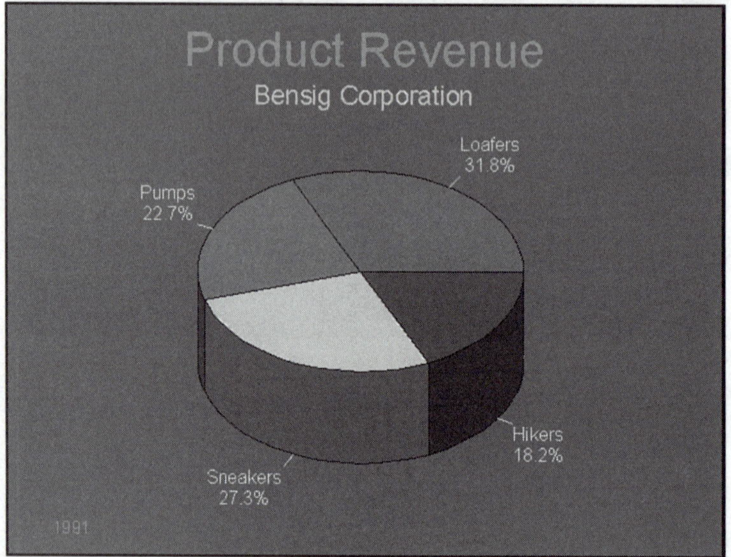

Fig. 8.11
A thick pie chart.

Linking Pies for Break Downs

Linking two pie charts helps you provide secondary information about an individual slice in the first pie. In figure 8.12, the second pie, which is displayed as a column, shows the break down of Loafers sales in the four regions of the country. The Loafers slice is cut away and linked lines are drawn from the slice to the column, further emphasizing the relationship. See the section "Creating Linked Pies" in Chapter 6, "Creating Pie Charts," for more information.

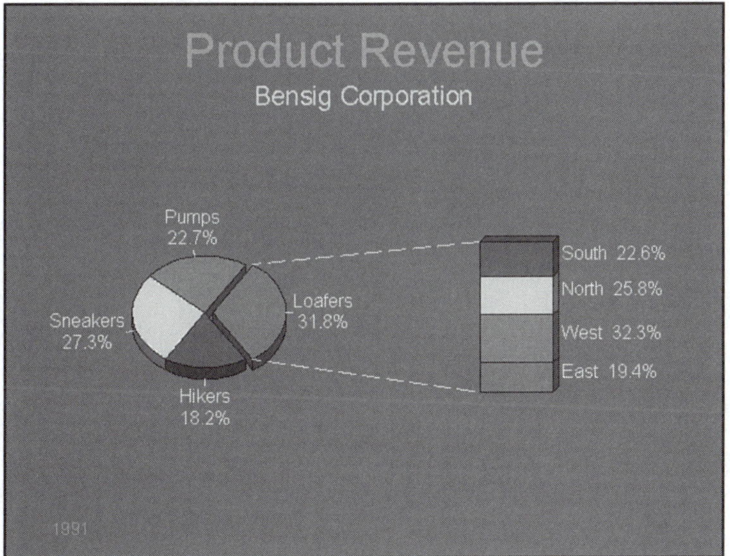

Fig. 8.12
Two pie charts linked together.

From Here...

This chapter presented many examples of charts you can create with Harvard Graphics. These examples showed you interesting and creative ways to present data with a chart. Along with each example, you read a brief description of the example, including how you can use the chart and where you can find information on creating the chart in other chapters of the book. The next chapter discusses Chart Makeovers, which turn a bland, simple chart into an effective and appealing chart.

Chapter 9

Chart Makeovers

Most of the chapters in this book explain how to use the many features of Harvard Graphics for Windows. These chapters are filled with instructions, tips, and advice to help you become an expert user, but creating effective presentations sometimes requires more than just drawing a box or modifying chart options. The default options for different slide types are designed to create appealing and presentable slides. Sometimes, however, your data just doesn't look right for these settings, and you end up with a slide that lacks features to grab your viewer's attention and present your information clearly. If you find yourself in this situation, your slide may benefit from a chart makeover.

In this chapter, you learn how to do the following:

- Transform a simple chart into an effective chart
- Evaluate your charts and then make improvements

Making over a chart involves examining the chart for fundamental problems and making changes to the data or chart options. This chapter shows you how to correct some basic problems by using three examples. You follow these examples that start with a simple bullet, bar, and pie chart, then improve the appearance of the chart to increase the effectiveness of the image. By reading this chapter, you learn the basic techniques for identifying problems and the types of changes you can make to help improve your chart. Even if your chart does not fit one of the three examples, you can apply the techniques you learn to almost any chart you create in Harvard Graphics.

To help you better evaluate the charts in this chapter, each chart is displayed in the color insert in this book. The same charts from the insert are displayed in black and white along with the steps and descriptions in this chapter. As you glance through the examples, you may wish to refer to the color charts to appreciate how the different options can exemplify your information.

Bullet Charts

A surprising number of slides in a presentation are text or bullet charts that present information such as sales goals or corporate objectives. On the surface, you may think that you cannot do much to improve a bullet chart except, perhaps, to change the font. Actually, you can do a great deal in addition to changing the font, including adjusting the wording, improving the colors, and adding graphics to visually improve the image. The chart in figure 9.1 is an example of a bullet chart that needs help. The chart is crowded with too much text and is generally unappealing.

Fig. 9.1
An unappealing bullet chart.

Sales Goals For The Bensig Corporation
For The Year 1991

- Increase Market Awareness For All Products
- Reach 110% of Sales Quota
- Obtain 5 New Accounts Per Region Of The Country
- Expand Into New Regions Throughout The Country

Design Note

Space and layout are two of the first areas you examine in a chart during a makeover. A crowded chart impairs the viewer's ability to discover the most significant information on the chart. Improving the layout also helps to focus attention on the most significant data.

The first change made to the bullet chart in figure 9.1 is to remove extraneous text. Your bullet items should be concise and to the point. You want your listeners to spend more time listening to you speak than reading the chart.

Also, if your viewers need to read too much during your presentation, they may become disinterested and bored. Figure 9.2 shows the same chart with much less text. To modify the text, double-click the chart body. See Chapter 7, "Working with Text," for more information on editing text.

Design Note

In any chart, use text that is precise and to the point. Your viewers should not have to read much or work too hard to comprehend the information on a slide.

Fig. 9.2
The same bullet chart with reduced text.

A bullet chart has nothing but text and bullet items. The next step in improving a bullet chart is to modify the text attributes. In Windows, use TrueType fonts for the best appearance when printing and displaying a ScreenShow on screen. Use colors that contrast well with the background and make sure the text is large enough to read from anywhere in your audience. Figure 9.3 displays the bullet chart with improved text and colors. With the **B**ackground command on the St**y**le menu, the chart background has been changed to a darker color, which makes the lighter text colors easier to see. The text has been changed to Times New Roman and the colors are more coordinated. All the text attributes were set with the A**l**l attributes... command on the **T**ext menu.

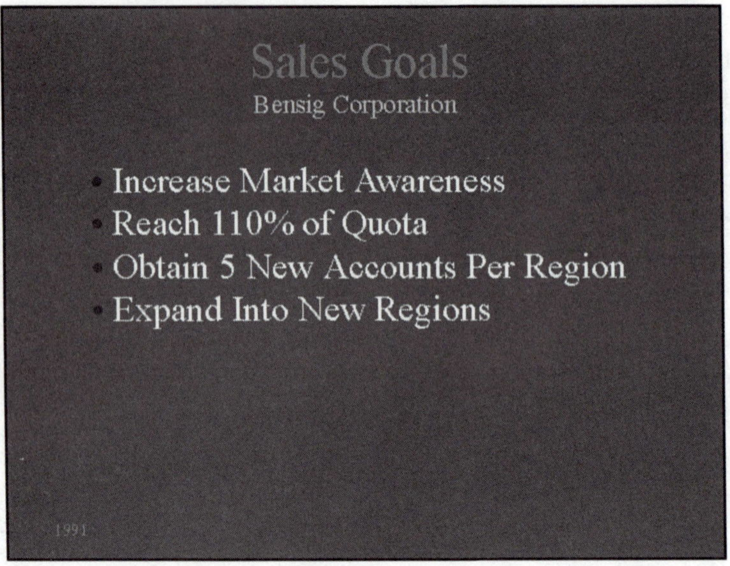

Fig. 9.3
A bullet chart with improved text attributes.

Notice in figure 9.3 that the bullets look out of place compared to the other colors and text on the chart. The bullets themselves are modified with the Set **b**ullet attributes... command on the **T**ext menu. With this command, you set the bullet size, type, color and the distance between the bullet and the text. Figure 9.4 shows the completed bullet chart. The bullet symbol has been changed to a triangle to make the chart a little more interesting. The color also has been changed to match other text in the chart.

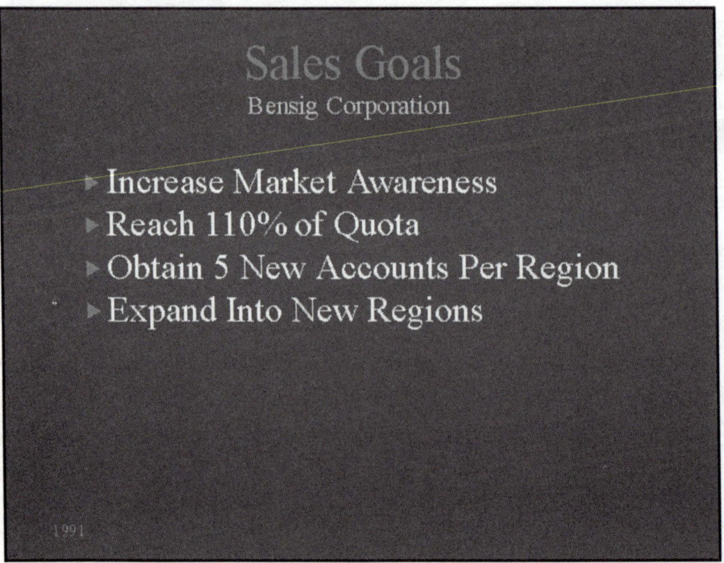

Fig. 9.4
A polished bullet chart complete with interesting bullets.

Vertical Bar Charts

A bar chart is one of the most common charts for presenting numeric data. Viewers interpret the data in the chart by comparing the heights of the bars. As opposed to bullet charts, you cannot always modify the data of a bar chart to improve the chart appearance. Therefore, most of the changes you make to a bar chart focus on cosmetic changes and modifying chart options. The chart in figure 9.5 is a bar chart created with the default Harvard Graphics options. The biggest problem with this chart is that it simply is plain and lacks some of the style associated with creations in a graphics product.

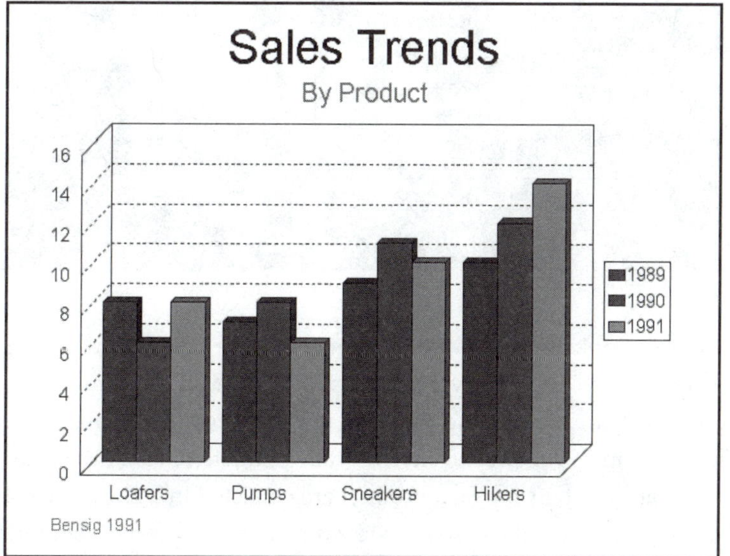

Fig. 9.5
A plain and unappealing bar chart.

Design Note

Use colors that are sharp and appealing. Brighter colors are easier to see. Make sure you stay with consistent colors such as reds and blues, pastels, or fluorescent colors. Just as a bland chart can be boring and difficult to read, mixing too many colors or using contrasting colors can make a chart difficult to read.

Figure 9.6 is the same bar chart with a different color scheme (see also the color insert). The colors are visually appealing and easy to see. To help emphasize the chart on the slide, the frame background of the chart is set to a lighter shade of gray. You can change the background color by selecting the chart and using the fill tool in the Slide Editor. You can change the bar colors using the **S**eries... command on the **C**hart menu, which is discussed in Chapter 5, "Creating XY Charts."

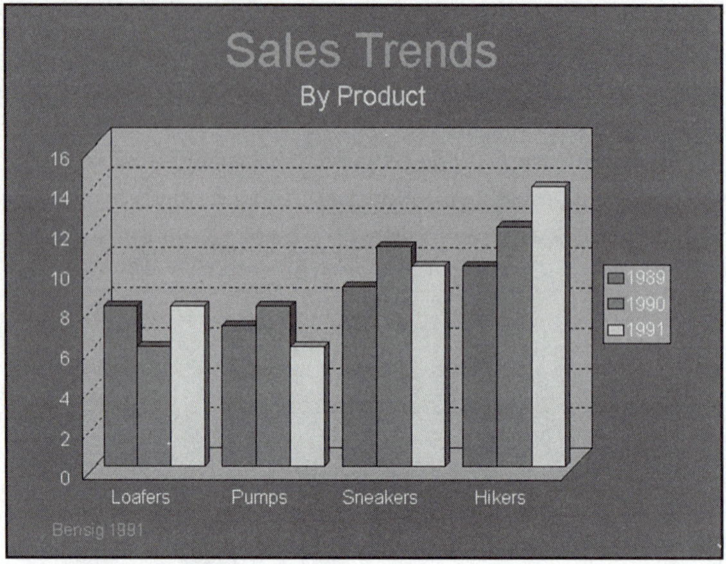

Fig. 9.6
A bar chart with appealing colors.

When viewers look at this chart, they can easily compare the sales for each product over the years. However, comparing all four products for a single year is not as easy. For example, the viewer may want to compare sales for Sneakers and Hikers in 1990. The bars in the chart in figure 9.6 are displayed in *cluster* format—the bars for each product are collected in a cluster. The bar chart in figure 9.7 uses the *overlap* style which creates a second method for comparing bars. You can examine product sales for any given year by comparing from left to right. You also can compare a single product over three years by comparing front to back. You change the bar style with the Chart **o**ptions... command on the **C**hart menu. With this command, you also set the depth of the floor, which was increased in figure 9.6 to make the bars in the back of the chart more visible. The bar depth and width also was modified to create the square bars in the chart. Information on changing all of these options is found in Chapter 5, "Creating XY Charts."

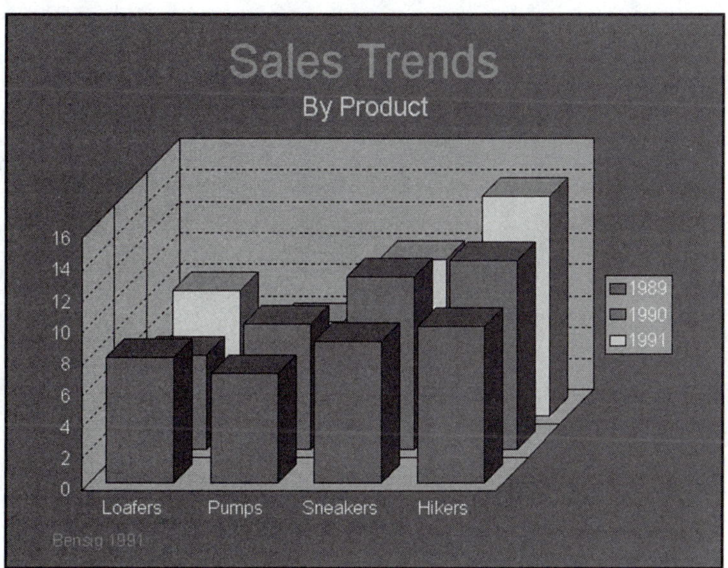

Fig. 9.7
A finished 3-D bar chart.

Pie Charts

Pie charts display data using slices. The larger the data value, the larger the slice in the pie. Of course, the slices do not mean anything without the labels displayed next to each slice. These labels identify the data behind the slice, like the products of the Bensig Shoe Corporation in figure 9.8. This chart suffers from problems similar to the other charts in this chapter. The chart is boring, colorless, and the entire slide has too much text.

With pie charts, the labels must share the same space as the pie. If your labels are too long, the pie chart must shrink to make room for the labels. The first change you should make is to edit the text. You double-click the chart to display the chart data form and edit the text. After you are finished editing, click the OK button to remove the data form.

Figure 9.9 is the same chart with reduced text. The viewers still can decipher what each slice represents. In fact, comparing the different slices is much easier because the size of the pie is larger. The next step is to improve the appearance of the chart by modifying chart colors. You easily can change the color for a slice by clicking one time to select the pie, clicking again to select a slice, and then using the fill tool to change the fill and outline colors for the slice (see fig. 9.10). See Chapter 6, "Creating Pie Charts," for more information.

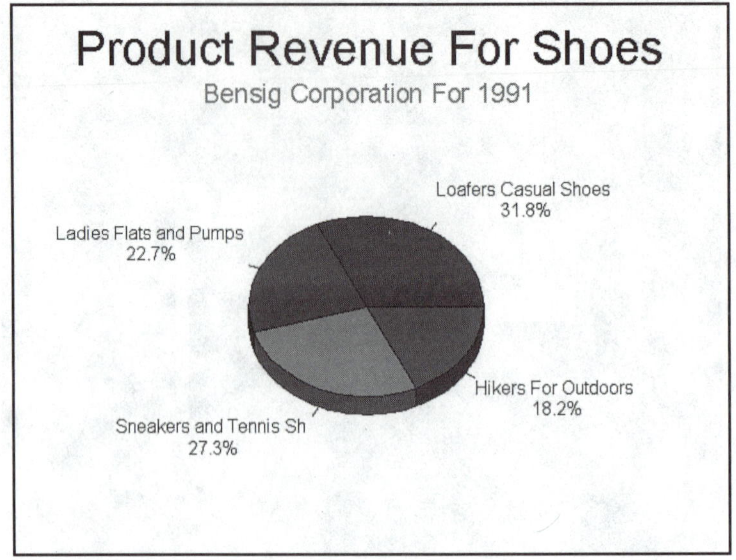

Fig. 9.8
A crowded pie chart with too much text.

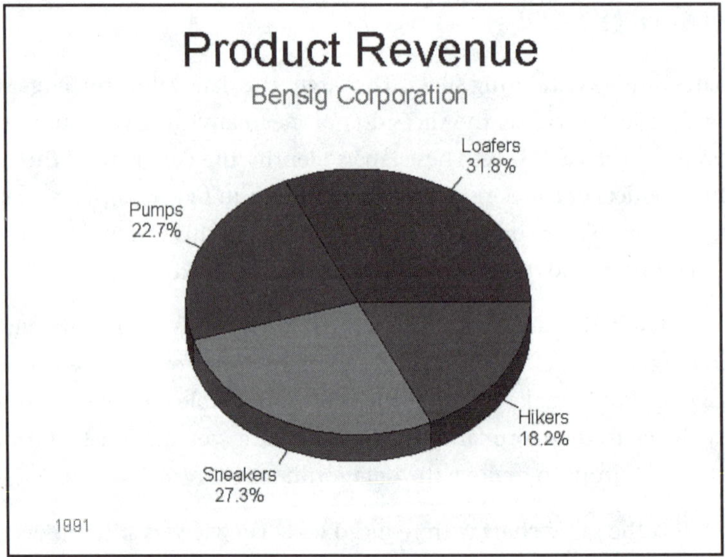

Fig. 9.9
An improved pie chart still somewhat bland.

Design Note

When modifying chart colors, make sure that you change the text as well to create a consistent appearance across all the elements of your chart.

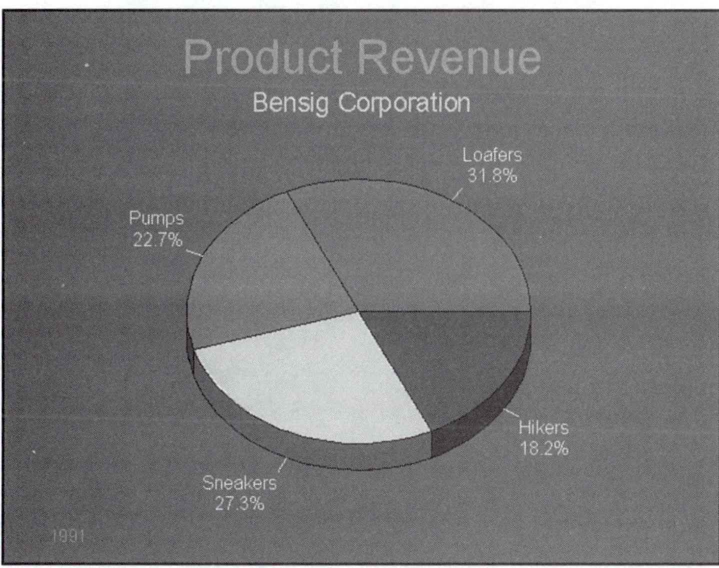

Fig. 9.10
A sharp pie chart with eye-catching colors.

Figure 9.11 displays one last modification to the original pie chart. The pointer drawn from each slice to the label is much longer than the pointers in previous examples. The longer lines further separate the labels from the slice and help spread the different chart elements throughout the slide. The chart is less crowded, which helps the viewers concentrate on the actual information.

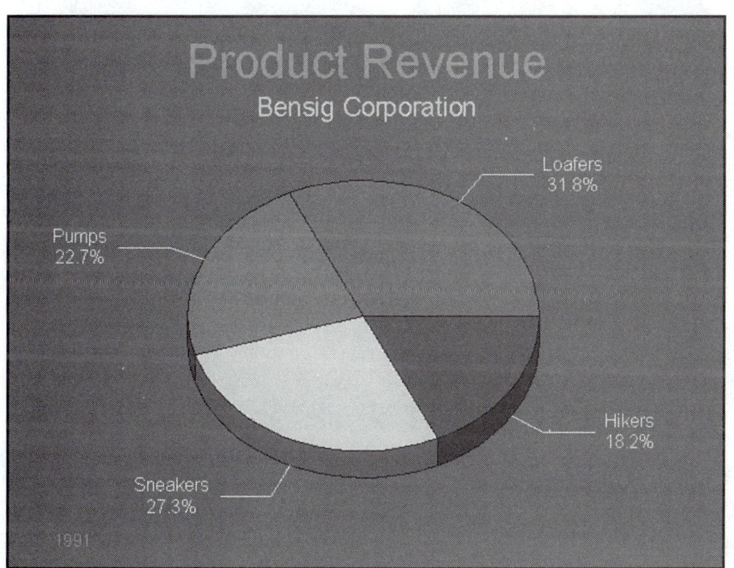

Fig. 9.11
A less-crowded chart with extended pointers.

From Here...

This chapter illustrates chart makeover techniques for improving chart appearance. For three different charts, you see how to identify problems in the chart. You learn how to correct these problems with different chart options to improve both the appearance and effectiveness of the chart. In the next part of the book, you learn how to use the slide sorter and outliner and how to draw and output with Harvard Graphics.

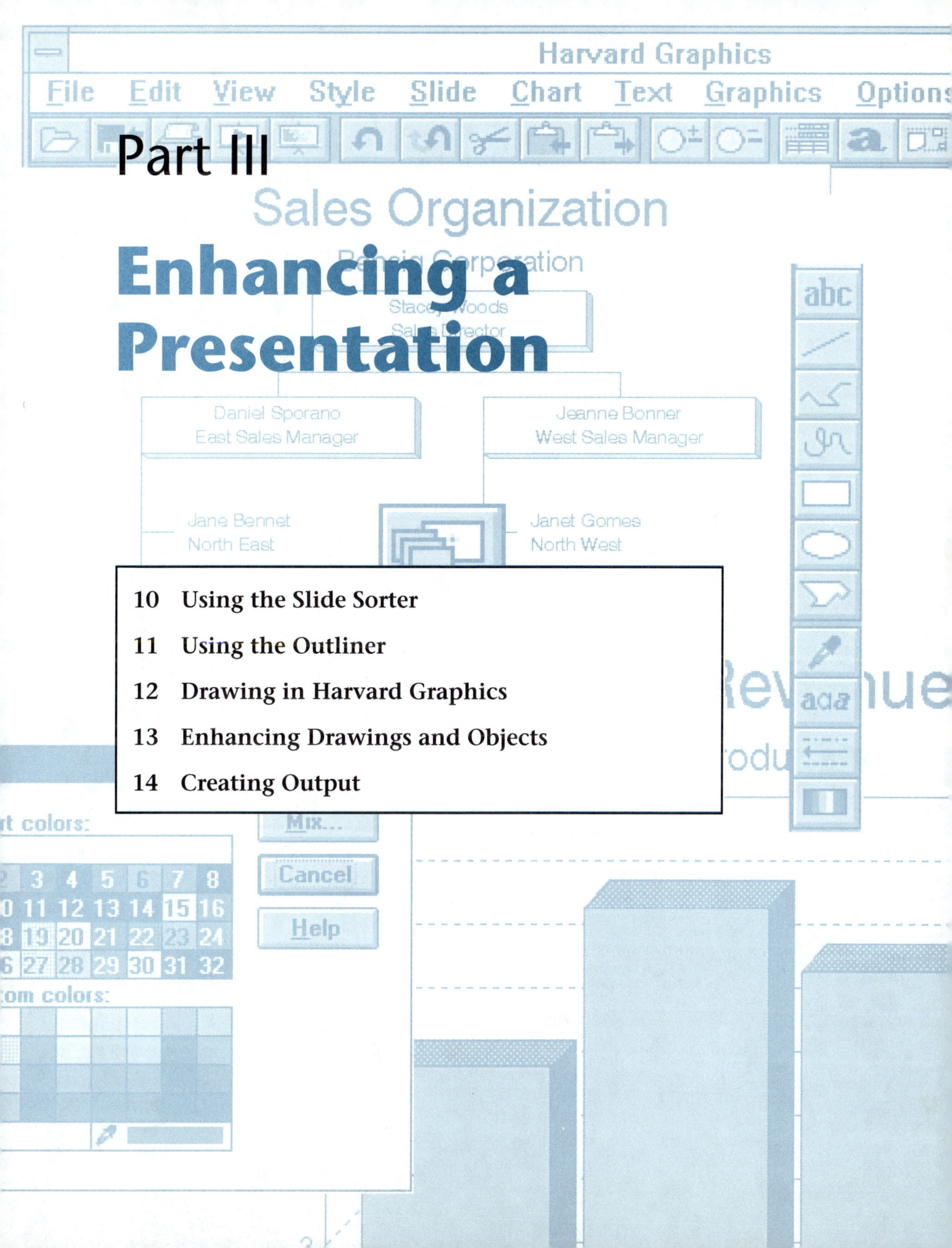

Part III

Enhancing a Presentation

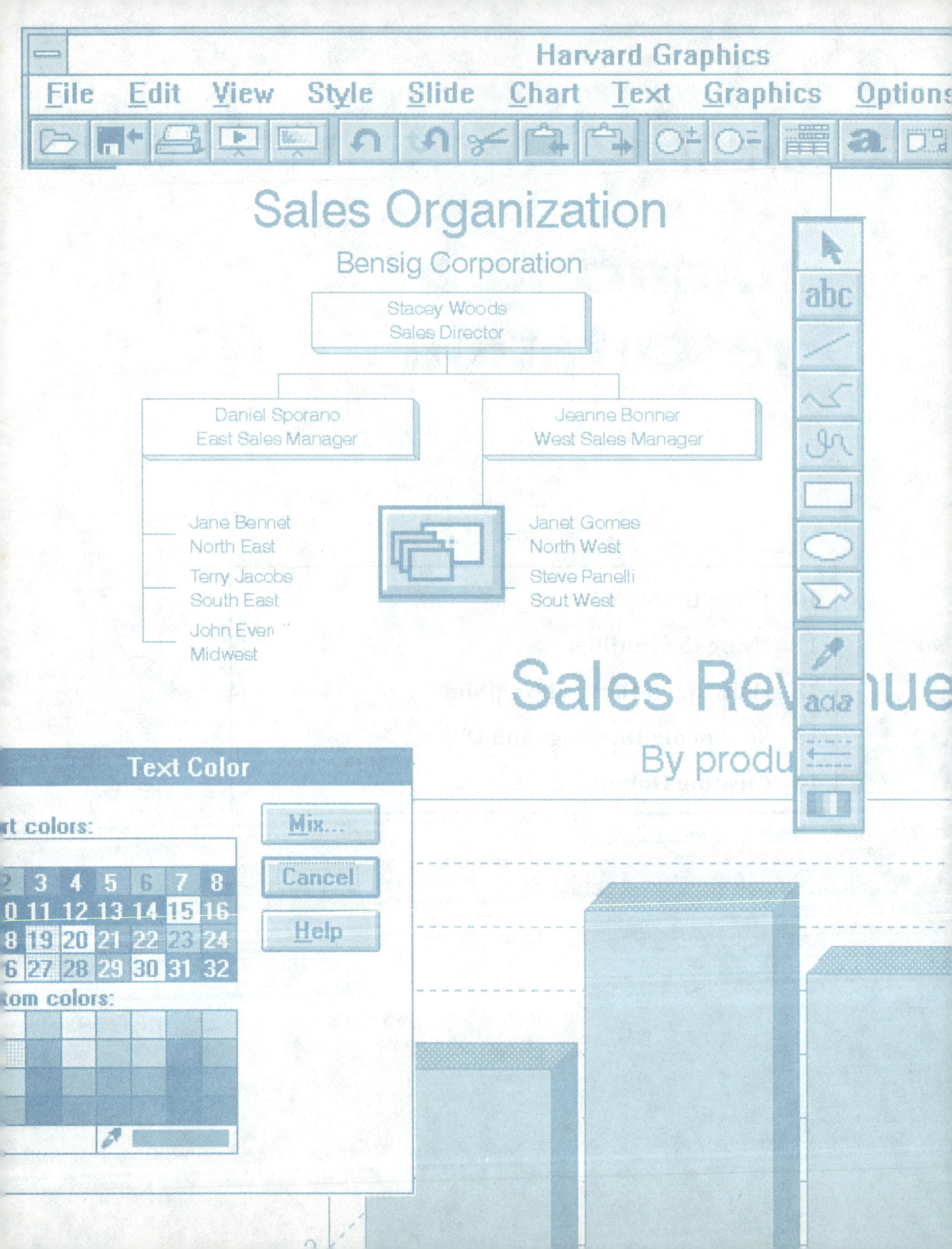

Harvard Graphics
File
Edit
View
Style
Slide
Chart
Text
Graphics
Sales Organization
Bensig Corporation
Stacey Woods
Sales Director
Daniel Sporano
East Sales Manager
Jeanne Bonner
West Sales Manager
Jane Bennet
North East
Terry Jacobs
South East
Midwest
Janet Gomes
North West
Steve Panelli
Sout West
Sales Rev
By produ
Text Color
Mix...
Cancel
Help

Chapter 10

Using the Slide Sorter

The *Slide Sorter* is a graphical environment that enables you to edit a presentation as you view the presentation slides. The Slide Sorter and the Outliner, discussed briefly later in this chapter and in greater detail in Chapter 11, "Using the Outliner," are the two features of Harvard Graphics in which you can edit an entire presentation.

In this chapter, you learn how to do the following:

- Edit a Presentation
- Use the Icon Editor
- Change the View

The Slide Sorter is analogous to the slide table you use with a slide projector. You place the slides in the projector in the order in which you want the audience to view the slides. You use a slide table to determine the order of the slides in the projector. The illuminated top of the table enables you to view many of the slides simultaneously. Harvard Graphics Slide Sorter is a computerized slide table. You can use the Slide Sorter to view many slides and to edit the order of the presentation.

Even though most text is too small to read, one advantage of using the Slide Sorter is that you can see all the information on each slide (the Slide Sorter window can contain miniature images for as many as 25 slides in a presentation) and evaluate the slide with a global view of the information. Another advantage of using the Slide Sorter is that you view all slides of your presentation, which gives you the opportunity to evaluate the effectiveness of your presentation's organization. The greatest advantage of using the Slide Sorter, however, is that it provides you with the opportunity not only to view your presentation, but also to rearrange, add, and remove slides from the presentation.

Figure 10.1 shows an example presentation in the Slide Sorter. In this figure, you easily can see the slides you create and the slide order in the presentation.

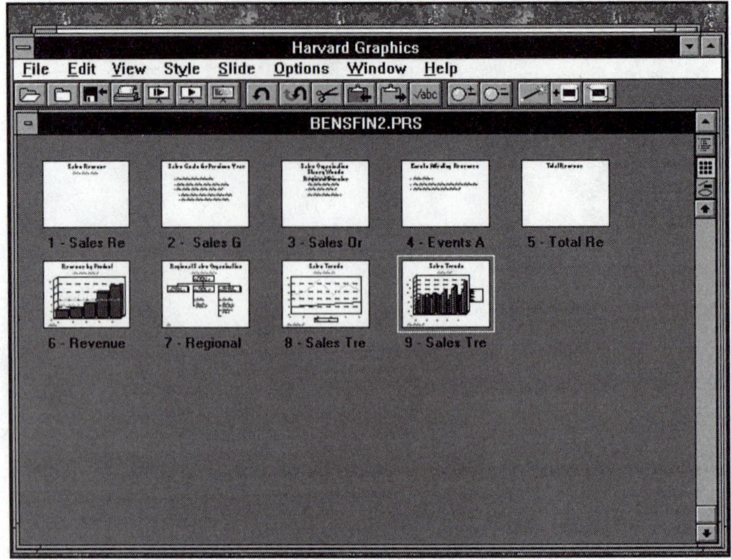

Fig. 10.1
A Slide Sorter

Understanding the Slide Sorter

In the Slide Sorter, which simplifies the process of editing your presentation, a miniature image of the slide represents each slide in a presentation. As you view the slides of your presentation, you can evaluate the organization of your presentation and change it if necessary. If you determine that a group of slides may be more effective near the beginning of the presentation, for example, you can drag those slides to the new location.

Figure 10.2 shows a typical slide presentation containing nine slides displayed in the Slide Sorter. Because of the graphical nature of the Slide Sorter, you easily can distinguish between text, organization, pie, and XY charts. Beneath each slide, Harvard Graphics displays the position number and the beginning of the slide's title. You can use the position number and the title to distinguish slides that are similar in appearance. In figure 10.2, the last slide in the figure is highlighted—surrounded by a box—indicating that this slide is the active slide.

With the Slide Sorter, you can see up to 25 slides of a presentation. If your presentation has more than 25 slides, you use the scroll bars on the right side of the window to scroll through the slides.

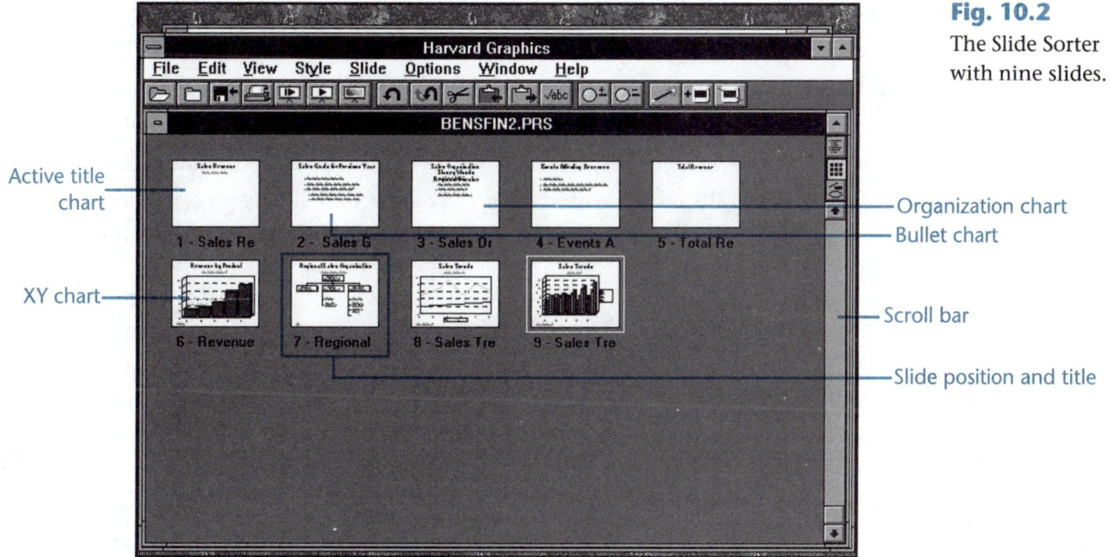

Fig. 10.2
The Slide Sorter with nine slides.

Editing a Presentation

You have several editing options in the Slide Sorter. You can edit the organization of your presentation by rearranging, relocating, or deleting selected slides. Editing in the Slide Sorter can be as simple as selecting a slide (clicking it) and moving the slide to a new location. In the Slide Sorter, you use common mouse techniques—clicking, double-clicking, and dragging—to edit your presentation.

In the Slide Sorter, you can change the arrangement and location of single or multiple slides. You can edit only active slides, however. This section explains how to make slides active and how to move, cut, copy, and paste slides in your presentation. In case you make a mistake while editing, this section also explains how you can undo your last action. (*Note:* The examples throughout this chapter make changes to the presentation shown in figure 10.2. Keep this in mind as you read the following sections.)

Selecting Slides

You can select one slide or a group of slides for editing in the Slide Sorter. To select a single slide, click the image of the slide. When you select a slide, Harvard Graphics highlights the image with a box. The slide surrounded by a box is the active slide.

Three methods of making multiple slides active exist: choosing Select all, Shift-clicking, and dragging a marquee. If you intend to select all slides in your presentation, the easiest way is to choose Select all from the Edit menu. Times may occur, however, when you want to choose several—but not all—slides in your presentation. If the slides you want to select are not adjacent, you can use the Shift-click method. You click each slide in the presentation while you hold down the Shift key. Using this method, you can select slides throughout the presentation.

The last method for selecting a group of slides involves dragging a marquee around the slides. The *marquee* is a dashed box that encompasses a group of objects (see fig. 10.3). With the marquee, you can select only adjacent slides.

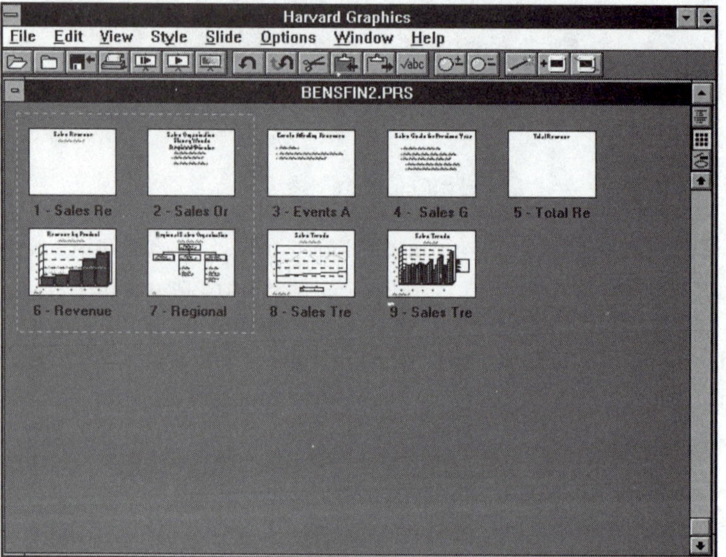

Fig. 10.3
Selecting a block of slides.

To select a block of slides by dragging a marquee around them, place the mouse pointer next to one of the slides in the group you intend to select. (Because the marquee begins at the location of the mouse pointer, you should place the mouse pointer on the outside edge of the first slide in the group.) Click and hold down the mouse button; then drag the marquee until the dashed line of the marquee touches—it does not have to encompass—all slides in the group. Release the button.

To select the slides in figure 10.3, for example, you click near the top left corner of slide 1; then drag the marquee diagonally across the other slides. Release the mouse button when slides 1, 2, 6, and 7 are within the marquee.

To deselect a slide or group of slides, you can click an unselected slide (the slide becomes active), or you click any empty area in the Slide Sorter window.

Rearranging Slides

You can rearrange slides in the Slide Sorter by dragging the slide to the new location. When you move the slide, the mouse pointer changes to a placeholder that resembles a small slide. Harvard Graphics displays the placeholder between slides to indicate the new position of the slide (see fig. 10.4). When you release the mouse button, the slide appears in its new location. Harvard Graphics rearranges and renumbers the other slides to accommodate the relocated slide.

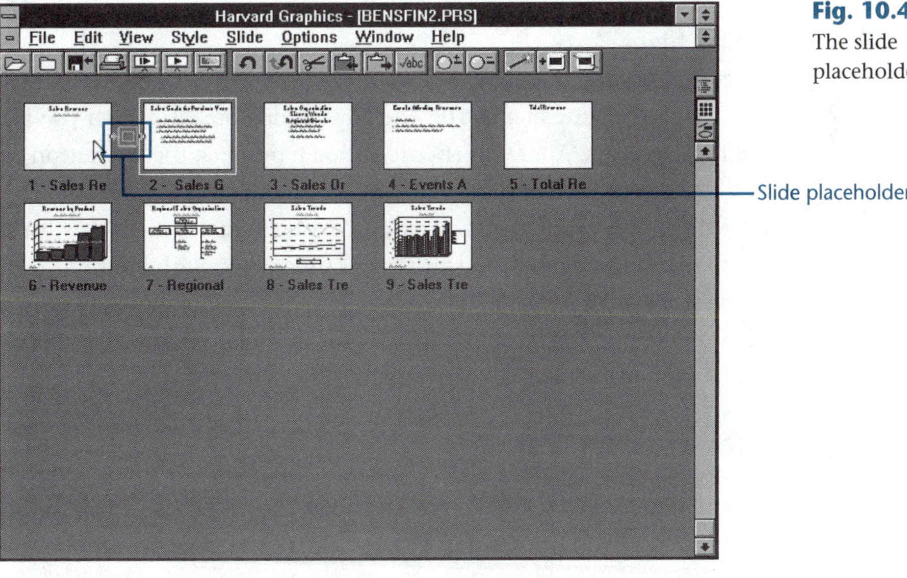

Fig. 10.4
The slide placeholder.

You can move more than one slide at a time. To move several slides, you first must select the slides. (For information on selecting a group of slides, see the preceding section, "Selecting Slides.") Although moving a group of slides is relatively easy, you can move only a group of *consecutive* slides. You cannot move the slides highlighted in figure 10.3, for example, because although they are adjacent, these slides are not consecutive. You could move the group, however, if the slides in positions 3, 4, and 5 also were selected.

To move consecutive slides, you use the same technique that you use to move a single slide. Place the mouse pointer on one of the group slides and drag the slide to the new location. The slide placeholder indicates the new location of the slides. When you release the mouse button, the group of slides appears in the new location.

If you want to move slides 2, 3, and 4 to follow slide 7 in the presentation, for example, follow these steps:

1. While holding down the Shift key, click slides 2, 3, and 4. As you click each slide, Harvard Graphics highlights the slide.

2. Place the mouse pointer on any of the slides and drag the mouse pointer until the placeholder appears between slides 7 and 8.

3. Release the mouse button. Slides 2, 3 and 4 appear in the new location.

Adding Slides

You can add slides to a presentation in the Slide Sorter by choosing Add slide... from the Slide menu. The Add Slide dialog box, in which you pick a slide type, appears. After you choose a slide type, click the OK button to add the slide to your presentation. Harvard Graphics places the new slide after the active slide in the Slide Sorter. Harvard Graphics creates the slide with sample data so that you can see how this type of slide works with your presentation. See the section "Adding Slides to a Presentation" in Chapter 2, "Learning Harvard Graphics for Windows Basics," for more information on this dialog box.

Deleting Slides

In the Slide Sorter, you can delete one slide or a group of slides. To delete slides, you first must select the slides. Unlike moving slides, however, the slides you delete do not have to be consecutive in the presentation. After you select the slides to be deleted, you must decide what method of deletion to use.

Two methods of deleting slides from a presentation exist: you can clear slides from the presentation, or you can cut slides to the Windows Clipboard. To clear the slides from the presentation, use the Clear command from the Edit menu or press Del; Harvard Graphics removes the selected slides from the presentation. To keep a copy of the slides in the Clipboard, however, you can use the Cut command from the Edit menu; Harvard Graphics removes the slides from the presentation and stores them in the Windows Clipboard.

Copying and Moving Slides

In the slide sorter, Harvard Graphics does not limit you to rearranging slides in a single presentation. You also can place copies of slides in the same presentation or transfer the slides to other presentations. To show a particular group of slides at the beginning of your presentation and again at the end of the presentation to recap the material, for example, you can copy the slides from the beginning of the presentation and paste them at the end. You also may want to copy a common set of slides between presentations to avoid creating the slides from scratch. In this section, you learn to use three commands from the Edit menu: Copy, Cut, and Paste. With these commands, you can duplicate and rearrange many slides in a presentation.

The Copy and Cut commands from the Edit menu are similar and easy to confuse. One important difference does exist, however. When you use the Copy command, Harvard Graphics stores a duplicate of the slide in the Clipboard, and the original slide remains intact. When you use the Cut command, Harvard Graphics removes (cuts) the original slide and places it in the Clipboard. Keep this important difference in mind as you read the rest of this section.

You must select the slides before you can copy or cut them. (Refer to "Selecting Slides" for instructions on selecting one or many slides.) You use the same technique to cut or copy slides. After you select the slides, choose Copy if you want the original to remain intact and a duplicate placed in the Clipboard. Choose Cut if you want to remove the slide from the presentation and store it in the Clipboard.

Caution

The contents of the Windows Clipboard remain intact only until you store something else in the Clipboard or exit Harvard Graphics, at which time all information stored in the Clipboard is lost.

After you use the Copy or Cut command to store a slide in the Clipboard, you can use the Paste command from the Edit menu to place a copy of the slide(s) in the original presentation or another presentation. When you use the Paste command, Harvard Graphics inserts the copied slides after the active slide in the presentation. If no slide is active, Harvard Graphics places the slide at the end of the presentation.

Follow these steps to paste a group of slides in the current presentation:

1. Select the appropriate slides as discussed earlier.

2. Choose **C**opy or Cu**t** from the Edit menu. Harvard Graphics stores the selected slide in the Clipboard.

   (Remember, if you choose **C**opy, the original slide remains intact; if you choose Cu**t**, Harvard Graphics removes the original slide.)

3. In the Slide Sorter, click the slide that the pasted slide should follow.

4. Choose Paste Slide(s) from the Edit menu. Harvard Graphics places the copied slide at the specified location.

You also can paste slides into other presentations. To transfer slides, you must open both presentations—the source and target presentation—using the Open command on the File menu. (See Chapter 2, "Learning Harvard Graphics for Windows Basics," for instructions on opening a presentation.) Both presentations—the target and source—must be shown in the Slide Sorter.

The Window menu lists all open presentations (see fig. 10.5). To access another presentation, choose the presentation's name from the Window menu; if the view of the active window is not the Slide Sorter, choose Slide Sorter from the View menu. To transfer slides between presentation, cut or copy the slides in the source presentation, switch to the target presentation, and execute the Paste command.

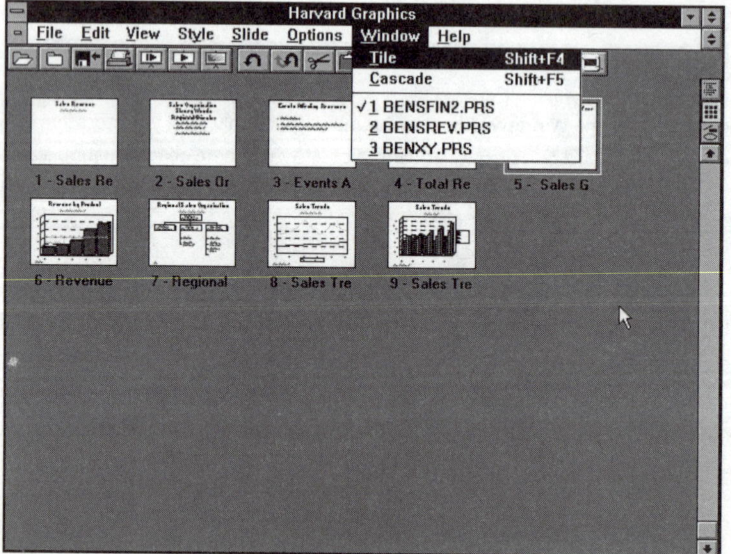

Fig. 10.5
The Window menu.

Follow these steps to transfer a slide between presentations:

1. Use the **O**pen command from the File menu to open both presentations, if you have not done so already.

2. Select the source presentation in the Window menu. The source is the presentation *from which* you copy or cut the slide.

3. If you are not viewing the presentation in the Slide Sorter, choose Slide Sorter from the View menu.

4. In the Slide **S**orter, select the slide you want to copy or move.

5. Choose **C**opy from the Edit menu to copy the slides from the source presentation; choose Cu**t** to remove the slides from the source presentation.

   Harvard Graphics stores the slide temporarily in the Clipboard. (Remember, the slide remains in the Clipboard until you store something else there or until you exit the program.)

6. Choose the target presentation in the Window menu. The target is the presentation *to which* you want to move the slide.

7. If you are not viewing the target presentation in the Slide Sorter, choose Slide **S**orter from the View menu.

8. Click the slide that the pasted slide should follow.

9. Choose Paste Slide(s) from the Edit menu. Harvard Graphics inserts the slide into the specified location in the target presentation.

When you copy a slide from one presentation to another, Harvard Graphics copies the background from the slide as well When you copy the slide, Harvard Graphics checks the target presentation to see whether a background with the same name as the slide's background exists. If Harvard Graphics finds a background with the same name, the Paste Background dialog box appears (see fig. 10.6). Using this dialog box, you change the slide's background or rename the background.

To rename the background, click the Rename button and type the name in the text box. To change the slide background to that of the presentation, click the use current presentation's background button. Then click OK to paste the slide.

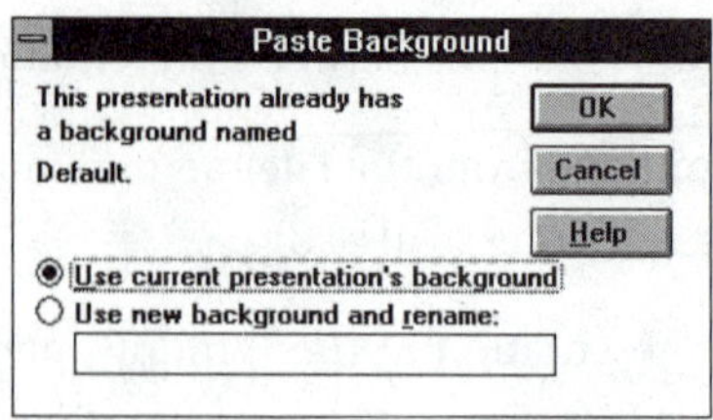

Fig. 10.6
The Paste Background dialog box.

Undoing a Change

As you work with a presentation, you may find that a change you made was not what you wanted. The Undo command on the Edit menu reverses the most recent change you made to a presentation. If you select a large group of slides and mistakenly clear them from the presentation, for example, you simply choose Undo from the Edit menu; the deleted slides reappear. Keep in mind, however, that the Undo command can reverse the *most recent* change only. All other changes are permanent.

Using the Slide Sorter Icon Bar

As presented in previous chapters, the icon bar is also available for use in the Slide Sorter. For example, to cut a slide and have it copied to the clipboard using the Cut icon:

1. Select the slide you want to copy to the clipboard.
2. Click the Cut icon (scissors). Please keep in mind that the slide you just selected will be removed from the current slide sorter display and placed in the clipboard, available for pasting in the current or another presentation.

Tip
To help you determine which icon you need, Harvard Graphics displays the name of each icon in the Window title when you first move the mouse over the icon.

Changing the View

Although you can perform many editing functions in the Slide Sorter, occasions may occur in which the Slide Sorter does not meet your editing needs. Other views—the Outliner and Slide Editor—are available.

You can use the Outliner to edit the slides of a presentation. The Outliner is like the Slide Sorter in that it enables you to see all the slides in your presentation; however, unlike the Slide Sorter, in the Outliner, you can only see textual information, such as the data in a bullet chart or the title of a pie chart. Chapter 11, "Using the Outliner," teaches you how to add slides and edit the data for text charts in the Outliner.

If the slides in your presentation are mostly text charts, you may prefer to use the Outliner to edit the presentation. If your presentations contain numeric charts, the Slide Sorter is more useful for editing the presentation.

The Slide Editor enables you to edit and add graphical objects to individual slides of a presentation. Unlike the Slide Sorter or the Outliner, in the Slide Editor, you can work with a single slide only. You access the Slide Editor from the Slide Sorter window by double-clicking the slide you intend to edit.

The View menu lists each view (Slide Sorter, Slide Editor, and Outliner). To change the view of a presentation, select the appropriate view from the menu. You also can change the view by using the view icons displayed on the right side of the Slide Sorter window. The Outliner and Slide Editor windows also display these icons, shown in figure 10.7. To change the view by using the icons, click the appropriate icon: to view the presentation in the Outliner, click the Outliner; to view the active slide in the Slide Editor, click the Slide Editor icon.

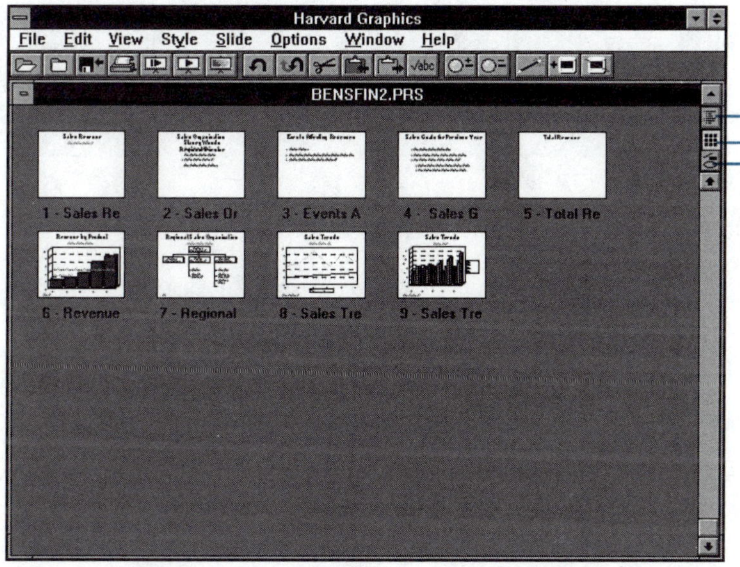

Fig. 10.7
The View icons.

Showing Slide Jackets

For slides shown in a projector, each slide is a photograph enclosed in a white jacket. You also can display jackets around the slides in the Slide Sorter. Figure 10.8 shows the Slide Sorter slides with jackets. One advantage of showing the jackets is that each slide has more space. The extra space is helpful for selecting and moving slides, and the jackets also emphasize the active slide, which is white in the figure. One disadvantage of displaying slide jackets, however, is that the Slide Sorter can display fewer slides.

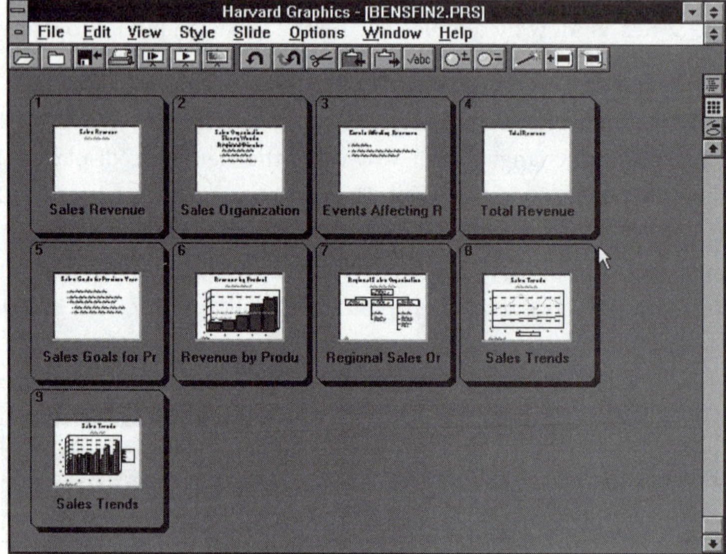

Fig. 10.8
The Slide Sorter showing slide jackets.

To view the jackets in the Slide Sorter, follow these steps:

1. Choose **D**isplay... from the Options menu. The Display Options dialog box appears.

2. In the Display Options dialog box, click the Show jackets in Slide Sorter box so that an X appears.

3. Click the OK button to accept the changes.

From Here...

This chapter covers the Slide Sorter, which you use to edit the organization of a presentation. In this chapter, you learned how to change the order of your slides and how to delete slides from a presentation. You also learned how to copy slides and how to move slides to a different presentation. The chapter ends with an explanation of how to change the view of a presentation and how to show slide jackets in the Slide Sorter.

The next chapter, Chapter 11, "Using the Outliner," explains how to create and edit a presentation in the Outliner, which is another view in which you can edit your entire presentation.

Chapter 11

Using the Outliner

When you create a presentation, you assemble a collection of slides that show, in one fashion or another, information relevant to your audience. Although an audience sees the finished product—a professional-quality slide show that illustrates your data and information—the audience does not see the process, the time, and the effort spent creating these images. You can use a program like Harvard Graphics, which enhances your ability to create presentations, to produce an effective and informative presentation with less effort.

Harvard Graphics provides a feature—the Outliner—that you can use to create presentations. The Outliner enables you to do more than simply create slides, however. The great advantage of the Outliner is that you use it throughout the entire creation process. You use the Outliner to store ideas as they come to you, reorganize and subordinate the ideas into topics, and—from these topics—create slides. In other words, you transform your thoughts and ideas into a presentation with the Outliner.

The primary difference between using the Outliner and the Slide Sorter—another Harvard Graphics slide creation feature—for example, is in the way you translate the information into slides. The Outliner enables you to take a free form approach to building presentations. Unlike other presentation views, you do not have to choose a slide type prior to creating the slides. With the Outliner, you enter information as topics in the outline; these topics ultimately become the titles and textual data in your slides.

The goal of this chapter is to introduce you to the Outliner. To demonstrate the concepts covered, a sample presentation is provided. Although this sample illustrates only one way you can use the Outliner, it gives you a solid foundation on which to expand your knowledge of the Outliner. You will learn how to create and edit a presentation, using common and

In this chapter, you learn how to do the following:

- Create a presentation by using the Outliner
- Add and move topics within your presentation
- Edit topics of your presentation in the Outliner

not-so-common Harvard Graphic features. When you complete this chapter, you will be able to create a professional-quality presentation.

Understanding the Outliner

You use the same basic steps to create a presentation whether you use the Outliner or pen and paper. You decide on an objective, gather data, organize the data as appropriate, enhance the slides, and critically evaluate your presentation. You can perform all these tasks within the Outliner. To use the Outliner effectively, you must understand the functions of the Outliner and the Outliner window.

Figure 11.1 shows a presentation in the Outliner. The Outliner numbers each slide, and the slide icon next to the number indicates the type of chart—text, organization, or data—the slide contains. A topic icon (the triangular symbol) indicates each topic, and subtopics are indented below a topic. The *active* topic is designated by a box that contains the insertion point. Notice in figure 11.1 that a box surrounds the first slide and that the insertion point immediately precedes the word Sales. The box and insertion indicate the *active* slide—the slide you can edit, move, or delete.

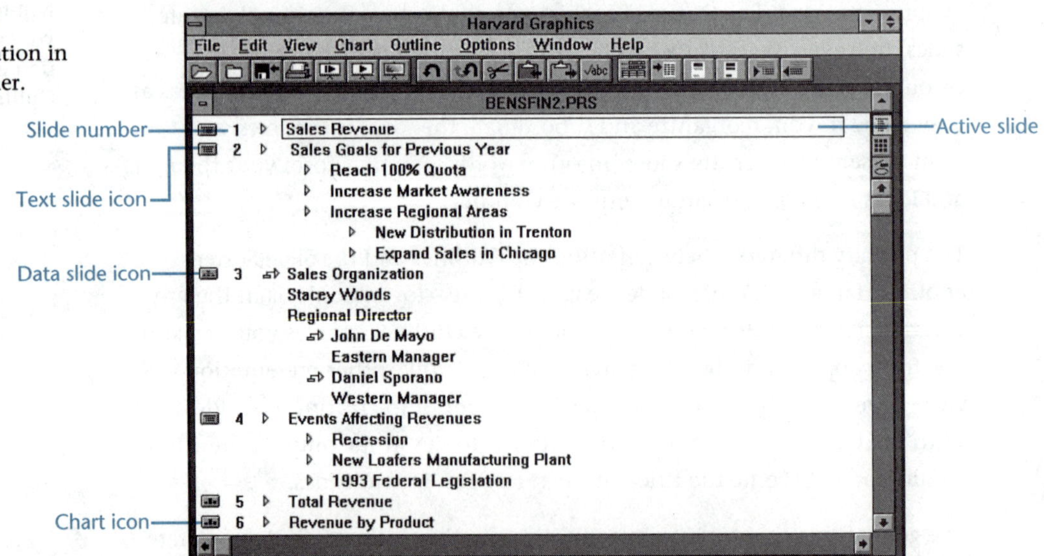

Fig. 11.1
A presentation in the Outliner.

You can understand a great deal about presentations in the Outliner by examining figure 11.1. The number and slide icons appear next to topics that are slides. You can tell the slide (chart) type—bullet, organization, data—by the slide icon. In figure 11.1, for example, an organization icon appears beside slide 3, and data icons appear beside slides 5 and 6.

Each line in the outline is a topic. In fact, topics, which comprise the body of your outline, represent the textual data in your presentation. In the Outliner, certain topics represent slides, and the topic's text is the title of the slide.

A topic's indentation determines its level. The leftmost topics are at the topmost level in a presentation, and indented topics are subordinate. All *subtopics* (indented slides) below a slide topic appear as the slide's data. Slide 2 of figure 11.1, for example, is a bullet chart, and the subtopics are the bullet items of the chart. Slide 3 is an organization chart, and the subtopics are the members of the organization.

Creating a Presentation

Your objective in using the Outliner is to create a presentation. Unlike the Slide Sorter or Slide Editor, in which you first must decide on a chart type and then enter the chart data, the Outliner enables you to lay out your presentation before determining the types of the slides.

This section presents a sample presentation created with the Outliner. As you read this section and study the accompanying figures, keep in mind that this sample is just an example of how a presentation can evolve in the Outliner. The flexibility of the Outliner enables you to be creative as you produce a presentation. When you become more proficient with the features of the Outliner, you may develop your own style of creating a presentation.

The first step in creating a presentation is "jotting down" all topics that are pertinent to your presentation. Because the Outliner enables you to rearrange your topics later, you should not concern yourself with organization at this point. In fact, worrying about organization may inhibit the free flow of ideas.

Figure 11.2 shows a list of random presentation ideas entered as topics in the Outliner. These topics, derived at a brainstorming session for a presentation on sales and revenues of the Bensig Corporation, must be covered in the presentation; however, not all the topics should become individual slides. As you create your presentation, you rearrange, combine, and elevate or subordinate your topics as necessary. In the example presentation, many of the topics shown in figure 11.2 will be combined in bullet charts.

The section "Adding Topics and Subtopics" explains how to enter ideas as topics in a presentation.

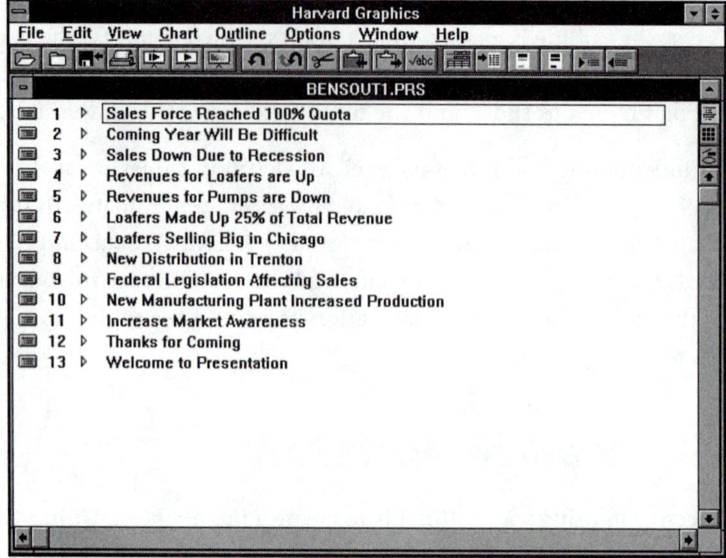

Fig. 11.2
The beginning of a new presentation.

The next step in creating a presentation involves arranging the topics into logical groups that follow a progressive order. Figure 11.3 shows one possible arrangement. (The blank topics were added to illustrate the division of groups.) The four topics that relate to sales achievements of the previous year are covered near the beginning of the presentation as an introduction to the revenue data. The three topics in the second group, factors that affected company revenue, are covered next. The revenue data is covered in the third group, and the presentation ends with projections for the next year.

Figure 11.4 shows a more complete version of the presentation, which now contains six slides. The first slide contains a title chart that introduces the theme of the presentation. The following slides provide information on sales achievements in the last year, events that affected sales throughout the year, and the year's revenue. The final slide is a bullet chart that presents closing remarks to the audience.

Using the Outliner, you can do more than rearrange your topics. You also can add and edit individual slides. Figure 11.5 shows the final version of the presentation on Bensig Corporation sales revenue, in which individual slides have been edited. Notice the changes in slide titles and subtopics.

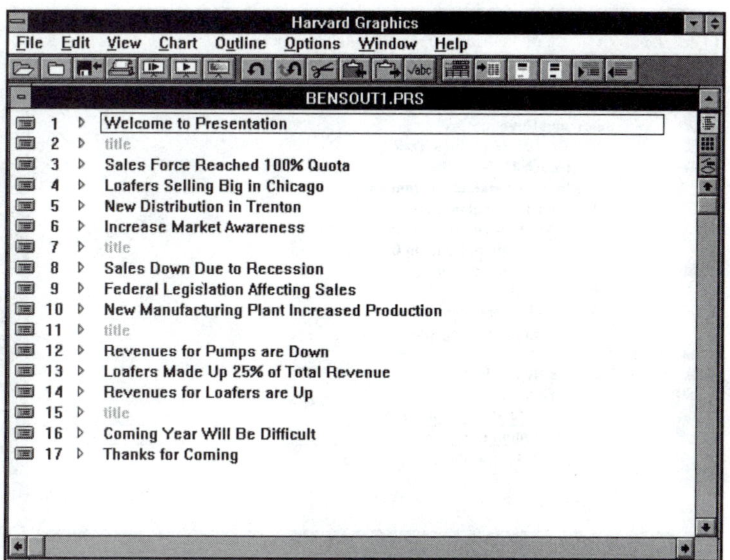

Fig. 11.3
A presentation with organized topics.

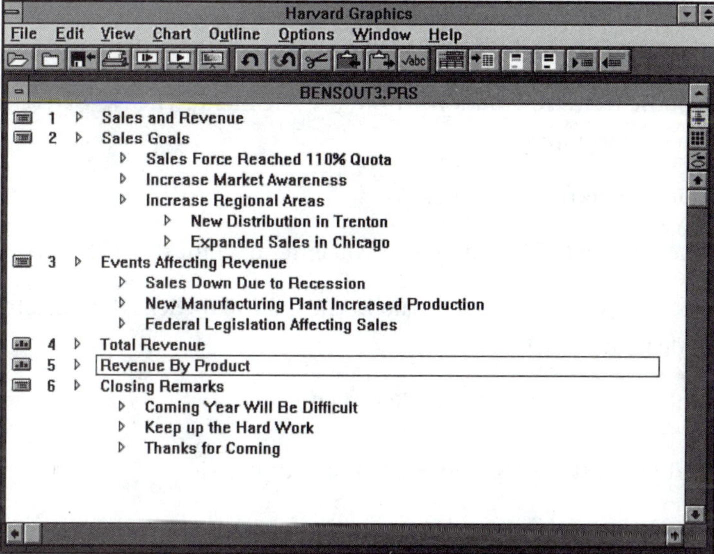

Fig. 11.4
A more refined version of the presentation.

In the following sections, you learn how to reorganize, edit, and add charts to your presentation so that your chart, although not the same in content, conveys the same professional quality as the sample presentation.

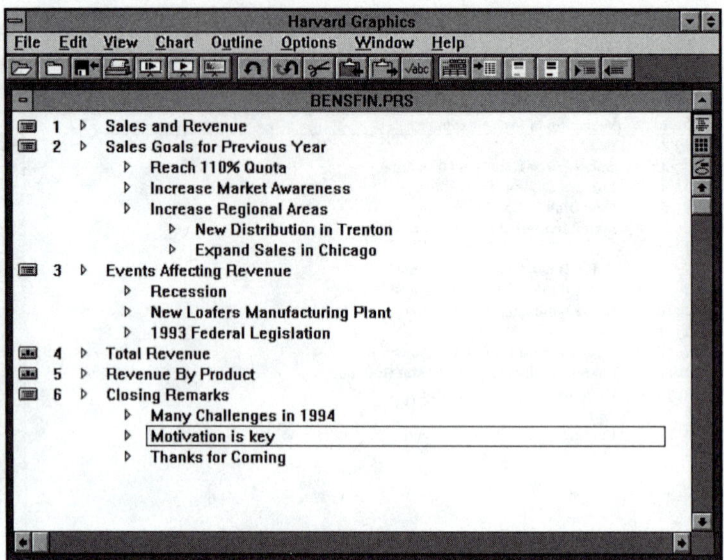

Fig. 11.5
The final version of the presentation.

Beginning a New Presentation

To start a new presentation in the Outliner, follow these steps:

1. Choose **N**ew Presentation... from the File menu. The New Presentation dialog box appears.

2. Click OK in the dialog box.

   The chart data form, in which you enter data for the first slide, appears.

3. Because you will enter all data in the Outliner, click OK to create the slide without data.

4. Choose **O**utliner from the View menu.

The chart you just created appears in the Outliner view.

Adding Topics and Subtopics

If you discover that the topics listed in your early outline do not cover fully the information you must convey, you can add new topics to the Outliner. Harvard Graphics inserts new topics below the active topic. By default, slides you create in the Outliner contain bullet charts; the main topic is the title and any subtopics are the bullet items. See "Adding a Chart to a Slide" for instructions on changing the chart type.

To create a new topic below the active topic, press Enter. If the active topic is at the topmost level, the new topic becomes a subtopic of the slide; otherwise, Harvard Graphics creates the new topic at the same level as the preceding topic. You can change the level of topics and subtopics; see "Changing the Level of a Topic" for more information.

If the active topic does not contain data, pressing Enter increases the level of the active topic; it does not create a new topic. You can add successive slides quickly by clicking a topic that represents a slide, pressing Enter once to create a new topic, and then pressing Enter a second time to increase the level of the topic and make a new slide.

Follow these steps to add topics to your presentation:

1. Click the topic that the new topic should follow. If you created a new presentation, click the first topic. The topic you click becomes the active topic.

2. Press Enter. Harvard Graphics creates a new topic.

   The topic you create is a subtopic of the preceding slide. You must elevate your new topic, which is now active, to a slide.

3. Press Enter until the topic is at the topmost level. At the top level, Harvard Graphics displays the slide icon next to the topic.

4. Type the text of the topic. Because the first topic is the title of the slide, type the title of your presentation.

5. Press Enter. Because the active slide contains text, pressing Enter here creates a subtopic.

6. Press the Enter key again to elevate the subtopic to a slide.

7. Type the text of the topic for the slide.

8. Repeat steps 5 through 7 for each slide in the presentation. For your sample presentation, you can create as many slides as you want.

Creating Multiline Topics

The topics you create in the Outliner can be more than one line long. When you enter text that exceeds the first line, Harvard Graphics automatically wraps the text to a new line. To create a new line without filling the preceding line, however, you must press Ctrl-Enter. When you press Ctrl-Enter, Harvard Graphics creates the line and moves all the text following the insertion point to the beginning of the new line.

Follow these steps to add a new line to a topic:

1. Click the topic to which you want to add a new line of text.
2. Press the End key to move the insertion point to the end of the topic. (If the insertion point is in the middle of the text, Harvard Graphics places the text following the insertion point on the new line.)
3. Press Ctrl-Enter. Harvard Graphics creates a new line.

You now can type information on either topic line.

Figure 11.6 shows a subtopic (New Loafers Manufacturing Plant) containing two lines of text. A topic symbol appears next to the first line only. This subtopic is a bullet item in a bullet chart. In the chart, only one bullet symbol appears for both lines.

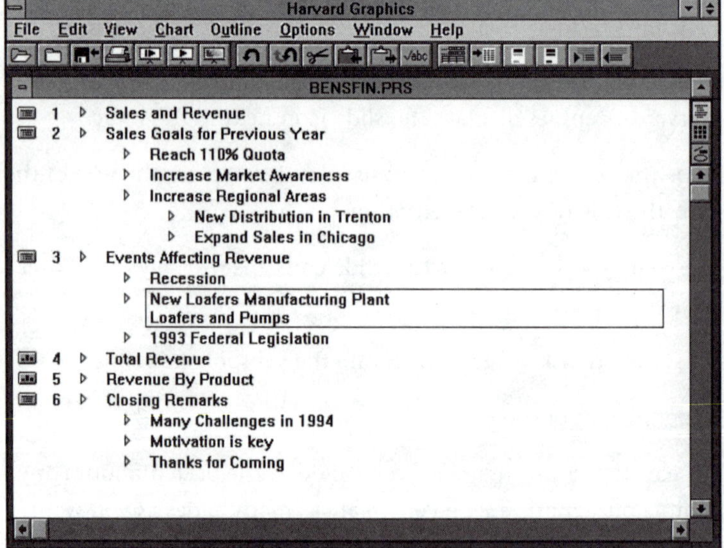

Fig. 11.6
A multiline subtopic.

Adding a Chart to a Slide

In previous chapters, you learned about the charts available in Harvard Graphics: *data charts*, which consist of pie and XY charts; *organization charts* on which you plot the organizational hierarchy of a business or association;

and *text charts*, which include title and bullet charts. Harvard Graphics enables you to enter any of these chart types into your presentation in the Outliner.

In the Outliner, you create bullet charts by adding subtopics to the outline, and you add organization charts by changing bullet charts (discussed in the following section, "Creating Organization Charts"). You add title and data charts by using the Add chart to slide... command on the Chart menu.

As explained in an earlier section, the slide icon shows the type of chart the slide contains. When you add a chart to a topic, the slide icon changes to reflect the new chart type. When you add a pie chart to a slide, for example, the slide becomes a data chart slide, and the slide icon changes to a data slide icon. In the sample presentation, slide 5 changed from a data slide icon to a text slide icon (see fig. 11.7). Although you can add more than one chart to a slide, the slide icon represents the first chart only.

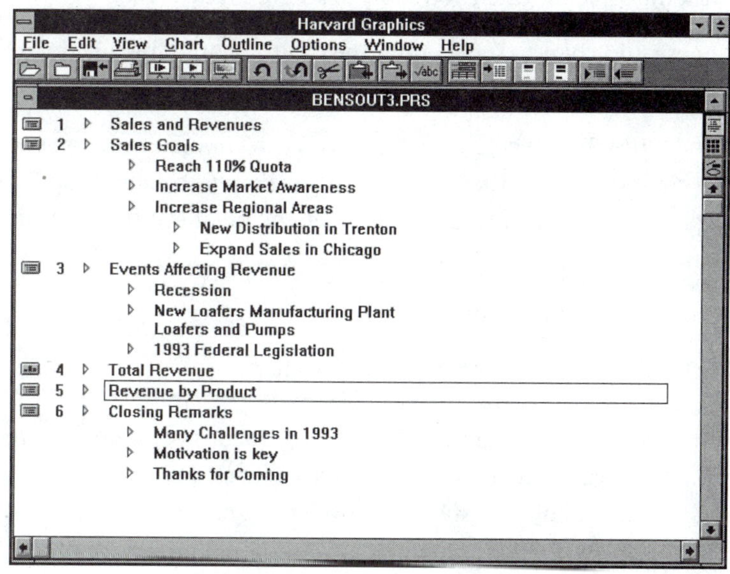

Fig. 11.7
An outline with data and text charts.

Most of the charts in your presentation probably will be data charts. To add a data chart, you use the Add chart to slide... command from the Chart menu. When you add a data chart to the slide, the topic becomes the title of the chart, and the slide icon changes to a data slide icon. Figure 11.7 shows the revenue presentation; in the presentation, slide 4 contains a data chart (notice the data slide icon).

Although you can add several charts to a slide, Harvard Graphics places restrictions on the type of chart you add to a slide. Table 11.1 summarizes which chart types you can add to particular slides.

Table 11.1 Acceptable Chart Types

Type of Slide	Acceptable Chart Type
A single topic	All chart types with no subtopics
A bullet slide	All chart types except bullet or organization
An organization slide	All chart types except bullet or organization
All other slides	Any chart type except title

Follow these steps to add a data chart to a slide in your presentation:

1. Click the topic to which you want to add the chart.
2. Choose Add chart to slide... from the Chart menu. A menu containing all the chart types you can add appears.
3. Choose the chart type; for example, you can choose Pie. If you choose any chart type other than bullet or organization, the appropriate data form appears. (You enter data for bullet and organization charts in the Outliner, not in a data form.)
4. Enter the appropriate information in the data form.
5. Click OK in the data form to create the chart.

You should avoid adding many charts to a single slide because the charts may display on top of each other. When you add a data chart to a bullet chart, for example, Harvard Graphics displays the two charts on top of each other. If your slide is a bullet or organization chart, you should not add another chart. If you do add a chart, make sure that the images on the charts do not collide.

Creating Organization Charts

You create organization charts in the Outliner by adding subtopics to a slide. When you add subtopics, the slide becomes a bullet chart. You must use the Change chart type... option on the Chart menu to change bullet charts to organization charts. (You also use this feature to change organization charts to bullet charts.)

When you change a bullet chart to an organization chart, the bullet items become positions in the organization, and the slide icon changes to an organization slide icon, as shown in figure 11.8. This figure shows the organization of the sample chart after a slide representing the members of the sales organization. The position icon appears next to the positions.

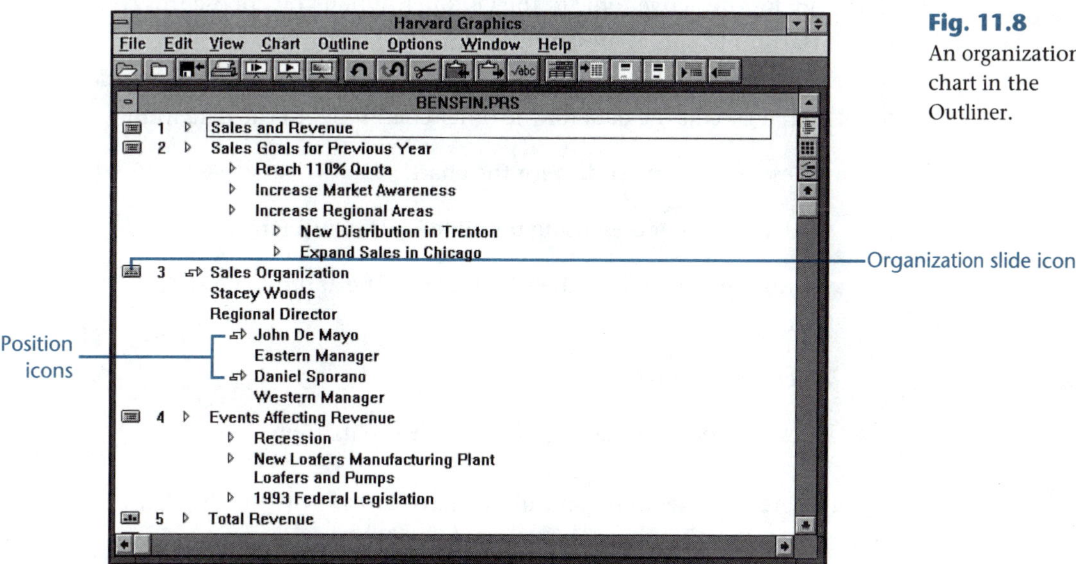

Fig. 11.8
An organization chart in the Outliner.

Follow these steps to create an organization slide in the Outliner:

1. Click the topic that you want the organization slide to follow.
2. Press Enter to create a new topic. A new line, which indicates a new topic, appears in the Outliner.
3. Press Enter until the topic becomes a slide. A slide icon appears.
4. Type the title of the organization chart and press Enter. Usually, for organization charts, the name of the organization is the title of the chart.
5. Choose **C**hange Chart Type... from the Chart menu. A pop-up menu appears.
6. Choose **O**rganization from the pop-up menu. The slide icon changes to an organization chart icon.

After you create the organization chart, you can enter the data for the chart directly into the Outliner. For more information on editing organization chart data, see Chapter 4, "Creating Organization Charts."

Editing Chart Data

By using the Edit Data... option on the Chart menu, you can modify the chart data for the active topic in the Outliner. When you choose this command, Harvard Graphics presents the data for the chart in the data form. Although you edit bullet and organization charts in the Outliner or the data form, you must edit the data for the other chart types in the data form.

Follow these steps to enter data for the chart:

1. Click the topic representing the slide in the Outliner.
2. Choose Edit **D**ata from the Chart menu. The appropriate chart data form appears.
3. Enter the chart data.
4. Click the OK button at the bottom of the data form.

If you created a bullet or organization chart, Harvard Graphics updates the outline with the new data. If you created another chart type, you see no change in the outline unless you changed the title of the chart.

Editing a Presentation

With the Outliner, you can edit an entire presentation. You can change the order of slides by dragging the topic of a slide to a new location. You also can move subtopics from one bullet chart to another, and you use the Edit Data... command on the Chart menu to edit the data for the charts. All these features make the Outliner a powerful tool for editing presentations.

Selecting Topics

Harvard Graphics enables you to edit only an active topic. You must select a topic to make it active. Depending on the method of selection you use, you can activate a single topic, a topic and its associated subtopics, or multiple topics.

The easiest way to make a topic active is to click the text of the topic in the Outliner. The topic is highlighted, and the insertion point appears where you clicked. You use this technique to edit the text of a topic. The Backspace key removes the character preceding the insertion point, and the Del key removes the character following the insertion point. To select a group of characters for editing, drag the mouse pointer across the text.

To make an entire topic and its associated subtopics active, click anywhere between the edge of the window and the first letter of the text for the topic. When you select a topic in this way, you select all the subtopics below the topic, as well (see fig. 11.9). Any editing command you choose affects the selected topic and the associated subtopics.

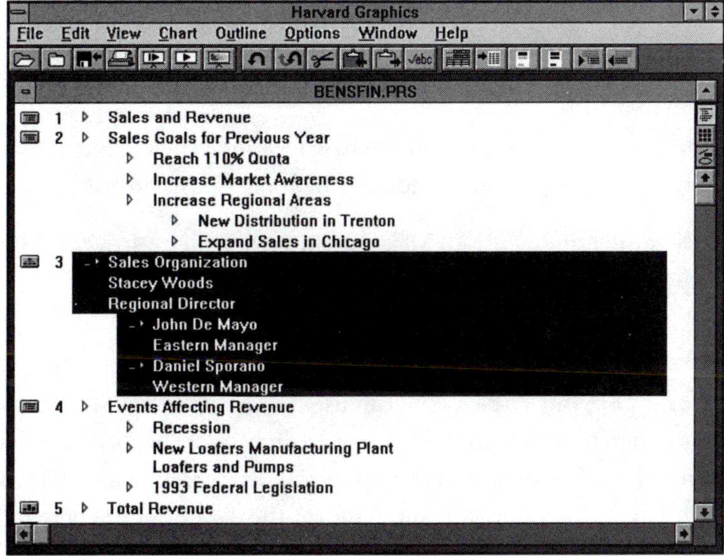

Fig. 11.9
An example of selected topics and subtopics in the Outliner.

You also can select the entire outline by choosing Select all from the Edit menu.

Moving Topics

An easy way to reorganize your outline is to move the topics. You can change the order of the slides by moving the topic that represents the slide in Outliner. You also can change the order of bullet items in a bullet chart or the position of members in an organization chart. Harvard Graphics does not limit you to moving topics within a presentation. You also can move topics to other presentations or to other applications.

Dragging Topics to a New Location. To move topics in the Outliner, you can drag the topic to a new location. Place the mouse pointer in front of the topic's text. Click and hold the mouse button. As you hold the button, the mouse pointer changes to a hand placeholder that points in the direction you move the topic. A red line that begins with a triangle also appears. The red line indicates the location and level of the topic you are moving.

You select a new location by dragging the topic up or down; you change the level of the topic by dragging the topic to the right or left. (For more information on changing levels, see the section "Changing the Level of a Topic" later in the chapter.)

Follow these steps to change the location of a topic in your outline:

1. Place the mouse pointer in front of the text on the topic line; then click and hold the mouse button. The mouse pointer changes to a placeholder.

2. Drag the topic up or down to the new location. The red line moves with the mouse pointer to indicate the topic's position and level.

3. Release the mouse button. Make sure that you align the level of the topic with the leftmost topics in the Outliner.

Harvard Graphics adjusts the outline to show the topic in its new position.

Cutting and Copying Topics. You can use the commands on the Edit menu to transfer topics to and from the Windows Clipboard. The Copy command copies data from the Outliner to the Clipboard, leaving the original intact in the presentation. The Cut command removes the data from the presentation and stores it in the Clipboard. After you issue the Cut or Copy command, you can use the Paste command to copy the stored data from the Clipboard to the Outliner presentation.

Caution

The contents of the Windows Clipboard remain intact only until you store something else in the Clipboard. If you exit Harvard Graphics, all information stored in the Clipboard is also lost.

To cut or copy topics, you must first select the topic in the Outliner. (Menu commands affect the selected topics only.) You can transfer topics to the Clipboard with the Cut command or copy the information with the Copy command. The Paste command copies the topics from the Clipboard to the Outliner. Pasted material appears below the active topic.

To copy several characters from one topic to another, follow these steps:

1. Place the mouse pointer in front of the text of the topic you want to copy; click and hold the mouse button.

2. Drag the cursor to the end of the text.

3. Release the mouse button. The text is highlighted.

4. Choose **C**opy or Cu**t** from the Edit menu. Harvard Graphics stores a copy of the text in the Clipboard.

5. Place the mouse pointer in the topic where you want to insert the text, and click the mouse button.

6. Choose **P**aste from the Edit menu. Harvard Graphics places the material in the specified location.

Copying Topics to Another Presentation. Harvard Graphics enables you to move topics between presentations and applications. When you issue the Copy or Cut command, Harvard Graphics temporarily stores the selected material in the Clipboard. You can transfer the data stored in the Clipboard to other presentations or other Windows applications by using the Paste command from the Edit menu. You can transfer slides to another presentation or copy text from an outline to a word processor, for example.

Follow these steps to copy the topics from one presentation to another:

1. Select the topics you intend to copy.

2. From the Edit menu, choose **C**opy to leave the original topic intact; choose Cu**t** to remove the topic from the outline. Harvard Graphics stores a copy of the selected material in the Clipboard.

3. You can copy the material to a new or an existing presentation. To copy to a new presentation, choose New... from the File menu. The New Presentation dialog box, which you use to create slides in a presentation, appears.

   To open an existing presentation, choose Open from the Edit menu; then choose the appropriate presentation from the list.

4. If you created a new presentation, click OK in the data form to add the slide. See the section "Editing Chart Data" earlier in the chapter for more information.

5. Choose **O**utliner from the View menu to see the new presentation in the Outliner.

6. Choose **P**aste from the Edit menu. Harvard Graphics places the topics after the active topic in the Outliner.

To copy topics to another application, you must open the appropriate application before you choose Paste from the Edit menu. The application you choose must have an Edit menu and be capable of supporting the Windows Clipboard.

Deleting Topics

In the Outliner, you can use the Clear command on the Edit menu to remove topics or text within a topic. This command operates on the active topic or the selected text in the Outliner. To use the Clear command, you click the topic or select the text to be deleted and choose Clear from the Edit menu. Harvard Graphics removes the topic or text.

In addition to the Clear command, you also can press Del to remove the active topic in the outline. You also can use the Cut command, explained in the preceding section, to remove topics.

Expanding and Collapsing Topics

When you work with a large presentation, you may have more topics in the chart than you can see in the Outliner. You can *collapse* topics—hide the subtopics—to make room in the Outliner window. Collapsing topics also makes editing easier because you can select a topic and its associated subtopics with a simple mouse technique.

You use the Collapse command on the Outline menu to hide subtopics. You also can double-click the topic icon (the triangle) displayed next to the topic. To collapse a single topic, double-clicking is easier; to collapse several topics, choosing Collapse from the Outline menu is easier. When you collapse a topic, the topic icon becomes solid, indicating that hidden subtopics exist.

When you hide subtopics, you do not remove the subtopics from the presentation. To create more room in the Outliner, Harvard Graphics combines hidden subtopics with the main topic of the slide. Commands that you use on the topic also affect the hidden subtopics. When you move a topic that contains hidden subtopics, for example, all collapsed subtopics move as well. If you select Cut from the Edit menu, Harvard Graphics removes the topic and collapsed subtopics from the Outliner and places them in the Clipboard.

Figure 11.10 shows the revenue presentation with the second slide, Sales Goals, collapsed (notice the solid triangle).

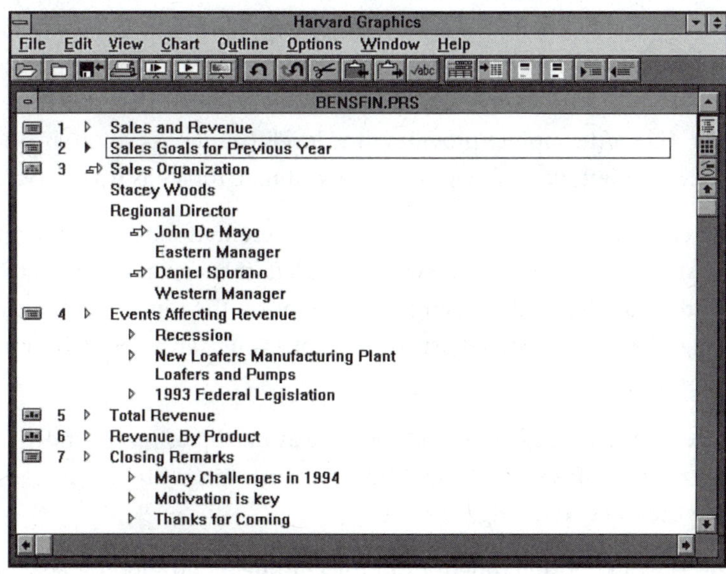

Fig. 11.10
A collapsed topic in the Outliner.

Follow these steps to collapse a topic:

1. Select the topic you want to collapse.
2. Choose Collapse... from the Outline menu. The Collapse pop-up menu appears.
3. Choose Topic from the pop-up menu to collapse the selected topic; choose All to titles to collapse all topics in the outline. Harvard Graphics hides the subtopics.

You use the Expand... command on the Outline menu to redisplay collapsed subtopics. You also can expand the data by double-clicking the topic symbol.

To expand the topic you just collapsed, follow these steps:

1. Select the collapsed topic.
2. Choose Expand... from the Outline menu. A pop-up menu appears.
3. Choose Topic. The selected topic expands to show the previously hidden subtopics. When you choose All from the pop-up menu, Harvard Graphics expands all collapsed topics in the presentation.

Changing the Level of a Topic

As you reorganize your presentation, you may discover that you must elevate some topics and subordinate others. In the Outliner, you can change the levels of topics by moving the topic right or left. When you move a topic to the left, you elevate its importance. A topic that you move to the leftmost point becomes a slide. Conversely, you subordinate any topic you move to the right. Harvard Graphics provides nine levels of subordination. By moving a topic right or left, you can elevate or subordinate topics as necessary.

You can change the level of any topic in the presentation. If you raise the level by shifting the topic all the way to the left, it becomes a slide in the presentation. Similarly, decreasing the level makes the topic a subtopic of the preceding slide. When you adjust the level of a topic, all associated subtopics change as well.

Three methods to change the topic level are available: using the Indent and Unindent commands from the Outline menu, pressing Tab or Shift-Tab, and dragging the topic to the right or left.

Pressing Tab or choosing Indent from the Outline menu subordinates the topic; pressing Shift-Tab or choosing Unindent elevates the level. You also can place the mouse pointer in front of the first character of the topic you intend to move and drag the topic right or left to the new level.

Follow these steps to drag a topic to a different level:

1. Place the mouse pointer in front of the first character of text of the topic you intend to move. Click and hold the mouse button. The mouse pointer changes to a hand placeholder, and a red line appears to indicate the new level.

2. While holding down the mouse, drag the mouse left or right to change the level. As you move the mouse, the inverted topic symbol shown at the end of the line indicates the new level.

3. Release the mouse button. The topic appears at its new level.

Subtopics you create appear initially as bulleted items on the slide. You can change the subtopic so that it represents a slide, however. If you elevate a subtopic to a slide, the text of the subtopic becomes the title of the slide, and indented subtopics comprise the bullet items.

To change a subtopic to a slide, select the subtopic. Then choose Change Topic To... on the Outline menu; from the pop-up menu that appears, choose Slide title. You can return a subtopic to a bulleted item by choosing Change topic to.. and Bullet.

Showing Subtitles and Footnotes

The first slide of a presentation is the title chart, which introduces the theme of the presentation. Other charts, even though they are not the title chart, also can contain a title, subtitle, and footnote. When you add a slide, the slide's topic shows only the title. You can make changes to the title by editing the text of the topic. To edit the subtitle and footnote, however, you must use the Show subtitle & footnote command from the Outline menu. With this command, you can display and edit the subtitle and footnote for any slide in the presentation.

Follow these steps to enter the subtitle and footnote into your title chart:

1. Select the topic in the Outliner.
2. Choose Show Subtitle & Footnote from the Outline menu. The subtitle and footnote appear below the title in the outline.
3. Click the subtitle, which is just below the title. If you have not entered a subtitle, grayed text indicates that the subtitle belongs in this line.
4. Type the subtitle for your presentation. The subtitle should complement the title and clarify the data.
5. Click the footnote.
6. Type the footnote for your title slide. Like the subtitle, the footnote should clarify the data on the slide.
7. To leave room in the Outliner so that you can view the data in the slides, choose Hide Subtitle & Footnote from the Outline menu to hide the title information.

Harvard Graphics does not remove the data from the presentation, but the titles no longer appear in the Outliner.

Using the Outliner Icon Bar

When working within the Outliner, you will find that using some of the icons will make the tasks you encounter much easier. For example, when working with an organization chart, you might find yourself using the Tab and Enter keys to create subordinates or to promote and demote positions. Using the appropriate icon, you can perform these tasks with the click of your mouse.

Changing the View

Harvard Graphics provides three views of a presentation: Outliner, Slide Sorter, and Slide Editor. In this lesson, you have been viewing your presentation in Outliner, which shows only textual information of the slides in your presentation. Like the Outliner, the Slide Sorter view displays all slides of a presentation; unlike the Outliner, however, the Slide Sorter shows graphical information and no text. The third view, the Slide Editor, displays one slide at a time. You can edit the content of individual slides in the Slide Editor.

You use the options on the View menu and the view icons, shown in figure 11.11, to switch between the Outliner, Slide Sorter, and Slide Editor views. For information on working with the Slide Sorter, see Chapter 10, "Using the Slide Sorter." For information on working with slides in the Slide Editor, see Chapter 12, "Drawing in Harvard Graphics" and Chapter 13, "Enhancing Drawings and Objects."

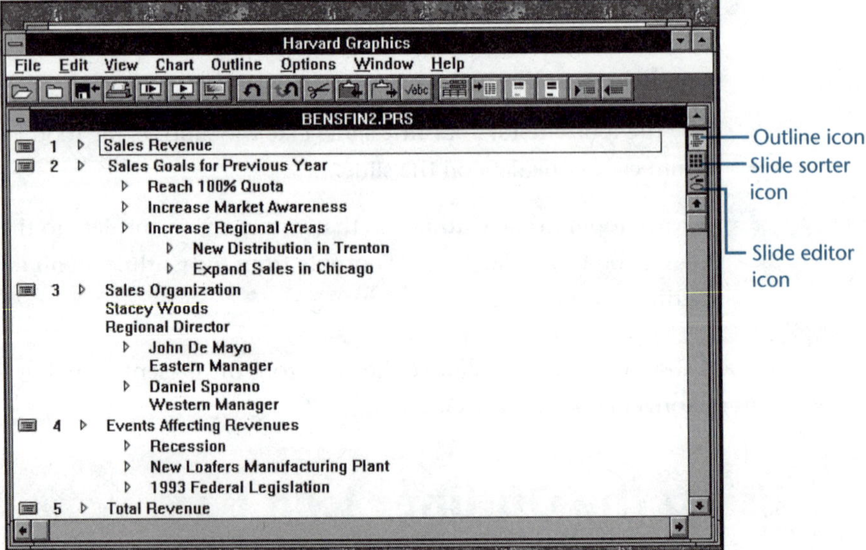

Fig. 11.11
The view icons.

To change the view, you can choose the Slide Editor, Slide Sorter, or Outliner from the View menu. Alternatively, you can click the appropriate icon from any of the three views (all views contain these icons). To view the revenue presentation in the Slide Sorter, for example, click the Slide Sorter icon.

Changing the Default View

When you first begin working with Harvard Graphics, the Slide Editor is the default view for creating, opening, and editing a presentation. If you prefer to work in the Outliner or Slide Sorter, however, you can change the default view that Harvard Graphics displays when you create and open a presentation. You use the Display Options dialog box, shown in figure 11.12, to set the default view for presentations. To see the available choices, click the down arrow next to the appropriate list box-View for New Presentation or View for Open Presentation. You can select a different view from the list that appears.

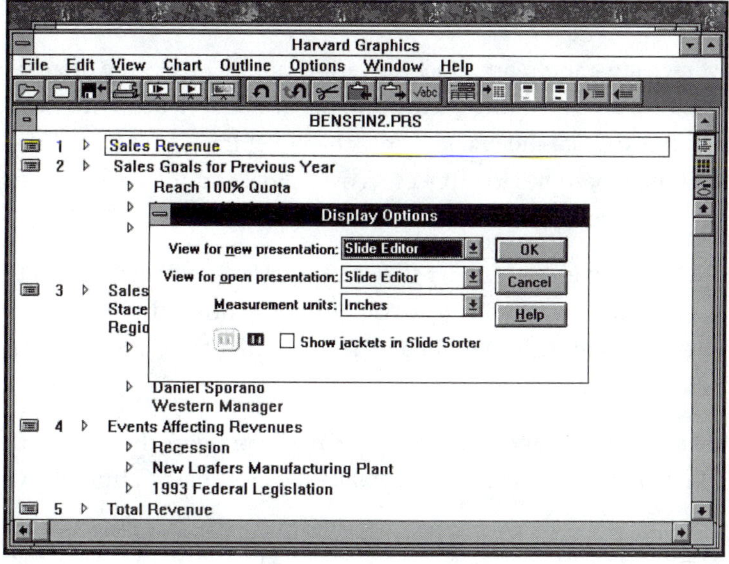

Fig. 11.12
The Display Options dialog box.

The views you use for the defaults depend on your personal preferences. Follow these steps to make the Outliner the default view for a new presentation and the Slide Sorter the default view for an open presentation:

1. Choose **D**isplay from the Options menu. The Display Options dialog box appears.

2. Click the arrow next to the View for new presentation list box.

3. Choose Outliner from the list to set Outliner as the default view for new presentations.

4. Click the arrow next to the View for open presentation list box.

5. Choose Slide Sorter from the list to set Slide Sorter as the default view for open presentations. When you open a presentation, the default view will be the Slide Sorter.

6. Click OK to accept the new preferences and exit the dialog box.

Creating a Slide Summary

If you have a complex bullet chart that conveys a great deal of information, you may want to create a slide summary. Summary slides spread the data of complex bullet charts across multiple slides so that audience members don't become overwhelmed with too much information on one slide.

When you create a summary slide, Harvard Graphics breaks the original slide into several slides, depending on the number of bullet items. With a slide summary, the original slide retains only the bullet items, not the sub-bullets. Each bullet item becomes the title of its own slide, and the associated sub-bullet items become the bullet items of the new slides.

Figure 11.13 shows a single bullet slide with two levels of subtopics in the Outliner. This slide conveys a great deal of information (three bullet items each containing sub-bullets) that could be presented more effectively on several slides.

To create a slide summary, select the topic that represents the slide's title for the original bullet chart; then choose Make slide summary... from the Outline menu.

Figure 11.14 shows the same presentation after a slide summary is made. At first glance, this figure may look identical to figure 11.13; however, when you study it more closely, you can see that slide icons indicate that new slides have been created. Instead of one slide containing three bullet charts, you see four slides: the title slide and three bullet slides.

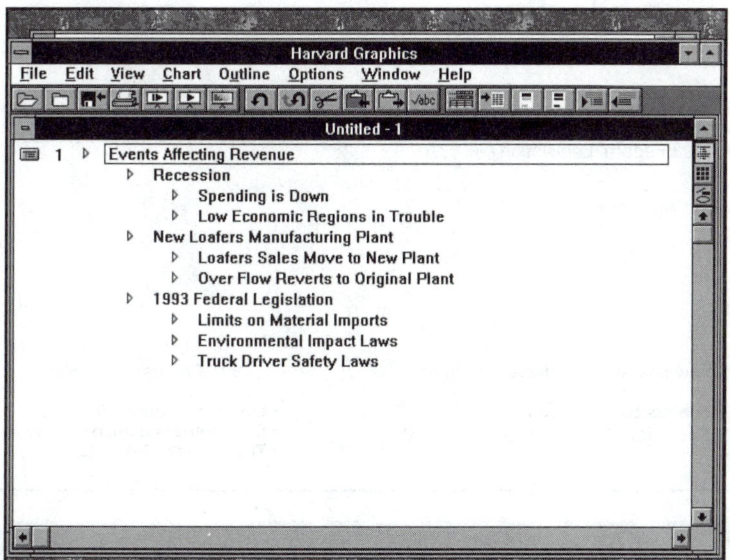

Fig. 11.13
A complex bullet list.

The four slides created with the summary are shown in figure 11.15. The first slide in the upper left corner is the actual summary slide. Notice that the bullets on this slide are also the titles of the three subsequent slides. This slide introduces the material displayed in the remaining slides of the presentation. The three remaining slides provide more detail about the events.

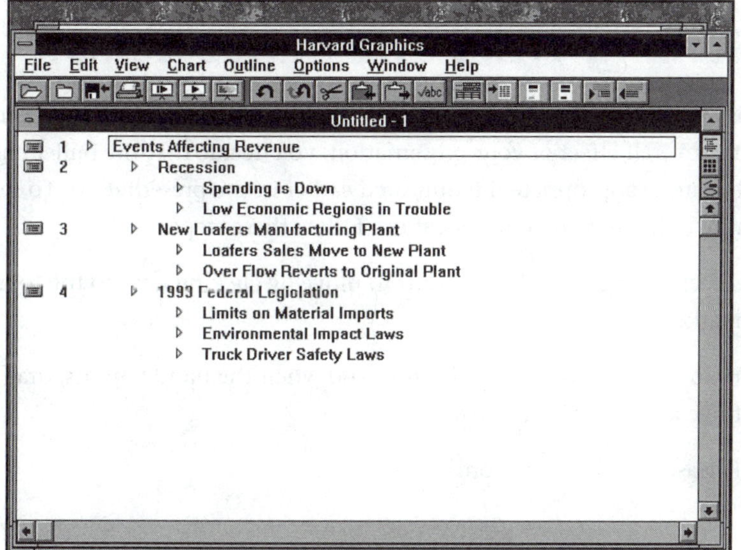

Fig. 11.14
The complex bullet chart with a slide summary.

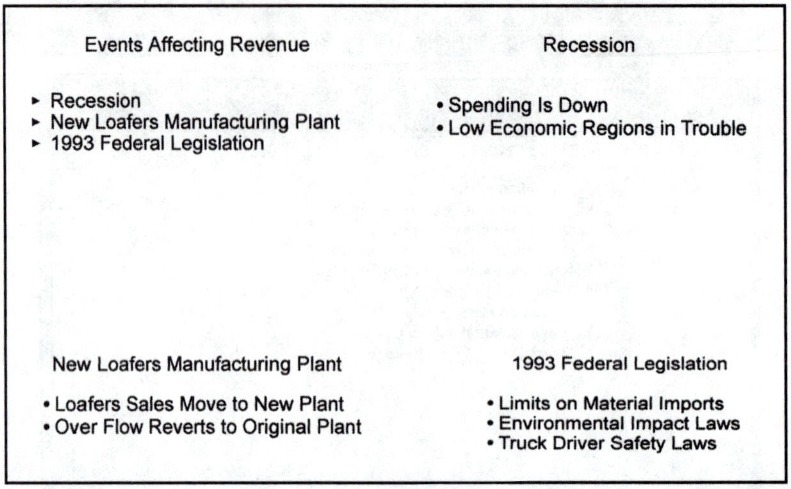

Fig. 11.15
Four slides created with the Make Slide Summary command.

Events Affecting Revenue

- Recession
- New Loafers Manufacturing Plant
- 1993 Federal Legislation

Recession

- Spending Is Down
- Low Economic Regions in Trouble

New Loafers Manufacturing Plant

- Loafers Sales Move to New Plant
- Over Flow Reverts to Original Plant

1993 Federal Legislation

- Limits on Material Imports
- Environmental Impact Laws
- Truck Driver Safety Laws

Design Note

With the slide summary, you can touch briefly on the events before moving into specific detail to prevent your audience from feeling overwhelmed as you communicate relevant information.

To remove the summary, select the original topic that represented the slide's title and choose Remove Slide Summary from the Outline menu.

Switching Titles and Bullet Items

Suppose you have incorporated into your outline a bullet chart. After examining the overall effect of your presentation, you decide that the bullet chart would be more appropriate if it appeared earlier in the presentation. To move the entire bullet slide to a new location, follow these steps:

1. Select the bullet topic you want to move by clicking next to the topic marker.
2. Hold down on the mouse button, and when the hand appears, drag the topic to its new location.
3. Release the mouse button.

From Here...

This chapter covers the many facets of the Outliner. In the beginning of the chapter, you are presented with an example of how to transform thoughts and ideas into a presentation. After this example, you learned how to add topics in the Outliner and how to create charts and slides. You then learned how to edit your presentation and how to create a slide summary.

The next chapter, "Drawing in Harvard Graphics," covers the features of the Slide Editor, which you use to enhance individual slides.

Chapter 12

Drawing in Harvard Graphics

The *slide* is the primary element of a presentation—a blank canvas on which you present the charts that represent your data. The Slide Editor provides tools you can use to enhance your slides with graphics objects. Squares, circles, and polygons are examples of graphics objects you can add in the Slide Editor. You can add arrows to emphasize a particular section of the chart, for example, or you can add text to explain the data.

This chapter teaches you how to add all these objects to a slide. You learn how to view the slides in different ways in order to see finer details of the images or to preview the slide on the entire screen. You also learn how to add charts to a slide so that you can display more than one chart per slide.

Figure 12.1 shows the Slide Editor with a slide containing several graphics objects. All these objects were created using tools in the toolbox at the left side of the window. Some tools in the toolbox are computerized equivalents of equipment that can be found in an artist's studio. For example, you can draw lines on a slide, using one of several Line tools as a "pencil." Harvard Graphics, however, also provides some tools with capabilities that are unique to a computer environment. For instance, changing the size or color of an object, a process that requires painstaking and time-consuming restarts or paint-overs when done by hand, requires only a few mouse clicks in the Slide Editor.

In this chapter, you learn how to do the following:

- Create graphics objects on a slide
- Add multiple charts to a slide
- Edit data on a chart

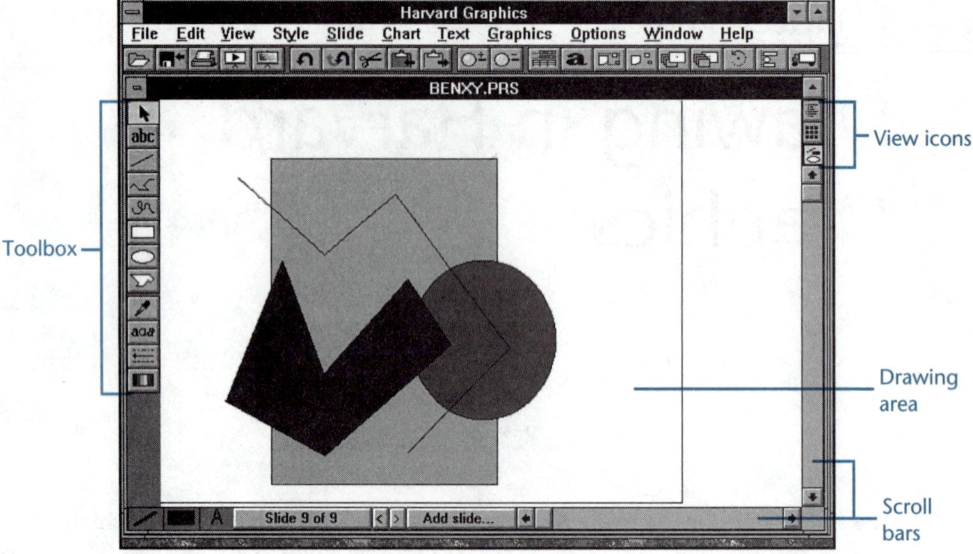

Fig. 12.1
The Slide Editor showing a slide containing graphics objects.

This chapter introduces you to the Slide Editor. First, you learn about the different components of the Slide Editor. This information should help you build a foundation for working with the different features of the Slide Editor. Chapter 13, "Enhancing Drawings and Objects," expands on the information in this chapter by explaining how to modify the objects you create.

Understanding the Slide Editor

The Slide Editor provides one of three ways you can view a presentation. You use the Slide Editor to make changes to a single slide. You use the Slide Sorter and the Outliner, covered in Chapters 10 and 11, respectively, to edit an entire presentation. To view the presentation in the Slide Editor, select Slide Editor from the View menu.

The Slide Editor window has three components (refer to fig. 12.1). The largest part of the screen serves as a drawing canvas. The toolbox at the left of the screen gives you a selection of tools for different operations you can perform. Scroll bars along the right edge and bottom of the screen enable you to view any objects that are not visible in the current view of the slide. The icons at the top right side of the screen are used to view the presentation in the Slide Editor, Slide Sorter, and Outliner. For more information about working with the Harvard Graphics tools, see "Understanding the Toolbox" in this chapter. For more information on the view icons, see "Changing the View" in Chapter 10, "Using the Slide Sorter."

You use the Add Slide button at the bottom of the Slide Editor window to add new slides to your presentation. For an explanation of how to use the Add Slide... button to add new slides to a presentation, see "Adding Slides to a Presentation" in Chapter 2. The field to the left of the Add Slide... button indicates the number of slides in the presentation and the slide you are working with in the Slide Editor. See "Moving to Slides" in Chapter 2, "Learning Harvard Graphics for Windows Basics," for more information about using this button to view different slides in the Slide Editor.

Understanding the Toolbox

The icons in the toolbox represent tools for adding graphics objects to a slide and for modifying the objects. Figure 12.2 shows the icons in the toolbox and their functions in the Slide Editor.

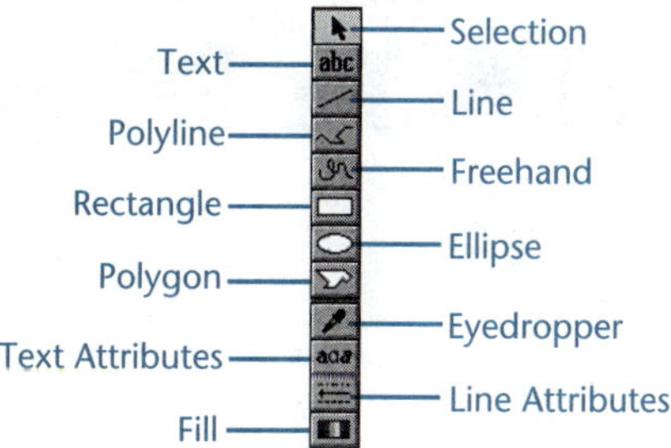

Fig. 12.2
The tool icons of the toolbox.

The first set of eight icons in the toolbox function primarily to create and select objects. The mouse-pointer icon is the Selection tool. (See "Selecting Objects" in Chapter 13, "Enhancing Drawing and Objects," for information on how to select objects in the Slide Editor.) The remaining tools in this section create the different graphics objects on a slide. Each of these tools is explained later in the chapter.

The Eyedropper icon can be used to change the appearance of objects in a slide in the Slide Editor. It is discussed in Chapter 13, "Enhancing Drawings and Objects."

The Text Attributes, Line Attributes, and Fill icons enable you to view and modify specific attributes of objects. The current settings for text, line and fill attributes, and the fill are displayed in the lower corner of the chart, directly below the toolbox (see "Setting the Line Style" and "Setting the Fill Style" in Chapter 13).

Using a Tool

To activate a tool, click the appropriate icon. The active tool is highlighted in a different color (notice the Selection tool in fig. 12.2). The tool that is active determines what actions are performed when you click in the drawing area.

Some tools in the toolbox have toolbars of more tools for performing specific actions. For example, the tool to create rectangles gives you a choice of square or rounded corners. Clicking the tool icon highlights the tool in the toolbox. To see the toolbar showing other available choices for a tool, click and hold down the mouse button. Figure 12.3 shows the two choices for the Rectangle tool. To select a tool from a toolbar, drag the pointer to the tool you want.

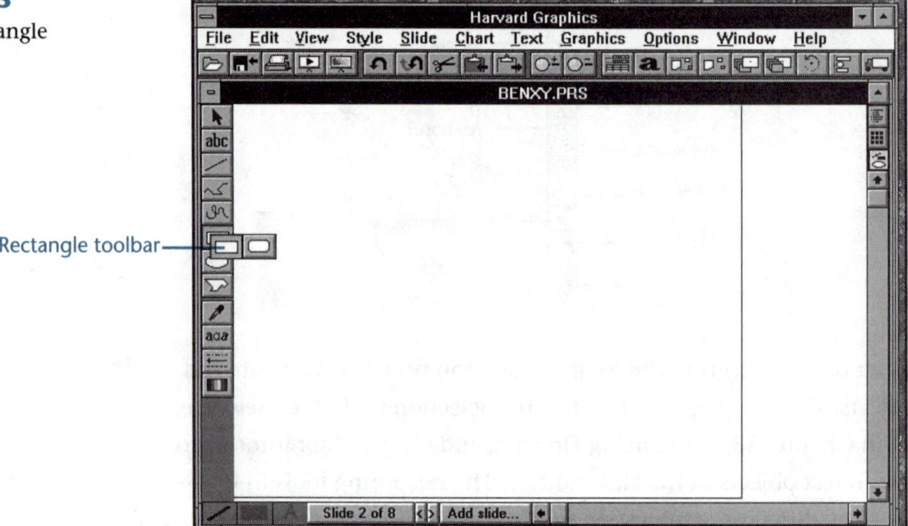

Fig. 12.3
The Rectangle toolbar.

Viewing Slides

You can view a slide in different ways in the Slide Editor. This capability helps you when you are editing the objects on the slide or evaluating the appearance of the slide. You can zoom in on a part of the slide to see finer detail. You can also zoom out of the slide to see more of the slide at one time. See the section "Zooming the Display" for more information. The section "Previewing the Slide" explains how to use the Preview feature to evaluate a slide's appearance. The section "Viewing Actual Size" explains how to work with a slide in actual size, in which objects are the same size on the Slide Editor as they are when you display or print the presentation.

Zooming the Display

The Zoom In and Zoom Out tools (see fig. 12.4) determine how much of the slide you can see in the Slide Editor window. When you zoom out all the way, the entire slide is visible in the window. As you zoom in, objects on the slide appear larger, and you can see more detail, but a smaller portion of the slide is visible. The purpose of the zoom feature is to enable you to work with small objects and in tight places on a slide. For example, if you want to move objects so that their edges touch slightly, zooming the display gives you more control over the distance between the objects.

Figure 12.4 shows a slide zoomed out, and figure 12.5 shows the same slide zoomed in. You can see less of the slide in figure 12.5, but you can see finer detail of what is visible.

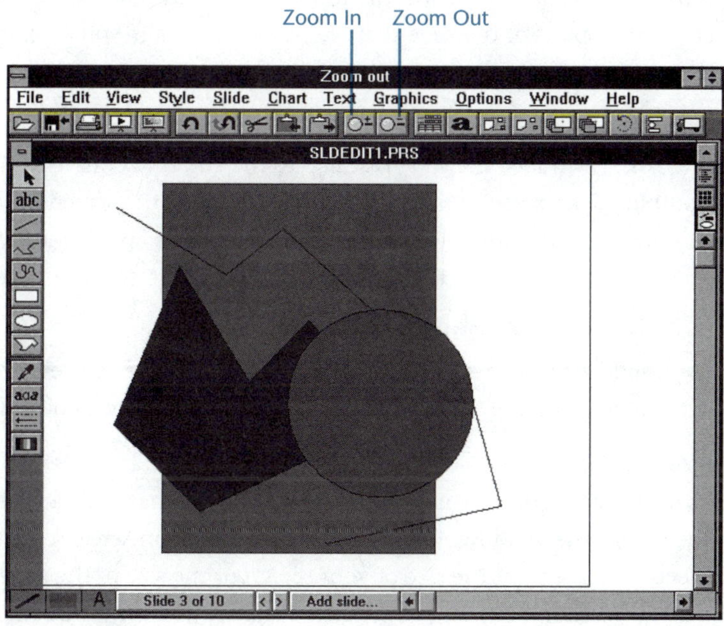

Fig. 12.4
A display zoomed out.

To zoom the display in or out, click the appropriate Zoom icon until the slide shows the objects at the level you want. You can also choose Zoom from the View menu and then choose Zoom In or Zoom Out.

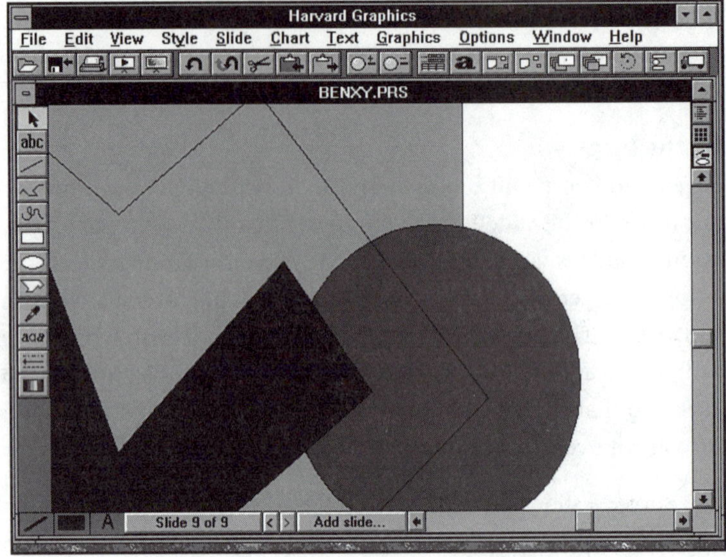

Fig. 12.5 A display zoomed in.

As you zoom in on a slide, objects at the top, bottom, and sides of the slide disappear. To view parts of the slide that are not visible while you are zoomed in, use the scroll bars.

Previewing the Slide

In the Slide Editor window, the slide is scaled to the current zoom level. In the final output of the presentation, the images use the entire screen or page. To see the entire screen so that you can evaluate the slide's appearance, you use the Preview Slide option on the View menu. Figure 12.6 shows a slide in preview.

To preview a slide, choose Preview Slide from the View menu, or press F2. After you finish viewing the slide, press any key to return to the Slide Editor.

Viewing Actual Size

The slides in the Slide Editor window are scaled down so that you can see the entire slide within the window. When you view the slide on-screen or print it, the objects increase to fit the size of your screen or the size of the page on which you are printing. You can use the Actual size option on the Zoom menu off the View menu to work with the objects at the size they will be when you display or print the presentation.

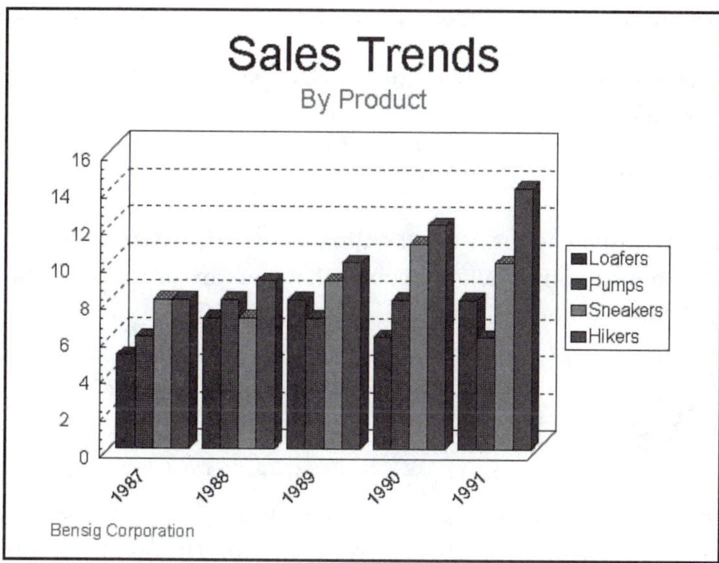

Fig. 12.6
Viewing a slide in Preview.

The Actual size option shows you exactly how the objects in your slide will appear in your output. The disadvantage of Actual size is that the complete slide cannot fit into the dimensions of the screen when you are fully zoomed out (see fig. 12.7). When Actual size is not set, you can zoom all the way out to see the entire slide. In any case, you can still zoom the display in and out. You must scroll to see parts of the slide that are off-screen if Actual size is set or if you are zoomed in.

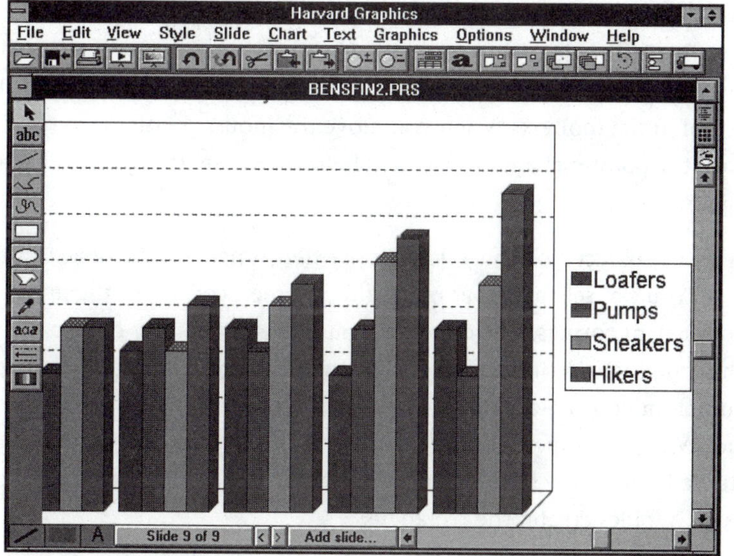

Fig. 12.7
A slide in Actual View.

To view your slides in actual size from the Slide Editor, follow these steps:

1. Choose **Z**oom from the View menu. Harvard Graphics displays the Zoom menu.

2. Choose **A**ctual size from the Zoom menu.

To return the display to the original setting, choose the Fit in Window option on the Zoom menu off the View menu so that you can see the entire slide in the Slide Editor window.

Adding Graphics Objects

The tools in the toolbox enable you to add squares, circles, lines, and free-hand drawings to a slide. The method for adding an object is fundamentally the same for each tool. You click to activate the tool. The pointer becomes a cross hair when you move into the drawing area. Then you click in the drawing area until the object is defined. A tool remains active until you select another tool or execute commands from a menu. This feature enables you to continue to add the same type of object without having to select the icon again for the object each time.

If you prefer to add one object at a time, see "Setting the Tool Lock," which explains how to change the Tool Lock setting so that the Selection tool becomes active after the object is created.

Creating Rectangles and Squares

You use the Rectangle tool (refer to fig. 12.2) to add squares and rectangles to a slide (see fig. 12.8). To draw a rectangle or square on a slide, select the Rectangle tool in the toolbox. When you move the mouse pointer into the drawing area, the pointer changes to a cross hair to indicate that you are creating an object.

To create the object, you must define opposite corners for the object in the window. You can set the upper right and lower left corners or the upper left and lower right corners. The direction you move the pointer determines which corners you define. You can click the first corner and drag to the opposite corner, or you can click once for the first corner and click again to set the second. With either method, the marquee is displayed as you move the pointer to indicate the sides of the object. After you set the second corner, Harvard Graphics creates the rectangle.

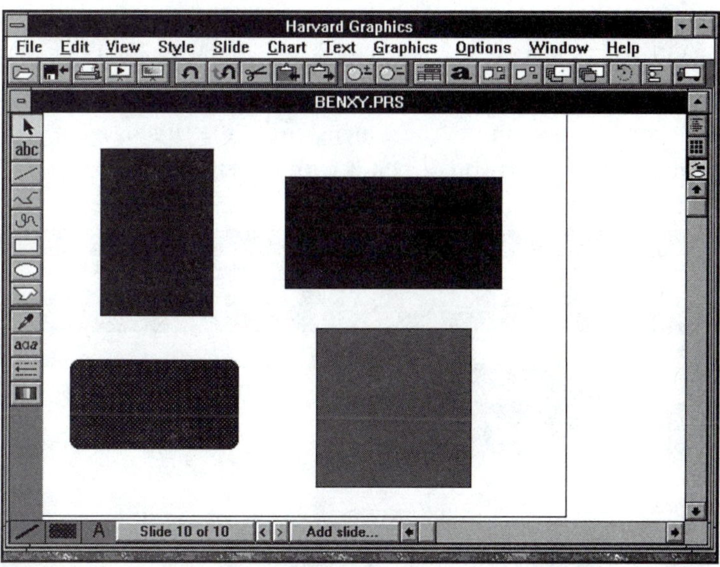

Fig. 12.8
Squares and rectangles in the Slide Editor.

To add a rectangle to a slide in the Slide Editor, follow these steps:

1. Click the Rectangle tool in the toolbox.

   When you click and hold down the mouse button, you see two icons that determine the shape of the corners of the object. The left-hand icon in the panel has square corners, and the right-hand icon creates rectangles with rounded corners.

2. To create a rounded rectangle, drag the pointer to the right-hand icon. After the tool becomes active, release the mouse button.

3. Move the pointer to the drawing area; the pointer changes to a cross hair to indicate that you are creating an object.

4. Click the first corner of the object and drag to the opposite corner.

5. Release the mouse button. Harvard Graphics creates the rectangle defined by the corners you clicked.

To create a square, press the Shift key while you move the mouse.

Creating Ovals and Circles

You use the Ellipse tool to create circles and ovals (refer to fig. 12.2). Circles and ovals are created the same way that squares and rectangles are created. For a circle, you define the two corners of a box. The circle touches the top and bottom and the sides of the box. To define the box, you can click once in the drawing area to define one corner and click again to define the other, or you can drag the mouse. As you move the mouse, the marquee indicates the size of the box that determines the dimensions of the circle. Figure 12.9 shows some of the objects you can draw with the Ellipse tool.

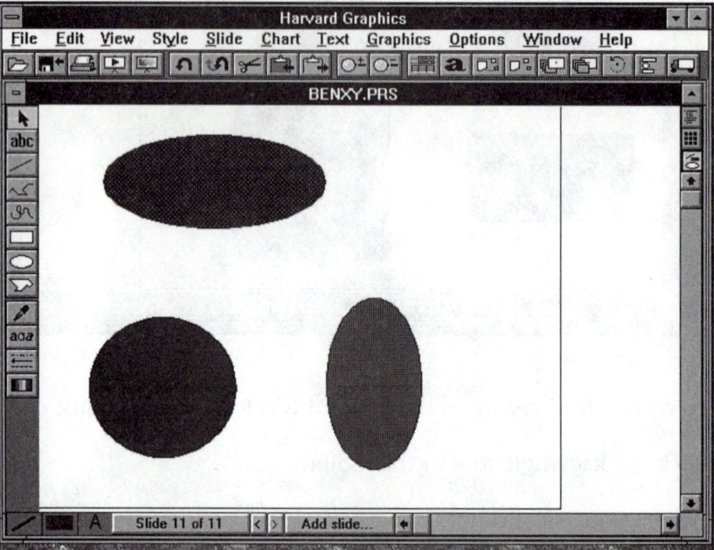

Fig. 12.9
Circles and ovals in the Slide Editor.

To add an oval using the Ellipse tool in the Slide Editor, follow these steps:

1. Click the Ellipse tool. When you move the pointer into the drawing area, the pointer changes to a cross hair to indicate that you are creating an object.

2. Click the first corner and drag to the opposite corner.

3. Release the mouse button. Harvard Graphics creates the oval within the corners you defined.

To create a perfect circle on the slide, press the Shift key while you move the pointer.

Creating Straight Lines

You use the Line tool to add straight lines to a slide. Figure 12.10 shows examples of lines you can draw with this tool. Each line is defined by its end points. To start a straight line, click in the drawing area. To draw the line, move the pointer to the location of the other point and click again. You can also define a straight line by dragging to the end of the line before you release the button. With either method, as you move the pointer, an image of the line is displayed to show just where the line will be drawn.

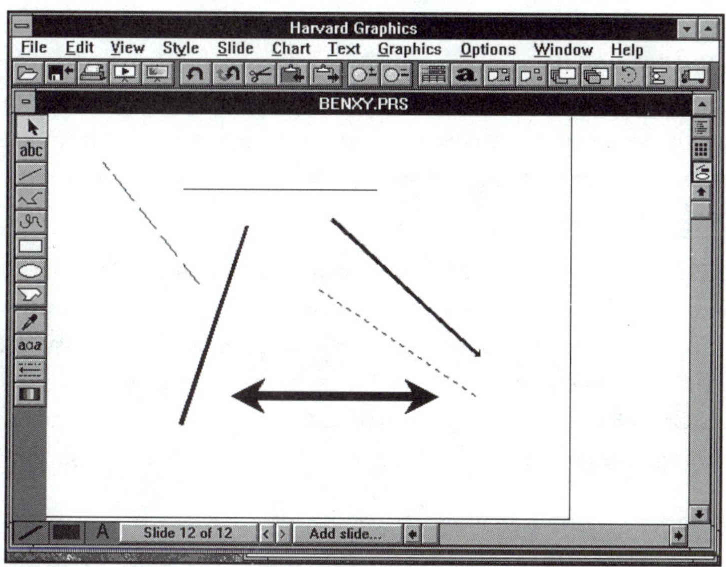

Fig. 12.10 Different styles of lines in the Slide Editor.

The section, "Setting the Line Style" in Chapter 13, "Enhancing Drawings and Objects," explains how to change the style for any line in a slide. For example, you can make broken lines or create arrows. You can change the style for individual lines or for lines that are part of an object—the outline of a rectangle, for instance.

To add a straight line to a slide in the Slide Editor, follow these steps:

1. Click the Line tool. When you move the pointer into the drawing area, the pointer changes to a cross hair to indicate that you are creating an object.

2. Click and hold down the mouse button at the beginning of the line and drag to the end of the line. You see a line between the point you clicked and the current location of the cross hair.

3. Release the button. Harvard Graphics creates the line.

Creating Polygons

Polygons are multisided objects that are filled with a color or image (a bit map, for instance). You define the sides of a polygon by clicking in the drawing area at each point where you want an angle of the polygon. As you click each point, a line is drawn from the preceding point to the current point. These two points determine a side. A line also is displayed from the cross hair to the first point of the polygon. When you double-click a point, you finish the polygon. Harvard Graphics then connects the last point to the first point and fills the inside with the current fill-style settings. For more information about these settings and about changing the fill of a polygon, see "Setting the Fill Style" in Chapter 13.

Figure 12.11 shows different types of polygons in the Slide Editor. The polygon on the left was created by clicking outside the polygon so that no two lines cross each other. For this object, the inside of the object is easy to determine. The other two polygons in the image have sides that cross. In this case, Harvard Graphics determines the inside of the polygon based on the number of times that lines intersect.

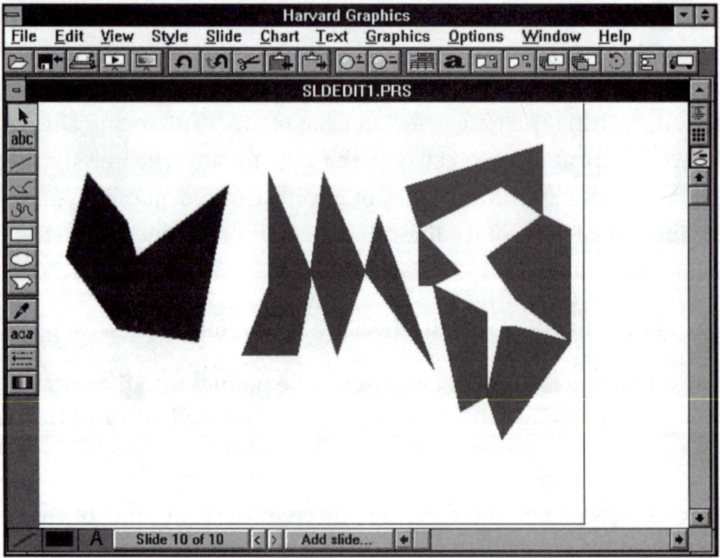

Fig. 12.10
Polygons in the Slide Editor.

To create a polygon in the Slide Editor, follow these steps:

1. Click the Polygon tool.

When you click and hold down the mouse button, you see two icons that determine the shape of the corners of the object. The left-hand icon in the panel has sharp corners, and the right-hand icon creates polygons with rounded corners, polycurves.

When you move the pointer into the drawing area, the pointer changes to a cross hair to indicate that you are creating an object.

2. Click in the drawing area to start the polygon.

3. Click each successive point to add additional sides to the polygon.

4. Double-click the last point to define the polygon.

Harvard Graphics creates the polygon and fills it with the style of the current fill settings.

Creating Polylines and Polycurves

Polylines and polycurves are lines made of multiple line segments connected end to end at points you define. With polylines, the segments are straight lines, as in the polyline on the left in figure 12.12. Polycurves are displayed as one continuous curve that passes through defined points (the right-hand drawing in fig. 12.12). Individual segments are much harder to distinguish in the curved line.

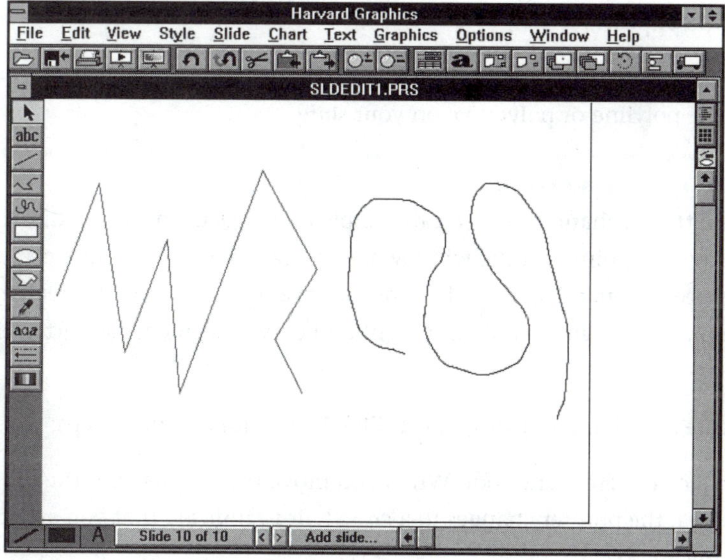

Fig. 12.12
A polyline and polycurve in the Slide Editor.

To create a polyline or polycurve, you use the Polyline tool in the toolbox (refer to fig. 12.2). When you hold down the mouse button, a toolbar shows the icons you can use to create a polyline or a polycurve. The icon on the left, with straight lines, is the Polyline tool. The other icon, with curved lines, is the Polycurve tool. To create a polycurve, drag to the Polycurve icon before releasing the button.

To create a polyline or polycurve in the Slide Editor, follow these steps:

1. Click the Polyline tool.

   When you click and hold down the mouse button, you see two icons that determine the shape of the corners of the object. The left-hand icon in the panel has sharp corners, and the right-hand icon creates polycurves. You drag the pointer to select the Polycurve tool.

   When you move the pointer into the drawing area, the pointer changes to a cross hair to indicate that you are creating an object.

2. Click in the window to start drawing the line.

   Harvard Graphics displays a line or curve from the point you click to the cross hair.

3. Continue clicking to add successive points. As you add points to the line, an image of the polyline or polycurve shows how the final line will appear.

4. Double-click the last point to define the polyline or polycurve. You see the polyline or polycurve on your slide.

Creating Freehand Lines

You use the Freehand tool to create simple drawings in the Slide Editor. You can move the pointer in the window much the same way you move a pencil on a piece of paper. Figure 12.13 shows an example of a scribble created with this tool. In the figure, you see straight and curved segments as part of the same line.

To create a freehand drawing in the Slide Editor, follow these steps:

1. Click the Freehand tool. When you move the pointer into the drawing area, the pointer changes to a cross hair to indicate that you are creating an object.

2. Click and hold down the mouse button in the drawing area.

3. Move the cross hair while holding down the mouse button to create the drawing.

4. Release the mouse button to stop drawing. You see your freehand drawing on the slide.

Fig. 12.13 A freehand drawing in the Slide Editor.

Editing Objects

You use the Edit Object option on the Graphics menu to alter the points of an object after the object has been created or to change the shape of the corners on a rectangle. You can adjust the rounding of a rectangle or square until the object looks like a circle or has 90-degree corners, or you can move any of the points that define polygons and polylines.

Changing Rounded Corners on a Rectangle

The Edit Object option on the Graphics menu enables you to change the rounding of the corners of a rectangle or square. When you select this item, an outline of the object is displayed, with a handle that you can use to make changes in the rounding. As you move the handle toward the center of the object, the rounding increases, making the object more oval. Dragging the handle toward the corner sharpens the corners—as in a square or rectangle.

To turn a rectangle into an oval, follow these steps:

1. Click the rectangle in the Slide Editor window.
2. Choose **E**dit Object from the Graphics menu. Harvard Graphics displays the outline of the rectangle as dashed lines. You use the handle to change the rounded corner.
3. Click and drag the handle toward the center of the object. As you move the handle, an image of the new object is displayed to indicate the rounding of the corners.
4. Release the mouse button when the image is correct.
5. Click the left mouse button, or press Esc to complete the change.

Changing the Points in a Polygon or Polyline

The Edit Object option on the Graphics menu enables you to move the points of a polygon, polyline, or freehand drawing. To edit the points, you click the object in the window and choose Edit Object from the Graphics menu. Figure 12.14 shows the edit handles that are displayed when you choose Edit Object. Harvard Graphics displays a handle for each point so that you can change the point. When you move the pointer over a handle, the pointer changes to a four-directional arrow, indicating that the handle can be moved. Click and drag the handles to change the locations of the points.

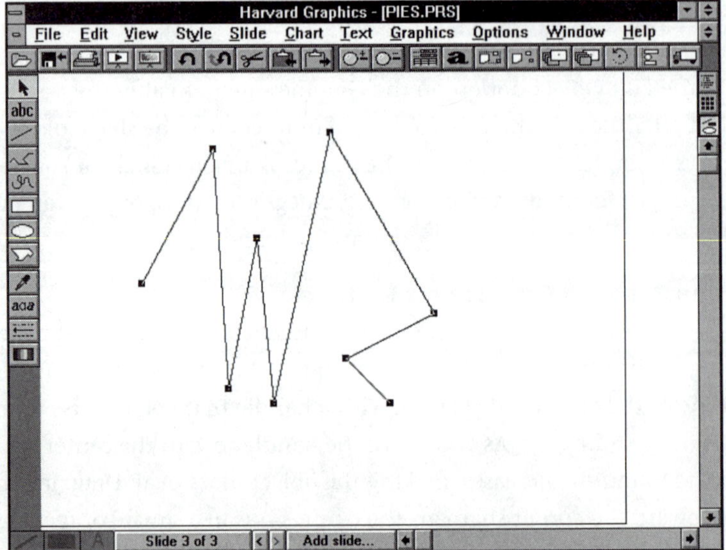

Fig. 12.14
The handles used to edit the points of a line.

To edit the points of a polygon, follow these steps:

1. Click the polygon in the Slide Editor window.
2. Choose Edit Object from the Graphics menu. You see the outline of the object as a dashed line with handles displayed for each point.
3. Click a point you want to edit and drag the point to the new location. The outline changes to show you how the object will look when you have finished editing.
4. Release the mouse button.
5. Repeat steps 3 and 4 for the other points in the polygon.
6. Click the left mouse button or press Esc.

Using the Slide Editor Icon Bar

The icon bar, present in all the different slide presentations, functions the same here as it does elsewhere. For example, to zoom the display in or out, click the appropriate zoom icon until the desired zoom level is attained. For more information on zooming using the View menu, refer back to the section Zooming the Display presented earlier in this chapter.

Many of the tools previously available from the toolbox have been moved to the tool bar. The zoom functions (discussed previously), along with align, rotate, group/ungroup, move to front/back, opening the symbol library and the data form now are accessed from the toolbar rather than the toolbox.

Note

To help you determine which icon you need, Harvard Graphics displays the name of each icon in the Window title when you first move the mouse over the icon.

Setting the Tool Lock

With the Tool Lock feature, a tool remains active until you select another tool or execute a command from a menu. This feature enables you to add the same type of object to your slide repeatedly without having to select the tool each time. The Tool Lock option in the Options Default dialog box determines whether the tool stays active after you create an object. An X to the left of Tool Lock indicates that is enabled. Locked tools remain active after the object is created. When Tool Lock is disabled, the Selection tool becomes active. By default, Tool Lock is on when you start Harvard Graphics.

With Tool Lock disabled, each time you want to use a tool from the toolbox, you must select it. For example, if you wanted to draw multiple rectangles on your slide, you must select the rectangle tool and draw your rectangle. To draw a second rectangle, you must again select the rectangle tool before you can draw the next rectangular object. If you were to place ten rectangles on a slide, you would have to select the rectangle tool ten times.

To disable Tool Lock, remove the X from the Tool Lock check-box, found in the Options Defaults dialog box. When the X is visible, Tool Lock is active. When no X appears in the check-box, Tool Lock is disabled, and you will need to select the appropriate tool from the toolbox each time you what to use it.

Working with Rulers and Grids

Rulers and grids are tools that help you create and move objects in the Slide Editor. Figure 12.15 shows the Slide Editor with rulers and grid lines. The rulers are displayed along the top and side of the window to help you judge the size of objects in the window. The grid serves two purposes in the Slide Editor. The lines of the grid combine with the ruler to help judge the size of objects. With the Snap to grid option, you can force all objects you create and move to be aligned with the lines of the grid. You set all these options by choosing Ruler/Grid from the Options menu.

Figure 12.16 shows the Ruler/Grid Options dialog box, accessed through the Ruler/Grid option on the Options menu. This dialog box shows the current settings for the rulers and grid lines. The top two list boxes on the menu, Vertical and Horizontal, determine how many tick marks are displayed between the inch markers on the ruler and between grid lines in the window. The Show Ruler and Show Grid options must be marked with an X for the rulers and grid lines to be displayed. The Show Position on Ruler option causes lines to be displayed in the ruler to indicate the position of the pointer. The Show text box ruler option allows for the appearance of a ruler above a textbox whenever a textbox is opened. The Snap to Grid option indicates whether objects are snapped to the nearest grid point when they are created and moved. When an object is snapped to the grid, all the points that define the object are defined on the grid. If you click a point that is not on the grid, Harvard Graphics moves the point to the nearest line of the grid. The sides of the rectangle, for example, snap to vertical and horizontal grid lines.

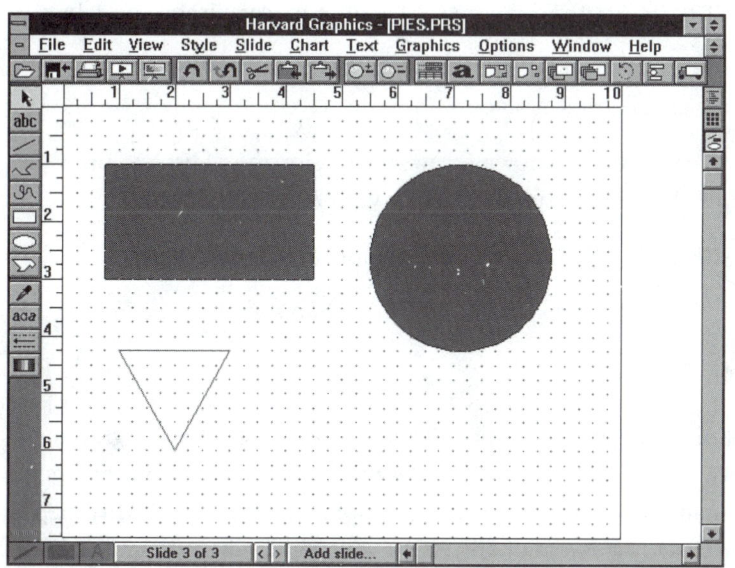

Fig. 12.15 The Slide Editor displaying rules and gridlines.

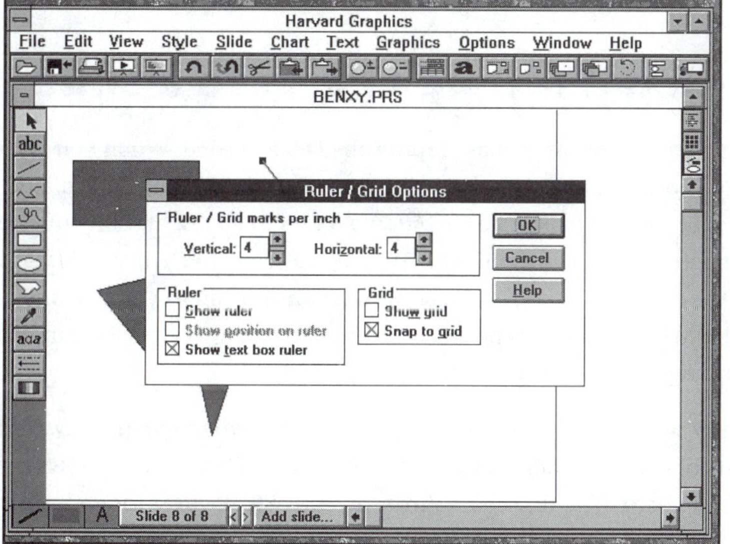

Fig. 12.16 The Ruler/Grid Options dialog box.

To show rulers and grid lines, follow these steps:

1. Choose **R**uler/Grid from the Options menu in the Slide Editor. The Ruler/Grid Options dialog box appears.

2. Click the Show Ruler item so that an X appears in the check box.

3. Click the Show Grid item so that an X appears in the check box.

4. Click the up and down arrows in the Vertical list box until the number of vertical grid lines you want is displayed.

5. Click the up and down arrows in the Horizontal list box until the number of horizontal grid lines you want is displayed.

6. Click Show Position on Ruler option so that an X appears.

7. Click the Snap to Grid option so that an X appears.

8. Click OK.

The Slide Editor window is now displayed with the ruler and grid lines. Harvard Graphics shows on the ruler the location of the pointer. The program snaps objects to the vertical and horizontal grid lines. This snap allows for the exact placement of objects on your slide. When the snap feature is enabled, any object that is created or moved is forced to align its upper left-most corner with the nearest grid dot.

Adding Multiple Charts to a Slide

You can add charts, as well as graphic objects, to a slide. When you create a slide in the Slide Editor, you pick a chart type from the Add Slide dialog box. (This dialog box is explained in "Adding Slides to a Presentation" in Chapter 2, "Learning Harvard Graphics for Windows Basics.") When the slide is created, the chart is a graphics object, which you can edit as you edit any other object on the slide. With the Add chart to slide item on the Chart menu, you can add multiple charts to a single slide.

You may want to use a slide with multiple charts when you have two different sets of data you want to present on one slide. Figure 12.17 shows a slide with two charts. The first chart shows revenue for the year for each product at Bensig Corporation. The second chart shows how much each product contributed to the total revenue.

Design Note

Make sure that all the charts on a slide complement each other well and do not make the slide look crowded.

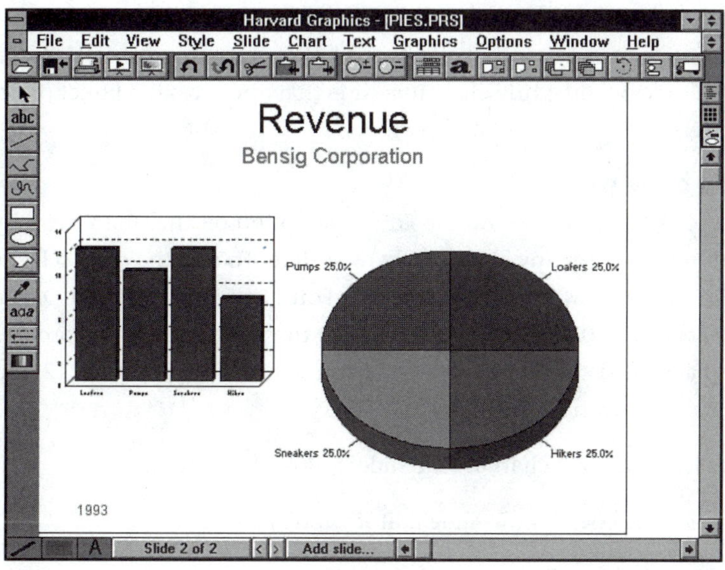

Fig. 12.17 A slide with two charts.

You use the Add chart to slide option on the Chart menu to create additional charts on a slide. You can add as many charts to a slide as you want. The following section explains how to add charts of different types in the Slide Editor. "Editing Chart Data" at the end of this chapter shows how to use the Data Form tool on the toolbar to edit the data for any chart.

Adding Charts to Slides

The Add chart to slide option on the Chart menu creates charts on a slide. When you choose this option, Harvard Graphics displays a menu from which you can choose the chart type you want. After you choose a type of chart, Harvard Graphics presents the data form, where you can enter the data for your chart. For more information on entering and editing chart data, see Chapters 3 through 6.

To add a chart to a slide from the Slide Editor, follow these steps:

1. Choose **A**dd Chart To Slide from the Chart menu. The chart types are listed in a menu.

2. Choose the chart type from the menu. Harvard Graphics displays the appropriate data form.

3. Enter the chart data.

4. Click OK to create the chart on the slide.

Harvard Graphics imposes some restrictions on the types of charts you can add to a slide. A slide can have only one bullet chart or organization chart, and you cannot add a title chart to a slide that already has a bullet or organization chart.

Editing Chart Data

With the Data Form tool and the Edit Data option on the Chart menu, you can edit the data for any chart object on a slide. To edit the data, select the chart in the window; then click the Data Form icon, or select Edit Data on the Chart menu. (Both choices accomplish the same result.) Harvard Graphics displays the data form for the chart you selected. (Refer to fig. 12.4 to see the Data Form icon in the toolbox.)

To edit the data for a chart on the slide, follow these steps:

1. Click the chart in the Slide Editor window.

2. Click the Data Form tool. Harvard Graphics displays the data form for the chart so that you can edit the data.

3. Edit the data.

4. Click OK.

From Here...

This chapter, the first of two chapters covering the features of the Slide Editor, explains how to create graphics objects on a slide. You learned how to create rectangles, circles, and lines by using tools from the toolbox and how to use rulers and grids as an aid in creating the objects. In addition, tools on the toolbar offering a swift method of performing certain tasks were discussed. The chapter also explains how to add multiple charts to a slide and how to edit the data for each chart.

Chapter 13

Enhancing Drawings and Objects

Many steps are involved in creating a presentation. You create slides that contain charts, and you enter data into the charts. Although many presentations contain nothing but charts, Harvard Graphics goes beyond the common chart presentation by enabling you to add graphics to a slide. By using Harvard Graphics features to enhance your drawings and objects, you can create artistic and effective slides without being a graphics artist.

In Chapter 10, "Drawing in Harvard Graphics," you learned how to use the toolbox to create drawings and objects in the Slide Editor (refer to Chapter 10 for a complete discussion of the available tools). In this chapter, which is an extension of Chapter 10, you learn how to edit and enhance the images you create. You learn how to move, resize, copy, and delete objects. The later sections of the chapter explain how to modify object attributes, such as the fill color or the line style.

Figure 13.1 shows a presentation slide in the Slide Editor window. In addition to the bar chart and legend, this slide contains graphics and text that enhance the appearance of the slide. Throughout this chapter, you learn about features you can use to modify and enhance slides you create.

In this chapter, you learn how to do the following:

- Select objects for making changes
- Move, resize, rotate, and manipulate graphic objects
- Make changes to graphic object attributes

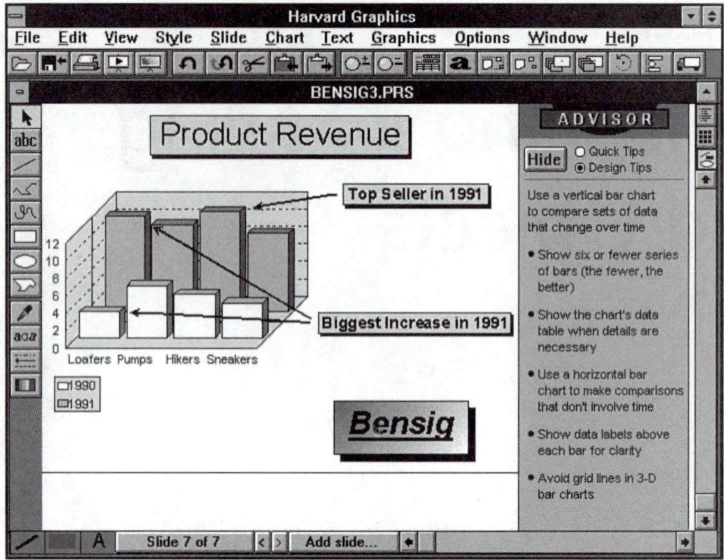

Fig. 13.1
An enhanced bar chart slide.

Selecting Objects

You modify slide objects in the Slide Editor. If you are not in the Slide Editor, click the Slide Editor icon, if available, or choose Slide **E**ditor from the **V**iew menu. To modify an object, you first must select the object using the Selection tool. The commands and options that you apply affect the selected object only. The easiest, and perhaps most common, method of selecting an object is to click the object. Handles appear on the selected object (see fig. 13.2).

Harvard Graphics does not limit you to selecting only one object at a time—you also can select several objects simultaneously. With a little more effort, you can select a hidden object or a single object within a group. No matter how you select an object, though, handles appear around the selected objects, which are the only objects affected by commands and options. The following sections describe these various selection techniques.

Selecting Multiple Objects

In the Slide Editor, you can select many objects simultaneously. When you select several objects together, any command you issue and any change you make affects all selected objects. Selecting multiple objects is helpful, for instance, if you want to delete several objects from a slide. Instead of selecting and deleting each object individually, you can select all objects and issue the Delete command one time.

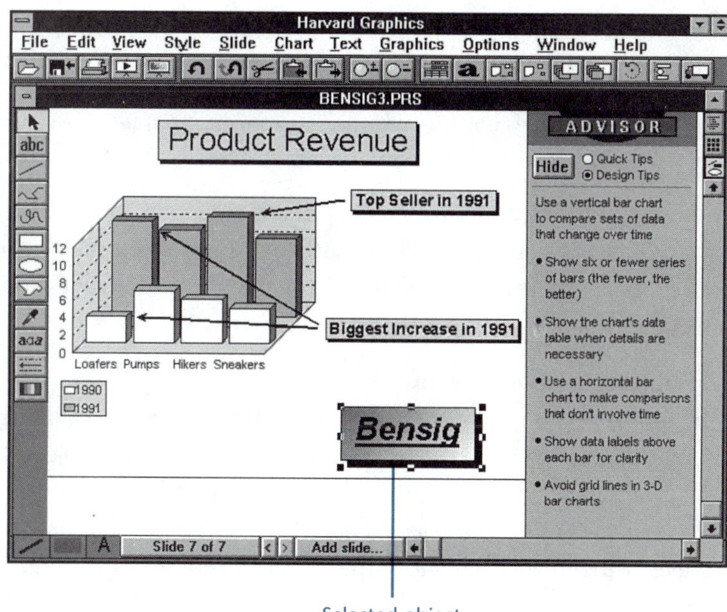

Fig. 13.2
An object selected in the Slide Editor.

Follow these steps to select multiple objects:

1. Hold down the Shift key and click each object you intend to select.

2. After you select your objects, release the Shift key. Handles appear on each object.

The biggest advantage of using the Shift-click method of selecting is that you can select objects on any part of the slide, whether the objects are adjacent or not.

Another method of selecting multiple objects is to drag a marquee around them. Selecting objects with a marquee enables you to select adjacent objects only. When you use this method, all objects within the marquee are selected. Selecting objects with a marquee is similar to selecting slides with a marquee in the Slide Sorter, as you did in Chapter 10, "Using the Slide Sorter."

To drag a marquee around objects, follow these steps:

1. Place the mouse pointer next to one of the objects in the group you intend to select. (Because the marquee begins at the location of the mouse pointer, place the pointer on the outside edge of the first object you want to select.)

2. Click and hold down the mouse button; then drag the marquee until it surround objects.

3. Release the button when the marquee surrounds all objects you want to select. All objects within the marquee are selected.

When you group objects, as explained later in the section "Grouping and Ungrouping Objects," you can select the entire group with one mouse click. To select a group, place the mouse pointer on any object within the group and click one time.

Selecting Objects within a Group

Although you may have grouped objects, as explained later in "Grouping and Ungrouping Objects," you still can select and change individual objects in the group. Commands you apply to the selected object do not affect the other objects in the group. The selected object remains part of the group, however, even though you may move the object to another part of the slide.

To change one object in a group, you must select the object. When you first select the object, the entire group is highlighted with handles. As you continue to click the object, a marquee remains around the group to indicate that the object is from a group, and handles appear on the selected item (see fig. 13.3).

Follow these steps to select an object in a group:

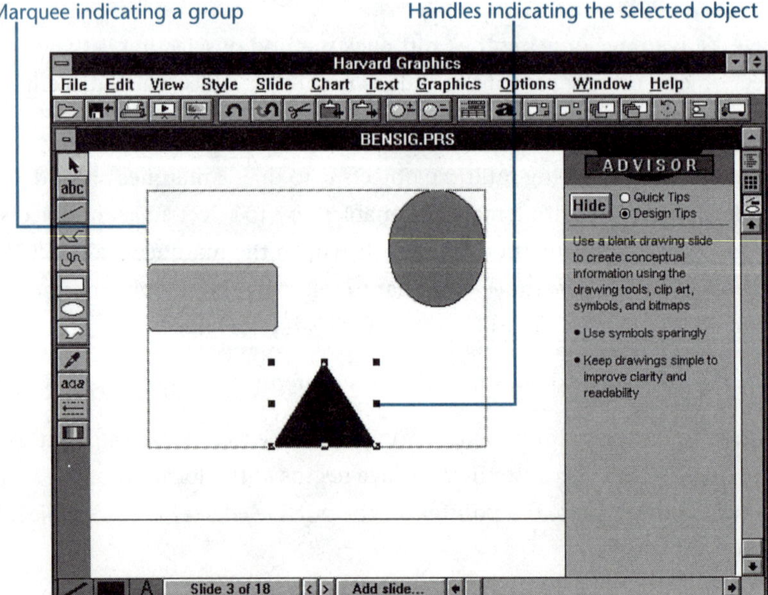

Fig. 13.3
An object selected within a group.

1. Click the object in the group. Selection handles appear on the entire group.

2. Click the object again so that handles appear on the specific object only.

Selecting Hidden Objects

Complex slides often contain many objects. As you add objects, parts of other objects may become hidden from view. In some cases, a new object may obscure completely other objects in the slide. You can select the hidden objects, however, by clicking the top of the object or clicking in the area where you think the object is located, even though the object is not visible. Continue to click until the handles surround the object. Figure 13.4 shows a hidden object that has been selected. The handles, which do not encompass the visible object, belong to the hidden object.

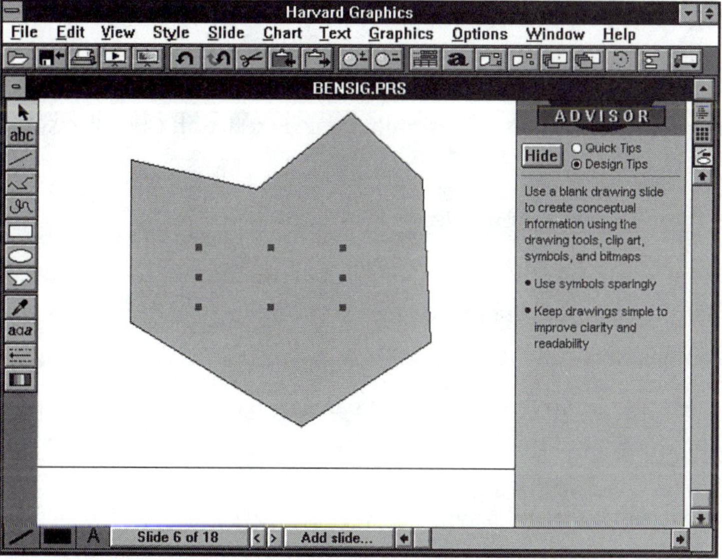

Fig. 13.4
Selecting a hidden object.

Manipulating Objects

In the Slide Editor, you can manipulate the location and dimensions of objects in your slides. To create an easy-to-read and well-organized slide, you can copy, cut, and paste objects to a new slide or new locations in the same slide. You also can flip, rotate, align, and center the object to achieve the best effect. And when all else fails, you can delete unsatisfactory objects. By grouping objects, you can perform these actions on several objects simultaneously. This section explains the many features that enable you to manipulate effectively the objects on your slides.

Grouping and Ungrouping Objects

You use the Group tool or the **G**roup command from the **G**raphics menu to group objects. When you group objects, you preserve the location of the objects relative to each other despite the changes you make. When you select a group, as explained earlier in "Selecting Multiple Objects," any command you apply affects all objects within the group.

Generally, you should use groups so that you can change the attributes of many objects to the same settings at the same time. Grouping objects enables you to move several objects without placing each object individually in the new location, and you also can simultaneously resize all the objects of a group.

Tip
Grouping is an editing convenience. Your audience cannot distinguish grouped objects on a slide.

Follow these steps to group objects:

1. Hold down the Shift key as you click each object in the window. Alternatively, you can drag a marquee around the objects. Handles appear around selected objects.

2. Click the Group tool in the Icon bar (see fig. 13.5). One set of handles appears around the grouped objects.

Harvard Graphics doesn't limit you in the number of groups you can have on a slide, and any object can be part of a group. One group, in fact, may consist entirely of smaller sets of grouped objects.

Times may occur, however, when you want to separate grouped objects. To edit a single object or to use objects in other groups, for example, you must separate the grouped objects. You use the **U**ngroup command on the **G**raphics menu or the Ungroup tool, which you see on the Icon bar.

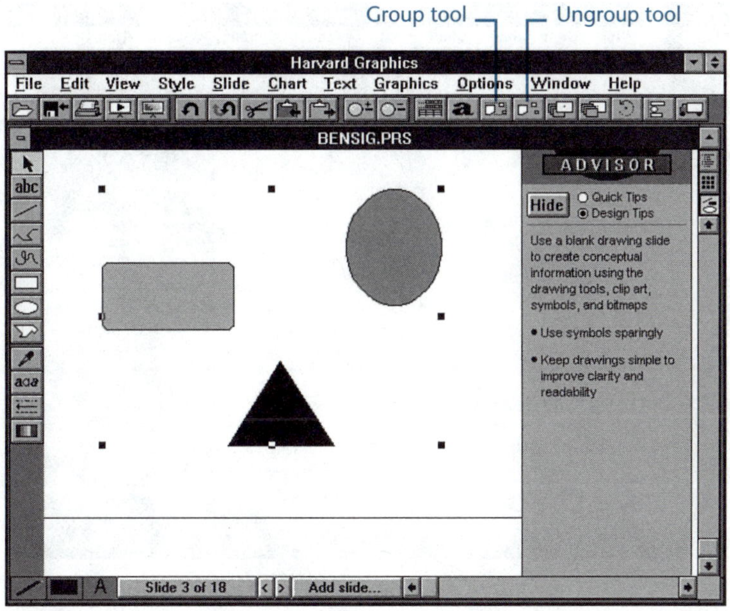

Fig. 13.5
The Group and Ungroup tools.

Follow these steps to ungroup objects in the Slide Editor:

1. Select the group in the Slide Editor window.

2. Choose the Ungroup tool in the Icon bar (see fig. 13.5).

Handles appear around each object to indicate the objects are no longer part of the group.

Moving Objects

You can move objects in the Slide Editor by selecting and dragging them to a new location. When you move the mouse pointer over a selected object, the pointer changes to a four-directional arrow, which you use to move objects. To move the object, click the object when the four-directional arrow appears; then drag the object to the new location. As you drag the object, an outline of the object follows to indicate the new position.

Tip
You can move many objects at the same time by grouping the objects or selecting multiple objects. See "Selecting Objects" in this chapter to learn how to select multiple objects. To move multiple objects, you must hold down the Shift key as you drag the objects.

Follow these steps to move an object in the Slide Editor:

1. Select the object.

2. Drag the object to the new location. An outline, indicating the new location, follows the object (see fig. 13.6).

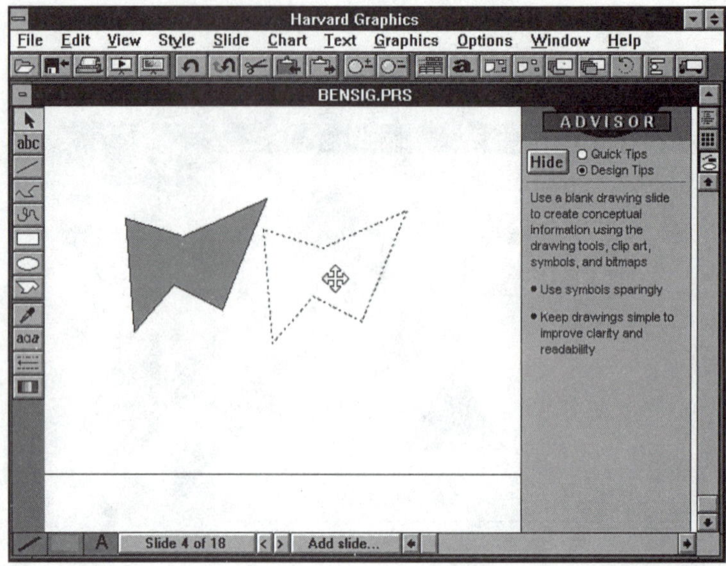

Fig. 13.6
A polygon moving to a new location.

3. Release the mouse button. The object appears in the new location.

Resizing Objects

You use selection handles to change the size of an object. By dragging a selection handle, you can change the size of an object in one of four directions: up, down, left, or right. To widen an object, for example, you drag any handle on the side of the object. By dragging a handle on the top or bottom of an object, you can lengthen the object. By dragging a corner handle, you change the width and length simultaneously.

When you click a selection handle, the mouse pointer changes to a two-directional arrow showing the directions in which you can drag the handle. To make the change, drag the object to the new size. An outline shows the current size of the object (see fig. 13.7).

Follow these steps to move the right side of an object:

1. Select the object in the Slide Editor; selection handles appear.
2. Click the handle on the right side of the object. The mouse pointer changes to indicate that you can drag the line to the right or left.
3. Drag the handle inward. An outline showing the change appears.
4. When the outline indicates the size you want, release the mouse button. Harvard Graphics redraws the right side of the object to the new dimensions.

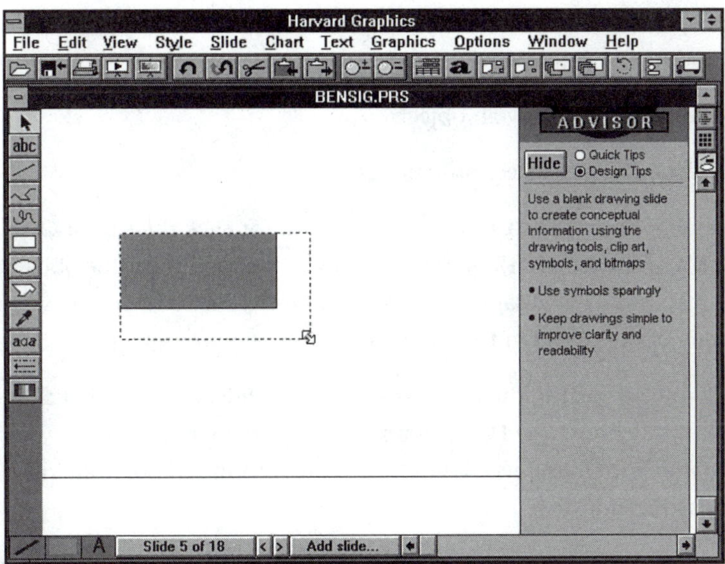

Fig. 13.7
Resizing an object.

To change the dimensions of any other side, follow the same procedure, using the appropriate selection handles.

Deleting Objects

To remove one object or several objects, select the object(s) and choose Cl**e**ar from the **E**dit menu or press Del. See "Selecting Multiple Objects" earlier in this chapter to learn how to work with more than one object.

You also can use the Cu**t** command from the **E**dit menu to remove an object. When you choose Cu**t**, Harvard Graphics removes the object from the slide and stores the object in the Clipboard, where the object remains until you store another object or text in the Clipboard or exit Harvard Graphics.

Copying and Duplicating Objects

As you work on your slides, you may create effective objects that you want to repeat in your presentation. You can copy these objects from the current slide to other slides in your presentation. If you decide that an object doesn't suit the purpose of the current slide but would look better on another slide, you can cut the images from one slide and paste them into another. You also can create duplicate copies of an object on the same slide.

To copy or cut objects on a slide, you must use the **E**dit menu's Cu**t** or **C**opy command. The **C**opy command copies the selected object to the Clipboard, and the original object remains intact. The Cu**t** command removes the object from the slide and stores the object in the Clipboard. To transfer the contents of the Clipboard to the slide in the window, you use the **P**aste command—also found on the **E**dit menu.

Follow these steps to copy an object:

1. Select an object; selection handles appear.
2. Choose **C**opy or Cu**t** from the **E**dit menu (or click the Cut or Copy tools in the Icon bar), depending on whether you want the object to remain intact or disappear from the original. Harvard Graphics stores a copy of the object in the Clipboard.

   (If you are pasting the object into another slide, move to that slide before you choose the **P**aste command. See Chapter 2, "Learning Harvard Graphics for Windows Basics," for more information on moving between slides.)
3. Choose **P**aste from the **E**dit menu or click the Paste tool in the Icon bar.

The new object appears partially on top of the original object. See the section "Moving Objects" earlier in this chapter to learn how to place the object in a different location on the slide. If you copy the object to a different slide, the object appears in the same location on the new slide that it appeared on the old slide.

You also can create a copy of the object on the same slide without using the Clipboard or the commands from the **E**dit menu. To duplicate an object quickly, hold down the Ctrl key as you move an object. When you use this method, you move a copy of the object; the original object remains intact.

Duplicating objects enables you to copy objects on the same slide without using the Clipboard. You cannot duplicate objects between slides, however. To move an object from one slide to another, you must use the Clipboard.

To duplicate an object, follow these steps:

1. Hold down the Ctrl key as you drag the object. An outline of the object shows the position of the duplicate.
2. Release the mouse button when the duplicated object is in the appropriate location. The copy of the object appears in the new location, and the original remains intact.

Aligning Objects

In the Slide Editor, you can align objects along the left, right, top, and bottom sides of a slide. You also can align objects by their horizontal and vertical centers. Aligning objects creates a uniform appearance. Figure 13.8 shows three sets of objects aligned to the left, center, and bottom. The left-aligned text gives the appearance of a margin. The objects on the right are center-aligned. The text aligned on the bottom appears to be sitting on the frame displayed around the slide.

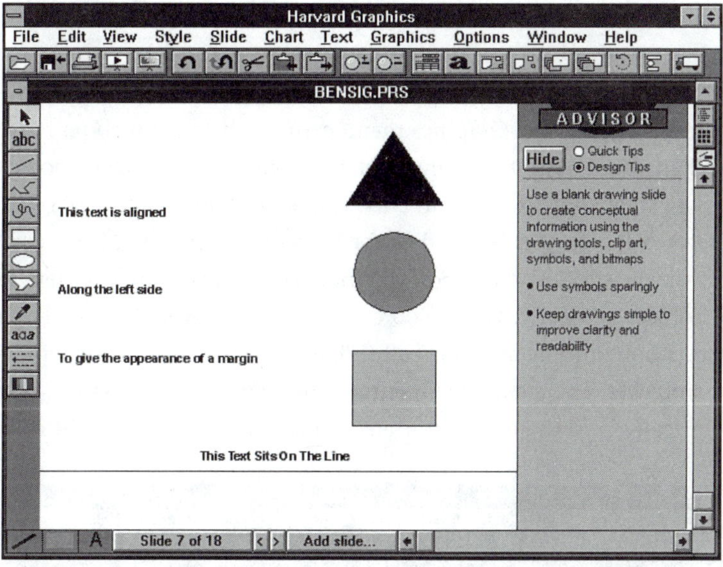

Fig. 13.8
Objects aligned to the left, center, and bottom.

To align objects, you can use the **A**lign command from the **G**raphics menu or the Align tool in the toolbox. When you select the Align tool, the Align dialog box, which contains the six alignment options, appears (see fig. 13.9). The options in the dialog box illustrate the alignment settings. The upper left option, for example, aligns objects to the left.

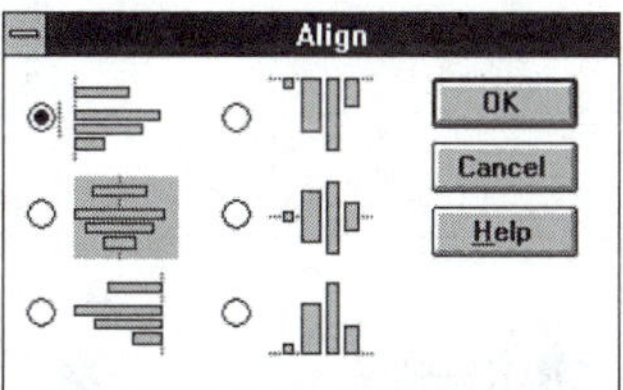

Fig. 13.9
The align dialog box.

Follow these steps to left-align objects on a slide:

1. Hold down the Shift key while you select the objects in the Slide Editor to be aligned. You also can drag a marquee around the objects.

2. Choose the Align tool in the Icon bar. The Align dialog box appears.

3. Choose the left align button in the upper left corner of the Align dialog box.

4. Choose OK. The selected objects align according to the setting.

Centering Objects

Harvard Graphics enables you to center objects on your slide. The **C**enter on slide command from the **G**raphics menu centers objects horizontally or vertically. When you choose this command, a pop-up menu in which you choose a centering style appears. You can choose **H**orizontally, **V**ertically, or **B**oth. With *horizontal centering*, Harvard Graphics centers the selected object horizontally on the slide. With *vertical centering*, Harvard Graphics centers the selected object vertically. When you choose **B**oth, Harvard Graphics centers the objects horizontally and vertically. Figure 13.10 shows a slide with three centered objects. The rectangle is centered horizontally; the triangle is centered vertically; and the oval is centered both horizontally and vertically.

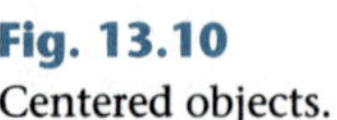

Fig. 13.10
Centered objects.

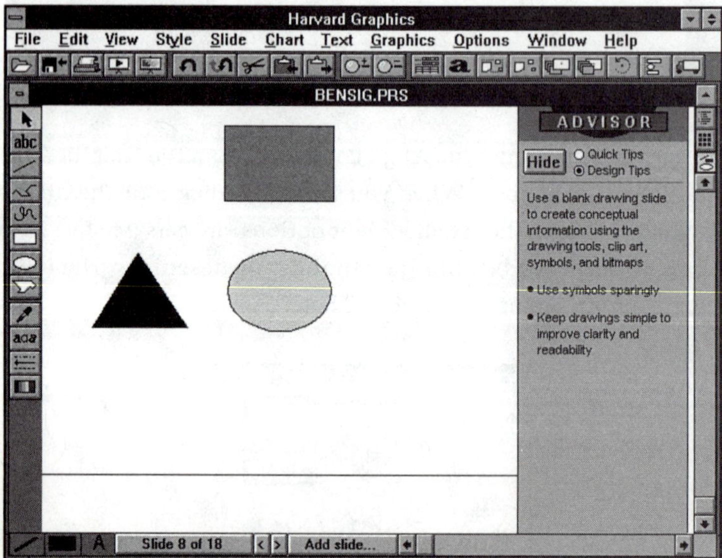

Follow these steps to center an object horizontally on a slide:

1. Select the object.
2. Choose **C**enter on slide from the **G**raphics menu. A pop-up menu, from which you choose a setting, appears.
3. Choose **H**orizontally from the pop-up menu. Harvard Graphics moves the object to the horizontal center of the slide.

You can center an object vertically or horizontally and vertically by choosing the appropriate command—**V**ertically or **B**oth—from the **C**enter on slide pop-up menu.

Rotating Objects

Rotating is one way you can use Harvard Graphics to create special graphic effects on your slides. You can rotate text so that it appears slanted, as shown in figure 13.11. To illustrate the point that airline maintenance costs are increasing, for example, you can rotate a graphic of a plane so that it appears to be taking off. You use the Rotate tool in the toolbox to rotate objects.

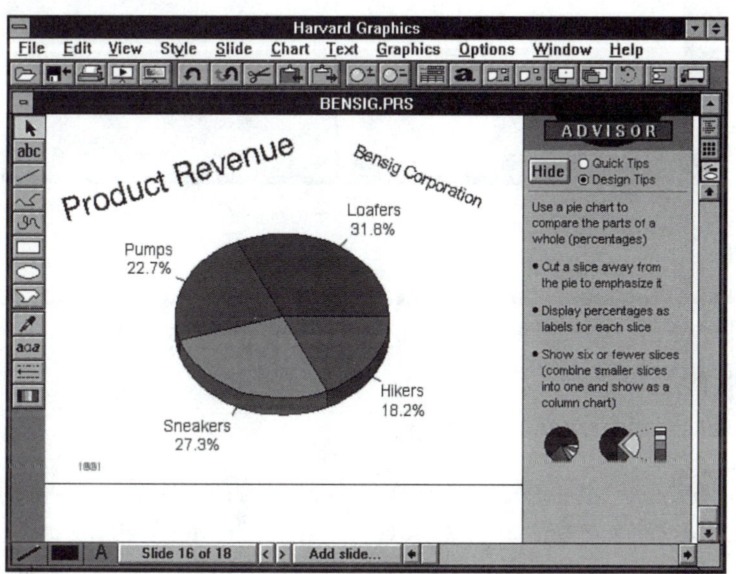

Fig. 13.11
Rotated text.

Follow these steps to rotate an object in the Slide Editor:

1. Select the object you want to rotate.
2. Choose the Rotate tool in the Icon bar to show the rotation bar on the object (see fig. 13.12). The mouse pointer changes to the rotation cursor.

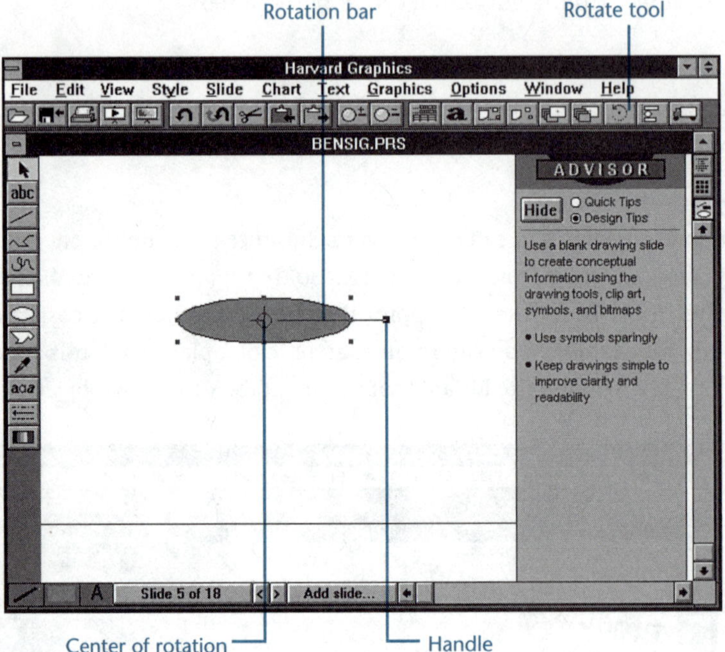

Fig. 13.12
Rotating objects in the Slide Editor.

3. Place the mouse pointer on the rotation bar's handle and drag the bar to the new angle. As you move the bar, an outline of the object indicates the rotated position.
4. Release the button.

Tip
If you hold down the Shift key while you rotate an object, the object rotates in 45 degree increments.

An object rotates around its center. When you select more than one object to rotate, the objects rotate around the center in the middle of all the objects. If you select objects in the four corners of the slide, for example, the objects rotate around the center of the slide.

You can change the center of rotation, however, so that the object(s) rotate in a different way. You can rotate one object around the center of the slide by moving the center of rotation to the slide's center. To move the center of rotation, drag the center of rotation symbol, shown in figure 13.12, to a new location. Figure 13.13 shows an object rotating around the center of the slide.

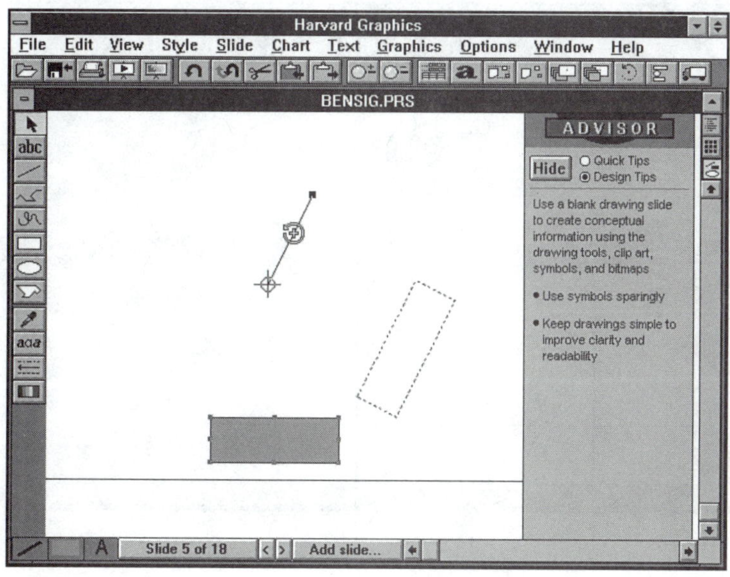

Fig. 13.13
A rectangle rotating around the slide's center.

To rotate an object around the center of the slide, follow these steps:

1. Select an object to rotate in the Slide Editor.
2. Choose the Rotate tool in the Icon bar. The mouse pointer changes to the rotation bar.
3. Click the center of the object. The mouse pointer changes to a four-directional arrow to indicate that you can move the center of rotation.
4. Drag the center of rotation to the center of the slide.
5. Rotate the object, as necessary.

When you release the mouse button, the object appears in its new position.

Flipping Objects

Flipping objects is another way you can create special graphic effects on a slide. You can make a duplicate of an object and then flip the duplicate to create a mirror image, for example. You use the Fli**p** command from the **G**raphics menu to flip objects horizontally or vertically (see fig. 13.14). The top object is the original. The object on the left is flipped horizontally. The object on the right is flipped vertically.

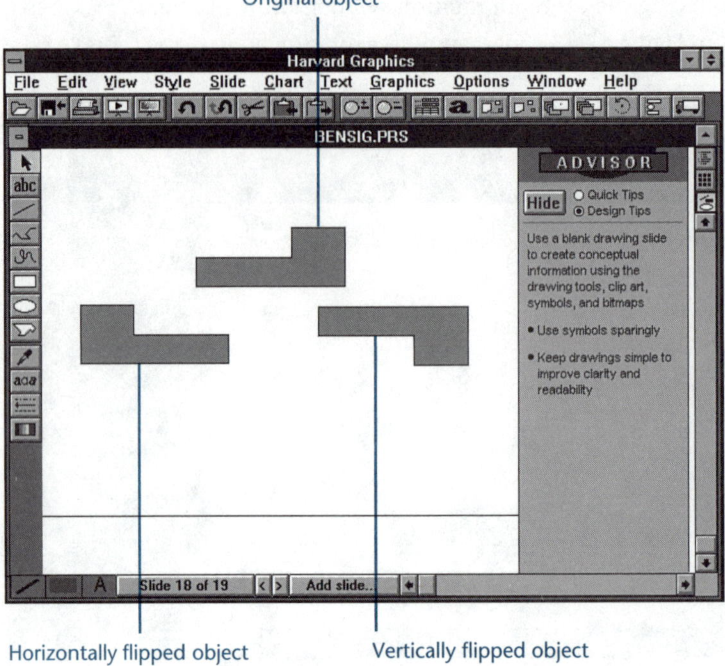

Fig. 13.14
Horizontally and vertically flipped objects.

Follow these steps to flip an object horizontally:

1. Select the object.

2. Choose Fli**p** from the **G**raphics menu. A pop-up menu appears.

3. Choose **H**orizontally from the pop-up menu. Harvard Graphics flips the object horizontally.

To flip an object vertically, you follow the same procedure, except you choose **V**ertically from the pop-up menu.

Changing the Object Order

When you create an object, the new object appears on top of the other objects in the slide; consequently, overlapping objects are common in complex slides. You use the **M**ove to front command on the **G**raphics menu to bring an object to the front so that it is clearly visible. In figure 13.15, the square was created first and the triangle last.

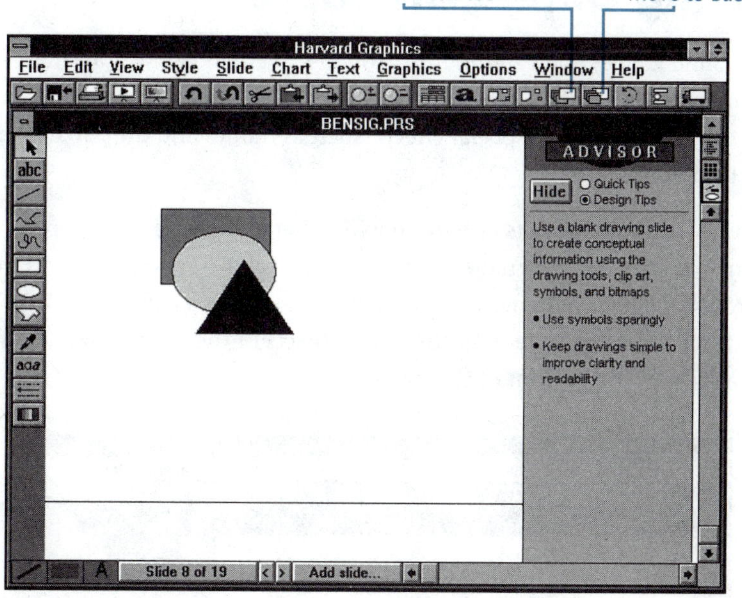

Fig. 13.15
The Move to Front and Move to Back tools.

By using the **M**o**v**e to front and Mo**v**e to back commands from the **G**raphics menu, you can rearrange the order of any stacked objects in a slide.

Follow these steps to move an object to the front:

1. Select the object to move.
2. Choose the **M**ove to front command from the **G**raphics menu. The selected object moves to the front.

The Mo**v**e to back command places objects behind other objects on the slide. To move the triangle behind the square, for example, you use the Move to back tool.

Follow these steps to move an object to the back:

1. Select the object.
2. Choose the Mo**v**e to back command from the **G**raphics menu. The selected object moves to the back.

Setting Object Attributes

In the Slide Editor, you can modify attributes to enhance the appearance of your objects. You can change the color, line styles, and fill patterns of an object. You also can add special effects, such as frames and drop shadows, to objects in your slides.

Figure 13.16 shows objects enhanced with several attributes. The top left rectangle is filled with a gradient and has a special drop shadow effect; the other rectangle has a frame. The polygon is filled with a pattern, and the oval has a thicker outline style than the other objects in the figure. Two styles of lines appear at the bottom of the figure.

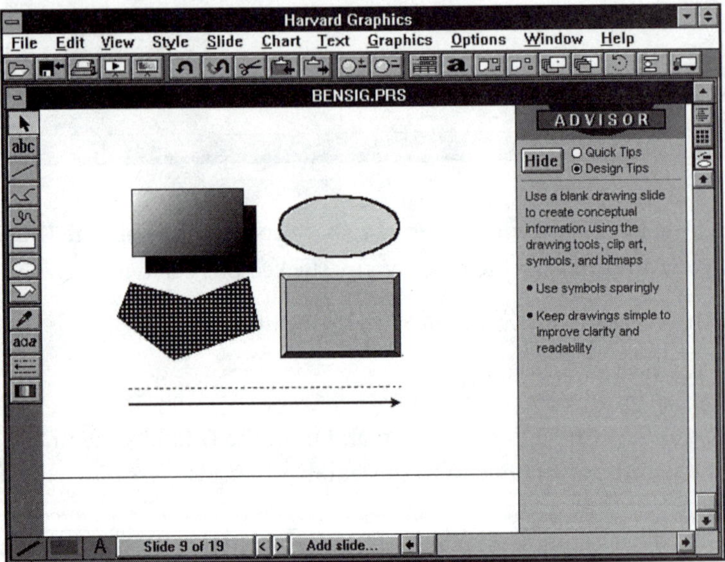

Fig. 13.16 Objects with different fill colors, style, and line attributes.

You can set the default attributes before you create an object, or you can modify the attributes after you create the object. To use the same attributes on several objects on your slide, you should set default attributes prior to creating the objects. Modifying the attributes after you create the object, on the other hand, enables you to evaluate how your changes affect the slide.

Setting the Line Style

Harvard Graphics supports many line styles. You can display dashed or solid lines. Using the Line Attributes tool, you can modify a line's thickness and add arrows to solid lines; you also can create a dashed line effect (see fig. 13.17). You use the Line Attributes tool to modify the lines of any object, including the outline of an object or the lines in a group.

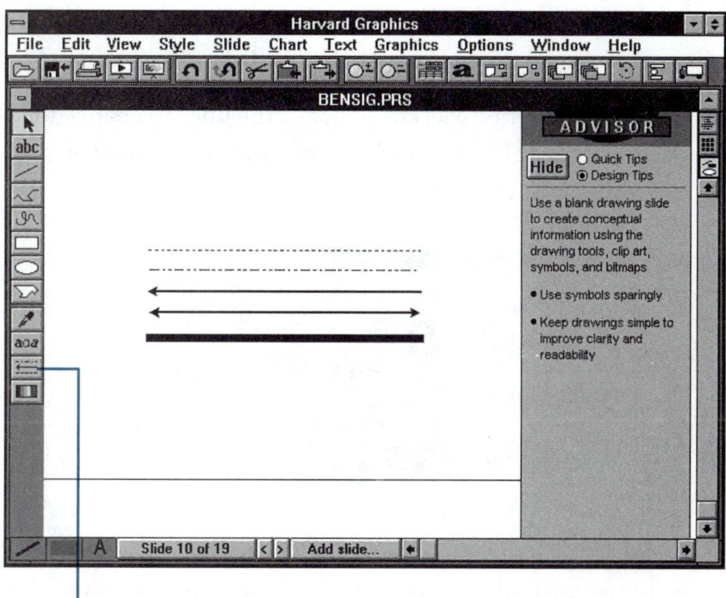

Fig. 13.17 Sample line styles and the Line Attributes tool.

To change the line style, select an object and choose the Line Attributes tool. The Line Attributes dialog box appears (see fig. 13.18). The Sample box provides an example of the line with the current settings.

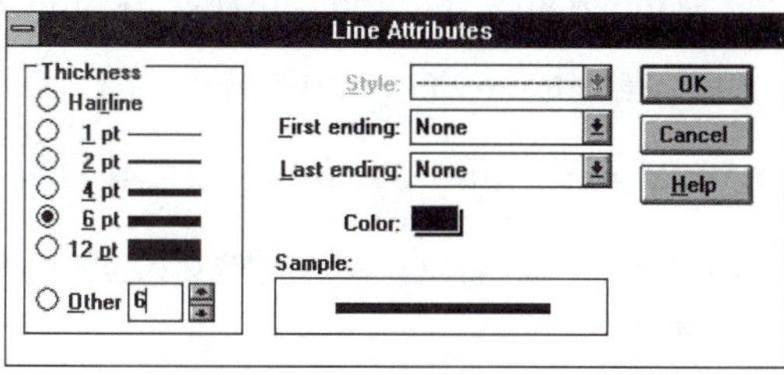

Fig. 13.18 The Line Attributes dialog box.

The Line Attributes dialog box contains options for the following settings:

- *Thickness buttons.* You use these buttons to set a line's thickness. You can choose one of the predefined thicknesses or enter a custom thickness in the text box following the last button in the list (**O**ther).

- *Style list box.* The Style list box controls the style for lines with hairline thickness. The styles range from a solid line to a combination of large and small dashes. To see the choices, click the down arrow next to the Style list box.

- *First ending and Last ending list boxes.* These boxes add arrows to the ends of a line. You can choose Large Arrow, Small Arrow, or None.

- *Color box.* The Color box sets the color of the line. To change the color, click the box and select a color from the Line Color dialog box that appears (see fig. 13.19).

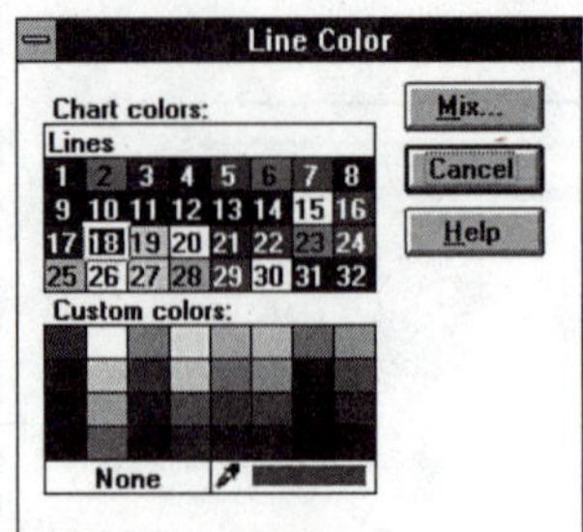

Fig. 13.19
The Line Color dialog box.

When you change the line style, your changes affect all lines in the selected object, including the outline of the object. If you do not select an object, the settings affect the next object you create.

Follow these steps to change the line attributes of a plain line to a thick, red line with arrows at both ends:

1. Select the line. Handles appear to indicate that the line is selected.
2. Choose the Line Attributes tool from the toolbox.
3. Click the **6** pt thickness setting to make the selected line 6 points thick.
4. Click the arrow next to the **F**irst ending: list box; choose Large Arrow from the list that appears.
5. Click the arrow next to the **L**ast ending: list box; choose Large Arrow from the list that appears.
6. Click the Color box. The Line Color dialog box appears.
7. Choose a red color in the dialog box.
8. Click OK in the Line Attributes dialog box.

The thick, red line appears in the Slide Editor window (see fig. 13.20).

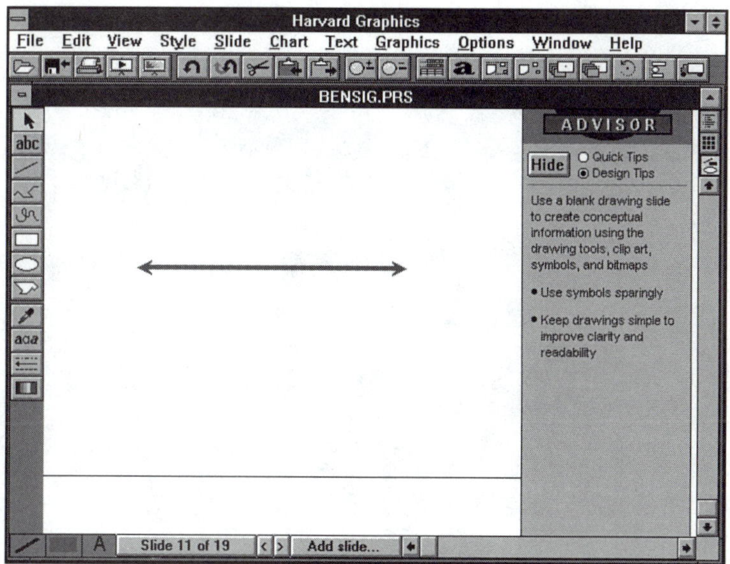

Fig. 13.20
A line modified in the Line Attributes dialog box.

Setting the Fill Style

The fill style determines how Harvard Graphics fills objects. A rectangle and circle are examples of objects you can fill with a color or pattern. In the Slide Editor, you can fill an object with a solid color or with a style that varies in color and pattern.

You use the Fill tool, shown in figure 13.21, to set the fill style for a solid object. The figure shows four rectangles, each containing a different fill style. The top left rectangle contains a solid fill; the top right rectangle contains a pattern/hatch fill; the lower left rectangle contains a gradient fill; and the final rectangle in the lower right contains a Windows bitmap fill.

To change the fill color of an object, click the Fill tool and hold down the mouse button. The pop-up toolbar, shown in figure 13.22, appears. You can choose any of the four fill tools that appear. The Fill tool sets the solid fill color, the Hatch/Pattern Fill tool sets the hatch and pattern fill style, the Gradient Fill tool sets the gradient fill, and the Bitmap Fill tool sets the bitmap fill.

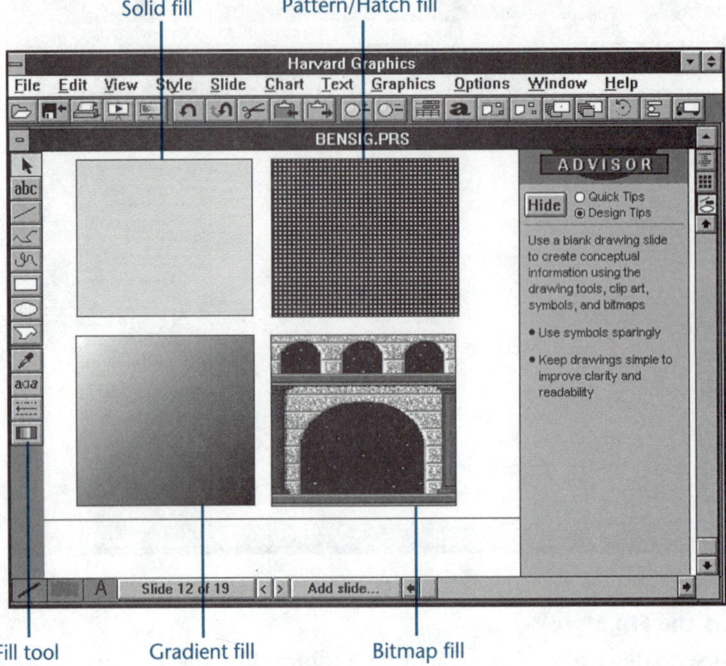

Fig. 13.21 Examples of the four fill styles.

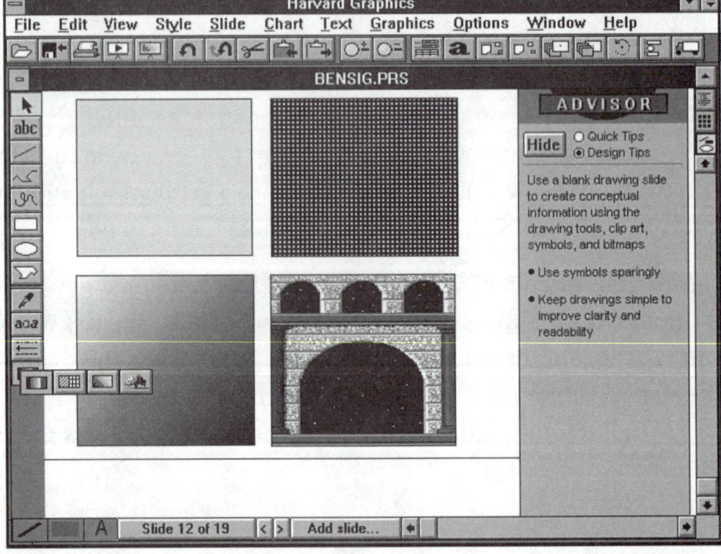

Fig. 13.22 The pop-up toolbar of fill styles.

Setting the Solid Fill Color

A solid filled object is an object filled with a single color. To set the solid fill color for an object, follow these steps:

1. Select the object.
2. Click the Fill tool.

   The Solid Color Fill dialog box appears (see fig. 13.23). This dialog box presents the colors available on the current color palette.

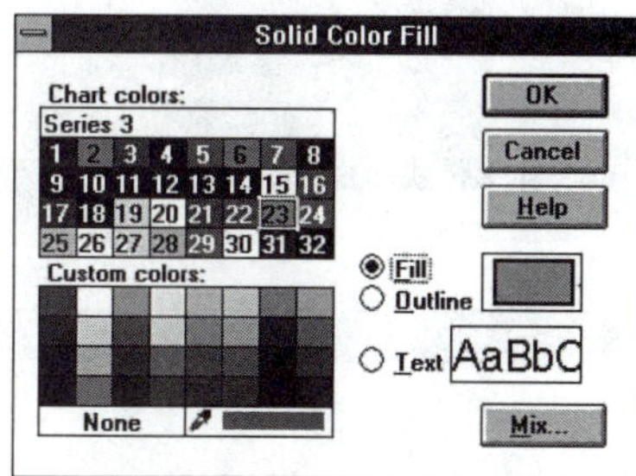

Fig. 13.23
The Solid Color Fill dialog box.

   Using this dialog box, you also can change the color for an object's line and the text. To change the line color, click the **O**utline button; then select a new color. To change the text color, click the **T**ext button; then select a color. You use the **M**ix button to create custom colors.

3. To change the color, click a color in the dialog box.
4. Click OK.

The fill color of the selected object changes to reflect the options you chose in the Solid Color Fill dialog box.

Setting Hatch and Pattern Fills. Hatch- and pattern-filled objects display a pattern in one color in the foreground and a solid color in the background of the object (see fig. 13.24). The rectangle in the upper left corner contains a hatch fill. Hatch fills, which consist of lines, are more effective on slides output to a plotter because plotters are limited to simple lines. The other rectangles contain pattern fills. Pattern fills use a special bit map to determine the parts of the object filled with the foreground color. Bit maps are not limited to the lines of a hatch fill.

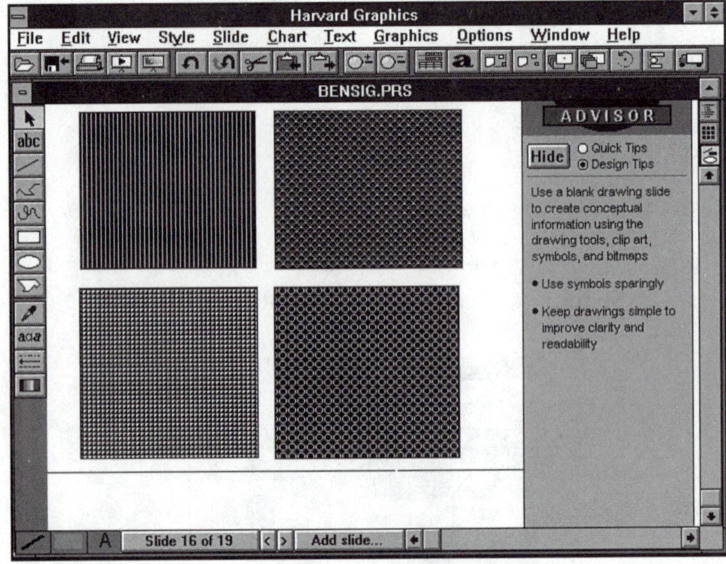

Fig. 13.24 Hatch- and pattern-filled objects.

Follow these steps to fill an object with a hatch or pattern:

1. Select the object you want to fill.
2. Choose the Hatch/Pattern Fill tool, the second icon on the pop-up toolbar.

   The Hatch/Pattern Fill dialog box appears (see fig. 13.25). In the dialog box, you can choose from 8 hatch fills and 56 pattern fills.

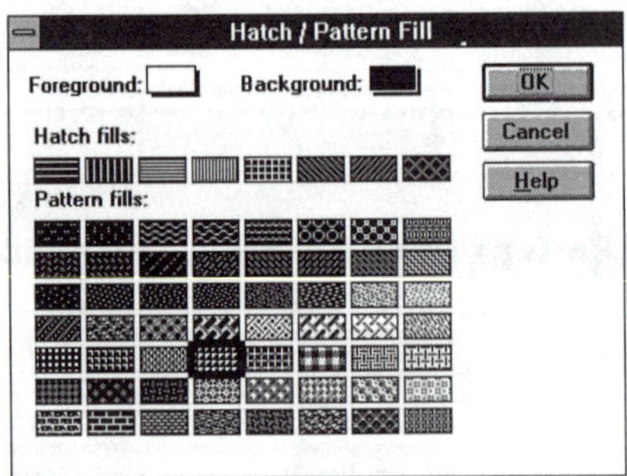

Fig. 13.25 The Hatch/Pattern Fill dialog box.

3. To hatch-fill an object, select a style from the Hatch fills: section of the dialog box. To pattern-fill an object, select a style from the Pattern fills: section of the dialog box.

   You have chosen only the hatch or pattern style. Now you must select the foreground and background colors of the object.

4. Click the Foreground: button. The Foreground Hatch/Pattern Color dialog box, in which you select a color for the foreground, appears.

5. Select a foreground color. When you change the color, the hatches and patterns appear with the new color.

6. Click the Background button. The Background Hatch/Pattern Color dialog box, in which you choose a background color, appears.

7. Select a background color. The Background Hatch/Pattern Color dialog box closes.

8. Click OK to return to the Slide Editor.

The selected object reflects the changes you made in the Hatch/Pattern Fill dialog box.

Setting Gradient Fills. A gradient fill blends from one color into another. In addition to setting the start and finish color, you also can control the angle of the fill. Figure 13.26 shows three objects with gradient fills at 0, 45, and 90 degree angles. A 0 degree angle displays the starting color on the left of the object and the ending color on the right. As you rotate the angle, the start color rotates around the object as well. A 90 degree angle starts the fill at the bottom of the object.

You use the Gradient Fill tool to set the gradient fill of an object. When you select this tool, the Gradient Fill dialog box appears (see fig. 13.27). The Sample box in the middle of the dialog box shows the current gradient fill settings. The Start color: and End color: boxes determine the colors of the fill. The **A**ngle: text box and dial determine the fill's angle. You can change the angle by typing the angle in the **A**ngle: text box or by dragging the arm of the dial to the new angle.

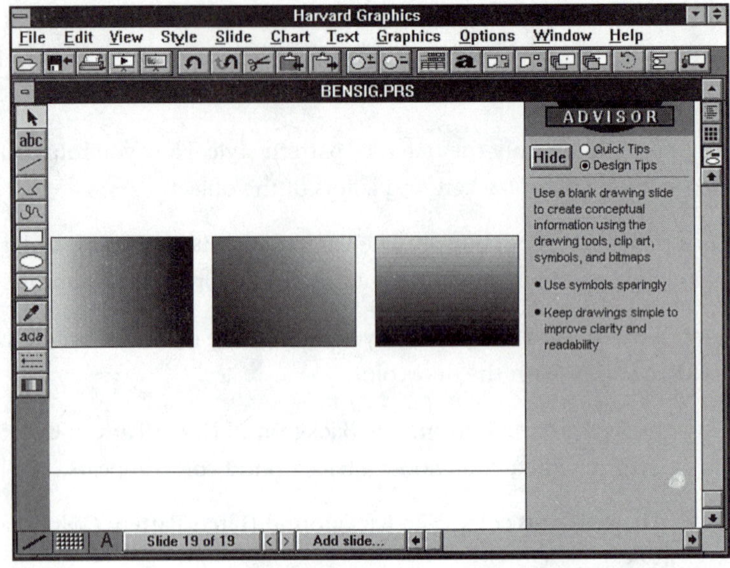

Fig. 13.26
Examples of three gradient fill angles.

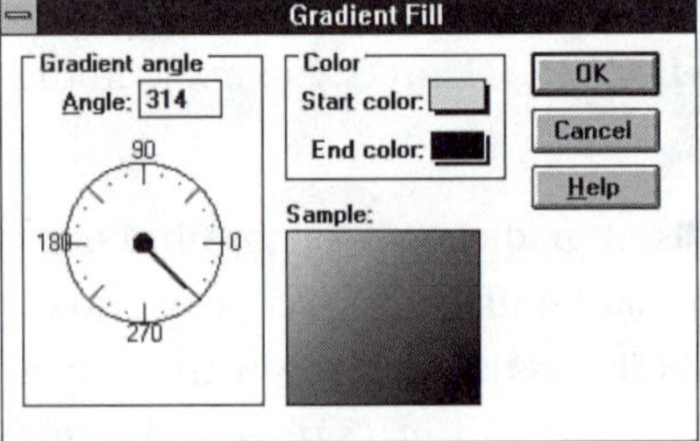

Fig. 13.27
The Gradient Fill dialog box.

Follow these steps to set a 45 degree fill:

1. Select the object.
2. Select the Gradient Fill tool from the pop-up toolbar. The Gradient Fill dialog box appears.
3. Click the Start color: box. The Start Gradient Color dialog box, containing the available colors, appears.
4. Choose a starting color in the dialog box. This dialog box closes, and the Sample in the Gradient Fill dialog box changes to the new color.
5. Click the End color: box. The End Gradient Color dialog box, containing the available colors, appears.

6. Choose an ending color. The dialog box closes, and the Sample in the Gradient Fill dialog box changes to the new color.

7. Drag the arm of the dial to the 45 degree angle. As you move the dial, the colors in the Sample box rotate. The current angle for the dial appears in the **A**ngle: text box.

8. Click the OK button to return to the Slide Editor.

The selected object appears in the Slide Editor with the gradient fill options you chose.

Setting Bit-Mapped Fills. A *bit map* is a picture stored in a file that uses a standard format. Harvard Graphics supports bit maps that use the BMP, PCX, PCC, GIF, and TFF formats. You can create bit-mapped images with a painting program, such as Windows Paintbrush, or with a scanner that converts pictures into bit-mapped images. You use the Bitmap Fill tool to fill a solid object with a bit-mapped image. Figure 13.28 shows a polygon filled with the bit-mapped image EGYPT.BMP, which comes with Windows.

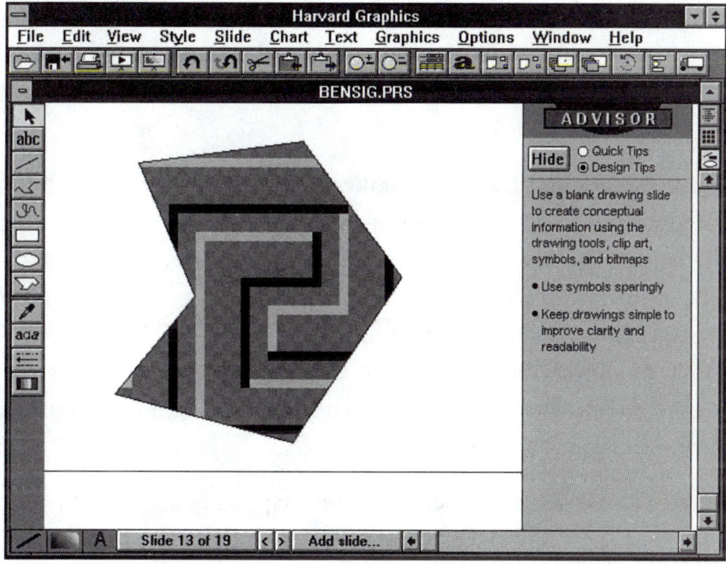

Fig. 13.28
An object filled with a bit-mapped image.

To fill an object with an image, select the Bitmap Fill tool from the pop-up toolbar. The Bitmap Fill dialog box appears (see fig. 13.29). The Bitmap source buttons (File and **C**lipboard) indicate whether the bit map comes from a file or from the Clipboard. To use the Clipboard, you must transfer the bit map to the Clipboard before selecting the Bitmap Fill tool.

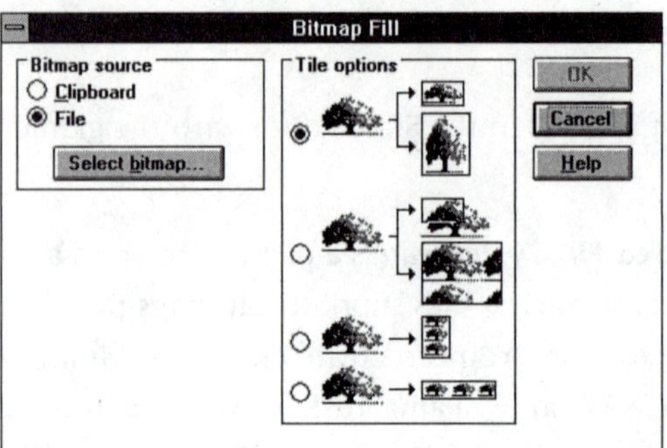

Fig. 13.29
The Bitmap Fill dialog box.

You use the Select **b**itmap... option to search for files on your hard disk. To locate the bit map file on your hard disk, click the Select **b**itmap... button to see the available bit maps. The name of the file appears next to the File button in the Bitmap source area. The next time you choose the Bitmap Fill tool, Harvard Graphics displays this name to indicate that this file is used in the fill.

You use the Tile Options buttons to indicate how the bit map should fill the object. Figure 13.29 shows examples of the four ways you can use the bit map to fill the object. The first option increases or decreases the size of the bit map to fit within the object; when you change the size of the object, the bit map also changes. The second option tiles miniature images of the bit map throughout the object. The third option keeps the height of the bit map but increases the width. The fourth option increases the height but keeps the width of the bit map the same.

Follow these steps to fill an object with a bit-mapped image:

1. Select the object.
2. Choose the Bitmap Fill tool from the pop-up toolbar. The Bitmap Fill dialog box appears.
3. Click the File button to fill the bit map with a file.

4. Click the Select **b**itmap... button. The Select Bitmap dialog box, in which you select a bit map file, appears. This dialog box resembles other directory dialog boxes used throughout Harvard Graphics, and is similar to the Window's File Open dialog box.

5. To see the available bit-map types, click the arrow next to the list box.

6. Select EGYPT.BMP from the Windows directory. (The directory on your system is based on your Windows installation.)

7. Choose the Save bitmap with presentation file option to save the actual bit-mapped file with your presentation.

8. Click the OK button in the Select Bitmap dialog box. You return to the Bitmap Fill dialog box. The name of the file—in the example, EGYPT.BMP—appears next to the File button.

9. Click the OK button on the Bitmap Fill dialog box to accept the changes and return to the Slide Editor window.

The selected object reflects the options you set in the Bitmap Fill dialog box.

Adding Special Effects

To add a frame, drop shadow, or sweep to an object, you use the **S**pecial effects... option on the **G**raphics menu. Figure 13.30 shows each of these effects. The rectangle in the top left has a three-dimensional frame. The bottom rectangle has a drop shadow. The oval sweeps from a lighter to a darker color.

To add an effect, select an object; then choose **S**pecial effects... from the **G**raphics menu. The Special Effects dialog box appears (see fig. 13.31). The selected object appears in the Sample box. To add a special effect, click the down arrow next to the **E**ffect: list box and choose an effect from the list. (You can apply only one special effect to each object.) When you choose an effect from the list, the object in the Sample box reflects the current setting.

Fig. 13.30
Examples of special effects.

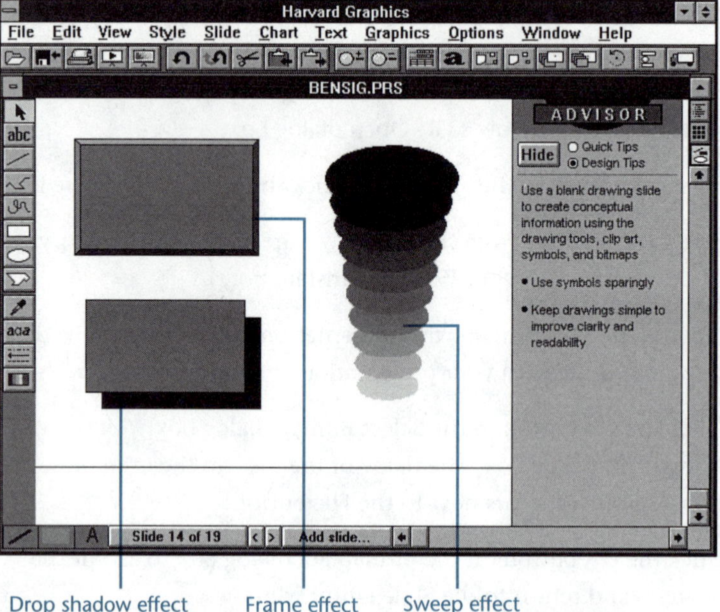

Fig. 13.31
The Special Effects dialog box.

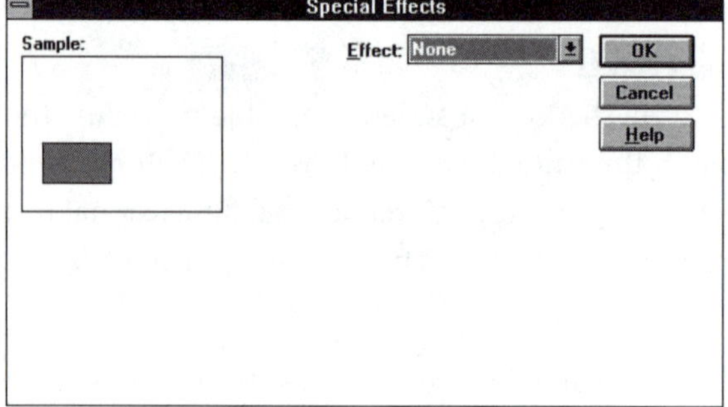

Adding a Frame. The first option in the **E**ffect list is the Frame option. When you choose Frame from the list, the frame options appear in the Special Effects dialog box (see fig. 13.32). You set the color of the frame in the Color box by clicking the Color button and choosing a color from the dialog box that appears.

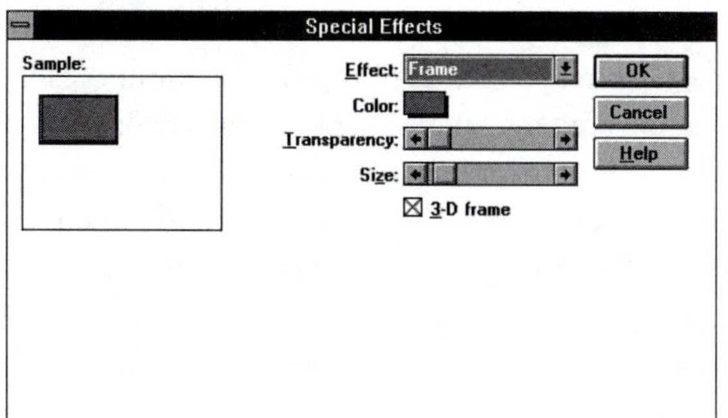

Fig. 13.32
The Special Effects dialog box with the Frame options.

You use the **T**ransparency: slider to adjust the transparency of the frame, affecting the visibility of objects beneath the frame. If you drag the slider to the right, you make the frame more transparent and the object beneath the frame more visible. If you drag the slider to the left, you make the frame less transparent and the object beneath the frame less visible.

You use the Si**z**e: scroll bar to change the thickness of the frame. By dragging the slider to the right, you make the frame thicker; dragging the slider to the left makes the frame thinner. By toggling the **3**-D frame check box, you determine whether the frame is two-dimensional (no X in the box) or three-dimensional (X in the box).

Follow these steps to create a frame:

1. Select the object.
2. Choose **S**pecial effects... from the **G**raphics menu. The selected object appears in the Sample box in the Special Effects dialog box.
3. Click the down arrow next to the **E**ffect: list box. A drop-down list of special effects appears.
4. Choose Frame from the list.
5. Click the **3**-D frame box. An X appears.
6. Click the OK button to remove the Special Effects dialog box and add the effect to the object.

The object in the Slide Editor window appears with a 3-D frame.

Adding a Drop Shadow. The Drop shadow option displays a color shadow behind any object. When you choose Drop shadow from the Effect list in the Special **E**ffects dialog box, the Drop shadow options appear (see fig. 13.33). You can set the color and the transparency of the shadow much like you set these options for a frame. With a drop shadow, however, you also can change the position of the shadow. In the Sample box, you can change the location of the shadow by dragging the shadow to a new location. When you move the mouse pointer over the box, the pointer changes to a four-directional arrow.

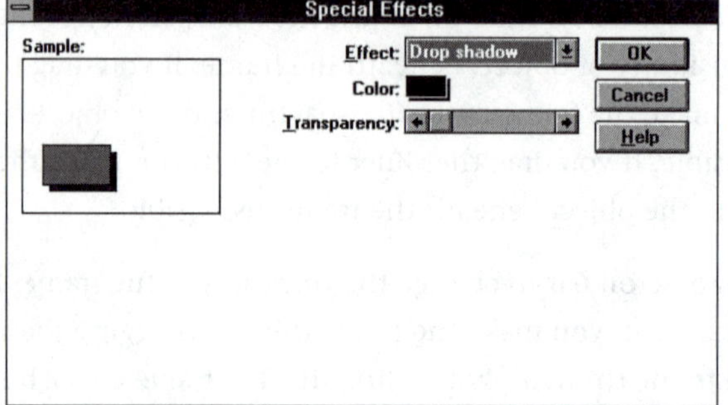

Fig. 13.33
The Special Effects dialog box with the Drop shadow options.

Design Note

A lighter transparency enhances the effect of the shadow by enabling the objects behind to appear in the shadow of the object.

Follow these steps to create a drop shadow:

1. Select the object.
2. Choose **S**pecial effects... from the **G**raphics menu. The selected object appears in the Sample box of the Special Effects dialog box.
3. Click the down arrow next to the **E**ffect: list box and choose Drop shadow from the list that appears. The drop shadow options appear in the dialog box.
4. Click the Color: box and choose the shadow color from the Shadow Color dialog box.
5. Click the right scroll arrow of the **T**ransparency: slider to make a more transparent shadow.

6. Change the location of the shadow by dragging the shadow of the object in the Sample box to the right of the object.

7. Click the OK button to remove the Special Effects dialog box and add the effect to the object in the Slide Editor.

Adding a Sweep. You use the Sweep effect to create copies of an object evolving from one color to another. With a sweep, multiple copies of the object appear on the slide. You can set a starting color for the first copy and an ending color for the last. Harvard Graphics colors the middle objects much like a gradient. The sweep effect is ideal for creating the illusion of movement.

The Special Effects dialog box, shown in figure 13.34, shows the Sweep options when you choose Sweep from the list. The Color: and End color: boxes control the starting and ending color of the sweep, respectively. The *starting color* is the color of the copy displayed directly below the original object. The *ending color* is the color of the copy farthest from the original.

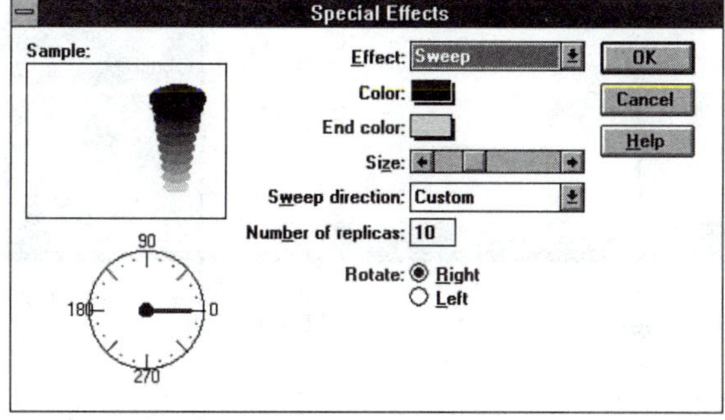

Fig. 13.34 The Special Effects dialog box with the Sweep options.

The Size: slider determines the size of the last copy, which is the farthest from the original object. By clicking the right scroll arrow, you increase the size of the object. The starting size of the object in the sweep depends on the original object. The sizes of the middle copies gradually increase or decrease from the original size to the last copy.

The Sweep direction: list box determines whether the objects evolve in a predefined or custom direction. To see the choices, click the arrow next to the Sweep direction: list box. The first option in the list is Custom. You can set the custom sweep by clicking the end of the sweep in the Sample box and dragging the object to a custom location.

The choices for predefined directions include Left, Right, Up, Down, and Out. These options sweep the copies of the object to one of the four directions. The Out option places each copy of the object on top of the next, with the original on top. (If you choose this option, make sure that the last copy is larger than the original.) Figure 13.35 shows a predefined sweep to the left and a custom sweep down and to the left.

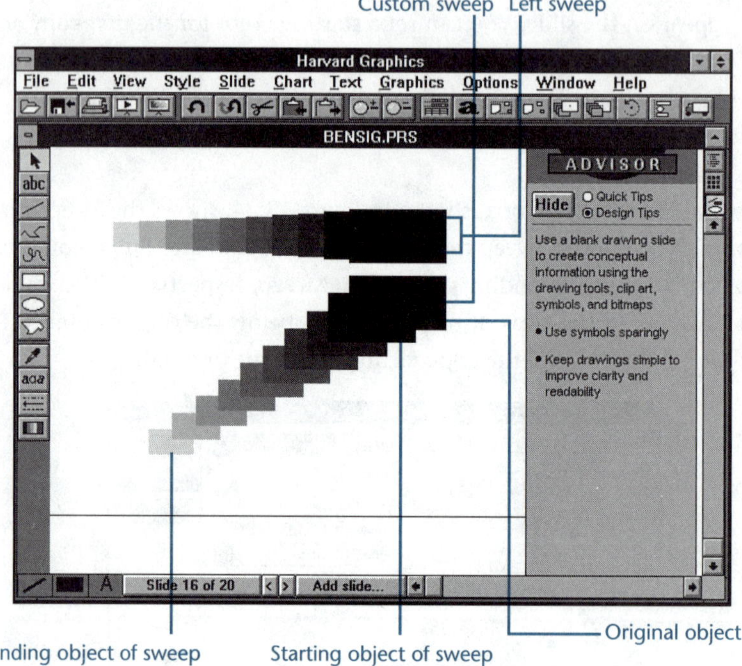

Fig. 13.35
Left and custom sweeps.

The Num**b**er of replicas: option determines how many copies of the object Harvard Graphics uses in the sweep. By default, Harvard Graphics creates the sweep with 10 replicas of the object; however, you can set this option to any number 2 through 20.

You can rotate the copies of the objects to the right or left. The Rotate buttons—**R**ight and **L**eft—determine in which direction the objects rotate, and the dial determines how much each object rotates. You can rotate each copy of the object 0 through 360 degrees.

Figure 13.36 shows a custom sweep with the objects of the sweep rotated to the right. The End color is lighter than the starting color. Nine objects appear in the sweep, and the final object is much smaller than the original object.

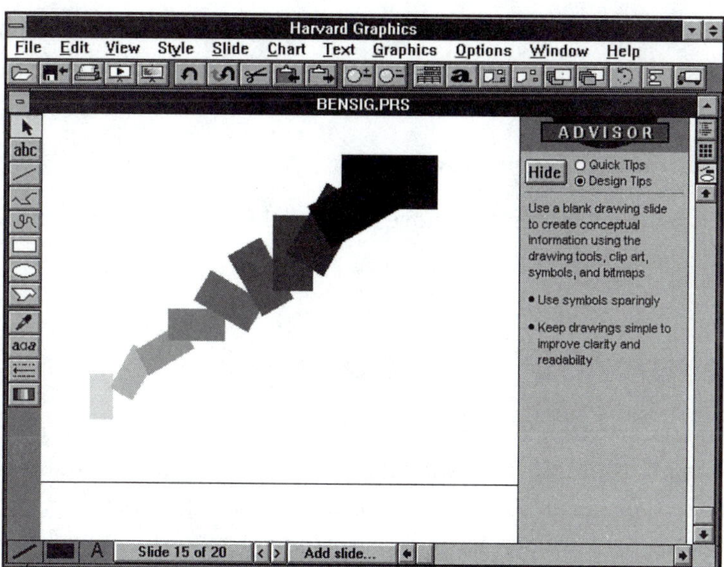

Fig. 13.36 A custom sweep with rotated objects.

Follow these steps to create a sweep:

1. Select the object.
2. Choose **S**pecial effects... from the **G**raphics menu. The selected object appears in the Sample box.
3. Click the arrow next to the **E**ffect: list box. A drop-down list appears.
4. Choose Sweep from the list. The Sweep options appear in the Special Effects dialog box.
5. Click the Color: box and choose a color from the Shadow Color dialog box.

   Pick a color that is similar to the original object so the sweep appears to evolve into the final object.
6. Click the End color: box and choose a color from the Shadow Color dialog box.
7. Click the left arrow of the Si**z**e: slider to decrease the size of the ending object.
8. Change the degree of the angle by dragging the arm of the dial to the 45-degree angle.

9. To move the end of the sweep, place the mouse pointer in the Sample box. The pointer changes to a four-directional arrow, indicating that you can move the end of the sweep.

10. Drag the object to the new location.

11. Click the OK button to remove the Special Effects dialog box and add the sweep to the object.

Copying Object Attributes

After you set the attribute, you can use the Eyedropper tool to copy attributes, such as the line style and fill color, from one object to another (see fig. 13.37). Copying attributes from one object to another enables you to avoid setting the attributes for each object individually. You also can copy the attributes so that the subsequent objects you create contain the attributes.

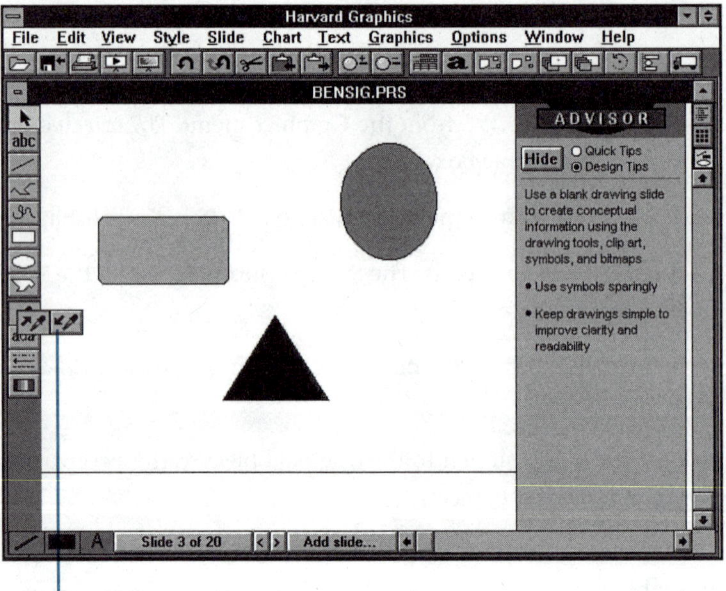

Fig. 13.37
The Eyedropper pop-up toolbar.

When you click and hold down the mouse button on the Eyedropper tool, a pop-up toolbar appears. You use the left icon (which contains the arrow pointing upward) to copy the attributes; you use the right icon (which contains the arrow pointing downward) to transfer the attributes to a new object.

Follow these steps to copy attributes from one object to another:

1. Select the object whose attributes you intend to copy.
2. From the pop-up toolbar that appears when you select the Eyedropper tool, choose the icon that contains the arrow pointing upward.
3. Select the object to which you're copying the attributes.
4. Choose the Eyedropper tool that contains the arrow pointing downward.

The copied attributes appear in the selected object.

From Here...

This chapter covers the Slide Editor features that you use to modify and enhance the objects on a slide. The chapter explains how to select objects in the window and how to edit the objects. The section on editing objects includes instruction for transferring objects to the Windows Clipboard and moving objects in the window. After explaining how to edit objects, the chapter covers the features you use to modify an object's appearance. You learned how to set the line and fill style for an object and how to add special effects.

The next chapter, "Creating Output," explains how you can print a presentation.

Chapter 14

Creating Output

While you prepare the slides of a presentation, your work exists only in your computer's memory and on your hard disk. With the **F**ile menu's **P**rint command, however, you can transfer the images on your slides to another medium, such as transparent pages or film. The printing capabilities of this product complete the tools you need to transform ideas and information into a final presentation.

In this chapter, you learn how to do the following:

- Print a presentation
- Create handouts
- Create speaker notes

Harvard Graphics enables you to present your data on various media. By using transparencies with an overhead projector, for example, you can present your ideas on a screen much larger than your computer monitor. For color output, you can use any color printer or plotter that Windows supports. You also can record your presentation on film and then use a slide service, such as Autographics, to create slides for a slide projector. This chapter explains how to output your presentations using any of these media. You also learn how to create handouts so that your audience can follow along with the presentation.

Printing a Presentation

Harvard Graphics can print your slides on any output device, such as a printer or a plotter, that Windows supports. An *output device* is any device that transfers information and images from your computer to another medium—paper, for example. You must load the device with the medium you intend to use; for example, load your printer with paper or—if your printer supports it—transparencies.

You use the **P**rint command to transfer your presentation to a printer and from there, to paper. Make sure that you set up your printer before you choose **P**rint.

To print the presentation, follow these steps:

1. If the presentation is not in memory, load the presentation by using the **O**pen command on the **F**ile menu.

2. Choose **P**rint from the **F**ile menu.

   You see the Print dialog box (see fig. 14.1). The Select a de**v**ice: list box lists the current output device. The default options in the dialog box are set for basic printing of an entire presentation. The following section, "Changing Print Options," contains information about print settings.

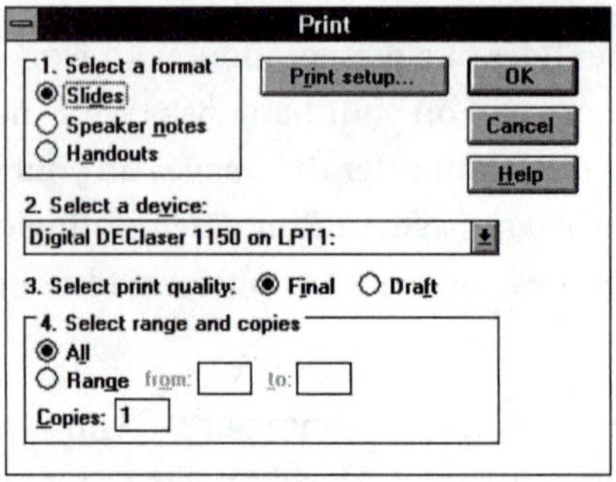

Fig. 14.1
The Print dialog box.

3. Click OK.

Harvard Graphics prints the presentation.

While your slides are printing, Harvard Graphics displays the status box shown in figure 14.2 to communicate the progress of your output. This status box indicates which slide of the presentation Harvard Graphics is printing. To cancel the print job, click the Cancel button in the status box.

Fig. 14.2
The output status message box.

Changing Print Options

The options in the Print dialog box are designed to produce quality output for different types of devices. You also can set these options to output quick draft copies of your slides or final high-quality output. Some options, such as **C**opies: and Ran**g**e, determine how many copies or what slide range to print.

The first option, Select a format, enables you to print one of the following types of output: the Sli**d**es of your presentation, Speaker **n**otes that show each slide along with notes you enter, or H**a**ndouts that enable you to combine many slides on one page for handing out to your audience. See the section "Generating Speaker Notes" later in this chapter for more information on setting up and printing your notes. See "Generating Handouts" later in the chapter for more information on handouts. The P**r**int setup... button enables you to change options that affect the appearance of your printed presentation. See the section "Modifying Print Setup Options" later for more information.

Choosing an Output Device. The Select a de**v**ice: list box lists the current output device. With Windows you can set up many output devices at one time. To see all the devices, click the down scroll arrow next to the list box. (See "Adding New Devices" later in this chapter to learn how to set up new devices with Harvard Graphics.) If the device you want is not the current listed device, choose the device from the list that you wish to use when printing.

Printing Multiple Copies. You use the **C**opies: text box on the Print dialog box to determine how many copies of the presentation to print. The default value is 1, indicating that Harvard Graphics will print one copy of the presentation. To print more than one copy, click this box and type the value for the number of copies you want.

To print more than one copy of a presentation, follow these steps:

1. Choose **P**rint... from the **F**ile menu. The Print dialog box appears.
2. Click the **C**opies: text box.
3. Press the Del key to clear the box.
4. Type the number of copies that you intend to print.
5. Click OK.

Harvard Graphics prints the specified number of copies.

Printing a Range of Slides. The A**l**l and Ran**g**e options on the Print dialog box determine what slides in the presentation to print. To print the entire presentation, click the A**l**l button. To print a range of slides, click the Range button.

If you choose the Range button, the from: and to: text boxes are enabled. The from: text box determines the first slide to print and the to: text box determines the last slide.

Follow these steps to print the second, third, and fourth slides of a presentation:

1. Choose **P**rint... from the **F**ile menu. The Print dialog box appears.
2. Click the Ran**g**e button. The from: and to: text boxes become enabled.
3. Click the from: text box and type **2**.
4. Click the to: text box and type **4**.
5. Click OK to start printing.

Harvard Graphics prints the specified range of slides.

Producing a Draft-Quality Printout. The Dra**f**t button of the Select print quality: option in the Print dialog box enables you to quickly produce a hard copy of your presentation. With a draft copy, you quickly can examine the flow between slides or allow others to edit a draft of your work. Dra**f**t printing is faster than F**i**nal printing, although the quality of the output is less polished. To print a draft-quality copy, click the Dra**f**t button before printing.

Modifying Print Setup Options. The P**r**int setup options affect the appearance of the slides when you print your presentation. You display these options by choosing P**r**int setup... from the **F**ile menu or clicking the P**r**int setup... button in the Print dialog box shown in figure 14.1. Figure 14.3 shows the Print Setup dialog box. The Select a format section enables you to set default options for printing Sli**d**es, Speaker **n**otes, and H**a**ndouts. To set options for each of these three types of output, click the radio button before setting other options in the dialog box. The Select a de**v**ice: and Select print quality: options are identical to the options in the Print dialog box. When you set options in the Print Setup dialog box, you set the default options displayed in the Print dialog box before you print.

The remaining options in the Set print options box affect the appearance of the printed output; you do not affect the appearance of the original slides. An X in the check box indicates that the option is enabled. The following list explains these options:

- *Print text black.* The Print text black option forces all the text on a slide to become black in the output, regardless of the color of the text on the slide.

Design Note

Light-colored text may be difficult to read on some output devices. You can set the Print text black option to ensure that all your text is clear and readable.

- *Use **B** & W palette.* The black-and-white palette contains color settings designed specifically for printing on a black-and-white device. For example, the dark colors of some palettes may not contrast well on your device, and the colors on this special palette may be easier to see.

- *Fast patterns.* This option uses shades of gray when printing patterns rather than the colors displayed on your slide. Many printers can produce slides faster without color.

- *Convert fills to white.* This option changes all filled objects to solid fills of white. Printing a white fill is quicker than printing other types of fills—such as gradient or pattern—on the page. This option helps to increase the speed of the output when printing draft copies of your presentation.

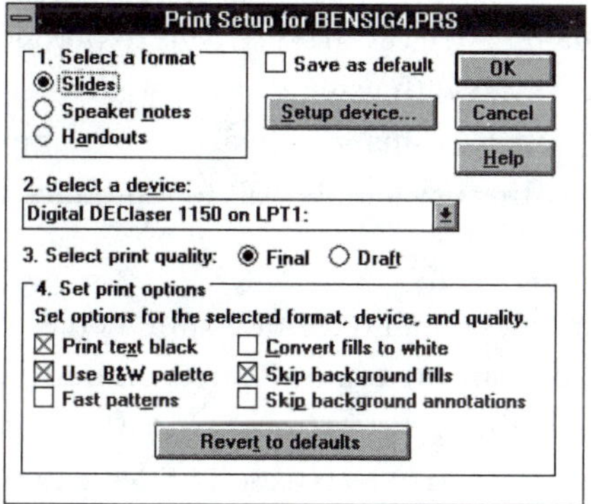

Fig 14.3
The Print Setup dialog box.

- *Skip background fills.* The background fill is a fill or color displayed behind the slide images. If you choose to skip the background fill, you may lessen the time required to print a slide on some devices, such as a color printer.

- *Skip background annotations.* As with the preceding option, skipping background annotations shortens printing time by not printing graphics that you have added to the background of a slide.

Follow these steps to modify the Print Setup options:

1. Choose Print setup... from the **F**ile menu. The Print Setup dialog box appears.
2. Change the options in the dialog box according to how you want to print your presentation.
3. Click the OK button to remove the dialog box. The next time you print, your output will reflect the new settings. When you save the presentation, your new settings are saved as well.

When you modify the setup options, your changes are saved with the current presentation. If you click the Save as default box before clicking OK, Harvard Graphics uses these settings when you create a new presentation as well.

The **S**etup device... button enables you to access the device options available within Windows for your particular output device. See your device documentation or your Windows documentation for more information.

Plotting a Presentation

Plotters, which are ideal for producing high-resolution output in a variety of paper sizes, are specialized devices that use pens to produce output. Because of the technology involved with using pens, however, certain types of fills are not possible with a plotter. Bit-mapped images, for example, often have many shades of color or gray that are too difficult to reproduce with the limited set of plotter pens.

Harvard Graphics cannot plot all types of graphics objects—such as filled objects—that you can create on a slide. Plotters outline bit-mapped filled objects, for example, but they cannot produce the bit-mapped image. A plotter prints gradient-filled objects as solid-filled with the first color of the gradient. Plotters also convert pattern-filled objects to solid fills.

To print a presentation on a plotter, follow these steps:

1. Choose **P**rint... from the **F**ile menu. The Print dialog box appears.
2. If the Select a device: list box does not list the plotter, click the box's down scroll arrow and choose the plotter from the list.

You cannot set options for a plotter the way you can for a printer. In fact, Harvard Graphics ignores options you try to set.

3. Click OK to start plotting the presentation.

Generating Handouts

As you plan and produce a presentation, you may decide that audience members may benefit from a handout of the presentation slides. Harvard Graphics enables you to create such a handout.

Figure 14.4 shows an example of a handout in the Slide Editor. The three placeholders show the positions of three consecutive slides in the presentation. The right side of the handout contains a graphics object, which Harvard Graphics prints on every slide. The handout shows the company logo and provides room for the audience to keep notes.

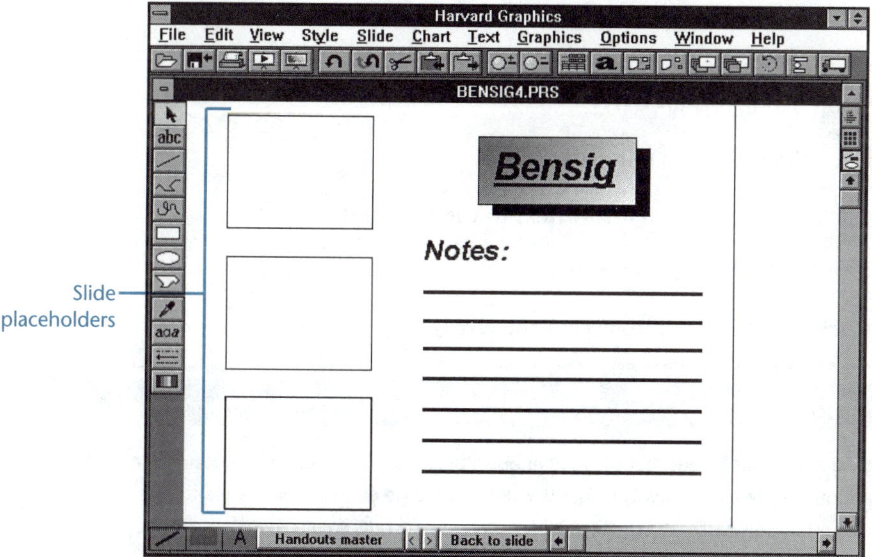

Fig. 14.4 A handout in the Slide Editor.

Choosing a Handout Design

The handout layout determines how many slides to print on a single page and where to locate the slides on the page. You can display one, two, three, four, or six slides on a single page. For three slides on a page, you can display the slides in the center of the page or on the left. Figure 14.5 shows layouts for the different handout styles.

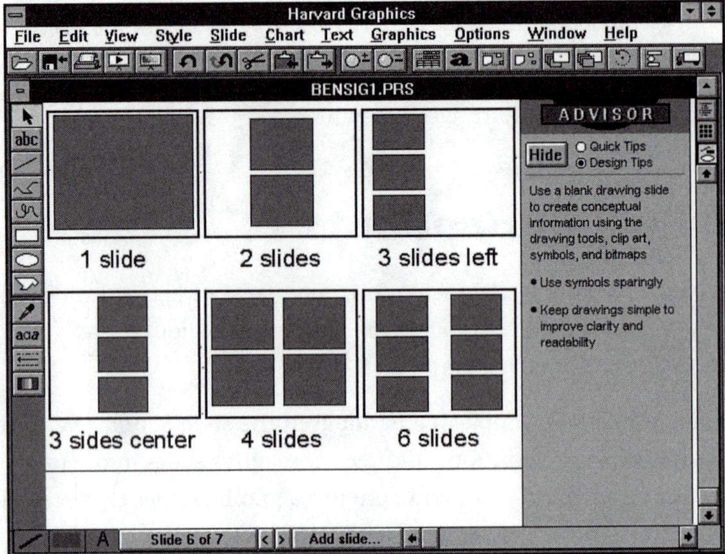

Fig. 14.5 Examples of the different handout styles.

Follow these steps to set the layout design:

1. Choose Presentation se**t**up... from the **F**ile menu. The Presentation Setup dialog box appears.
2. Click the Handouts button.
3. Click the down scroll arrow next to the Handouts list box.
4. Choose the layout from the list.
5. Click the OK button to accept the changes.

Design Note

Choose a handout layout that displays enough presentation slides to function well as a handout. Make sure, however, that the slides are large enough for readers to see clearly. A handout with two or three slides on a page works well.

Adding Graphics to Handouts

Often, when you create handouts, you want to include items in the handouts that you do not include on the presentation slides. You can use the Slide Editor to add graphics and text annotations to any slide and to your handouts. Figure 14.4 shows a handout with graphics added in the Slide Editor. In this figure, lines for notes have been added to the handout so that your audience can take notes on the presentation as you explain the slides. A company logo also appears on the handout.

When you print your presentation with the handout, Harvard Graphics prints the graphics you add on each page. The Edit handouts master command on the St**y**le menu displays the current handout in the Slide Editor. You can create and change the same objects on a handout as you do on a slide. However, you cannot move or resize the slide placeholders.

To enhance your handouts, follow these steps:

1. If you are not viewing the presentation in the Slide **E**ditor, choose Slide Editor from the **V**iew menu.

2. Choose Edit **h**andouts master from the St**y**le menu. The handout appears in the Slide Editor.

   After the handout appears, the Add slide... button at the bottom of the Slide Editor window changes to the Back to slide button.

3. Enhance the handout by using the tools of the Slide Editor. See Chapter 12, "Drawing in Harvard Graphics," for information on using the Slide Editor to enhance your slide.

4. After you finish making your changes, click the Back to slide button.

Printing Handouts

The H**a**ndouts button on the Print dialog box causes your slides to print using the current handout style. When you print the presentation, the handout style determines the number of slides printed on the same page and the locations of the slides on the page. See the section "Choosing a Handout Design" for more information.

Follow these steps to output a presentation using the current handout style:

1. Choose **P**rint... from the **F**ile menu. The Print dialog box appears.

2. Click the H**a**ndouts button.

3. Click OK to start printing.

Generating Speaker Notes

Speaker notes are intended to provide reference and other helpful information while presenting your slides. Each slide has a single speaker note. A representation of the slide is displayed in a box on your speaker notes to help you associate the slide with the notes. You can add textual prompts about information you need to cover when you present the slide to your viewers, or you can add graphics that you may need to draw on a white board to help illustrate a point. Speaker notes do not appear when you display a presentation on-screen, nor do they print when you print your slides. Instead, you print a separate copy of your presentation with your notes using the **P**rint... command on the **F**ile menu. Figure 14.6 shows an example of speaker notes for a pie chart on Product Revenue. The notes remind the presenter to cover products in a specific order and to mention profits before releasing the audience for a break.

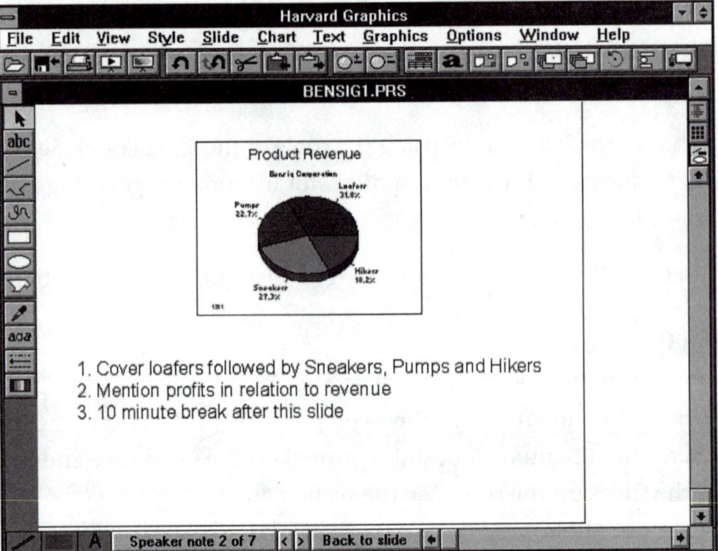

Fig. 14.6 Speaker notes for the Product Revenue slide.

Editing Speaker Notes

The **E**dit speaker notes command on the **S**lide menu displays the speaker notes for the current slide in the Slide Editor. You can create and change the same objects as you do with a slide. You add text and other graphics to help you when you give your presentation. You even can move or resize the image of the slide on the notes to make room for additional information.

To edit the notes for a slide, follow these steps:

1. If you are not viewing the presentation in the Slide Editor, choose Slide **E**ditor from the **V**iew menu.

2. Choose **E**dit speaker notes from the **S**lide menu. The Speaker notes for the current slide appear in the Slide Editor. The Add Slide button at the bottom of the Slide Editor window changes to the Back to Slide button.

3. Enhance the notes by using the tools of the Slide Editor. See Chapter 12, "Drawing in Harvard Graphics," for information on using the Slide Editor to enhance your slide.

4. After you finish making your changes, click the Back to Slide button.

Printing Speaker Notes

The Speaker **n**otes button on the Print dialog box causes your speaker notes to print rather than your slides. Follow these steps to output a presentation using the current handout style:

1. Choose **P**rint... from the **F**ile menu. The Print dialog box appears.

2. Click the Speaker **n**otes button.

3. Click OK to start printing.

Modifying Presentation Setup Options

You use the Presentation se**t**up option on the **F**ile menu to set the basic output options when printing slides, handouts, and speaker notes. After you choose this command, the Presentation Setup dialog box appears for you to set options for orientation, paper size, and margins (see fig. 14.7). Orientation determines how the presentation prints relative to the length and width of the page. With ***Landscape*** orientation, Harvard Graphics prints the slides horizontally across the longer axis of the page. ***Portrait*** orientation, which is the default orientation, prints the top and bottom of the slide along the width and the sides of the slide along the length.

The Select a paper si**z**e: list box enables you to print your presentation on many different paper sizes. You can print on the large paper associated with some plotters or on standard Letter 8.5 x 11 paper used with most laser printers. The margins you set in the Set margins box are based on how much of the page you want to use for the slide. Larger margins leave more blank space on the edge of the pages and less room for slide images. Smaller margins, on the other hand, leave more room for slide images. The defaults for these options enable the slide to use most of the page without reaching the edges.

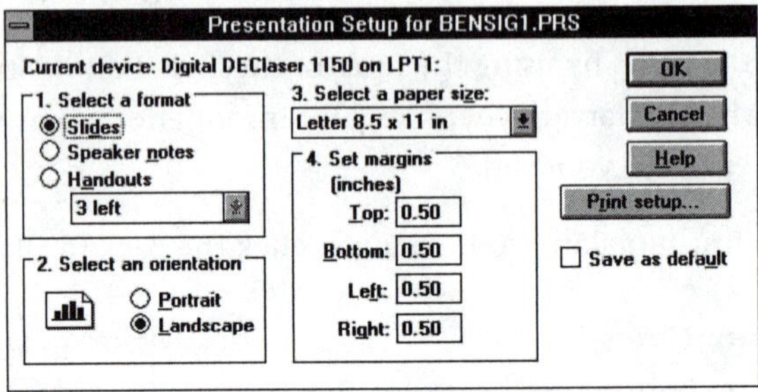

Fig. 14.7
The Presentation Setup dialog box.

Follow these steps to change the settings for printing slides:

1. Choose Presentation se**t**up... from the **F**ile menu. The Presentation Setup dialog box appears.
2. Click the Sli**d**es button to set output options for printing slides.
3. Click the orientation you want to use in the Select an orientation box.
4. Click the left arrow next to the Select a paper si**z**e: field and click the size you use with your device. The size you select appears in the field.
5. Click each of the margin fields for the four sides of the page and set the margins you want to use.
6. Click the OK button to remove the dialog box and save your changes.

When you save your presentation, these settings are saved as well. If you click the Save as defa**u**lt box, these settings will be the default when you create a new presentation.

From Here...

This chapter covers the output capabilities of Harvard Graphics. In the chapter, you learned how to print your slides on any device that Windows supports. You then learned how to set printer options and to print a presentation with handouts and speaker notes. The latter parts of the chapter explain how to set the default printing options and how to set up output devices. The next chapter covers important topics related to importing and exporting data and graphics with Harvard Graphics for Windows.

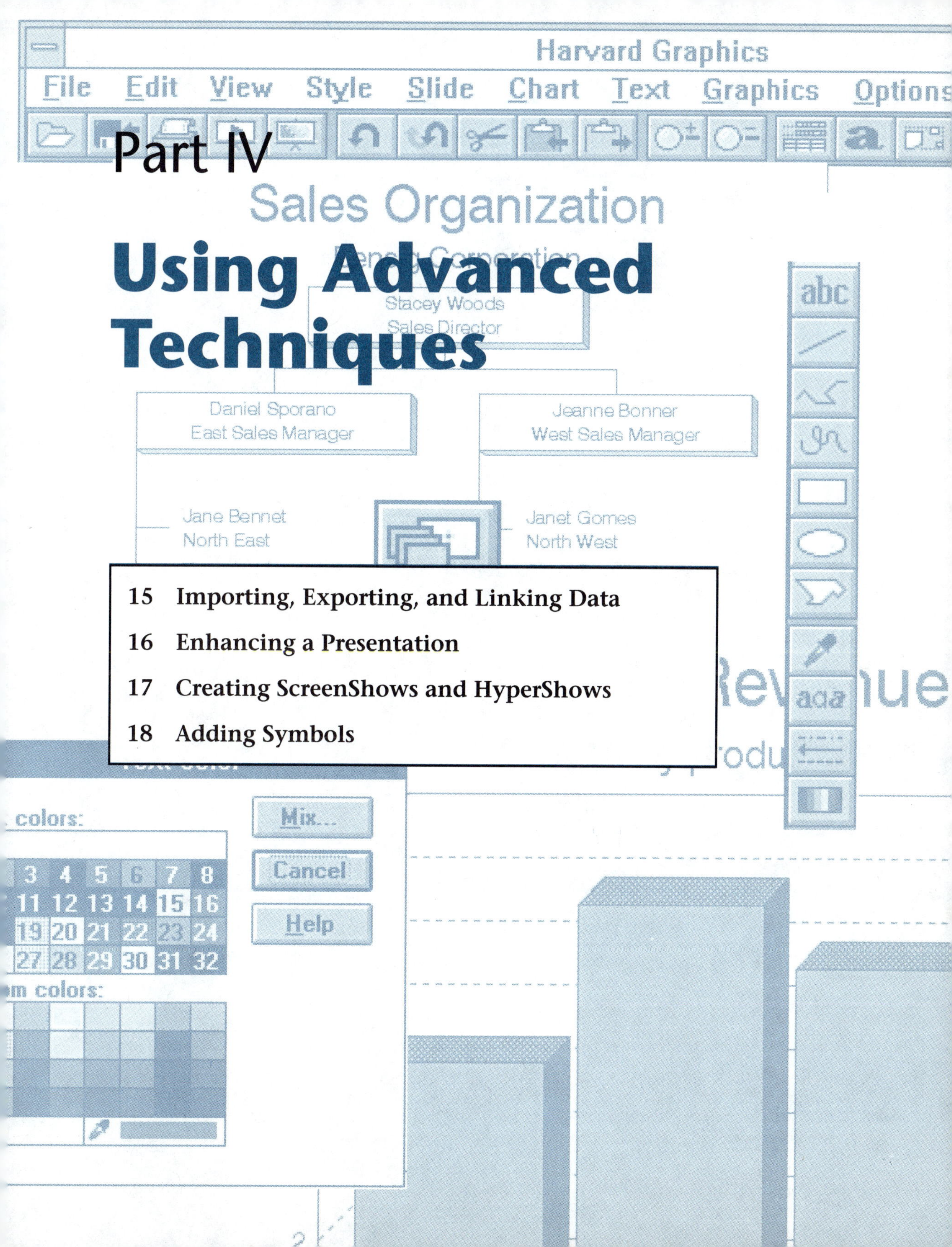

Part IV

Using Advanced Techniques

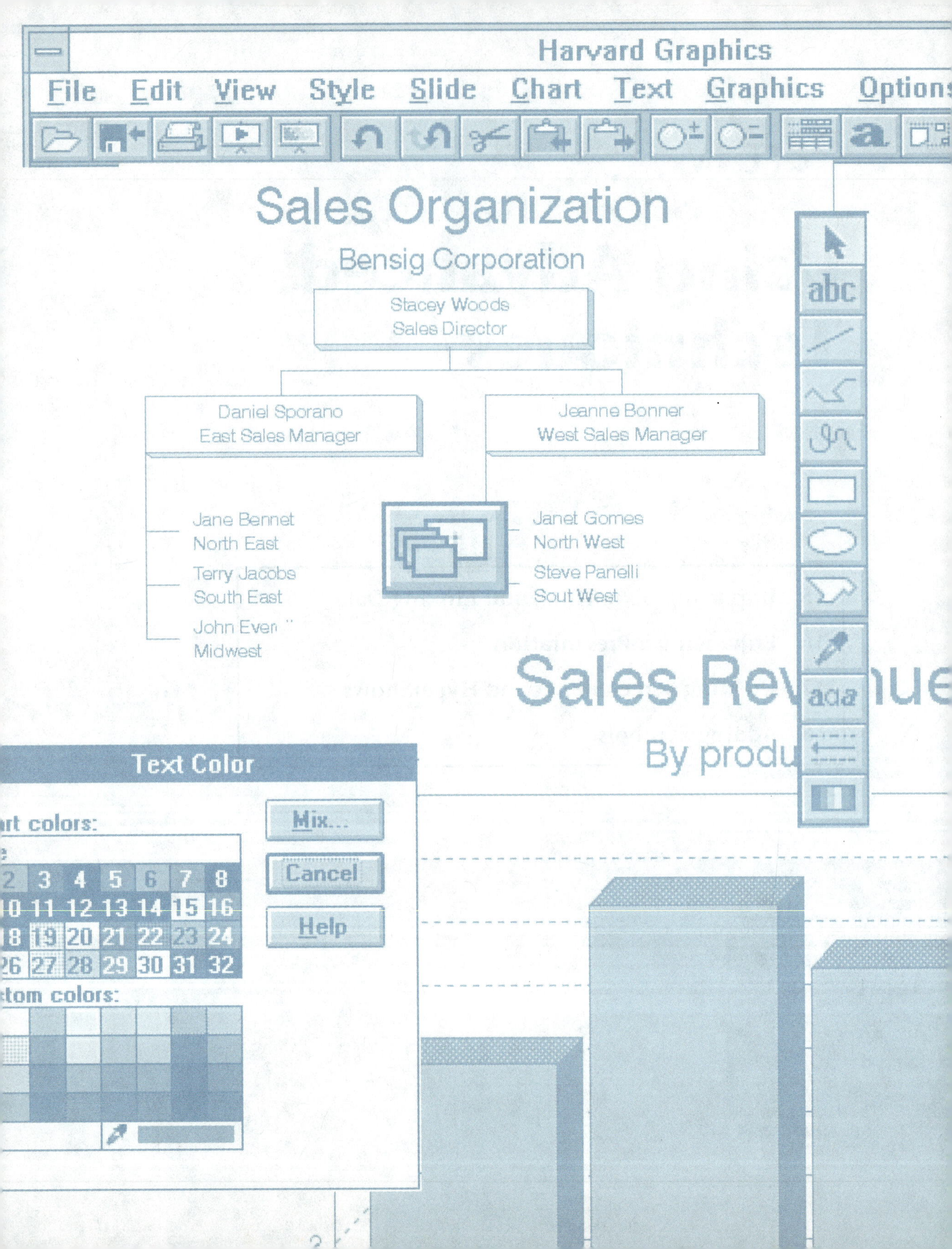

Harvard Graphics
File Edit View Style Slide Chart Text Graphics Options
Sales Organization
Bensig Corporation
Stacey Woods
Sales Director
Daniel Sporano
East Sales Manager
Jeanne Bonner
West Sales Manager
Jane Bennet
North East
Terry Jacobs
South East
Midwest
Janet Gomes
North West
Steve Panelli
Sout West
abc
Text Color
Mix...
Cancel
Help

Chapter 15

Importing, Exporting, and Linking Data

In this chapter, you learn how to do the following:

- Import data and graphics
- Export data and graphics
- Link together multiple documents using DDE and OLE

When you build a presentation, you create slides that communicate ideas and information in graphics images. Because slides generally combine information from various applications—such as spreadsheets, word processors, and graphics—the capability to transfer images between applications is essential in detailed slide creation. To bridge the gap between programs, Harvard Graphics enables you to import a variety of data and images from other Windows and DOS applications to your slides. When you *import*, you transfer data and images *into* your Harvard Graphics presentation from other programs or applications. For example, you can calculate financial data in a spreadsheet and import the data to a chart or table.

Similarly, you can *export* information *from* the Harvard Graphics presentation to other programs or applications. You can export charts you create in Harvard Graphics to a document you produce in a word processor, for example. Because Harvard Graphics uses a variety of export formats, you can export data to other programs easily.

A *link* is a connection between two files or data items that enables a change in the original file to occur in the other file. When you import or export data, the link to the original program is not maintained. If you do not link the files, the data in the original file may change, but the file that received the original data remains unaltered. Harvard Graphics enables you to create links, which resolve this problem.

This chapter explains how to import and export data from various applications and programs to and from Harvard Graphics. You also learn how to use the Windows Clipboard to transfer data and images between Harvard Graphics and other Windows applications. Finally, you learn how to establish a link from another Windows application directly to Harvard Graphics.

Importing Data

To import data and images from other applications into your presentation, you use the **I**mport command on the **F**ile menu. You can import charts and presentations from the DOS versions of Harvard Graphics, as well as images created in other Windows applications.

The information you can import depends on the current view—Outliner, Slide Sorter, Slide Editor, or chart data form—of the presentation. In the Slide Sorter, for example, you can import presentations and charts from Harvard Graphics for DOS. In the Slide Editor, on the other hand, you can import Harvard Graphics DOS files plus bit maps and drawings from other programs. Table 15.1 lists the files you can import into the different views.

Table 15.1 Files Harvard Graphics Imports

View	Files
Slide Editor	Harvard Graphics Chart 2.x
	Harvard Graphics Show 2.x
	Harvard Graphics Template 2.x
	Harvard Graphics Chart 3.x
	Harvard Graphics Show 3.x
	Harvard Graphics Template 3.x
	Adobe Illustrator
	Windows bit-mapped
	Computer Graphics Metafile
	Micrografx Drawing
	GIF Bitmap

View	Files
	Macintosh PICT
	PC Paintbrush bit-mapped (PCX)
	PC Paintbrush bit-mapped (PCC)
	SPC Interchange
	TIFF bit-mapped
	Windows Metafile
	WordPerfect Graphics
Slide Sorter	Harvard Graphics Chart 2.x
	Harvard Graphics Show 2.x
	Harvard Graphics Template 2.x
	Harvard Graphics Chart 3.x
	Harvard Graphics Show 3.x
	Harvard Graphics Template 3.x
Outliner	ASCII
Chart data form	Excel
	Lotus
	Delimited ASCII

When you choose **I**mport from the **F**ile menu, the Import dialog box appears (see fig. 15.1). You use the Import dialog box to indicate what data you intend to import. The dialog box contains the following options:

- *File **t**ype:*. This list box determines the type of file you are importing. The data you can import depends on the file. For example, only numeric data can come from a spreadsheet, but both data and images come from Harvard Graphics DOS 3.x charts. In figure 15.1, the File **t**ype: box indicates that you can import Harvard Graphics 2.x charts. To see the other formats available for import, click the down arrow next to the list box. To import a different type of file, select a file format from the list that appears.

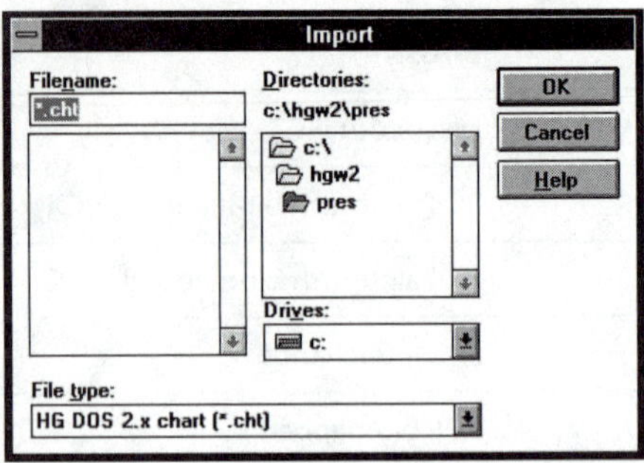

Fig. 15.1
The Import dialog box.

- *Filename:*. This text box contains the name of the file you are importing. To import a file, type the file name in the File**n**ame text box or double-click the name in the Filename: list box. The list box contains the names of files that match the extension for the current import file format. If the file you intend to import is in a directory other than the directory identified at the Directories prompt, you can change directories by typing the drive and directory—not the file name—in the File**n**ame text box.

- ***D**irectories:*. This prompt shows the current directory. To view files in different directories, you can change the current directory by double-clicking the directory in the list box. As mentioned, you also can type the directory in the File**n**ame text box. When you change the directory, Harvard Graphics displays the files of the specified type that are contained in the new directory.

- *Dri**v**es:*. This field shows the current drive. To view files on different drives, you can change the current drive by clicking the down arrow next to the field and then clicking a new drive.

Importing a Harvard Graphics for DOS Chart

You can import files from the DOS versions of Harvard Graphics to use previously created charts or to share files created with these versions. When you import a chart from a DOS version, you import the data from the chart along with the chart option settings. See Chapters 3 through 6 for information about chart options.

Follow these steps to import a Harvard Graphics 3.x chart from the C:\HG3\DATA directory (the directory that contains the chart may be different on your system):

1. If you are not viewing the current slide in the Slide Sorter, choose Slide **S**orter from the **V**iew menu.
2. Choose **I**mport... from the **F**ile menu. The Import dialog box appears.
3. Click the down arrow next to the File **t**ype: list box to see the available formats.
4. Choose Harvard Graphics Chart 3.x from the list that appears. If this format is not visible, click the scroll arrows until the Harvard Graphics 3.x format appears; then select it.
5. Click the File**n**ame: text box. If the text box is not empty, press the End key to move to the end of the box; then press the Backspace key until the text box is clear.
6. To change the directory, type **C:\HG3\DATA** in the File**n**ame: text box and click OK. The **D**irectories: prompt indicates that the current directory is C:\HG3\DATA.
7. In the File**n**ame: text box, type the name of the file you want to import.
8. Click OK to import the file.

Harvard Graphics creates a new slide with the data and images from the imported file.

Importing a Harvard Graphics for DOS Presentation

You can import Harvard Graphics for DOS presentation files in the Slide Sorter or the Slide Editor. In the DOS version, the slides in a presentation are stored in individual chart files. When you import, each chart file becomes a slide in your Harvard Graphics for Windows presentation.

To import Harvard Graphics for DOS files, you must view your presentation in the Slide Editor or Slide Sorter. In the Import dialog box, which appears when you choose **I**mport from the **F**ile menu, select the version and file type in the File **t**ype: list. See "Importing Data" earlier in this chapter to learn how to import files from different directories.

Follow these steps to import a Harvard Graphics 3.x presentation from the C:\HG3\DATA directory (your directory may be different):

1. The current view of your presentation must be the Slide Sorter or the Slide Editor. If you are not in one of these views, choose Slide **S**orter or Slide **E**ditor from the **V**iew menu.

2. Choose **I**mport... from the **F**ile menu. The Import dialog box appears (refer to fig. 15.1).

3. Click the down arrow next to the File **t**ype: list box. A list of available formats appears.

4. Select Harvard Graphics Show 3.x from the list. If this format is not visible, click the scroll arrows until the Harvard Graphics 3.x format appears; then select it.

5. Click the File**n**ame: text box. If the text box is not empty, press the End key to move to the end of the box; then press the Backspace key until the text box is clear.

6. To change the directory, type **C:\HG3\DATA** in the File**n**ame: text box and click OK. The **D**irectories: prompt indicates that the current directory is C:\HG3\DATA.

7. In the File**n**ame: list box, double-click the name of the file you want to import.

When you import files from Harvard Graphics for DOS, the data from the original file remains intact although the appearance of the slide may change. For example, some of the colors may be different in the Windows version. With templates, you can modify the appearance of your imported files to make them more consistent with the slides in your presentation. See the section "Applying Templates" in Chapter 14, "Creating Output," for more information on working with templates.

Tip
Most chart types, except for title, bullet, and organization charts, accept data from spreadsheets. The Import... option on the File menu is not enabled for chart types that cannot accept imported spreadsheet data.

Importing Spreadsheet Data

You can import data from spreadsheets into the chart data form. With this feature, you can avoid retyping the data that has already been entered or calculated in your spreadsheet. You can import the entire spreadsheet or a range of cells on the spreadsheet. Harvard Graphics imports data from Lotus 1-2-3 and Microsoft Excel.

To import data from a spreadsheet, choose Edit **d**ata from the **C**hart menu to display the chart data form. Because Harvard Graphics enters the imported data into the data form from the active cell's location, you must activate a cell in the data form before you import the spreadsheet information. Open the Import dialog box by choosing **I**mport... from the **F**ile menu (see fig. 15.2).

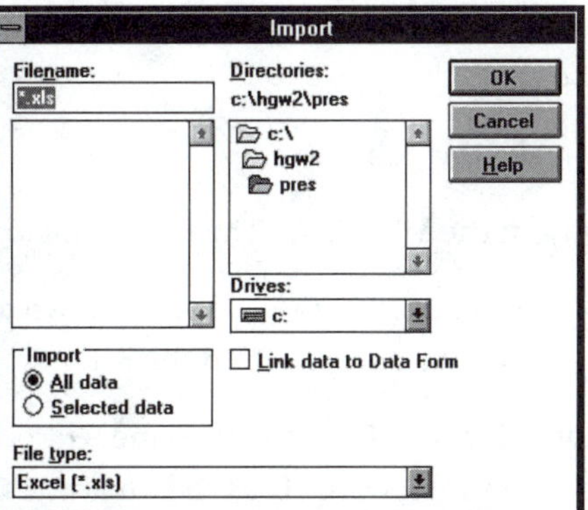

Fig. 15.2
The Import dialog box for importing spreadsheet data.

This dialog box is only slightly different from the dialog box discussed in the section "Importing Data." The dialog box in figure 15.2 contains buttons for specifying the type of spreadsheet import. You indicate whether you are importing the entire spreadsheet or a range of specified cells by clicking the appropriate button—**A**ll data or **S**elected data.

Tip
You can import data by clicking the Get data... button on the data form.

Importing the Entire Spreadsheet. You can import an entire spreadsheet into the chart data form so you save the time needed to enter the spreadsheet data cell by cell. Only data values—no formulas—import from the spreadsheet. The value of the formula from the last calculation of the spreadsheet is the value imported. The next section, "Importing a Range from a Spreadsheet," explains how to import specific parts of the spreadsheet.

Suppose that you are importing the Microsoft Excel spreadsheet REVENUE.XLS from the C:\EXCEL directory into cell A1 of the data form. Follow these steps:

1. If you are not viewing the presentation in the Slide Editor, choose Slide **E**ditor from the **V**iew menu.

2. Choose **A**dd slide... from the **S**lide menu. The Add Slide dialog box opens for you to create a new slide. (See the section "Adding Slides to a Presentation" in Chapter 2, "Learning Harvard Graphics for Windows Basics.")

3. Click the type of slide you want to import *into*. Remember, you cannot import spreadsheet data into title, bullet, or organization charts.

4. Click OK in the Add Slide dialog box to create the slide and display the data form for the chart.

5. Click cell A1 to make this cell active.

6. Choose **I**mport from the **F**ile menu. The Import dialog box appears.

7. If Excel is not the current file format, click the down arrow next to the File **t**ype: list box and choose Excel from the list.

8. Type the directory **C:\EXCEL** in the File**n**ame text box and click OK. The directory changes to C:\EXCEL, as shown at the **D**irectories prompt.

9. Click the **A**ll data button to import the entire spreadsheet.

10. Type the name of the spreadsheet in the File**n**ame: text box. For this example, type **revenue.xls**.

11. Click OK. Harvard Graphics imports the spreadsheet into the chart data form at cell A1, the active cell.

After data is imported, you can edit it on the data form without affecting the original spreadsheet. You can make changes to the data or chart just as if you had typed the data directly into the data form.

Importing a Range from a Spreadsheet. The **S**elected data button in the Import dialog box enables you to import a range of cells or a named range from any spreadsheet. That is, you can import a section of the spreadsheet without importing an entire sheet. *Named ranges* define by name a range of cells in the spreadsheet. For example, you can specify the name *Revenue* for cells A1 through D1 on the spreadsheet. With the **S**elected data button, you can import a named range, like *Revenue*, or a specific range, such as A1 through D1.

Before importing the range into the data form, Harvard Graphics opens the Select Data dialog box (see fig. 15.3). In this dialog box, you use the **F**rom cell: and **T**o cell: text boxes to specify the range of cells to import. Type the first cell from the range in the **F**rom cell: text box; then type the last cell in the **T**o cell: text box.

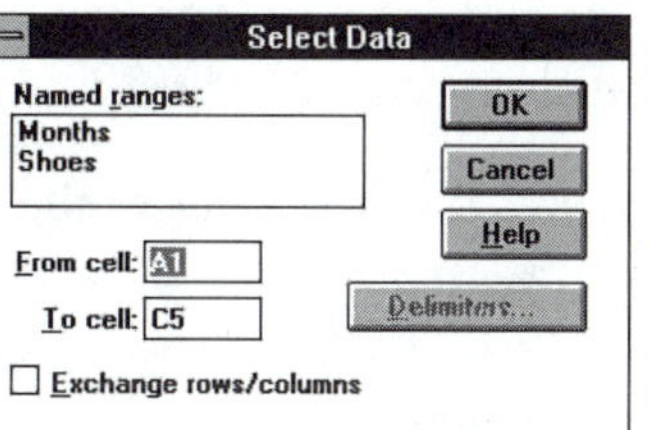

Fig. 15.3
The Select Data dialog box.

You use the **E**xchange rows/columns option to transpose the information in the rows and columns of the spreadsheet. The swap is made when the data is imported. If you do not set this option, the spreadsheet data appears with the same rows and columns in the data form. If you set the option, the rows and columns switch.

In the Select Data dialog box, named ranges from your spreadsheet appear in the Named **r**anges: list box. To import the range, select the name of the range from the Named **r**anges: list box. When you select the range name, Harvard Graphics displays the starting and ending cells, which define the range, in the **F**rom cell: and **T**o cell: text boxes, respectively. This display helps you determine what part of the sheet is importing.

Follow these steps to import a named range of cells from a spreadsheet into the data form starting at cell A1:

1. If you are not viewing the presentation in the Slide Editor, choose Slide **E**ditor from the **V**iew menu.

2. Choose **A**dd slide... from the **S**lide menu. The Add Slide dialog box opens for you to create a new slide. (See the section "Adding Slides to a Presentation" in Chapter 2, "Learning Harvard Graphics for Windows Basics.")

3. Click the type of slide you want to import *into*. Remember, you cannot import spreadsheet data into title, bullet, or organization charts.

4. Click OK in the Add Slide dialog box to create the slide and display the data form for the chart.

5. Click cell A1 to make this cell active.
6. Choose **I**mport... from the **F**ile menu. The Import dialog box appears.
7. Choose the import format in the File **t**ype: list box. For example, to import from Lotus 1-2-3, choose Lotus from the list.
8. Click the **S**elected data button to indicate that you are importing a *range* from the spreadsheet, not the entire spreadsheet.
9. In the File**n**ame: text box, type the name of the file.
10. Click OK.

    Before Harvard Graphics imports the data, the Select Data dialog box appears.
11. Select the range in the Named **r**anges: list box. The beginning and ending cells of the range appear in the **F**rom cell: and **T**o cell: text boxes, respectively.
12. Click OK. Harvard Graphics imports the specified range to cell A1 of the data form.
13. Click OK to create the chart with the data.

You can modify the data and chart directly without affecting the original spreadsheet.

Importing Delimited ASCII

Delimited ASCII files are text files in which delimiting characters, such as commas or double quotation marks, separate the labels and data items in the file. Delimited ASCII files are text files you generate with programs like Microsoft Excel or dBASE. When you create the file, you specify a *delimiter*, or character, to separate the items in the file. When you import these files into Harvard Graphics, you must specify the correct delimiter character. You import delimited files into the chart data form.

To import a delimited ASCII file, choose **I**mport... from the **F**ile menu while you are viewing the chart data form. In the Import dialog box, choose Delimited ASCII as the file type.

Before Harvard Graphics imports the data, the Delimiters dialog box appears (see fig. 15.4). You use this dialog box to indicate what delimiter separates the labels and data in the file. You can use a comma, tab, or custom character as the delimiter. You click the appropriate Field separator button to set the delimiting character.

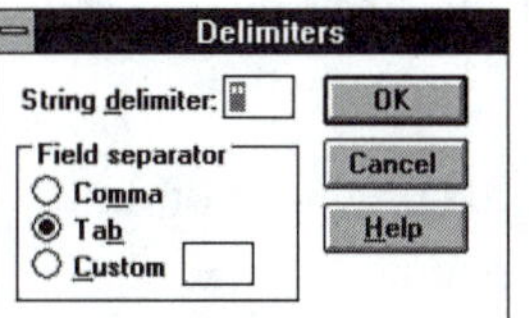

Fig. 15.4
The Delimiters dialog box.

Commas and tabs are the two most common delimiters. If your delimited ASCII file was not created with comma or tab delimiters, choose the **C**ustom button and specify the character in the text box next to the button. Figure 15.5 shows a sample ASCII file delimited with commas.

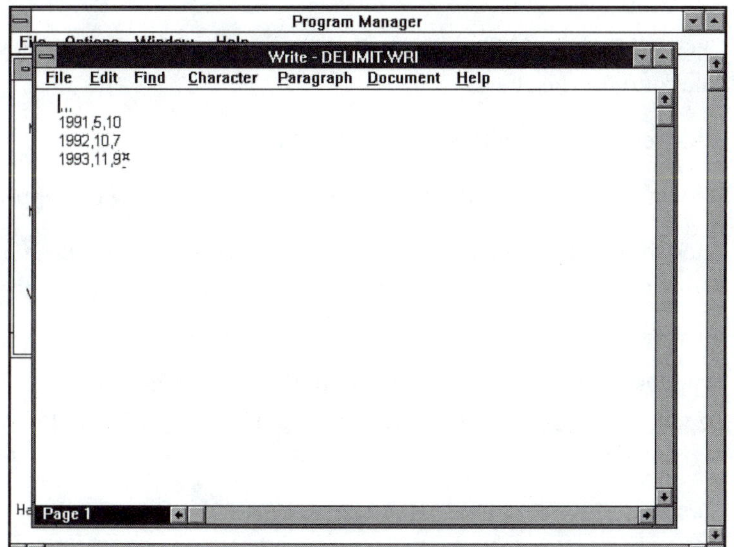

Fig. 15.5
An ASCII file delimited with commas.

If commas delimit your file and you use a comma in a number (such as 1,507), Harvard Graphics imports the number as two separate values (1 and 507). Strings in a delimited ASCII file, however, override the delimiter. A *string* is a group of characters that are specially marked to indicate that they belong together (as with the number 1,507). If you place string characters around the number, Harvard Graphics imports the number correctly. You use the String **d**elimiter: text box to define the string character. As with the delimiter, you must use the same string character that was used to create the file. A common string character is the double quotation mark. For the number 1,507, the file contains the string with quotation marks around the number: "1,507".

To import a delimited ASCII file, beginning at cell A1 in the chart data form, follow these steps:

1. If you are not viewing the presentation in the Slide Editor, choose Slide **E**ditor from the **V**iew menu.
2. Choose **A**dd slide... from the **S**lide menu. The Add Slide dialog box opens for you to create a new slide. (See the section "Adding Slides to a Presentation" in Chapter 2, "Learning Harvard Graphics for Windows Basics.")
3. Click the type of slide you want to import *into*. Remember, you cannot import spreadsheet data into title, bullet, or organization charts.
4. Click OK in the Add Slide dialog box to create the slide and display the data form for the chart.
5. Click cell A1 to make this cell active.
6. Choose **I**mport... from the **F**ile menu. The Import dialog box appears.
7. Click the down arrow next to the File **t**ype: list box and select Delimited ASCII from the list. The Delimited ASCII format appears in the File **t**ype: list box.
8. Type the name of the file you are importing in the File**n**ame: text box. To select a file from another directory, refer to "Importing Data" earlier in the chapter.
9. Click OK. The Delimiters dialog box appears.
10. Click the Co**m**ma button in the Field separator section of the dialog box. If your delimited ASCII file was created with string separators, type the separator in the String **d**elimiter text box.
11. Click OK. Harvard Graphics imports the data, beginning at the active cell.

Figure 15.6 shows data from figure 15.5 after importing in the data form.

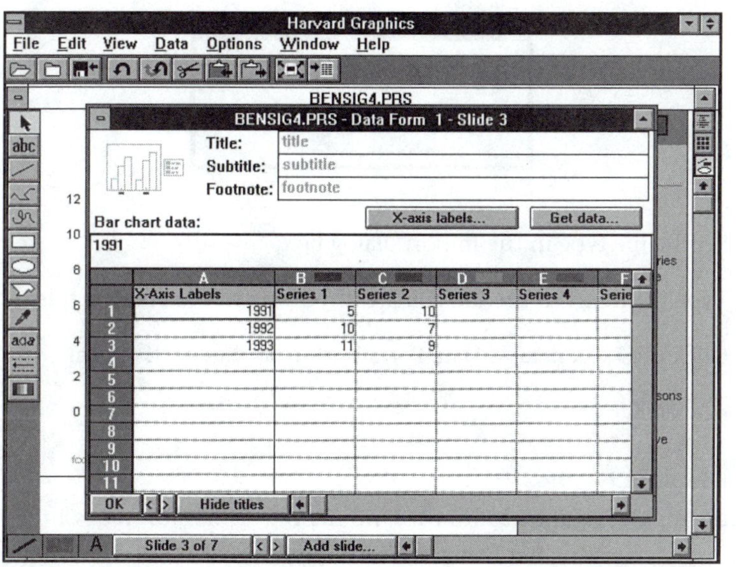

Fig. 15.6 Data imported from an ASCII delimited file.

Maintaining Links To Import Files

When you import data into the chart data form, Harvard Graphics copies the data from the import file to the chart and saves the data in the presentation. Although the data from the original file may change between the time you import the file and the time you open it again, the imported file does not reflect the change. You can solve this problem by creating a link between the original and imported files. As explained in a previous section, a link enables a change in the original file to occur in the other file. You can create a link from an Excel, Lotus 1-2-3, or Delimited ASCII file to the data in a chart.

If you activate the **L**ink data to Data Form button in the Import dialog box before you import the data, you can maintain the most up-to-date information from the import file. To create a link when you import a file, click the **L**ink data to Data Form button before you click OK in the Import dialog box. When you open a presentation with linked data, Harvard Graphics opens the dialog box shown in figure 15.7. Choose **Y**es or **N**o to indicate whether to update the links by retrieving the most recent data from the file.

Follow these steps to create a link between a slide and an imported file:

1. Choose Edit **d**ata from the **C**hart menu. The chart data form appears.

2. Choose **I**mport... from the **F**ile menu. The Import dialog box appears.

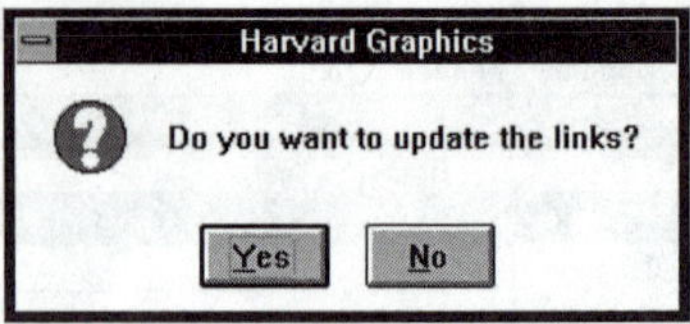

Fig. 15.7
The Update Links dialog box.

3. Set the file type in the Import dialog box.
4. Type the name of the file you are importing in the File**n**ame: text box.
5. Click the **L**ink data to Data Form button so that an X appears.
6. Click OK.

Importing ASCII Files

You can import ASCII files into the Outliner only. An *ASCII* file is a text file that contains nothing but characters and numbers. ASCII files are similar to just the text from a word processing file without any special character or page formats. In fact, most word processors, including Microsoft Word, can save a file as an ASCII or text file. Importing the ASCII file saves you the time and effort of retyping the information in the Outliner. With an ASCII file, as opposed to a Delimited ASCII file, special characters do not separate individual items in the file. Figure 15.8 shows a sample ASCII file. When imported, each line in the ASCII file becomes a new slide in the Outliner. Harvard Graphics inserts the slides after the active topic in the presentation.

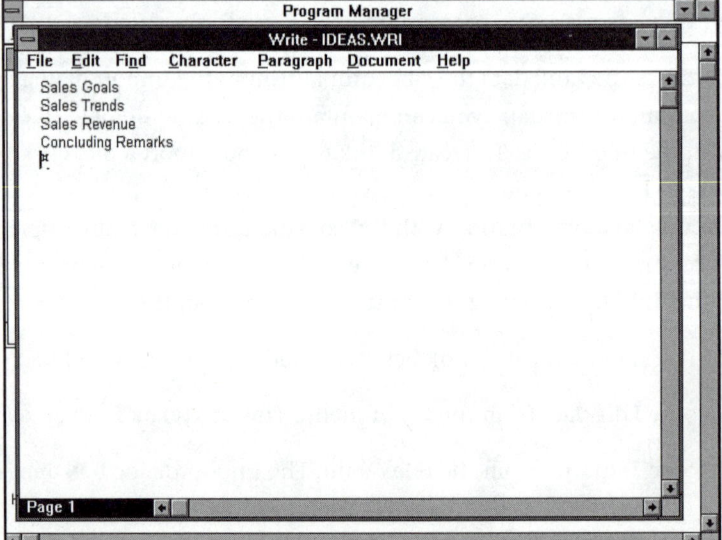

Fig. 15.8
A sample ASCII file.

Follow these steps to import an ASCII file:

1. If you are not viewing the presentation in the Outliner, choose **O**utliner from the **V**iew menu.

2. Activate the topic after which you want to insert the imported ASCII file.

3. Choose **I**mport... from the **F**ile menu. The Import dialog box appears.

4. Type the name of the file you are importing in the File**n**ame: text box.

5. Click OK. Harvard Graphics imports the ASCII file below the active topic in the Outliner.

Figure 15.9 shows an outline after importing the file shown in figure 15.8.

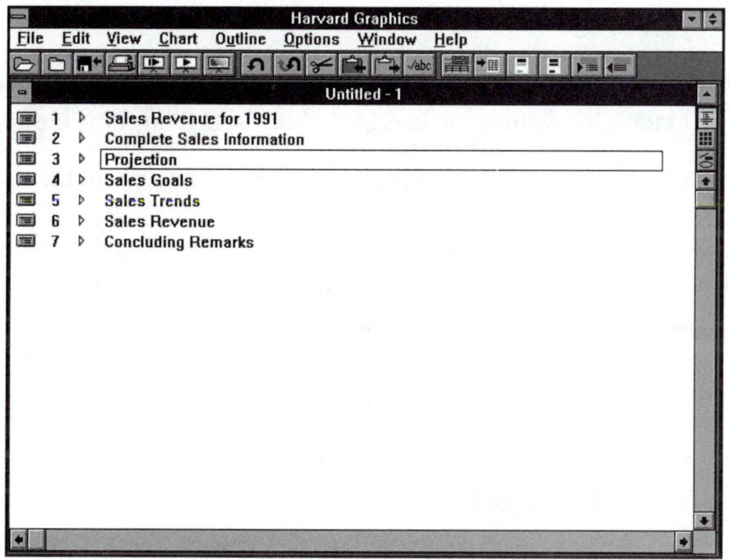

Fig. 15.9
An example of an imported ASCII file in the Outliner.

Importing Bit-Mapped Files and Graphics Images

You can import bit maps and images in a variety of graphics formats into a slide in the Slide Editor. A *bit-mapped file* is a picture stored in a file, much the same way a photograph is stored on film. An *image file* is a set of instructions that tell the program how to draw a picture. When you import a bit-mapped file, the image appears directly on the slide. When you import an image file, Harvard Graphics follows the instructions in the file to display the image on the slide. For bit-mapped files, you can import Windows bit-mapped (BMP),

GIF Bitmap (GIF), PC Paintbrush bit-mapped (PCC or PCX), and TIFF bit-mapped (TIF) files. For image file formats, you can import Computer Graphics Metafiles (CGM) and Windows Metafiles (WMF). The imported bit-mapped or image file appears directly on the slide.

Follow these steps to import a Windows bit-mapped file to the Slide Editor from the C:\WINDOWS directory:

1. If you are not viewing the presentation in the Slide Editor, choose Slide **E**ditor from the **V**iew menu.

2. Choose **I**mport... from the **F**ile menu. The Import dialog box appears.

3. Click the down arrow next to the File **t**ype: list box and select the Windows bit-mapped format.

4. To change the directory, type **C:\WINDOWS** in the File**n**ame: text box and click OK.

5. Select the file you want to import in the files list box. If the file name is not visible, click the scroll bars beside the list box until the file appears.

6. Click OK. Harvard Graphics imports the bit-mapped file to the slide.

After Harvard Graphics imports the bit-mapped or image file, you can manipulate the object the same way you manipulate other objects, using the tools on the toolbox. For more information on working with objects in the Slide Editor, refer to Chapter 12, "Drawing in Harvard Graphics," and Chapter 13, "Enhancing Drawings and Objects."

Exporting Data

The **E**xport... command on the **F**ile menu enables you to transfer data and images *from* Harvard Graphics *to* other programs. You can export the images on a slide to another type of graphics file that other applications can read. For example, you can export your chart to a common graphics file format and then read the file from your word processor. You also can export slides and presentations to Harvard Graphics DOS files to use with the DOS version. The type of file you can export depends on your current view of the presentation. From the Slide Editor, you can export a single slide or a Harvard Graphics presentation file; from the Slide Sorter, you can export a presentation, which may contain several slides and export to several files. You also can export your presentation outline to an ASCII file in the Outliner. Table 15.2 lists the views and the files that can export from each view.

Table 15.2 Files Harvard Graphics Exports

View	Files
Slide Editor	HGW runtime presentation
	Harvard Graphics Chart 3.x
	Harvard Graphics Show 3.x
	Windows bit-mapped
	Computer Graphics Metafile
	CGM Harvard Graphics
	CGM Lotus Freelance Plus
	GIF Bitmap
	Macintosh PICT
	PC Paintbrush bit-mapped (PCX)
	SPC Interchange
	TIFF bit-mapped
	Windows Metafile
	WordPerfect Graphics
Slide Sorter	HGW runtime presentation
	Harvard Graphics Chart 3.x
	Harvard Graphics Show 3.x
	Windows bit-mapped
	Computer Graphics Metafile
	CGM Harvard Graphics
	CGM Lotus Freelance Plus
	GIF Bitmap

(continues)

Table 15.2 Continued

View	Files
	Macintosh PICT
	PC Paintbrush bit-mapped (PCX)
	SPC Interchange
	TIFF bit-mapped
	Windows Metafile
	WordPerfect Graphics
Outliner	HGW runtime presentation
	ASCII

If you export from Harvard Graphics, the program creates a new file using the export file format. If you export a presentation, Harvard Graphics appends a number to the name of each slide in the presentation. If you type **Bensig** as the file name, for example, Harvard Graphics exports the first slide to the file BENSI001, the second file to BENSI002, and so on.

The Export dialog box, shown in figure 15.10, appears when you choose **E**xport... from the **F**ile menu. In the File**n**ame: text box, type the name of the file you want to create when you export. The File **t**ype: list box lists the export formats. To change the format, click the down arrow next to the File **t**ype: list box and select the correct format.

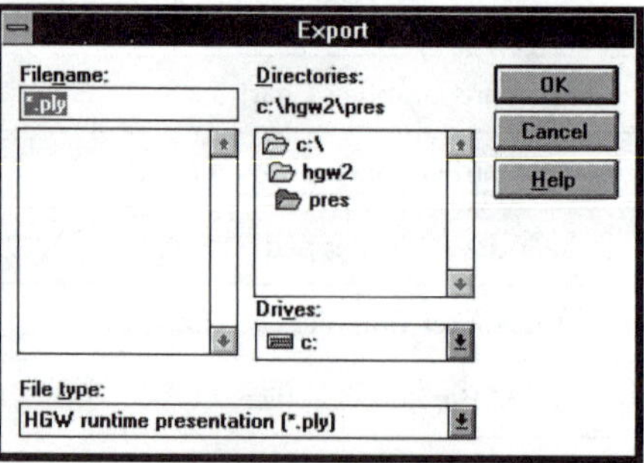

Fig. 15.10
The Export dialog box.

You can use the Export dialog box to export files into different directories. The current directory appears in the **D**irectories: prompt. The other available directories appear in the list box below the prompt. To change the current directory, double-click the directory in the box. You also can change the directory by typing the name of the directory—not the file name—in the File**n**ame: text box and clicking OK. If you change the directory, the files matching the export format appear in the list box below the File**n**ame: text box. The current drive appears in the Dri**v**es field. To select a different drive, click the down arrow next to the field and select a new drive from the list that appears.

Follow these steps to export the slides of a presentation to Harvard Graphics 3.x charts:

1. If you are not viewing the presentation in the Slide Sorter, choose Slide **S**orter from the **V**iew menu.
2. Choose **E**xport... from the **F**ile menu. The Export dialog box appears.
3. Click the down arrow next to the File **t**ype: list box and select Harvard Graphics Show 3.x from the list of formats. The selected format appears in the File **t**ype: list box.
4. In the File**n**ame: text box, type the file name for the file that you want to create when you export. When the slides export, Harvard Graphics appends a slide number to the end of the file name created for each slide in the presentation.
5. Click OK. Harvard Graphics exports the file.

During an export, Harvard Graphics displays a status box to indicate the process of the export (see fig. 15.11). In the status box, you can see the current slide and the total number of slides exporting. You also can see the percentage of the processing completed with the current slide. Click the Cancel button in the status box to cancel the export operation. You may want to cancel the export if you accidentally export the wrong presentation or choose to export to the wrong file format. The files you created before choosing Cancel remain on your hard disk.

Exporting Harvard Graphics 3.x for DOS Files

You can export Harvard Graphics 3.x files from the Slide Editor. Harvard Graphics 3.x presentations or shows consist of individual chart files. The chart files are equivalent to the slides of a Harvard Graphics for Windows presentation. If you export to a Harvard Graphics 3.x chart, the program creates a chart file from the data and images on the slide. From the Slide

Sorter, Harvard Graphics creates a chart file for each slide in the presentation. If you export a Harvard Graphics 3.x show in the Slide Editor or Slide Sorter, the program creates a chart file for every slide in the presentation.

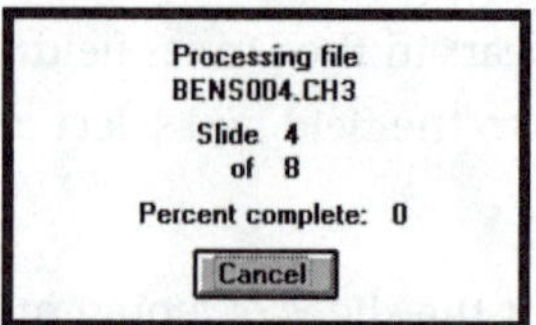

Fig. 15.11
The Export status box.

In addition to the chart files, the program creates a Harvard Graphics 3.x show file. This file contains the names of all the chart files along with information on how these charts are used in the presentation. For example, the chart file created from the first slide in the Harvard Graphics for Windows presentation is the first chart file listed in the Harvard Graphics 3.x show file.

Follow these steps to export your presentation to a Harvard Graphics 3.x show in the C:\HG3\DATA directory:

1. If you are not viewing the presentation in the Slide Sorter or Slide Editor, choose the Slide **E**ditor from the **V**iew menu to export a slide to a single chart file, or choose the Slide **E**ditor to export the presentation to a show file.

2. Choose **E**xport... from the **F**ile menu. The Export dialog box appears.

3. Click the down arrow next to the File **t**ype: list box and select Harvard Graphics 3.x Show or Harvard Graphics 3.x Chart from the list. The format you choose is listed in the File **t**ype: list box.

4. Type **C:\HG3\DATA** in the File**n**ame: text box and click OK to change the directory.

5. Type the name of the chart or show file in the File**n**ame text box. If you are exporting using the show file format, this file names all the charts. Each chart has the first five letters from the show file name, followed by the number of the slide position in the presentation.

6. Click OK to start exporting.

The Export status box, discussed in the section "Exporting Data," indicates the progress of the export.

Exporting Graphics Images

With the Export command, you can export slides and presentations using graphics image file formats. You then can import the files you create into other programs, such as a word processor or spreadsheet. The list of supported formats includes Computer Graphics Metafile (CGM), CGM Harvard Graphics (CGM), CGM Lotus Freelance Plus (CGM), Macintosh PICT (PCT), Windows Metafile (WMF), and WordPerfect Graphics (WPG).

To export a graphics image, make sure you are viewing the presentation in the Slide Sorter or Slide Editor and choose **E**xport from the **F**ile menu. If you export from the Slide Editor, Harvard Graphics exports only the current slide with the specified file format. (This slide is visible in the Slide Editor.) From the Slide Sorter, Harvard Graphics exports the entire presentation, and each slide becomes a separate file.

Follow these steps to export a slide from the Slide Editor to a Windows Metafile:

1. If you are not viewing the presentation in the Slide Editor, choose Slide **E**ditor from the **V**iew menu.

2. Choose **E**xport... from the **F**ile menu. The Export dialog box appears.

3. Click the down arrow next to the File **t**ype: list box and select Windows Metafile from the list of file formats.

4. In the File**n**ame: text box, type the name of the file you want to create when you export.

5. Click OK to export the slide to the file.

Exporting PCX Files

The *PCX* bit-mapped file format represents bit-mapped images in black and white or color, using a variety of resolutions and sizes. You can export a slide into a bit-mapped file and read the bit mapped file into a paint program, such as PC Paintbrush. From there, you can make further enhancements to the file using the features of the paint program. To export a PCX bit-mapped file from Harvard Graphics, choose **E**xport from the **F**ile menu while you are viewing the presentation in the Slide Editor or the Slide Sorter. Before you export PCX files, Harvard Graphics opens the PCX File Export dialog box in which you set the color, resolution, and size for the bit-mapped file (see fig. 15.12).

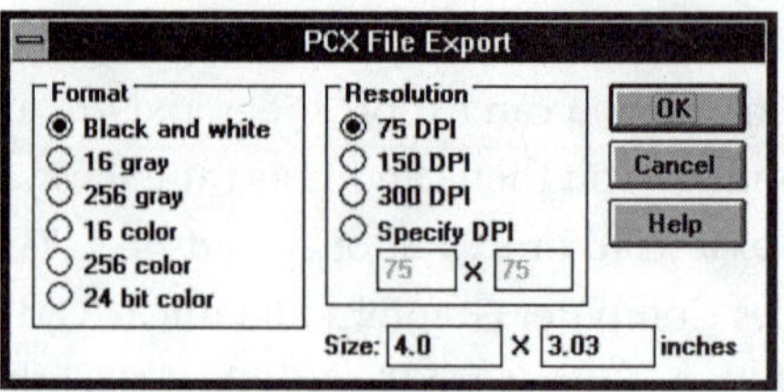

Fig. 15.12
The PCX File Export dialog box.

The color scheme of the bit map determines the basic format of the export file. Bit-mapped files change depending on the color scheme. The color scheme determines the colors that are stored in the file. These colors determine how the bit map appears when viewed in other programs. You can export black-and-white files, files that use between 16 and 256 colors or shades of gray, or files with 24 bits of color. The 16 color button creates a 16-color bit map compatible with the default color palette of PC Paintbrush.

The bit-map resolution is determined by how many dots per inch (dpi) represent the bit map. More dots provide better resolution in the file. In the dialog box, you can specify 75, 150, or 300 dpi, as well as a custom resolution. For bit maps displayed on-screen, 75 dpi is sufficient to produce a clear image; the other settings suit printers that support higher resolutions than a computer screen. The Size: text boxes enable you to control the height and width of the bit map.

Follow these steps to export a PCX file for use with PC Paintbrush:

1. If you are not viewing the presentation in the Slide Editor or Slide Sorter, choose one of these views from the **V**iew menu.
2. Choose **E**xport... from the **F**ile menu. The Export dialog box appears.
3. Click the down arrow next to the File **t**ype: list box and select PC Paintbrush (PCX) from the list of file formats.
4. Type the name of the file you want to export in the File**n**ame: text box.
5. Click OK. The PCX File Export dialog box appears.
6. Click the 16 color button in the dialog box.
7. Click OK to export the file.

Exporting TIFF Files

As with PCX bit-mapped files, the TIFF bit-mapped file format can create bit-mapped files in black and white or color, using different resolutions and sizes.

As with PCX files, you can import a TIFF bit map into other programs to make further enhancements. You also can create a compressed file to control the size of the bit-mapped file. Compressed files store the image in a more compact format without affecting the appearance of the image.

To export a TIFF bit-mapped file, make sure you are viewing the presentation in the Slide Editor or Slide Sorter and choose **E**xport... from the **F**ile menu. Click the down arrow next to the File **t**ype: list box, and select TIFF Bitmap from the list of formats. Before exporting the file, Harvard Graphics opens the TIFF File Export dialog box, in which you set the color, resolution, size, and compression used to create the bit-mapped file (see fig. 15.13).

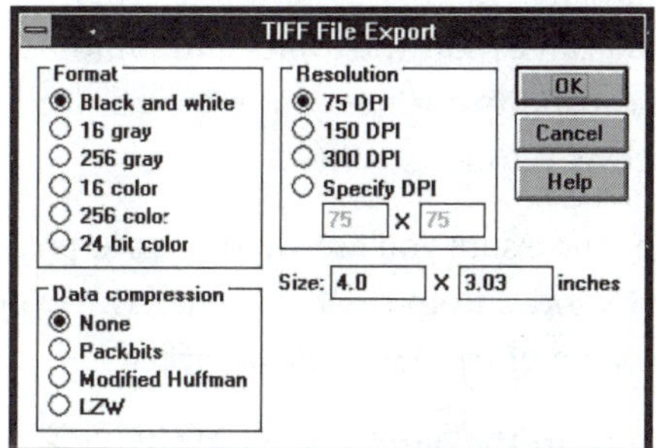

Fig. 15.13
The TIFF File Export dialog box.

The color scheme of the bit map determines the bit-map format. You can export black-and-white TIFF files, files that use between 16 and 256 colors or shades of gray, or files with 24 bits of color.

The bit-map resolution is determined by how many dots per inch (dpi) represent the image. More dots provide finer control over the image and better resolution in the file. In the dialog box, you can specify 75, 150, or 300 dpi, as well as a custom resolution. For bit maps displayed on-screen, 75 dpi is sufficient, although many printers can support higher resolutions than a computer screen. The Size: text boxes control the height and width of the bit map. The Data Compression buttons create smaller bit-mapped files without affecting the clarity of the image.

Follow these steps to export a TIFF file for use with a high-resolution black-and-white printer:

1. If you are not viewing the presentation in the Slide Editor or Slide Sorter, choose one of these views from the **V**iew menu.

2. Choose **E**xport... from the **F**ile menu. The Export dialog box appears.

3. Click the down arrow next to the File **t**ype: list box and select TIFF Bitmap from the list of file formats.
4. Type the name of the file in the File**n**ame: text box and click OK. The TIFF File Export dialog box appears.
5. Click the 256 gray button in the TIFF File Export dialog box.
6. Click the 300 DPI button.
7. Click OK in the Export dialog box to clear the dialog box and begin exporting the file.

Exporting an ASCII Outline

From the Outliner, you can export the topics and subtopics of your outline to an ASCII file. This capability enables you to view and edit the outline in another program, such as Windows Write.

To export the outline, make sure you are viewing your presentation in the Outliner and choose **E**xport... from the **F**ile menu. The Export dialog box, in which you enter the name of the ASCII file, appears.

Follow these steps to export the outline to an ASCII file:

1. If you are not viewing the presentation in the Outliner, choose **O**utliner from the **V**iew menu.
2. Choose **E**xport... from the **F**ile menu. The Export dialog box appears.
3. Type the name of the ASCII file in the File**n**ame text box.
4. Click OK to export the outline.

Using the Clipboard

The Windows Clipboard provides one of the easiest methods for transferring information between Windows applications. Windows' capability to switch between applications enables you to copy the information without creating an export or import file. You don't need to start one program to perform the export and then exit that program so that you can import into another program. Using the Clipboard, you can copy cells from a spreadsheet and paste them directly into the chart data form, and you can copy topics in the Outliner and paste them into a word processor, such as Windows Write. Most Windows applications can communicate directly with the Clipboard.

The applications of each combination work together to produce the best result when you transfer information. If you select a range of cells in the chart data form and paste them into a spreadsheet, for example, each cell in the data form becomes a cell in the spreadsheet. If you paste the same information into a word processor, each row of chart data becomes a line in the document. In this section, you learn how to copy the contents of the Clipboard into Harvard Graphics and how to transfer information from Harvard Graphics to the Clipboard. For more information on the Windows Clipboard, consult the Windows documentation.

Importing from Windows Applications

You use the **P**aste command on the **E**dit menu to transfer the contents of the Clipboard to a Harvard Graphics slide or chart. The result of the **P**aste command depends on the current view of the presentation. In the Slide Editor, the **P**aste command creates objects on the slide. In the Outliner, text from the Clipboard becomes topics in the outline. The Slide Sorter can accept only slides from the Clipboard. If the contents of the Clipboard are incompatible with the current view, the **P**aste command is disabled on the **E**dit menu.

To copy an object from another application to the Slide Editor using the Clipboard, follow these steps:

1. Copy the objects from another Windows application to the Clipboard by selecting the object and choosing **C**opy from the **E**dit menu.

2. Activate Harvard Graphics within Windows by clicking in the Harvard Graphics window or double-clicking the Harvard Graphics icon. (For more information on working with multiple applications in Windows, consult the Windows documentation.)

3. If you are not viewing the presentation in the Slide Editor, choose Slide **E**ditor from the **V**iew menu.

4. Choose **P**aste from the **E**dit menu. Harvard Graphics pastes the object from the Clipboard into the Slide Editor window.

Design Note

With the Paste **s**pecial... command on the **E**dit menu, you can paste different parts of items you copy. The items you paste depend on what you copy and from which application. For example, if you copy a slide, you can paste the slide as a picture of objects or as a graphic bit map on another slide.

Exporting to Windows Applications

You use the Cut and Copy commands on the Edit menu to transfer data and images from Harvard Graphics to the Windows Clipboard. The Copy command copies the information from Harvard Graphics and leaves the original presentation intact. The Cut command, on the other hand, removes the information from the presentation before placing the data in the Clipboard. After you issue the Cut or Copy command, you can paste the contents of the Clipboard into other Windows applications.

Harvard Graphics transfers the information in the manner most appropriate for the other application. If you select cells in the pie chart data form, for example, you can paste the data into the cells of a spreadsheet.

Follow these steps to copy information to the Windows Clipboard:

1. Select the objects or data in Harvard Graphics.
2. Choose Cut or Copy from the Edit menu.
3. Activate the other application by clicking its window or double-clicking its icon.
4. Choose **P**aste from the **E**dit menu.

Using DDE Links

Dynamic Data Exchange (DDE) enables Windows applications to communicate information directly. With DDE, changes made to one application appear automatically in the linked application. You can create a DDE link between the cells in a spreadsheet and the bars of a chart in Harvard Graphics, for example. As the data in the spreadsheet changes, the bars of the chart grow and shrink accordingly. As opposed to the links discussed in an earlier section, "Maintaining Links to Import Files," DDE links require both applications to be running in Windows.

You use the Paste special... command on the Edit menu to create a DDE link between Harvard Graphics and another Windows application. You can create a DDE link from the data form for any chart type except title, bullet, and organization charts; you can link only to another program that supports DDE, such as Microsoft Excel. To start the link, select the data in the Windows application and choose Copy from the Edit menu. In the data form for the Harvard Graphics chart, choose Paste **s**pecial... from the **E**dit menu. The Paste Special dialog box opens (see fig. 15.14). In this dialog box, you see a list of different ways you can paste the items you copied. In the figure, the copied items can be pasted as text or as a DDE Link. To create the link, click the Link item in the dialog box. Then click the Paste **l**ink button to paste the link.

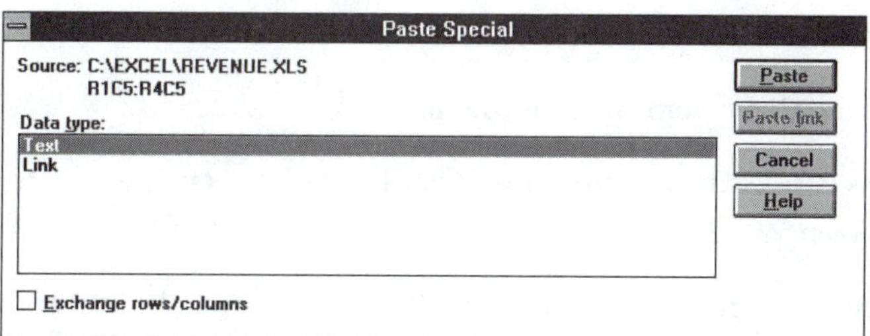

Fig. 15.14
The Paste Special dialog box.

Figure 15.15 shows a Pie chart data form with a DDE link. The edit line shows the syntax for a DDE link in a cell that was created using the Paste **s**pecial... command. The information in the data form comes from cells R1C5:R4C5 in the REVENUE.XLS Excel spreadsheet.

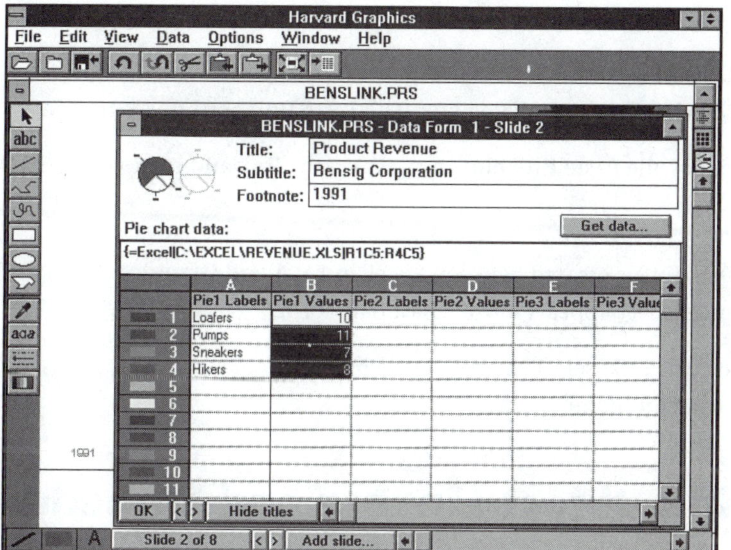

Fig. 15.15
A DDE link in an XY chart data form.

Suppose that you want to create a link between Harvard Graphics and Microsoft Excel. To create the link, Harvard Graphics and Microsoft Excel must be running in Windows, the Excel spreadsheet must be open, and a slide with a vertical bar chart should have been created in Harvard Graphics.

Follow these steps to create a DDE link between Microsoft Excel and Harvard Graphics:

1. In the spreadsheet, select the cells you want to link.
2. Choose **C**opy from the **E**dit menu.
3. Press Ctrl-Esc to show the Task List. The task list enables you to switch between Windows applications.
4. Select Harvard Graphics from the list of tasks. You also can click the Harvard Graphics window or double-click the Harvard Graphics icon.
5. Choose Edit **d**ata from the **C**hart menu in the Slide Editor to display the data form for the chart.
6. Click the cell where you want to create the link. For the example, click A1.
7. Choose Paste **s**pecial... from the **E**dit menu. The Paste Special dialog box opens.
8. Click Link in the dialog box. The Paste **l**ink button is activated.
9. Click the Paste **l**ink button to set up the link and remove the dialog box.

The DDE link is created between Excel and Harvard Graphics. The data from the spreadsheet appears in the chart data form.

To clear the link, select the affected cells in the data form and choose Cl**e**ar from the **E**dit menu.

Using Object Linking and Embedding

Files created with various Windows applications are becoming more complex and powerful. Using the Windows Clipboard covered earlier, you can create charts in Harvard Graphics and then paste those charts in Microsoft Excel or another Windows application. The files you create can have many objects created with several different applications. *Object Linking and Embedding* (OLE) is a feature that Windows supplies to help ease the creation and maintenance of these compound files while ensuring that the different parts are up-to-date and look sharp.

Similar to DDE, OLE supports a link between an object created in one application and pasted into another. The difference is that when you double-click an OLE object, the creating application is launched and the object is loaded into the application. The application then determines the behavior based on its own OLE settings. For example, if you embed an object from PC Paintbrush, double-clicking the bit map allows you to quickly edit the bit map in PC Paintbrush. Likewise, you can embed Harvard Graphics presentations into other applications that support OLE. Based on the OLE settings discussed in the next section, double-clicking the object in the other application either displays the presentation as a ScreenShow or loads the presentation into Harvard Graphics for editing.

Figure 15.16 shows the Bensig company logo in the bottom right corner of the slide. This logo is actually a bit map embedded from PC Paintbrush. Because Harvard Graphics does not enable you to edit bit maps, embedding the bit-map object allows you seemless access to bit maps. You can double-click the object to edit just like you would double-click other objects on a slide. All objects appear on the slide whether or not they were created with Harvard Graphics. In fact, you can even resize the object by clicking the object handles and dragging the marquee to a new size.

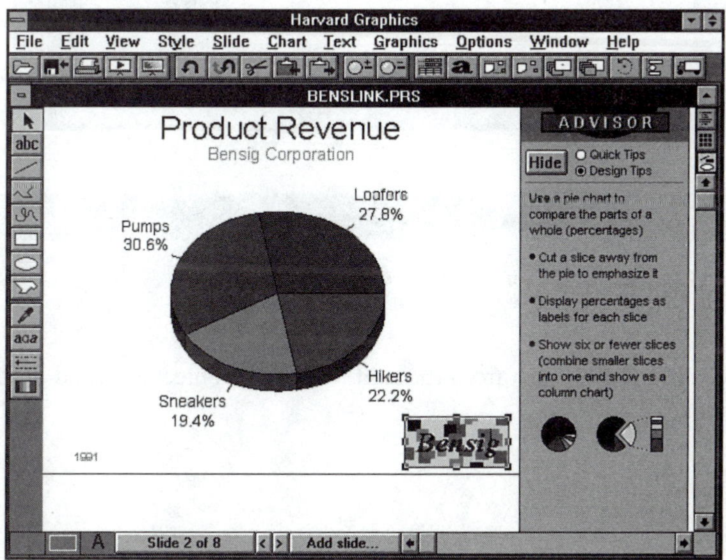

Fig. 15.16
The Bensig logo as an OLE object.

Follow these steps to embed an object in Harvard Graphics:

1. In the creating application, select the object you want to embed.
2. Choose **C**opy from the **E**dit menu.
3. Press Ctrl-Esc to show the Task List. The task list enables you to switch between Windows applications.
4. Select Harvard Graphics from the list of tasks. You also can click the Harvard Graphics window or double-click the Harvard Graphics icon.

   The **E**dit menu's **P**aste command changes to display the name of the application followed by the word *object* (see fig. 15.17). This command informs you that when you **P**aste the object, you create an OLE link.

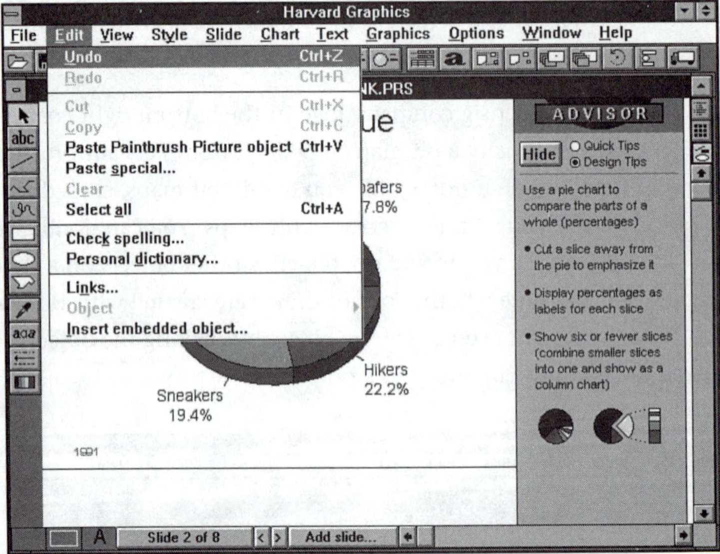

Fig. 15.17
The **E**dit menu with the **P**aste object command.

> **Note**
>
> To avoid OLE links, use the Paste **s**pecial... command.

5. Choose **P**aste object from the **E**dit menu. The object is pasted onto the slide.

To embed Harvard Graphics objects in other applications, select the objects you want to embed and choose **C**opy from the **E**dit menu. Then make the other application active and follow the steps necessary for that application to embed OLE objects (generally, you use a Paste command on the Edit menu).

Setting DDE/OLE Options

The DDE/**O**LE... command on the **O**ptions menu enables you to control the behavior of Harvard Graphics when creating OLE and DDE links. This dialog box is shown in figure 15.18. If you want Harvard Graphics to prompt you before updating links in a presentation, check the box labeled **P**rompt to update links when opening a presentation. If you don't mark the box, the links are automatically updated.

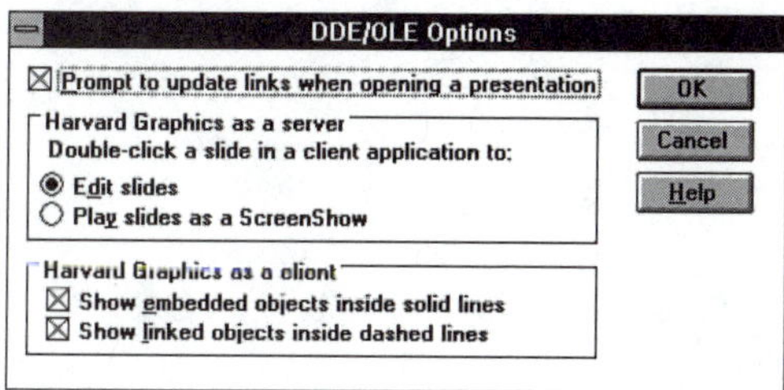

Fig. 15.18
The DDE/OLE Options dialog box.

The box labeled Harvard Graphics as a server determines the behavior of Harvard Graphics when you click a Harvard Graphics object that is embedded in another application. If the E**d**it slides button is marked, double-clicking the object loads the presentation for editing. The Pla**y** slides as a ScreenShow button displays the presentation on-screen. The Harvard Graphics as a client box determines how embedded and linked objects appear within Harvard Graphics. You can choose to Show **e**mbedded objects inside solid lines and Show **l**inked (DDE) objects inside dashed lines. Follow these steps to set DDE/OLE options:

1. Choose DDE/**O**LE... from the **O**ptions menu. The DDE/OLE Options dialog box opens.
2. Set the options you want to use in the dialog box.
3. Click OK to remove the dialog box and save the settings.

From Here...

This chapter explains how to transfer data and images to other applications. The chapter also covers Harvard Graphics import capabilities, which enable you to import files from other programs, including the DOS versions of Harvard Graphics. The sections on exporting explain how to save slides and presentations in files that use a variety of formats. At the end of the chapter, you learned how to create DDE links to other Windows applications for automatic updating of information and how to work with OLE objects.

The next two chapters cover the presentation features of Harvard Graphics, which you use to modify the appearance of the entire presentation or to display presentations on your computer screen.

Chapter 16

Enhancing a Presentation

Harvard Graphics provides several features to help you enhance a presentation and give your slides a consistent appearance. You can change the color for all the bars in your charts or display a common background behind the data in your slides, for example. You can use the features explained in this chapter to change the appearance of your presentation without editing each individual slide.

In this chapter, you learn how to do the following:

- Create and edit presentation backgrounds
- Work with templates and color palettes
- Create and use a presentation style

All the slides in a presentation display a *background* behind the slide's data. The section "Working with Backgrounds" explains how to create and use backgrounds in a presentation, for example, to display a company logo on every slide.

Templates control the default settings for slide items, such as a title or chart, when you create a slide. You also can use a template to change the appearance of an existing slide. The section "Working with Templates" explains how to create a template and how to use a template to change the appearance of a slide.

Color palettes determine the available colors to use with your slides. When you create charts, for instance, the colors in the charts change when you change the palette. The section "Using Color Palettes" explains how to change the palette and how to edit the colors.

By combining these features—backgrounds, templates, and color palettes—you can create a *presentation style* to use with many different presentations. Presentation styles save templates, backgrounds, and color palettes on the same file, which you can then apply to a presentation. Presentation styles enable you to save in one file a consistent presentation look to use with all the presentations you create.

Working with Backgrounds

Backgrounds add consistency to a presentation by displaying the same color and images as the backdrop of presentation slides. When you create a presentation, each slide you create displays a background titled *default*. Changes you make to the default background affect all the slides that use this background. The section "Editing a Background" explains how to make changes to a background.

Figure 16.1 shows a presentation with a gradient fill background. This background provides a consistent look for all the slides by showing the same images behind each slide.

Fig. 16.1
A presentation with a background gradient fill.

When you create a slide, the default template for that slide type determines the background. The section "Working with Templates" in this chapter explains default templates and how they affect slide creation. You are not locked into using the default template, however. After you create the slide, you can change the template and, as a result, the background style.

Also in this chapter, the section "Editing a Background" explains how to add graphics to the background and how to fill the background with different fill styles. "Creating a Background" explains how to create different backgrounds in a presentation, and "Applying a Background" explains how to change the background for one slide or an entire presentation.

The Background Images dialog box displays all the backgrounds available for your presentation. Figure 16.2 shows an example of the dialog box with three different backgrounds. The three listed in the Background: box include Company Logo, Default (which is created with the presentation), and Gradient. Since Gradient is selected, and the Show background option is checked, you see the actual background in the dialog box in the figure. You can use the dialog box to view different backgrounds, to create and edit new backgrounds, and to apply backgrounds to different slides in your presentation.

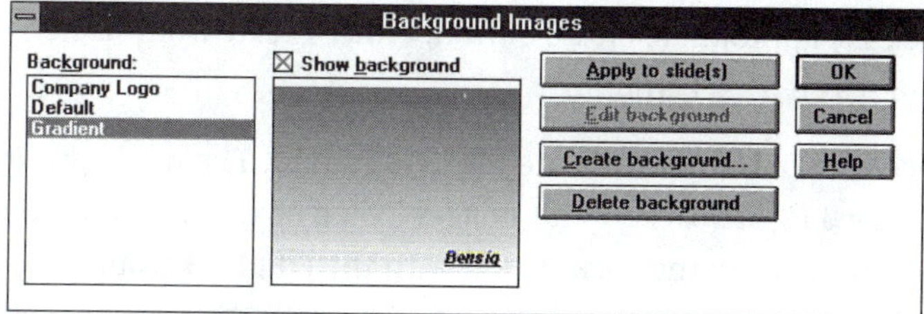

Fig. 16.2
The Background Images dialog box.

Creating a Background

To create a new background for a slide, you use the Create background button on the Button Images dialog box, which you access through the Images... command of the Background pop-up menu on the Style menu. Creating a new background enables you to have different backgrounds for slides in your presentation. To create a new background for a slide, you complete the following steps:

1. If you are not viewing the presentation in the Slide Editor, choose Slide Editor from the View menu.

2. Choose Background from the Style menu. A pop-up menu containing the background commands appears.

3. Choose Images... from the menu to display the Images dialog box.

4. Click the Create background... button to create a new background. The Create Background dialog box appears (see fig. 16.3).

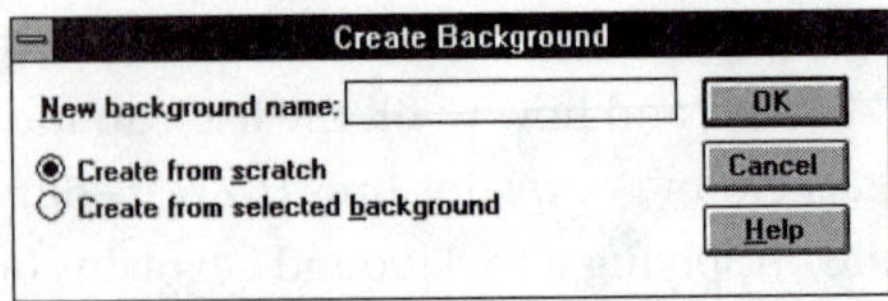

Fig. 16.3
The Create Background dialog box.

5. Type the name of the background in the New background name: text box.

   The Create from scratch button enables you to create a background without any existing images or colors. The Create from selected background duplicates the selected background in the Images dialog for the new background. You use this option as a starting point for the new background, for example, if you have one background you like and you wish to create another with some minor changes.

6. Click the appropriate create button, either Create from scratch or Create from selected background.

7. Click the OK button to create the background. The new background is displayed in the Background Images dialog box. From here, you can make changes to the background with the Edit background button and then apply the background to your slides with the Apply to slide(s) button.

8. Click the OK button to remove the Background Images dialog box.

Editing a Background

To edit a background, you use the Edit background button on the Background Images dialog box. When you click the button, the background selected in the dialog box appears in the Slide Editor. You use the Slide Editor tools to change the background. If other slides share the same background, changes made for one slide appear on all the others. To learn about the toolbox and tools that are available in the Slide Editor, read Chapter 12, "Drawing in Harvard Graphics," and Chapter 13, "Enhancing Drawings and Objects." Figure 16.4 shows a background in the Slide Editor. At the bottom of the Slide Editor window, you can see the name of the background and the Back to slide button. When you finish editing the background, click the Back to slide button to return to the slide.

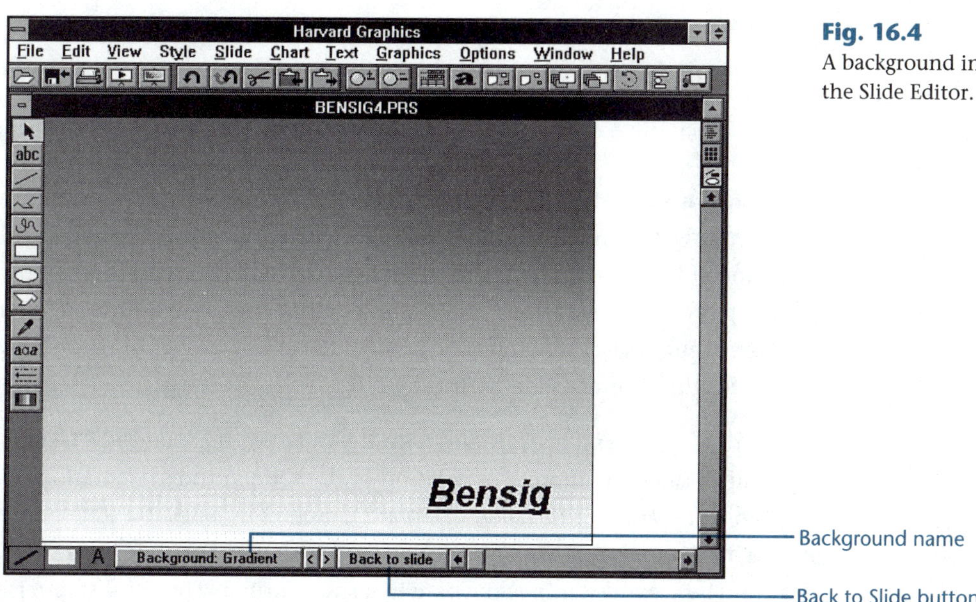

Fig. 16.4
A background in the Slide Editor.

Adding Graphics to a Background. In the Slide Editor, you can add to a background the same objects that you can add to a slide. You can add squares, circles, or polygons, for example. You cannot add charts of any type to the background, however.

The changes you make to the background appear when you return to the Slide Editor. You can view the background with the slide, but you cannot edit the objects of the background.

Follow these steps to edit the background for a slide:

1. If you are not viewing the presentation in the Slide Editor, choose Slide Editor from the View menu.

2. Choose Background from the Style menu. The Background pop-up menu appears.

3. Choose Images from the pop-up menu. The Background Images dialog box appears.

4. Click the background you wish to edit in the Background: box. The item you click is highlighted.

5. Click the Edit background button. The background appears in the Slide Editor.

6. Create the graphics objects on the background using the tools of the Slide Editor.

7. Click the Back to slide button to accept the changes; the slide reappears.

Adding a Text Stamp. *Text stamps* on a background display information that changes. You use a stamp to display the number of each slide, the date in one of two formats, and the current time. The data used in each type of stamp is determined when you display or print the presentation. If you move slides around, Harvard Graphics changes the slide number in the text stamp to reflect the correct slide position.

Figure 16.5 shows a background with the different text stamps. The first stamp is the slide number or position of the slide in the presentation. As you change the order of the slides, Harvard Graphics updates the slide number text stamp so that it displays the correct position of the slide in the presentation. The second stamp is the date in a short format. The third stamp is the date in a longer format, and the fourth stamp is the current time. Harvard Graphics updates the date and time stamps when you view a different slide in the Slide Editor, print the presentation, or view the presentation on-screen.

Fig. 16.5 The four different types of text stamps on a background.

You create text stamps in text annotations. You can add a stamp to an existing annotation or create a new annotation for the stamp. While editing a text annotation, choose one of the four stamp types from the Add Stamp pop-up menu of the Text menu. Text attributes that you set for a text annotation affect a text stamp, as well. For more information on text annotations, see Chapter 7, "Working with Text."

Follow these steps to create a text stamp that shows the slide number and the date on the background:

1. If you are not viewing the presentation in the Slide Editor, choose Slide Editor from the View menu.
2. Choose Background from the Style menu. The Background pop-up menu appears.
3. Choose Images from the pop-up menu. The Background Images dialog box appears.
4. Click the background you wish to edit in the Background: box. The item you click is highlighted.
5. Click the Edit background button. The background appears in the Slide Editor.
6. Click the Text tool in the toolbox. See Chapter 12, "Drawing in Harvard Graphics," for information about the toolbox.
7. Click the area on the slide where you want to place the stamp. Click the bottom of the slide to show the date and slide number at the bottom of each slide, for example.
8. Choose Add Stamp from the Text menu. The Add Stamp pop-up menu containing the different text stamps appears.
9. Choose Slide Number from the pop-up menu. The slide number of the current slide appears.
10. Press the space bar twice to separate the slide number stamp and the stamp you create in the following steps.
11. Choose Add Stamp from the Text menu. The Add Stamp pop-up menu containing the stamp types appears.
12. Choose Long Date from the pop-up menu. The date in the long format appears in the annotation.
13. Click the Back to slide button.

The text stamp appears on all slides that use the background.

Setting the Background Fill. The background fill controls the colors and patterns displayed behind all the objects on a slide. With the Background option on the Style menu, you can change the color of the background or use different fill styles, such as solid, gradient, hatch/pattern, or bit-map fills while viewing a slide with the background in the Slide Editor or while editing the background to add graphic images. Figure 16.6 shows a slide with a bit-map fill on the background.

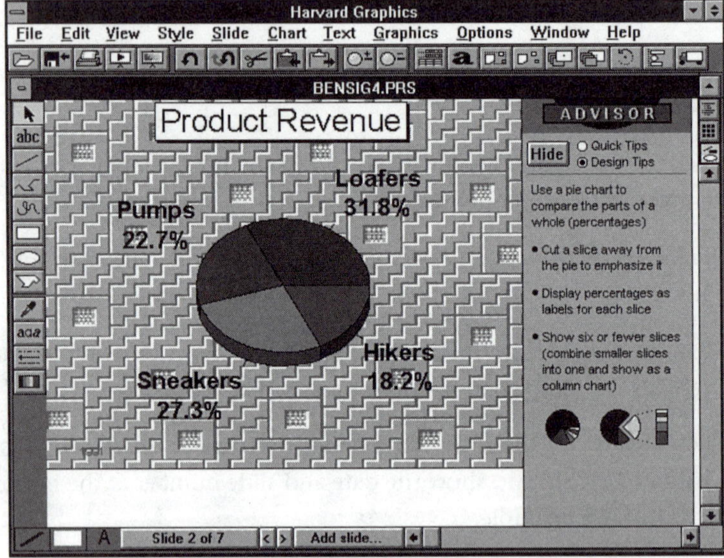

Fig. 16.6
A bit-map filled background.

Follow these steps to set the background fill to a solid color:

1. If you are not viewing the presentation in the Slide Editor, choose Slide Editor from the View menu.

2. Choose Background from the Slide menu. The Background pop-up menu appears.

3. Choose Solid.... The Solid Color dialog box, in which you choose a fill color, appears.

4. Choose the color in the Solid Color dialog box.

5. Click the OK button.

The background of the current slide and all slides that share the background display the color you selected.

Applying a Background

Harvard Graphics stores the backgrounds you create with the presentation. Any slide in the presentation can use any background. To use a background with a slide, you must apply the background. You use the Apply to slide(s) on the Background Images dialog box to apply the background to a slide. If you display this dialog box within the Slide Editor, the background is applied to the slide you are viewing. To apply a background to more than one slide, view the presentation in the Slide Sorter and click all the slides that you wish to display with the background. See Chapter 10, "Using the Slide Sorter," for more information. Follow these steps:

1. Choose Background from the Slide menu within the Slide Editor or Slide Sorter. The Background pop-up menu appears.

2. Choose Images... from the pop-up menu. The Background Images dialog box appears.

3. Click the background you wish to apply in the Background: box. The item you click is highlighted.

4. Click the Apply to slide(s) button. Your background is applied to your slide or slides.

5. Click the OK button to remove the Background Images dialog box.

Removing a Background

You use the Delete background button on the Background Images dialog box to remove backgrounds from a presentation. This command does not remove the background from an individual slide. To remove a background from a slide, you must apply a new background to the slide. The Remove command removes the background so that you can no longer apply the background to any slide in the presentation. Before you can remove a background from a presentation, you must make sure that none of the slides in the presentation uses the background.

Follow these steps:

1. Choose Background from the Slide menu within the Slide Editor or Slide Sorter. The Background pop-up menu appears.

2. Choose Images from the pop-up menu. The Background Images dialog box appears.

3. Click the background you wish to remove in the Background: box. The item you click is highlighted.

4. Click the Delete background button. Your background is removed from the list of backgrounds.

5. Click the OK button to remove the Background Images dialog box.

Working with Templates

Templates save the style and appearance of a slide under a unique name in a presentation. The items in a template control the default settings for slides when you create the slides. You can also use a template to change the appearance of an existing slide by applying the template to the slide.

A template contains the location and text attributes for the title, subtitle, and footnote of the chart. When you apply the template, the title, subtitle, and footnote change to the new settings.

In addition to title information, the template also contains the type and options for the chart on the slide, graphic objects created in the Slide Editor, the slide background, the color palette, and any HyperShow links created on the slide.

You create all the slides of a presentation from a template. Every presentation contains one template for each type listed in the Add Slide dialog box (see fig. 16.6). These templates are the default templates for the slide type. When you create a new slide, the default settings for the slide are determined by the template with the same name. For example, the template named Vertical Bar contains the default vertical bar slide settings. The section "Replacing an Existing Template" explains how to replace the individual templates, such as the default template, of a presentation.

Like backgrounds, Harvard Graphics stores templates with the presentation. Each presentation contains templates for each slide type as well as any templates you create. See the section "Creating a Template" for more information.

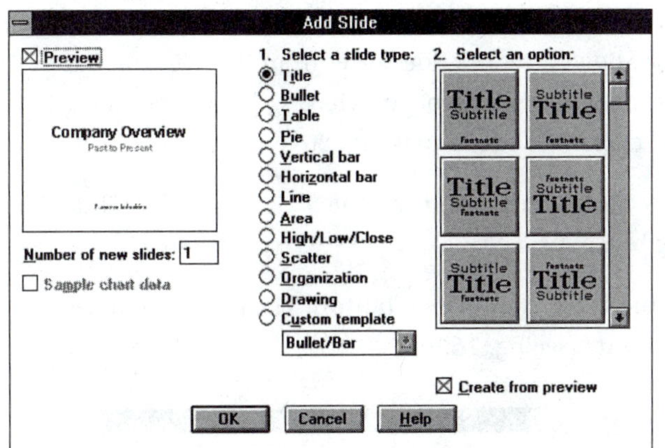

Fig. 16.7
The Add Slide dialog box.

The Slide templates... command on the Style menu provides access to the Slide Templates dialog box shown in figure 16.8. From within this dialog box, you create and edit templates, and also apply existing templates to slides you have already created. The Slide template box on the left side of the dialog box lists all the templates available in your presentation. To see a preview of the template with some sample data, click the template in this list. If you click the Show slide template option such that an X is not displayed, you will not see a preview of the template, for example, if you are in a hurry.

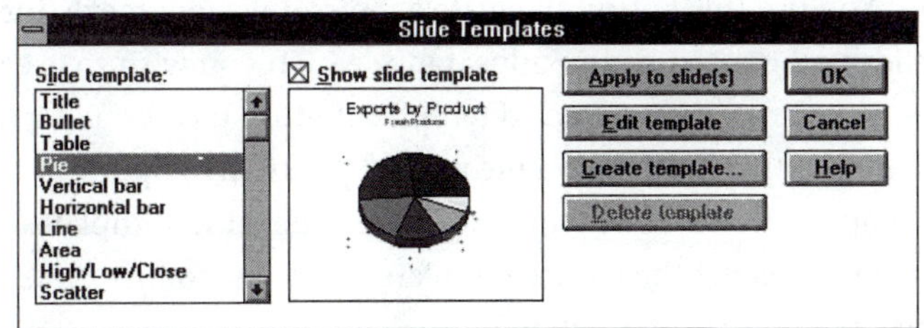

Fig. 16.8
The Slide Templates dialog box.

Creating a Template

You create a template to save a graphic look or chart appearance that you wish to reuse with other slides in your presentation. You first create the template with the Create template... button on the Slide Templates dialog box. Next, you modify slide options and chart layout with the Edit template button on the Slide Templates dialog box. See the section Editing a Template for more information. Follow these steps:

1. If you are not viewing the slide in the Slide Editor or Slide Sorter, choose Slide Editor or Slide Sorter from the View menu. In the Slide Editor, make sure that you are viewing the correct slide. In the Slide Sorter, click the slide to make it active.

2. Choose Slide template... from the Style menu. The Slide Templates dialog box appears.

3. Click the Create template... button. The Create Slide Template dialog box appears (see fig. 16.9).

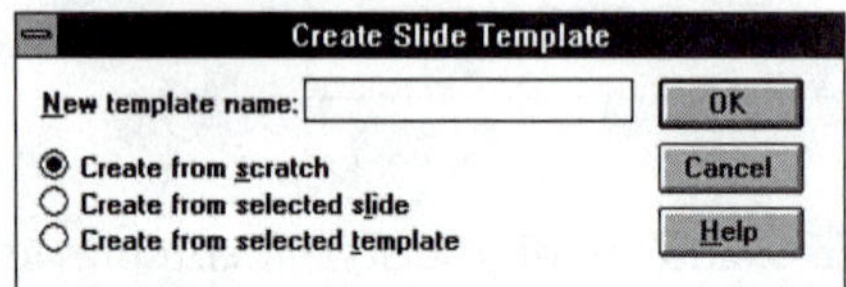

Fig. 16.9
The Create Slide Template dialog box.

In the Create Slide Template dialog box, you first enter the name for the template and then choose how the initial options, such as chart type and title placement, for the template will be set. The Create from scratch button sets the options according to the Harvard Graphics defaults. The Create from selected slide button uses the options from the slide you were viewing before selecting Slide templates... from the Style menu. You use this option to create a template from an existing slide if the slide you created has an appearance which you wish to use for other slides. The Create from selected template button creates one template from another for much the same reason. To use this option, you select the Template in the Slide template: box in the Slide Templates dialog box before clicking the Create template... button. Follow these steps to create a template from scratch:

4. Type the name of the slide in the Slide Template Name text box. Use a name that reveals something about the appearance of the slide, for example, *3d Pie with Legend.*

5. Click the OK button to remove the Create Slide Template dialog box and create the template. The template name appears in the Slide Template dialog box.

6. Click the OK button to remove the Slide Templates dialog box.

Once you have created the template, you can make additional changes to improve the appearance and then apply that template to other slides.

Editing a Template

To edit a template, you use the Edit template button on the Slide Templates dialog box. When you click the button, the template selected in the dialog box appears in the Slide Editor. You use the Slide Editor tools and commands on the Chart menu to change the template. For example, to change a 2-dimensional pie chart to a 3-dimensional pie chart, you use the Chart options... command on the Chart menu. If other slides share the same template, changes made for one slide appear on all the others. To learn about the toolbox and tools that are available in the Slide Editor, read Chapter 12, "Drawing in Harvard Graphics," and Chapter 13, "Enhancing Drawings and Objects." Figure 16.10 shows a template in the Slide Editor. At the bottom of the Slide Editor window, you can see the name of the template and the Back to Slide button. When you finish editing the background, click the Back to Slide button to return to the slide.

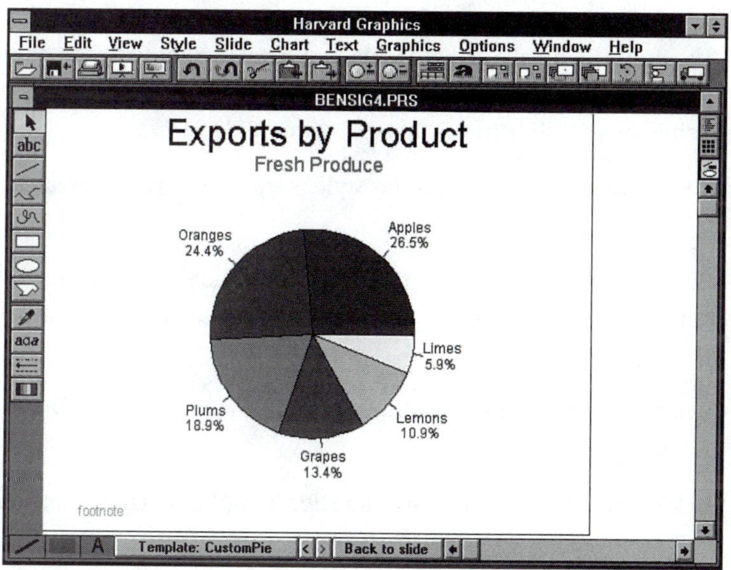

Fig. 16.10
A template in the Slide Editor.

Follow these steps to edit a template:

1. Select Slide templates... from the Style menu. The Slide Templates dialog box appears.

2. Select the template you wish to edit in the Slide template: list. If the Show slide template: option is marked with an X, you see a preview of the template in the box.

3. Click the Edit template button. You see the template in the Slide Editor.

4. Make changes to the template using the tools of the Slide Editor. You also modify chart options using the command on the Chart menu. All your changes are displayed in the slide in the Slide Editor.

5. Click the Back to slide button to finish making changes and to return to the Slide Editor.

Applying Templates

You can change the appearance of a slide with a template after you create the slide. You can apply one of the default templates to reset the chart to the default settings. You can also apply a template you created to give a similar appearance to many slides. To apply a template to a single slide, you must view the slide in the Slide Editor or the slide must be selected in the Slide Sorter. You apply a template to many slides by selecting them in the Slide Sorter. To apply a template, choose Slide templates... from the Slide menu, select a template and click the Apply to slide(s) button. Follow these steps to apply a template to a slide in the Slide Editor or Slide Sorter:

1. Select Slide templates... from the Style menu. The Slide Templates dialog box appears.

2. Select the template you wish to apply in the Slide template: list. If the Show slide template: option is marked with an X, you see a preview of the template in the box.

3. Click the Apply to slide(s) button. Your slide or slides are modified with the settings of the template.

4. Click the OK button to remove the Slide Templates dialog box.

Removing Templates

You can remove a template by using the Delete template button on the Slide Templates dialog box. You cannot remove any of the default templates from the presentation, however. Follow these steps:

1. Select Slide templates... from the Style menu. The Slide Templates dialog box appears.

2. Select the template you wish to remove in the Slide template: list. If the Show slide template: option is marked with an X, you see a preview of the template in the box.

3. Click the Delete template button to remove the template from your presentation.

4. Click the OK button to remove the Slide Templates dialog box.

Creating a Slide from a Custom Template

The Custom Template button on the Add Slide dialog box enables you to create a slide from a template that is not a default template. You click the arrow next to the field below this button to list all the templates you have created in your presentation. You then click a template in the list to use when creating the slide. See the section "Creating a Template" earlier in the chapter for information on creating a template. Figure 16.11 shows the Add Slide dialog box with the Custom Template button selected and the template CustomPie displayed in the field. For more information on creating slides, see the section "Adding Slides to a Presentation" in Chapter 2, "Learning Harvard Graphics for Windows Basics."

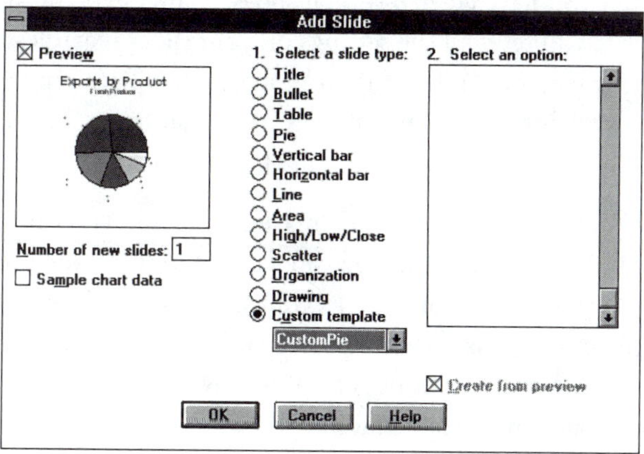

Fig. 16.11
The Add Slide dialog box listing custom templates.

Follow these steps to create a slide from a custom template:

1. If you are not viewing the presentation in the Slide Editor or Slide Sorter, choose Slide Editor or Slide Sorter from the View menu.

2. Choose Add Slide from the Slide menu. Harvard Graphics displays the Add Slide dialog box.

3. Click the Custom Template button.

4. Select a template from the list box below the Custom Template button.

5. Click the OK button to create the slide from the template.

Working with Master Templates

Master templates provide an easy method for setting the layout, color, and background for all the slides in your presentation regardless of the chart displayed on the slide. Regular templates, on the other hand, control the appearance of different slide types. Each presentation has a single master template which controls the placement and text attributes of the slide title, subtitle, and footnote. The master template also sets the location of the chart, the options of your background fill and the color palette used for all of your slides. You can even add graphics to a master template and those graphics will be displayed behind all of your slides.

Master templates actually affect your slides in two ways. First, the master template controls the settings for the items listed above when you create a new slide. After you have created several slides, changes you make to the master template will reset all the settings on your slides regardless of other changes you have made. In this way, your master template can insure a consistent look for all your slides by making sure similar items, such as the font of the title or the location of the chart, are the same on each slide.

There are two facets to working with a master template. You can make changes or edit the template and you can also determine which parts of the master template are actually applied to your slides. The section "Editing a Master Template" explains how to make changes to the template. The section "Setting Master Template Options" explains how you choose which parts of the master template affect your slides.

Editing a Master Template

You edit a Master Template in the Slide Editor using the same tools that enable you to modify and add graphics to a slide. The Edit master template command on the Style menu displays the master template in the Slide Editor. You then make changes to the template. For example, to change the location of the slide title, you click the Title placeholder and drag it to a new location similar to the way you move an actual slide title. You drag the placeholders for other chart elements such as the subtitle, footnote, and chart to new locations or click these items and change their appearance, for example, to change the font. Figure 16.12 shows a master template in the Slide Editor. In the figure, you see the different placeholders. When you are finished making changes, you click the Back to slide button at the bottom of the Slide Editor window.

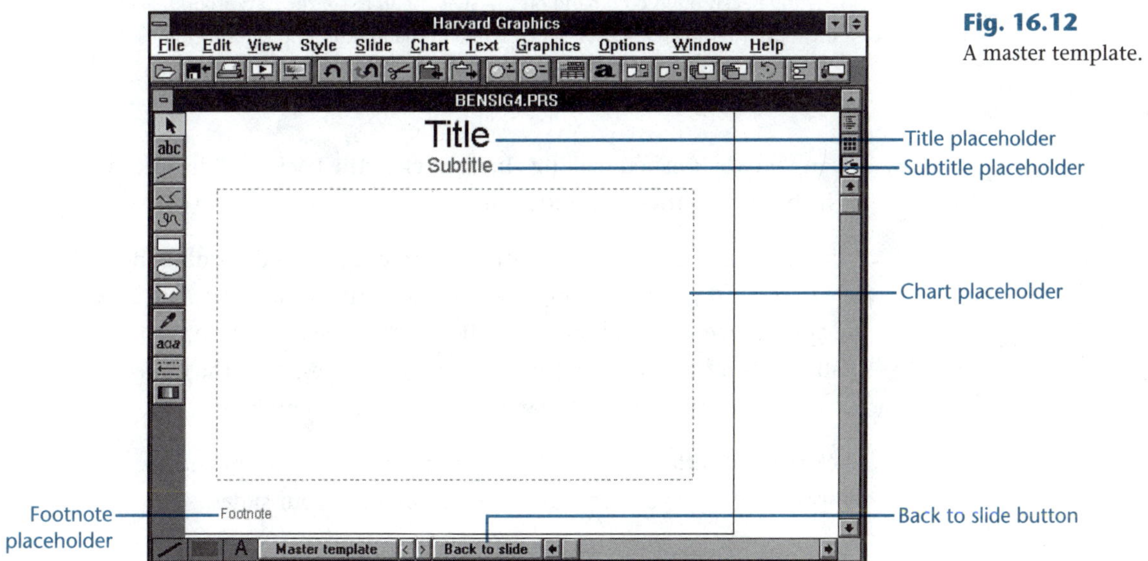

Fig. 16.12
A master template.

Follow these steps to make changes to the master template:

1. Select Edit master template from the Style menu. The master template is displayed in the Slide Editor.

2. Make changes to the slide using the tools of the Slide Editor.

   As an example of using a master template, you could increase the text size of the slide title and display the title on the left side of your slide. Follow these steps:

3. Click the title placeholder to select it. Handles appear around the placeholder.

4. Select Size from the Text menu and select a larger size from the pop-up menu which displays various sizes. The text on the master template changes to the size you selected.

5. Click the title placeholder and drag the text to the left side of the slide. As you drag, a marquee box displays the location of the text. To place the text, release the mouse button.

> **Design Note**
>
> Use the Background command on the Style menu to set the background fill of the master template. See the section Setting the Background Fill earlier in the chapter for more information.

6. When you are finished making changes, click the Back to slide button at the bottom of the Slide Editor window.

   When you click the button, Harvard Graphics displays a warning message to remind you that changes you make to the master template affect the appearance of all of your slides. If you click the No button, your changes are not saved. To return to making changes, click the Cancel button to return to making changes to the master template.

7. Click the Yes button to accept the changes you made to the master template. You see your changes reflected in all of your slides.

Setting Master Template Options

Despite the advantages of the consistent appearance you can create with a master template, you may not always wish to modify all your slides with all of the settings of the master template. For example, you could use a master template to change the location and text attributes of a slide title without changing the location of the chart on each slide. To determine which parts of a master template affect your slides, you use the Master Template Options dialog box shown in figure 16.13. For each part of a master template, an X in the dialog box indicates that the item from the master template will affect your slides. You click the box to enable the item or remove the X to disable the item. Follow these steps to set the master template options:

1. Select Adopt master template... from the Slide menu. The Master Template Options dialog box is displayed with your current settings.

2. Click the boxes for the different options to enable and disable specific elements of the master template.

Fig. 16.13
The Master Template Options dialog box.

3. Click the OK button when you have finished making changes. The dialog box is removed.

Using Color Palettes

The color palette determines the color scheme for the items on your slides, such as the bars of a bar chart or the color of a text annotation. The palette also provides the choices for changing the colors of objects on a slide, such as the fill color of a solid rectangle. Figure 16.14 shows a palette in the Solid Color Fill dialog box. You use this dialog box to set the color of filled objects, such as rectangles and circles. A similar dialog box appears when you change the color for an object on a slide.

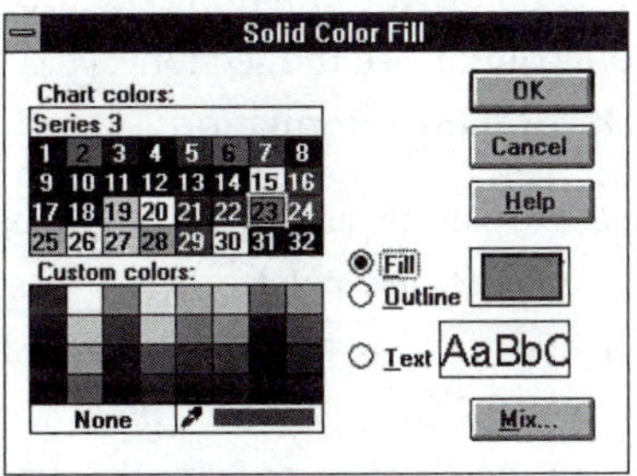

Fig. 16.14
The Solid Color Fill dialog box with the colors from the current palette.

The dialog box in figure 16.14 shows all the colors from the current palette. The colors listed in the top set of colors are the chart colors from the palette. These colors are available for the items in a chart, such as the title color or the color of pie slices. When you change the color palette, any objects that use the colors in this palette change to the colors in the new palette. The section "Understanding Chart Colors" explains the chart colors of the color palette and tells which colors affect which parts of the chart.

The second set of colors refers to the custom colors. You use custom colors to color an object so that the color does not change if you change the color palette. The color of the object can be changed only by explicitly setting a new color for the object.

Each slide in a presentation can use a different palette. The section "Selecting a Color Palette" explains how to change the color palette for a single slide. This section also lists all the palettes that are installed with Harvard Graphics. The section "Editing a Color Palette" explains how to change the colors in a palette. The section "Saving the Palette" explains how to create a new palette that you can apply to other slides and presentations.

Understanding Chart Colors

Chart colors determine the default colors for the objects in a slide that are part of the chart. The chart colors are numbered to identify the different colors in the palette (refer to fig. 16.14). Color 23 in the color palette sets the color for the third series of a bar chart, for example. In figure 16.13, the highlighted color is color 23 and the name Series appears above the chart colors. In addition to the number, chart colors can have a name.

You use the Fill, Outline, and Text buttons to set the color for these parts of an object. See the section "Setting the Fill Style" in Chapter 13, "Enhancing Drawings and Objects," for more information. The Mix button enables you to change the colors on the palette. See the section "Mixing Custom Colors While Filling an Object" for more information.

When you change the color palette, any item in the chart that uses a chart color reflects the color from the new palette. These items also include objects that use a chart color. You can create a rectangle on a slide and fill the rectangle with a chart color-color 2 (red) for example. If you change the palette, the rectangle appears with the chart color from the new palette-still color 2, but in this palette, color 2 is blue. See the section "Applying a Color Palette" for more information.

Table 16.1 lists the items that are set by the 32 chart colors in a color palette. These items determine the default colors when you create the chart. The palette determines the default color. The default for titles, for example, may be red in one palette and blue in another.

Table 16.1 Chart Colors

Chart Color	Color Name	Chart Item
1	Title	Chart title
2	Subtitle 1	Chart subtitle
3	Subtitle 2	Alternate subtitle
4	Text	Basic chart text
5	Text High	Highlighted chart text
6	Text Dim	Dimmed chart text
7	Footnote	Chart footnote
8	X Label	X-axis labels
9	Y1 Label	Y1-axis labels
10	Y2 Label	Y2-axis labels
11	X Title	X-axis title
12	Y1 Title	Y1-axis title
13	Y2 Title	Y2-axis title
14	Frame	Frame and legend outline
15	Frame background	Frame fill
16	Bullet	Bullet symbol
17	Bullet dim	Dimmed bullet text
18	Lines	Lines
19	Shadow	Shadow color
20	Legend	Legend fill
21	Series 1	Series 1 or 1st pie slice
22	Series 2	Series 2 or 2nd pie slice
23	Series 3	Series 3 or 3rd pie slice
24	Series 4	Series 4 or 4th pie slice
25	Series 5	Series 5 or 5th pie slice

(continues)

Table 16.1 Continued

Chart Color	Color Name	Chart Item
26	Series 6	Series 6 or 6th pie slice
27	Goal Y1	Y1-axis goal range fill
28	Goal Y2	Y2-axis goal range
29	Draw	Default solid fill
30	Background 1	Background fill
31	Background 2	Background gradient end
32	Outlines	Bar, line, and slide outline

Selecting a Color Palette

You can change the colors for a slide by selecting a new palette for the slide. Harvard Graphics stores color palettes in individual files, which you can share among different presentations. When you select a palette, you change the colors that are available for the objects on a slide. Objects that use chart colors change to represent the new palette. You can apply one of the many predefined palettes that come with Harvard Graphics. Palettes can be selected from the Slide Editor or Slide Sorter. In the Slide Sorter, you can select a palette for many slides at the same time by selecting all the slides in the Slide Sorter before selecting your new palette.

To select a new palette, choose Color Palette from the Style menu; then choose Select... from the pop-up menu. The Select Color Palette dialog box appears (see fig. 16.15). Type the name of the palette file in the Filename: text box and click the OK button. The Filename: list box shows the palettes in the current directory. To apply a palette from the list, choose the name from the list and click the OK button.

Follow these steps to select a palette from the default palette directory:

1. If you are not viewing the presentation in the Slide Editor or Slide Sorter, choose Slide Editor or Slide Sorter from the View menu.

2. Choose Color palette from the Style menu. The Color Palette pop-up menu appears.

3. Choose Select... from the pop-up menu. Harvard Graphics displays the Select Color Palette dialog box.

4. Type the name of the palette in the Filename: text box.

5. Click the OK button. The objects in the slide that use chart colors change to the color of the new palette.

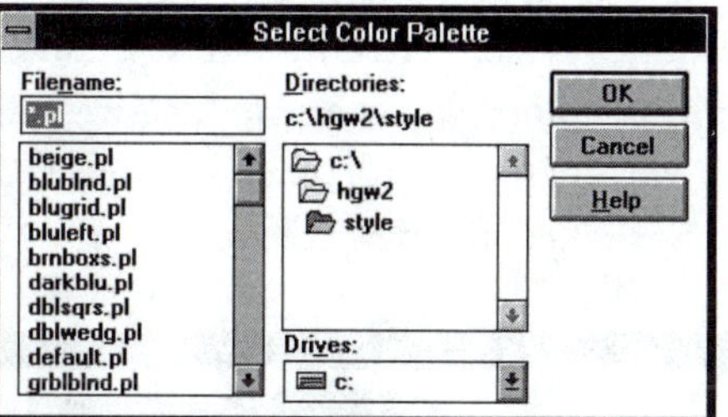

Fig. 16.15
The Select Color Palette dialog box.

You also can use the Select Color Palette dialog box to search your hard disk for palette files in different directories. The current directory appears below the Directories: prompt in the dialog box. Other directories on your hard disk are listed below this prompt. To search other directories, double-click the directory in the list. You also can change the directory by typing the drive and directory into the Filename: text box, without typing the name of a file, and then clicking the OK button. The Drives: field lists the current drive you are viewing. To search other drives for color palettes, select a new drive from this field.

Harvard Graphics installs a variety of palettes in the default palette directory. When you apply a template, you can choose a predefined palette or create a new palette. The section "Editing the Color Palette" covers how to change the colors in a palette. The section "Saving the Palette" explains how to create a palette file from the colors of your current palette.

Editing the Color Palette

You change the colors in a palette by mixing colors in the Edit Color Palette dialog box (see fig. 16.16), which you display by selecting Color palette... from the Style menu, followed by Edit... from the pop-up menu. To edit the palette for a slide, you must view the slide in the Slide Editor or select the slide in the Slide Sorter. The chart and custom colors from the palette appear on the left side of the Edit Color Palette dialog box. To change a color, click the color in the dialog box. The color appears in the color box in the top middle of the dialog box.

Harvard Graphics provides two methods for changing a color. These methods, called *mixing methods*, are based on different models for determining color values. The first mixing method is based on the *Hue Saturation Value* (HSV) color model. The section "Mixing HSV Colors" explains how to mix colors based on brightness and color spectrum. The second method uses the *Red Green Blue* (RGB) model. The section "Mixing RGB Colors" explains how to change colors by adjusting the levels of red, green, and blue. To pick a mixing method, click the HSV or RGB button in the Edit Color Palette dialog box. When working with colors, you can switch between the two methods as you adjust a color. If you change chart colors, the objects on the current slide that use the chart colors reflect the new colors.

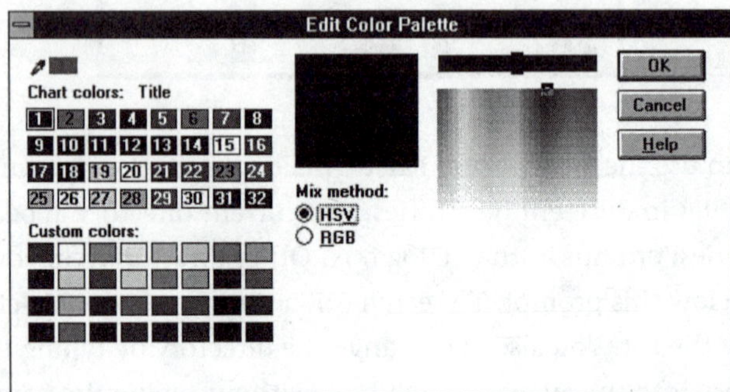

Fig. 16.16
The Edit Color Palette dialog box.

Follow these steps to change the colors for the palette of the current slide:

1. If you are not viewing the presentation in the Slide Sorter or Slide Editor, choose Slide Sorter or Slide Editor from the View menu.
2. Choose Color palette... from the Style menu. The Color Palette pop-up menu appears.
3. Choose Edit... from the pop-up menu. The Edit Color Palette dialog box appears.
4. Click the chart or custom color you want to change.
5. Change the color using the HSV or RGB mixing method. See the sections "Mixing HSV Colors" and "Mixing RGB Colors" for more information on mixing colors.
6. Repeat steps 4 and 5 for all the colors you want to change.
7. Click the OK button to change the colors for the palette.

Mixing HSV Colors. The HSV method for mixing colors involves picking a color from a color spectrum and adjusting the brightness of that color.

The Hue and Saturation determine the spectrum and the Value determines the brightness. Figure 16.17 shows the Edit Color Palette dialog box with the tools for mixing colors in the HSV model. To display these tools, click the HSV button for the mixing method.

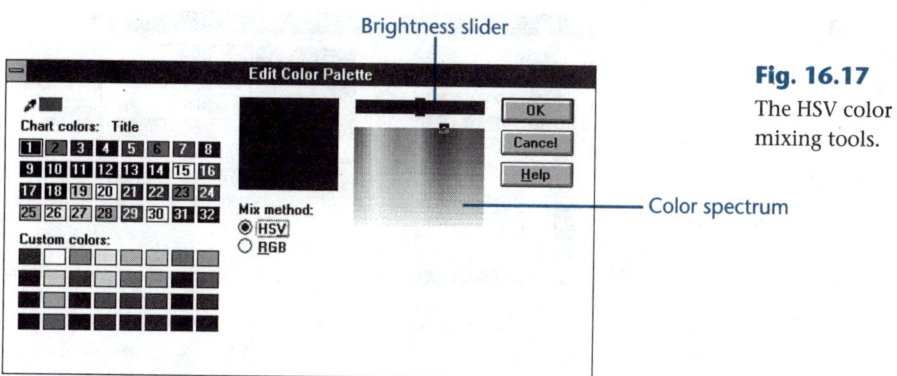

Fig. 16.17
The HSV color mixing tools.

The spectrum of colors appears on the right side of the dialog box. In the figure, the square in the spectrum indicates the current color. To change the color, click the new color in the spectrum. The slider above the spectrum shows the current brightness for the color. To increase the brightness, click the handle of the slider and drag it to the right. To decrease brightness, drag the handle to the left.

Follow these steps to change a color in the Edit Color Palette dialog box with the HSV mixing method:

1. Click the HSV button.
2. Click a chart color or a custom color. When you choose the color, the color box changes to show the color you selected.
3. Click a color in the color spectrum. The new color appears in the color box and in the original image of the color.
4. Adjust the brightness with the slider. As you change the brightness, the brightness in the color box changes.
5. Repeat steps 2 through 4 for the colors you want to change.
6. Click OK to accept the changes and exit the dialog box.

Mixing RGB Colors. The RGB color-mixing method involves adjusting the levels of red, green, and blue used to make the color. The different levels combine to form a particular color; for example, blue and red together make purple. Figure 16.18 shows the Edit Color Palette dialog box with the tools used to mix colors in the RGB model. The figure shows a slide bar for each of the three colors in the RGB model.

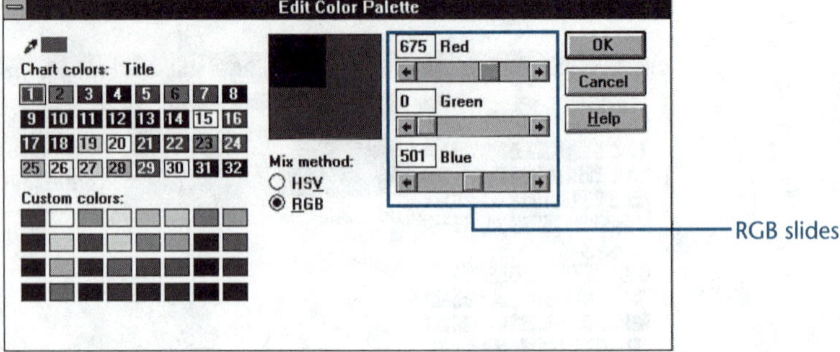

Fig. 16.18
The RGB color mixing tools.

To change a level, click the handle of the slider and drag it to a new level. You can also change the level by clicking the value box and typing the new level. The values for the three colors range from 0 through 999.

Follow these steps to change a color in the Edit Color Palette dialog box, using the RGB method:

1. Click the RGB button for the Mix Method.
2. Click a chart color or a custom color.
3. Click the handle for one of the three primary colors.
4. Drag the handle to the new value. As you adjust the level, the representation of the color in the dialog box changes to the new color.
5. Repeat steps 2 through 4 for the colors you want to change.
6. Click OK to accept the changes and exit the dialog box.

Copying Colors

In the Edit Color Palette dialog box, you can copy any color in the palette from one location to another. This capability is helpful for creating different shades of the same color or for starting a new color based on a previous one. For example, you can copy the color yellow to a new location and then use the HSV mixing method to produce a lighter or darker shade of yellow.

To copy a color, drag the color to the new location. When you copy the color, Harvard Graphics removes the previous value from the palette.

Follow these steps to produce a lighter shade of a color in the palette in the Edit Color Palette dialog box.

1. Click and hold down the mouse button on a dark color in the palette.
2. Drag the color to a new location. As you drag the color, a small marquee indicates that you are copying the color.
3. When the marquee is over the new location, release the mouse button.
4. Click the HSV button for the Mix Method.
5. Click the handle of the brightness slider.
6. Drag the handle to the right to make the color brighter.
7. Click OK when you finish your changes.

Copying Colors from an Object

You use the Eyedropper tool in the Slide Editor to copy the attributes from one object and apply them to another object. You can copy the text size and color from one text annotation to another, for example. For more information on using the Eyedropper tool, see the section "Copying Object Attributes" in Chapter 13, "Enhancing Drawings and Objects."

You also can copy the color of the object using the Eyedropper tool. After you copy the attributes, you can add the color to the current palette with the Edit Color Palette dialog box. You may have colored an object with a color from the palette, but cannot remember which color you used. You can copy the color, using the Eyedropper tool, to the color palette, even though you may not remember the position—especially if the colors in your palette are similar. Figure 16.19 shows the Edit Color Palette dialog box with the color of the object from which attributes were copied.

Follow these steps to copy a color from an object to the color palette:

1. If you are not viewing the presentation in the Slide Editor, choose Slide Editor from the View menu.
2. Select the object on the slide.
3. Choose the Eyedropper tool.

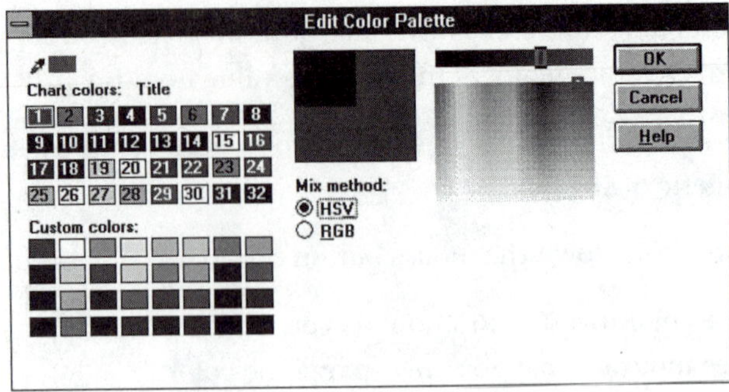

Fig. 16.19 The color copied with the Eyedropper tool.

4. Choose Color Palette from the Style menu.
5. Choose Edit... from the pop-up menu. The Edit Color Palette dialog box appears.
6. Click and hold the mouse button on the color copied from the object.
7. Drag the marquee over the new location of the color in the palette.
8. Release the mouse button.

The color appears in the new location.

An easy method of copying a color from an object to the color palette is dragging the number of the object to the new location.

Mixing Custom Colors While Filling an Object

You use the Fill tool in the Slide Editor to set the colors for an object on a slide. The Solid Color Fill dialog box appears when you choose this tool (see fig. 16.20). In the dialog box, you can set the color for the outline, fill, and text of the object. If the color you need is not available with the current palette, the Mix button enables you to edit the custom colors of the palette. To edit the colors, click the Mix button.

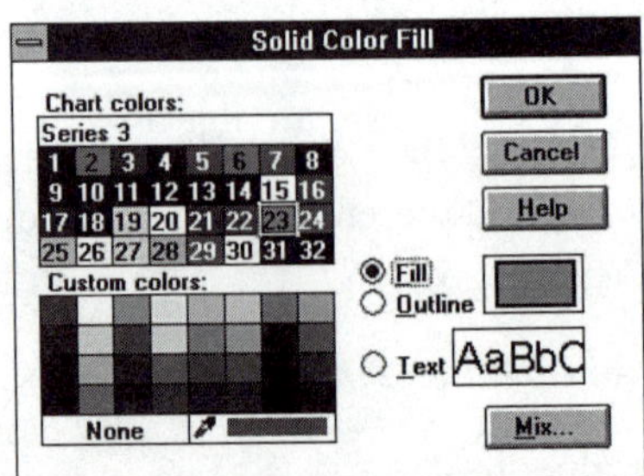

Fig. 16.20 The Solid Color Fill dialog box.

The Mix Custom Colors dialog box, in which you change the custom colors, appears (see fig. 16.21). This dialog box is identical to the Edit Color Palette dialog box. For more information on mixing colors, see the section "Editing the Color Palette" earlier in this chapter. In the Mix Custom Colors dialog box, you can edit only the custom colors for the palette.

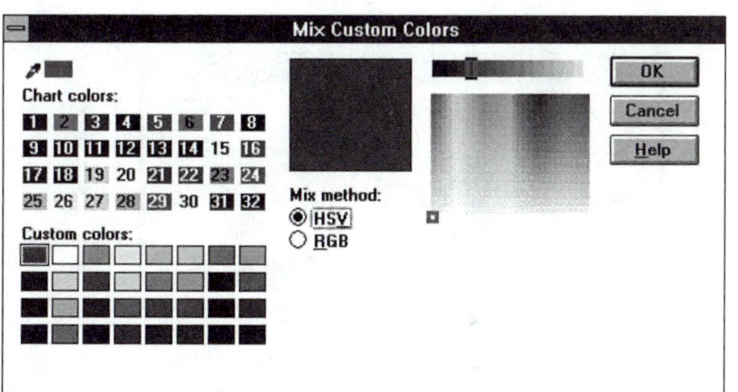

Fig. 16.21
The Mix Custom Colors dialog box.

Saving the Palette

As you change the colors for a palette, you may want to save your changes in a new palette to use with other presentations. From the Slide menu, you can select the Save item on the Color Palette pop-up menu to create a palette file from the colors in the current palette.

Follow these steps to save the colors in the current directory:

1. If you are not viewing the presentation in the Slide Editor or Slide Sorter, choose Slide Editor from the View menu.

2. Choose Color palette... from the Slide menu.

3. Choose Save... from the pop-up menu.

   The Save Color Palette dialog box appears (see fig. 16.22).

4. Type the name of the file in the Filename: text box. Use a name that reveals something about the palette. The file name BLUERED indicates that the palette contains shades of these colors, for example. Remember, however, that file names cannot exceed eight characters.

5. Click the OK button.

You can use the Save Color Palette dialog box to save palettes in any of the directories on your hard disk. The other drives on your machine appear in the Drives: list, while the other directories available appear in the Directories:

box. To change the directory, double-click the directory in the Directories: box or select a new drive in the Drives: field. You also can change the directory by typing the drive and directory in the Filename text box without typing the name of a file, and then clicking the OK button. When you change the directory, Harvard Graphics saves the palette in the new current directory.

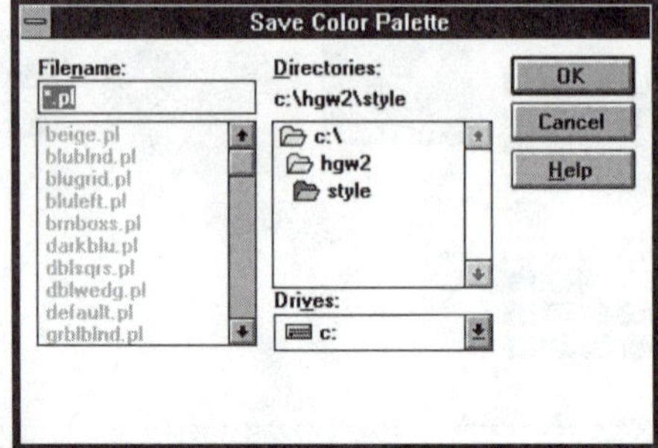

Fig. 16.22
The Save Color Palette dialog box.

Working with Presentation Styles

Presentation styles combine templates, color palettes, and backgrounds in one file. You use presentation styles to control the overall appearance of a presentation. The default templates that determine the initial settings for a slide are part of the style. Harvard Graphics saves the color palettes and backgrounds used with these templates in the style as well. When you create a presentation, the presentation uses the defaults from the default style as specified in the program preferences. The section "Setting the Default Style" in this chapter explains how to change the styles from which presentations are created.

After you create the presentation, you can apply a style to change the overall appearance. Harvard Graphics contains a variety of predefined styles. The section "Selecting a Presentation Style" explains how to use one of these styles (or a style you create) to change the appearance of a presentation.

You do not have to use a presentation style. With a style, however, you can create a consistent look for all your slides by using one command.

Selecting a Presentation Style

Use the Select presentation style... command of the Style menu to select a style for your presentation. When you select a style, Harvard Graphics applies the templates in the style to slides that use the same template. For example, each presentation has a template named Vertical Bar, which determines the default settings for a vertical bar chart. When you select a presentation style, Harvard Graphics applies the Vertical Bar template in the style to the slides created from that template. Every presentation style has a template for each slide type. These default templates were covered in the section "Working with Templates" earlier in this chapter.

To select a presentation style, choose Select presentation style... from the Style menu. The Select Presentation Style dialog box appears (see fig. 16.23). The dialog box shows the styles available in the current directory in the Filename: list box. The current directory appears below the Directories: prompt. To apply a style, type the name of the file in the Filename: text box, and click the OK button. You also can apply a style by double-clicking the name of the file in the Filename: list box.

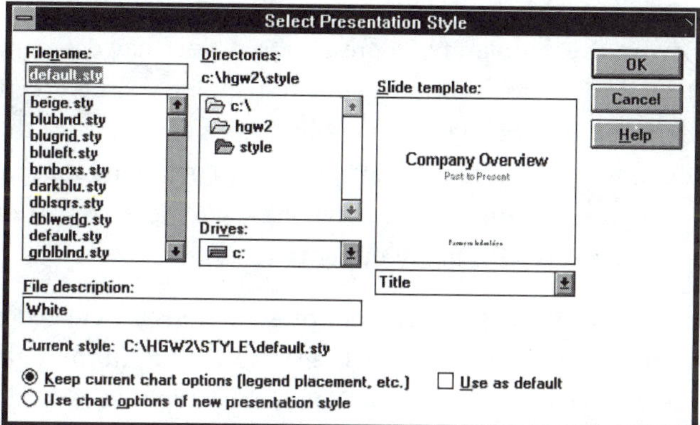

Fig. 16.23
The Select Presentation Style dialog box.

You can preview the templates of a style in the Slide template: box in the Select Presentation Style dialog box. You select a style in the Filename: list. Then, to view a template, you click the arrow next to the template field below the Slide template: box and select which template you wish to preview. The template you select appears in the box. The options at the bottom of the dialog box determine if the chart options in each template be applied to your slides when you select a style. Click the Keep current chart options button to leave your charts unmodified if you only wish to use basic options such as the color palette and backgrounds from the style. Click the Use chart options of new presentation style button to apply all the settings in the new style to your presentation.

Follow these steps to apply a style from the default palette directory:

1. If you are not viewing the presentation in the Slide Editor or Slide Sorter, choose Slide Editor from the View menu.
2. Choose Select presentation style... from the Style menu. The Select Presentation Style dialog box appears.
3. Type the name of the style in the Filename: text box. For example, type BEIGE which is the name of a predefined style.
4. Click the OK button.

Harvard Graphics applies the presentation style to your presentation. The appearance of your slides changes to show the palette, template, and backgrounds from the style.

Creating a Presentation Style

As you work with the templates of a presentation, you may develop a set of default templates that work well with your system. For example, certain colors and options may appear cleaner on your output device. With these templates, all the slides you create will have the same consistent appearance from presentation to presentation. You can save these templates as part of a style to use the same defaults with many presentations.

If you set the style as the default, all your presentations are created with the same appearance. The section "Setting the Default Style" in this chapter explains how to change the default style. You also can apply the style to existing presentations to change the overall appearance to match the defaults. See the section "Selecting a Presentation Style" in this chapter.

To save the current templates in a style, choose Save presentation style... from the Style menu. The Save Presentation Style dialog box appears (see fig. 16.24). Type the name of the file in the Filename: text box. Harvard Graphics creates the file in the directory shown below the Directories prompt. Other presentation styles in the directory appear in the Filename: list box. To save the style, click the OK button.

Follow these steps to create a presentation style from the current presentation:

1. If you are not viewing the presentation in the Slide Editor or Slide Sorter, choose Slide Editor from the View menu.

2. Choose Save presentation style... from the Style menu.

3. Choose Save from the pop-up menu. The Save Presentation Style dialog box appears.

4. Type the name of the style in the Filename text box. Be descriptive with your name, but remember that you can use no more than eight characters.

5. Click the OK button.

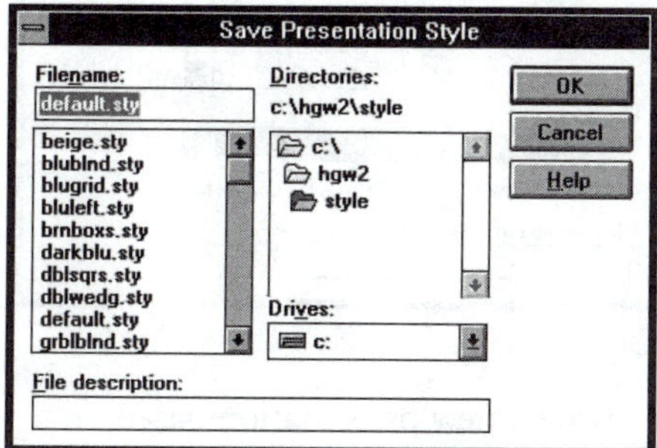

Fig. 14.24
The Save Presentation Style dialog box.

You can use the Save Presentation Style dialog box to save a style in any of the directories on your hard disk. The other drives on your machine appear in the Drives: list, while the other directories available appear in the Directories: box. To change the directory, double-click the directory in the Directories: box or select a new drive in the Drives: field. You also can change the directory by typing the drive and directory in the Filename text box without typing the name of a file and then clicking the OK button. When you change the directory, Harvard Graphics saves the style in the new current directory.

Creating a New Presentation from a Style

You use the Open... command on the File menu to load an existing presentation into memory for further changes and enhancements. You also can use this command to open a presentation style. When you open a style, Harvard Graphics creates a new presentation based on the templates in the style.

To create a new presentation by opening a style, choose Open... from the File menu. The Open dialog box appears (see fig. 16.25).

The File type: list box in the dialog box determines the type of file that will be opened. To see the available types, click the down arrow next to the box. HGW Presentation Style is one of the types you can open with this dialog box. To open this file, choose HGW Presentation Style from the list. For more information on working with the Open dialog box, see the section "Opening an Existing Presentation" in Chapter 2, "Learning Harvard Graphics for Windows Basics."

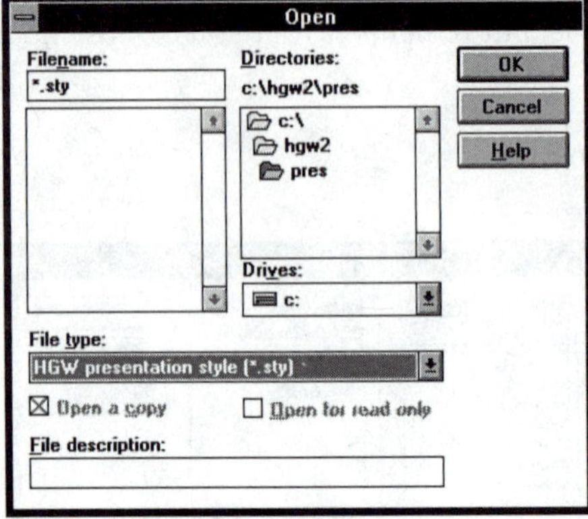

Fig. 16.25
The Open dialog box.

Follow these steps to create a new presentation based on a presentation style:

1. Choose Open... from the File menu.

2. Click the down scroll arrow next to the File Type: list box.

3. Choose HGW Presentation Style from the list of file types.

4. Click the Filename: text box.

   Harvard Graphics store the predefined styles in the Style directory which was created when you installed the program. You may have to change the directory to locate a style. The following steps assume you installed the program in the C:\HGW directory. If you did not, you will have to type a different directory for step 5. Follow these steps:

5. Type C:\HGW\STYLE in the Filename: field and click the OK button. Harvard Graphics changes to the style directory and lists the available styles in the Filename: list box.

6. Type the name of the file in the text box. Make sure to include the path indicating where Harvard Graphics stores your styles.

7. Click the OK button.

Harvard Graphics creates a new presentation using the style.

Setting the Default Style

The default style is the presentation style used when creating a presentation. This style determines the default templates that control the initial settings for your slides. To change the defaults, choose Defaults... from the Options menu. The Defaults dialog box, in which you set the default options for Harvard Graphics, appears (see fig. 16.26). To change the default style, click the Presentation style: field and type the name of the new style. In the Defaults dialog box, you can also set the default setting for the Tool lock. When Tool lock is enabled, tools you create objects with stay selected after the object is created.

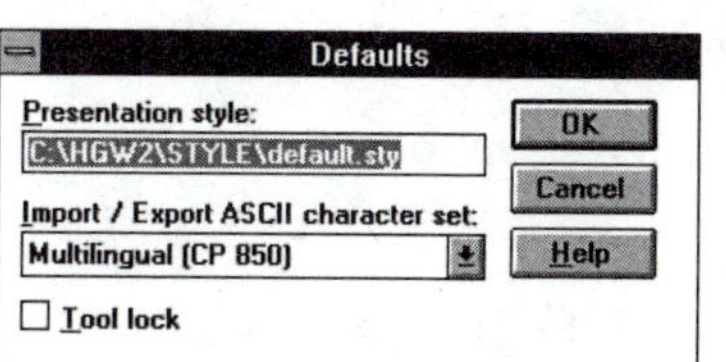

Fig. 16.26
The Defaults dialog box.

Follow these steps to change the default style:

1. Choose Defaults... from the Options menu. You see the Defaults dialog box.
2. Click the Presentation style: text box.
3. Press the End key to move to the end of the field.
4. Press and hold down the Backspace key until the previous default is removed.
5. Type the directory and file name of the new style.
6. Click the OK button to change the preferences and close the Preferences dialog box.

Changing the Default Style/Palette Directory

In addition to setting the default presentation style, you can also set the default directories for presentation styles and palettes. The default style/palette directory determines the initial directory for applying and saving a palette or style.

The Paths dialog box appears when you choose Paths... from the Options menu (see fig. 16.27). To change the default palette and style directory, click the Style/Palette directory: text box. Type the new directory and then click the OK button.

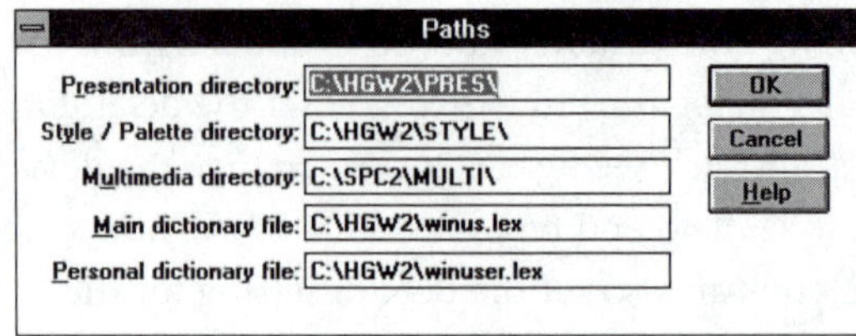

Fig. 16.27
The Paths dialog box.

Follow these steps to change the default style and palette directory to C:\HGW\NEWSTYLES:

1. Choose Paths... from the Options menu. You see the Options dialog box.
2. Click the Style/Palette directory: text box.
3. Press the End key to move to the end of the field.
4. Press and hold the Backspace key until the previous default is removed.
5. Type the new directory in the text box.
6. Click the OK button to change the preferences and remove the Preferences dialog box.

Setting the Presentation Font

The Change presentation font... item on the Style menu enables you to change all the fonts of a presentation to the same font. All the labels in your chart and text annotations, for example, appear in this font. For more information on fonts, see Chapter 7, "Working with Text." This option provides a consistent appearance for all the slides.

To change the fonts in a presentation to a single font, choose Change presentation font... from the Style menu. The Change Presentation Font dialog box appears (see fig. 16.28). You choose a font for the presentation from this dialog box. To change the font, choose a font from the list and click the OK button.

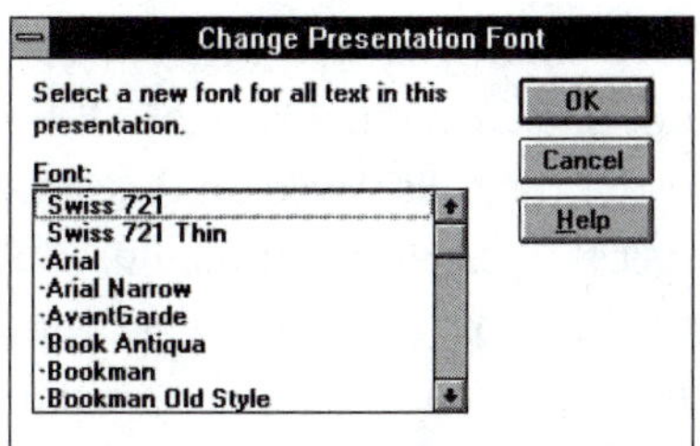

Fig. 14.28
The Change Presentation Font dialog box.

Follow these steps to change the font for all the text in a presentation to Swiss 721:

1. If you are not viewing the presentation in the Slide Editor or Slide Sorter, choose Slide Editor from the View menu.
2. Choose Change presentation font... from the Slide menu. You see the Change Presentation Font dialog box.
3. Click Swiss 721 in the list of fonts.
4. Click the OK button.

Harvard Graphics uses the new fonts in your presentation.

Creating Autobuilds

Autobuilds allow you to present a slide in a gradual manner where each successive image builds upon the next. Each image of the build presents a new element of the chart slowly revealing the complete slide. For example, an autobuild with a bullet chart displays each bullet item in the order it appears on the chart. For pie charts, you see the first slice, followed by the next slice, and so on until the entire pie is displayed. Autobuilds help you present information in two ways. First, you focus attention on the new item displayed for the chart making sure to fully explain or cover the item once it is displayed. Second, you prevent your audience from jumping ahead of you to read and think about information you have not yet covered. You can even use autobuilds to create suspense by hinting that the final piece of information, such as the final largest slice of a pie chart or the final point of a bullet chart, is the most significant. Because of the way autobuilds are displayed, you can only view an autobuild when you display a ScreenShow. See Chapter 17, "Creating ScreenShows and HyperShows," for more information.

To create an autobuild for a chart, you view the slide in the Slide Editor. Then, you select the Autobuild... command on the Slide menu to display the Autobuild dialog box for the chart displayed on the slide. Figure 16.29 shows the dialog box for Pie charts. To create an autobuild, you click the Use Autobuild option in the dialog box. When you click the Build type buttons become enabled. For build type, you can create a sequential build which as described above, reveals a new part of the slide on each image of the autobuild. Highlight autobuilds show the entire slide for each image and highlight the particular item you are discussing (actually, the other items are dimmed). Click the Both button to combine a sequential and highlight build.

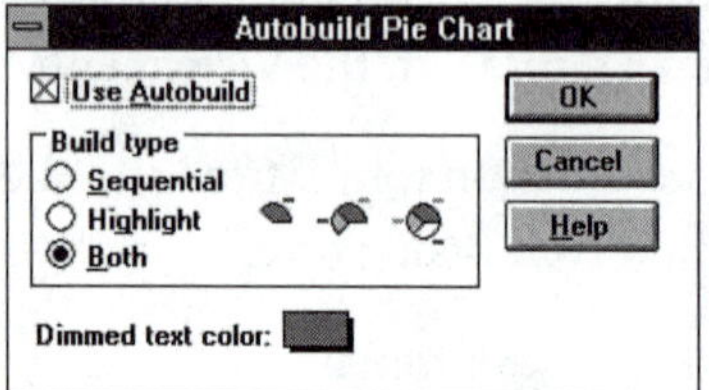

Fig. 16.29
The Autobuild dialog box for pie charts.

You click the Dimmed text color: box to set the color for dimmed text of an autobuild. As stated above, in a highlight autobuild, items in the chart are dimmed to emphasize the actual item you are discussing. Follow these steps to create an autobuild from the slide you are viewing in the Slide Editor:

1. Select Autobuild... from the Slide menu. The Autobuild dialog box is displayed.
2. Click the Use Autobuild option to enable the autobuild. The Build type buttons are enabled.
3. Click the Build type you wish to use.
4. Click the OK button to remove the dialog box and create the build. Remember, you will only see the autobuild when you display a ScreenShow.

From Here...

This chapter covers features that enable you to change the appearance of an entire presentation. You first learned how to create a background for a slide and how to change the background for a slide or for a presentation. You then learned how to work with templates to change the appearance of a single slide and to control the default options when you create a slide. After templates, you learned how to work with color palettes to change the colors on a slide. You learned how to mix colors of the palette and how to save a palette on your hard disk. The chapter ends with presentation styles that combine templates, backgrounds, and color palettes in a single file. You learned how to apply a style to change the appearance of a presentation and how to create a new presentation from a style. The next chapter addresses more advanced features of presentations including displaying a presentation on screen with a ScreenShow.

learned how to work with a template, to change the appearance of a slide, and to manipulate the default options when you add a slide. And you [illegible] places, you learned how to work with color schemes to change the colors on a slide. You learned how to add colors to the palette and how to save a palette on your hard disk. This chapter ends with presentation tricks that combine techniques: how to merge color palettes in a single file, how to [illegible] to apply a style to change the appearance of a presentation and how to [illegible] a new presentation from a style. The next chapter addresses more advanced features of presentations, including slide shows and [illegible] presentations.

Chapter 17

Creating ScreenShows and HyperShows

In this chapter, you learn how to do the following:

- Create a ScreenShow with transition effects
- Create a HyperShow with keys and buttons

Harvard Graphics provides all the features you need to build powerful slides that communicate data effectively. The extensive charting capabilities enable you to present data in a wide variety of charts and graphs. The print feature of Harvard Graphics enables you to produce output of your slides to use with a slide or overhead projector. You don't have to be content with these features, however. By using the Harvard Graphics ScreenShow and HyperShow features, you can turn your computer into a projector and show high-resolution images directly on-screen.

ScreenShow enables you to do more than present one slide after another on your computer screen, however; you also can enhance your presentation by adding special effects that make the transition from one slide to another more interesting. With transition effects, you can scroll a slide showing increased revenue off the top of your display, for example. If the focus of a slide is the flood of sales, for instance, you can create a transition effect in which falling rain forms the slide image. The ScreenShow provides several transition effects that enable you to assign a different *draw effect* (placing the slide on the screen) and *erase effect* (removing the slide from the screen) for each slide in your presentation.

HyperShow goes beyond the special effects of ScreenShow in presenting information. HyperShow keys and buttons enable you to control the flow of your presentation spontaneously, without editing the original slide order. With HyperShow links, you can jump back to a previous slide to reinforce a point, for instance, or you can skip ahead to slides that are more relevant to an idea or question from the audience. The capability of viewing slides in any sequence turns an order-driven presentation into a presentation driven by information. Best of all, you can tailor the information to accommodate the interests and focus of the members of your audience.

When you complete this chapter, you will be able to display and manipulate a ScreenShow, add ScreenShow effects, create and manipulate HyperShow links, and create self-running presentations.

Displaying a ScreenShow

When you use the Harvard Graphics ScreenShow feature, you have the capability to maneuver through your presentation, begin the presentation with a slide other than the first slide, and add special effects that enhance the appearance and quality of your presentation. You also can determine the length of time that a slide remains visible. This section explains how to use the ScreenShow to produce a professional and visually interesting presentation.

To display the ScreenShow from the beginning, you first must open your presentation file. If your presentation is not in memory, choose Open... from the File menu; then follow these steps:

1. Choose ScreenShow from the File menu. The pop-up menu containing ScreenShow commands appears.

2. Choose From beginning from the pop-up menu. The first slide in your presentation appears.

3. You press the space bar or Enter key to proceed through the slides, one slide at a time, until the presentation is finished.

Tip
You can also click the Display ScreenShow from beginning icon in the icon bar.

After all the slides have been displayed, you return to Harvard Graphics.

You also can display the show from the current slide, which is the slide in the Slide Editor window. In the Outliner, the first active topic indicates the current slide. In the Slide Sorter, the first active or highlighted slide is the current slide.

To display the presentation from the current slide, choose ScreenShow from the File menu; then choose From Current Slide from the pop-up menu that appears. You can also click the Display ScreenShow from current slide icon in the Icon bar within the Slide Sorter or Outliner. Harvard Graphics displays the current slide and all subsequent slides.

Moving Around in a ScreenShow

Harvard Graphics provides default keys that give you extra control when you display a ScreenShow. You can return to a previous slide to reiterate a point, for example, or you can restart the presentation from the beginning.

The keys you use to move around in a ScreenShow are *default keys*. Default keys enable you to jump to a slide other than the next slide in the presentation. When you press a key that is not a default, the next slide in the presentation appears.

Using the default keys, you can move back and forth between the slides in your presentation. You can move backward in the presentation by pressing the left-arrow key, for example, or you can return to the first slide and begin the presentation again by pressing the Home key. You also can use the left and right mouse buttons to move forward or backward in the presentation. Table 17.1 lists the functions of the default keys and the mouse buttons. For an explanation of how to change the default keys, see "Setting Default HyperShow Links" later in this chapter.

Table 17.1 Default Keys for Displaying a ScreenShow

Default Key	Function
Home	Go to the first slide
End	Go to the last slide
Left arrow or Left mouse button	Go to the preceding slide. If you show slide 4 and then slide 7, for example, pressing the left arrow or left mouse button returns you to slide 6.
Esc or Break	Stop the ScreenShow
Backspace	Go to the last slide *shown*. If you show slide 4 and then slide 7, for example, pressing Backspace returns you to slide 4.
F2	Redraw slide to remove lines drawn with On-Screen Chalk (see the next section).
All other keys and Right mouse button	Go to the next slide

Using On-Screen Chalk

On-Screen Chalk enables you to highlight certain parts of the slide during your ScreenShow. You can circle a significant bar in a chart or draw an arrow to the largest slice in a pie chart while the slide is displayed on your computer screen. You draw on the slide similar to the way you draw lines in the Slide Editor by clicking the mouse down and moving the mouse. As you move, Harvard Graphics displays the lines you draw.

Adding ScreenShow Effects

You can add flair to your ScreenShow presentation by using special ScreenShow effects. One ScreenShow effect in particular—the transition effect—can enhance your presentation greatly. The various transition effects for drawing (*draw effect*) and erasing (*erase effect*) slides provide interesting and eye-catching ways of getting slides on and off the screen. If you use the scroll effect, for instance, you can scroll a slide across the screen until it is entirely visible; then, as an erase effect, you can continue to scroll the slide off the opposite side of the screen.

Harvard Graphics provides many ScreenShow transition effects from which you can choose. You can add different transition effects for each slide, or, by using default effects, you can ensure that Harvard Graphics uses the same transition effects to draw and erase the slides of your presentation.

Setting Transition Effects

All presentations you create have transition effects. The default draw transition effect is the Replace effect. With Replace, the current slide completely replaces the preceding slide in one smooth action. The default erase transition is None. Harvard Graphics does not remove the slides; the current slide appears on top of the preceding slide.

To set transition effects, follow these steps:

1. Choose ScreenShow from the File menu. A pop-up menu appears.
2. Choose Edit ScreenShow Effects from the pop-up menu. The Edit ScreenShow Effects dialog box, in which you set ScreenShow effects, appears (see fig. 17.1). You can also click the Edit ScreenShow effects icon in the icon bar.

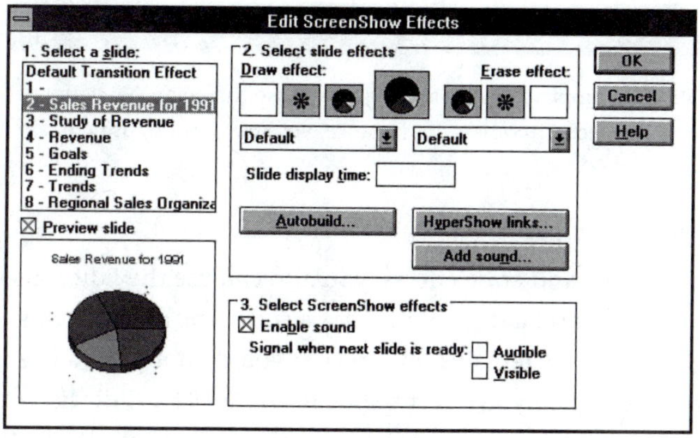

Fig. 17.1
The Edit ScreenShow Effects dialog box.

The slides in the presentation appear in the Select a slide: list box. Harvard Graphics reserves the first entry in the Slide List box for the Default Transition Effect. The section "Setting Default Effects" explains how to use the Default Transition Effect to set effect defaults for a ScreenShow.

3. To see the effects for a particular slide, select the slide from the Select a slide: list box. The current transition effects of the selected slide are highlighted in the Draw effect: and Erase effect: fields. In figure 17.1, for example, slide 2 (Sales Revenue for 1991) uses the default draw effect and the default erase effect. The Preview slide box displays the slide you selected. If you are in a hurry, click the Preview slide option to disable the preview.

4. To change an effect, choose a new transition in the Draw Effect or Erase Effect scroll boxes. Table 17.2 lists and defines the transition effects. When you select a transition, the images above the setting display a representation of the transition to help you see how the transition will appear in your ScreenShow.

5. Choose OK to accept the effects and exit the dialog box.

Design Note

When selecting draw and erase transitions, try to select effects that work well together. If you use a scroll right effect to draw a slide, for example, you can use a scroll right effect to erase the slide so that the image scrolls onto the screen from the left edge and scrolls off the right edge of the screen.

Design Note

Use transitions to emphasize your message. To make the point that your sales department will be flooded with orders, for instance, you may want to use the rain effect.

Setting a Display Time

In addition to draw and erase effects, you also can use the Edit ScreenShow Effects dialog box to set a display time for a slide. The display time determines how long a slide remains on-screen if you do not press a key to move to the next slide. When you select a slide in the Select a slide: list box, the current display time for the slide appears in the Slide display time: text box.

The default for the time is blank because Harvard Graphics continues to display the slide until you press a key. You can set a display time, however, by typing a time in the Slide display time: text box. You can enter the time in seconds or in minutes and seconds separated by a colon. Entering *23*, for example, sets the display time to 23 seconds; entering *1:30* sets the display time to 1 minute and 30 seconds.

Table 17.2 ScreenShow Transition Effects

Effect	Appearance of the Effect
Blinds	Draws or erases the slide vertically or horizontally with strips that resemble Venetian blinds
Close	Draws or erases the slide from the vertical or horizontal edges of the screen
Fade	Draws or erases the slide in small, random squares
Iris	Draws or erases the slide with a square that starts in the center of the screen and moves out or starts at the outside edge of the screen and moves in
Open	Draws or erases the slide as a vertical or horizontal line that expands from the center of the screen to the edges of the screen
Overlay	Draws a slide by overlaying the current slide on the preceding slide while leaving visible the unobstructed parts of the preceding slide
Rain	Draws or erases the slide in random vertical lines that resemble raindrops
Replace	Draws or erases the entire slide in one quick action (This is the default draw effect.)

Effect	Appearance of the Effect
Scroll	Draws or erases a slide by scrolling the current slide on or off the screen from one of the four sides
Wipe	The slide is moved on- or off-screen from one of the four edges while the previous image remains in the same position
Default	Draws or erases the slide, using the current default

Signalling for the Next Slide. Depending on the power and speed of your computer, Harvard Graphics may need time to prepare the next slide in the presentation before displaying it. The Signal when next slide is ready: options in the Edit ScreenShow Effects dialog box enable you to activate an audible signal (a beep) and visual signal (a small arrow in the bottom right corner of your screen) to indicate when the next slide is ready. To enable either of these signals, follow these steps:

1. If you are not in the Edit ScreenShow Effects dialog box, access it by choosing ScreenShow from the File menu; then choose Edit ScreenShow Effects from the pop-up menu that appears.
2. Click the Audible button so that an X appears, indicating that Harvard Graphics will signal you with a beep when the slide is ready.
3. Click the Visible button so that an X appears, indicating that Harvard Graphics will signal you with an arrow when the slide is ready.
4. Click the OK button to accept the changes and return to Harvard Graphics.

Setting Default Effects. Although you can use any transition effect to draw or erase the slide in your presentation, using a default transition effect provides consistency for your ScreenShow presentation. When you set a default transition, Harvard Graphics uses the same effect to draw and erase all slides.

In the Edit ScreenShow Effects dialog box, you set the transition and time display defaults and indicate which slides use the default effects. The Default Transition Effect is the first item in the Select a slide: list in the dialog box. If you are not in the Edit ScreenShow Effects dialog box, access it by choosing

ScreenShow from the File menu; then choose Edit ScreenShow Effects from the pop-up menu. When the dialog box appears, follow these steps to change the default effects and time display:

1. Select Default Transition Effect in the Select a slide: list box.
2. Select a new draw effect from the Draw effect: scroll box.
3. Select a new erase effect from the Erase effect: scroll box.
4. Click the Set display time: text box and type the default display time. If you do not set a time, the slides remain on-screen until you press a key. Refer to the section "Setting a Display Time" for more information.
5. Click the OK button to accept the default and return to Harvard Graphics.

To use the default display effects you just set, you must set the slide's effect to default. For more information on changing the effect for an individual slide, refer to "Setting Transition Effects."

Creating HyperShows

A HyperShow is a ScreenShow that you control with keys and buttons. The features of a HyperShow are similar to the default keys of a ScreenShow. Beyond default keys, HyperShows enable you to *define* (create) buttons that the viewer clicks on a slide.

HyperShows are more interactive than ScreenShows because viewers control what slide appears next. You use HyperShow keys and buttons to go to any slide in the presentation. The relationship between the key or button and a slide is the *HyperShow link*. You can set up *absolute links*, which branch to specific slides in the presentation, and *relative links*, which move to relative positions in the presentation—such as back one slide or forward one slide. You even can link a key or button to another Windows application, such as a spreadsheet, for quick viewing of the original information and formulas during the HyperShow.

Setting HyperShow Links

You can create a HyperShow link between a key or button and a presentation slide or destination. The link between a key and a slide is probably the most familiar. You can link the letter A to the first slide in the presentation and the letter B to the second slide, for example. When you press A, the first slide appears; when you press B, the second slide appears. Harvard Graphics also enables you to use objects on your slides as links. Any slide object—for example, a rectangle or text annotation—can be a button. In addition to keys and buttons, you can define a link that determines the length of the slide display time.

Two components are required to create a HyperShow link: the key or button and the slide or destination. You can use any letter or number, all function keys, and many other common keys as keys in a link. You can link a key or button to a specific slide. If you change the order of the slides, Harvard Graphics updates the links automatically. You also can link a key or button to one of the destinations listed in table 17.3.

Some of the destinations in the list indicate relative positions in the presentation. Previous Slide, for example, returns you to the preceding slide in the presentation order. Others, such as the First slide or Last slide, take you to absolute positions in the presentation—the first or last slide—even though you may change the slide order.

Table 17.3 HyperShow Destinations

Destination	Result
Next slide	Moves to the next slide in the presentation
Previous slide	Moves to the previous slide in the presentation
First slide	Moves to the first slide in the presentation
Last slide	Moves to the last slide in the presentation
Back up	Moves to the last slide shown on-screen
Iqnore	Ignores the key so that nothing happens when you press a key
Launch application	Starts a Windows application from within the ScreenShow
Play sound file	Plays a sound file within the ScreenShow
Stop sound files	Stops sound files which were started from a previous HyperShow link

(continues)

Table 17.3 Continued

Destination	Result
Start OLE action	Sends information to another Windows application along with a file to perform some action (see the section "Using OLE" in Chapter 15, "Importing, Exporting, and Linking Data")
Redraw slide	Redisplays the current slide to remove any lines drawn with On-Screen Chalk (see the section "Using On-Screen Chalk," earlier in this chapter)
Stop	Stops the ScreenShow

Creating HyperShow Links with Keys. To define a link, you must select a key and an associated destination by doing the following:

1. Choose ScreenShow from the File menu; then choose Edit ScreenShow Effects from the pop-up menu. The Edit ScreenShow Effects dialog box appears.

2. Select the slide in the Select a slide: list box to define a link for this slide. To use the link, the viewer must view this slide.

3. Click the HyperShow links... button in the Edit ScreenShow Effects dialog box. The Slide HyperShow Links dialog box, in which you create and edit HyperShow links, appears (see fig. 17.2).

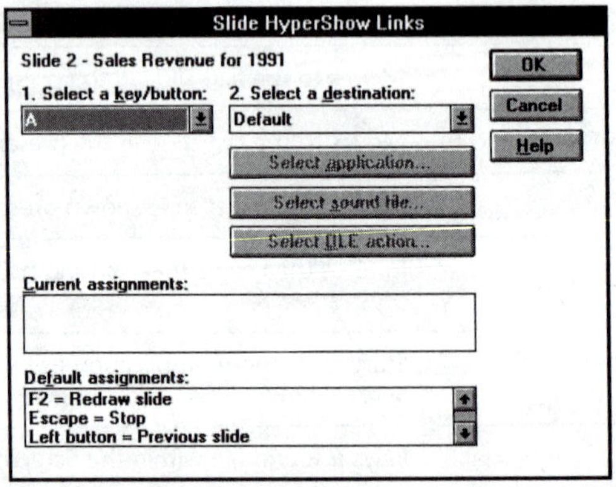

Fig. 17.2
The Slide HyperShow Links dialog box.

The name of the selected slide appears at the top of the dialog box. You use the Select a key/button: list box to indicate what key or button to use in the link.

4. To see the available keys and buttons, click the down arrow next to the Select a key/button: list box; then select a key or button. (The section "Creating a HyperShow Link with Buttons" explains how to create a button in the Slide Editor.)

5. You use the Destination: list box to select a destination to be associated with the key you just selected. To see the choices for the destination, click the down arrow next to the Destination list box.

   All the slides in the presentation appear at the end of the list. You can choose a destination or a slide. Refer to table 17.3 for an explanation of the destinations in this list.

6. Select a slide or destination from the list.

   When you define a link, the key or button and the destination appear in the Current assignments: list box.

You can use HyperShow links to create slide menus that link menu options to presentation slides. Figure 17.3 shows a sample slide menu. The instructions on the slide tell you to press a key or click a button to see the linked slide. If you press A, for example, you access the revenue slide; if you press B, you access the profits slide; and so on.

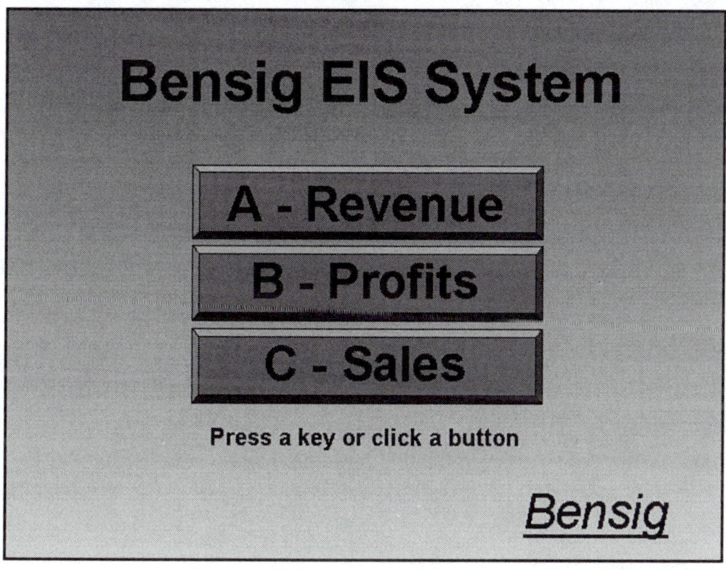

Fig. 17.3
An example HyperShow slide menu.

Follow these steps to create a link between the first menu option and the Revenues slide, using a key:

1. Choose ScreenShow from the File menu; then choose Edit ScreenShow Effects from the pop-up menu. The Edit ScreenShow Effects dialog box appears.

2. To define HyperShow links for the slide, select the slide in the Select a slide: box. The viewer will be viewing this slide as he or she presses a key or clicks a button.

3. Click the HyperShow Links button. The Slide HyperShow Links dialog box appears.

4. Click the down arrow next to the Select a key/button: list box; then select a key or button from the list. For the example, select the A key.

5. Click the down arrow next to the Select a destination: list box, and select a slide from the list. For the example, select the Revenue slide.

   The link appears in the Current Assignments list box.

6. Click the OK button on the Slide HyperShow Links dialog box to accept the link and return to the Edit ScreenShow Effects dialog box.

7. Click the OK button on the Edit ScreenShow Effects dialog box to return to Harvard Graphics.

Using the link you created in these steps, you can access the Revenue slide by pressing the A key while you view the slide you selected in step 2.

Creating HyperShow Links with Buttons. You create HyperShow buttons in the Slide Editor. Any object on a slide—a graphics object, a text annotation, and a chart—can be a button. To jump to another slide in the HyperShow, the viewer clicks this object.

Design Note

Make sure that the user is able to recognize the object as a button. Provide a hint or instructions, if necessary, to help the user distinguish buttons on a slide.

To create a button from an object, do the following:

1. Select an object from a slide in the Slide Editor.

2. Choose Button attributes... from the Graphics menu. The Button Attributes dialog box, in which you name the button and set a destination, appears (see fig. 17.4).

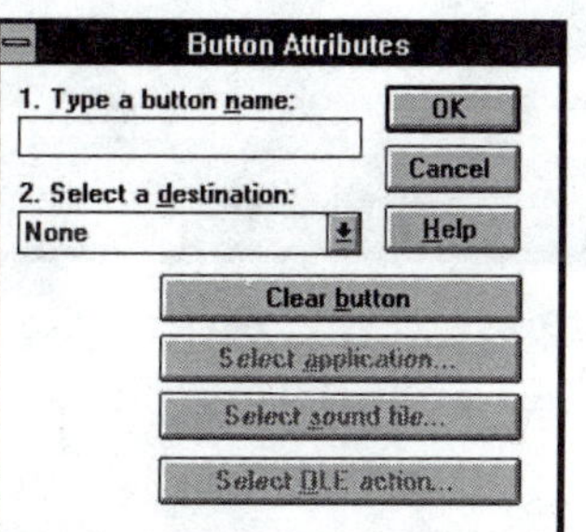

Fig. 17.4
The Button Attributes dialog box.

3. Type the button's name in the Type a button name: text box. You should use a name that reveals something about the purpose of the button. You can use the name *RevButton* for a button that jumps to the Revenue slide, for example.

4. To set the destination, click the down arrow next to the Select a destination: list box, and choose a destination from the list. See the section "Setting HyperShow Links" for more information on the elements of a link and the Slide HyperShow Links dialog box.

The slide in figure 17.5 is an example of a menu slide in a HyperShow. The instructions on the slide tell you to press a key or click a button to see information on the corresponding slide. To see the Sales slide, for example, you press C or click the appropriate button.

You saw this figure in the preceding section when you created a link between a key and a slide. In this section, you create a button from an object on this slide; then you link this button to a slide so that you can access a slide by clicking a button.

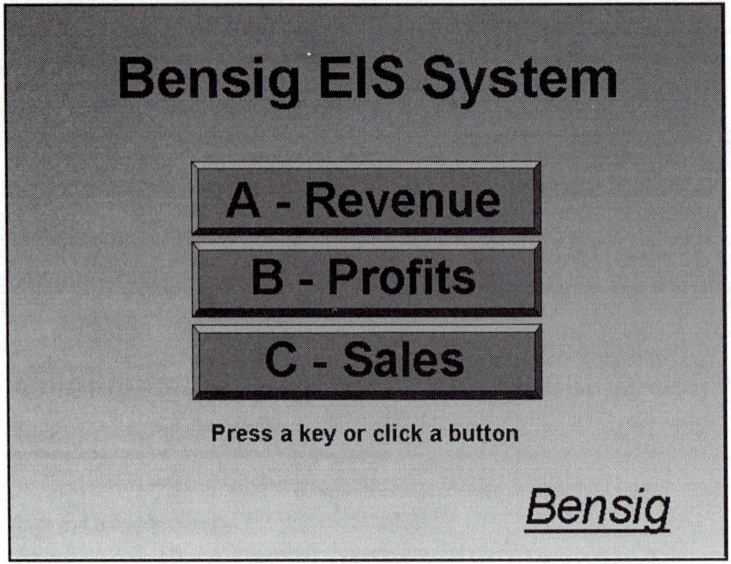

Fig. 17.5
A HyperShow menu slide.

Follow these steps to create and link a button from an object on the menu slide to a slide in your presentation so that, by clicking the A-Revenue button, you access the Revenue slide:

1. In the Slide Editor, click the object you intend to use as a button. From figure 17.5, for example, you can select the rectangle containing the words A-Revenue.
2. Choose Button attributes... from the Graphics menu. The Button Attributes dialog box appears.
3. Type the name of the button in the Type a button name: text box. For the example, type **Revenue**.
4. Click the down arrow next to the Select a destination: list box; then select the destination for the button from the list that appears. For the example, select the Revenue slide.
5. Click the OK button to accept the button and link and return to the Slide Editor window.

You use HyperShow buttons just as you use other buttons—you click them.

Changing a HyperShow Link

The Current Assignments list box in the Slide HyperShow Links dialog box displays the links defined for a slide. After you define a link, you can change the link's destination or remove the link. To change a link, follow these steps:

1. Choose ScreenS**h**ow from the **F**ile menu; then choose Edit ScreenShow Effects from the pop-up menu that appears. The Edit ScreenShow Effects dialog box appears.

2. Select the slide in the Select a slide: list box to define HyperShow links for the slide. This is the slide the user views when he presses the key or clicks a button.

3. Click the HyperShow links... button. The Slide HyperShow Links dialog box appears.

4. In the Current assignments: list box, click the link you want to change. The Select a key/button: and Select a destination: list boxes show the information about the selected link.

5. Click the down arrow next to the Select a destination: list box, and select a new destination from the list.

6. Click the OK button to accept the change and return to the Edit ScreenShow Effects dialog box.

7. Click the OK button in the Edit ScreenShow Effects dialog box to return to Harvard Graphics.

Setting Default HyperShow Links

The Default assignments: list box of the Slide HyperShow Links dialog box lists the presentation's default links. Harvard Graphics uses default links when you press a key or button that is not defined for a link on the slide. If a slide has a link for the letter B only and you press the letter A, for example, Harvard Graphics uses the default link for the letter A to determine the new slide.

The difference between links and default links is that you define links for an individual slide; default links are defined for an entire presentation. You should use default links for keys that cause the presentation to jump to a specific slide, regardless of which slide is visible on-screen. From the earlier example, the link for letter A exists for all slides. Pressing A accesses the default link unless you have defined a link between an individual slide and the letter A.

To set a default link, access the Edit ScreenShow dialog box, and then do the following:

1. Choose Default Transition Effect from the Select a slide: list box in the Edit ScreenShow effects dialog box.

2. Click the HyperShow Links button. The Default HyperShow links dialog box, in which you define default links, appears (see fig. 17.6).

   Keys for a default link appear in the Select a key: list box.

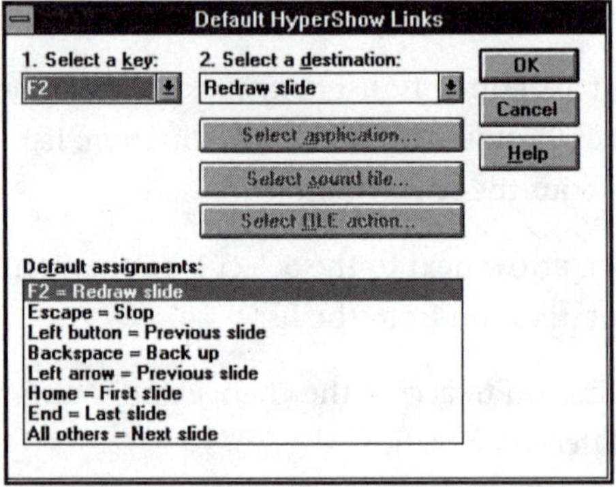

Fig. 17.6 The Default HyperShow Links dialog box.

3. To set a link for a key, click the down arrow next to the list box and choose a new key.

4. To set the destination, click the down arrow next to the Select a destination: list box, and choose a new destination. The link appears in the Default assignments list: box.

   (Refer to table 17.3 for a list of destinations. See also the section "Setting HyperShow Links" for more information on the types of links.)

Clearing a HyperShow Button

You use the Button Attributes dialog box to define, modify, and remove HyperShow buttons. In an earlier exercise, you defined a button. To modify or remove a button, you must select the button in the Slide Editor; then choose Button attributes... from the Graphics menu. The Button Attributes dialog box appears with the name and destination of the button.

To remove the button, click the Clear button option; Harvard Graphics removes the name of the selected button and sets the link to None. To modify the button, type a new name in the Type a button name: text box and specify a new destination in the Select a destination: list box. Click OK to accept the removal or modification and close the dialog box.

Launching Applications

HyperShow links turn a normal presentation into a dynamic collection of information. These links connect slides in unique ways that enable you to change your presentation in front of an audience. You also can use HyperShow links to connect your presentation to other Windows applications. With a link, you can launch an application, for example, to modify the data in a spreadsheet or view dates in a scheduler. A link to other applications or slides can make all the data that you present readily available.

You set links to applications the same way that you set other HyperShow links. Suppose, for example, that you want to be able to launch Microsoft Excel with the REVENUE.XLS spreadsheet from the C:\EXCEL directory by pressing the E key. To establish a link so that you can launch this program, do the following:

1. Choose ScreenShow from the File menu; then choose Edit ScreenShow effects. The Edit ScreenShow Effects dialog box appears.

2. In the Select a slide: list, select the slide for the link. This slide is the one from which you launch an application.

3. Click the HyperShow Links button. The Slide HyperShow Links dialog box appears.

   The Select a key/button: list box defines the key or button of the link, and the Select a destination: sets the action for the key or button.

4. To link a key or button to an application, click the down arrow next to the Select a key/button: list box; then choose a key or button from the list. For the example, choose E.

5. Click the down arrow next to the Select a destination: list box and select Launch Application from the list. Harvard Graphics enables the Select application... button.

6. Click the Select application... button to select the application to be launched. The Application to Launch dialog box appears (see fig. 17.7).

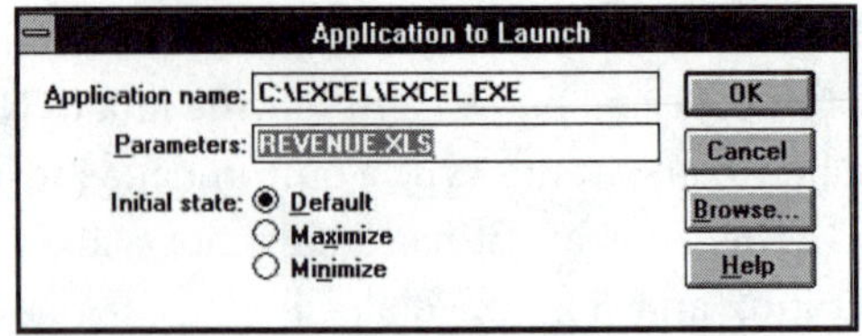

Fig. 17.7
The Application to Launch dialog box.

7. Type the name of the application in the Application name: text box. If the application does not exist in a directory in your path, you must type the full directory in addition to the application's name. For the example, type **c:\excel\excel.exe**.

   If you cannot remember the name or directory of the application, you can click the Browse... button in the Application to Launch dialog box. The Select Application dialog box, containing the applications from the current directory, appears (see fig. 17.8).

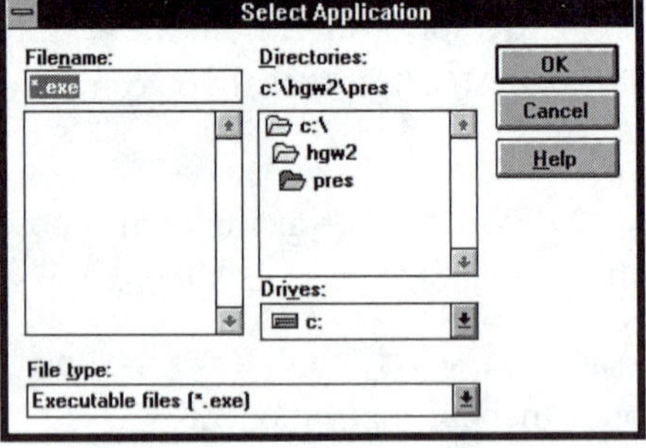

Fig. 17.8
The Select Application dialog box.

- *File type:*. This list box determines the type of application you are launching. You can launch executable files, com files, or batch files.

- *Filename:*. This text box contains the name of the application. Type the file name in the File**n**ame text box or double-click the name in the Filename: list box. The list box contains the names of files that match the extension for the current application file format. If the program you intend to launch is in a directory other than the directory identified at the Directories prompt, you can change directories by typing the drive and directory—not the file name—in the File**n**ame text box.

- *Directories:*. This prompt shows the current directory. To view files in different directories, you can change the current directory by double-clicking the directory in the list box. As mentioned, you also can type the directory in the File**n**ame text box. When you change the directory, Harvard Graphics displays the files of the specified type that are contained in the new directory.

- *Drives:*. This field shows the current drive. To view files on different drives, you can change the current drive by clicking the down arrow next to the field and then clicking a new drive.

8. Type any parameters or command line arguments in the Parameters text box. The name of a spreadsheet is an example of a parameter. For the example, type **revenue.xls**.

9. Click an Initial state: button.

   You use the Initial State buttons to set the state of the window in which the application is launched. The Default button launches the application, using the application's settings. The Maximize button launches the application in a maximized window. The Minimize button minimizes the launched application.

10. Click the OK button in the Application to Launch dialog box to accept the link and return to the Slide HyperShow Links dialog box.

11. Click the OK button in the Slide HyperShow Links dialog box to return to the Edit ScreenShow Effects dialog box.

12. Click the OK button in the Edit ScreenShow Effects dialog box to return to Harvard Graphics.

Creating Self-Running Presentations

Self-running presentations automate your ScreenShow by displaying the slides for a specified length of time before the next slide appears—pressing a key is not necessary. At the end of the presentation, a HyperShow link causes the ScreenShow to start over from the beginning. The presentation continues until you press the Escape key.

To create a self-running presentation, you must set the display time for the slides and create the link that begins the presentation again. You set links and display times in the Edit ScreenShow Effects dialog box.

To show the dialog box, choose ScreenShow from the File menu; then choose Edit ScreenShow effects from the pop-up menu that appears. You enter a slide's display time in the Slide display time: text box. You can set a different time for each slide or a default time for the entire presentation. To set a default time, click Default Transition Effect in the Select a slide: list box; then type the time in the Time text box. For more information on default effects, see "Setting Default Effects" earlier in this chapter.

You must set the link that restarts the presentation on the last slide, use the Time-out key for the link, and specify the first slide as the destination of the link. The Time-out key is a special key that defines the destination when the display time for a slide is finished. When time runs out, the presentation jumps back to the first slide.

To create a self-running presentation, access the Edit ScreenShow Effects dialog box, and then follow these steps:

1. In the Edit ScreenShow dialog box, select Default Transition Effect in the Slide List box.

2. Click the Slide display time: text box.

3. Type the display time for all the slides. For the example, type **20** to display each slide for 20 seconds.

4. In the Select a slide: list box, select the last slide in the presentation. You set the link that restarts the presentation on this slide.

5. Click the HyperShow Links button. The Slide HyperShow Links dialog box appears.

6. Click the down arrow next to the Select a key/button: list box, and select Time-out from the list of keys.

7. Click the down arrow next to the Select a destination: list box; then select First Slide from the list.

8. Click the OK button in the Default HyperShow Links dialog box to accept the link and return to the Edit ScreenShow Effects dialog box.

9. Click the OK button in the Edit ScreenShow Effects dialog box to return to Harvard Graphics.

When you display the ScreenShow, each slide remains on-screen for 20 seconds before the next slide appears. When time runs out for the last slide, the first slide reappears, and the ScreenShow begins again.

Controlling HyperShows

Before presenting your HyperShow, you may want to create links that keep people who use the HyperShow on track. If you press an *unexpected key* (a key that is not linked), the presentation may become less effective because you view too many slides in an unexpected order.

Because you define a destination for a button when you create the button, buttons are less likely to cause problems. With keys, however, you may not have defined a link for every key available. You can use a special key—the *All Others* key from the Slide HyperShow Links dialog box—to control unexpected key presses. Setting a link with the All Others key determines the destination when you press a key that does not have an explicit assignment. The All Others key controls the HyperShow by ensuring that every key the viewer presses uses a specific link in the HyperShow. You can control the show by setting a destination for this key.

All slides in the presentation appear in the Select a destination: list of the HyperShow Links dialog box. If you define a link with the All Others key for the Default Transition Effect, you can set an action for unexpected keys throughout the presentation. If you set the Destination for the All Others key to Ignore, unexpected keys have no effect on the HyperShow.

Follow these steps to create a default link for the All Others key:

1. Choose ScreenS**h**ow from the **F**ile menu; then choose **E**dit ScreenShow effects from the pop-up menu. The Edit ScreenShow Effects dialog box appears.

2. Select Default Transition Effect in the Select a slide: list box.

3. Click the HyperShow Links button. The Default HyperShow Links dialog box appears.

4. Click the down arrow next to the Select a key: list box; then select All Others from the list.

5. Click the down arrow next to the Select a destination: list box; then select Ignore from the list.

6. Click the OK button on the Default HyperShow Links dialog box to accept the link and return to the Edit ScreenShow Effects dialog box.

7. Click the OK button on the Edit ScreenShow Effects dialog box to return to Harvard Graphics.

When the viewer presses a key that does not have an explicit link, Harvard Graphics uses the destination of the All Others key. Because the destination of this key is Ignore (as determined by the preceding steps), pressing an unlinked key has no effect on the show.

Adding Sound to Presentations

When computers were first created, programmers and users were excited over monochrome displays and the ability to display very basic graphics. Over time, we have seen how high resolution graphics, the mouse, and other technological advancements enhance your ability to create, store and present information. The latest advances are found on the promising new frontier of multimedia, which is loosely defined as the combination of the computer with other media such as video and sound on the desktop.

Sound files in a presentation can have a variety of uses. For example, a self-running presentation enhanced with sound can provide verbal information about the data or provide instructions that are easier to explain than to write. A presentation distributed to your coworkers might be returned with voice annotations which provide more accurate feedback of the effectiveness of the presentation.

In Harvard Graphics, each slide in a presentation can have an associated sound (.wav voice or .mid Musical Instrument Digital Interface MIDI file). When the slide is displayed in a ScreenShow, Harvard Graphics plays the sound file for the viewers to listen to. You can create your own sound files or use existing prerecorded files of various sounds. You add sound to a presentation with the Edit ScreenShow effects dialog box where you add other special effects to a ScreenShow as well. Follow these steps:

1. Select ScreenShow from the File menu to display the ScreenShow pop-up menu.

2. Select Edit ScreenShow effects... from the pop-up menu. The Edit ScreenShow Effects dialog box is displayed.

3. Click the Enable sound box in the Select ScreenShow effects box until an X appears in the Enable sound box. This enables sounds to be played while viewing your ScreenShow.

4. Click the slide in the Select a slide: list that you wish to add sound to. The slide you click is highlighted and the image of the slide is displayed in the Preview slide box. Make sure you preview the slide before you add sound to the slide to insure you add the correct sound to the correct slide.

5. Click the Add sound... button to create a new sound file or add an existing one. The Add Sound dialog box is displayed with the slide number in the title. Figure 17.9 shows the dialog box for slide 2 of the current presentation.

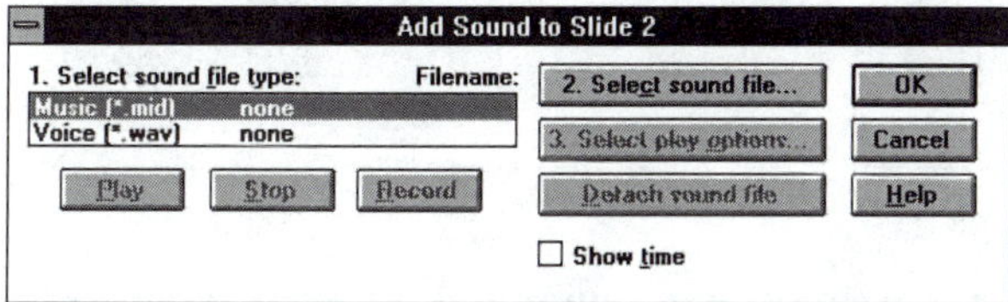

Fig. 17.9 The Add Sound dialog box for adding sound to slide 2.

In the Add Sound dialog box, you can create new sound files or select files you have already created for the current slide. For a new file, see the section Creating a Sound File. If you already have a sound file you wish to use, see the section "Selecting an Existing Sound File."

Creating a Sound File

The simplest way to add sound to your presentation is to record the sound from within Harvard Graphics. You can only record .wav files. Follow these steps to record a sound file from the Add Sound dialog box:

1. Click the Record button.

2. If you have previously added a sound file to the slide, Harvard Graphics displays a warning to ask if you wish to record over the file. If you do, click Yes and skip to step 4. Otherwise, click Cancel and read the section "Removing a Sound File," later in this chapter.

3. If you have not previously added a sound file to the slide, you see the Select Sound File dialog box which is a standard Windows dialog box. Type the name of the sound file you wish to create and click the OK button.

4. Speak into your microphone or follow the instructions of your sound hardware to record the sound. Harvard Graphics displays the time of your recording in the Add Sound dialog box.

5. When you have finished recording, click the Stop button in the Add Sound dialog box. The name of your new sound file is displayed in the dialog box. In figure 17.10, you see the recorded file PIE.WAV for slide 2.

6. Click the OK button to remove the Add Sound dialog box.

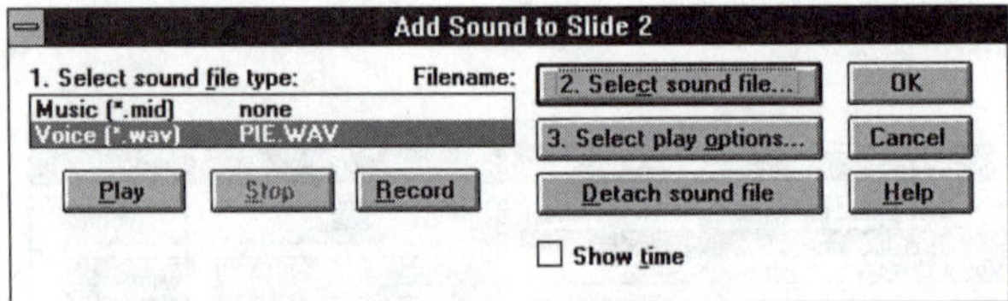

Fig. 17.10
The file PIE.WAV has been added to slide 2.

If you make a mistake recording your sound file, you can repeat the steps in this section to record over your previous file.

Design Note

You can create sound files for a slide while viewing the slide in the Slide Editor. You select Add sound... from the Slide menu to display the Add Sound dialog box.

Selecting an Existing Sound File

In addition to recording new files, you can also add existing sound files to a slide. These files can be ones you previously recorded or even professional recordings made by someone else. From the Add Sound dialog box, follow these steps:

1. Click the Select sound file... button. You see the Select Sound File dialog box which is a standard Windows dialog box.

2. Type the name of the sound file you wish to add and click the OK button. The name of the file is displayed in the Add Sound dialog box.

3. Click the OK button to remove the Add Sound dialog box.

Design Note

You can select sound files for a slide while viewing the slide in the Slide Editor. You select Add sound... from the Slide menu to display the Add Sound dialog box.

Setting Play Options

When you add a sound file to a presentation, the sound is played while the slide is displayed on your screen. In fact, the slide remains on-screen until the sound has finished. With the Play Options for sound, you cause the sound to stop playing when the slide is erased or even keep the sound playing until a later slide of your presentation is erased. To set play options for a slide from the Add Sound dialog box, follow these steps:

1. Click the Select play options... button in the Add Sound dialog box. The Play Options dialog box is displayed (see figure 17.11).

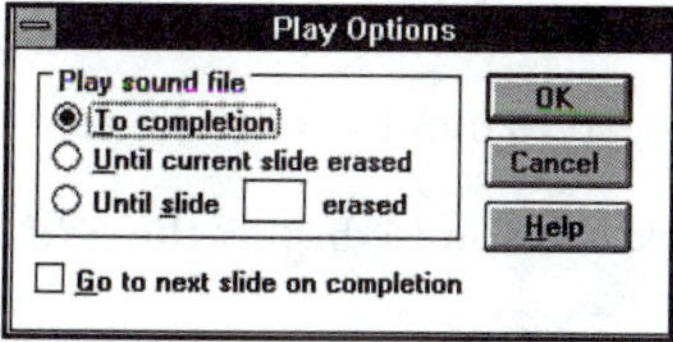

Fig. 17.11 The Play Options dialog box.

In the Play sound file box, you have three choices which determine how long the sound file is played. The To completion choice plays the entire sound file. The Until current slide erased option will play the sound until some other event, such as a keypress or time running out, causes the slide to be erased. The option allows you to better synchronize your presentation with these events. The Until slide option allows you to play a single sound file during the display of many slides. The sound plays until the slide you specify in the erase box is removed from your screen. The Go to next slide on completion option allows you to coordinate the display of your slides with your sound files. If this option is set, the slide is erased when the sound finishes playing. Follow these steps:

2. Click the Play sound file option you wish to use. If you clicked the Until slide option, type the slide number in the erased box.

3. Click the Go to next slide on completion option to erase the slide when the sound finishes playing.

4. Click the OK button when you finish setting these options to remove the Play Options dialog box.

5. When you finished adding sound files and setting play options for all of your slides, click the OK button in the Edit ScreenShow effects dialog box to return to your presentation.

Removing Sound Files

After adding sounds to a presentation, you may need to remove sound files to display the presentation without sound. For example, some of the sounds may be feedback from others reviewing your work. Once you listen to the feedback, you can remove the sounds with the Detach sound file button on the Add Sound dialog box. Follow these steps:

1. If you are not viewing the Edit ScreenShow Effects dialog box, select ScreenShow from the File menu and select Edit ScreenShow effects... from the pop-up menu.

2. Click the slide you need to modify in the Select a slide list box.

3. Click the Add sound... button to display the Add Sound dialog box.

4. Click the Detach sound file button to remove the sound file. The name of the file is removed from the dialog box and the sound will no longer be played.

5. Click the OK button to remove the Add Sound dialog box.

6. Click the OK button to remove the Edit ScreenShow Effects dialog box.

Conferencing

If your company has computers, chances are your company also uses a network to share files and other resources among those computers. You may currently use *e-mail* (electronic mail) and other network services to increase group productivity. Sharing information across a network, in the form of a presentation, is made easy with the conferencing feature of Harvard Graphics. Once you create a presentation, you can present your slides in a ScreenShow across a network as a conference for other users to view.

You control the flow of your ScreenShow so that everyone sees the same slides as you and can then provide feedback through messages.

As the person who created the presentation, you are the moderator of the conference. You determine the name of the conference and start the conference from your computer. See the section "Setting Up a Conference" for more information on how you prepare your system for conferences and the section "Starting a Conference" for information on how to begin the conference. Once you start your conference, others can join in by simply knowing the name of the conference. As you advance the ScreenShow on your computer screen, their screen displays the same slides.

Setting Up a Conference

Before starting a conference, you must create and save your presentation, and you must set the conference setup options that determine where on your network the conference information is stored. Harvard Graphics needs a common network drive which others can access to save the conference information. Each system which joins the conference uses this information to display the slides and keep the conference running smoothly. If you are not familiar with networks, you should confirm with your network administrator that the location of the conference information is generally available to users of the network and that you have read/write/create access to the network at this location.

Figure 17.12 shows the Conference Setup dialog box which is displayed when you select Conference setup... from the Options menu. You enter the common network path in the Network path: field. This is where the conference information is stored. The Current drive connections: list box displays network drives currently available for you to use for your conference in case you cannot remember the path. You can select a drive in the list instead of typing the path in the field. You type your password for your network in the Network password: field. You only need to enter a password if you normally enter one when you connect to your network. You click the Require users to type password box if you wish other members of the conference to enter their network passwords when joining the conference. If this option is not checked, others can join the conference without entering a network password.

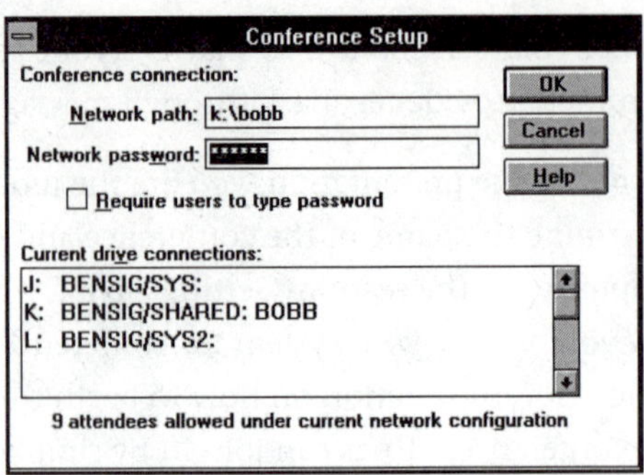

Fig. 17.12
The Conference Setup dialog box.

The bottom of the Conference Setup dialog box shows how many viewers may join your conference. In figure 17.12, you see that only nine viewers or attendees can join the conference. Follow these steps to set up a conference:

1. Select Conference setup... from the Options menu. The Conference Setup dialog box is displayed.

2. Type your network path or select a path from the Current drive connections: list box.

3. If your network requires a password, type the password in the Network password: box. As you type, Harvard Graphics displays an asterisk to prevent others from seeing your password.

4. Click the Require users to type password if you wish others who join the conference to enter their network passwords before joining.

5. Click the OK button to remove the dialog box and save your changes.

Starting a Conference

Before you start a conference, you must create and save your presentation, and the presentation must be the one you are viewing in Harvard Graphics. You must also set your conference setup options. When you are ready to start, select Conference from the File menu and select Start... from the pop-up menu to display the Start Conference dialog box (see fig. 17.13). In this dialog box, you enter your user name, which identifies you to others in the conference. You enter a name for the conference and an optional phone number which others who join the conference must enter before they join. In the figure, user bobb is starting the conference Bensig with the phone number 123456.

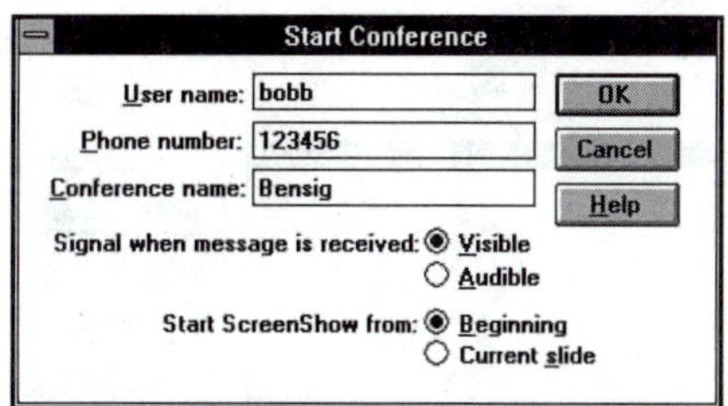

Fig. 17.13 The Start Conference dialog box.

The Audible and Visible buttons determine how attendees are notified of messages sent during the conference. See the section Sending Messages later in the chapter for more information. The Start ScreenShow from: buttons determine where the ScreenShow begins either at the current slide you are viewing or from the very beginning. Follow these steps to start a conference:

1. Select Conference from the File menu and select Start... from the pop-up menu. The Start Conference dialog box is displayed.

2. Click the User name: field and type the name by which other attendees will identify you.

3. Click the Conference name: field and type the name of your conference. Try to use a name that is easy to remember such as the name of your group, company, or a keyword which identifies the content of the presentation.

4. Click the OK button to start the conference.

   When you first start a conference, you see the Conference Moderator Commands dialog box as shown in figure 17.14 for the Bensig conference. You use this dialog box to control the conference, to send and receive messages, and to stop the conference. See the next section, "Moderating a Conference," for more information. When you click the OK button, you are returned to the conference where you use the same keystrokes as for a ScreenShow to advance the slides. After removing the initial dialog box which is displayed when a conference is started, you display Conference Moderator Commands dialog box by pressing the Escape key. To continue with your conference, follow these steps:

5. Click the OK button to remove the dialog box and continue the conference.

6. Press the Enter key to advance each slide of the conference.

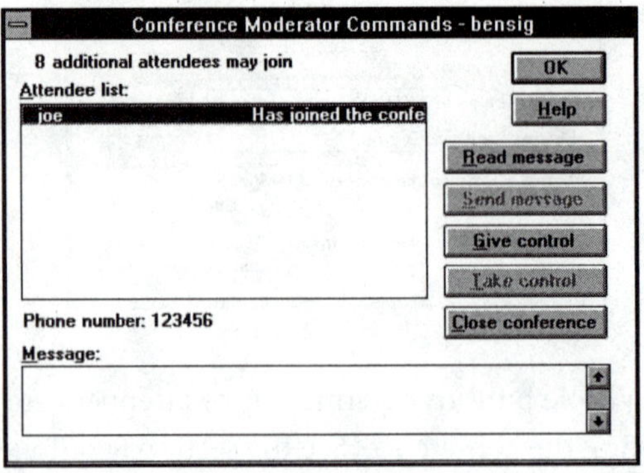

Fig. 17.14
The Conference Moderator Commands dialog box for the Bensig conference.

As others join the conference, a message is displayed on your screen to let you know they have joined.

Design Note

If you use On Screen Chalk during a conference, the chalk is displayed on the screen of all other attendees. With chalk, you can emphasize different elements of a slide or respond to messages. See the section "Using On-Screen Chalk," earlier in the chapter.

Moderating a Conference

The main functions of the Conference Moderator Commands dialog box are to control the conference and to handle messages. You display this dialog box by pressing the Escape key. In the dialog box, the OK button returns you to the conference. The Close conference button ends the conference and returns all attendees to editing a presentation. The Attendee list: box lists all users currently participating in the conference. At the top of the dialog box, you see how many attendees can join—which in the figure is 8.

The Give control button allows you to relinquish control of the presentation to any other attendee. That attendee determines when slides are advanced. To give control, you select an attendee in the list and click the Give control button. You can regain control at any time by clicking the Take control button. You use the Read message and Send message buttons, and the Message: box to communicate with other attendees. See the section "Sending Messages," later in this chapter.

Joining a Conference

Any user with access to your network can join an existing conference by selecting Conference from the File menu and then selecting Join... The Join dialog box is displayed for you to enter your user name which identifies you to others in the conference (see fig. 17.15). You must know the conference name and optional phone number to then join the conference. The Visible and Audible buttons determine how you will be notified when messages arrive. Once you enter this information and click the OK button, the current slide of the conference is displayed on your screen. From this point, the moderator has control of the ScreenShow until you leave the conference.

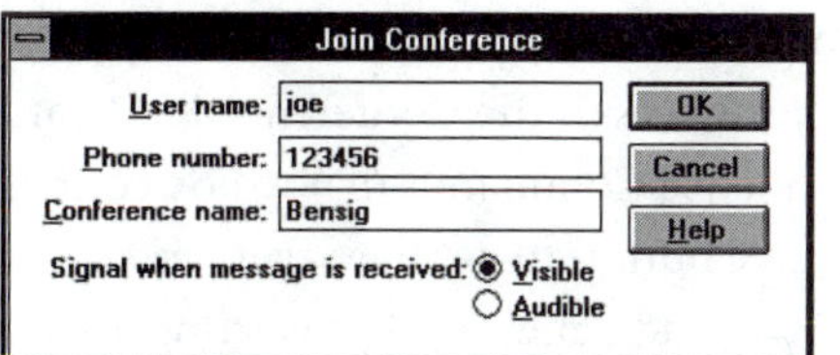

Fig. 17.15
The Join Conference dialog box.

Follow these steps to join a conference:

1. Select Conference from the File menu and select Join... from the pop-up menu. The Join dialog box is displayed.
2. Click the User name: field and type the name by which other attendees will identify you.
3. Click the Conference name: field and type the name of your conference.
4. Click the OK button to join the conference.

While participating in a conference, pressing the Escape key displays the Conference Commands dialog box, which you use to exit the conference and to send messages. Figure 17.16 shows the dialog box for the Bensig conference. You click the OK button to return to the conference. You click the Leave conference button to regain control of your system and return to making changes on your local presentation. The Attendee list: box displays other conference attendees. In the figure, you see one other attendee bobb. The text displayed after the attendee name is the beginning of the last message sent from the attendee to yourself. See the next section, "Sending Messages," for more information.

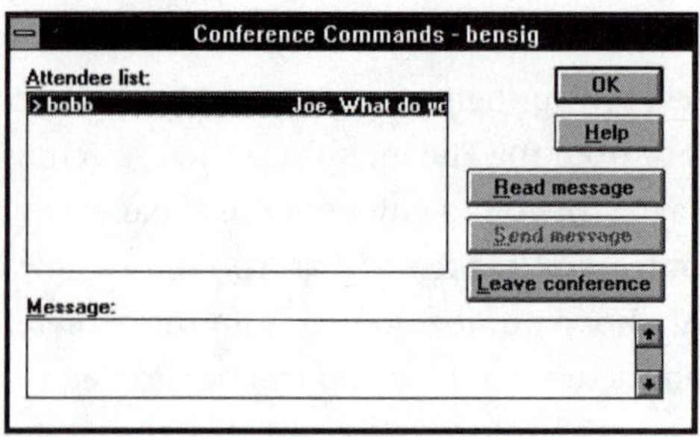

Fig. 17.16
The Conference Commands dialog box for the Bensig conference.

Sending Messages

In a conference, you can send messages to any other attendee to communicate your thoughts on the slide you are both viewing or to provide feedback to the presentation creator. Both the Conference Moderator Commands dialog box and the Conference Commands dialog box contain a Send button to send messages, a Receive button to get messages, and a Message: box to enter and view messages. You send a message by selecting an attendee in the Attendee, typing your message in the Message: box, and clicking the Send message button. Figure 17.17 shows the Conference Commands dialog box with a message from the user bobb.

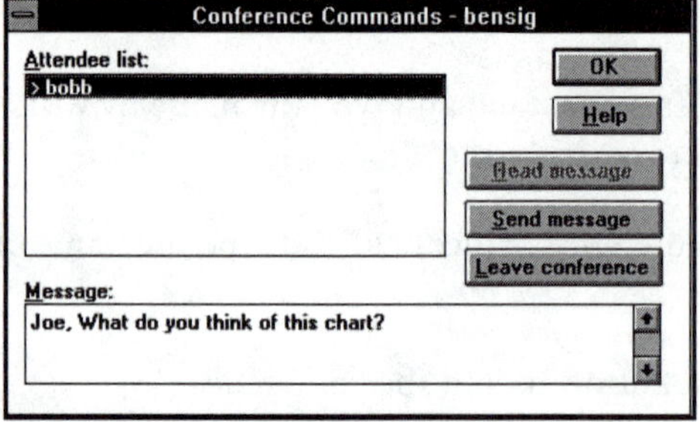

Fig. 17.17
The Conference Commands dialog box displaying a message from bobb.

When the message arrives, the attendee is notified with either a visible or audible cue depending on the option chosen when joining the conference. An arrow is displayed next to the name of the attendee to alert you that there is a message. To read the message, you click the name in the Attendee list and click the Read button. The message is displayed in the Message: box.

From Here...

This chapter explains the facets of Harvard Graphics ScreenShow and HyperShow features. You learned how to display a ScreenShow from any slide in the presentation and how to add special effects to the transitions from one slide to the next. You learned how to create links to your presentation slides from a key on the keyboard or an object on a slide. The chapter also provides special tips for creating HyperShows.

The next chapter, "Adding Symbols," explains how to add and manipulate symbols in your slides.

Chapter 18

Adding Symbols

In this chapter, you learn how to do the following:

- Add Clip Art symbols to your slides
- Create custom libraries of symbols

Symbols are clip art images that you use to enhance a slide. Harvard Graphics includes a complete set of symbols so that even people who are not artistically adept can add professional-quality drawings to their slides. If you have an artistic flair, you can save images that you create in a Symbol Library Manager file. Then, rather than creating the symbol again, you can copy it to other presentations. See the Harvard Graphics *Symbols, Palettes, and Presentation Styles* booklet for illustrations of the symbols.

Figure 18.1 shows the Symbol tool in the icon bar and a slide containing symbols. When you click the Symbol tool, the Symbol Library Manager window appears. You can copy symbols from the library to the Windows Clipboard and, from there, paste the symbols into your slides. The three starbursts in figure 18.1, for example, were copied from the STAR.SYW symbol file.

When you complete this chapter, you will be able to manipulate the Symbol Library Manager by doing the following:

- Adding symbols to a slide
- Opening and exiting the Symbols Library
- Creating and saving a symbol file
- Copying and renaming symbols
- Changing the Symbol Library Manager default view and directory

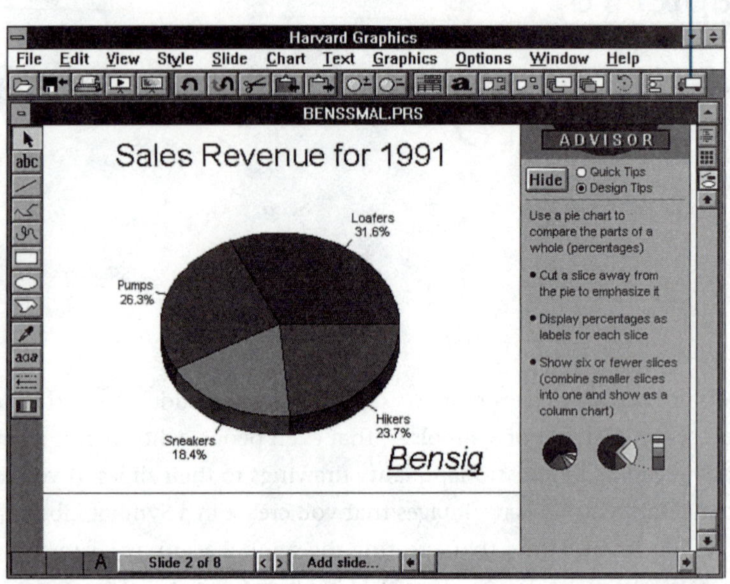

Fig. 18.1
A slide containing symbols and the Symbol tool.

Adding Symbols to a Slide

You use the Symbol tool in the icon bar within the Slide Editor to access the Symbol Library Manager. You can copy images to and from the library; in fact, you can copy the images from the library to other Windows applications, such as Windows Write or Harvard Draw.

Figure 18.2 shows the Symbol Library Manager, which begins the first time you click the Symbol tool. After you start the library, clicking the Symbol tool brings the Symbol Library Manager to the front. The symbols from the current library appear within the Symbol Library Manager window.

Follow these steps to open the Symbol Library Manager window:

1. If you are not viewing the presentation in the Slide Editor, choose Slide Editor from the View menu. The Slide Editor window appears.

2. In the Slide Editor window, click the Symbol tool in the icon bar (refer to fig. 18.1). The Symbol Library Manager window appears.

   (If you started the Symbol Library Manager earlier, clicking the Symbol tool brings the Symbol Library Manager window to the front of your screen.)

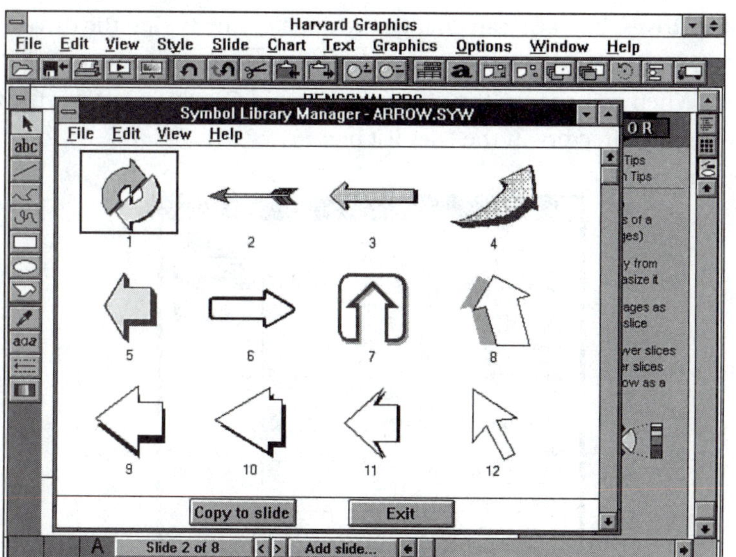

Fig. 18.2
The Symbol Library Manager window.

Opening a Symbol File

When you start the Symbol Library Manager, the Open Symbol File dialog box appears (see fig. 18.3). You use this dialog box to load a symbol file into the library. From the Symbol Library Manager, you can open an existing symbol file (Harvard Graphics stores all symbols within symbol files) or build a new file with images you create. For more information on creating symbol files, see "Creating a Symbol File" later in this chapter. If you already have started the library, choose **O**pen... from the Symbol Library Manager File menu to show the Open Symbol Library dialog box.

The Filename: list box in the Open Symbol File dialog box lists the symbol files contained in the current directory; you can choose a file to open from this list. Another way to open a file is to type the file name in the Filename: text box. The name of the current directory appears below the Directories: prompt. A simple description of the file's contents appears in the File description: text box.

You can use the Open Symbol File dialog box to search for symbol files on your hard disk. The directories available on the hard disk appear in the Directories: list box. To view files in a different directory, you can change the current directory by double-clicking the appropriate option in the list box. The Drives: field lists the current drive and you can use this field to view files on different drives. You also can change the directory by typing the drive and directory—not the file name—into the Filename text box and clicking the OK button. When you change the directory, Harvard Graphics displays the files found in that directory in the Files list box.

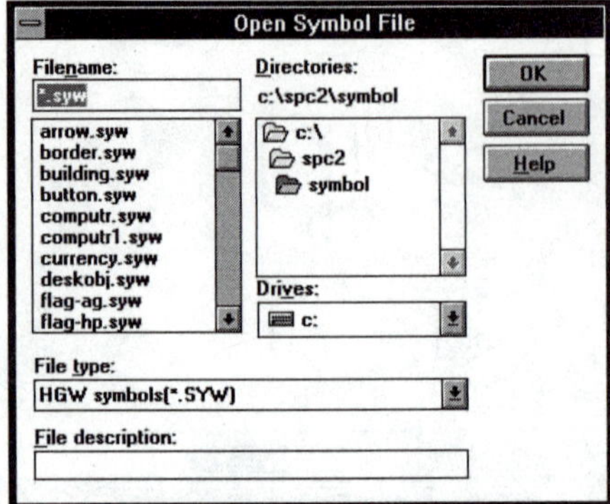

Fig. 18.3
The Open Symbol File dialog box.

Follow these steps to open a symbol file that contains arrow symbols:

1. If the Symbol Library Manager window is not visible, click the Symbol tool in the Slide Editor. The Symbol Library Manager window appears.

2. If the Open Symbol File dialog box does not appear, choose Open... from the File menu.

3. In the Filename: text box, type the name of the symbol file; for example, type **arrow**. Alternatively, select ARROW.SYW—which is one of the symbol files that comes with Harvard Graphics—in the Files list box.

4. Click the OK button. The symbols contained in the ARROW file appear in the Symbol Library Manager window.

When you open a symbol file, Harvard Graphics loads the symbols from the file into the Symbol Library Manager window.

Copying a Symbol

After Harvard Graphics loads symbols into the Symbol Library Manager, you can copy the symbols to the Clipboard and paste them into your slides. You use the Copy command from the Symbol Library Manager Edit menu to transfer a selected symbol to the Clipboard. You can also click the Copy command to slide button to quickly copy a symbol to the slide displayed in the Slide Editor. The commands on the Edit menu affect the active symbol only.

Figure 18.4 shows the symbols contained in the ARROW.SYW symbol file. To help you distinguish between similar symbols, the name of each symbol appears below the image (in some symbol files, the names are numbers). The box around the first symbol indicates that this symbol is active. To make another symbol active, click the symbol. To see other symbols in the file, scroll through the file by clicking the scroll arrows.

After you copy a symbol to the Clipboard, you can use the Edit menu's Paste command to transfer the symbol from the Clipboard to the active slide.

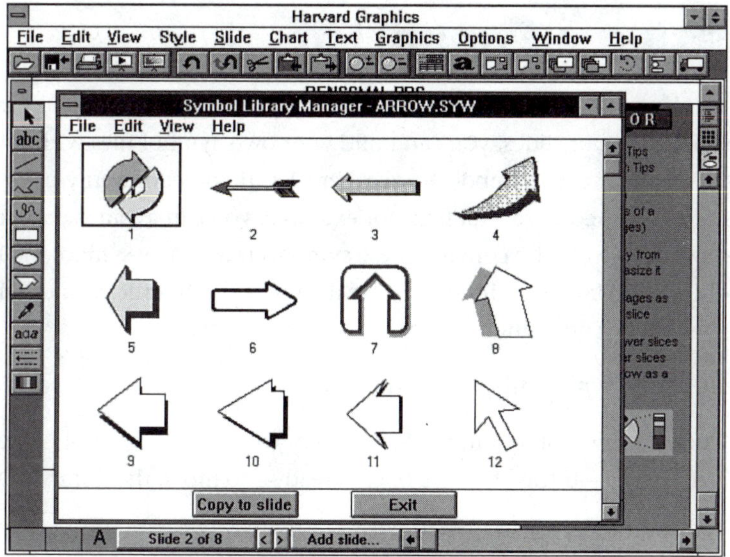

Fig. 18.4
The Symbol Library Manager containing symbols from the ARROW.SYW file.

Follow these steps to add an arrow symbol from the ARROW.SYW file to a slide:

1. If the Symbol Library Manager is not the front window, click the Symbol tool in the Slide Editor to move the window to the front.

2. If the Open Symbol File dialog box does not appear, choose Open... from the File menu.

3. Type **arrow.syw** in the Filename text box; then click the OK button. The contents of the ARROW.SYW file appear in the Symbol Library Manager window.

4. Click the arrow symbol you want to add. A box surrounds this symbol to indicate that it is active.

5. Choose Copy from the Edit menu of the Symbol Library Manager. Harvard Graphics copies the selected arrow to the Clipboard.

6. Click the Harvard Graphics window to make it active.

7. Choose Paste from the Slide Editor Edit menu. Harvard Graphics pastes the symbol stored in the Clipboard in the Harvard Graphics window. You can edit or change the symbol as you can edit any object in the Slide Editor.

Creating a Symbol File

Although Harvard Graphics contains a variety of symbol files that you can use to enhance your slides, you can build your own symbol files with images that you create or with symbols from other files. If you commonly use symbols that are located in several files, for example, you can avoid switching between multiple files by copying these symbols into a new symbol file in the Symbol Library Manager window. To create a new symbol file, you use the File menu's New command.

To create a new symbol file, follow these steps:

1. Click the Symbol tool in the Slide Editor to open the Symbol Library Manager or—if the library is open already—to move the library to the front.

   If you are starting the Symbol Library Manager, Harvard Graphics displays the Open Symbol File dialog box. Click the Cancel button to remove this dialog box.

2. Choose New from the Symbol Library Manager File menu. Harvard Graphics removes all symbols from the preceding library from the Symbol Library Manager window.

Now you are ready to add symbols to and save the new file. The following sections explain how to transfer symbols to a symbol file and how to save files you create or files you change so that you can use them again.

Adding Symbols to the Symbol Library Manager

You use the Cut, Copy, and Paste commands from the Edit menu to edit the contents of a symbol file. The Copy command copies the active symbol from the library to the Windows Clipboard, and the Cut command removes the symbol from the library and stores it in the Clipboard. You use the Paste command to copy the Clipboard image to the Symbol Library Manager. You also can paste symbols from other libraries or images from other applications into the Symbol Library Manager.

Follow these steps to copy an image from the Slide Editor to the new symbol file you created earlier:

1. In the Slide Editor, select the image to be copied. Handles appear around the selected object.

2. Choose Copy from the Slide Editor's Edit menu.

3. Click the Symbol tool to bring the Symbol Library Manager window to the front. (If you have not created a new symbol file, see "Creating a Symbol File" earlier in the chapter.)

4. Choose Paste from the Symbol Library Manager's Edit menu. The Paste Symbol dialog box, in which you enter the name of the symbol, appears (see fig. 18.5).

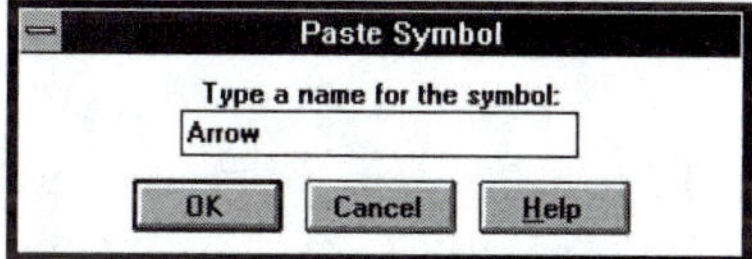

Fig. 18.5
The Paste Symbol dialog box.

   If the symbol you are pasting was copied from another symbol file, the name of the symbol appears in the dialog box; otherwise, the text box is empty, and you must enter the symbol's name.

5. Type the name of the symbol in the Paste Symbol dialog box.

6. Click the OK button. The symbol, with the name below, appears in the Symbol Library Manager window.

To paste symbols into an existing symbol file, follow the preceding steps, but do not create a new symbol file. You must save the file on your hard disk to add the symbol permanently to the file, however.

After you paste a symbol in the library, you can change the name of the symbol with the Rename... command on the Edit menu. When you choose this command, the Rename Symbol dialog box, which contains the symbol's current name, appears (see fig. 18.6). To change the name, type the new name in the text box and click the OK button.

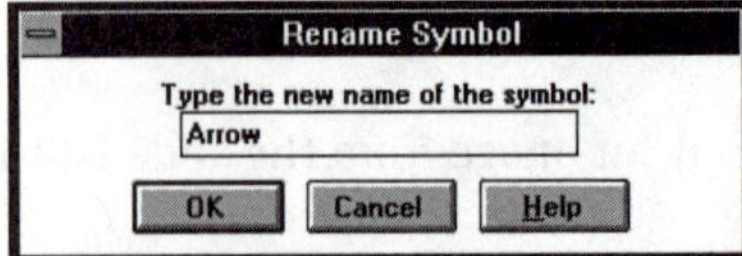

Fig. 18.6
The Rename Symbol dialog box.

Saving a Symbol File

After you create a symbol file or make changes to an existing file, you can use the Save and Save As... commands on the File menu to save the file to your hard disk. When you choose Save As... from the Symbol Library Manager File menu, the Save As Symbol File dialog box appears (see fig. 18.7). In the dialog box, you specify the name and directory of your symbol file. You also set the symbol file type in the File type: text box so that you can save symbols in Harvard Graphics for Windows 1.0 or Harvard Graphics for DOS 3.x formats. In the bottom of the dialog box, you can type a description to help you identify the contents of the symbol file. When you open symbol files, the description is displayed in the Open Symbol File dialog box shown earlier in figure 18.3.

With the Save As Symbol File dialog box, you can save the file to any drive or directory on your hard disk. The directories available on the hard disk appear in the Directories: list box. To view files in a different directory, you can change the current directory by double-clicking the appropriate option in the list box. The Drives: field lists the current drive and you can use this field to view and save files on different drives. Alternatively, you can change the directory by typing the name of the drive and directory—not the file name—into the Filename text box and clicking OK. When you change the directory, Harvard Graphics displays the symbol files contained in the specified directory in the Files list box.

To save a new symbol file, choose Save As... from the File menu. Type the name of the file in the Filename: text box and type a simple description in the File description: text box. To create a Harvard Graphics for DOS 3.x symbol file, click the down arrow next to the File type: list box; then select HG DOS 3.x from the list of file types. Click the OK button to save the file.

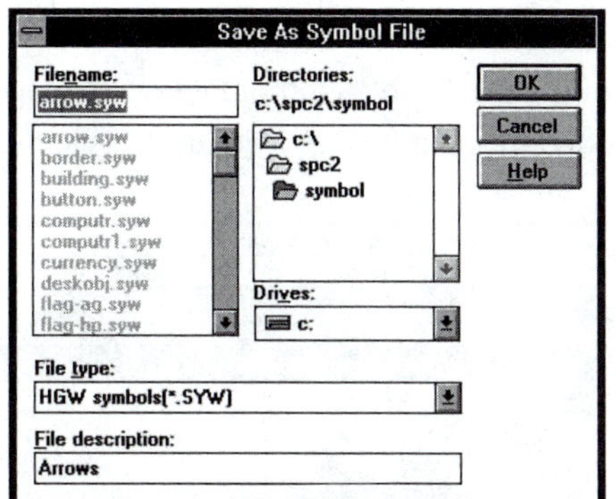

Fig. 18.7
The Save As Symbol File dialog box.

Follow these steps to save a new symbol file in the symbol file directory:

1. Choose Save As... from the File menu. The Save As Symbol File dialog box appears.
2. Type the name of the file in the Filename: text box. When you save a file, Harvard Graphics appends the SYW extension to the file name.
3. Type a description of the symbol in the File description text box.
4. Click the OK button. Harvard Graphics saves the new file under the name and directory you specify.

The Save command, executed by choosing Save from the File menu, saves the symbol file based on the settings—file name and directory, for example—that you established the last time you saved the file. If you have not saved a new file, however, the Save As dialog box appears when you choose the Save command.

Viewing Symbols

The default view in the Symbol Library Manager is the thumbnail view; a thumbnail image of the symbols appears in the library window (refer to fig. 18.4). This image enables you to view many of the symbols in the file at the same time.

You can change the view, however, by choosing another view option from the View menu. To see an enlarged version of the symbol, choose the Zoom symbol view; to see names instead of images, choose the List names view. The following sections describe these alternative views.

The Zoom Symbol View

The Zoom symbol command on the Symbol Library Manager View menu enables you to see individual symbols in finer detail (see fig. 18.8).

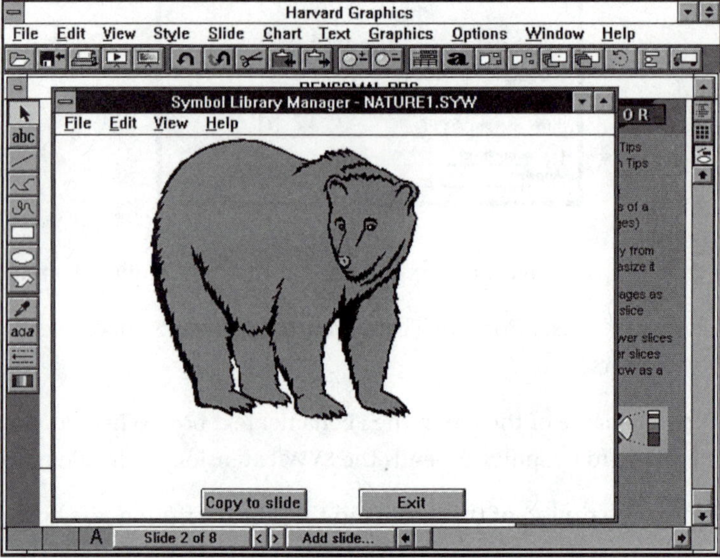

Fig. 18.8
The zoomed view.

To zoom a symbol, follow these steps:

1. Select the symbol in the Symbol Library Manager.
2. Choose **Z**oom symbol from the **V**iew menu.

When you zoom symbols, you can see only one symbol at a time. You must use the **P**revious and **N**ext commands on the View menu to flip through the zoomed symbols. To move forward in the symbol file, choose **N**ext from the View menu. To move backward, choose **P**revious. To return to the thumbnail view, choose Thumbnail view from the Symbol Library Manager View menu.

The List Names View

You use the List names command on the View menu to view symbol names rather than symbol images in the Symbol Library Manager. To view a symbol file by name, choose List names from the View menu.

Figure 18.9 shows a symbol file in the List names view. The name for each symbol appears on the left of the Symbol Library Manager window. A box highlights the active symbol, and an image of the active symbol appears to the right of the list. To change the active symbol, click the name of another symbol in the list. When a new symbol becomes active, the image for that symbol appears.

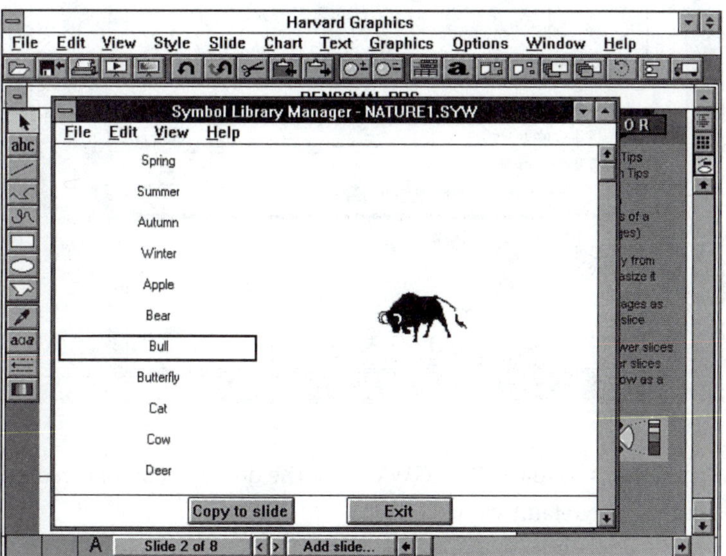

Fig. 18.9
A symbol file in the List names view.

Changing the Default Symbol Directory and View

When you first open the Symbol Library Manager, the Open Symbol File dialog box displays the files in the default symbol directory, which Harvard Graphics uses when you first open and save symbol files. All the files you also open and save go to this directory by default. You use the Options command on the Symbol Library Manager File menu to set the default directory. When you choose this command, the Options dialog box appears (see fig. 18.10). To change the default directory, type another directory name in the HG symbol directory: text box.

You also use the Options dialog box to change the default view (Thumbnail) of the Symbol Library Manager. The Default view: list box determines the view that appears when you first start the Symbol Library Manager. In the list box, you can choose between the three views on the View menu: Thumbnail view, List names, and Zoom symbol. To change the default view, click the down arrow next to the Default view: text box and select a new view from the list that appears.

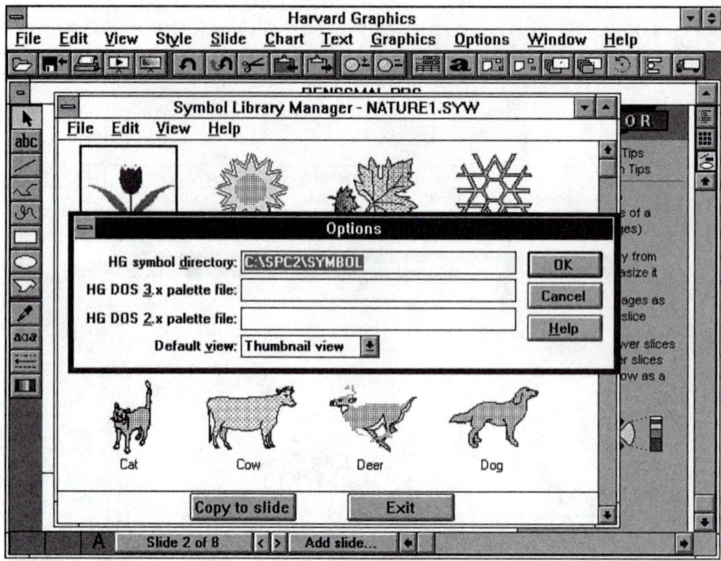

Fig. 18.10
The Options dialog box.

Follow these steps to make C:\HGW\DATA the default symbol directory and Zoom symbol the default view:

1. Choose Options... from the File menu. The Options dialog box appears.
2. In the HG symbol directory: text box, type **c:\hgw\data** to make C:\HGW\DATA the default directory.
3. Click the down arrow next to the Default view: list box and choose Zoom symbol from the list that appears.
4. Click the OK button.

The default directory is C:\HGW\DATA, and the default view is Zoom Symbol.

Exiting the Symbol Library Manager

You use the Exit command on the Symbol Library Manager File menu to close the Symbol Library Manager. If you changed the current symbol file but did not save the changes, the Symbol Library Manager displays a message asking whether you want to save the changes before you leave the library. Click Yes to save the changes of the symbol file. The Symbol Library Manager closes automatically when you exit Harvard Graphics.

From Here...

This chapter covers the features of the Symbol Library Manager. You learned how to start the library and how to transfer symbols to slides in the Slide Editor. You also learned how to add, edit, rename, and save symbol files in the library.

Appendix A

Installing Harvard Graphics 2 for Windows

The Harvard Graphics for Windows files are compressed so that the entire program can fit on ten disks. Because the files are compressed, you cannot copy the files to your hard disk. To install Harvard Graphics on your hard disk, you must use the INSTALL.EXE program, which is on the first disk. This program decompresses and copies the program files to a directory you specify.

Besides copying and decompressing files, the install program sets up a directory structure for the different file types that come with Harvard Graphics: program files, fonts, styles, palettes, filters, symbols, quick-start files, and other program files.

The install program copies each file into a different directory on your hard disk, except for styles and palettes, which share a directory. The installation program also creates the configuration file that indicates to Harvard Graphics where the files are installed.

Understanding System Requirements

To operate and install Harvard Graphics for Windows, you must have the following hardware and operating system software:

- An IBM or 100 percent compatible computer with an 80286, 80386, or 80486 processor
- A graphics card—listed on the Harvard Graphics package—with a minimum of 256K

- A hard disk with 21M free (or 8M for the minimum installations)
- A Microsoft-compatible mouse
- DOS 3.0 or later
- Microsoft Windows Version 3.1 running in Standard or 386 Enhanced mode

Installing All or Minimum Files

The first step in the installation process is starting INSTALL.EXE. Make sure that you have all the disks available before starting the program. Follow these steps to start installation:

1. Place disk 1 in drive A or B.
2. If you have not done so already, start Windows.
3. Choose Run from the Windows File menu to run applications within Windows.

   The Run dialog box appears.
4. In the Windows Run dialog box, type **a:install** if you insert the disk into drive A; type **b:install** if you insert the disk into drive B.
5. Click OK to start the installation.

   The main Harvard Graphics Installation dialog box appears (see fig. A.1). The Install To text box shows the default directory to which you copy the program files. To install Harvard Graphics in a different directory, type the new directory in the text box.
6. Choose an appropriate installation option—Install All Files, Install Minimum File Set, or Install Selected Files—from this dialog box. *Note:* If you choose Install Selected Files, go to the section "Installing Selected Files" for instructions on completing these steps.
   - *Install All Files.* You click this button to install all the files.
   - *Install Minimum File Set.* If you have a limited amount of hard disk space, you may choose to install a subset of the files required to run the program. This option requires 8M, rather than 21M, which you need to install all the files.

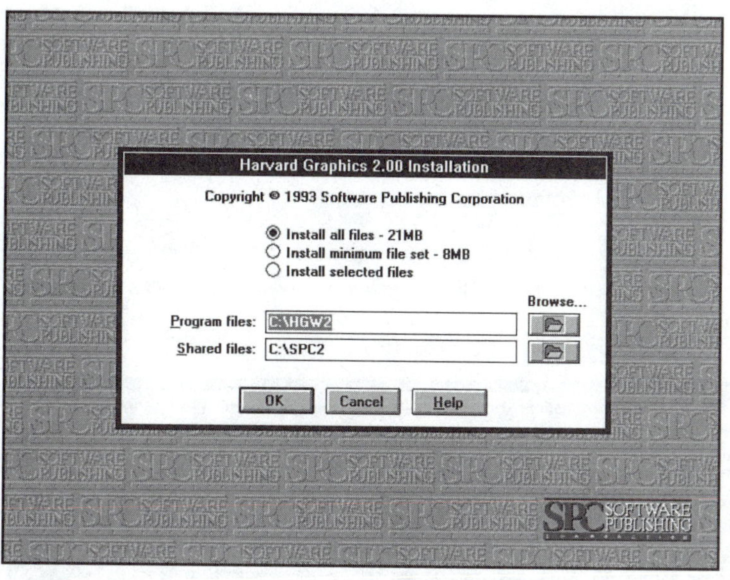

Fig. A.1
The Harvard Graphics Installation dialog box.

- *Install Selected Files.* You can use this option to recover erased or damaged files. See the section "Installing Selected Files" for more details about the files you can install.

7. Click OK. The installation program copies and decompresses the files, and the Harvard Graphics Installation status box, shown in figure A.2, informs you of the progress of the installation. To abort the installation procedure, you can click Cancel.

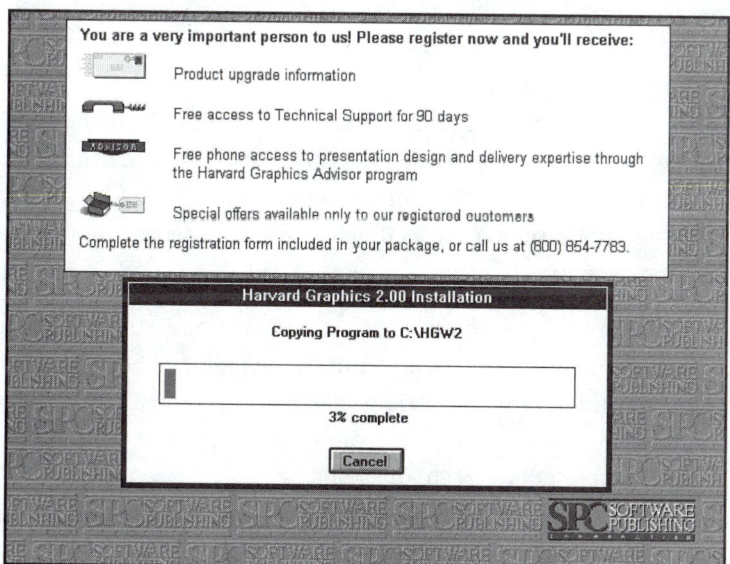

Fig. A.2
The Harvard Graphics Installation status box.

Appendixes

8. After Harvard Graphics installs all the files on a disk, the message box shown in figure A.3 appears and prompts you for the next disk. Insert the specified disk and click OK.

   If you stop the installation process by choosing Cancel, the files that were copied remain on your hard disk.

After you install the last disk, you add the Harvard Graphics icon to a Windows program group. The following section explains how to add a Harvard Graphics icon.

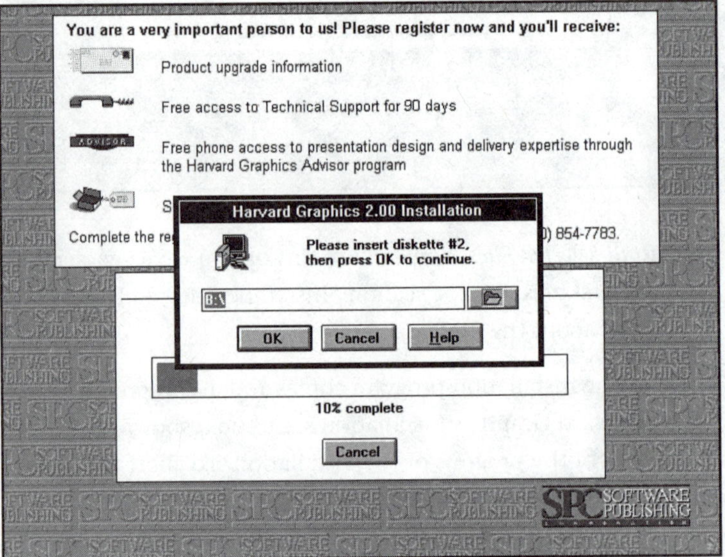

Fig. A.3
The message box prompting you to insert another disk.

Adding Harvard Graphics Icons

If you install all or the minimum Harvard Graphics files, the final installation step involves setting up the Harvard Graphics icons and other icons. You add these icons to the Windows Program Manager so that you easily can start Harvard Graphics. Figure A.4 shows the dialog box for setting up the icons; this dialog box appears after the last disk is installed.

Type the name of the new icon in the Icon text box for each icon. The installation shows the default name that identifies the program. Select a program group for the location of the icon from the Program groups: list box. The list box shows the names of all program groups available in the Windows Program Manager. Click OK to create the icons.

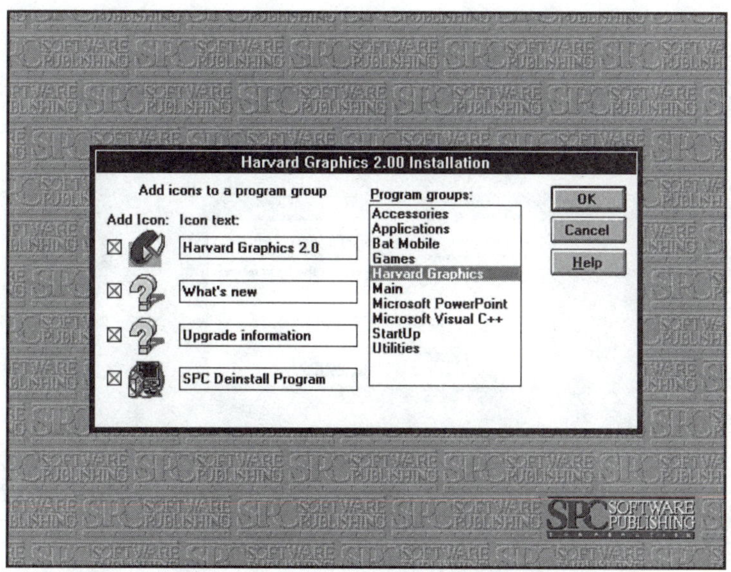

Fig. A.4
Setting the program icons.

Follow these steps to create the icons in the Windows Applications program group:

1. Choose the appropriate group in the Program Group list box for the Harvard Graphics icon. For example, choose Windows Apps to add the Harvard Graphics icon to the group containing Windows applications programs in the Windows Program Manager.

2. Click OK.

Finishing the Installation

After the installation is complete, the install program displays the Installation Completed message box, which shows the directory in which Harvard Graphics was installed (see fig. A.5). To complete installation, click OK.

Installing Selected Files

If you choose the Install Selected Files option in the Harvard Graphics Installation dialog box, you can install individual Harvard Graphics files without installing the entire program. Using this option is especially useful if a program file becomes damaged on your hard disk. By installing selected files only, you can replace the damaged file from the install disk without repeating the full installation.

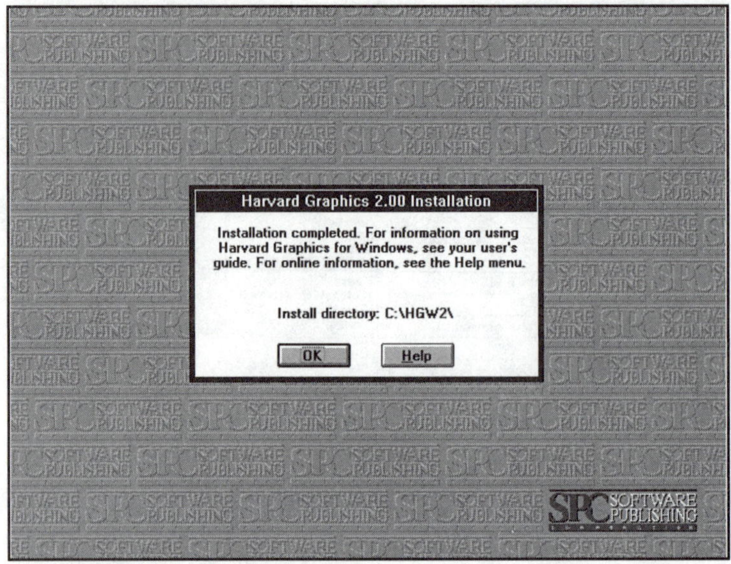

Fig. A.5
The Installation Completed message box.

For each file group, the install program enables you to pick the files you want to copy. After you choose Install Selected Files and click OK, the program displays the Install Selected Files dialog box, from which you choose the file groups to install (see fig. A.6). Common files are placed into groups—font files, symbol files, and so on—so that you can choose easily the files to install.

In this dialog box, specify whether you want to install none, all, or some of the files in a file group. If you don't want to install any program files, for example, you click None. To install only some Symbols group files, click Some for this file group.

To install selected files, follow these steps:

1. Choose the appropriate radio button next to the group whose files you want to install.

   To install files of an entire group, click the All button next to the group name.

   The Some radio button, which appears next to the Styles and Palettes..., Filters..., Symbols..., and Utilities... groups only, enables you to choose individual files from these groups. When you click the Some button, a corresponding dialog box appears. Refer to the following sections for instructions on installing individual files from a file group.

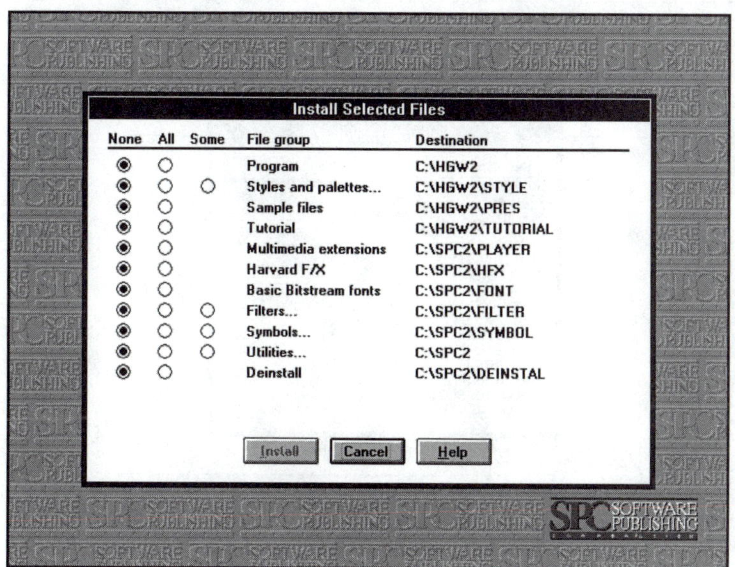

Fig. A.6
The Install Selected Files dialog box.

2. Click the Install button.

   The Harvard Graphics Installation status box informs you of the progress of the installation. To abort the installation procedure, click Cancel.

3. After Harvard Graphics installs all the files on a disk, the message box prompting you for the next disk appears. Insert the specified disk and click OK.

4. When the installation is complete, the install program displays the Installation Completed message box. To complete installation, click OK.

Choosing Style and Palette Files

Harvard Graphics treats Style and Palette files as one file group during installation. You can install all palette and style files or a selected subset of the files.

When you click the Some button next to the Styles and Palettes... group, the Styles and Palettes dialog box appears (see fig. A.7). To choose a file, click the file in the Styles and Palette list box. To deselect the file, click the file again. To select a group of files, drag the mouse pointer over the group.

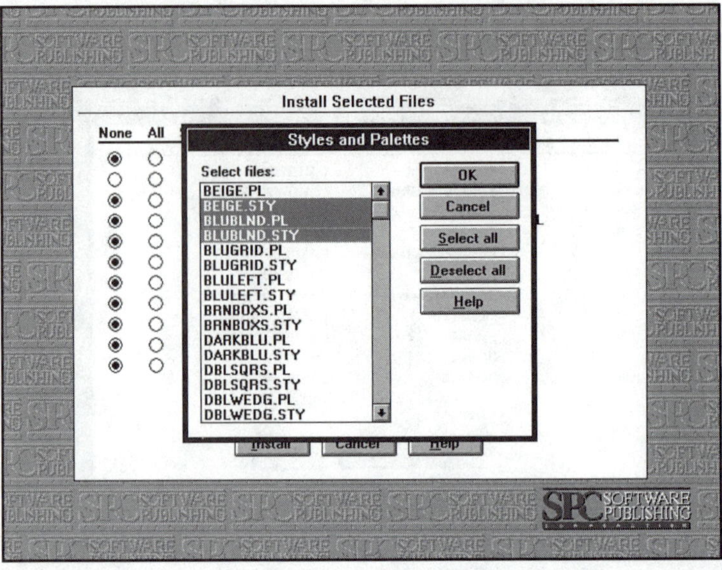

Fig. A.7
Choosing palettes and styles for installation.

Choosing Filter Files

Filters determine what types of files you can import and export with Harvard Graphics. You can install a filter to import Excel spreadsheets or TIFF bit-mapped files, for example.

When you click the Some button next to the Filters file group, the Filters dialog box appears (see fig. A.8). Separate options exist for Adobe Illustrator files, MicroGrafx Draw files, PICT files, and WPG files. The Basic Filters file group includes Harvard Graphics DOS files, Windows bitmapped files, and Windows metafiles.

To install selected filters, click the All button for the filters you want to install; then click OK to accept the filters. You cannot change the destination of filters.

Choosing Symbol Files

You can install a selected subset of the symbol files to save room on your hard disk. When you click the Some button next to the Symbols prompt, the Symbols dialog box appears (see fig. A.9). To choose a file, click the file in the Symbols list box. To deselect the file, click the file again. You can select a group of files by dragging the mouse pointer across them.

To install selected symbol files in the Symbols dialog box, click the files you want to install in the list box; then click OK.

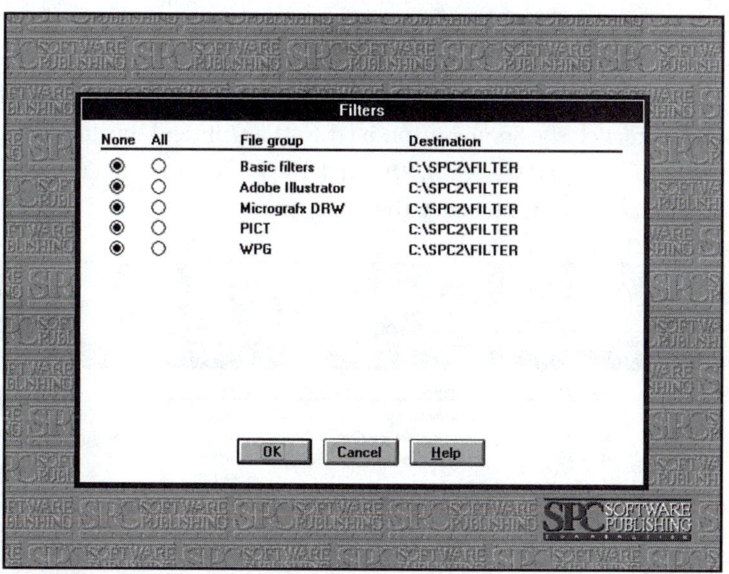

Fig. A.8
Choosing filters for installation.

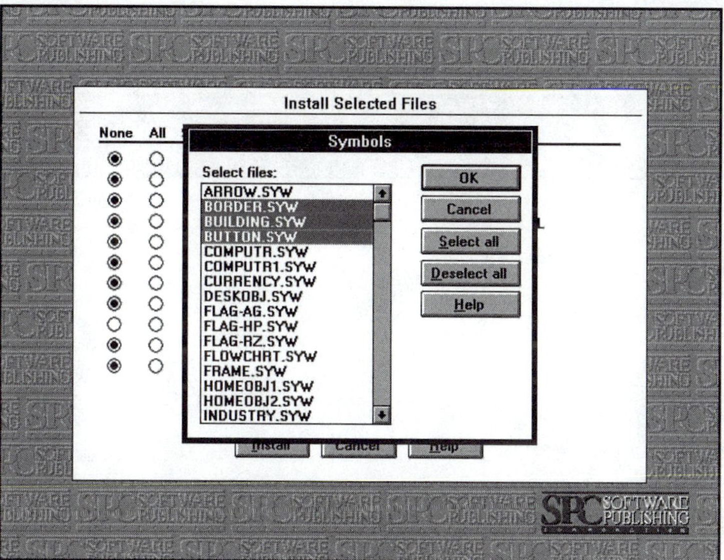

Fig. A.9
Symbol files for installation.

Choosing Utilities

You can install each of three separate utilities that come with Harvard Graphics. When you click the Some button next to the Utilities... button, the Utilities dialog box appears (see fig. A.10). Click the button next to each utility you want to install and then click the OK button.

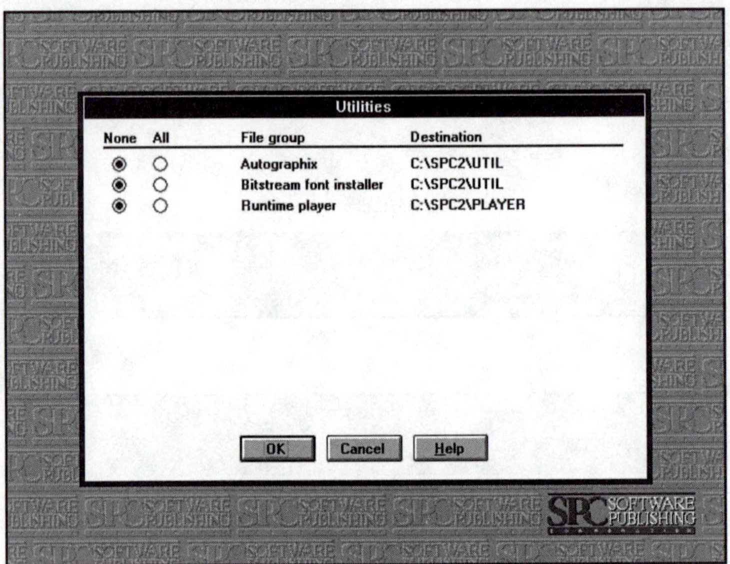

Fig. A.10
Utilities for Installation.

Appendix B

Speed Keys in Harvard Graphics

File Commands	
Ctrl-N	Create new presentation
Ctrl-O	Open an existing presentation
Ctrl-S	Save the presentation
Ctrl-P	Print the presentation
Ctrl-F2	Display ScreenShow from beginning
Alt-F4	Exit Harvard Graphics
Alt-F2	Display ScreenShow from current slide

Edit Commands	
Alt-Backspace	Undo an edit
Shift-Del	Cut an item to the Clipboard
Ctrl-Ins	Copy an item to the Clipboard
Shift-Ins	Paste an item from the Clipboard
Ctrl-A	Select all the objects in the window
Del	Clear (or delete) an item or character

Graphics Menu Commands	
Ctrl-G	Group objects together
Ctrl-U	Ungroup objects that were grouped
Ctrl-E	Edit an object or a cell in data form
Ctrl-H	Center on slide horizontally

Text Commands	
Ctrl-B	Boldface text or remove boldface
Ctrl-I	Italicize text or remove italic

Text Edit Commands	
Backspace	Delete the character before the insertion point
Del	Delete the character after the insertion point
Home	Move the insertion point to the beginning of the text
End	Move the insertion point to the end of the text
Ctrl-left arrow	Move the insertion point one word to the left
Ctrl-right arrow	Move the insertion point one word to the right
Ctrl-Enter	Add a new line of text

Chart Commands	
F8	Chart options

Outliner Commands	
Tab	Decrease the level of a topic
Shift-Tab	Increase the level of a topic
Ctrl-Home	Move the insertion point to the beginning of the first topic
Ctrl-End	Move the insertion point to the end of the last topic

View Commands	
F2	Preview the current slide

Window Commands	
Shift-F4	Tile windows
Shift-F5	Cascade windows

Appendix C

Formulas

Formulas are used with charts to define relationships in the data; for example, you use formulas to sum all the values in a series on an XY chart. For more information about formulas, see Chapter 5, "Creating XY Charts," and Chapter 6, "Creating Pie Charts," to learn how to enter data as formulas in XY and pie charts.

Numeric Formulas

Keyword:	ABS(*value*)
Description:	Returns the absolute value for the value
Examples:	ABS(-10) is 10 ABS(C2) is 5 if the value of C2 is 5 or -5
Keyword:	AVERAGE(*range*)
Description:	Returns the average of the range of cells
Examples:	AVERAGE(B1:B4) is 5 for values of 4, 7, 3, 6 in B1 through B4 Alternate formula: AVG(*range*)
Keyword:	COUNT(*range*)
Description:	Returns number of cells in the range of cells
Examples:	COUNT(B1:B4) is 4 Alternate formula: CT(*range*)
Keyword:	EXP(*power*)
Description:	Raises the value of *e* to the power
Examples:	EXP(3) is 20.0855 EXP(C2) is 22026.47 if the value of C2 is 10
Keyword:	INTEGER(*value*)
Description:	Returns the value rounded down to the nearest integer
Examples:	INTEGER(4.2) is 4 INTEGER(C2) is 10 for a value in C2 of 10.56 Alternate formula: INT(*value*)
Keyword:	LN(*value*)
Description:	Returns the logarithm base *e* of the value
Examples:	LN(20) is 2.9957 LN(C2) is 1.0986 if the value of C2 is 3

(continues)

Numeric Formulas Continued

Keyword:	LOG(*value*)
Description:	Returns the logarithm base 10 of the value
Examples:	LOG(3) is 0.4771 LOG(C2) is 2 if the value of C2 is 100 Alternate formula: LOG10(*value*)
Keyword:	MAVG(*cell,preceding,following*)
Description:	Calculates the moving average for the cells starting at the preceding number of cells before the cell to the following number of cells after the cell
Examples:	MAVG(C3,2,2) calculates the moving average from cell C1 to cell C5
Keyword:	MAXIMUM(*range*)
Description:	Returns maximum value of the cells in the range
Examples:	MAXIMUM(B1:B3) is 10 if cells B1 through B3 have values 7, 10, 3 Alternate formula: MAX(*range*)
Keyword:	MINIMUM(*range*)
Description:	Returns minimum value of the cells in the range
Examples:	MINIMUM(B1:B3) is 3 if cells B1 through B3 have values 7, 10, 3 Alternate formula: MIN(*range*)
Keyword:	MOD(*numerator,denominator*)
Description:	Returns the modulous, or remainder of the numerator divided by the denominator
Examples:	MOD(12,5) is 2 MOD(B2,B3) is 5 if the value of B2 is 15 and B3 is 10
Keyword:	SQRT(*value*)
Description:	Returns the square root of the value
Examples:	SQRT(25) is 5 SQRT(B3) is 2.6458 if the value of B3 is 7
Keyword:	STDEV(*range*) or STD(*range*)
Description:	Returns the standard deviation for the range using the population or biased method
Examples:	STDEV(B2:B4) is 2 if cells B2 through B4 have the values 10, 12, 8
Keyword:	SUM(*range*)
Description:	Returns the sum of the cells in the range
Examples:	SUM(B1:B3) is 20 if cells B1 through B3 have values 7, 10, 3
Keyword:	VARIANCE(*range*)
Description:	Returns the population variance of the cells in the range
Examples:	VAR(B1:B3) is 12.3 if cells B1 through B3 have values 7, 10, 3 Alternate formula: VAR(*range*)

Geometric Formulas

Keyword:	ACOS(*value*)
Description:	Returns in radians the angle whose cosine is the value
Examples:	ACOS(-0.2) is 1.7721 ACOS(C2) is 1.3387 if the value of C2 is 0.23

Keyword:	ASIN
Description:	Returns in radians the angle whose sine equals the value
Examples:	ASIN(-0.2) is -0.02014 ASIN(C2) is 0.5236 if the value of C2 is 0.5

Keyword:	ATAN(*value*)
Description:	Returns in radians the angle whose tangent equals the value
Examples:	ATAN(-0.2) is -0.1974 ATAN(C2) is 0.4636 if the value of C2 is 0.5

Keyword:	ATAN2(*x*,*y*)
Description:	Returns the arctangent of the *x* and *y* values in radians
Examples:	ATAN2(5,10) is 1.1071 ATAN(C2,C3) is 0.7854 if the value of C2 and C3 is 15

Keyword:	COS(*angle*)
Description:	Returns the cosine of the angle in radians
Examples:	COS(30) is 0.1543 COS(B2) is -0.9673 if the value of B3 is 72

Keyword:	PI
Description:	Returns the value of pi, which is 3.14159

Keyword:	SIN(*angle*)
Description:	Returns the sine of the angle in radians
Examples:	SIN(30) is -0.988 SIN(B2) is 0.2538 if the value of B3 is 72

Keyword:	TAN(*angle*)
Description:	Returns the etangent of the angle in radians
Example:	TAN(20) is 2.2372

Appendix D

Working with the Icon Bar

The Slide Editor in Harvard Graphics is an intuitive and efficient interface for modifying graphic objects. Tools, presented as icons, allow you to quickly execute an action by clicking the tool and then clicking in the drawing area to complete the task. With Version 2.0 of Harvard Graphics, the ease-of-use associated with icons has been expanded throughout the product in the form of an icon bar. Figure D.1 shows the icon bar in the Slide Editor. The icon bar is a set of icons or tools located just below the menu bar. These tools provide quick access to common features in the different parts of Harvard Graphics including the Slide Editor, Slide Sorter, and Outliner.

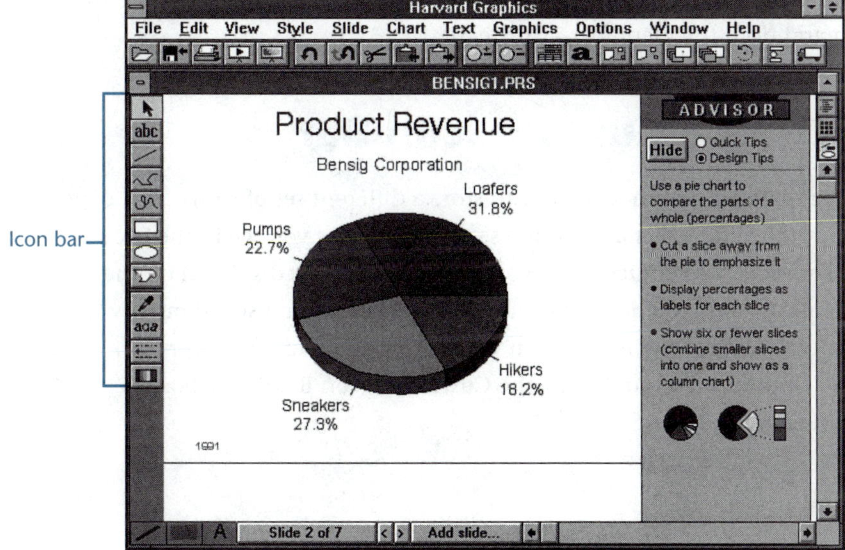

Fig. D.1
The icon bar in the Slide Editor.

Tip
To learn the function of an icon you don't recognize in the bar, just move the mouse cursor over the icon. Harvard Graphics temporarily changes the window title to the name of the icon to reveal the icon function.

The icon bar in each part of the product provides those tools used most often for each part of Harvard Graphics. For example, the Slide Editor icon bar contains tools to group, ungroup, and align graphic objects. The Slide Sorter icon bar shows tools used to cut and paste slides, which you commonly do in the Slide Sorter. When you first install Harvard Graphics, the icon bars in the product display the most common features for each area. The section "Using the Icon Bar" explains how to use these tools. If you decide there are other tools you use more often than the ones provided by Harvard Graphics, the section "Customizing the Icon Bar" explains how to add and remove icons from the bar. The section "Icons Available in Harvard Graphics" provides a complete list of the icons, which you can refer to when using and customizing the bar.

Using the Icon Bar

You use the icon bar the same way you use the tools in the Slide Editor or the toolbox. You click the icon and then finish the action the same way as if you executed the command from the menu bar. For example, the Cut icon will remove an object from a slide in the Slide Editor and place the object on the Windows Clipboard. You can achieve the same result by selecting Cut from the Edit menu in the Slide Editor. Some icons, such as the align icon, require additional actions. With align, for example, clicking the icon displays a dialog box for you to select which side of the graphic objects you wish to align. More simply stated, clicking an icon in the icon bar is equivalent to selecting a command from the menu bar—only easier!

Creating a Custom Icon Bar

Each area that displays an icon bar can store a different set of icons. The icons you see in the Slide Sorter are not the same as the ones you see in the Slide Editor. For each different icon bar, you can edit the icons displayed on the bar to remove icons you don't use and add ones you often use. To modify the icon bar, you change to the view you want to modify and select Icon bar... from the Options menu to display the Customize Icon Bar dialog box, as shown in figure D.2.

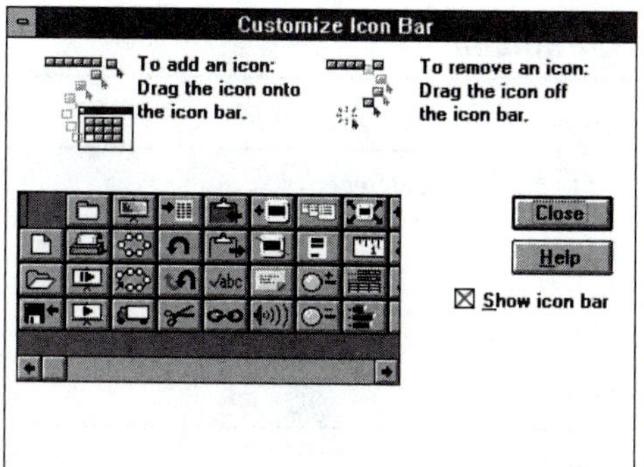

Fig. D.2
The Customize Icon Bar dialog box.

The Customize Icon Bar dialog box shows the icons you add to the icon bar you're modifying in the icon area in the middle of the dialog box. To add an icon from this area, you click the icon and drag it to the icon bar to the location where you want to place the icon. To see all the icons, click the left and right scroll bar arrows to scroll the icons in the dialog box. To remove an icon, you click the icon in the icon bar and drag it anywhere on-screen not directly over the icon bar. You can even move icons around on the bar by clicking and dragging them to a new location. For example, follow these steps to add an icon in the Slide Sorter:

1. If you are not viewing your presentation in the Slide Sorter, choose **S**lide Sorter from the View menu. You see the presentation in the Slide Sorter.

2. Choose **I**con bar... from the Options menu. The Customize Icon Bar dialog box appears.

3. Click the icon you want to add in the dialog box and drag it to the location on the icon bar.

4. Release the button to add the icon.

5. When you're finished making changes to the **I**con bar, click the Close button in the dialog box to return to the Slide Sorter.

Icons Available in Harvard Graphics

The following table lists all the icons available in Harvard Graphics. Refer to this table to locate icons in the bar and to help when creating a custom icon bar.

Icon	Command
	Close
	Edit ScreenShow effects
	Import
	Copy
	Add slide
	AutoBuild
	Preview slide
	Create new presentation
	Print
	Start conference
	Undo
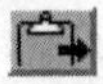	Paste
	Delete slide
	Add title, subtitle, footnote
	Change ruler/grid options
	Open
	Display ScreenShow from beginning
	Join conference
	Redo
	Check spelling
	Edit speaker notes
	Zoom in
	Display data form
	Save
	Display ScreenShow from current slide
	Open Symbol Library
	Cut
	Edit links

	Add sound
	Zoom out
	Change chart options
	Add chart to slide
	Align text left
	Special effects
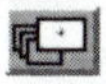	Move to front
	Flip horizontal
	Edit color palette
	Bold
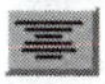	Align text center
	Change button attributes
	Send to back
	Align
	Italic
	Align text right
	Group
	Rotate
	Edit object
	Underline
	Justify text
	Ungroup
	Flip vertical
	Change presentation style
	Indent topic
	Add organization chart
	Unindent topic
	Show subtitle and footnote
	Hide subtitle and footnote

Index

Symbols

A

D

E

F

G

H

I

J–K

L

P

Q–R

S

T

U